OXFORD POSTGRADUATE
1963-1966

Alan Macfarlane

For Keith Thomas

With my highest respect, admiration and affection

Contents

Preface

This description of my postgraduate years doing a Doctorate at the University of Oxford from 1963 to 1966 builds on a number of earlier accounts. In *Indian Infancy* I describe my roots, both my ancestors who went to India and also my first five years there from 1941-1947. Then I describe the move to England and my home life aged six to twelve in *Dorset Days*. Aged eight I was sent to a preparatory boarding school in north Oxford, which is described in *Becoming a Dragon*. In my last year at the Dragon School we moved to north Lancashire. Life there from 1954 to 1960 is described in *Lakeland Life*. From our home in Wordsworth's valley, I was sent to a boarding school in Yorkshire from 1955-1960, described in *Sedbergh Schooldays*. I then went read history at Oxford University from 1960-1963, described in *Oxford Undergraduate*. The current volume takes the story from there.

There was much continuity with my undergraduate life. I was still attached to Worcester College, where some of my undergraduate friends had stayed on. My parents were still, for my first two years, away on a tea plantation in Assam. Yet there were also large changes. I was living for two years in 'digs' out of College. I had a 'supervisor' in another College. I was now starting to learn how to do research and how to prepare a long piece of work which I would submit for my doctorate.

By the time I returned to Oxford to undertake a research degree in history in October 1963 I was in many ways an adult. This makes the volume different from the preceding ones. They were concerned with all aspect of my growth – physical, emotional, social, spiritual, intellectual. So they contain a good deal of material on my games and hobbies, emotional attachments, religious strivings and social ties. By the age of nearly twenty-two, I was now more or less mature. So the main focus of this volume will shift to the intellectual side.

Until I began the research degree my intellectual education had been carefully supervised and consisted largely of tasks set me by a series of teachers, often on a weekly basis. I had moved from class teaching up to 'O' level at sixteen, to supervision (one or two to one) teaching from sixth form through the years as an undergraduate, but I was still closely directed.

The purpose of the postgraduate experience was to launch me into a new, unexplored, sea of facts and impressions where, with a little guidance every few months, I would explore for myself. I was to make 'an original contribution to knowledge', which in effect meant that I should find out things which no-one else, including my supervisor and some of the best thinkers in my field (history) had not known before I discovered them.

I was to do this not merely to produce a long and sustained (100,000 thousand word maximum) thesis or dissertation on a particular subject (which might be published as a book), but also to learn the method of making discoveries. The latter was essential to do further original research and also enable me to guide my students if I became a university teacher.

This explains the different nature of this volume. Although I had a number of minor love affairs and towards the end of my time as a postgraduate met the girl who would become my first wife, I have omitted the materials relating to this aspect of my life unless the letters throw serious light on my intellectual progress. Likewise I have omitted a number of letters to and from a circle of friends, as well as a certain amount of ephemera of a religious and social kind.

Instead I have concentrated on what it is like to try to explore and discover new worlds. I have tried to convey the bewilderment, uncertainty, frustrations, excitements and triumphs. As far as I know, there has never been any detailed analysis, based on contemporary documents including letters and extracts from the research materials, of how one learns to do a doctorate. Since many hundreds of thousands of people around the world have now undergone this process it is perhaps strange that this seems to be the first account of this kind. Yet for those who have done a doctorate, or plan to take a higher degree in the Arts, Humanities and Social Sciences, it may be of interest to see how one young historian moved from the undergraduate to graduate world.

Of course, both the discipline as well as the methods of doing research, have changed hugely in the half century since I did my degree. In particular I was working in a pre-computer age and so this account is of an older, pre-digital, world which has largely gone. Yet the basic structure of how one goes about trying to solve intellectual questions remains today. I have tried to summarize this process in three short books, particularly written for a Chinese audience, namely *How to Discover the World*; *On How to Investigate Mysteries; How to Study the World*, which provide the analytical conclusions of what I learnt from the process.

Though I have copies of all the working notes and drafts of the process, these would have been dry and not very illuminating about what I was feeling and thinking on their own. I have the good fortune to have several sets of letters that give the context of the work and the intellectual progress. Most important are the letters between my mother Iris and myself. My mother was in India for most of the first two years of my research project and we wrote to each other almost weekly. Over half our letters survive. Iris herself was starting to do research and write on Indian history, so we shared our experiences. This provides a unique source for my intellectual development.

In the third year, when I was living at home and writing the thesis and my parents were back, I have other letters. These are to my fellow researchers, eminent scholars and particularly to my former undergraduate tutor, Lady Clay, whom I had been meeting regularly after I graduated.

This was also a period of saying good-bye, for both myself and my parents. I had first come for six months to north Oxford from India when I was six. I had returned to the same part of Oxford for five years of boarding life at the Dragon School. After that we moved north and I spent five years at a northern boarding school, returning again to Oxford for my three years as an undergraduate and three years postgraduate study.

By my twenty-fifth birthday, I had spent almost half my life in Oxford. It was full of memories and associations from. When I finished I went off to London for further courses and then to Cambridge for the rest of my academic life. Oxford was my childhood, boyhood, adolescence and early adulthood. Leaving its beauty and excitements, where my heart and mind were opened and trained, was a wrench.

At the same time it was the end of twenty-five years' experience for my parents too, again half their lives. They had married in India in 1941, were there throughout the war and from 1946 lived together on several tea estates in Assam where my father was a manager. For my mother, who found that she was suddenly leaving India in late 1965 as a result of illness and the Pakistan-India war, it was an even greater wrench than for me. She had given birth to her three children and brought them up in India. She had come to love and admire the country, while also being highly critical and often miserable. Leaving at a time when the imperial world she had been brought up in was rapidly vanishing was also a saying good-bye.

So this account explores at different levels. There is the strange, repulsive yet intriguing world of historical witchcraft, the delight of finding new records no-one had ever used before and the excitements of discovering a new discipline (anthropology) which became a surrogate for orthodox religion. There was the challenge of working closely with a superb and involved supervisor, Keith Thomas, and of becoming an intellectual partner and deep friend with my mother. At the same time it was the next stage in saying good-bye to an often enchanted and meaningful youth, and finding myself in the complex and lonely world of adult compromises and moral relativity.

The study itself turned out to be influential. In the introduction to the Second Edition of the book re-published in 1999, Professor James Sharpe wrote:

> There are not many history books which entirely change the perception of their chosen field of study. One such was Alan Macfarlane's *Witchcraft in Tudor and Stuart England: A Regional and Comparative Study*, which was first published in 1970. The work originated as an Oxford University D.Phil. thesis completed under the supervision of Keith Thomas, then fellow of St. John's College, whose own magisterial study of popular beliefs in the sixteenth and seventeenth centuries, *Religion and the Decline of Magic*, appeared a year later. The treatment of witchcraft in the latter book, where it constituted a major theme, overlapped with Macfarlane's, and one can imagine how ideas about the subject had flowed between student and supervisor in an intense and fruitful intellectual exchange... *Witchcraft in Tudor and Stuart England* represented a remarkable methodological and conceptual breakthrough in the study of a particularly intractable, and much misunderstood, historical problem and although more recent research has challenged and to some extent overtaken it, it remains a classic in its field.

So this book is both a biographical study of my life, but also gives hints of how the creative process works in exploring a new set of ideas.

1963

In the study of my school years I separated off the life at school and at home in the Lake district. In my undergraduate years at Oxford the text was divided into terms, and the social life and letters were separated from the essays and work. This type of arrangement does not work for postgraduate life. Terms are much less important as most of my time was either in Oxford, Essex or the Lakes and did not keep to the term boundaries. Furthermore the intellectual work and my letters and social life are fused together and really inseperable.

So I have arranged the materials in strict chronological order, except for the last chapter on storage technologies. Occasionally it has been necessary to place a letter or piece of writing a little out of order as it straggles across the months, but almost always it is possible to place it within a particular monthly time frame.

1963 - October

I moved into digs at 19 Chalfont Road, Oxford, about 20 minutes' walk north of Worcester College. I imagine that the housing was arranged through the College. I do not remember searching for it or having difficulty in finding it. Meals could still be taken in College and the structure of what the College provided is evident. The battels for my first term as a postgraduate show what use I was making of College facilities, and the cost of tuition and other items.[1]

---

[1] 'H.T.' refers to the Hilary (Spring) Term, 'M.T.' to the Michaelmas or autumn term.

WORCESTER COLLEGE, OXFORD

Battels for Michaelmas Term, 1963

A. D. J. Macfarlane, Esq

	£	s.	d.
Inclusive charge for Board and Lodging			
Meals in Hall	4.	4.	0
Guests Meals			
Guests Accommodation	4.	0.	0
Boat Club Dinner			
Debating Society Dinner			
Hockey Club Dinner			
Kingsley Club Party			
Buttery Account			
Kitchen Account			
Coupons			
Gratuities			
Laundry		11.	6
Heat			
J.C.R. Art Fund			
Postage and Messenger		1.	4
J.C.R. Scholarship		10.	0
Damage			
Library-book Fines			
Junior Common Room	1.	0.	0
College Clubs	4.	0.	0
College Dues	15.	0.	0
University Dues	4.	15.	0
Library Dues	1.	10.	0
	35.	11.	10
Tuition Fee	18.	0.	0
Key Deposits			
B.U. Provident Association			
Oxford Society			
Debtor Balance brought forward ...			
Prepayment for H.T. 1964	25.	0.	0
	78.	11.	10

Credit:	£	s.	d.
Prepayment for M.T. 1963 ...	9.	1.	7-
Credit Balance of last account			
Scholarship			
Exhibition	44.	5.	0-
Ministry of Education ...			
Local Authority			
Cash			

	£	s.	d.
Balance Due to the College £	25.	5.	3*

The College meets for next term on Friday, 17th January, 1964.

If these battels are not paid by 25th January 1964 a fine will be imposed unless permission has been obtained from the Domestic Bursar for postponement of this payment.

The whole of this form, with the appended slip completed, should be forwarded with your remittance for the exact amount to National Provincial Bank Limited, 32, Cornmarket Street, Oxford. Cheques should be made payable to Worcester College, Oxford.

I had spent the summer in the Lake District thinking a good deal about what I would like to pursue in my intellectual life whether I went on to University or not. At the heart of this was an interest in the sixteenth-and-seventeenth century growth of what I thought of as a split between the head and the heart, the 'dissociation of sensibility' as T.S. Eliot called it. I felt that at the end of my undergraduate days I was losing that sense of childhood which I had clung onto, and was now entering a world of relativity, where magic and enchantment were being lost. I was going through the Wordsworthian transition to adulthood and was trying to come to terms with this through reading and thinking.

So when I found that I would have the opportunity to go on to do two or three years serious research I wanted to find a subject that would carry on this interest. At first it seemed to me that one way into a huge topic which encompassed the rise of science, the rise of capitalism and modernity, etc., was through taking one small part – educational change. So when I arrived back in Oxford I started to investigate the possibility of doing my research on education, particularly primary education, in the sixteenth and seventeenth centuries.

I wrote almost immediately to the Regius Professor of History at Oxford, Hugh Trevor-Roper, who would become one of my chief correspondents during this period.

Hugh Trevor-Roper, Later Lord Dacre

2.10.63 Worcester College, Oxford

Dear Professor Trevor-Roper,

I graduated with a 2nd. class degree this summer & have been awarded a State Studentship. I hope to receive permission to study for a B.Litt. on C17-C16 history & am informed that you interview applicants for such study. I wonder, therefore, if you could kindly see me sometime at your own convenience. I apologise for leaving this so late, but I have only just been informed by the Ministry that I cannot postpone my award for a year.

Yours sincerely,

Alan Macfarlane

1963

One of those whom I turned to for advice was Brian Harrison. Brian was then into the later part of his D.Phil. on the temperance movement and I was already heavily in his debt in several ways. He had lent me all his wonderful undergraduate files of notes which I had largely re-typed, and shown me his filing system – little cards of a subject index – which transformed my life. He also gave me a piece of general advice when I arrived back.

"The Cottage", 18a, Pembridge Place, W2.

5 Oct

Dear Alan:

How kind of you to write! I'm so glad you're staying on. I'd do a D.Phil. if I were you, but I'm sure nobody would stop you doing a B.Litt. It all depends what you want to do afterwards: B.Litt is good for teaching – width but no depth: D.Phil is good for researching – depth but no width (though I don't really see why chronological width is a virtue). But we can talk about this. Of course I will talk about methods of research, though it's rather an individual matter, and I'm geared to the typewriter. How about coming to St. Antony's for dinner on Friday 18 Oct, in my room by 7? Let me know at St. Antony's after I get back on Sunday 13th Oct, or here before then. Why not write for Hist.Today yourself? Brian

I heard from Trevor-Roper's secretary arranging a time for an interview.[1]

8th October, 1963

Dear Mr. Macfarlane,

---

[1] Adam Sisman very kindly provided a copy of this and other letters from Trevor-Roper's archive in Oxford.

Professor Trevor-Roper has asked me to write and thank you for your letter of the 2nd October seeking for an interview with regard to your proposed advanced degree. Could you please call on him here, in this Library, at 9.30 A.m. on Friday, 11th October? If this is not convenient perhaps you would let me know and we could arrange some other time. Yours sincerely, ... Secretary

Notes in Trevor-Roper's hand:
viva'd for First
F.P [Foreign Paper] 1494-1648
Sp Sj Commonwealth
wants to teach
interested in econ hy, lit: educational history: e.g. on secondary & elementary teaching in England in C17 ? perhaps in N. England
supervisor ? Hill

My mother wrote from Cherideo Tea Estate, Assam, on October 9th 1963.

So glad to hear you have come to roost safely in Oxford, full circle to St Margarets Road or almost. It is lovely to think of you settling down in front of another fire with your typewriter and your tapes, you haven't said what your thesis is going to be about yet or how long it will last. We have just read Robert Graves "Goodbye to all that" and enjoyed it enormously, is he still at Oxford? I see one of his prep schools was Copthorne about which he is gently scathing. I have finished "I Claudius" and am reading the sequel now, a little ponderous in parts and I get muddled with the relationships but am enjoying it all the same. Interesting that J. Caeser, Alexander and Akbar were all epileptic – perhaps there are more – subject for a thesis there? ... Creative work <u>is</u> very tiring, even though it is stimulating, perhaps because. I have started dabbling with my oils again but I find it the most soothing of occupations, knowing I am not good I have no standards to strive for whereas in my writing I'm always falling short and suffering. No thats not true really, it's the struggle for adjectives that tires me, I have now got a notebook full of adjectives which I riffle through when I'm stuck, all wrong I'm sure but in history one is constantly describing people and trying to find new words to do it with. .. No news about my article, perhaps they have shelved it after all, do hope I get paid for it in time for Christmas!... Thank you for sending the money to Anne, I presume your grant has arrived and you are all right for the time being? We shall be sending money home every month, but are hoping to be able to have a little put by for our leave so that we can go to Manchester for the afternoon without breaking out in a sweat of anguish every few minutes – shall always remember that last trip with did with Felicity and David Porter and not enough money to give them a decent meal! ... I am on my last Moghul book so hope to hear something from the national library soon, I really should mug up the whole of Indian history to get the perspective right but keep putting it off.

Have a happy term (?), Much love from us both, Mummy

My mother wrote from Cherideo on 18th October 1964:

Thank you for a letter yesterday, explaining your programme - I hope the sense of purposelessness has left you and also your headaches. If there is nothing wrong with your eyes these are probably due to nervous tension and will disappear as soon as you see your way clear - you have had quite a lot to cope with this year in the way of ordeals, interviews etc. and it is quite likely that your nerves have got jangled in the process. On the other hand if you have doubts about having chosen the right course it might be that. I think your restless uncertain feeling is almost inevitable and will recur to bother you at intervals but the only thing is to plod on and wait for it to pass. One must have a sense of fate (or divine guidance perhaps) and the fact that you were offered the studentship would surely be a pointer that that is the road you are supposed to tread. I suppose it is a bit primitive to look for "signs" but I have found it a comfort. I do hope you get Hill as your supervisor, I'm afraid I've never heard of him,

I think a study of education might be indeed very useful and anyway I don't think study is ever wasted, it leads you into so many unexpected byways and forms new contacts that are always enriching.

I will refund you the £10 that F. didn't, we would like to give you a course of driving lessons and when we come home will try to get some sort of car for you – you could take the lessons at Oxford it would be easier, if you will let us know what they cost we will make it a birthday present. Presume your grant has come? ... You were born in Shillong by the way and were there again from four to five – you had your tonsils out there – don't you remember it at all? I hope to do some browsing in the library there this time, I'm coming to the end of my books, I think I will send you a list of the ones I chiefly want and Blackwells might be able to get them, only I insist on paying for them....Richard sent me a parcel of books for my birthday, at the moment I'm reading "Orlando" by Virginia Woolf which is very odd – the hero goes to sleep and wakes up as a woman – I'm sure it is terribly significant but what of eludes me. Very well written of course. Have just finished the "Claudius" books and liked them though I thought they were too long and detailed, it had a soporific effect in the end. Mysticism is still claiming some of my attention too, I could never be a real mystic because to deny the senses would be to lose the best and most beautiful of life's experiences – but I envy them their ability to break through to the reality that is just out of reach. What they chiefly lack is a sense of humour it seems, they take themselves so seriously, one of them even rejoices when her husband and children die because they are distracting her! ... Your descriptions of autumn in Oxford remind us of that last day we spent trailing our feet through leaves in Worcester Coll. gardens – autumn is always the time of having to go away and leave you all and rather a terrible time to me for that reason, last year I remember the trees opposite the flat we left Anne and Felicity in and the wet roads on the way back from Manchester and the smell of fires, all so sad, so sad. Next autumn will be the last leave-taking though.

The fullest account I have of my feelings at this exact point of time is in a letter on 24th October to Felicity Cowan, my godmother's daughter and later my sister Anne's flatmate, who had gone to South America, a girl I had known since we were both children. I explained my predicament in some detail.

Term began nearly two weeks ago but it doesn't make much difference to me – except that there are many more distractions. I decided just before it began that I would have a campaign to meet some nice girls & thus joined several unlikely clubs such as the 'Communists' 'Humanists' etc. The attempt exceeded my expectations. On Monday last I met a sweet (tho' I didn't find her physically attractive) girl called Georgina who knows Gavin Maxwell & likes all the right things – poetry, animals, children's stories. Then on Tuesday I went to the "Heritage" guitar club where amid a terrible crush and with my voice almost gone I managed to make friends with a sweet young Dutch girl called Dorothy. She has long blond hair (not as nice as yours) and an innocent but serious expression & is at one of the tutorial colleges at Oxford before going to Leyden Univ. We arranged vaguely to meet at a Ballet club talk the next evening but since she didn't arrive within half an hour of its starting I went off to a Mozart opera instead – 'The Marriage of Figaro'.

There I came across a strange girl called Helen who I had been rebuffed by last term this term she was more friendly & I took her out to dinner & a film on Thursday & she came around with a friend called Peter to sample my cooking (imagine me preparing chips, mushrooms, chips, tomatoes, mixed veg, soup etc on a tiny "baby Belling" !) – surprisingly we were still friends & I saw her on Sunday evening at her room in St Annes. All the time I was feeling a bit mean since though she is very sweet etc I was only half attracted to her & didn't want to hurt her (when I tell this to friends they all say I'm conceited, that a girl is very careful before getting committed, but perhaps I'm morbidly sensitive but I know that if a girl paid me attentions & didn't really mean it I'd be hurt). Anyway on Monday I bumped into (almost literally) an American girl – Simone – who had just arrived in England & we went to see "The Devil's Eye" by Bergman – a comedy ("A woman's chastity is a sty in the devil's eye" – so Don Juan is sent up to remove the trouble). On Tuesday on the vague hope of meeting Dorothy at the guitar club I went along about an hour after it had started. I found her there talking to another MAN! Having mentally sunk through the floor into the bar-parlour below & refreshed myself with a stiff drink I awoke in time to find her standing talking to me. So we walked home singing Tom Lehrer etc. Then I had to go home – catching a train up to Windermere one day & back again the next.

Yesterday evening I found myself in a complicated, but amusing in retrospect situation. I had said to Helen that I would see her on Thursday but now, of course, I wanted to see Dorothy. "Half beast & half God" that I am like all men, I decided on compromise. I was also asked to a History Society meeting – I would go to Helen & if she wasn't in I would go round to Dorothy. If H was in I would ask her to the meeting – if she didn't want to come I would go & see D. She was in & didn't want to come but I hadn't foreseen two things a) that she was much nicer & more unprotected than I remembered b) I would have to tell a lie viz that I was going round to the meeting when really going to see Dorothy. So I stood & dithered & looked indecisive until I had quite infuriated her. In the end with burning mouth I told my lie – found Dorothy was not in & sought propitiation by going to work for an hour sticking on labels at OXFAM. I don't know why I bore you with all this - - please forgive me, but it helps to purge me of my guilty feelings & will show you what petty, deceitful & over-serious people we (I) are!

My work is not going too smoothly since I still don't have much idea what I will be doing or even if I have been officially accepted – let alone an official supervisor. I may have told you that there is a possibility that I might get Christopher Hill who is perhaps the most brilliant & certainly one of the nicest historians on the C17 in England. The more one thinks about subjects of course the more there appears to be done. Once I have started I will probably bore you to tears by trying to describe what I am doing. It is one of the tragedies that one becomes so specialized that there is no-one – except perhaps one's supervisor – to whom one can talk about one's subject with. One is cut off from the rest of humanity in an unshared absorption. The danger is, of course, that any charity etc one has will also be destroyed. I must copy down that text of St Paul's. 'Though I speak with the tongues of men & of angels, & have not charity, I am become as sounding brass, or a tinkling cymbal. And though I have the gift of prophecy and understand all mysteries, and all knowledge; … and have not charity, I am nothing."

It is very difficult here where intellect counts for so much and when one is just beginning to realise the joys of disinterested thought, when one is just beginning to be able to criticize other eminent writers and see their basic prejudices clearly not to become conceited, academic, or at the least slightly "superior". To smile with slight disdain at the "people" or those in the past who were wrong. Humility is so hard – so is a continued contact with the things in life which really matter – love, beauty, God, sorrow, sympathy. That's why I wanted to get away from all this for a year because one can positively feel human feelings being dried out of one – like a wet garment steaming in front of a fire. Perhaps one is soggy & sentimental & escapist before – one believes in things, hates things, rejoices in things etc – but is this worse than being a dried parchment on which "the moving hand has write & then moves on?"

I am still thinking of doing "education" as my topic but hoping to approach it from a slightly new angle. Most books on the subject up to now have been school histories, narrative & political with a touch of the economic background. If I stress the economic & the factors allowing the remarkable growth of education in the C16 and C17 and also the emotional factors – the clash with old superstitions and rites, the breaking down of old ideas and beliefs, the psychological & anthropological aspects in fact I might be able to give a depth & humanity to facts which can so easily become stale.

Sunday 27th October 1963 Worcester College, Oxford

Dear Mummy and Daddy,

Thank you very much for your letter of the 18th which gives the first hint of the cold weather. The feeling of purposelessness and the headaches have gone at the moment and I am dazed with the excitement of a whole new field of ideas. I expect that part of the trouble was starting hard work after a longish rest. I still don't feel I'm doing enough - about 5 hours a day - & suddenly have an outburst of horror at the thought of the petty-minded & dry person this specialization may turn me into. But the struggles become weaker & I turn again with joy to the intricacies of myths & superstitious in the C16. I still haven't heard who my supervisor is, am still praying for Hill, tho' won't hope for too much.

Thank you very much for the offers about driving. I have always been rather reluctant to learn as you know - or rather too lazy. For myself I would be more than happy to doodle around on a motorbike or bus all my life, but I suppose I must learn to bear my responsibilities in our modern society instead of sponging on the charity of others. Please don't think of buying me a car, I might buy some kind of motorized transport tho' since I want to be able to visit all the beautiful churches, forests & houses round Oxford. I would like to put off driving lessons until you're back & I can co-ordinate them with practices under Daddy's tuition. My attitude to cars at the moment is rather the same idealistic & immature one I have towards marriage - i.e. it complicates life & brings all sorts of new responsibilities. I don't think I am too afraid of the responsibilities etc, but at the moment the hampering of personal freedom is uppermost in my mind. Badly explained but a healthy adolescent 'student' emotion I expect! ...

Yes, my grant has come - tho' it is disappearing at an alarming rate. This wasn't helped by having to go up North last week to collect the rest of my stuff for £5 and then having my graduate gown (£4) stolen from the college. The visit to Field Head went off smoothly despite the sprained ankle. Granny & Grandpa seemed on good form & I was sorry not to be staying longer. They said that Fiona was superficially very tired when she came up the previous week-end, but a bath & some good food worked wonders. I can understand her situation for though I am much quieter & less energetic I sometimes get into the same rushing life from which she suffers. It is the penalty of having too many friends & interests & it means that I eat a bit irregularly - often fish & chips between one place & another. But it has many compensations - a wealth of activities & ideas crammed into a small space. I am told I am looking a bit tired, which wasn't helped by forgetting to put my alarm back an hour this morning & emerging bleary-eyed for communion at 7 p.m. instead of 8 p.m!

About the books you mention. Do send a list of books you want. I might be able to get some of them cheap since I know several girls who work with the O.U.P & at a bookshop in Oxford. I will be collecting my parcel of books for your Christmas presents soon so tell me a) if there is anything either of you would like especially in this line b) if you would prefer to have something other than books. I haven't read 'To Kill a Mockingbird', tho' I saw the film in a rather dazed way in Burnley with Jean. Am just about to start what looks like a delightful book - 'Arthuro's Island' by Elsa Morante - have you read it? Also have you read 'The Little Prince' by Saint-Exupery - one of the greatest children's/adult books ever written I suppose. And also have you read Lampedusa's 'The Leopard' which has been leant me? What with this, Arthurian literature, C17 literature, Anthropology I am a bit dazed! Graves is lecturing three times this term - on 'Personal Experience in Poetry'. Unfortunately I won't be able to go - still they'll all be printed. Apparently he has a series of dazzling daughters - one of whom is the toast of Oxford as I may have told you, a sort of Zuleika Dobson.

My love life still throbs in its chaotic way. On Tuesday I went to the guitar club about an hour after it started in the vague chance of seeing Dorothy that Dutch girl there. The place was steaming with rank humanity packed in gaping hordes & one thought several cruel & Laurentian things about 'how beastly are the bourgeoisie' etc. Actually the singing was very good. Anyhow I discovered Dorothy there & we went & had a coffee & walked back to St Clare's thro' the romantic evening mist with the dim north-Oxford street-lamps casting a mysterious glow on the late roses & autumn leaves; I am hoping to see her again today or tomorrow. I saw Helen last night & in a suitably ideal situation - candles, wine, a delightful mess-up cooked by your honourable son - listened to Schubert Lieder. It makes my Puritan conscience feel sickly to have every sort of carnal pleasure around me - while the millions suffer in silence. I don't think I would ever be a successful sensualist sadly.

You will have been to Shillong when you get to this. I hope it went well. Much love to you both,
Alan

My mother wrote again from a cottage in Shillong on 31st October 1963

My dear Alan,

I'm afraid I didn't write last week. I suddenly found the post office shut for days & days & on the Monday we left to come up here. Your letters will all be piling up too - I hope.

We wondered whether we were doing a dotty thing in setting off on leave with no accommodation booked – and so much to arrange in the way of pruning programmes, dogs, digs & packing away of books & linen to stop the rats eating them – but have found ourselves in the most delicious little log cabin among pine woods with Khasis yodelling all round us and the golf course only 10 minutes away.

.... I shall come here to write my book when I eventually finish my notes on it. My only regret is I haven't got the dogs who would have adored it, but by the time we had piled bedding, stoves etc. in the car there was very little room left.

We spent a night in the rest house at Gauhati & were chewed alive by mosquitos which bored through the sheets like little drills – none here, but the nights are icy, four blankets & all the windows closed & I still wake up at 5 a.m. frozen but Daddy is ready to get up & brew up tea. Everything tastes & feels so good & all the little worries & frustrations of Nazira P.O. have been forgotten.

I've joined the library & am reading a book on Warren Hastings but rather spasmodically. Hope you're settled into your routine. Will write again - at length. Much love, Mummy

Christopher Hill

My hope that I would get Christopher Hill as a supervisor looked as if it would be realized, as I was summoned to meet the great man. As an undergraduate Hill's books had been an inspiration and part of my desire to go on to do research was the wish to be supervised by him. My first letter from Hill gives a nice indications of his almost unreadable, but friendly and egalitarian hand-writing when he was already Master of Balliol.

Balliol College,
Oxford.

[For those who cannot read the his handwriting, it says: 'Dear Mr. MacFarlane, The History Board has asked me to discuss your research with you. Could you see me at 11.15 a.m. to-morrow (Friday)? Failing that, 12.0 noon on Tuesday? Yours sincerely, Christopher Hill]

I went to see him and remember he explained that the subject of education at the primary level, which I was thinking would be a good research topic, was probably impossible due to shortage of a serious set of records. He asked me what else I was interested in. I remember answering myth (Arthurian), sexual relations and witchcraft and his quipping that his former pupil Keith Thomas was the person I should go to see – he knew more about sex (in the seventeenth century anyway) than he did. I was perhaps disappointed for though I had been to Keith's very good undergraduate lectures on political theory, and he had been on the board that gave me a viva at the end of my undergraduate Finals, he was young (only eight years older than I) and I knew little about him.

1963 - November

Keith Thomas

St. John's College
Oxford

Telephone 47671/2

13 Nov
1963

It looks as if I may be supervising you after all! Could you call in sometime – next Monday (18th) at 12.15 would suit me.

KVT

I am not sure what the 'after all' refers to – perhaps I had been in touch with him earlier and been dissuaded, or there was still a chance of Christopher Hill for a while.

As for my good fortune in being Keith's first student, I shall dwell on that later as I devote a good deal of attention to our relationship, which became one of the half dozen most important in my life, and certainly the most important intellectually at Oxford.

My mother wrote from Shillong on Nov 6th 1963

My dear Alan,

No letters have reached us here yet, so I feel very cut off but I expect there's been the usual hitch somewhere. Such a beautiful day, I'm sitting outside the golf-club looking over the wooded hills & watching hooded Khasi women carry bundles of wood up the green snake of a road that slides from here down into a valley & then up again to our little hut...

This is the next day & we are having a lunch picnic beside an emerald green river with pine trees coming down to white sandbanks and water frothing over elephant grey boulders exactly like the Duddon but bigger – a cloudless day although we are nearly at Cherrapungi, the wettest place in the world (?). We're both burnt to cinders from golf & it is all quite perfect & J.S. seems a million miles away & quite unimportant.

I've read & made notes on "Warren Hastings" since I've been here to feel it hasn't been frittered time completely – Daddy has been a bit on edge but feeling happier that things have come to a head, one of our ex-planters & a great friend of his has been around to talk to, he has a Khasi wife & has retired up here – seems to be happy but I wonder if one can ever really settle in a foreign country. I don't think I could. Daddy wants to move on so must leave this blissful place – will post this in Shillong.

Don't worry about us, we might all be together for Christmas - sometimes I feel it would be the best thing for us all. No letters have come to us here so hope all is well with you.
Much love, Mummy

In a letter of November 24 1963 from Cherideo my mother wrote:

My dear Alan,
A rather sad letter from you written on a wet Sunday evening - I agree that Sunday evenings are sad (the Assamese would have a word for it!). I think it's something to do with school, I always remember feeling overcome by a sort of pleasant but heavy gloom after chapel on Sunday evening, in that case probably a combination of evensong and an empty stomach as we never had much to eat for lunch - but the nostalgic feeling has lasted and I always want to listen to music or poetry and brood. I'm sorry you have broken with Dorothy, alas no relationship can stand still and usually leads sooner or later to an impasse. I hope you will find someone else to fill the void, I'm glad the work is interesting anyway, I shall certainly come and look at the Indian art and would also be helped by seeing your system of cross reference and filing - my little cards are already cram jam full and I shall have to reorganize them soon. I shant have much time for work for the next month or so as I have this young girl to entertain, I've sent for some books from Calcutta library so if they don't come or I think of anything I'll let you know.... We are all shocked and saddened by the Kennedy affair,[1] *without Television or wireless we haven't probably felt the full impact of it as you have at home but it does seem a fearful waste and makes one wonder for the millionth time who is running this crazy world. We had Father James staying with us at the beginning of the week, I would have been interested to talk it over with him but the Catholic answer is always the same and one envies them the discipline of their faith. ...*

Let me know when you go home and for how long - it will be little cabins on the landing for all I fear as the house is groaning at the seams or will be unless Beryl can help. Fiona's last letter was full of resolutions to live a more regulated life but she finds people come bursting in the whole time and stay half the night and all is as before. Anne will be quite close to you at Sutton Coldfield so will perhaps be able to come over occasionally..... Don't forget to send me Penny's address.
With much love from us both, Mummy

Finally, there is a letter from my history schoolmaster from Sedbergh, Andrew Morgan, who had played the key role in getting me prepared to go to Oxford. As this is such an important link, which continued until Andrew's death, I will include a scan of the letter which was obviously a request for any information he had about witchcraft.

[1] The assassination of President John Kennedy on 22nd November.

SEDBERGH SCHOOL
SEDBERGH
YORKSHIRE

25th November '63

My dear Alan,

How delightful to hear from you. I had heard yr good news from Robert but had not known what you were intending to choose as your subject. My congratulations to you on your research studentship.

I'm afraid I'm going to be a completely broken reed for your purposes. I have absolutely no knowledge of any witchcraft beliefs in Sedbergh — though I do believe that we have no Room 13 either! You refer to the sad case of Mrs. Bailey. She is still with us. She is indeed a foreigner — French married to an Englishman who left her. Dogs and cats have now left us, but she, pathetically, still gathers her herbs and brews brews and scrounges food where she can. Now she may think of herself as being regarded by others as a witch, but this is a classic case of persécution mania. Never have I heard any of the locals express anything suggesting that they thought her a witch: squalid a nuisance, a scrounger, smelly thieving filthy, insanitary — yes, all these, but never ascribing nefarious talents to her. No, alas, poor Mrs. Bailey is too easily explained as an outsider who has kept her highly 'foreign' ways and has refused to be assimilated with the local community. (Four Poles for examples have been assimilated & are highly respected members of the community)

About 10 days ago (just about the time you wrote, I think) there was an item in the Yorkshire Post (front page) about a contemporary Yorkshire witch — she complaining that there were so few of her sort now. Alas, I know no more.

Rather lamely I'm going to wish you great joy in your hunt & leave you in the lurch. I'm sorry to be so inadequate but I'll certainly let you know if I come across anything. Best wishes, Andrew Morgan.

1963 - December

My mother wrote on December 7th 1963 from Cherideo

Crack of dawn and I'm trying to get my letter written in the swirly early morning mist, I have a fifteen year old guest and somehow find myself occupied from dawn to dusk in listening to Cliff Richard chatter or in otherwise occupying her. She has taken the dogs out for a walk now so I hope I can finish this. Thank you for your letter, I'm glad you and Dorothy are friends again (or perhaps not, my remarks are always slightly of date!). I hope you'll be able to find a satisfying pattern for your relationship, not easy ever. the work sounds fascinating, as you say the field is almost limitless, I find the same in my meagre way, I should know all about the different religious sects which figure largely in Indian history, and every character mentioned ought to be investigated, and then theres architecture and medecine and so on. Actually I'm feeling most depressed about it at the moment as I've just had a letter from the library in Calcutta saying they can' supply any of the four books I wrote for as they are "out of print". All of them were on the library catalogue, so it's obvious that none of the book I want will be available. I feel like giving up, it is so hopeless trying to get any help here, I can see now why Indian students are so frustrated. I will make a list out for you and perhaps you can get a few of them – the trouble is I can't afford to buy them all as they will be expensive books and some of them I will probably need only to skim through. Anyway enough of my tiny personal problems, Christmas is hardly the time to air them, I always find it a bit depressing these days to be indulging in orgies of eating and drinking when half the world is hungry and lonely and unwanted – this is not the Spirit I know, but it is the one time I would really like to go out and do something helpful and perhaps boring and unpleasant, but instead I always follow the old routine and sink in guilt and indigestion. While we're on the subject, I have sent a cheque for £35 to your bank, could you please send or give £10 to Anne for a present and pocket money, keep £10 for yourself for your birthday and Christmas and give Fiona £5 for her Christmas. The remaining £10 is for you and F. to use as you need during the hols (I have paid Granny for your keep separately). I hope this will be enough, I am imagining that you have some grant left, let me know how that is going. I have a strong feeling you should get a suit, a nice one, perhaps on the never never?[1] *... I stayed up till midnight last night reading "The Unicorn" by Iris Murdoch, a fascinating book. My proof copy arrived several days ago but I haven't had time to correct it yet, as usual they have removed quite a lot of the choicest bits and drastically pruned the rest, very disappointing to find a carefully balanced sentence with the two most important words taken out but it's best not for me to argue, I suppose they know best.*[2] *My Peter Quennell has been busy editing William Hickey and writing a book on Shakespeare so I don't suppose he had anything to do with it.*[3] *Your books for Daddy have arrived and he is writing to thank you, I've read the Goshawk which is delicious but very sad, I wish I could write a mixture of T.H. White and Forster....*

My mother wrote again from Cherideo on December 12th 1963

Daddy got his birthday greetings off yesterday he says, so I hope one of us will hit the nail on the head. I feel this should be a very auspicious year, 22 being my lucky number and the 22nd year of our marriage as well (Sir J. Frazer would have some crushing revelations on the subject of lucky numbers). Anyway, I hope you will have a happy day, Granny will see to the food side of it I know, and will not spend it wishing that someone who isn't there was. We shall be thinking of you and wishing as usual that we weren't separated again, half my life seems to have been spent sitting round moping about lost

---

[1] The 'never never' was a popular term for hire, or delayed, purchase.
[2] Iris Macfarlane, 'An English Ambassador at the Court of the Great Moghul; The Embassy of Sir Thomas Roe 1615-1619', *History Today*, November 1964.
[3] Peter Quennell was, along with Alan Hodge, the editor of *History Today*.

occasions. The only comfort we have is that in spite of almost continual separations we don't seem to have drifted too far apart as a family, in this case distance has lent freshness to our relationship I think, if Fiona is around to read this she will have some caustic remarks to make on my laborious birthday philosophizing! The happy thought has just struck me that you will all be together for a few days so that my Christmas letter won't have to be thrice repeated, it will arrive in a couple of days I hope. I haven't sent my immediate family cards I'm afraid, they arrived too late to send by Sea Mail! I have a vivid picture of Field Head at the moment with cooking smells and Christmas cards propped up among the Staffordshire cows and Fiona leaping about knocking nails into the beams for the holly and the usual panic about the lights and the decorations, which will be unearthed from the bottom of the compost heap eventually or the lowest box in the shed. The nicest part was the walk across the dawn fields to church with pink frost and Hawkshead in a mist and Fiona going green and having to be chased out. One is inclined to forget the acres of greasy plates and tangerine peel under the beds for days afterwards. Here nothing could be less festive... Would you like me to make any investigation on Assamese brand witchcraft or have you enough on your plate? ....I wonder how Stephen Grieve is, perhaps you will see him during the holiday, he was always my favourite among the young. this is a very boring birthday letter, I'm sorry, I haven't had time to work and our conversational level for the whole last week has stuck at pop stars and I feel slightly soggy mentally – but you know all the things I would like to say and how we are bursting with pride at your achievements and full of confidence in your future. I wrote you a poem on your first birthday and feel faintly like writing another now, but my standards being higher I seldom attempt to reach them.[1]

I was starting to plan what I might try to research, as these first pages show. This became somewhat more refined in later plans, which I typed out in December, either in Oxford or the Lakes.

[1] The poem on my first birthday, along with further poems to me, my father and others, are published in Iris Macfarlane, *Love's Legacy: Selected Poems* (2017).

LIST OF TOPICS. 12/63.

I.GENERAL.

✓ Puritanism & witchcraft.
Educational changes & witchcraft.
Differences between English & Scottish witchcraft (also continental)
Robin Hood & the witches.
The sects & the witches.
Oliver Cromwell & the witches.
Economic changes & witchcraft beliefs.
Plague,medicine & witchcraft.
The Civil War & witchcraft.
Mathew Hopkins.
Class & professional attitudes to witchcraft.
Witchcraft & superstitions in towns & villages contrasted.
Witchcraft & the scientific societies.
Witchcraft & the Royal Society.
Witchcraft & the royal family.
Witchcraft & psychic phenomena.
Witchcraft & insanity.
Witchcraft & the relationships between the sexes.
Witchcraft in the C17 & C19s.
Witchcraft, historical & contemporary.
Statistics of witchcraft.
Fairies + witches.
Arthur + the witches.
Literature + witchcraft – light on C17 'dissociation'.
Witchcraft + the place of women in C17.

II.INTERPRETATIONS OF WITCHCRAFT.

The historiography of witchcraft study.
The value of the anthropological approach.
The value of a study of witchcraft.
The sources for a study of witchcraft.

TOPICS.(ii)

EVI.ECONOMIC.

What clues does the study of economic history offer ?
A comparison of different geographical & temporal areas in economic terms.
Economic & social factors in 1640-1660 witchcraft.
Famine, economic depression & witchcraft.
The growth of industry & towns & witchcraft.
(How much did the new trades,by bringing the West into contact with Oriental & African ideas allow in new witch beliefs - cf at Salem where the scare was started by a negro maid. Were trade connections & consequent intercourse responsible for the similarities between French & Scottish witchcraft e.g?)

My justification for what I was doing, clearly written at the same time, gives further insight into the central theme of the disenchantment of the world.

THE STUDY OF WITCHCRAFT.

Introduction.

"For my part, I have ever believed, & do know, that there are witches". (Sir Thomas Browne)

The value of a study of witchcraft in the C17 is that it allows one to peer into dim borderlands of sex, religion & belief which are usually covered. It allows an analysis of the point where many levels of experience & thought converge & where accepted & often unconscious forces break into view. Using attitudes to witchcraft & the statistics of witch trials as a thermometer one can measure from a new angle many of the problems which continue to vex historians. The decline of belief in witches throws into more detail the clash between older religious concepts & the new scientific ideas; the decline of belief in 'supernatural' causation and the emphasis on 'natural' causes with its severing of organic & emotional ties with an 'otherworld' of dark & unmeasurable spiritual forces illustrates the process somewhat notoriously known as the 'dissociation of sensibility'. Attitudes of various religious groups & outstanding theologians throws further light on the ethical differences of 'puritans' & 'the rest'. More factually one is given an insight into medical practices & the opposition to new medical ideas, on the extent of mental unbalance & the antecedents of psychic experience. Hints as to the relationship between economic changes & popular beliefs, between plague, political upheaval &

One final list of questions gives another way in:

Witchcraft.

Problems.

How, when, where, why was.......

The worst outbreaks.
The highest percentage of convictions.
The types of offences.
The most women convicted.
The higher classes involved
Ordeals & tests most often used.
"Familiars" most often used in evidence.
Popular opinion roused.
Roman Catholicism involved.
Puritanism or sectarianism involved.
Plague involved.
Economic distress involved.
Politicial tensions involved.
Class interests involved.
Differences from county to county.
Differences from country to country.
Differences in different years.
Differences from modern witchcraft.
Differences between educated & uneducated opinion.
Differences in the views of different professions - clergy, lawyers!..
Changing attitudes of the monarchy.
Effect of scientific ideas(esp. medical')
Effect of theological ideas.
Relationship to general myths, legends & underworld of belief.

Various angles.
Economic....
Political...
Sociological...
Anthropological....
Theological.....
Literature & culture...
Biographical.....
Constitutional...
Religious.....
Legal.....
Medical.....
Philosophical...
Psychological & psychic.....

One of the first books I read in my new field was K.M. Briggs *Anatomy of Puck.* My somewhat niggly review of the former is one of my first writings on the subject. Later I met her and warmed to her work and recommended her books strongly to my Extension Lectures students. For the record, here is my first book review, and the one letter I have from this erudite and delightful lady, as I recall her.

REVIEW. K.M.BRIGGS. 'ANATOMY OF PUCK'. (Dec.1963)

Most useful for references. Clear, sensible & competent her failing is not that she loses her way, but that the way she sets herself is so plain & easy. She is content to narrate & not to question very deeply, thus leaving aside most of the difficult & interesting problems. For instance she never really asks if writers really believed in the fairies they wrote of; how beliefs changed with time & what caused the changes both in general & in detail; how fairy beliefs were related to other thought, religious, social, political etc; what ideas replaced the dying anthropomorphism, how much of the older structure remained & how great was the vacuum; why fairy-beliefs differed geographically; what function fairy beliefs served etc.

Her method is partly responsible for this narrowness since it is the comparative one whose archetype is the 'Golden Bough'. This tends to mean a heterogeneous collection of examples from differing regions & times, with no adequate examination of real differences, in the attempt to show what 'C17 man' thought about 'mermaids' or 'monsters' or 'elves' etc. The evidence is almost purely literary which tends to give the impression of unreality & placidity of belief, almost insincerity.

Miss Briggs tends to over-simplify the Puritan re-action to fairies, explaining the merging of witch & fairy beliefs by ascribing to all Puritans a horror-struck reaction to all 'superstitions'. which turned innocent fairies into devils. From Baxter's recognition of fairies as spirits half-way between men & angels we can see that the relationship between fairies & witch-beliefs has more complex origins.

It also seems strange that in a book which deals with basic beliefs which must often have contained coarse gains, even if we reject the fertility origins of the spirits, there is scarcely a reference to the sexual element in folk-beliefs.

Thus we are left with a delightful picture, but a picture which hardly makes us aware of the logic of fairy lore & hardly understanding the depth of fairy-belief.

BRIGGS

The Barn House
Burford
Oxford

Burford 3289

June 5th 1965.

Dear Mr McFarlane,

Here is the book whose title you wanted: Oral Tradition A Study in Historical Methodology by Jan Vansina, Routledge & Kegan Paul, 30s. [not in Bodly] Here also is a card of this season's programme. I will let you have next season's when it is out; but this gives you a notion of the kind of subjects covered.

I very much enjoyed meeting you the other day, and feel that we had only begun our exploration into what can be done to extend the philosophic grasp of folklore study. I feel that you may have something very well worth while to give to the world on that. At present we are trying to work towards greater academic recognition for Folklore.

I hope we may meet again soon.

Yours sincerely,

Katharine M. Briggs.

1964

1964 - January

Iris to Alan, Cherideo on 1st January 1964.

My dear Alan,
This should be a philosophical letter full of speculations and resolutions but don't worry, it won't be. I'm half asleep after getting home at 3 a.m. this morning… I've been lent Graves's "The Greek Myths" which no doubt you will have red, fascinating though I find myself wondering if some of his conclusions aren't a little far-fetched if one had the scholarship to argue. The more I think about it the more I feel you ought to come out here for a year of your thesis and live amongst a community who are practising witchcraft and the mother goddess worship from which it sprang – would anybody give you a grant – or would they let you have your whole grant in a lump sum which would more than pay your passage and you could do some teaching and article writing to keep you going when you arrived. The primitive communities of Assam are being rapidly assimilated, Christianised and ironed out and now is the time to catch them, the Garos or Khasis as the two matriarchal societies would be the best bet, and very little organised study has been made of either of them. I am going to join the Hakluyt society and will be able to get quite a few of my books from them, the ones I really want are the memoirs of the first three Moghul Emperors, Baba, Humayon and Jehangir – these have all been translated and edited by Beveridge but can't be borrowed from any library it seems, and I doubt if you will find them but your friend in the Bodleian might know if there is any way I could get them. I particularly want the Babar-nama. We are going to form a historical association and read each other papers, at least that's the idea but like all ideas here it will probably peter out, we being some of my Assamese friends. Please note any thesises you read or see on Assam as I have promised them that I will try to do some research for them when I come home though quite when I shall find the time I don't know only I do feel for them not being able to get at any reference books or manuscripts. ….Do wonder how you all got on in Field Head or where you laid your heads, you are probably glad to be back to the peace of your own Oxford room. Let us know if you need money to tide you over until your next bit of grant comes in. …

One event of that holidays is brought back in a letter of January 8th from my mother. My Uncle Robert, then a clerk in the House of Commons, had asked me to be god-father to his third daughter, Charlotte, who was to be baptized before Christmas in the Chapel in the House of Commons. I was possibly reasonably dressed underneath an ancient duffle coat, but had long hair and probably battered shoes (and the ancient fishing haversack to which my mother refers below). So when I presented myself outside the House, the policeman was reluctant to let me in, until an embarrassed Robert came and vouched for me. I remember it, in the end, as a happy occasion, though I proceeded to be a useless god-father.

Thank you for a most amusing letter written after Christmas, it made us laugh like mad to think of you arriving with your fishing haversack at the H of C crypt, Julia must have just about died – actually she said you were looking very nice so perhaps you managed to stuff it and the duffle coat behind Big Ben?! Where did you get a suit or was it hired? Really will have to fit you up with some clothes next year but there always seem more important things to spend money on and I do terribly want to get that croft too. ... Your wonderful parcel of books arrived last week, we were horrified to tot up and see how much you spent on them but they were very welcome and I didn't know which to read first. I have actually read "Arturo's Island" which is an absolute classic, quite unlike any childhood portrait I've read before, reminds me of "The Leopard" which I also loved though nobody else here did. Now I'm, half way through "The Nabobs" which is also fascinating and particularly so for me as I'm studying the period. Daddy is reading "Zorba" which he says is very good too, you can't imagine how welcome books are, specially now that we have resigned from the library, but this doesn't mean you are to spend your precious grant on sending us parcels please. I have sent you £20 this month but let me know if you want more. I couldn't be more contented than I am at present.... Like you though I feel pangs when I think of Calcutta and remember the children picking over dustbins and fighting over what they find with starving dogs. I wish I had thought of collecting for Oxfam at Christmas, though Hard-bitten planters would probably not have been very impressed.... I am studying my Assamese fairly hard and soon I hope to go out into the village and will try to collect some folk stories and anything I can on witchcraft. There is talk of starting a historical society too in Nazira but I don't know if it will come to anything... I hope Dorothy will be back soon and nothing will have changed, it was nice to hear Stephen Grieve was himself again but odd that all the rest were either engaged or married, who did David marry?

I wrote a very long letter to my Sedbergh School friend, Ian Campbell in Canada, which summarizes much of what had happened in my first term.

Letter to Ian Campbell on 12th January 1964

My dear Ian,

At last I've stopped procrastinating and answered the awful summons. Each time I write one of these confession sheets I feel as if my whole worthless life is being showed to me by some recording angel, but here goes. I'm not sure if I owe you a letter since I've left all your correspondence in a neat little file at Field Head. Excuse me Therfore if I don't answer vital questions etc.
(I then ask several questions about his life, including *'How is the 'loved one' – is it still Joice & how are your thoughts running on those old topics – God, woman, career etc?) ... My parents will be home this summer so I will probably be staying in England most if not all of the time. They have one more session in India...*

I heard in about July that I'd just missed a first & a bit later that I'd been awarded a State Studentship with which to do research. I wasn't allowed to put off the start of the research so came back up to Oxford – after some delightful weeks working in a Youth Hostel on Ullswater.

I spent about six weeks looking around for an interesting subject on which to do research and for some time thought I would do something on educational history with a view to teaching someday – perhaps in an underdeveloped country. Anyhow the idea was squashed by the various dons I visited on the grounds that the evidence in the C16 and C17 was too dispersed. They asked me for other suggestions & for some inexplicable reason – tho' I've been mildly interested in the subject for a while I suggested doing 'Witchcraft in C17 England' of which they heartily approved. So I'm gradually working my way into a B.Litt. which I would like to turn into a D.Phil (Ph.D.) if I could – but more of that later.

My only other major activity last term was going out with a pretty & sensitive Dutch girl called Doortje or translated badly – Dorothy. (Have I already told you all the above – I have a nasty suspicion I have!) Anyhow my affair with her will come under the heading Sex – para. 1. § - or something to that effect! So I spent the term either working, reading poetry or making love (not in the strictly technical sense as you will learn later & be glad to hear) – with occasional intervals for sleeping & eating.

Last holiday went very quickly – hardly surprising since I only had about 2 weeks (I'm only allowed to be at home 8 weeks of the year). I went to three parties, had a little skating on Tarn Howes (I know it sounds stupid of Canada, but Vancouver is pretty warm – do you get skating. Talking of Vancouver reminds me that I'm reading a book by Ruth Benedict called 'patterns of Culture' in which she describes at length the culture of the 'Kwakiutl' of Vancouver Island, presumably they've been 'absorbed' by now – but it's a most fascinating account) and, to continue after that digression, ate far too much. But my grandmother is still wonderfully active & it was pleasant to have Fiona & Anne around. Fiona (the elder if you remember) is now in her second year at Manchester Art College – Anne who has been au pering in Germany goes to Domestic Science college next year.

And now I'm back here again though in a different & warmer room – surrounded by an impressive array of filing cabinets, paper-racks & other office gadgets which I hopefully collect in the vain delusion that it will somehow make my life more organized, purposeful & successful & reduced the chaos of thoughts & passion over which I, like others, walk, to some kind of order. Like the desperate attempt to pigeon-hole people and to work out 'systems' both of knowledge and for our own private lives these attempts are narrowing & cramping but one would go mad, I suppose, if one didn't order one's existence and try, at least, to correlate the various strange phenomena that come our way. Here endeth the first philosophical dissertation!

I've only vaguely gathered the activities of our Sedbergh contemps – you will learn more from Boggis' column in the Luptonian if you still get the magazine; very sad A.T.I.B's retiring. Geoffrey [Bromley] *is into his last year at Cambridge & so is Charles* [Vignoles] *– but you'll know this & I know no more. I met Alan Barnes who is doing textiles at Manchester – playing rugger for the 2nd XV & whose sister has been married for 3 years. Rupert Merrer I also met.*[1] *He is going out with my sister Fiona – in a desultory way & working at A.E.I. as an engineer or something to that effect in a similarly unenthusiastic manner. He went on a 7 week cruise as 6th engineer up the Great Lakes & got as far as Chicago. He saved over £100 & enjoyed himself very much. He told me that Dave Badger has thrown over his farming & is on a contract to rubber-plant in Malaya for about 10 years; earning pots of money but a bit lonely. Bob Pears is back from Australia but that's all I know of him. David Porter came over here to play rugger. After doing very well in his final exams he's cramming for 6 months before going into father's business – I heard a rumour that Stewart Black was engaged – but only very vague one – Dave OP. is, apparently, getting dangerously serious over a girl. To show what rumours are I heard that Mark Sykes had tried to commit suicide – it might be true in this neurotic atmosphere tho I saw him less than a month ago & he seemed fine then.*

II. WORK.

(a) *My thesis. This is fascinating of course though it entails not only a historical study of the C17 documents relating to witch trials and of propaganda documents arguing for & against the existence of witches also a passable knowledge of C16-C17 literature & 'climate of opinion'; psychical phenomena; psychology with special reference to mental derangement leading to fits & trances & voluntary confessions as well as the psychology of dreams, for instance the impression of flying; anthropology/sociology – for instance the ways in which a swiftly-changing society attacks new ideas or seeks outlets for frustration & fear by seeking a scapegoat and of course a knowledge of modern witchcraft in Africa & Haiti – if only to make comparisons which show their differences; a general knowledge of the history of the time – social, legal, political, economic etc – and so one goes on. This outside reading on subjects I haven't touched before is part of my justification for wasting another two or three years. I think I'm too young to do much about 'world problems' at the moment anyhow – I ought to learn to think first.*

(b) *Generally I am still conscious, though this consciousness is often blunted, of the misery of the millions but one becomes more aware every day of the problems & less confident of the solutions – one can't decide, for instance whether to take the Romantic approach and judge goodness by intentions – e.g. Blake's*
"He who would do good to another, must do it in Minute Particulars,
General Good is the plea of the scoundrel, hypocrite & flatterer."

---

[1] Rupert Merrer was a boy a couple of years ahead of me at Sedbergh, who had also become friends with my sister Fiona.

The approach which is essentially spiritual & religious & poetic & sees more good in the widow's mite than in all the dishonestly garnered & guiltily given millions of a Rockefeller or Nuffield – or the reverse, which prompts one to get power or learning or money as a means to a good end. Does the end, however good, justify the means. Can one sit around in warmth and fully-fed when millions die in the slums etc? I don't get as worked up as much as I used to since I enjoy my work too much & also begin to realise the difficulties much more. One of these, as you know, is "security" which begins to loom large as one grows older. The Romantics hate it of course – for instance here is a passage I read recently from E.E. Cummings' "Six Non-Lecture" (p.43) which is terrific.

"This inwardly immortal world of my adolescence recoils to its very roots whenever, nowadays, I see people who've been endowed with legs crawling on their chins after quote security unquote. "Security?" I marvel to myself "what is that? Something negative, undead, suspicious & suspecting; an avarice & an avoiding; a self-surrendering meanness of withdrawal; a numerable complacency & an innumerable cowardice who would be 'secure'? Every and any slave" – and so on – and I cry out to them with sympathy. But the Romantic solution begins to recede and one is torn in half by a growing fissure, all or nothing, no compromise, sacrifice everything, love entirely and without thought – or start calculating and weighing-up, in fact become 'adult' in the opprobrious sense, used by Saint-Exupery & all the other good children's story writers & become welcomed by other grown-ups, but lose any hope of real sensitivity and fulfilment. I hope this doesn't sound too rambling, it's a tricky subject & deserves a much longer space. Anyhow I hope when this degree is over to <u>get the hell out of here</u> and have a wander around to see what needs <u>doing</u> & then train specifically to <u>do</u> that.

On my little list of headings for my letter I've still got "Religion, Poetry & Sex" to cover but it's getting late & each of them need a million million pages at least sufficient to say that on Religion I still conform & pray & believe intermittently but feel pretty uncertain & more than ready to tolerate other viewpoints. I still believe the solution of "why" to be the most important thing in one's life & I still have moments of wonder at the mystery of it all, but like Wordsworth's 'Intimations of Immortality' my golden age of belief tends to fade into duller grey & though 'the rainbow comes and goes & lovely is the rose' I am slowly experience since it opens up a world of new ideas which I had never dreamt of amidst the childish undergrowth.

As to poetry I have gone thro' a Yeats stage & then Robert Graves – but here is a delightful Elizabethan-type poem by Michael Roberts I've just picked up

<u>*Question & Answer*</u>

'How do you love me, with silver and gold?'
'How do you love me, with kisses untold?'
'How do you love me?' again and again.

'I love you with passion & fury & pain,
With death at the elbow & none to explain.
The pain & the passion, where out in the rain
A love lies dreaming of silver & gold,
And cold heavy raindrops & kisses untold.'

Which covers Sex too – where my views are the same, the same clash between the pursuit of ideal beauty & the union of souls etc & the bitter compulsion of lust which drives me on. I hope to go out with Dorothy this term – but don't know how she feels. Been pseudo analysing myself for Oedipus etc but you're spared my agonizings here since I've come to the end of the page & probably your patience.

Write if/when you have time. Give my regards to all the family & thrive yourself. Alan

One of the pleasures of staying on to do a D.Phil. at Oxford, which I had known well but had to rush through my history course, was to be able to continue going to lectures and talks by interesting people. I imagine that I continued to do this through the two years while I was resident, though perhaps decreasingly as I became buried in my thesis. But certainly in my second term I marked a number of potential lectures in the one lecture list for this period which I have kept.

I have lecture notes which tie-up with some of the courses marked for the second term (Spring or Hilary Term 1964) of my course. It is interesting to see the rather thin fare on research methods we were offered – but this was more than compensated by some interesting general lectures, and in particular the stellar array for the G.M. Young lectures. I would many years later meet George (Dadie) Rylands, the last of the Bloomsbury group, when I became a Fellow of King's in 1971.

FACULTY OF MODERN HISTORY

Lecture List for Hilary Term 1964

Subject	*Lecturer*	*Time*	*Place*
BRITISH HISTORY			
The European Iron Age: Continent and British Isles	Professor C. F. C. Hawkes	M. W. 6	Institute of Archaeology (34 Beaumont Street)
English Church History 870–1066	Dr. W. A. Pantin	T. Th. 12	Schools
England and the Continent 1050–1215	Professor Southern	Th. 12	"
The Royal Demesne 1066–1399	Mr. H. M. Colvin	F. 10	St. John's
Church and State 1089–1170	Dr. E. Stone	Th. 10	Keble
Stubbs' *Select Charters* (from the early twelfth century)	Dr. J. F. A. Mason	W. F. 10	Christ Church
Personalities and Policies 1154–1216	Mr. J. O. Prestwich	W. F. 11	Schools
The Fourteenth-century English Background	Mr. A. G. Mathew	F. 11	Balliol
Religious Movements and the Universities: the Friars to the Tractarians	Dr. V. H. H. Green	M. 10	Lincoln
English Economic History 1485–1600	Mr. W. G. Hoskins	Th. 10	Schools
English Economic History 1485–1730 (*class*)	Professor Habakkuk and Mr. J. P. Cooper	T. 5	All Souls
Tudor Foreign Policy (*three or four lectures to conclude*)	Professor Wernham	M. 11	Schools
The English Reformation: Edward VI to Elizabeth I	Dr. T. M. Parker	M. 10	University
Science, Medicine, and Politics 1540–1660	Mr. J. E. C. Hill	T. 10	Balliol
The Early English Separatists 1550–1620	Dr. B. R. White	T. 9	Regent's Park
Prothero and Gardiner Documents	Mr. W. G. Barr	M. W. 11	Schools
Aspects of English Economic History 1600–1730 (*four lectures*)	Mr. W. G. Hoskins	Th. 12	"
The Puritan Revolution	Professor Trevor-Roper	F. 12	"
Men and Politics 1660–1721	Dr. G. V. Bennett	W. 11	New College
Social Doctrines of the Churches: eighteenth and nineteenth centuries	Mrs. J. Hart	T. 12	Schools
English Economic History since 1760	Professor Habakkuk	M. 11	All Souls
Constitutional Developments since 1780 (Costin and Watson, vol. II)	Mr. J. Steven Watson	W. 11	Christ Church
King and Ministers 1782–1832	Mr. C. H. Stuart	T. 12	"
British Foreign Policy 1815–1939: a critical analysis	Mr. M. C. Hurst	Th. 10	St. John's
Origins of the Commonwealth: Imperial Defence and Colonial Nationalism 1815–1939	Mr. D. K. Fieldhouse and Professor R. A. Preston	F. 10	Rhodes House
Parliamentary Reform 1830–85	Mr. M. G. Brock	W. 10	Corpus Christi
British Constitutional History 1830–1914	Miss S. E. Crowe	M. S. 10	Schools
†Reaction and Reconstruction in English Politics 1832–52 (*six lectures*)	Professor N. Gash (*Ford's Lecturer in English History*)	F. 5	"
History of English Local Government since 1832	Mr. B. Keith-Lucas	F. 12	"
The Conservative Party from Peel to Macmillan	Mr. R. N. W. Blake	M. Th. 10	Christ Church
Politics and the Economy 1870–1914	Mr. M. Shock	M. 10	University
The British Constitution 1914–53 (Le May Documents)	Professor Beloff	W. F. 12	Schools
British Economic History 1918–39	Dr. R. M. Hartwell	W. 11	Nuffield

Subject	Lecturer	Time	Place	Course begins
ARTISTIC AND OTHER ASPECTS OF HISTORY				
The Russian Ikons: their Art and Doctrine (*with slides*)	Dr. N. Zernov	W. 5	Ashmolean	W. 29 Jan.
§Illustrations to Plato	Professor Wind	W. 11.30	35 Beaumont Street	W. 5 Feb.
‡Rubens, Impresario (*three lectures*)	Mr. A. M. Jaffé (*King's College, Cambridge*)	F. 5	Ashmolean	F. 31 Jan.
§The Discourses of Sir Joshua Reynolds (*class*)	Professor Wind	Th. 11.30	35 Beaumont Street	Th. 6 Feb.
Problems in Iconography (*informal instruction*)	„	To be arranged	To be arranged	
**L'Art de la Reliure en France et l'action des Bibliophiles: quelques aspects de la question (*three lectures to be delivered in French*) (*continued in Trinity Term*)	M. Jacques Guignard (*James P. R. Lyell Reader in Bibliography*)	T. Th. 5 (20, 25, 27 Feb.)	Ashmolean	
Problems in Seventeenth-century Science (*class*)	Mr. A. C. Crombie and Mr. R. Harré	W. 5	All Souls	
Problems in Nineteenth-century Biology (*class*)	Mr. A. C. Crombie	W. 11–1	„	
ADVANCED HISTORICAL TEACHING				

The attention of supervisors is drawn to the board's regulation requiring the attendance of Probationer B.Litt. Students at these classes (see Examination Statutes, 1963, p. 314).

Subject	Lecturer	Time	Place	Course begins
††Further Sources in Research, and some problems in writing a Thesis	Dr. A. F. Madden and others	T. 5.15	Nuffield	
Medieval Colloquy	Professor Southern	M. 8.30 (*fortnightly*)	All Souls	M. 27 Jan.
Palaeography of Books and Documents written in England 1300–1500	Mr. Ker	T. 5, F. 10	History Faculty Library	
†Sources of Medieval Anglo-Jewish History (*class*)	Dr. C. Roth	To be arranged	To be arranged	
The English Royal Chancery (*continued*)	Mr. P. Chaplais	W. F. 11	History Faculty Library	
English Local History: Problems and Sources (*class*)	Mr. W. G. Hoskins	W. 5	All Souls	
Commonwealth History (*graduate seminar*)	Professor Gallagher, Dr. A. F. Madden, Mr. G. Bennett, Mr. D. K. Fieldhouse, and Mr. C. W. Newbury	F. 5	Rhodes House	
Indian History (*graduate seminar*)	Mr. K. A. Ballhatchet	Th. 5	Oriental Institute	
International Communism 1918–43	Warden of St. Antony's and Mr. H. T. Willetts	F. 5	St. Antony's (1 Church Walk)	
State and Party under Stalin and Khrushchev	Mr. G. Katkov	T. Th. 11	Schools	
Contemporary Latin America	Mr. R. Carr and Mr. J. Maiguashca	T. 5	St. Antony's	
Middle Eastern Seminar	Mr. A. H. Hourani	T. 4.45	137 Banbury Road	
East Africa (*seminar*)	Mr. G. B. Masefield and Mr. G. Bennett	M. 5	Queen Elizabeth House	
Case Study in Group Relations: British Central Africa	Professor Kirkwood	T. 11	St. Antony's	
Race Relations and African Affairs (*seminar*)	„	Th. 5	„	
German Foreign Policy since 1949	Professor Headlam-Morley and Mr. J. B. Joll	Th. 5	St. Hugh's	
Seminar in International Relations: Disarmament	Mr. D. E. T. Luard and others	Th. 5	St. Antony's	

§§The Victorian Age (*G. M. Young Lectures*)	Mr. John Woodward and others	W. 5	Playhouse, Schools	

* Lectures begin on the first possible day after the beginning of Full Term (Sunday, 19 January), unless otherwise stated in this column.

† Those interested should communicate with Dr. Roth at the Oriental Institute.

** Th. 20 Feb. Les premières reliures royales
T. 25 Feb. La Renaissance et les premières reliures de Grolier en France
Th. 27 Feb. Quelques amateurs du XVIIème siècle

§ Those wishing to attend should call on Professor Wind at 35 Beaumont Street on Wednesday, 29 January, between 2 and 3 p.m.

‡ F. 31 Jan. The Origins of the Studio
F. 7 Feb. Rubens, Van Dyck, and Jordaens
F. 14 Feb. Rubens and the print-makers

§§			
W. 22 Jan.	Mr. John Woodward	The Pre-Raphaelite Brotherhood	Playhouse
W. 29 Jan.	Dr. Graham Hough	The Novel as Metaphor: three Philosophic Romances	Schools
W. 5 Feb.	Mr. John Betjeman	Victorian Architecture	Playhouse
W. 12 Feb.	Mrs. Cecil Woodham-Smith	The Founding of Irish America	Schools
W. 19 Feb.	Mrs. Joan Bennett	From *Oliver Twist* to *Our Mutual Friend*	Schools
W. 26 Feb.	Mr. Roy Jenkins	From Gladstone to Asquith: Political Leadership in the Late Victorian Age	Schools
W. 4 Mar.	Mr. George Rylands	'Weaker Vessels': the Novelists' Problem	Schools

Members of the University are asked to take their places before 4.50 p.m. If there is room, members of the public will be admitted thereafter

††		
T. 21 Jan.	Professor Gibbs	Some Twentieth-century Sources
T. 28 Jan.	Mr. R. Cobb	Some French Sources, Local and National
T. 4 Feb.	Dr. R. M. Hartwell	Problems in the use of Sources for Economic History
T. 11 Feb.	To be arranged	
T. 18, 25 Feb.; 3, 10 Mar.	Dr. A. F. Madden	Some problems in writing a Thesis

TIME TABLE

	9 a.m.	10 a.m.	11 a.m.	12 noon	Afternoon
Monday		Mr. Blake Professor Callcott Mr. Cowdrey Miss Crowe Dr. Green Dr. Parker Mr. Shock Mr. Thompson	Mr. Barr Mr. Brown Mr. J. Campbell and others, 11.30 Professor Habakkuk Mr. Lewis Professor Wernham	Mr. Armstrong Mr. Bueno de Mesquita Professor Gallagher	Mr. Aston and Dr. Stone, 5 Professor Hawkes, 6 Mr. Mackesy, 5 Mr. Masefield and Mr. Bennett, 5 Dr. Roth, 5 Professor Southern, 8.30 Dr. Whiteman, 5
Tuesday	Dr. White	Professor Berlin Mr. Hill Miss Reeves	Mr. Hourani Mr. Katkov Professor Kirkwood Professor Vandiver	Mrs. Hart Dr. Pantin Mr. Stuart Dr. Zernov	Mr. Carr and Mr. Maiguashca, 5 Professor Habakkuk and Mr. Cooper, 5 Mr. Hourani, 4.45 Mr. Ker, 5 Mr. Hurst and Mr. A. E. Campbell, 5 Dr. Madden and others, 5.15 Dr. Parker and others, 5 Mr. Pitt and others, 5 Professor Vandiver and Mr. Pelling, 5
Wednesday		Mr. Brock Mr. Holmes Mr. Joll Dr. Mason Professor Wernham	Mr. Barr Dr. Bennett Mr. Crombie Mr. Chaplais Dr. Hartwell Mr. Prestwich Mr. Steven Watson Professor Wind, 11.30	Professor Beloff Mr. Carr Mr. Crombie Professor Gallagher Mr. Mackesy Dr. Roberts Dr. Zeldin	Mr. Carr, 6 Mr. Crombie and Mr. Harré, 5 Mrs. Dick and Mr. Brock, 5 Mr. Evans, 5.30 Professor Hawkes, 6 Mr. Hoskins, 5 Mr. Woodward and others, 5 Dr. Zernov, 5
Thursday		Professor Berlin Mr. Blake Mr. Cobb Mr. Hoskins Mr. Hurst Dr. Stone	Mr. Katkov Dr. Schenk Professor Vandiver Professor Wind, 11.30	Mr. Caute Mr. Hoskins Dr. Pantin Professor Southern	Mr. Ballhatchet, 5 Mr. Brown, 5 Mr. Fieldhouse, 5 Professor Headlam-Morley and Mr. Joll, 5 Professor Kirkwood, 5 Mr. Luard and others, 5 Professor Seznec and others, 5 Miss Smalley and Mr. Leyser, 5
Friday		Mr. Ballhatchet Mr. Colvin Mr. Fieldhouse and Professor Preston Mr. Joll Mr. Ker Dr. Mason Professor Wernham Mr. Willetts	Mr. Chaplais Mr. Hourani Mr. Lewis Mr. Mathew Mr. Prestwich	Mr. Armstrong Professor Beloff Professor Headlam-Morley Mr. Keith-Lucas Dr. Macartney Professor Trevor-Roper	Warden of St. Antony's and Mr. Willetts, 5 Professor Gallagher and others, 5 Professor Gash, 5 Mr. Jaffé, 5
urday	Mr. Ramsay, 9.30	Miss Crowe	Mr. Mathew		

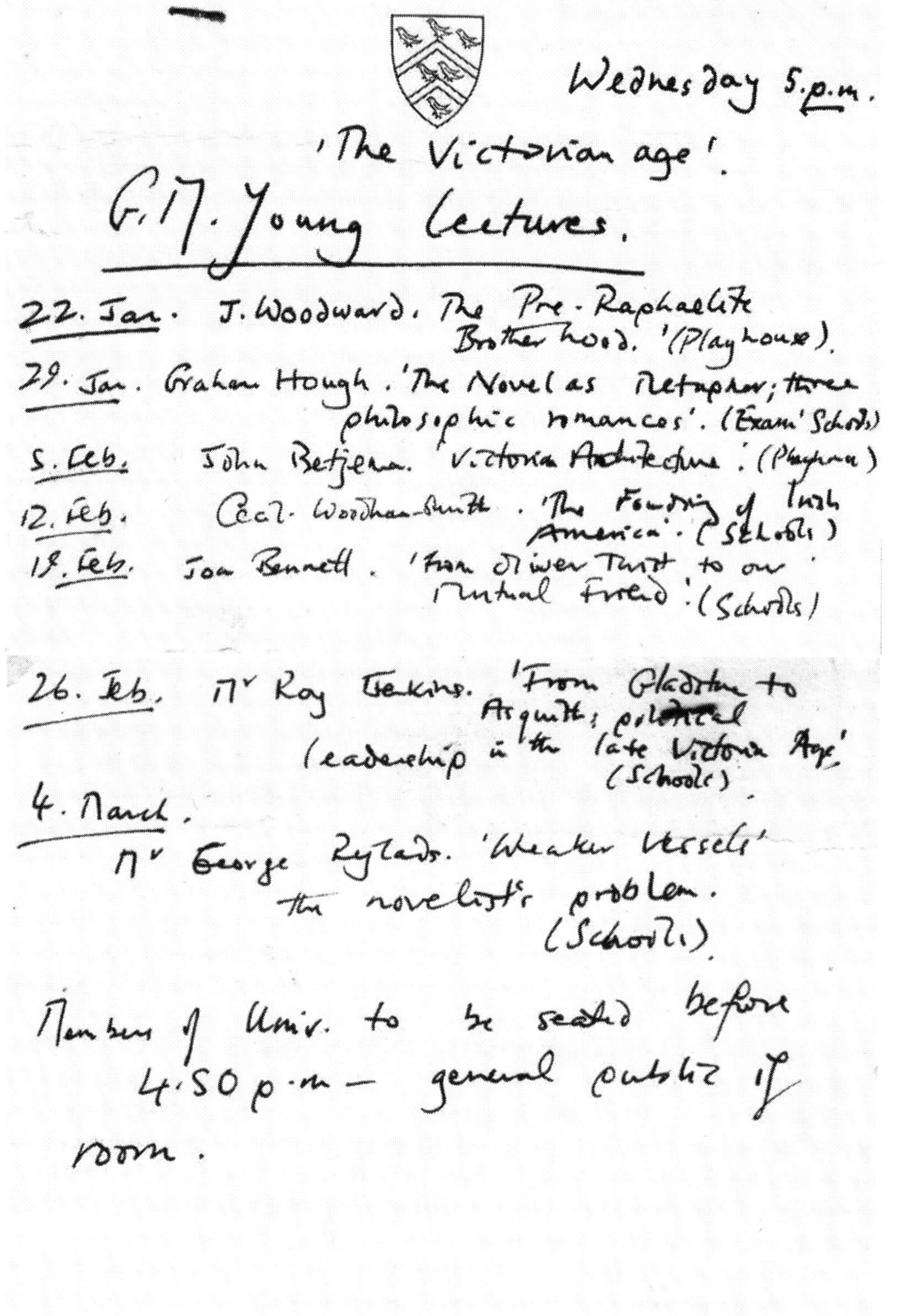

Wednesday 5.p.m.

'The Victorian age'.

G.M. Young lectures.

22. Jan. J. Woodward. The Pre-Raphaelite Brotherhood.' (Playhouse).

29. Jan. Graham Hough. 'The Novel as Metaphor; three philosophic romances'. (Exam' Schools)

5. Feb. John Betjeman. 'Victorian Architecture'. (Playhouse)

12. Feb. Cecil Woodham-Smith. 'The Founding of Irish America'. (Schools)

19. Feb. Joan Bennett. 'From Oliver Twist to our Mutual Friend'. (Schools)

26. Feb. Mr Roy Jenkins. 'From Gladstone to Asquith; political leadership in the late Victorian Age' (Schools).

4. March. Mr George Rylands. 'Weaker Vessels' the novelist's problem. (Schools)

Members of Univ. to be seated before 4.50 p.m – general public if room.

I have my lecture notes on Christopher Hill's lectures on 'Medicine, Science and the Puritan Revolution'. Whether I went to the lectures of W.G. Hoskins, Hugh Trevor-Roper and Norman Gash I am not sure. Nor can I remember whether I attended any of the special seminars on 'Advanced Historical Teaching'. I marked Dr. A.F. Madden on 'Further Sources in Research, and some problems in writing a

Thesis'. I may have been to one or two – as I starred them again, but don't suppose I went to Cobb or Hartwell. '

*

It is difficult to find much evidence of what I was doing at this time, but as I remember it, and is hinted at above, it consisted of three strands. I was reading round the subject to see what interpretations there were of the witchcraft trials and witchcraft in general, both from historians and anthropologists. A particularly strong theory in relation to the whole historical phenomenon was that of the archaeologist Margaret Murray. Over the Christmas holidays and mid-January 1964 I undertook a very detailed analysis of her two major books, *The Witch Cult in Western Europe* (1921 and re-published as an Oxford Univ. Press paperback in 1962) and her *The God of the Witches* (first published in 1931 and republished in paperback by an Essex publisher also in 1962). The republication of both her books in the year before I started my research shows a revival of interest in her work and I remember that Christopher Hill, as we shall see Trevor-Roper also noted, had more or less swallowed her whole thesis – that witchcraft was the survival of an ancient fertility religion which had been victimized by the church, that the survivors did meet in covens etc.

Anyway, here was my first chance to do a long analysis as a prelude to the theoretical introduction which a thesis would need, and I clearly enjoyed the exercise and entered into it with gusto. It was this piece which Keith acknowledged receipt of on 31 January.

It is a very long piece, probably about 15,000 words or so, some 32 pages of foolscap argument. It was based on breaking the book into tiny pieces and re-assembling her evidence. This is shown in one of the workings preceding the writing of the piece:

Chapters = after each chapter (pre-1100 cases are omitted). Continuity of religion. The God.

((Ch. IX is omitted in Ch. V + VI. note in Rites are together.)

(0 Evidence from [illegible] used)

— N.B. ag. of susceptibility of [illegible] evidence of [illegible] — see p. 35.

Nos from each country (+ sources)

Generalization = *

TOTAL

Cases + Source.

Accusation [illegible]

England. Pierce of Inverkeithing. (23). Bp of Coventry accused of doing homage to Devil. (23)

Northants witches. Agnes Browne & daughter. Jane Shaw + Tomy Phelps.

Margaret Johnson. Chelmsford 1556 (from [illegible])

York witch. Alice Huson. (1664)

Anne Armstrong. (1673)

Mongh of Dunstaple. 1649

Alice Goodridge. 1597.

Eliz. Sawyer witch of Edmonton.

East Anglia. 1645. Ellen Greenliefe. Rebecca West.

R. Scot. [illegible] Clarke. Rebecca Jones.

Cooper Pleasant Treatise.

Leicester 1618 — Joan Willimott.

Sutt. 1584.

John Walsh. Dorsetshire.

Anne Chattox. (Lancs.)

Eliz. Southern.

Yarmouth witch. 1644.

Hunt. Joan Wallis of Keiston 1646.

Essex trial 1645 (Hopkins)

Suffolk. 1665-6. Rose [illegible]. Richard [illegible]. Bust [illegible]

Somerset 1664.

Ilbre Gruneset. Bury St Edmunds Suff. 1665. Susanna Edwards. 1682.

Scotland. Full Tryal of Aberdeen witchcraft.

Major Weir. Jean Weir.

Aberdeen witches. 1596. Marion Grant. Ellen Gray.

Isobel Gowdie.

Janet Rendall. (Orkney) (1629)

Bute. 1662. Janet Stewart.

Ayrshire. 1576. Bessie Dunlop (from [illegible])

Ayrshire. 1605. Patrick Lowrie. Janet Hunter.

Fifeshire. Alison Peirson. (1588)

Perth. Isobel Haldane. (1607)

North Berwick.

Barbara Napier.

Agnes Sampson.

John Fian. Effie McCalyan.

Janet Stewart. (Edin. 1597)

Mc Gill. (Dessing N. Berwick)

W. Barton. Edin. 1655.

Maggie Tempill. Aberdeen.

Paisley. 1678. Annabil Stuart. John Stuart. Maggie Jackson.

Eliz. Anderson. Jas. Lindsay. Dalkeith 1662. Isobel Rutherford. Bessie Halburton. Robert Wilson. Bessie Neil. Agnes Hay. Agnes Brugh. Janet Paton. Kin Grieve. [illegible] Marie Lamont (1662) Innerkip.

Janet Watson, Dalkeith. 1661. Edin. Janet Kerr. Helene Casse. Isobel Ramsay. Janet Miller.

Kian Mitchell. Marion Grant.

Forfar Witches. 1661. Helen Guthrie. H. Porter. Isobell Smith.

Janet Howat.

Thurso. 1719. Margaret Nin-Gilbert.

Janet Rendall of Orkney. 1629.

Alexander Hamilton. (East Lothian) 1630.

Eymouth. 1634. Bessie Bathgate.

Marie Halburton of Dirlton. 1649.

Margaret [illegible] of Bute 1662

Sassie Hunter. (East Lothian) 1649.

Robert Grieve. (Lauder) 1649.

Janet Brown. (Broomhills) 1649.

Bute (1658)

Allan Witches. 1658. Margaret Duchall. Katherine Rigg.

Isobel Adams. 1704 (Pittenweem).

Isobel Crawford. Trials Court. Old Scotland.

France. Joan of Arc. 1431. Gilles de Rais 1440. executed.

Boguet. De Lancre. Bodin. Boulanger. Danaeus.

Estebène de Cambrue.

Sir Geo. Mackenzie. Forbes. Bute 1662.

ENG? no

Cannaert. Zuccalmaglio. Pouzet. Jeanette Cellag. Boguet. Françoise Secretain.

Pierronne. follower of Joan [illegible] put to death (1430)

Van Elven. La Tradition (no name or place given)

Abbé Guibourg (Ravaisson).

Boguet.

Michaelis. Discourse.

Puy de Dôme. Jean Bordeaux. (Hutchinson)

Chartier. Guillaume Edeline. 1453.

Lamothe. La Tradition (Michelet)

Sinistrari.

Fournier. 1615 (Burke)

Monsieur (Madam Wallace)

Law. Jean Tacquet (Arras) 1460.

Sec. p. 137 for open discussion of generalization.

Lorraine. Remigius.

Sweden. 1670

New England. Mary Osgood. Salem. Mary Lacey. Martha Carrier. (Connecticut) 1662. 1671.

Cotton Mather remarks. Goodwife Foster. Sarah Carrier. (B)

Ireland. Trial of Dame Alice Kyteler 1337.

Lapland. 1767. General.

Switzerland. Nider. Formicarius. 1337.

Papal Decrees.

I shall just give two pages out of the 32 to give a glimpse of my first sustained piece of research writing, albeit a critique of secondary sources.

The first page started to lay out her argument and why I thought it was important to take her seriously.

(16/1/64)

MISS MARGARET MURRAY'S USE OF EVIDENCE.

I. THE GENERAL ATTACK ON MISS MURRAY.

a). Her thesis outlined.

A summary of Miss Murray's thesis can be found in the fourteenth edition of the Encyclopaedia Britannica: (Under 'Witchcraft')

> She says: "When dealing with the records of the medieval witches, we are dealing with the remains of a pagan religion which survived, in England at least, till the eighteenth century, 1,200 years after the introduction of Christianity....The number of witches put to death in the sixteenth and seventeenth centuries is a proof of the obstinate paganism of Europe. Whole villages followed the beliefs of their ancestors; and in many cases the priests, drawn from the peasant class, were only outwardly Christian and carried on the ancient rites; even the bishops and other high ecclesiastics took part. As civilization increased and Christianity became more firmly rooted, the old religion retreated to the less frequented parts of the country and was practised by the more ignorant members of the community.....It was only when the new religion had gained sufficient strength that it ventured to try conclusions with the old. Backed by the civil law, it overcame the old religion, not only by persuasion but by the use of force."

This is further elaborated in her 'The Witch-Cult in Western Europe' first published in 1921 and republished as an Oxford Paperback in 1962 with a forward by Sir Steven Runciman. Sir Steven warns us not to judge this book by later volumes - "Dr Murray herself did not disarm criticism by introducing later books, notably The God of the Witches (1933) and, more recently, The Divine King in England, in which she somewhat recklessly pursued her theories further." (1) he continues that "The accusation of extravagance cannot, however, be brought against The Witch-Cult in Western Europe". As we will see critics hostile to the Murray thesis sometimes refer slightingly to her later books(2) but it is on 'The Witch-Cult....' that her thesis rests.

1) Murray: The Witch-Cult in Western Europe (1962 Ed'n).p.4-5.

(2) See Appendix B.(b) p.30.b.

My review of her was not just dismissive. While I showed that she had created a fictional coven organization and false interpretation, I applauded the fact that she took the phenomenon seriously and did not just dismiss it, as many of her Victorian predecessors had, as crazy superstition and illogical thought. What I found in her was the anthropological message, preached by Tylor, Frazer, Lang and others, that however different other people's beliefs were, we should look at their internal logic and premises, and treat them with some respect.

This premise had led to what I think is the best anthropological work on the philosophy of witchcraft, Evans-Pritchard's *Witchcraft, Oracles and Magic among the Azande* (Oxford, 1937) and I shall give just one other example from my essay which shows that I had read that book and absorbed its message. Much of my thesis would was influenced by Evans-Pritchard and I was enormously fortunate to get to know him in his last years and to have him as my D.Phil. examiner.

(26)

were accused of, and therefore redeem their accusers from the position of complete fools or bigots; or else a rejection of witchcraft and hence the train of argument which has been described above which runs in terms of 'superstition' and ignorance. It seems, however, that there is a third approach somewhere between the two, which avoids the credulity of writers like Summers and perhaps Miss Murray and also the over-rigidity of the other approach. The following diagram may shed some light on this synthesis:

It is in the work of modern anthropologists that such an approach is most often found, an attitude which rejects the basic tenets of a culture-pattern yet is prepared to study that pattern sympathetically and to admit that it had validity and coherence for those who abide by it. This approach, which would see witchcraft-beliefs not in terms of 'right' and 'wrong' but in terms of function, is ably demonstrated in the work of Professor Evans-Pritchard, especially in his '<u>Witchcraft, Oracles and Magic among the Azande</u>' (1937), for, while the author points out that witchcraft is 'an imaginary offence because it is impossible. A witch cannot do what he is supposed to do and has in fact no real existence." - yet he is concerned to find out <u>why</u> people believed in them, without immediately assuming that they were temporarily or permanently blinded by some perversion. Miss Murray started from this latter conviction - that a sympathetic approach was necessary - and it is only unfortunate that through subtle selection she reached the conclusion that since witchcraft-belief was patently such a widespread belief and held by so many people who were far from being insane or particularly biased, therefore it must have an actual substratum. If she had merely gone as far as showing that this was what people really believed and left the question of whether it really happened open she would not have been derided, and with our growing awareness of the equal value of beliefs about actions to the

The main and increasingly intense relationship was with my supervisor, Keith Thomas. On 18th January I wrote from Worcester

Dear Mr Thomas,

I hope your expedition to Herefordshire is proving fruitful. You asked for a rough agenda of my future activities which I enclose. I also enclose a Quarter Session reference to a disciple of William Lilly. ... Perhaps we could meet sometime in the fourth week, or whenever is convenient? Saturdays are usually a good day for me.

My mother wrote from Cherideo January 19th 1964

No letter since Christmas, but this is probably to do with the prophet's hair, we are always seeing pictures in the paper of the vast pile of mail bags in the Calcutta post offices. A letter from Anne yesterday in which she said you had given her a lift home with someone called Ralph, delivering Fiona on the way, so at least I know Field Head hasn't disappeared under a snow drift. I haven't had a word from Granny, expect she is still rallying from the strain though she usually enjoys a houseful. I'm glad your party was a success, more than ours was but I've forgotten it all now. My amoeba have quietened down somewhat... I went on an expedition to have tea in a village last week, was rather surpassed when I found the dear old Assamese lady entertaining me was called Ruth Andrews, a Baptist, and descendant of one of our General Managers!
I am going to paint her, and will try to get some folk lore at the same time.

My other historian friend is writing a thesis on Folklore and Mythology for some degree, and is giving me the names of various books. His chief reference is the fourth Veda which is full of magic and witchcraft, but I suppose there is a limit to the scope of your studies, and you have to stick to a country and period? I wonder how you are getting on and if you have achieved a sense of direction. I'm reading Christopher Hill at the moment and agree that he is wonderfully clear and interesting, particularly the second part of the book where he takes various characters and through their writings illuminates the scene, I am thinking of copying the idea if I ever get my book written – at the moment I don't see much chance of it, haven't had a word from the library about the books I sent for three weeks ago. I see Roseberry was chosen as the best Biography of the year by the D.T.[1] *which is jolly good, have you read it?...*

I hope Dorothy is back and you still find pleasure in each other's company, have you heard how Penny likes York? What about Felicity, what are her plans? haven't heard a word from Pat this Christmas. It is so beautiful here now, wish we could waft you all out for a week or two away from the fog and smog, ... Please let us know if you want more money next month.

My mother wrote again from Cherideo January 27th 1964

My dear Alan,

Thank you for a letter when you returned to Oxford, I expect you have quite settled in with your witches again and Christmas a dim memory. Granny wrote me a long and most amusing account of the preparations for the party, exaggerated I suspect, I particularly liked the bit when you set off into the night looking like refugees from Skopje strung around with brass cauldrons full of cider cup. It was very good of your friend to drive everyone everywhere, I hope we shall be able to do the same for him one day. I think the idea of commuting between the Lakes and Oxford is wonderful, Daddy says he would love to go back and watch cricket in the park and I can't wait to get my hands on those Moghul thesises. Dr Bhyans book I have, he is still alive though very old, I hope to meet him soon. There seems to be a sort of revival of interest in the Moghul's, I see there is a big exhibition of their art and handwork in America, perhaps I can cash in on it but I've got a feeling someone much more

[1] The Daily Telegraph

knowledgeable and influential is going to pip me at the post. Two books from the National Library arrived a couple of days ago, but I have hardly had time to open them, maddening, I've been waiting a month for them and now they come when I have the Leetham children coming to stay[1]... I read "The Spy Who came out of the Cold" this week and thought it very good and most moving, refreshing to find someone with the courage to announce spies instead of glorifying them a la Fleming. My little guest Rosemary[2] sent me down two poetry books from Shillong from her father's collection of ancient books I imagine, Siegfried Sassoon and Wilfred Owen, the latter quite wonderful with some I had never read, I think he moves me more than any poet, I can hardly bear to read some of his poems even though I nearly know them by heart. To think that a whole generation like him died to make the world safe for the Beatles... I was most distressed to see that T.H. White had died.

Keith wrote the on the 31st January 1964

Dear Alan,

1) *Many thanks for your piece on M. Murray. I don't promise to let you have it back immediately; I must refresh my memory of M. Murray first.*
2) *Here's your letter from Mr. Srigley. I'd go cautiously on this one. Don't give away all your info until you've found out a bit more about him, but do try to find out more specifically just what he is writing about. It may be that you overlap more than you think.*
3) *Christopher Hill asked me to tell you that he is holding an informal class on 17th century history this term. It will consist of papers and discussions led by his various research students on their own subjects. You'd be very welcome to come if you were free. I thought I might go to a few of them myself. In particular they'd like you to come to the one on roman Catholic scares in England 1639-42 as it is obviously in some ways a parallel subject. The programme is (from memory)*
   4th week (1st meeting) Rise of Arminianism.
   5th week RC scares[3]
   6th Education and Inns of Ct.
   7th County government
   8th Coleman St.
   All at Mondays at 5 in Balliol. Let me know if you can go. No need to tell C.H. Just turn up.
   Yrs Keith Thomas
   P.S. Yes do let me see the other R[ecord] O[ffice] letters.

The special seminars which were such an important part of our social and intellectual life, where we met other young researchers and gave our first papers, were still largely informal and held at the will of Christopher Hill and, later, Keith. And there was also Trevor-Roper's seminar.

[1] Children of a neighbouring tea planter couple.

[2] Rosemary was a young Anglo-Indian girl whom my parents befriended and later helped to settle in the U.K.

[3] RC scares, fears of Roman Catholic

1964 - February

Cherideo February 6th 1964 Iris to Alan

My dear Alan,

What a surprise and a thrill to get your enclosures from that agent,[1] *and how sweet of you to have had faith in my book – in fact the only person who has read it! I will write to the agents of course & see if something can be fixed to please the publishers when I get home, though I'm loath to just "extract" the stories, if that's all they want can produce lots more but there so many books of legends & stories I would have thought. Anyway, it is very encouraging & very sweet of you, Daddy is terribly bucked too. I have quite lost interest in "fame" but am still interested in money I fear, I justify it by pretending it's not for myself but that's rather roundabout as I will get the pleasure from giving it away! …. I heard from the Hakluyt Society which I am joining & that will help a lot with my books. When do you go to Borstal? Thought of spending about ten days in Oxford after I arrive, but could arrange it for later if it suits you better. I'm getting so excited about it already, and getting away from this crazy, petty, backbiting atmosphere. Just read "The Towers of Trebizond" by Rose Macaulay which I loved. Am keeping your books & making them last. Hope you are less lonely, the penalty of the scholarly life. Much love, Mummy.*

I sent further materials to Keith and he wrote again on Sunday 9th Feb

Dear Alan,

Another very interesting haul. Many thanks for letting me see them. Once you've decided on the area I think you'll need to do the same ecclesiastical records (I expect you know the Pilgrim Trust report in Duke Humphrey), but obviously they won't be much help for the 1640s.

I told C. Hill you'd like to go to his class.

Did you see that they are auctioning Margaret Murray's books? (Advert in T.L.S. about ten days ago I think.) Yrs. Keith Thomas

Keith refers to 'another very interesting haul'. What I remember doing was going through all the guides to local and national archives in the Duke Humphrey library of the Bodleian. I abstracted everything I could, particularly about the whereabouts of good Quarter Sessions[2] records. I became so interested that I wrote it up as an article which I sent to the National Records Association as a possible useful survey or pamphlet for them. They did not quite know how to react, as I recall, suggesting that it was perhaps not necessary as many of the Guides were already available.

What they had perhaps missed was that as well as the written guides, I had written to almost every county record office to check what was published and to ask for estimates of unpublished quarter sessions materials. I did indeed get back long and helpful letters and it was these which I lent to Keith. What I was trying to do was to find out which part of England to concentrate on, and the Quarter Sessions were one of the best possible sources. The other main source were the Assize records, of which there was a calendar in the Essex Record Office, the best organised and most efficient Record Office in the country. It was because of this efficiency, and the richness of these and other records, as well as the fact that I had already learnt that Essex was

[1] The agent was A.P.Watt, who remained her agent for some years.

[2] Quarter Sessions was a county level court, for example the Essex Quarter Sessions, which met at the county town every three months, or quarterly.

particularly prone to witchcraft accusations at this period, that I chose that county for my study.

My mother wrote from Cherideo T.E. on February 13th 1964

My dear Alan,

Thank you for writing so nobly when you must be fed up with paper and pen by the end of the day, but the sight of an Airgraph in the dak bag makes my day. I am sitting back sipping cold milk and feeling blissfully relaxed with my guests gone and no more conversations to make or meals to plan and then apologise for. Actually they were both very nice and good company but it is always a strain having people for days on end, particularly here when you don't have anything to offer in the way of entertainment. ...

Brenda will be delighted with all the fish information, she has now started lecturing at Sibsagar college twice a week and there is a fish farm there right on the spot so she can give them a hand with it as its pretty neglected looking. I'm very glad she has got something to do and she is thrilled and they are thrilled with her so let's hope the hot weather wont damp everyones enthusiasm. I would have liked to do something like that but not having a degree they wouldn't have taken me, anyway its twice as far from here. ...

After that I'm looking forward to sinking back into my rut and picking up the Moghuls again, I don't think my article is ever coming out.

I had a letter from John Lampitt yesterday, he is getting married at Stratford on August 8th so we might fit that in with my Oxford visit and then I'll go on to meet Daddy at Amsterdam afterwards...

I wrote to the agents and said I would be coming home in July and would be glad to discuss my book with anyone who is interested, tried not to sound too Keen, slightly cool and offhand but not too, hope something comes of it.

I envy you your life, but don't ruin your eyes – let us know how much you need for March – Much love – Mummy

My mother wrote from Cherideo on February 22nd

Thank you for a letter yesterday, I agree that it would be a bit wasteful to keep your flat on all summer if you won't be going back before October. I will definitely come and keep it warm while you're at Borstal and then stay around till Daddy wants to avoid Bank holiday week end so was planning to arrive about August 8th, but this might be difficult if you want to hand the flat over from the 1st. Would they let you keep it on for half that month do you think? If not Daddy will have to come a week earlier, at the end of July. Let us know. If you have a friend who will take it till September it might be then worthwhile to pay the month's rent so as to save the trouble of looking around for something else, and we could pop down occasionally during September and Fiona might like to too. My plans are to go straight to Manchester, where I hope both F and A will be and after a few days there onto Field Head and then down to Oxford on 11th, or perhaps a day or two earlier so as to see something of you, but I don't know how much room there is? Have to visit my publishers! They say they want a sort of junior Arabian Nights, sounds a pretty corny idea to me but still if that's what they want I suppose they know best. there is certainly a limitless supply of folk story and legend here. ...

Glad the witches are absorbing, the funny thing is that almost any subject is if you start examining it at depth, Brenda's snails are absolutely fascinating when you realise what goes one in their stomachs, I didn't even know snails had stomachs before.[1]

---

[1] Brenda Finney was a close friend of my mother's in Assam, a trained zoologist and the wife of a Tea Garden scientist, John Finney.

Trevor-Roper was born in 1914, so he was fifty and in his prime when we met, and had been Regius Professor of History for seven years. From other letters, it is clear that I liked him– his mixture of arrogance and insecurity, and the trouble he took to discuss with me in long conversations in his elegant flat near Christ Church where he told me a good deal about the history and myths related to the historical profession. He treated me with confidence and was one of those, on the same level as Lady Clay, who made me aware of the rich oral history of academic life, which has interested me ever since.

Later Trevor-Roper wrote a book on witchcraft and we fell out over it – but that is another story. Here it is the relationship of a patron and client, or famous and upper-class Regius Professor and a humble research student.

From The Regius Professor of Modern History

History Faculty Library,
Merton Street,
Oxford.
Telephone 43395
25th February, 1964.

Dear Mr. Macfarlane,

Roger Howell tells me that you would like to consult me on some matter. Do, of course, come and call on me at any time. I am going abroad for a few days from tomorrow, but will be back next week and am generally here; so is the Faculty Secretary, Miss Edwards, who could make an appointment if you like.

Yours sincerely,

Hugh Trevor-Roper

A. D.J. Macfarlane, Esq.,
Worcester College,
Oxford.

My mother wrote from Cherideo on February 29th

A postal holiday yesterday so your letter has not reached us yet, but a catalogue from Blackwells arrived and I have been poring over it and covering it with ticks in red ink. It has a lot of books I want but most of them are very expensive and I shall see if I can find them in libraries before launching out and buying them. One I would like though, perhaps for an early birthday present?! is Berniers journal of the Moghuls, I'll look up the number later. Thank you so much for sending this, little by little I shall manage to read everything though it'll take years.... I've been working on some more folk stories and have written to someone at Gauhati who is an expert so they will come pouring in I expect. Dr Verrier Elwin who wrote that nice letter about you died suddenly last week which was sad as I had hoped to meet him next time I went to Shillong. I didn't realise that he had been a Fellow at Oxford and gave it up to become a disciple of Gandhis and it was Gandhi who sent him to spend his life among the tribes. He had also worked for a bit at trying to reconcile Hinduism and Christianity but was buried with Buddhist hymns being sung around him – a man after my own heart and it is sad we never met. ... I have just finished "Zorba the Greek" which is fascinating, a most unusual book and a wonderful character study. Have still got "The Grapes of Wrath" and the Evelyn Waugh study of Ronald Knox left.

I have sent £30 for this month but let us know how things go and when you get your next grant. I hope your time at Lee Abbey is truly reviving,[1] *is it a high church establishment or non-denominational? I hope to be taken round one of the local monasteries soon, establishments for the pries of the religion of Sankara Deva whose life story I wrote an article on once, I think you read it, a purified non-idolotrous form of Hinduism with Krishna as the one god.*

---

[1] Lee Abbey, founded in 1946, is an ecumenical Christian community between Woody Bay and Lynmouth in Devon, England. It runs 'retreats', that is short periods for reading, walking and discussing religion. For me, was in many ways a more relaxed continuation of my earlier yearly visits to the evangelical Varsities and Public Schools boy's camps at Iwerne Minster.

1964 - March

My mother wrote to me from Cherideo on March 7th

Thank you for your letter, hope the £30 will help towards your overdraft and you will be financially as well as spiritually boosted by now, but let us know about the money. I wonder if rest from responsibility in beautiful surroundings with fellow spirits is really a good way to find satisfaction. I have a feeling that the sense of well-being it gives would be only temporary, and it is hard, boring frustrating acts of renunciation that are truly fulfilling. However you have tried this course before and found it stimulating so there must be something to be said for it – the ideal of course is when one has a centre of rest within and doesn't have to take "courses" of it, but this is very difficult to achieve, particularly in the hurly burly of making ones way in the world and so on.

I'm glad your work is coming on, more than can be said for mine as I am out of books at the moment, but I think I will have to get down to a job which I've been avoiding, Indian History down to the Moghuls of which I only have the sketchiest idea. We went up to Jorhat on Thursday and I scoured the shops for Assamese folk stories but without success, hope the man I wrote to in Gauhati will answer, not that there is any shortage of Indian stories but it is the original ones I'm looking for....

I read "The Castles and the Crown" which came from the Nazira library and I only kept for a day, it was excellent, I think the teaching of history through personality instead of events would be an advantage at least a combination of the two instead of the "cause-and-effect" method which still seems to be used – as half the causes had different effects in different parts of the world this is illogical as well as dull. For instance the plague was always cited in English history as the cause of the rise of the middle classes, but in other places, particularly the east, plagues and famines had the exactly opposite effect. It seems to me that history is as wildly unpredictable as the people who make it, and should be taught as such, starting with the people. Anyway that is how my history will be written if it ever is.

My mother wrote again from Cherideo on March 15th

I have another young guest and find it hard to get time to write... I have one of yours to thank you for telling of Penny's visit, I'm sorry she is a bit disappointed with York and her history, my idea of heaven would be to do what she is doing with time and books and a lovely place like that to live in but perhaps she built up too glamorous a picture in her mind of what it would be like. You will have heard from Fiona, I am torn between disappointment that she isn't going to finish her course, and approval at her sense of responsibility and desire to do something useful, I've told her to write to various organisations like the Pestalozzi place to see if she can get in, I really don't think I can ask Daddy to start training her in something else though as she will definitely not get another grant! ...I wonder if you are snow bound and gale wrecked like the rest of England, it will kill all the flowers and blossom I suppose, I hope the A.P's [aged parents] aren't suffering too much as they don't seem to be very fit.'

I wrote from Worcester College on Sunday 22nd March 1964

Dear Mummy and Daddy,

Since I had two letters last week I didn't expect one when I arrived back from Lee Abbey yesterday evening. There were several waiting for me - including one from Anne and Fiona so I can't complain about being neglected by the family. Fiona confirms that she will wait and talk over her restlessness with us all; she is planning to go to Paris for a flying visit but passport problems - aided and abetted by Granny perhaps - may prove insuperable. I will be very sad not to be up in the Lakes for Easter & begin to realize what you feel away from it all. How is everything with you both? How are the animals, book, General Manager etc? Won't be much longer till you can tell me in person.

I'm feeling a little melancholy after a really wonderful week in Devon - a sadness which is obviously accentuated at not having Dorothy here to greet me for she went back to Holland on Friday. The turbulent sea and moorland wind was just what I needed - though I didn't do much more than go down and watch the waves breaking on the rocks. Most of the times I spent making friends and talking - things which I have tended to overlook for the last few months. There were a host of nice people and among them some very pretty girls, usually, unfortunately, members of the community. Although one is occasionally annoyed at stupidity or complacency there is little bigotry or intolerance and a considerable amount of gentleness and humour. I spent quite a time asking members of the community about the tensions and difficulties of living in a closed society geared to high moral principles and though it is obvious that all tensions cannot, and perhaps should not, be ironed out yet it works though it is easy to say that 'it's all very well to live a cosy, sheltered Christianity without coming up against the suffering and compromises of ordinary life' etc. I suppose most of the community - which is an open [underline] one by the way - will not stay for more than six months. They are usually people from fairly simple jobs, nurses, secretaries, mechanics, etc and as far as I could see were not suffering from any particular complexes which drove them into seclusion from the world. But the very fact that I feel disorientated when I return to the world does mean that it provides some kind of shelter I suppose. The blend of Christianity put across is, for me, an attractive synthesis of enthusiasm & tolerance, reason & emotion, evangelicism and catholicism. In the end one just knows that most of these people are good and sensitive - and it doesn't too much matter whether they became Christians because of that or whether they were made into that by being Christians.

I'm not yet certain what my plans for this vacation are. I arrived to find a letter from the Essex Record Office informing me that the office will be shut from about 13th April for about five weeks. As it is vital that I go for a week at least it looks as if I will have to buzz off next weekend. There are various complications - for instance my next grant doesn't come in until April etc & Bill said he was coming here from 4th-8th April & I had said I would be here, still, perhaps another jaunt will cure my melancholia. If I am going to have to buzz over to Essex frequently I would like to get a small scooter or something - costing about £30. I wonder if you could possibly advance me this? I won't need the loan until about the end of May & will pay you back in July.

I enclose a) a not very good photo of Dorothy - I'm having a better one copied & will send that later (could you return this one) b) an article which is interesting chiefly because it suggests that an insight into my subject might be given by living in one of the Mediterranean countries. The only books I read at Lee Abbey were on anthropology and they added to my conviction that that discipline can help historians a good deal by showing the close interrelationships between human activities which are usually treated as separate subjects - thus economic exchange also provides social & political links and incorporates religious elements. Still, I'll work this out in more detail later. As it is I agree with your idea that it might prove very helpful to study a primitive society whether in Italy or the Naga hills even if one is primarily interested in C17 England. (Don't bother to send the cutting back as I have a copy.)

When is Roe appearing?[1] *Felicity should be hitting England in a week or two. Hope all goes well.*

Much love to you both. ,

Alan

My mother wrote to me from Cherideo on March 24th

Two letters from you (the first took 13 days) and also the book for Brenda which arrived yesterday and which I know she'll be thrilled with. The college she teaches in has a fishery place just next door so I'm sure she could work in some sort of project with her lectures in zoology. I browsed through it and found it very interesting if involved, the thing here is to get through the blanket of apathy that smothers every new idea and also try to collar some of the money that is supposed to go into rural Development but in fact goes straight into the various ministers' pockets. I have been re-reading the

[1] The article in *History Today*, which was finally published in November 1964.

Bhagavad Gita (got the paperback edition by Isherwood but the best part of it is Huxley's introduction) and its insistence that the action should be disassociated from its fruit, and work should be done without any thought of reward or result is the only answer here. I feel it is an extremely comforting philosophy anywhere, and rids one of the feeling of frustration one so often has that work isn't "leading" anywhere. The perennial philosophy is for me, but I find myself quite unable to meditate, simply cannot rid my mind of all the thoughts that clutter it up and when I try am simply conscious of the effort and nothing else. Perhaps one day I shall reach that beautiful pose between action and inaction like the lotus leaf that rests on the water but is not wetted – the "holy indifference" of the Christian mystics. T. S. Eliot has borrowed most of his ideas on the subject from Indian thought and writing I'm sure, that bit you quoted to me could almost have been a bit of Buddhist psalm.

I hope your week at Lee Abbey sent you back to your witches a New Man, I was interested in your interview with Trevor-Roper, I can understand why he is unpopular but he writes so well, I have cut out and kept all his articles on the rise of Christendom. My history if it ever gets written will be trivial and feminine, I haven't the knowledge or insight to see grand movements, it all seems capricious and unpredictable to me. They're taking so long to print my article I'm wondering if the proof copy ever got back to them. ... I think you under-estimate Fiona's ideals, she may be bored with Manchester but I think it goes deeper than that, she genuinely wants to fulfil herself in a way she feels is more worthwhile – I think most women do but it takes years to realise it usually and by then they have got immersed in other things. I've told her to write to various places for advice and also see if she can't find something to do that would fit in with her art, it is the round of coffee drinking and parties that gets her down I think.

The £30 is not to be paid back, the £100 extra we said we could give you still has about another £40 to run so I'll send another £20 for April as I don't know when your grant will arrive, unless you'd like more? I wonder how much you could get an old car for nowadays, though driving round Oxford is somewhat of a nightmare, still it would be nice in the summer and wouldn't be tied to weekends. Have a look round, we still owe you a 21st birthday present.

I had given Trevor-Roper some materials on witchcraft, a subject he was starting to research for a book he would write over the next couple of years.

From The Regius Professor of Modern History

History Faculty Library,
Merton Street,
Oxford.
Telephone 43395

26th March, 1964.

Dear Macfarlane,

I have suddenly realised that I did not give you back your papers when I saw you yesterday. I will not trust them to the post or the messenger, but will keep them here and give them to you next term. I hope there is no hurry about them.

I am afraid the documents quoted by the Occult Review stink to me of 18th century forgery.

I am leaving Oxford now till next term but I look forward to seeing you again then and hope you may even come to my class.

Yours sincerely,

H. R. Trevor-Roper.

A. D. J. Macfarlane, Esq.,
Worcester College,
Oxford.

My mother wrote to me from Cherideo on March 31st

Thank you for the letter and the picture of Dorothy, she looks sweet, an interesting face too and rather like Penny. Has she gone for good... I don't know what has happened to Roe, I wonder if the proof copy ever got back to them, but surely they would have let me know if it didn't? If it doesn't come out soon perhaps I should write and ask, they may be having difficulty getting illustrations. I'm sending another batch of folk stories home with the Higham children at the end of the month, the agents are very nice and helpful and say they are sure that if this publisher falls by the wayside they can find another. Can't get any sense out of the National Library, I've just read a book on the Mutiny in which he acknowledges the help given by its curators but he obviously had more winning ways or perhaps introduction. It is a vivid book, resting on a mass of new material from diaries and letters but never misses to mix a metaphor or produce a sun like molten brass or the sound of bugles smiting the ear drums and has some perfectly terrible "O" level common errors of the English Lang. it surprises me that such obvious howlers can get past proof readers and such. Still I enjoyed it for it impartiality and because it was all about a part of India I know, it was called "The Sound of Fury" by Richard Collier....

I was interested in the witchcraft article, there is masses of that sort of thing here, but if you are thinking of living in a primitive community the Mediterranean would be more comfortable, here it would take years to learn the language, but one constantly gets the feeling that if only there was someone around who could organise, the intentions are there and often the money but everything is frittered and muddled away. … Don't know why Granny is so against her [Fiona's] French venture, she seems to forget that at her age I was doing vast journeys across India with you and dogs and cats and on my own – the only thing I worry about is the driving capacity of the people from whom she takes lifts. Yes of course we shall let you have the money for a scooter in May, wish it could be a car but I suppose they are hard to come by at a price we can any of us afford. … It is very beautiful and lush, particularly in the milky early mornings when the leaves are soaked in a blue dew, I quote Laurie Lee to myself as I take the dogs for a walk and chew the bitter buds of the new growth.
P.S. Leave Bernier till I come, not worth sending.

1964 - April

There is then a considerable gap in what I have until a letter from Keith dated 12th April:

Dear Alan,

I hope you have had/are having a rewarding trip to Essex. We never got to the Lake District in the end, alas, but are enjoying a week in the Cotswolds as a second best.

I write now to ask whether you could introduce a discussion on witchcraft (whichever aspect currently interests you most) at next term's graduate class in Week 2 i.e. on Monday 4th May. Nothing very elaborate – just enough to get us started. I hope this isn't too short notice & I don't want you to waste time on it in advance – use some of your existing material if you'd prefer.

Yours, Keith

My mother wrote to me from Cherideo on April 17th

Thank you for a letter from your Essex doss house, I see the keeper of the archives there has written a book on the subject so is probably one of the best people in the country to help you.[1] *Great fun, I should love to poke among graveyards and church records. Re. transport, we think a new, or fairly new scooter would be the best buy, then I can take it off you when we come home or one of the girls. If we sent £30 next month you could put that down as a first instalment and we could get the bank to pay off the rest monthly. ... One would need plenty of that "nerve of failure"*[2] *here, according to the Hindu conception "nerve" doesn't really come into it – total indifference to success or failure, a stage of being suspended above ones actions, is the thing to aim at. Indifference isn't the right word either as it implies lack of interest, the two words most often used are renunciation and release, the one leading to the other with absolute inevitability, renunciation of course not being a negative "giving up" but a positive fight against self-interest. You know all this from the Perennial Philosophy of course, all religions say the same but we conveniently ignore them. Pain and the suffering of others is the hard thing to fit in, as Menander says "Poor mortal never pray to have not griefs, Pray to have fortitude" and that's about the best one can do.... Can't get a word out of the National Library.*

My mother wrote again from Cherideo on April 26th

I'm afraid this is a couple of days late. I suddenly realised that the Highams were off and I hadn't done my folk-stories for them to take home so spent Saturday on that. Your friends mother in Harrods might come as a help in boosting the book if it ever gets into print, what a nice job, just the sort of thing I'd like to do if I didn't live a million miles away. I can understand your feelings about your witches, perhaps you could get a teaching or other job for a couple of years and then go back to study some more on the proceeds? It's not the age that matters, a lot of people are in their late twenties before they know what they want to do, it's the finance really. I feel the same about my little researching, avenues are forever waiting to be explored and stones to be turned over and I'm sure the National Archives in Delhi are piled high with fascinating manuscripts, the only this is they would probably be in Persian. I have at last had four more books from the library, huge thick volumes which I'm supposed to have back in a fortnight but obviously wont. ... Are you planning to ask anyone home – actually it won't be too bad as there will be the Troutbeck house as an overflow – I'd like to have Felicity if she's free, I wonder if she's back yet.

---

[1] Hilda Grieve, *Examples of English Handwriting*, see below.

[2] A phrase I had quoted from David Riesman's work, *Individualism Reconsidered* (1955) p.48

Will send £30 for an instalment on scooter.

The problem of palaeography, or the reading of old scripts, was a really serious barrier at the start. The problem was a double one. Often the abbreviations and writing style are difficult enough, but this is compounded by the fact that until one knows how the organization that produced the records worked one cannot make much sense of what is written down.

I remember that when I first visited the Essex Record Office I was overwhelmed with the difficulty of using the original documents. Fortunately there were many good transcripts, and even more fortunately Hilda Grieve was one of the leading experts on early writing and was in charge of the Search Room. I became good friends with her and exchanged a number of letters. with her over the years. It was she who started to teach me how to read the documents, with patience and with the aid of the excellent booklet which she had published in 1954.

EXAMPLES
OF
ENGLISH HANDWRITING
1150—1750

With Transcripts and Translations

PART I : FROM ESSEX PARISH RECORDS
PART II : FROM OTHER ESSEX ARCHIVES

By
HILDA E. P. GRIEVE, B.E.M., B.A.,
formerly Senior Assistant Archivist

PUBLISHED BY THE ESSEX EDUCATION COMMITTEE
ESSEX RECORD OFFICE PUBLICATIONS, No. 21
1954

Fourth impression, 1974

Sixty Pence

There were degrees of difficulty. The Quarter Sessions Records with which I started were often in English and that helped, but parts were in Latin. The following is a Quarter Sessions deposition taken from Hilda Grieve's book, with her transcription.

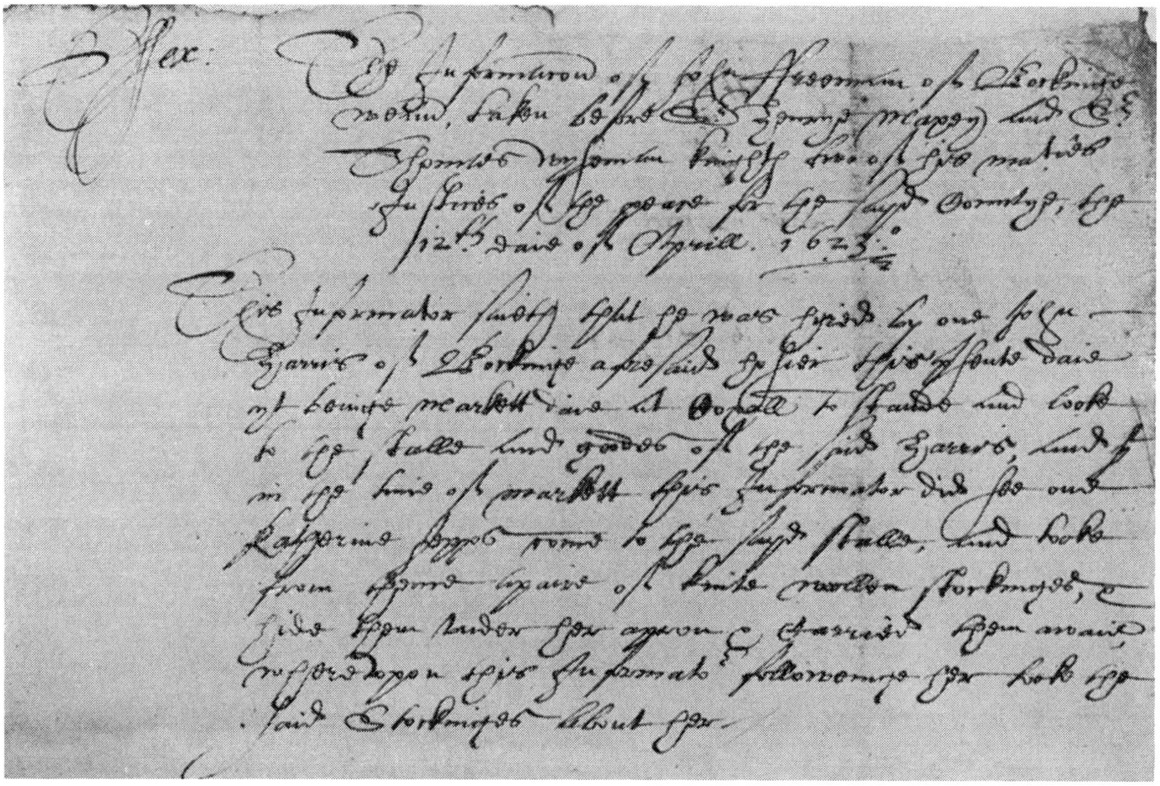

Essex: The Informac[i]on[1] of John Freeman of Bockinge weau[er], taken before S^{r}. Henrye Maxey and S^{r}. Thomas[2] Wyseman knight[es] two of his ma^{ties}. Justices of the peace for the sayd Countye, the 12th. daie of Aprill. 1623:[3]

This Informator saieth that he was hired by one John —— Harris of Bockinge aforesaid hosier this p[re]sente daie y^{t}[4] beinge markett daie at Coxall' to stande and looke to the stalle and goodes of the said Harris, and y^{t}[5] in the time of markett this Informator did see one Katherine Jepps come to the sayd stalle, and tooke from thence apaire of knite woollen stockinges, & hide them vnder her apron & Carried them awaie, wherevpon this Informato^{r} followeinge her tooke the said Stockinges about her./

[1] *Note omission of* i *in ending* -cion. *See also p.28 l.7 and note on p.ii.*
[2] *Note awkward appearance of* a *followed by* s, *almost suggesting an* e; *see also* was, *l.6. The form of this* s *can be seen clearly in* Harris, *l.9, and* this, *ll.10, 14.*
[3] *i.e.* Millesimo sescentesimo vicesimo tercio.
[4] *Here* y *stands for* i; *cf. n.5.*
[5] *Here* y *stands for* th, *i.e.* [th] [a]t; *see p.7 n.3.*

DEPOSITION TAKEN BY JUSTICES OF THE PEACE, 1623

One of the duties of Justices out of Sessions was to examine persons brought before them suspected of felony, and to take down the information against them. From the Quarter Sessions Rolls it appears that Katherine Jepps, accused above, was indicted for stealing the stockings, valued at 8d., at the following Easter Sessions on 24th April. She and her sureties failed to appear, and the recognizance was estreated.

In order to help in the reading, Hilda gave the following from an old book on legal and court hand.

A general Alphabet of the Old Law Hands.

ALPHABETS from A. Wright's *Court Hand Restored* (5th ed., 1818, plates 18, 19), illustrating a variety of forms of letters, mainly but not entirely from 16th and 17th century Legal and Chancery hands.

The most important documents for my study were those which brought a suspect to court in the Assize courts. The following are an indictment and then an inquisition presented to the court

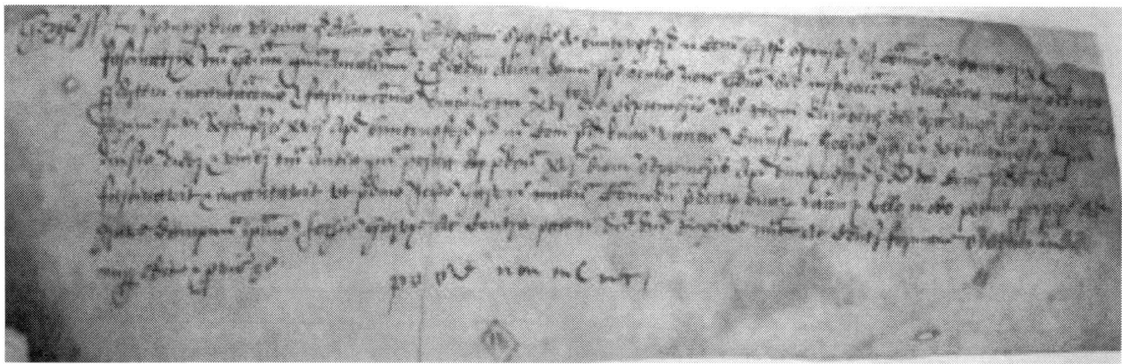

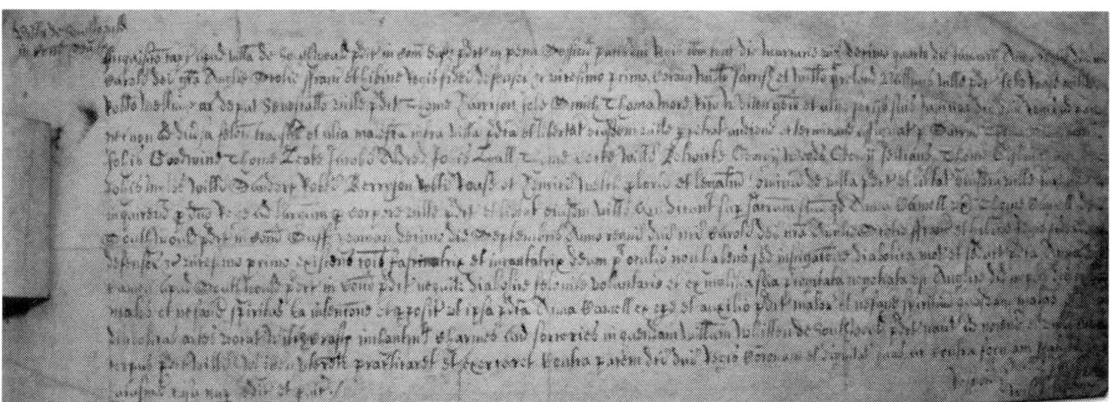

My reaction when seeing documents like this was dismay and a feeling that I would never be able to read them and I was to encounter even more difficult records when I started to work on the ecclesiastical court materials almost a year later.

Keith wrote to me from St John's on 29th April.

Dear Alan,

Many thanks for your most interesting letter & transcripts. I'm sure to prove a broken reed so far as palaeography is concerned, but it will be nice to see you again. Would Saturday 8th May at 11.30 be possible? Keith

1964 - May

Apart from learning my way around the records, and how the administrative and legal system of England worked, my other parallel task was to deepen my understanding of the theoretical framework. This consisted of two parts, the anthropological approach and the historical accounts.

On the anthropological it seems that it was really during this term that I began to seriously immerse myself in the subject. This consisted both of spending time with anthropologists and going to lectures in the Institute of Anthropology, and starting to read and index a wide variety of books on the anthropology of witchcraft.

In relation to lectures, I see that I have notes on three lectures in May, two by Lienhardt and one on Sir Henry Maine by Evans-Pritchard Here are parts of the notes I made.

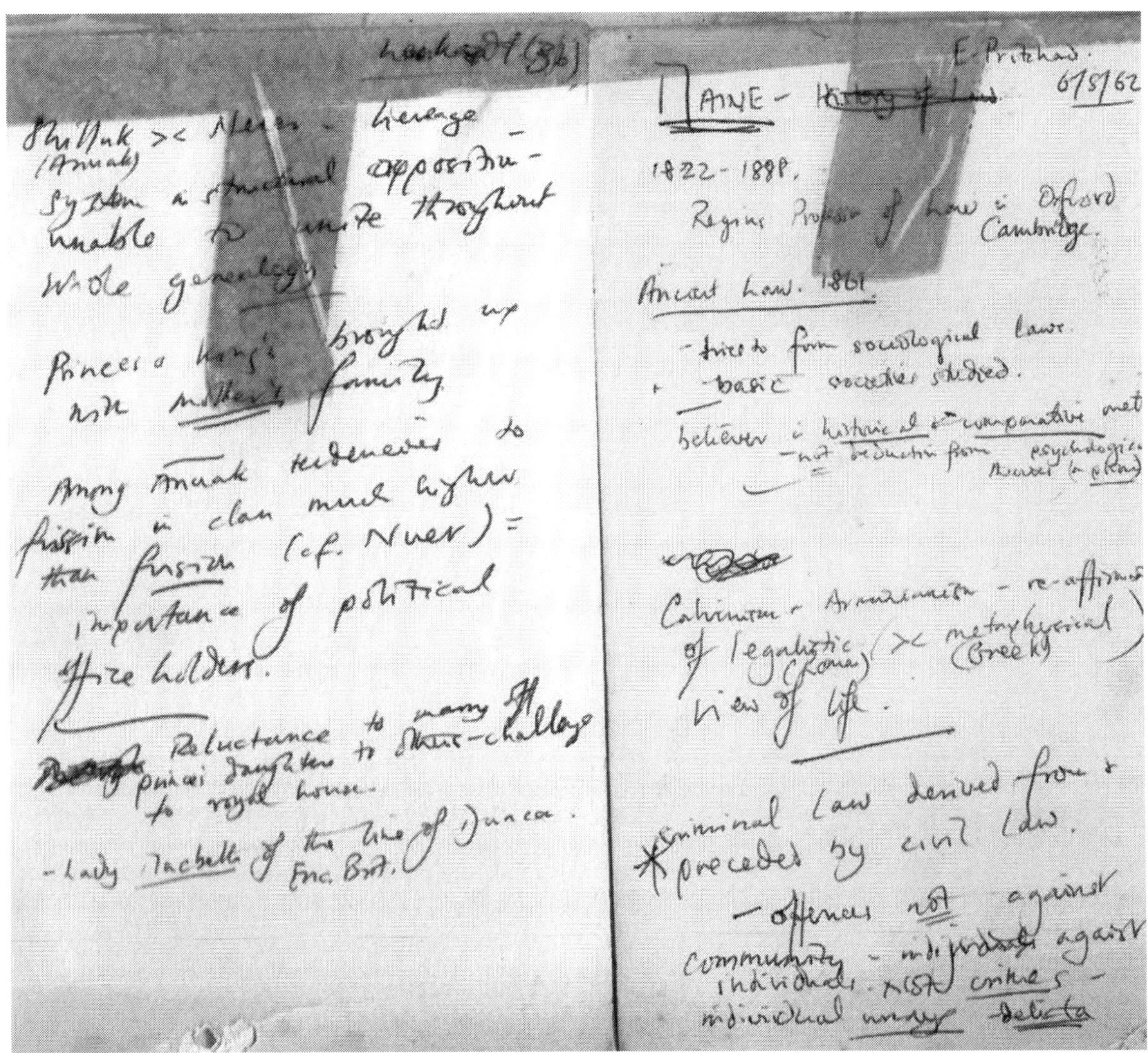

Lienhardt (86)

Shilluk >< Nuer - lineage - (Anuak) system a structural opposition - unable to unite throughout whole genealogy

Princes a king's brought up with mother's family

Among Anuak tendencies to fission in clan much higher than fusion (cf. Nuer) = importance of political office holders.

Reluctance to marry [illegible] princes' daughters to [illegible]-challenge to royal house.

- Lady Macbeth of the line of Duncan. Enc. Brit.

E-Pritchard. 6/5/62

MAINE - ~~History of Law~~

1822-1888.

Regius Professor of Law in Oxford Cambridge.

Ancient Law. 1861

- tries to form sociological laws.
+ basic societies studied.

believer in historical + comparative method - not deduction from psychological theories (a priori)

Calvinism + Arminianism - re-affirmation of legalistic (Roman) >< metaphysical (Greek) view of life.

Criminal law derived from + preceded by civil law.

- offences not against community - individual against individual. [illegible] crimes - individual wrongs - delicta

Keith had asked me in a letter previously quoted to give a talk to his graduate class on Monday 4th May on 'Problems in the Interpretation of Witchcraft' - 'Nothing very elaborate'. I took it seriously, however, and typed out twelve pages of foolscap. Here are three paragraphs that show how I was starting to incorporate serious anthropology into the work. The first extract shows how I set out the purpose and structure of the talk.

Introductory.

Of all subjects 'witchcraft' is the most difficult to approach objectively. With its tortures which equal or outdo the worst fiendishness of the last war, with its extraordinary accounts of devils and sabbaths and its obscene parodies of normal life it has attracted the attention of those ready either to revel sadistically or to point disgustedly at the beastly superstitions of the middle ages and of a repressive Church. Since my later approach will be, I hope, far from sensational it is perhaps worth reminding ourselves of one or two of the facts, including a few of the details which have made scholars too often lose their self-control & throw up their hands in horror, uttering streams of abuse.

I would like, therefore, to divide this paper into three parts. First a very brief outline of some of the facts about the distribution of witchcraft. Second to summarize some of the movements in the historiography of witchcraft and indicate a few of the suggestions made by anthropologists working on the same subject. And thirdly to suggest one or two of the main problems as I see them, and also a few of the ways in which a study of witchcraft might contribute to an understanding of the sixteenth and seventeenth centuries.

Towards the middle I described some of the anthropological interpretations.

It is this 'functional' approach which I would like now to examine, as treated in three monographs - *Nupe Religion* (1954) by S.F.Nadel, Professor Evans-Pritchard's *Witchcraft and Oracles among the Azande* (1937) and Clyde Kluckhohn's *Navaho Witchcraft* (1944).It could, and indeed has been, argued that the comtemporary findings of anthropologists are completely irrelevant to a discussion of C17 European witchcraft, thus R.H.Robbins' in his recent *Encyclopedia* argues that witchcraft is a specifically Christian heresy,limited in area & time with no real afinity with what he calls 'sorcery' which is universal.No-one would disagree that comparison is dangerous and that there are elements manifest in the European phenomenon & completely lacking in,for instance tropical Africa. Thus it might be asked whether we can compare the Navaho, where witches are usually men and usually rich, with the poor old women witches of England; or the Azande where people are not interested in witches as 'witches' until some disaster happens needing explanation, which seems, if anything the opposite to what happened in England where an old woman was disliked and misfortunes began to be focused onto her. Nevertheless the real test is whether anthropological studies prove helpful,giving us more sympathy,suggesting theories, and teaching us to ask new questions. I believe that it does.

At the end I turned to the wider question of the ways in which the study of witchcraft was more broadly valuable for the historian – giving an early insight into how I was exploring a whole new area, what the French had called mentalité, and hence opening up new worlds. My excitement was palpable.

One of the historian's basic problems is that the things he is most interested in - the common assumptions and bonds of a society, what it values most and takes for granted - are precisely those things which will not appear in the normal records. People will not go around saying 'We believe in monogamy, we believe in patrilineal descent & matriclocial inhabitation, we believe that one should only eat certain kinds of flesh, that the home is sacred' &tc. But, if I might suggest very tentatively, beliefs in witchcraft act as a unique mirror to these basic assumptions. In them we discover all the things a society abhors & which it fears may be attacking its precious roots. Thus witches dance naked, commit incest, fornicate freely, look like Puritan clergy, act like followers of the covenant theology, or of Roman Catholicism, worship idols, profane the Sabbath, have cannibalistic orgies, cause awful disease & sterility in men & animals and so on. In Sweden & Scotland they indulged in adult baptism, in New England they were organized similarly to the congregational system. There are special dangers in deducing facts from the reflexion they find in myths & ideologies but it may be possible to pursue this line. Thus for example witchcraft may throw considerable light on the family & home - why was it that Navaho witches were never believed to carry on their witchcraft in their homes, while they did so in England? What were the permitted hostility relationships within an English village - was it the same as among the Azande where for various reasons one did not accuse members of one's own family, nobles or children ? Kluckhohn suggests that his study will throw light on 'how Navahos think' - what they consider as evidence, what types of connections between events they infer, what are the unstated premises of their logics etc and also that is sheds interesting light on what types of envy recur - data which could be utilized to infer the types of motivation which influenced the individual Navaho (of given status) most strongly.

My mother wrote from Cherideo on May 8th

I don't think I've had a letter this week, but I've rather lost track. I sit every evening waiting for a letter from one of you and after about three days I start moaning that I never hear and Daddy points out that I've already heard that week. The last one told of your motor bike purchase,[1] hope it has turned out a success, it doesn't matter about a scooter, I don't suppose I should ever learn to ride one anyway. It sounds so lovely at home now, I wish I could be there, its lovely here too and I've just been watching a golden oriole chasing a myna away from what I imagine must be its nest. ... Had a letter from my agent saying he had got the folk tales so it now remains to see whether the publisher wants them. I'm sure "Country Fair" would take anything you liked to send on the subject of looking up old records and so on, they wouldn't pay much but it would be a start. ...I was wondering whether to bring the records home for you to tape, or are they too corny? What happened to the gramaphone by the way, Anne is always saying she wants one. Was wondering if you could book us some seats for a Stratford play on August 9th, thought we might come down to John Lampitts wedding and then have a day at Stratford (could distribute ourselves round on various reluctant friends for the night or your room) he is being married there on Aug. 8th. If you could let me know what it costs. Anne is going up to stay with Felicity so can report on her maturity or otherwise, we must have her to stay. Am plodding on with my Moghuls, get into quagmires sometimes and all the interest goes out of the subject but this is quite common I know, T. H. White describes the feeling very well. ... I haven't done any reading this week except Assamese and The Golden Bough, my speech is to be "Folklore of the East and West" can't remember any from the west thats the trouble.

My mother wrote again from Cherideo on May 15th

Two letters this week, I'm so glad your D. Phil. thing has been cleared up,[2] a feather in your cap that the great Trevor-Roper is on your side (he was never on Roberts!). Do hope you will get a bigger grant too as I feel things are pretty tight at the moment, specially with that enormous rent to be paid. I'm sorry about the bike, and hope you won't be stung for a whole lot more, you should have got some expert advice before buying it really... Am coming to the end of my latest Moghuls, pretty stiff going this lot, from 1761 to 1788 when the last real emperor was blinded, and a mass of intrigues and battles which nobody could make interesting. Do you have to "book" reading in the Bodleian and will I even be allowed in? I want to study the diaries of the emperors particularly, and any other original journals of the period, perhaps you could pull some strings for me? I wrote to Robert congratulating him on his successes, his new venture on the history of the British empire will involve a lot of Indian research I should imagine, quite a vast task in fact. I expect it is jealousy but though Robert writes entertainingly I wouldn't have called his books "literature" would you? Don't seem to find much time for light reading these days, as I struggle with Assamese short stories in the intervals of everything else, they are touching and rather childish but give one an insight into the way of life of the people... It's depressing to find how many words I still don't know, I'm too old and forget so quickly.

I do not recall how the talk went, but from comments three months later, it seems that Keith was impressed by my preparations in terms of interpretation.

I also wrote an overview paper on witchcraft in western Europe. I introduced the 20 pages of foolscap paper thus.

---

[1] My second motorbike was a 250 c.c. bsa. motorbike.

[2] I had originally been entered for a two year M.Litt, and this refers to the approval for a three year D.Phil.

WITCHCRAFT IN WESTERN EUROPE: FACTS & INTERPRETATIONS.

Introductory.

The study of witchcraft is notoriously difficult. The accounts of tortures and the confessions of witches seem, at first sight, so beastly & insane that the mind is revolted. Some historians of the subject, for instance R.Trevor Davies end up in mental asylums, others like Miss.Margaret Murray become completely obsessed with an interpretation and oblivious to criticisms, others, like the Rev.Montague Summers are learned cranks. 'Witchcraft persecution' becomes a valuable intellectual weapon - a dirty activity to be attributed to whichever group the historian happens to dislike - thus, for example, the Puritans, or the Roman Catholic inquisitors, or the Presbyterian clergy have in term been blamed for stirring up & using this 'weird superstition'. In this paper I would like to discuss some of the interpretations so far suggested, but first it is necessary to see what witchcraft really meant in the C16 & C17.

Later I put down a few of the known facts about the distribution.

<u>The Distribution of Witchcraft.</u>

Geographically witchcraft was distributed throughout Europe & North America. Germany & Scotland are especially notorious for their trials and Spain & Holland for their tolerance with England coming half way inbetween. France was ~~especially notorious~~ famous for its possessed convents such as Louviers & Loudun, and North America for its intense outbreak at Salem in 1693. Sweden had an intense outbreak in 1669 while Italy suffered severe ~~outbreaks~~ persecution up to about 1540 when the Roman Inquisition, as in Spain - according to H.C.Lea, exercised a moderating influence. The wildest guesses have been made as to the numbers involved in the period 1484-1700. Thus H.C.Lea guessed (i) that there were some 90,000 victims in Britain alone and Maurice Ashley accepts that 'many thousands were condemned & burnt' in the first twelve years of James I's reign, perhaps deriving his information from Robert Steel who says that 70,000 witches were hanged in England under the Act of James I of England(2). In fact, according to the most reliable figures yet given it is very doubtful if over 1,000 people were executed in the whole history of witchcraft in England. This kind of exaggeration makes one slightly sceptical of the figures bandied about when talking of Europe. Thus Lea & Burr accept that 100,000 persons were executed in Germany & a German writer Ohle calculates that between 1575 & 1700 no less than a million persons were charged with witchcraft. Robbins' suggests, accepting the Burr-Lea number, that there were probably some 200,000 victims in Europe (3). The fact is that these are pure guesses, based on literary evidence which grossly exaggerate the probable numbers. ~~This Thomas has estimated that~~ (cf. Essex. 1560-1660. about 490 cases in 3/4 Assize records. 2nd only to theft)

Later in the essay I introduced the historical approaches thus:

Interpretations of witchcraft.

The two central problems for the historian of witchcraft are: why did such beliefs -apparently so irrational & beastly - arise & dominate the European mind when in many fields it was shaking itself free of medieval conceptions, and what were the forces which broke down the witchcraft-system? Necessarily our answers to these questions will be linked and will depend on our assessment of witchcraft itself. Thus, for example, if we believe witchcraft to be the product of sadistic church inquisitors we will argue that it arose when the Church gained a tighter grip over society & declined when secular interests emerged in their own right. If we hold that witchcraft is a continuation of deep-rooted paganism we may argue that its persecution arose when the Church grew powerful enough to drive deep into the popular mind and that the persecution only ended with the eradication of the pagan cult. Let us briefly examine three of the major theories which have been suggested so far.

Then after a brief summary of the anthropological approach, I concluded with a criticism of functionalist approach.

What seems to me the main defect of this 'functional' approach is that is is static. It can tell us what witchcraft does in a certain society but since anthropologists are usually concerned with a society at a certain point in time (& historians with how it changes) of necessity they do not have the material for showing why a particular pattern emerges rather than another. To take the anxiety-theory for instance, was it that people were more anxious in the centuries after about 1500 or was it that the methods of channelling that anxiety, persecution of other minorities or Job-like acceptance were no longer satisfying? Did anxiety decrease after 1660 with the growth of insurance, law & order, medical improvements - if there were any - and so on or was it that the energy found new outlets? Thus the problems solved seem to raise as many new ones.

Thus by the end of the summer term I had started to sketch out a framework for analysis and already encountered some of the difficulties of working on hitherto untouched legal records.

In late May I participated in the summer production by the Worcester College dramatic society, the Buskins. I was asked to sing 'Take oh take those lips away...' in Shakespeare's 'Love's Labours Lost'. I remember it a pleasant, but stressful, event as I could never learn the lines properly and some of the audience were not happy with my improvisations.

By kind permission of the Rev. the Vice-Chancellor, the Right Worshipful the Lord Mayor, and the Provost and Fellows of the College.

Worcester "Buskins" present

LOVE'S LABOUR'S LOST

by

William Shakespeare

FERDINAND, *King of Navarre*	David Stanton
BEROWNE } *Lords attending the King*	Roger Whitehouse
LONGAVILLE	Nick Roddick
DUMAIN	Colin Rowland
DON ADRIANO DE ARMADO, *The Braggart*	Geoff Shaw
MOTH, *A Boy, his Page*	Nicky Mitchell
SIR NATHANIEL, *The Curate*	Ralph Houlbrook
HOLOFERNES, *The Pedant*	Phillip Darnton
DULL, *The Constable*	Michael Wood
COSTARD, *The Clown*	Robert Osborn
JAQUENETTA, *A Countrey Wench*	Jenny Ormond
THE PRINCESS OF FRANCE	Susan Bevan
ROSALINE } *Ladies attending the Princess*	Julia Evans
MARIA	Susan Plimmer
KATHERINE	Maureen Knight
BOYET } *Lords attending the Princess*	Nicholas Wilson
FORESTIER	Michael Symes
MARCADE, *A Messenger from France*	Peter Taylor

MUSICIANS :

Descant and Treble	Robin Wilson, Rodney Shewan
Treble	Peter Ward-Jones
Tenor	Robert Crofts
Bass	Richard McNicol
Crumhorn	Robin Wilson

CHORUS :

Helen Perry, Elizabeth Jacobs, Clare Roskill, Jane Caplan, Alison Franks, Alan McFarlan, Otto Uttenthal, Paul Fisher, Richard Hemingway.

DANCER: David Raston.

MUSIC by Taverner, Dowland, Holborne, Morley, etc.

There will be one interval of fifteen minutes during which Coffee and Hot Dogs will be available.

My mother refers to this performance in her next letter.

My mother wrote again from Cherideo on May 27th

I'm afraid this is a few days late, there seem to have been a mass of postal holidays this last week and every time I send for a form I find the P.O. for which Nazira is famous is shut! I got yours yesterday and was relieved to hear the bike was back and hadn't been too expensive to mend. Are you all right for money for June? I'm glad to hear Julie is quite recovered, sad news about Felicity having found her Man isn't it – at least I'm glad for her but perhaps you are sad?! This I believe is not to be passed on to Granny for the time being. I gather you aren't going to Borstal in July after all so perhaps there won't be room for me in your rooms then? I don't want to arrive and disorganise you, but can't afford to go to a hotel either, it might just happen that a friend has an empty room for week or two. I haven't quite grasped who Peter is, a college friend? It sounds so blissful at home now... I have finished my books so am trying to go through all my notes and make some sort of date chart, dates have always been my weakness. If my article isn't out by the time I get home I shall drop them a line I think, what is your thesis for Trevor-Roper on specifically and are going to read it or what? I read somewhere that more and more people are staying on to do post graduate research, I shouldn't fret too much about youth flying past, it is a pretty elastic quality which can't be tied down to years, some people never have it at all and others keep its essential wonder and surprise all their lives. Most of the young men out here are so old they have lost the use of all their senses and are to all intents and purposes dead already. ... I do wish I could see you being yokelish and playing your lute or is it lyre, has the white witch proved interesting? Did you read the long thing in the Sunday Times about the "W.H" of Shakespeare's sonnets? I must say I wasn't convinced, but it was amusing. I don't seem to be doing much reading these days except Assamese short stories which take a long time and are very quaint and old fashioned, full of death bed scenes of saintly girls etc....only three more letters I think, I really can't believe it.

I wrote again to Professor Trevor-Roper at the end of the month.

Worcester College, Oxford 31.5.64

Dear Professor Trevor-Roper,

Thank you so much for letting me attend your most profitable and enjoyable seminars on Intellectual History: I am only sorry that they had to end so early.

As you will be only too well aware it is a constant temptation to those doing research to become engrossed in dredging some minor historical tributary – especially when one salvages such strange objects as those incorporated in 'witchcraft' beliefs! One soon becomes incapable of dealing with wider historical problems etc. Though seminars have draw-backs – they involve a preparation which is not always possible – yet they seem a sensible way of combating over-specialization.

I wish you joy in 'Schools' and thank you once again for your help with regard to 'witchcraft'.

Yours sincerely, Alan Macfarlane

1964 - June

This summer is chiefly memorable for the return of my parents for the summer, my mother returning in late June and my father in August. This was their last leave before retiring in autumn 1965 and it was a precious time with the family re-united. Because we were mostly in England, the number of letters between us is diminished and hence there is less information about our lives. But there are still some strong traces of what was a beautiful and emotionally charged summer and a productive one for my writing.

My mother wrote again from Cherideo on June 6th 1964

A nice long letter yesterday which cheered me after rather a sad afternoon delivering one of my kittens to its new home ... I have got the "Memoirs of William Hickey" from Calcutta which is priceless, I expect you have read it. I have given up any idea of time with my Moghuls, shall probably still be tapping away on my typewriter about them in twenty years, with you working on your witches in the other corner! Anthropological theories of witchcraft sounds fascinating and this would be just the place for it, ever since the beginning of time Assam has been known as the land of magic and witchcraft, and this links up with their sakti Hinduism, which in turn takes one back to the mother goddess, sakti being the female principle. … I will certainly keep an eye open for animals, the folk stories are full of them but mostly odd creatures called "tail snatchers" or "toe nibblers" nothing very romantic. There is one theme running through all the stories of girls who for various reasons have to marry an animal, who of course is a prince in disguise – like the frog prince, I wonder what this Signifies?

I can't believe this will be almost my last letter, so much seems to have happened since I left England like running away from the chinese, it seems centuries since I saw you all. Anne has decided against Domestic drudgery which I think is a good thing, it sounded vastly boring and having to work in that hideous toast rack building in Manchester would be agony too. We'll have to find something else for her... Are you going to be away from July 11th I will carry on with my plan to come down then, if it's too much of a squash after you get back I can spend a week visiting all the friends and relations round about and we can all go back north together, probably need two shifts to get your books back. I'm spending a couple of nights in Manchester with all fifteen of Fiona's friends who are obligingly turning out of their beds for me, knowing how cold and tired I always feel when I first arrive it may prove a trying ordeal all round!

My mother wrote again from Cherideo on 16th June.

Really and truly my last letter, I leave a week to-day, the monsoon is late in breaking this year, it would be, and will probably follow me and my planes all over India Its damp and quite cool here, Daddy has a heavy cold which he will probably give me just before I leave too so I expect to arrive a wreck but some English air will soon put me right. Thank you for a letter I got on Saturday, I'm afraid I haven't quite grasped what this new job you hope to get is but you can explain it all to me. Brenda got your long letter and she and John were most impressed at your clear logical mind! They have been having great fun trying to find the answers to some of your questions, especially the one about the average amount spent on food etc. by the average working man. It is almost impossible to get a straight answer to any question here, they say the thing they think you want to know and you are supposed to be able to decide for yourself whether it is the truth or not and make the necessary adjustments, a curious trait that was irritating Sir T. Roe in 1611 and still drives us mad. I don't know what has happened about my article but shall write to them when I get back. I am busy trying to finish the four Vols of William Hickey, it's great fun but horrifying too, the nepotism, graft, and coldblooded unfeelingness of the White Man in Bengal from Warren Hastings down chills one's own blood even now. They all spent their time screwing huge sums out of the "opulent natives" and occasionally noticing the corpses on the roadsides when the local famines became very severe. One of the clergymen, in business with the undertaker, looked forward to the "harvest" period of November and December and gave minute instructions as to how much to screw out of the bereaved, the greater their sorrow the more they could be expected to spend. And so on ad nauseam. I suppose the England of George III wasn't too different, but it seems worse when set against the suffering poor of India. I am reading "Ronald Knox" by Waugh, I like it but somehow the problems and lives of he and his friends seem rather "precious" and uninvolved, endlessly debating whether bread was brad or Bread and the Holy Ghost was a second form of breathing and all those elegant cosy teas and the huge sum of money he left at the end of it – imprisoned again by his times I suppose and his Eton–Balliol upbringing but he gives the impression that the only important thing in life is being a Catholic and once you are safely "in" the rest of the world can struggle along somehow... I don't seem to have done any packing but it's just a question of flinging a few rags in to a case, I spend several hours in Amsterdam but will probably be too frozen to move out of the airport as I haven't got a warm coat. I'm due at Manchester at 5 p.m. on Sunday and will try and ring you up that evening if anyone knows your number. Till then keep your fingers crossed for me, the most dangerous part of the journey will probably be the road trip to Gauhati. Longing to see you. Much love, Mummy.

I wrote to my father from Worcester College on Sunday 21st June

Dear Daddy,

Just a scribble since you must be a little lonely with Mummy gone. By the time you get this she will be shivering in Manchester, hustled around by five thousand of Fiona's friends. I will try to get up to meet her - depending on whether my motorbike electric fittings have been repaired by then, the battery keeps running down - I suppose it's either not re-charging or shorting: wish I knew something about these machines! I think really it's quite a good bargain actually, but little things have been going wrong.

As you will have gathered I have a fairly chaotic programme for the summer - the only fixed point being the 11-25th July when I will be amidst the bogs of Yorkshire with the Borstal camp. As I write this I'm listening to the Beatles - or rather tape-recording them - so that I can learn a few of their songs & be "with it". Of course, you've missed the 'Beatle mania" - you'll have to spend the first week listening to them - getting used to the new, post Beatle world! They're very good really. Anyhow I expect you've had them on 'Radio India' endlessly.

I don't seem to do much at the moment except wander among piles of typed sheets of paper scouring for witches; actually I've chosen a fascinating subject but look forward very much to getting away from it for a while. The Borstal Camp is on the Aire or some river with good trout fishing. We must get over to the Duddon & see if we can't get a few sea-trout. I wonder if we could go off on the motorbike & a tent for a few days to Scotland or the Yorkshire dales?

Look after yourself - see you soon.

Best love, Alan

My grandfather's diary records that 'Sunday 28 June Iris arrives at Manchester'. The next day my mother wrote amusingly to my father about us all, having not seen any of us for nearly two years (my parents had returned to India in October 1962).

Iris to Mac from 153, Mauldeth Road, Manchester, 29 June 1964.

Darling,

A brief respite in the chaos that is Art to tell you I'm safely home as you probably guessed – arrived ten minutes late yesterday, the 10 mins being me holding the plane up! I was sitting in the wrong

"lounge" & would have been there still if a stewardess hadn't happened to check upon on me – honestly you'd think they'd have loudspeakers in every room. Had to sprint like mad & arrived gasping & sobbing to find all the other passengers strapped into their seats & looking very frigid as they had been held up by me, felt quite a fool! We had a good trip and the girls were at the airport to meet me, both in good form & very fat! Especially Anne who is like a pudding. Of course I started moaning about Fiona's hair straight away, she is fearfully scruffy, no make-up etc. but when I went to the art college this morning found everyone looked exactly like her. The flat is incredible, nobody ever puts anything away and it is a mass of clothes, dirty cups, paintings, cigarette ash & records. I complained weakly to start with but have given up – just concentrate on keeping my few little belongings from being swamped in the tide. I looked at Fiona's paintings which were rather odd but so were everyones, the only ones I really liked I found the artist was considered so bad he had just been thrown out! F is considered to be doing well and seems now to want to go on & finish which is a good thing though how she can bear to go on living like this I can't imagine! At about 6 Alan arrived, so we had a lively homey evening with the guitar & two bottles of Guinness! Alan is just the same, wearing the same black jeans & the same shoes we left him in – I went out & bought him a new pair of each this morning! We had a hectic morning shopping in the sales, I got a dress, skirt & jeans & shoes so there. Also underclothes & a haircut for us all – this last in the face of violent protests from F who already looks better. Great excitement here over topless dresses, one of the girls here asked to try one on to-day & was followed round by a troop of drooling reporters! They are very nice girls all of them, all north country and 3 of them very pretty under the sheets of hair. I'm going home to-morrow & will write again in a couple of days to let you know about Field Head, will you let me know again what day you arrive at Amsterdam? Can't really concentrate with the noise – but am thinking of you darling and hoping all is well with you all & longing to see you again.

My grandfather then records on Tuesday 30 June 'Iris arrived here. Alan arrives' The gap here is caused by the fact that my mother and Anne came up by train and I by motorbike.

1964 - July to September

My mother wrote to my father on 2nd July from Field Head.

Home at last – arrived the day before yesterday on a beautiful day and it was bliss to be back. The house looking very nice & tidy, poppies & roses blooming, the first strawberries ripening and the hay being cut in the front fields. It was a heavenly day yesterday and we went for a walk down Black Beck & I got hay fever but it was still lovely. M & D are both looking very well and are full of energy, doing the same things as when we left, racing papers all morning & Telly in the afternoon – we've been watching Wimbledon & saw some Test Match this p.m – unfortunately I.T.V. is on strike & B.B.C. very poor & streaky in the afternoon. I was very depressed by Fiona's flat which was unbelievably squalid, they're clearing out at the end of this term so I hope will find somewhere less congested – I suppose being tired after the journey it got me down particularly. Anne & I came back by train, the taxi from the station cost us as much as the rail fare but I'll indent for both! This morning I went into the bank & was immediately recognized & greeted which was nice, Anne opened an account with the money she made out of her job. Everything is exactly the same, same people in the shops & on the bus, terribly restful. All the gardens are looking lovely, the Barrs Farm is just a shell surrounded by rubble but the formidable Rev. Woodall hasn't appeared yet. I spoke to Beryl over the fence but she didn't sound very rapturous to see me, perhaps imagination. Alan is still working very hard, he has his typewriter in the shed and taps away all morning & some of the afternoon. He & Anne went to a "do" at the rifle club last night, you should have seen us trying to find something presentable for him to wear, he is just as vague about clothes as ever, & loves the black shirt I bought in Calcutta as he reckons it will never need washing & will see him through his D.Phil easily! I don't think I'll go down to Oxford till about 20th, can't be bothered to pack up again yet awhile. Could you please send your salary thing for F's grant? So sorry about the animals darling – I should stop the ointment in Dinah's eye & just use Boric Acid Cotton. I'm, missing you terribly & am longing to see you.

My mother then went off the next day to visit my father's brother and his wife in Scotland, my grand-father noting in his diary on Friday 3 July 'Iris left for Scotland'. She wrote to my father from Wishaw on July 7th.

As you see I'm up staying with Alan & Jean – I rang them up soon after I arrived & they were very anxious for me to come up & stay for a few days before they go off to Ireland for a month & the kids go back to school – so I'm here till the end of the week. Came up by bus, an easy trip after a slightly chaotic start. Mummy said there was an 11.50 bus at the end of the road but after waiting 20 mins we realised there wasn't & I'd miss my connection in Ambleside – so Alan had to rush back for his motor bike, fling a few necessary clothes into my air bag & off we set – me blue with cold & fright & whispering "slower Alan" through clenched teeth! We got there with 5 minutes to spare & then I let the bus come in & go out again because it had "Blackpool" stuck on the windows. However I got another one which caught up with it at Keswick & after that it was a lovely sunny trip & Alan met me at Hamilton. They are all exactly the same here, the children a bit larger & quite nice – the girls that is, John comes back to-morrow. Alan & Jean look blooming & Jean is endlessly cooking us all vast meals. We had a lovely first day but since then the weather has been drizzly, not that I mind, we've watched Wimbledon & the Test Match & there is golf to-day, apart from sport. I find Telly terribly dreary but perhaps I shall get used to it again. We haven't done much, went over to visit some friends who have just bought a vast new house one evening, otherwise just pottered, eaten & slept – shall be vastly huge by the time I see you. The silly clots have made out my ticket from Manchester to Amsterdam so shall have to have it changed as soon as I hear your arrival date. Am not going to Oxford till about 20th July, that will give me 2 weeks & will fit in with Anne's refresher course in London. I left Rs 190 with Mr Hannah in Calcutta, he's probably told you, so that should see you through. He was very kind & helpful. I'm quite happy but missing you lots & doggies & Bird & everything. I hope they have all settled down and Suet Pud isn't driving you silly & the factory working – it all seems terribly remote now & I feel I've been home for months instead of 10 days, my tummy aches all gone, have lots of new clothes, all I need now is you to tell me I look nice in them. Keep cheerful darling. Love you lots *- Totty*

The epic motorbike ride with my mother on the back was seen from another angle in a letter I wrote to my father two days later on 9th July, which also contains other news of my doings.

Dear Daddy,

I am just about off to spend two weeks in the wilds of Yorkshire and in one of H.M's borstals so I thought I'd drop you a line before I lost contact with civilization completely - also you will be leaving Cherideo T.E. soon. Hope everything goes well with you - Mummy tells me that you are very busy. As you will know she has gone to Scotland for a few days, a pity as she is missing the beginning of the strawberries & raspberries which are magnificent (I will miss the bulk of them unfortunately). I steamed up to meet her on my motorbike - it went beautifully with bits & pieces tied all over it - but of course she had told me the plane arrived at 5 p.m. thinking that was the same as 1500 hours! Still we met up at the "flat" and I must say you have *been looking after her well; I can't remember seeing her looking better. The usual chaos when we saw her off to Scotland - the Hawkshead bus was half hour late & so I drove her, clutching whitely on the back, to Ambleside - muttering "there's no hurry" through clenched lips every time the speedometer registered over 15 m.p.h! We arrived in plenty of time- but I foolishly left her to catch the bus alone & she watched it come in & go out, without moving, apparently! You will have heard this story from her - I wonder if the versions tally!*

You may have heard that we went to a party last Saturday with Anne Johnson, Dusty & Jane etc. The bike played up a bit - my fault really since I had left the battery a bit loose & suddenly found myself stalling in the dark with the battery swinging by one lead against my leg! I have left it with a lad in Hawkshead who is supposed to be an expert, hope he is as I have got to take it round England - or rather it's got to take me.

I've been busy practicing the latest 'pop' tunes on my guitar - a great social asset with these boys I'm told.

Went fishing in Black Beck the other day - masses of tiddlers of 4-6 inches but nothing worth keeping.

Look after yourself & see you in Oxford in early August.

Much love, Alan

On 11th July, according to my grandfather's diary, I left for the Oxford-Borstal camp. Just before I went, I left a message for my mother as follows:

Dear Mummy,

So sorry to miss you - but will see you in a few days. Hope everything went O.K. in Scotland. Granny has my addresses & dates - here are a list of miscellaneous things.
1) Enclosed a cheque for my board & keep for 10 days - if you could pay it to Granny.
2) Enclosed some letters - could you post them on Monday or Tuesday - could you censor the letter to Daddy & make sure I haven't said anything indiscreet about Scotland etc.
3) Here is all the stuff I'd like you to take to Oxford if you would - file, 1 book & hole-machine.[1]
There are also some things for you - map of Oxford, key (remember that Miss Faraday will expect you

---

[1] First reference to punch card Cope-chat cards

to get a key from her as I'm not supposed to have a duplicate) & letter for the Bodleian - to be handed to the librarian when you meet him.
4) Library & work. Write to Mr Beesley, Bodleian Library saying the date when you would like to start (remember library closes Sat 1.p.m & Sunday) saying that I've mentioned you to Mr Webster (who is at the moment on holiday) & asking if you could see him (& specify that you want to work at my desk in the typing room &, if you can, any books etc. you would like to work on).
Also included two addresses - I would suggest Mr Davies as your best bet - drop him a card saying you will be down in Oxford & could you see him.
Use anything in my room you want - tape-recorder (get Linda to show you how etc)
Digs My digs are 19, Chalfont Rd - Miss Faraday lives next door in 21, Chalfont Rd (?17? - same house) & may want you to have a room in her house. Arrange about money when I come down as I think she may have a temporary fill in for my room - drop her a line as to when you'll be arriving. The house is thus.

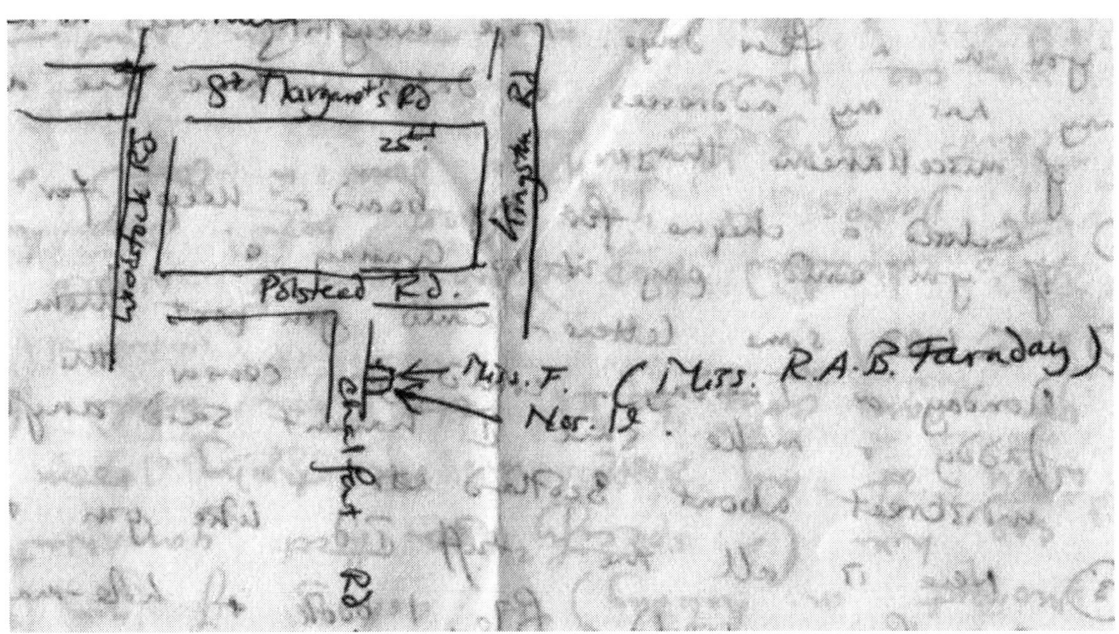

If you have any trouble about digs contact Linda S. who I hope you'll see anyway - she lives at the top of Nos. 19 & is perhaps rather lonely.

If you have any trouble about the library ring up (or go to see) Mr H.G. Pitt, Worcester College (Dean) who wrote the letter. (you could tell him Robert has accepted the fellowship at all Souls).
Also if you have time the following expect to see you.
Lady R. Clay. 121A Woodstock Rd - an invalid & very nice - just nearby - interested in history - related to Mitchisons/Mitfords & keen on Robert.
Rosemary 10 Hearnes Rd (Oxford 58391) - very sweet - social worker - mother in children's books - interested in Arthurian legend
Bill Caldwell. 24, Frenchay Rd. (end of Chalfont Rd) - hemophiliac, lonely, American

I will arrive on 25th I hope - write to Borstal etc if you have any questions. Hope all goes well - get a new reel for typewriter (ask Anne about how it jams). See you then, Much love, Alan

This is a revealing letter, as it mentions several new characters who played a considerable part in my further life in Oxford: Linda, my next girlfriend, Lady Clay, my undergraduate tutor, Rosemary Collins, married to my undergraduate friend Roy – I would lodge in the same house with them in my second year – and Bill Caldwell at whose flat I would stay on visits to Oxford from the Lake District. It also shows my attempt to help my mother's research for her book.

My mother went to Oxford via London (where my sister Anne was working) as planned. She wrote to my father on her birthday, the 22nd July, from 19 Chalfont Road, Oxford

I arrived here last night after a 13-hour journey – it took me 6 hours from Birmingham as I had to get local buses via Stratford with hours to wait – but finally got in at 9.30 p.m. & was met by Alan's landlady, a very bubbly lady but very kind. It's a v. nice room with a tiny stove, bookshelf, big table to work on & two huge leather arm chairs, at present I'm in bed with a bottle after a day getting myself organised. Went to the New Bodleian, then the old where a very exquisite intelligent girl made me take an oath before giving me a reading card, kept asking me if I was taking a Higher Degree and was most pained & suspicious when he found out I hadn't a degree at all. However I finally got myself & my typewriter settled at a table in the Indian Institute which has <u>all</u> the books I want & nearly went mad trying to decide which to go to first. I had a bottle of Guinness & sandwiches in a pub next door, shall be able to go there every day, felt a bit conspicuous as everyone else was either hairy undergraduate or part of a loving couple but still I got a lot of amusement out of listening to them talking, a young man next to me was saying to another "My dear, it changes key <u>three</u> times in the first few bars, can you imagine anything more EXCITING?" Oxford is just the same, very crowded, a peculiar man outside the pub asked me the way & then asked me to have a drink with him & yesterday a peculiar woman on the bus told me how lonely she was & when we arrived I couldn't shake her off. Finally got into a taxi & left her standing on the pavement, so there seem to be lots of peculiar people about! Still haven't heard from you your arrival date, nor had my ticket back from K.L.M. but hope to have both within the next couple of days, this will probably be my last letter to you, though I'll send another in case, can't think why I didn't check up properly about Amsterdam but will get there somehow darling – go to the K.L.M. desk when you arrive in case there's a message from me, that is if I'm not there myself but I just might not to be able to make it until the evening or something. Do hope the hand over goes off all right and no last minute floods or hitches occur – longing to see you darling – Hugs till then Totty

It would appear that finally my parents did manage to meet in Amsterdam, as the following postcard written to my sisters show.

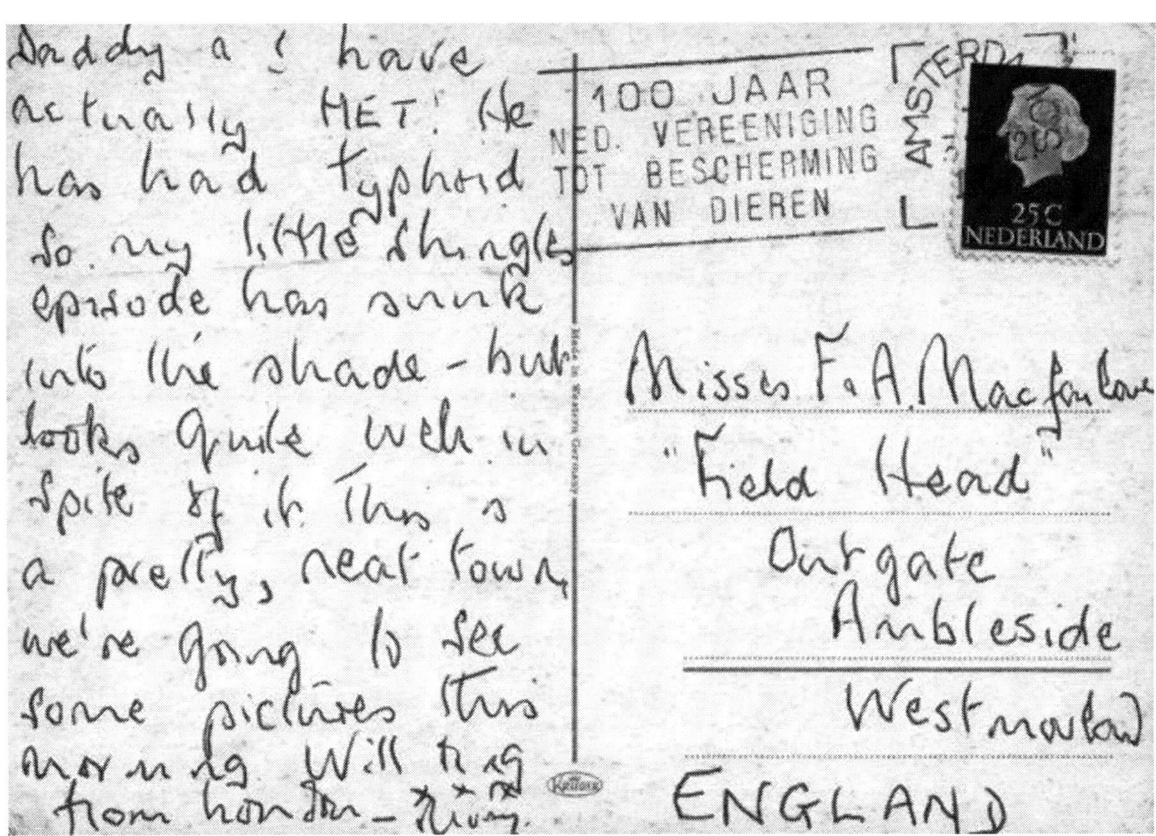
Daddy a I have actually MET! He has had typhoid so my little shingles episode has sunk into the shade - but looks quite well in spite of it. This is a pretty, neat town, we're going to see some pictures this morning. Will ring from London - Xxxx

100 JAAR
NED. VEREENIGING
TOT BESCHERMING
VAN DIEREN
AMSTERD
25 C
NEDERLAND

Misses F. A. Macfarlane
"Field Head"
Outgate
Ambleside
Westmorland
ENGLAND

With the imminent arrival of my father, my grandparents moved out temporarily into a house which I was owned by the daughter (Jane) of our neighbour Beryl Buckmaster. This was Browhead in Troutbeck, where we would visit for parties at a later date. My grandfather records on 24th July in his diary 'Came to Browhead' and then, on Saturday 8th August, 'Mac arrives'.

The only record I have of the ten weeks of my father's stay is in photographs, of my father, a visit to the sea and lounging on the front lawn at Field Head.

Only one poem from this vacation has survive. It must have been written in a moment of leisure while on the Borstal camp as it is dated 26.7.64

To be poised in and out of time,
To feel still uncertain of the movement
of things, to feel unsure that the rose will ever die.

To kiss the rose and not to know goodbye
To hear music in the silences
And the distant trumpets of a loftier moment
When all the majesty, all the misery
Of this world gathered itself to a greatness
And struck in fury and pain on the rock
Thinking the fair moment with its spray
Its lights, and dancing desires and
The sound of bells in the deep.
This is the stillness in the storm
The unravelled moment of the poet
The affirmation that 'all is well'
The answering voice in the dark.
Not an answer to a query
Not a certainty amidst doubt
Not even shelter, but a certain
Timelessness.

In the three months from July to September I continued to work on the theoretical background to the thesis. I met Keith at least once, on August 3rd.

Keith wrote from St John's on 4th August

Dear Alan,

What a pity I hadn't read these before we met yesterday. I think they are excellent – particularly the Sociological Approaches & the Recent Interpretations. I think you are now very well equipped to extract the maximum interest from your Essex findings. It is a pity the anthropologists are so unhelpful on the fundamental problem – why witchcraft & why then? But if it can be solved you are in a better position than anyone else to do so.

I look forward to seeing you again at the end of the vac. Yrs Keith Thomas

P.S. I have made a few pencilled notes on the text itself, but none are of very great interest. I thought the style much better, if I may say so!

I have the carbon copies of the two essays which Keith referred to, but not the originals, so do not have his markings. Here are a few samples from each just to show how my thinking was developing and also my methodology.

I wrote a parallel text. In the main body, double-spaced, I outlined the questions and theories of anthropologists. I then used this as a stimulus to write some first impressions of what the sources and answers for such questions might be.

(1)

THE SOCIOLOGICAL APPROACH TO WITCHCRAFT.

Introductory.

Specific people are accused of being witches,other people are named as their victims.These are observed facts and can be analysed,unlike the 'ideology of witchcraft' which can only be interpreted.The two basic facts we must ascertain are the position,sex,age & other details of witch & victim & their relationship to each other.The study of the second of these has especially attracted anthropologists recently for it illuminates not only the tensions which precipitate witchcraft accusations but,more generally, indicates the major stresses in the inter-personal relationships of a society.

The older approach, that followed by Kluckhohn & Evans-Pritchard on the whole, was to see what personality,occupational or other types were involved as witch or victim.We will start by following this,but it should throughout be remembered that each detail of the victim's age,sex, or otherwise must be related to that of the witch and vice versa.Thus it is not enough to learn that Nupe witches are old women, we must also remember that their victims are usually young men under their influence (1).

On this I commented as follows.

The historical study of the 'sociology of witchcraft' has not, as far as I am aware, proceeded beyond a few generalizations about the fact that women were usually accused of being witches, often old women at that, and that children were often their supposed victims. It has been noted that not all witches were old, ugly & poor everywhere (Robbins, Encyclopedia, p.16), but beyond this little detailed work has been done on either the witch/victim in themselves or on their relationships. This is because, as has been pointed out, historians of the subject, exclusively concentrating on literary evidence which only dealt with occasional sensational trials have been primarily interested in 'the ideology of witchcraft'. C.L.Ewen's studies however allow us to analyse in detail those involved, their background, personal characteristics etc. & combined with the pamphlets & Gifford this should allow us to form a clearer picture of how witchcraft prosecution actually worked – what relationships were resolved in these terms, what personality types accused etc.

The 25 foolscap pages of the essay on 'Recent Interpretations of Witchcraft/Sorcery' included the following.

WITCHRAFT AS EXPLANATION.

Witchcraft as an explanation of personal misfortune.

The Azande says that "Death has always a cause, and no man dies without a reason" (4) and death is not the only misfortune which needs explanation. Of every misfortune the Azande ask "why did it happen to a certain person at a certain time"? For instance when an elephant and a man meet it is obvious that the natural cause of death – the 'how' of the death if one likes – was the elephant – but they also seek the metaphysical cause – the 'why' of the death. Thus witchcraft as a metaphysical explanation does not exclude rational observation of the natural world. Nor does it exclude human responsibility, for it is only when human skill & human goodness has been used to the uttermost that witchcraft can be

(1) Kluckhohn, 1944, p.40. (2) Nadel, 1954, p.206. (3) Evans-Pritchard 1951. p.102.
(4) Evans-Pritchard, 1937, p.111.

The advantage of the anthropologist in being able to actually live with witchcraft are balanced by two advantages which the historian possesses. The first is that he can study witchcraft diachronically – watch it evolved & undermined in a society, see what it replaced & what destroys it. Apart from the observations (see later) on the recent effects of westernization on African societies anthropologists are almost unable to do this. Kluckhohn attempts, and apart from a few remarks about the effects of Fort Sumner on the Navaho, admits defeat. (see p.41 & p.64) Thus a historical survey should be able to test what are still theories – that witchcraft serves certain functions – by investigating the 'before' & 'after' of witchcraft.

Secondly there is far more information for a study of European witchcraft, statistically analysable material, than for the most witch-haunted of modern societies where witchcraft, usually unrecognized in law, goes underground. Thus Nadel's elaborate theorizing is built on 10 observed cases, Fortes' on less than ten (1949, p.33) & even Kluckhohn's elaborate figures have nothing like the amount of material that the 500 odd cases in the Essex Assize records alone /11/ give the

Another section shows the way in which I questioned the rather conservative and functionalist interpretation which was forced on anthropologists by the nature of their data.

The fact that witchcraft can be used to preserve a group's or a society's equilibrium by keeping all disruptive elements in control (6) & by encouraging such virtues as'good neighbourliness' & general charity (7) has frequently been pointed out. We are told that it is in the idiom of witchcraft that the Azande"express moral rules which lie mostly outside criminal & civil law" (8); that it is a sanction upholding the rights of age-mates among the Bugisu (9);that among the Nupe the witch is the person who openly & successfully sets aside the social values of the 'good' society, while among the Mesakin, the witch is the person who cannot live up to the social values yet cannot openly rebel against them (10); that the threat of

(1)Middleton,p.217.(2) Kluckhohn,1944,p.63. (3)Middleton,p.93.
(4)Kluckhohn,1944,p.63.(5) Evans-Pritchard,1937,p.100.(6) ~~[illegible]~~ Kluckhohn, 1944,p.63-4; see also Gluckman,1963,p.94,Middleton,p.156,p.92,Nadel,1952,p.28.

On this I comment in the parallel essay at the bottom.

It is usually assumed by anthropologists that witchcraft is,on the whole, a conservative force, preventing deviation,experiment etc. It's very foundation is the organic view of man, that each is intimately involved with another, that one man cannot rise without another falling (a conception which seems to lie,e.g., behind much of the Tudor economic legislation) that our actions somehow influence others & that our very thoughts, even unspoken ones, may have an harmful effect on others. Evil intentions, as Hobbes,Bayle & Selden (Briggs,Pale Hecate,47,Kittredge,Witchcraft in Old/New England,p.350) were punishable it was thought - but not just because such evil intentions should be discouraged since they might lead one day to evil action but because somehow,mystically, they harmed society.It is in the distinctions between visible & invisible activities, between mind & matter, prayer & action; in the application of the Cartesian disociation, the 'disociation of sensibility' that we must look for the <u>intellectual</u> changes which helped make those in power sceptical. But had there been some subtle shifting, a blurring of distinctions which is possibly the basis of magical activity also, which had occurred somewhere towards the end of the middle ages ? How does P.K, placebos, psycho-somatic illness etc. effect our

Both essays summarized a number of theories and analyses in anthropology. I had about ten key books by Evans-Pritchard, Nadel, Kluckhohn, Marwick and others, and I carefully went through them and made a subject index on small cards (5 by 3 inch cards cut in half). Here is a sample of that index, part of what I extracted on the sex of the supposed witch.

Females & witches
- suggested reason
(females always impure)

Hertz, Right Hand, 97

Sex ratio of sorcerers -
different in theory/practice.

MARWICK
Sorcery p 96

Women as witches - reason why

White, Luvale Beliefs, 66

Will of the male is permissive in witchcraft activity - in not preventing witches.
Nupe; 169.

Witch may be a member of either sex among Amba!

W/Sorcery in E.Africa. 280 n.

Sorcerer among Bunyoro may be of either sex.

W/Sorcery in E.Africa.29.

Analysis of Cewa witchcraft cases indicates that there is an equal sex ratio among 'witches' (contradicts theory - that most witches are women).

Marwick. n.n. 400.(b)

Women, and occasionally men, believed to be able to have the evil eye. (Gisu)
W/Sorcery in E.Africa.
194.

Women alone are evil witches.
Nupe; 169.

In all ten known cases of witchcraft accusations among Tale the accused was a woman.

Fortes. n.n. 474.

Many witches elderly women among Gusii.

W/Sorcery in E.Africa. 226.

Women, weaker in personality, not such strong witches as men among Bugisu.
W/Sorcery in E.Africa.
215.

Keith had been very pleased with my two essays on anthropological approaches in August, but was more critical of a piece which I sent him in early October on 'The Historiography of Witchcraft'. I had planned this piece out rather carefully, as two plans drawn up in the summer show.

I. DEFINITIONS OF WITCHCRAFT.

II. GENERAL INTERPRETATIONS.

a) By authors. (Kluckhohn)

Williams. Evans-Pritchard. Preserved Smith.
Briggs. Notestein Christina Hole.
Robbins. Ewen. Kittredge. (Rago for tout.)
(Murray) Trevor-Davies. Burr.
(Parrinder) Oxford Histories Lea.
(Summers) Lecky. Scot.
Pennethorne Hughes. Ewen.

b) By types of interpretation.

(5) Economic & social.
(4) Anthropological/sociological. literary/anthropological – 2 worlds views conflict.
(3) Religious/ theological/ [illegible].
Historical
– Political.
(2) Local events.
(1) Medical/psychological (sexual etc)

Perhaps divide interpretation chronologically e.g. Romantic (Michelet) Rationalist (Lecky) Anthropological etc.

weakness when tested against facts.

Kinds of question asked & answers expected.

(Addenda: Some implicity & explicit comparisons examined; e.g. Nazis, Jews, Voodoo – Haiti, Africa)

III. SUGGESTED INTERPRETATIONS SO FAR UNUSED.

IV. TYPES OF EVIDENCE SO FAR ADDUCED.

(a) Type of evidence – (see sources for study. *).
(b) Who used it & with what effect.
(c) Nature & dangers of evidence.
(d) How might this further be used.

– see use of
(1) Distortions caused by present evidence.
(2) Gaps which might be filled.
(3) Necessary lacunas.
(4) Evidence from unlikely sources which might be used.
(5) Relative imp. of various kinds of evidence.

V. METHODS OF HANDLING EVIDENCE.

VI. MY AIMS & METHODS.

VII HOPKINS & EAST ANGLIA.

SOURCES FOR STUDY. *

Central.

Admin.

Parlty attitude. (State Papers)
Commissions of Oyer & Terminer.

Legal.

Laws.
Activities of central cts – esp. Privy Council.

Local.

~~Records~~ Town records.
County records; ¼ sessions etc.
Ecclesiastical records ? – visitation returns ?
Parish records.
Inventories post mortem.
Family papers, biographies etc.
Gaol records.

Literary.

Accounts of trials.
Witch-pamphlets & theoretical
General literature – plays, poetry etc
Secondary sources – local historians etc.

APPROACHES TO THE STUDY OF WITCHRAFT.

SOURCES.

i. Literary.
ii. Historical.

APPROACHES.
a) Anthropological - through a study of modern anthropological techniques.
b) Sociological - " " " sociological techniques.
c) Political& constitutional - " "

INTERPRETATIONS.
1. a) Political,constitutional - vide Trevor Davies & Burr, but do they distinguish causes from effects ? Even if it can be shown that Puritans were anti-witchcrat etc & this helped cause the civil war, why were they anti-witchcraft?
~~b) Religious~~ The above , as suggested by Notesteing, does perhaps explain the Mathew Hopkins Outbreak when political events released popular hatred from the bonds of authority.
2 b) Religious & theological.
This equates Puritanism esp. with rising belief in witchcraft - but there are many inconsistencies - eg why was Calvinist Holland so free from it ?
3 c) Regional.
Certain regions (Essex,Lancashire) more prone to it than others. One can trace a definite spreading outward from London from 1560. But not much has been said as to ~~whether~~ why these regions should be worst- usually half-baked ideas about Puritanism are cited.
4. d) Local situations. Eg Notestein who stresses that no overall theory can be held to account for all the events & stresses the importance of personal factors - the energy of Hopkins, personal rivalries, the views of James I etc. A sane but in the end unsatisfactory explanation.
5. e) Economic. This theory is held more about the Inquisition etc abroad than in England. It suggests that the Inquisition started up a class who became financially dependent on the torture & conviction of rich victims. This comes nearest to realisation in England in Hopkins & the Scottish witch-finders of the mid-C17 (see Notestein).
6 f) Sexual.
See esp. Preserved Smith on the sadism of frustrated clerics.
7 g) Anthropological/ folklore.
That witchcraft was serving a necessary purpose - attacks on witchcraft were attacks on infiltrating ideas, on the new science & medicine.
That there really was a secret pagan superstition in hostility to the orthodox religion - see Margaret Murray.
8 h) Sheer hatred.
See Montagu Summers etc(?) & those who argue that the whole phenomenon was a monstrous creation on the part of the authorities with no basis in fact.
9. j) Literary/anthropological.
That there was a conflict between two 'world views' & that the witch scare was one of the symptoms. Renaissance man was challenging the old Catholic universe where man was helpless & in the stage before he discovered the natural causes of phenomena such as sickness he blended the spiritual & material by saying that the Devil brought sickness through people. Thus neither was the the spiritual explanation utterly rejected, nor the human one entirely accepted.

BASIC FACTORS TO ASCERTAIN.
a) All facts relating to number & details of witch-trials.
b) Views of contemporaries.
Classify historiographical treatment.
Cf with other areas & countries & times.
Basic methods & questions of anthropology.
Relationship between various factors - political,economic, social etc & witchcraft.
Theories concerning literature & ideology in C16 & C17.

Psychological } interpretations recently ? esp re. education.
Psychiatrical } children.

I then wrote a preliminary version. This was read by my mother who made a few minor suggestions.

(1)

It is not surprising that ~~witchcraft~~ the history of witchcraft with its curious & gruesome details should have ~~has~~ attracted considerable attention~~, both from serious & less scholarly students.~~ Containing much that is brutal, much that is perverted & much that seems at first sight either ludicrous or fantastic to our eyes it has been more than usually difficult to remain objective. As a result there have arisen (polemical divisions split) apparently irreconcilable interpretations. There are disagreements over all the fundamental problems; when witchcraft began & ended; whether there really were 'witches'; whether prosecution was really justified on occasions; why witchcraft was prosecuted more fiercely during the sixteenth & seventeenth centuries in Europe; whether one can draw any analogies with modern witchcraft in primitive societies, and what forces led to its lighter treatment towards the end of the seventeenth century. ~~It is hoped that~~ An examination of the various interpretations so far ~~suggested~~ (~~the assumptions on which they are based & the evidence that is adduced in support of them~~) ~~will demonstrate~~ suggests that many of the collisions are caused by different questions being asked & different definitions being used. [The bracketing of several authors within one 'interpretation' necessarily does injury to their total contribution and can only be excused on grounds of brevity.] Paras 8 & 9 here, followed by a listing of the various interpretations. 1.

The 'Rationalist' approach.

This interpretation includes among its exponents such notable historians as W.E.H.Lecky (1),H.C.Lea (2), G.L.Burr (3),A.D.White (4), & Preserved Smith (5). It has recently found expression in the learned Encylopedia of Witchcraft & Demonology (London,1958) by R.H.Robbins and its assumptions are the basis for the controversial work of R.Trevor Davies on this subject(6). It has amassed a vast amount of material & is undoubtedly the most powerful school working at the moment. An extreme statement of this interpretation illustrates, if a little unfairly, some of its basic tenets of this approach. R.H. Robbins argues that "If witchcraft had never 2.

(1) W.E.H.Lecky. History of the Rise & Influence of the Spirit of Rationalism in Europe.(London,1865).
(2) H.C.Lea. History of the Inquisition of the Middle Ages.(London,1888)
Materials Towards a History of Witchcraft.(Philadepphia,1939,ltd.ed. New York,1957)
(3) G.L.Burr. Selections from his Writings.(ed. Lois Oliphant Gibbons.Ithaca.1942)

I then retyped a second version in late autumn which was 37 pages long, some 10-15,000 words. I sent it to Keith and he read it with great care and attention. This is the most meticulous set of comments I think I have from him, and it led him to write me a set of instructions on how I should write. It shows how a highly engaged and careful "master" can teach his "apprentice" student, I shall include a few of the most heavily annotated pages to show what he felt I was doing wrong. Over half the pages had no comments on them. (Some of the general comments and markings are my own)

THE HISTORIOGRAPHY OF WITCHCRAFT.

It is not surprising that the history of witchcraft with its curious and gruesome details should have attracted considerable attention. Containing much that is brutal, much that is perverted and much that seems at first sight either ludicrous or fantastic to our eyes it has been more than usually difficlt to remain objective. As a result there have arisen opposed and apparantly irreconcilable interpretations. There are disagreements over all the fundamental problems; when witchcraft began and ended; whether there really were 'witches'; whether prosecution was really justified on occasions; why witchcraft was prosecuted more fiercely during the sixteenth and seventeenth centuries in Europe; whether one can draw any analogies with modern witchcraft in primitive societies, and what forces led to its lighter treatment towards the end of the seventeenth century. An examination of the various interpretations so far suggests that many of the collisions are caused by different questions being asked and different definitions being used.

Very broadly studies of witchcraft fall into two groups, the 'rationalist', which includes the work of W.E.H.Lecky, R.H.Robbins and Trevor Davies, and the 'early anthropological', with its ablest exponent Margaret Murray. These are supplemented by other, miscellaneous, interpretations, varying from the sweeping and hysterical generalization of Montague Summers, to the careful and almost purely factual works of C.L.Ewen. Historically the development has been from the nineteenth century approach which saw witchcraft persecution as part of the struggle between progress and superstition. Then through a period at the beginning of this century when the influence of Sir James Frazer's theories of the sacrifice of the God and the importance of fertility cults led to attempts to reconstruct witchcraft as the surviving "old religion". Up to the present, where a host of interpretations jostle with each other, borrowing for that purpose psychological or anthropological findings.

There are considerable difficulties in defining 'witchcraft', 'magic', 'sorcery' and similar terms. It is arguable that differences in such definitions are the primary reason for the major divisions were the worst persecutions? Which class or group was responsible? What was their motive? Why did they choose certain victims and not others? What had the accused in fact done to earn them hatred? How was it possible for otherwise intelligent men to fall into this lapse from reason? How were the supposed 'confessions' of witches obtained? What were the forces which finally undermined this 'superstition'? Very broadly the answers build the following pictures. The worst persecutions took place between about 1480-1680, flaring up into sudden 'outbreaks', and spreading like 'epidemics'. Witchcraft, though known in some of its forms before 1400 lacked the distinctive 'compact with the Devil' and was hardly persecuted. After 1680 there were only intermittent 'panics' in backward areas such as Scotland and parts of Germany. In England, it was originally argued that James I was largely responsible for introducing prosecutions (1) but more recently the date has been pushed back to the first years of Elizabeth's reign. Attempts are made to correlate centres of witchcraft prosecution with religious divisions - for instance it was once argued that New England, East Anglia, Sweden and Calvin's Geneva suffered far more than Catholic Italy and Spain, because of the intolerant and Devil-obsessed Puritans.(2) This opinion has been modified recently because it is realized that no such simple division can be made to include the tolerant Dutch and the intolerance of many Catholic German princedoms. It is now more generally argued that Northern Europe suffered more than Southern and that wherever there was persecution Churchman, of whatever official orthodoxy, took the lead. Thus to the question - which group was 'responsible' for the outbreaks? It is answered primarily the clergy, aided and abetted by profiteering lawyers and magistrates. The motives for their persecuting activity were varied. In very general terms witchcraft is seen as a bi-product of the struggle between two world-views, the scientific and religious and thus those who persecuted were

---

(1) For an attack on the earlier theory of James I's personal responsibility see G.L.Kittredge, Old & New England (op.cit.) ch.XVII. which has received statistical support from the figures of C.L.Ewen in his Witch Hunting & Witch Trials (London,1929).
(2) W.E.H.Lecky, Rise & Influence...(op.cit.) vol.1. pp.8-9; R.T.Davies, Four Centuries (op.cit.), passim. But see the powerful counter-arguments of G.L.Kittredge, Old & New England, ch.XVIII. & my Appendix

The general comment on the piece are contained in a typed letter from Keith dated 20th October and were a very useful guide for my writing as it gathered pace.

as from St.John's College,
Oxford.

20 October 1964

Dear Alan,

I have read the enclosed with great interest and I am very happy about your general approach. I think you have a good idea of what the problems are and are well placed to extract the maximum value from your Essex findings. So don't worry too much about the criticisms I shall now proceed to make or about the scribbles on the paper itself(above the line as well as below I fear); almost all of them relate to the method of presentation you have adopted and not to the general argument, which I think very sound.

Can I first set out some very general do's and don'ts for thesis writing(not necessarily for other sorts of writing)?

Avoid loose rhetoric and 'journalistic' writing.

Define your terms very carefully and aim at the maximum precision.

Take one question at a time and deal with it exhaustively. Then move on to the next one. Avoid false starts, 'see below's,etc.

Take the maximum care over your footnotes and references and have a standardised style(I can let you have one of the guides to conventions issued by the historical journals if you like).

Do not appear to have prejudged the question. Never make un-disclosed assumptions or invoke evidence which has not yet been set out.

When discussing other authors avoid being personal about it. It's their approach or their findings you are concerned with. When criticisng their findings be careful to separate their <u>assumptions</u> from their actual <u>method</u> and <u>evidence</u>,

If you look at your chapter in the light of all this I think you'll see what I mean. It is rather loosely, sometimes even carelessly written, and tends to open up subjects without dealing with them properly. You keep leaping ahead to invoke evidence which has not yet been disccussed. You never define your terms and this makes for apparent imprecision. Finally you are too rhetorical when discussing other writers. Always go for a matter of fact style. Outline rival theories coolly and baldly. If they are patently absurd they won't need your interpolated criticisms.

As I see it the purpose of this chapter is to justify the approach you propose to follow in the main body of the thesis. I think it should take the following course.

a) Define witchcraft , sorcery etc, and make it clear what subje you are proposing to investigate. ~~I might avoid it best to discuss Essex at this stage.~~

b) Outline the various approaches to the study of witchcraft which have been current hitherto (If you are going to talk about it then a brief survey of the anthropologists' work should come here). Explain as coolly as possible the strengths and weaknesses of these various approaches as methods.

c) Outline the method you propose to adopt. (I think your presesn paragraphs on this are very good).

d) Explain that you have chosen Essex and why. Indicate the sources you ~~xxxxxxxxxxxx~~ propose to use and discuss in particular the problem of the survival of assize records etc so that we have some idea in advance about how much weight to attach to you findings.

e) THE ESSEX DATA

f) Their interpretation and the light they throw upon exist ~~xxxxxx~~ theories(e.g. Puritanism and w., medicine and w.)

g) Your conclusion.

[handwritten margin beside d)–g): This of course would be the rest of the thesis]

Appendicex

Statistical tables,etc.
Bibliography.

At the risk of being schoolmasterly may I just repeat the most important point as far as exposition is concerned. TAKE IT SLOWLY;DEAL WITH ONE QUESTION AT A TIME: PROCEED FROM THE KNOWN TO THE UNKNOWN.

I realise that this is very difficult to do, but you must avoid presupposing any knowledge on the part of the reader and you must be particularly careful to avoid pre-supposing knowledge of what you are going to say in the next chapter. And never pronounce upon any topic without having first produced exhaustive evidence in support of your conclusion. In this chapter you tend to mix up expostion of other people's ideas with a prior taste of your own.

One tiny and unrelated point. How much attention are you going to devote to the <u>beliefs</u> side so far as Essex is concerned?

So there it is. If you think you've been hard done by you must tell me so! If there are any of the pencilled notes you can't decipher we can go over them when we meet next. I am in Wales at the moment but will be back in Oxford by thefourth week of term.x A meeting in say the fifth week might be a good idea, but do say if you'd prefer meet sooner. I can hardly wait to know what the results of the Essex calculations are going to be. It should be most exciting.

Yours,

Keith Thomas

x St. John's will forward mail, if you put a stamp on it!

1964 - October

I returned to Oxford at the end of September, to my new digs at 38 Park Town, a small flat in the basement of a house part of which was rented by Roy and Rosemary Collins. Roy I had met when he was studying history at Oxford under Keith Thomas. I prepared to give my first lecture for the Extra-Mural Department, which I had to give for a course on social history on 28th September , so I went down a little earlier to prepare. This was my first experience of lecturing to serious audiences, apart from the odd history society, was the course of lectures I gave for the Extra Mural Delegacy (what I incorrectly referred to as the W.E.A. [Worker's Educational Association], a different organization).[1] Over a period of two terms and bit terms, in 1964-5. There is a good deal about this in my letters and also my memories are quite strong.

I had done this for the money mainly – some £120 in the end, about a quarter of my grant. It was also good experience and a chance to try out my ideas. I remember going to the Central Library and the Bodleian and trying to get as many slides as possible as I was aware of the value of audio-visual aids. I remember starting by allocating just one day before the lectures, and creating notes on my little filing cards. Yet it was not very successful and the organizer obviously had complaints and took me for a drink in a pub near Worcester to enquire what I was doing. I then prepared more carefully, with more extensive notes, and it got better. Part of the problem, I think, was one rather knowledgeable man who left after a couple of lectures – he was expecting something different. Another was my rather novel anthropological approach. Another was that I had absolutely no training and was, no doubt, nervous. By the end, in the following summer, the audience were clearly enjoying it. They consisted mainly of retired, male, middle class local historians in Eynsham near Oxford, to which I used to travel on my motorbike. I took over this role from a research student in the year above me.

I prepared a booklet in advance in the autumn. It contains a good deal of my wider interests and philosophy of history as I encountered anthropology seriously for the first time and includes many themes which I would develop over the rest of my life.

---

[1] This was part of what would later become the Oxford University Department for Continuing Education (OUDCE). The University of Oxford was one of the founders, in the late 19th century, of the so-called 'extension' movement, wherein Universities began to offer educational opportunities to adult learners outside of their traditional student base. The 19th Century saw an awakening social awareness to the needs of working-class people generally, and Oxford University signalled an educational responsibility to the general community by sending lecturers into towns and cities across Victorian England, bringing university culture to a diverse adult audience. The first of the early "Oxford Extension Lectures" was delivered in 1878. (Summarized from Wikipedia)

OXFORD UNIVERSITY DELEGACY
FOR EXTRA-MURAL STUDIES

EYNSHAM SESSIONAL CLASS

Syllabus for a course of study on

SOCIAL HISTORY

by A. D. J. MacFarlane, B. A.

to be held at St Bartholomew's School
Eynsham

beginning Monday 28 September
at 7.15 pm

Oxford 1964

Introductory

The period 1566-1714 saw the transformation of England: we shall attempt together to trace why and bow that trans- formation occurred- Studying various changes to normally separated fields, we will try to link economic, artistic, political, social and religious factors - thereby creating an integrated picture of a society to transition; of its worries and pleasures,, its hopes and fears. Its ideals and hatreds, its weaknesses and strength. Leaving for the most part the 'great" and affairs of state, we shall try to discover now ordinary men lived and died - what they ate, now- they spent their leisure, what they wore, what their houses were like. We will study those aspects of their lives which are nearest to our own, their health, their children's education, their Jobs,

In all this we will try to relate general problems to a local setting - Eynsham and Oxford. Our 'basic materials will be contemporary wills, letters, pamphlets and law-cases. The effort will necessarily be co-operative since the type of problems we will be discussing will be on the borderline of orthodox history and thus the material, though plenteous, has been little sifted and the topics little studied.

I. POLITICAL, CONSTITUTIONAL AND FOREIGN

Our period starts with the accession of Queen Elizabeth in 1558 and ends with the death of Anne in 1714. It witnesses the gradual growth of opposition to the monarchy, erupting in the turbulence of the Civil Wars, the 'restoration and re-expulsion of the Stuarts, and establishment of the Orange family. In this process the Commons eclipses both Crown, Church and Lords as the fount of power. These political upheavals find both a cause and reflection in the economic, religious and intellectual life of the time: 'Puritanism', 'Population', 'Legal Reform' are words, just as Hobbes, Bacon and Milton are names, which cannot be omitted when discussing the events of the time.

Abroad the Counter-Reformation and Thirty Years War, the defence against the Turks, the opening up of the East and America, the rise of France and decline of Spain, the writings of Descartes, Copernicus and Calvin all influence England in a thousand ways. She repulsed the Armada, accepted William of Orange and brooded over the humanistic and scientific writings which were flooding from Continental presses. Every sphere of life was influenced in subtle ways by events and discoveries taking place many hundreds of miles away; the peasant was touched by such discoveries as clock-making, salt-refining, ship-building or textile weaving as he was by the influx of American gold into Spain. It is a truism to say that England, as Donne was to say of Man, was 'a part of a continent'. 'Splendid isolation' was far in the future.

II. ECONOMIC CHANGE

a) Agriculture

The period saw further enclosure of land and conversion from arable to pasture - though the actual details of the change are still blurred and vary with each region. There were experiments with new crops and fertilisers, with three field systems and livestock breeding which in many ways anticipated the 'agricultural revolution' of the 18th century. Forests were growing scarce - which in turn influenced the development of the coal and other industries. - and fens and marshes were beginning to be drained. England was still predominantly rural to the end of our period and weather and harvests were of extreme national concern. But there was growing specialisation of agriculture and growing commerce between regions - especially to the London market. Agricultural changes were closely linked to.. .

b) Population

Though exact figures are impossible to obtain, it is generally assumed that the population of England from 1530-1720 grew from about three to five million. Certainly London increased enormously during the same period, from about fifty to three hundred and fifty thousand. This had complex effects on all fields of life - from colonization to price changes. Its causes and effects, like those of the late 18th century rise, are a subject of controversial discussion. It has been argued that population increase, by cheapening labour, was a major factor in.

c) Industrial progress

J. U. Nef in several books has argued for the existence of 'an industrial revolution of the C16'. Certainly the greatly expanding cloth trade, the production of commodities like glass, soap, coal, iron and so on are of considerable interest. Defoe's picture of England in the 1720s shows a country already exporting considerable quantities of coal and manufactured goods, and a country with a developing banking system based on credit. We may discuss the vexed question of economic growth up to the late 18th century and its relationship to religious, political and social activity. The whole topic of industrial growth is intimately linked with. . .

d) Commercial expansion

It was during our period that Europe really opened up her contacts with the East and America and England, with the Dutch, led the race. But English goods also found expanding markets nearer home in the Baltic and Mediterranean. Commercial changes were reflected in England not only in increased prosperity and building, in improvements in internal communications, but also in the growth of the Western ports - especially Bristol and Liverpool (at the end of our period) and London, and the decline of some of the Eastern, such as Ipswich, though Newcastle with its salt, coal and Eastland trade was the second port in the kingdom. Trade was often conducted by big companies whose struggle for monopolies such as those of the Merchant Adventurers was intimately connected with..

e) Government regulation

The State was increasingly aware of the advantages and obligations with regard to economic expansion. It regulated prices and wages, enforced customs and monopolies, encouraged and dissuaded invention and enterprise. The extent of state control was a constantly controversial point throughout our period, a powerful factor in the strained relations leading up to the Civil War and the Restoration and finding a temporary balance in the 'laissez-faire' at the end of the 17th century. One of the major problems which faced Tudor and Stuart governments was. . .

f) The poor

It was during our period that the State began to undertake responsibility for the poor and vagabonds, though its activities were still not far in advance of the whipping treatment which had been normal in the Middle Ages. Professor Jordan has examined philanthropic giving in microscopic detail, showing how merchants played a growing part in charity and how their gifts tended to be more 'practical' than those of their pre-Reformation forefathers. But while people were more aware of the problems caused by expanding population, price fluctuations, enclosure and so on, their answer was often harsher than might be expected - 'if they do not work they do not eat' - was a favourite phrase. Closely allied to this problem of the poor was that of the aged and of children, especially paupers. The latter were involved in one of the most interesting and little studied features of this period,

g) Educational reform

There is no doubt that both in methods and in numbers affected here was considerable educational advance in our period. Universities doubled their numbers or more, pupils in the grammar schools were beginning to be taught English as well as Latin; but the causes and effects of the changes are little known, nor has much interest been shown as to how these changes affected the lower strata of society. In this subject, as in so many others, we see a number of strands coming together. The Reformation and Puritanism influenced education by stressing the necessity of reading the Bible and understanding sermons: economic changes allowed more money to be invested in what is, after all, a long-term policy, and also encouraged the teaching of mathematics and foreign languages; the religious wars on the Continent encouraged educational reformers such as Comenius to visit England; political upheavals led to the purging of the universities during the Interregnum.

III. SOCIAL CHANGE

a) The individual

There are a host of changes in the physical environment of the individual, changes which are largely determined, of course, by where he lived and what social group he belonged to. Thus if we look at a yeoman we will find his food improving, his house acquiring windows and furniture, his farm growing and better equipped. We may ask numerous questions about his activities; what did he do in his leisure? How did he regard his family and neighbours, his Church and his God, his king and his gentry superiors? One of the least explored, but most interesting of these problems is how did he fit into,

b) The family

Is it true that this period saw changes in the status of women, increasing tolerance to children, a great movement of families from place to place? How many families had servants? How big were families, and did they change in size and structure during our period? What were the ceremonies and beliefs surrounding births, marriages and deaths? Who inherited the property and what happened to 'the unmarried' and younger sons? What were the differences between families in a town such as Oxford or London and a market town such as Eynsham? All families belonged to.. .

c) Class

The growth of 'the middle class' has often been seen as one of the major features of our period, and an important factor in the origins of the Civil War. More recently emphasis has been laid on a decline in the power of the aristocracy and on the rise of a prosperous yeomanry. It has been held that the 'yeoman' is the backbone of England' and was destroyed by the Industrial Revolution. If this is so it will be worth examining this class in its zenith. We may also examine what were the causes and effects of changes in the relationships between the different classes; did the Reformation and/or Civil War have profound social consequences? Did economic change favour one class more than another? Was Puritanism the philosophy of a new class? Class structure is based on horizontal divisions, but there were also interesting perpendicular divisions in..

d) The professions

It has been said that there was a growing lawyer class during our period - litigation and the Inns of Court flourished in a society subject to a new intellectual and economic fluidity. Likewise this was a great period for the country parson, often ignorant and underpaid as he was. The Reformation - for instance the introduction of clerical marriages - and economic changes altered both the status and the functions of this profession. How well did they respond to the new demands and what were their relations to other classes? To take one more example we have the merchants and clothiers, busily travelling round the country, buying their way into the landed classes and investing in culture, education and at the end of our period - with the Bank of England - the State.

IV. RELIGION AND CULTURE

a) Doctrine

Our period saw the change from what has been called the medieval 'world-picture' to the scientific, mechanistic, universe of the 18th century. The rise of 'modern science' and the decline of medieval Catholicism is the central feature of the emotional and intellectual history of our time. Over-simply, leading thinkers became more interested in 'How' things happened rather than 'Why'. The orthodox approach to a study of this problem has been to study the doctrinal changes of the period, the works of the Puritans and Arminians, of Cambridge Platonists and Newton. Excellent studies have been made of Puritanism, of the radical sects during the Civil War and the Anglicans and Nonconformists of the later 17th. The struggles of Protestants and Catholics, of Presbyterians and Independents, of Church and State will have to be examined but we must also notice a new field which is just opening and promises rich rewards, the study of...

b) Myths and ideologies

Myths, in a complicated way, both reflect and shape their age; and the beliefs about the Millenium, the 'Norman Yoke', the 'Golden Age', Fairies, Witches, folk heroes such as Arthur and Robin Hood and animals and plants give us valuable and exciting insights into a vanished age. If we refrain from dismissing the beliefs in sorcery and astrology, in magical cures and strange animals, in Lost Continents and Sleeping Heroes as ludicrous but treat them with sympathy, attempting to feel the assumptions on which they were based and seeing how each belief fulfilled a genuine need and was logically connected to the intellectual and physical environment, we will be richly rewarded. We will share the dreams and ecstasies, the visions and fears of a people who were reluctantly shedding their old assumptions before the bitter breath of scientific and economic change and we will find that the old rituals and myths were superseded by new ones more appropriate in the changing society. It is in the realms of custom and folklore that we will discover how people reacted to disease and misfortune, how they adapted themselves to what was physically often a very painful existence.

c) Certain aspects of this problem

In dealing with these popular assumptions, we will consider the basic, unquestioned, factors in life; how one spends one's leisure - country sports and pastimes (maypoles, festivals, feasts, seasons), the major events in life and attitudes to them - birth, marriage, death and the ageing process, how one regulates one's life by clocks or cock-crows, how one treats animals or lunatics, preoccupation with the weather or with property. The material for this kind of question will predominantly come from ballads, broadsides, children's stories and other 'folklore' sources. But it will also be found in the last of our major divisions..

IV. LITERATURE AND ART

Christopher Hill has called the 17th century 'the greatest age in English literature' and certainly if we add such Elizabethans as Sidney, Spenser and Shakespeare it would be difficult to rival our period. The fine efflorescence of the Elizabethans gave way to the anatomizings, the tensions and the melancholies of the 'metaphysicals' to be superseded by the brisker, more sophisticated wit of the post-Restoration. These generalizations cover gems such as the sweetness of Sidney, the tense doubts of Donne, the melancholy majesty of Milton and the jests of Aubrey. The art, like the poetry and philosophy, reflected and influenced the political, economic and religious tensions and like the numerous letters, books of moral advice, sermons, biographies, histories and essays, illuminates a really fascinating period of English history.

READING LIST

Basic introduction

*Bindoff, S. T.	Tudor England. 1950
Hill, J. E. C.	The Century of Revolution, 1603-1714. 1961

General

*Clark, Sir G. N.	The Seventeenth Century. 2nd ed. 1
*Hill, J. E. C.	Puritanism and Revolution. 1958
Notestein, W.	The English People on the Eve of Colonization, 1603-1630. 1954
Trevor-Roper, H. R.	Historical Essays. 1957

Hexter, J. H. Reappraisals. 1961
*Ashley, Maurice England in the Seventeenth Century. 1952
Hoskins, W. G. The Making of the English Landscape. 1953
*Tawney, R. H. Religion and the Rise of Capitalism. 1936
Holdsworth, Sir W. A History of English Law. 1924. vols. iv, vi
Neale, Sir J. E. Essays in Elizabethan History. 1958

<u>Economic and social</u>

Hoskins, W. G. The Midland Peasant. 1957
Hill, C. Economic Problems of the Church. 1957
Ramsay, G. D. English Overseas Trade during the Centuries of Emergence. 1956
Tawney, R. H. Business and Politics under James I. 1958
Unwin, G. Industrial Organisation in the C16 & C17s. 1904
Tawney, R. H. The Agrarian Problem of the C16. 1916
Fisher, F. J. (ed) Essays in the Economic & Social History of Tudor & Stuart England. . . 1961
Ernle, Lord English Farming Past & Present. 1922
James, M. Social Policy during the Puritan Revolution. 1930
Hoskins, W. G. Leicestershire Essays
Campbell, M. The English Yeoman. 1942
Ashton, T. S. The Industrial Revolution. 1948
Rowse, A. L. The England of Elizabeth: The Structure of Society. 1950
Judge, A. V. The Elizabethan Underworld. 1930

<u>Political and constitutional</u>

Hill, C. Oliver Cromwell (Hist. Assn. Pamphlet 1958)
*Brailsford, H. N. The Levellers. 1961
Tanner, J. R. English Constitutional Conflicts of C17. 1928
Willson, D. H. James VI & I. 1956
Neale, J. E. Queen Elizabeth I. 1934
Mattingly, Garret The Defeat of the Spanish Armada. 1959
Clark, G. N. The Later Stuarts. 2nd ed. 1955

<u>Religion and ideas</u>

Allen, J. W. English Political Thought 1603–44. 1938
Butterfield, H. The Origins of Modern Science 1300–1800. (1949
*Haller, W. The Rise of Puritanism. 1938
Jordan, W. K. Philanthropy in England 1480–1660. 1959
*Willey, B. The 17th Century Background. 1934
*Tillyard, E. M. W. The Elizabethan World Picture. 1943
Lewis, C. S. English Literature in the C16 – excluding drama (Oxford His. 1953)

12

Grierson, H.	Cross Currents in English Literature of the Seventeenth Century. 1929

Art and architecture

The Oxford History of Art - relevant volumes

Summerson, J.	Architecture in Britain: 1530-1830
Waterhouse, E.K.	Painting in Britain: 1530-1790

Biography

Wedgewood, C.V.	Strafford
Trevor-Roper, H.R.	Laud
Buchan, John	Cromwell
Hexter, J.H.	King Pym, The Reign of. 1941
Bryant, Arthur	Samuel Pepys
Churchill, Winston	Marlborough
Strachey, Lytton	Elizabeth and Essex
Slater, M.	Englishmen with Swords. 1949. A novel

Contemporary

Plays - of Shakespeare, Marlowe, Jonson, Middleton, Wycherley, Congreve

Poems - of Spenser, Sidney, Donne, Herbert, Milton, Marvell, Dryden

Essays - of Bacon, Addison, Steele

Letters & papers - of Dorothy Osborne & the Verney family

Works - of Winstanley, Raleigh, Bunyan, Defoe, Swift, Browne, Burton

Memoirs, histories & diaries - of Pepys, Ludlow, George Fox, Clarendon, Burnet, Evelyn and Aubrey

Philosophy - of Bacon, Hobbes, and Locke

More detailed references to the literature of the period will be given on request; for detailed bibliographies and a good general introduction see the relevant volumes of the Oxford History of English Literature and The Pelican History of English Literature.

I wrote a postcard to my mother in the Lake District on 8th October from Chelmsford.

Dear All,

*Thank you v. much for your letter – glad your Tour & visit to P*bl*sh*rs went so well. Must get down to see the Sussex clan. the second W.E.A. class went o.k – on the Parish Church & clergy with a film strip. Am now in Essex 'witching'. Have met the girl who is working on it – she's a poppet. Will be going to her sister's 21st on Saturday. do stay for 14th/15th if you feel you can bear the scrum – I think Daddy might prefer it to Miss F!*

The reasons for my parent's visit was see me receive my B.A. from the University.

Connected to this event, I received an invitation from my undergraduate tutors at Worcester.

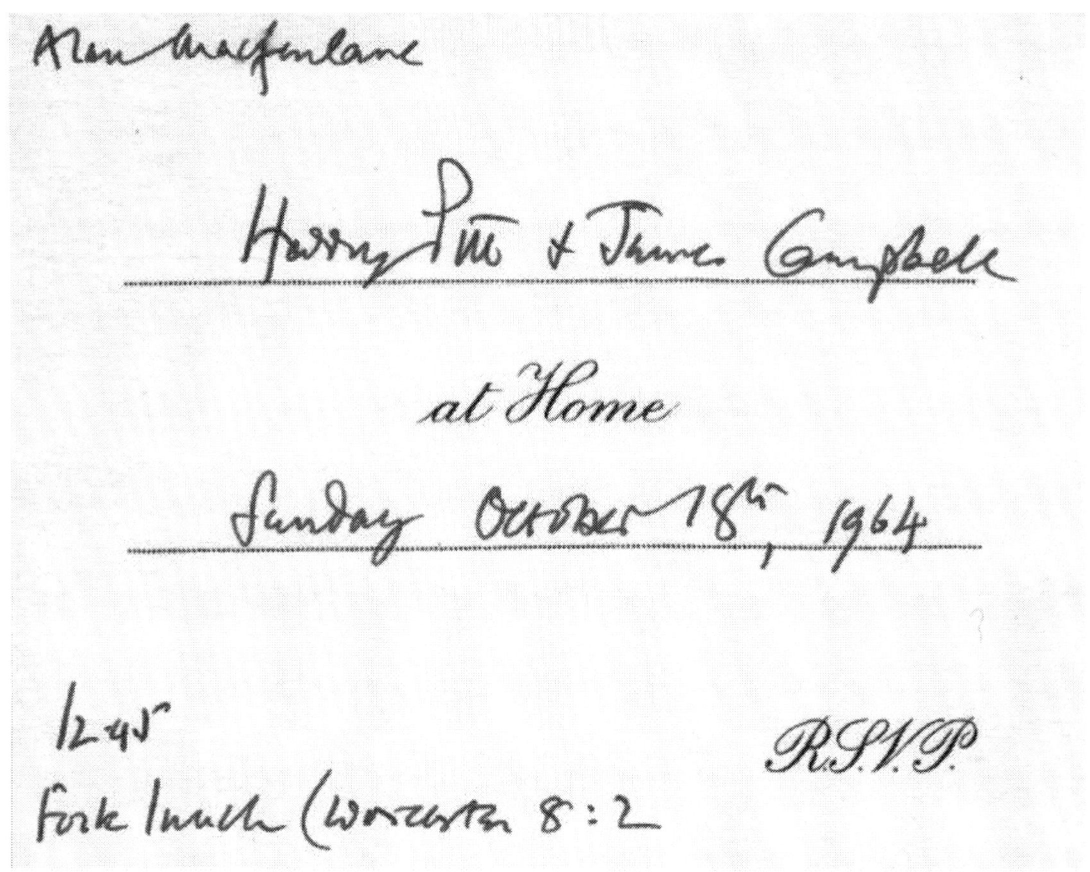

Alan Macfarlane

Harry Pitt & James Campbell

at Home

Sunday October 18th, 1964

12.45

Fork lunch (Worcester 8:2

R.S.V.P.

I sent a postcard to my sister Fiona after the lunch.

Dear Fish,
Many thanks for the invitation to the party – so sorry I couldn't come. I would have if the bike had been working properly. But had an important lunch on Sunday & there are no early buses back. Perhaps you or I could make use of Larrie – who as I told you goes up to Manchester every week – mid-week for 2 or 3 days. I'll find out details. I hope the Party was swinging. It was marvellous having Mummy & Daddy down here for my ceremony. They said the house is beginning to look like home. Stick this on the kitchen wall & I'll send some more in the series – I think they're tremendous.[1]
Give my love to all the gang – Val, Heather, Jan etc – I miss them all; all come down to see me?
Love and look after yourself, Alan

My mother wrote to me from Field Head on 19th October

A sad, wet Sunday evening which makes me feel the angst (?) you always do. I took the dogs for a walk through misty rain & wet fallen leaves after tea & thought of all the things we haven't done on this leave and came back to a programme on mentally retarded children. Perhaps a large lunch with Granny contributes to my heavy, depressed disposition – anyway, that's enough of that.

[1] The Sixth Seal, from the Douce Apocalypse series, Bodleian Library postcard.

We loved our short time in Oxford, really unforgettable, one of those experiences that will ripen with time. I'm absolutely thrilled with my books. I'm trying not to read them but have dipped into the anthropology one which is going to be revolutionary when I show it to my Assamese friends. Did you read the article on Verrier Elwin in the Sunday times? Makes me even sadder I never quite met him.

We got back in 5 and a half hours without a single fight which was miraculous. I sat down to your typewriter at the first opportunity and it gave a loud snap and refused to space between words. Daddy was watching Olympics so I battled on all afternoon holding the tension thing with one hand & typing with the other – very back aching and slow, but thank goodness its now mended & I was able to get quite a lot of work done this afternoon. I hope they don't throw it back at me, somehow all these agents & publishers don't seem real at all, just figments of my imagination (what actually is a figment?)

I do hope your class went off well, don't get too depressed if numbers are down, on cold wet nights its inevitable. Hope the lunches went off well too, your brown suit will be quite worn out – I don't know what our plans are for leaving, I rather feel that having made the break I'd rather not do it again – what do you feel? I so hate partings, I want to see you but can't bear to say goodbye again. Anyway I'll write again in a day or two. Much love – Mummy

They then went for a flying visit to Scotland – going on 23rd and returning on 24th according to my grandfather's diary. My mother wrote to me from Field Head on 26 October, and the same day my grandfather noted: 'Mac and Iris leave for India'.

Just before they left, I wrote to my parents, agreeing that it would be best not to repeat the pain of parting.

I wrote to my mother from Worcester College on Sunday October 26th

Dearest Mummy & Daddy,

*Thank you very much for your letter; I agree that it would make things worse if you came to Oxford on your way out - though I would love to see you. Do come if you feel like it - I leave the decision to you. The melancholy autumn splendour here would make it all worse. It is very glorious. I went out to Blenheim this afternoon on the bike (which by the way seems <u>fully</u> repaired at a cost of £1) and the greens were, well one can't give them higher praise than by saying that they were like those in the canon's drive [*Canon Bradley*] or at the Tarns. The Parks are superb too. The blaze and fire is indescribably pathetic. There are frosts, and the edges of buildings are beginning to show through the elms & chestnuts. The softness is going.*

Yes, I saw the article on Elwin (by Mortimer). He sounded a wonderful man. Will you be getting the book for the Cherideo library, or would you like it as part of the Xmas bundle? If the latter, I could read it before I sent it out! If you ever need books, do let me know. But you realize that. I enclose some pictures on film-strips etc. Rather expensive, keep it if you want. There are some wonderful colour strips in the Bodleian, medieval demons etc; I must have a look. You don't have a slide projector in India do you? - in case I found any on the Moghuls. You said you wanted another book on the Moghuls for Mrs Manby - so include one here - a leaving present. Please excuse me from getting one for you Daddy. Anything that makes Mummy happy also pleases you! You must have had an exciting time with the Olympics - and nearly won 10/-. We did marvellously didn't we?!

Jack[1] has stayed here since you left & is possibly leaving tomorrow, to head north. It is depressing that such a sensitive, friendly & intelligent person should be unable to find a niche. I wish I had my island for 'lost souls'. Perhaps I'll start hunting for that big house on the West Coast soon - 'Macfarlane College'.

---

[1] My Patterdale Youth Hostel, autumn 1963, boss, Jack]

I will be working in Essex next week (Nov. 3rd on) for a week. I've had a bad cold (despite all my pills) so haven't done much work this week.

It was wonderful seeing you both. Thanking you for making it so happy; and for sweating so many years to give me this incredible opportunity. All that I have you have given me. But, as Fiona would say, enough slop! Have a wonderful journey. I will be thinking of you. It'll be no time until it's all over... Fondest love, Alan

My mother wrote from Europe Hotel, Cromwell Road on 28th October

My dear Alan,

Just heading off for the Airport & feeling a bit grim but trying to disassociate myself from it all.

Anne spent the night with us here, she seems very cheerful, hasn't fixed flats or jobs yet, but is on the point of doing both. I've told her to head for you if she's in trouble You might be of mutual benefit to each other actually.

I shall think of you wrapped in your grey rug poring over those fascinating maps – only wish I'd read more of your work, where did the summer go? The plan for my Moghul book has fallen into my mind. Will explain it later.

Have a good year, it'll be nice if Robert Joins you. Our best love, darling. Mummy

Let us know if you want a loan ever.

My mother wrote from Calcutta on 30 October

My dear Alan,

Back to the filth & starving dogs, one always hopes by some miracle things will have improved but they get worse. The journey was good… I went to the National Library this morning to find it closed because a minister has died – around to that bookshop advised by Blackwell to be told the manager was away & nobody else had any idea where anything was – the frustrations of trying to get anything done here are almost too much until one unwinds & adjusts oneself! The bookshop actually turned out to be a hovel down a filthy lane miles from anywhere, I crossed a grimy courtyard & climbed some dark stone steps with a strong feeling that the taxi driver was a white slave trader, but finally reached a tiny room with books piled up to the ceiling, all over the floor, all over a little desperate man prodding at a typewriter – probably wonderful bargains amongst them but one would have needed a day to sort them out. So my Moghuls look like receding into the background again, unless I can make a book with what I've got… Feel disorientated & rather depressed at the moment but I expect will settle & find plenty to do, the problems always seem so gigantic when one first comes back & insoluble.

I felt happier about Anne after seeing her, she didn't seem too flustered by London, & will be happy for a bit I think. Keep thinking of you all in your little rooms, Val too on her mattress, when I get back here it seems as if I've never been away. We fly up to-morrow morning, shall be glad to take my conscience away from this ghastly spot, though sorry not to have explored it a bit. Much love, Mummy

1964 - November

On 3rd November I had a note from Keith, clearly referring to materials on York archives which I had lent him.

Dear Alan,

It's most kind of you to let me see these. A lot of my labours in York could have been avoided if I'd known about them sooner, but I suppose it's always best to do these things oneself.

What about Saturday 14th Nov for our next meeting. Would 2 p.m. be a possible time? Yrs, Keith Thomas

My mother wrote to me from Cherideo on 3rd November

This time last week we were driving down to Oxford, it seems at least five years ago. I expect you've heard by now of our grisly journey, at least the last stages. As far as Calcutta the flight was absolutely smooth but all the way I was haunted by the fact that the wheels were going to stick so that when it actually happened wasn't at all surprised, merely petrified! Trust me to be sitting next the window right on top of where the wheel was supposed to appear, Daddy and the others had no idea that anything was wrong, and I was too rigid to turn round and tell them. My companion kept saying helpfully "My God now we are <u>really</u> in trouble" and when we got down we found Gauhati airport all ready with fire engines, but that was all they had got ready, nothing at all was arranged as to how we should finish our journey.... I picked up some tummy trouble on the way, and returned to find my lovely compound under a foot of grass, I've never seen anything like it. Some of the shrubs have disappeared completely, some are dead and the whole place will take months to recover. It's a funny thing, on the plane I thought "If I get out of this I'll never complain about anything again" but I've been doing nothing else since. The two big dogs terribly thin and covered with sores and fleas so I doubt one way and another I shall get my history of the Moguls written. Anyway there is no question of being bored, it'll take the whole of eighteen months to get this lot sorted... Actually thinking of you in that nice cosy room with the logs switched on in the grate is my one comfort at present, I still worry a little about Fiona. We found our way to London Airport quite easily but were terribly confused when we got there, millions of lights and tunnels and Daddy rapidly coming to the boil. The man was waiting to collect the car and we found the girl we were escorting out, we flew by Geneva, Istanbul, Beirut, Bagdad and Karachi and arrived two and a half hours late at Calcutta so that we didn't get into bed till two in the morning and slept till 11.30 next day. Calcutta was very cool we met Liz Leetham at Dum Dum next morning, poor thing she had just got off the London plane and had lost a suitcase with all her jewels, new shoes, handbags etc. in it. John Lampett has resigned and everyone here is sunk in gloom, ah well, I think of that croft in Barra & feel more peaceful. I really will get down to my history and my painting & teaching as soon as I have sorted myself out. Don't work <u>too</u> hard (are you listening?) & get those calories down yourself won't you. Will write more cheerfully next time I hope. Much love - Mummy

My poetic efforts continued, and I even found a muse, the fair Antonia of whom I can remember nothing.

To Antonia 4/11/64

It is not easy to rhyme to you;
Beauty cannot be invoked for your
Beauty is still a mystery unknown
Too passing even for the leaf to notice.

It is a recollection of eyes & hair
Set in a childish candour of innocence,
Of level eyes & golden hair
And the rapture of a shared smile.
Your grace of movement and
Our serious concentration are your art.
I remember this; but no more.
Nor can Love be wooded
In all its melancholy meaninglessness,
For the love I have is all
For the shadow princess in
My own soul and not for you.
And what is Truth? Is it true
That this day is lonely, and that
Spring buds grow in the midst of
Autumn leaves, it is sure
That midst the last fine fire
Our hearts & souls will remain unquenched? All that I
Can offer is the still, sad, Musings of a love-lorn
Wight, a glimpse into the
Formless, shapeless complexities
Of a restless child who seeks
To hold your hand and gaze
In terror at the darkening night.

A week later, on Sunday 8th November, I wrote an apologetic letter to my father, having missed his birthday on 31 October.

Dearest Daddy,

I'm ashamed to admit, as you must have realized, that I completely overlooked your birthday. Perhaps the excuse that the rush of your departure drove it from my mind will partly explain my failure. Where were you on the day? All that I can do is to wish you a very happy year ahead & to say that I was thinking of you - as I would have been doing as you were on your journey. Not even a present I'm afraid. But perhaps you can claim one of my Christmas books as a present - a dullish selection and a bit high-brow, but I didn't know what to get. It seems best to get books that you will want to keep - rather than light, though throwable-awayable ones.

How is the Garden? Mummy says that you and another manager have been made Deputy General Managers - congratulations! What exactly does this mean? More work/money/freedom/office jobs? Anyhow I hope it goes O.K.

It was marvellous seeing you both in the summer - especially, perhaps in Oxford. Extraordinary how quickly it went. If this time 'out' goes anywhere as fast you will be back seeing me get another coloured hood in no time!

Look after yourself and Mummy and hank you a million times for the wonderful start you have given me in life, with all the sacrafices you have made. My love as always, Alan

My mother wrote to me from Cherideo 10th November

Your letter written before we left is the only communication that has braved the barriers of Nazira P.O. – it was very welcome of course. I know Anne has written, she bought an Airgraph at London Airport which she was going to send off next day but it has never arrived and of course I'm worrying like mad about her though unnecessarily I'm sure, she can always come and use your sleeping bag if she is desperate and homeless. Sorry to hear about your cold, you must increase the pills and try and get out into any sun there is.

I have settled down fairly happily now, the weather is perfect which helps and the pleasure of birds and animals is constant and consoling. There is an absolute pageant of birds all day long, it makes one realise how scarce they are in England now and how shy, here they come and dangle on the shrubs a few inches away. I have been working in the morning and half the afternoon, making notes on my Burma books which are full of intersting information about the Shans who were Ahoms (or rather vice versa). "The Tribes of Highland Burma"[1] *is fascinating too although the anthropological language beyond me in places and I haven't quite grasped his dynamic new theory, I'll return it when I have shown it to my historian friend who I fear will be even more in the dark but it may give him an idea how to tackle the study of a tribe. Please don't dream of sending me anything for Christmas, the books you gave me have been more than enough, I'm going to take them and show them to everyone in Shillong who might be interested, connected with the north east frontier tract – with doubtful results I fear. …still feel quite disconnected from the "life" of the community, think of nothing but Moghuls and you all at home and my garden which I have been digging in fairly hard in the evenings, my books from the Hakluyt Society haven't yet arrived so I haven't much Moghul to go on but am re-indexing and filing according to your instructions with mountains of little cards piling up as a result. It was kind of you to say you owe everything to us but not true, your own exertions did most of it and still do and we are the grateful ones.*

Much love & regards to Roy and Rosemary. Mummy

On the same date I was gave a talk at the College history society known as the Thomas of Walsingham Society. I was in distinguished company since all the other speakers were established academics.

THE THOMAS OF WALSINGHAM SOCIETY

Michaelmas Term 1964

A.D. MacINTYRE — Thursday 29th October

'The Politics of Betrayal in 19th Century Britain'

A.D.J. MACFARLANE — Tuesday 10th November

'Witchcraft in Tudor and Stuart England'

R.R. WALZER — Thursday 19th November

'Medieval Islamic Philosophy'

R.H.C. DAVIS — Thursday 26th November

'How to be a Medieval King'

Staircase 5:6 — 8.15 p.m.

CLARET

[1] Edmund Leach's *Political Systems of Highland Burma*

'WHITE' WITCHCRAFT IN TUDOR AND STUART ENGLAND. (Walsingham Society, 12/11/64)

Introduction; definition of terms & field of scope.

The history of witchcraft may be divided roughly into three parts; an study of the ideas about witches and their deeds, investigation of the actual individuals involved in witchcraft cases and their motives, and an analysis of the actions which people take to avoid or cure witchcraft. It is the last of these that I want to talk about. I apologise to any who hoped to hear stories of sadism and vice, of Satanic orgies and underground 'covens', but of all aspects of witchcraft that has already received the most attention. There are several stimulating books on the subject, often replete with the most absorbing illustrations - among them the works of Miss Margaret Murray and Montague Summers. When a historian as eminent as Mr. Hill can write "...by the seventeenth century magic was already ceasing to be communal: or rather its communities - the witches' covens - were already voluntary and indeed underground organizations" (C.Hill, Society and Puritanism, London 1964, p1486.) it is a temptation to give a talk discussing the possibility of a secret 'witch-cult', which had been inherited from the Middle Ages and was only driven under in the Tudor & Stuart period, a rival religion to Christianity and based on fertility rites. Instead of this, however, I would like to turn for a while to the methods employed (by individuals and professionals) to prevent and cure witchcraft. This I have labelled 'white' witchcraft as opposed to 'black' because to many people, its ends seemed commendable. Both the methods it employed and the attitude of various groups in society towards it give, I believe, some interesting insights into the still largely unknown regions of popular beliefs in our period.

For Keith I wrote a paper on the witch's familiar and he again made a number of punctilious comments.

This was a mammoth piece, some 52 pages of foolscap which must be about 20,000 words at least. The plan for the piece was as follows.

THE WITCH'S FAMILIAR IN ESSEX: 1560-1680.

BACKGROUND.

1) Legal & contemporary definitions of 'familiar'.
2) Geogaphical distribution.
3) Temporal distribution.
4) Explanations so far suggested & aims of this article. — see Wilson Quote
(attitude to animals, responsibility of witch/Devil/God, relationship of spirit & matter; will & threat & intention etc.) : apply anthropology/throw light on witch. + C17.

FAMILIAR IN THE RECORDS & THE LAW.

The types of evidence used; Assize, Pamphlets etc. Literary.
Legal enactments & the familiar as evidence. (p.24. (25)) (children, etc)
The familiar as a part of witchcraft - its function.
(Animals & Witchcraft generally- 4 uses)
p.21.

FAMILIAR IN FACT: ESSEX.

The familiar in isolation.
Size, colour, number, name, residence, mobility, special characteristics.
Feeding, communication, moving & attacking.
cats - p.24 (28) → 23 (15) + 23 (17). → 23 (7) + 23 (4)
p.23. (13)

'colour bar' (Wilson)
see. 21 (2). Africa - certain animals traits associated with
24 (28) reflects character of witches.

The familiar in relationship.
To the Devil, fairies & animals, angels & spirits.
- 23 (5) + (6).

To the Victim; harms they do, ways in which observed (dreams etc) — milk cows 23 (8). — 24 (24).
counter-action against. (cunning-men) — 23 (11). — (Gifford 25 footnote).

To the witch; lycanthropy & physical relationship. → 22 (3).
benefits for the witch. — 22 (4) + 23 (9) + (10).
sexual. — 23 (12) + 23 (15) - familiar = witches "child"
food & rewards from witch.
hostility etc. — p. 23 (16).
authority & prime responsibility.
ways of obtaining(& passing on) spells, rites etc.
time & place when appearing.
pact, covenant etc.
to her family.

EXPLANATIONS.

As explanation of unnatural activity. — 24 (26)
Why animals ? Outsider, wild beast etc. — 24 (27)
Necessity in law - outward & visible sign = projected soul of witch.
medicines/magic/soul/familiar. - 21 (footnote).
Delusion, illusion & reality.
Folklore.
As reflection of contemporary society.
psychological.

(refs. to numbers = my essay on 'The Ideology of Witchcraft')

A page with one or two of Keith's comments is:

chief records are in Essex,Suffolk, and the other Eastern counties."(1) This is perhaps narrowing the area too much,though it cannot be disputed that Essex trial pamphlets are by far the most detailed existing accounts of this belief. In the first Lancashire trial of 1613 old Mother Demdike had a familiar like a dog which sucked her blood (1), of the witches who plagued the Fairfax family in 1621 in Yorkshire five had domestic familiars (3) and coming further south and east women arrested at Windsor in 1579 were believed to have familiars (2).The details of these familiars correspond very closely to those in Essex.

There have been few suggestions as to why the belief in familiars should have been limited to England(3) and it is not the purpose of this article to explore this problem directly.But it will clearly be easier to approach a solution when we know what function such a belief served in English witchcraft beliefs and what was its equivalent abroad, or in Scotland.

The temporal distribution of familiars.

The beliefs we are discussing were not particularly limited to the period 1560-1680, though it is at this time,primarily,that they led to accusations in a court of law. Familiar spirits were to be obtained from magicians in the middle ages (4) and the famous Witch of Berkely had her pet raven according to William of Malmesbury (5). Even the blood-sucking details are anticipated; a man had a familiar in Yorkshire in 1510 which fed on blood from his finger (6).After 1680

(4) M.Murray,Witch-Cult. p.209.See also W.N.Neill.'The Professional Pricker & his test for Witchcraft' in the Scottish Hist.Review.1922.vol. 19. p.212.
(1) M.Murray, Witch-Cult. p.209.(2) M.Murray,Witch-Cult,p.210-13.
(3) The only suggestion I have come across is the very tentative and somewhat improbable one that it was due to the Englishman's love of pets -

The fact that familiars can only be found in the trial pamphlets - they seldom remain in the actual indictments as we will see - means that those counties with good pamphlets, particularly those inspired by Hopkins (who seems to have made a speciality of this kind of evidence), give the impression of being far more steeped in beliefs about familiars than others.Whether this is any more than an impression cannot be decided as yet, but it seems likely that such beliefs were indigenous throughout England , though they seem to have grown more sophisticated during our period. There is obviously some connection between the Scottish fairies, who are closely associated with witchcraft in that country & much more 'real' than in England & the English familiar; this needs exploring.

Some of the footnotes were very long – for instance the following one, which was based on a B.Litt. thesis completed by my anthropologist friend Wendy James in the summer of 1964. I have five pages of typed notes on her thesis on 'Animal Representations and their social significance; with special reference to reptiles and carnivores among peoples of Eastern Africa'

14(b) (Addenda to footnote on p.14)

Why are certain animals associated with witchcraft – cont'd.

(All refs. are to Miss James' thesis, Animal Representation.....)

Wendy James makes several interesting points in regard to the relationship between witches and animals. She confirms a point made by Lévi-Strauss, Middleton & others that 'outsiders', 'strangers' and generally hostile people are thought of as akin to animals & hence it is not surprising if witches, who are traitors within the group should be seen to bear a resemblance to animals (p.138-9). She also illuminates the distinction made by primitive mentality between the human and animal world (p.2,13,156) and between different types of animal, domestic & wild, edible and inedible etc(22-27.) I am not sure, however, whether her acceptance of MacCulloch's theory that it is always "the fiercest and most dreaded animals" whose shapes are taken by witches(p.59.) is right. Her general argument is that "Wild and dangerous animals seem to represent power, neutral and abstract power which may be harnessed for good or for bad,....The same suggestion of latent potency underlies the wider associations of dangerous wild animals with witchcraft and sorcery.....".(p.50) Behind this and her discussion of why hyenas are especially withcraft animals (p.187-188) there rests the implicit assumption that it is the character the animal – its ferocity, uncleanliness etc. – which in the first place decides that it should be incorporated into witchcraft beliefs ; it is the relationship between villagers and certain animals which are analogous to those between the same people and witches, relationships of fear, disgust, horror etc. This is a satisfying thesis when we are dealing with a society which is faced by large numbers of wild animals, whose marauding needs explanation and whose activities seem to parallel those of witches. But in C17 England such animals were absent, but not beliefs in a relationship between witches & animals. The animals chosen were not, it seems, necessarily chosen for their intrinsically abhorrent nature – frightening night-animals, the mysterious owl or bat etc, were absent. Otherwise insignificant animals such as moles, rats, mice, dogs, weasils & other small vermin including bees ,butterflies and crabs were associated with witchcraft. This suggests that the function which the animal has to play in witchcraft beliefs is as important as anything in deciding which animals are chosen. In the English case the animals must be fairly common & be seen fairly often; they must be small so that a witch could keep them hidden and maintain them etc. Further, it was their association with witchcraft which gave them an aura of horror rather than vice versa. Gifford reported the feelings of a countryman thus; "when I goe but into my closes, I am afraide, for I see nowe and then a Hare; which my conscience giveth me is a witch, or some witches spirite, shee stareth so uppon me. And sometimes I see an ugly weasell runne through my yard, and there is a foule great catte sometimes in my Barne, which I have no limking unto." Dialogue, A.4. If one can separate the two – and James' rightly points out "that one cannot speak either of 'social imagery in the animal world' or 'animal imagery in the social world': the two concepts blend into and reinforce each other' (p.188) – it seems that it was the fear of witchcraft which lent horror & ugliness to the animal, rather than the

Wendy James read my essay and made her comments.

Some Comments (Wendy James)

Alan M.

p.3. Distinct btn. lycanthropy & familiars: what sort of it anyway.

p.12. Footnote: names in prim. soc.
See L-Strauss – Pensee Sauvage.
— Beattie (Nyoro Personal Names)
Middleton (Lugbara " ")
etc

p.15. ? no werewolves? see Eliot.

16–17 See point different

17 Footnote: generalis. – "Af. witchcraft" ×

31. sponsorship. food quest: beer, milk, blood – concept of body fluids – gen. relat. of fluid idea w. spirit, life.

I also asked Lady Clay to read and comment on it. The first of three pages of scribbled comments in her almost unreadable hand is:

Familiars || Lady S 27/11/07.

p.18 coldness of devil ; Russ
Rabbits as familiars
17. incubi & succubi Saxon Leechdoms
rubbing w. foxglove etc as giving sense
of movement – flight in air
Black dog at Rollbright,
Also in Africa cats.
p.18 'Amusing revelation of late 16c.
How much is Margaret Murray accepted?
p 22 like Rasputin
p.22 not tongues but tongs

Why are the witches called weird sisters?

What is the original meaning of Imp
p.27 by settling in her husband's shoe
& biting her??
Knots (Ballad & Saga)
27 Beer. New (ale old) but not butter
27 Note Read hers is a controlled?

In preparation for the supervisions I would prepare a set of thoughts and questions. I only have one set of these, which I typed out (as opposed to the abbreviated handwritten notes usual for the supervisions).

K.V.T. 14/11/64.

Papers. (pink file)
Corrected paper from K.V.T. - footnotes?
Familiars in Essex. -notes for w
('White witchcraft' -paper to Walsingham.
+ to write.

Books.
Ewen (1) obtained.
Scot.R. to buy?

To give Keith.
1) Ref. to Pope's article.
2) Cases from Archdeaconry.
3) More refs. to Augustine Draper (gent)?
4) 1582 Pamphlet.

To ask.
Ref. to E.Jordan - Suffocation of Mother in Bodley ?

(Robin Briggs - lines of research ?)
Book of K.V.T - how going.

To discuss.
a) Outline dates of theses - to 1736 ?
b) Meaning of 'sociological' - includes beliefs ?

During the meetings, where I often sat at the end of a long sofa and Keith sat at the other end, Keith would pour out ideas, references, comments. He would frequently leap up to bring a book from his superb library which stretched out of the room into the corridor outside. The wealth of a well-stocked mind was showered on me. Here are the notes I took on this session as an illustration of the kind of stimulus I received from these supervisions. (I shall give only one other example, some six months later. I have notes on about 8 of the sessions.)

Notes on the meeting of 14 November.

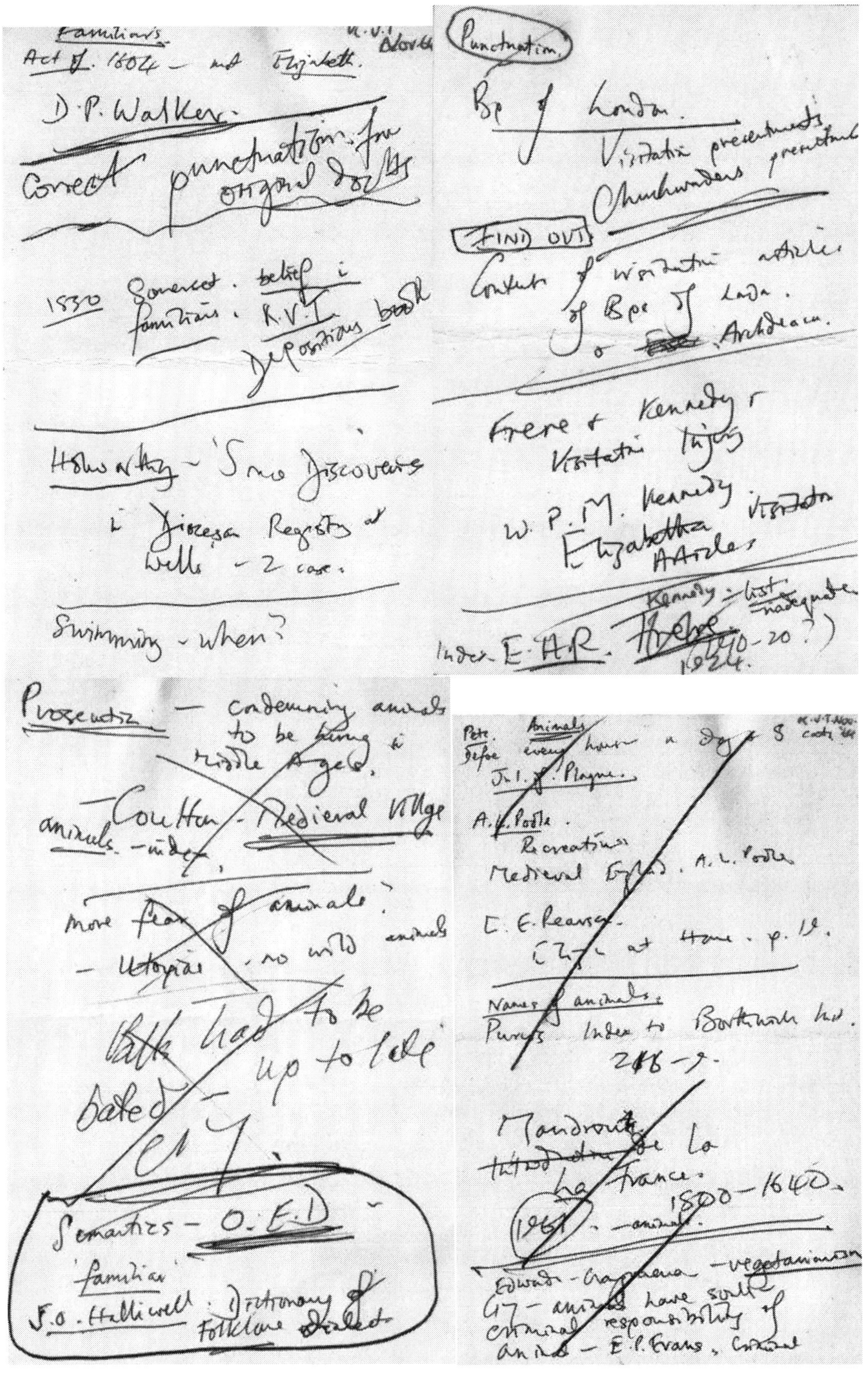

My mother wrote from Cherideo on November 15th 1964

Granpa said my article had appeared with a Moghul Emperor on the cover which is nice, shall welcome the cheque even more! Why don't you try a witch trial article, or History To-day a bit below your standards, it isn't actually anything more than tit-bits is it, but there's the money. The idea for my book which seemed wonderful at the time is really rather dull, I'm calling it "The field of Panipat", there were three momentous battles of Panipat and I'm dividing it into three parts, each one starting with the battle and then going back to describe everything that led up to it – not very original but gives me the "shape" to work on. For the cover I would like to photograph the Moghul miniature I saw in Calcutta which a gorgeous battle scene with lots of gay Moghuls on even gayer horses charging about. No books have come and no answer from the National Library so I think I shall start writing the book and add to it as my knowledge increases.I went to tea in a village on Friday and heard a couple of rather nice folk stories from a very drunk old man (my host) rather rashly said I would go and give English lessons there but more to get more stories than with any hopes of teaching them English I must admit... By the way how are your classes going, I hope they still are. Detect a longing note in your story of the lucky man who got the fellowship,[1] but there might be a chance of that afterwards mightn't there? The more I see of this place the more hopeless it appears and one could go on bashing one's head against the stone of its indifference and lethargy for a life-time without causing the slightest dent. … A blistering novel on the tea industry is called for some time I think.

I wrote to my parents from Worcester College on 15th November 1964

Again it is a wonderful sunlit autumn day and again I am writing from a bench by the Lake. Even since I last wrote there has been a great change - everything is showing through for the leaves are nearly all fallen; the lawns are carpeted with them and they pile up like brown snow against the fences and walls. Coming back into this dying season for a breath from my work always fills me with strange longings, to be doing better things and be among better men. But you know the feeling. Tomorrow I will be engrossed again.

No letter, but a <u>most</u> enjoyable article on Roe to thank you for. They gave you a pretty curt 'note on contributors' at the back - with no reference to Robert or M.R.[2] I see! But your actual article was by far the longest and they obviously thought it was good or they wouldn't have put the picture on the front. As a complete inexpert on the subject I found it both comprehensible & amusing. I wonder if anyone will write any letters about it? How is your other work going. I'm not sure what your concentration on - the Moghuls? - or fairy tales? or anthropology? If you get a parcel of books from Blackwell's don't open 'till Xmas as it's your present. I may have already warned you that you may have the hard-back in the Nazira library - if so I still don't think it's a waste getting it, as I'd like to read it!

I had a 2 and a half hr session with my supervisor in which, among other things, we went through my essay on 'Witch's Familiars', he seemed to find it interesting and gave me a load of references to attitudes to animals for instance to the fact that animals were <u>hung</u> as felons for certain offences in the Middle ages and all bulls, by statute, <u>had</u> to be baited to death before they could be sold by a butcher up to the end of the C17 - ugh! I would like to give a talk to my class about this. The last talk went o.k - on conjurors or 'white' witchcraft. I find it easier if I write the whole thing out & then improvise. Have you been doing any teaching? (which reminds me, Brenda Finney owes me a letter, I believe,) My supervisor put me on to a whole new chunk of material which may lengthen my thesis by about 3 months - I can see it turning into one of those interminable, perennial student, things!

---

[1] This was Robin Briggs, who was elected a Prize Fellow of All Souls in 1964.
[2] M.R. was the distant relative, M.R. James, ghost story writer and Provost of King's and Eton.

A fairly busy week as far as activities go; on Monday night W.E.A., Tuesday a talk (on Witchcraft of course, very long but not too badly received) to the college history society. On Thursday I had dinner with a friend (and lunch at All Souls - very pleasant, I envy Robert) & his girlfriend and on Friday went to 'The Crucible' with Linda. It's by Arthur Miller and about the Witchcraft trials at Salem (Massachusetts) 1692 - supposedly a veiled attack on McCarthyism. As a professional on the subject I thought it was a very good play well done - it was acted by undergraduates. Then last night was Mozart concert at Somerville college in which various of my friends were playing - included a piano concerto 'The Jupiter'. Look forward to hearing your new record when you return.

Anne seems happy in her new job. Granny tells me she has put 'The Curse of Cromwell' on the Rev. Wooddall [neighbour]. Apparently it worked last time she used it - we'll have to protect her from the police if he starts shrivelling up! Do you know what it is! Very foolish I think.

Hope all goes well on the garden, forgive this self-centred scrawl.

Much love, Alan

I wrote from Worcester College on 22nd November 1964

Dear Mummy and Daddy,

Thank you very much for your letter. I hope that my hurried request for a loan got through as I shall be rather sunk if it didn't. The situation could be a lot worse really and I hope it didn't worry you at all. I just can't understand where it all goes. I fear I shall have to keep an expenditure book soon. I don't regard myself as a person of luxurious tastes - I suppose it's books & thesis equipment & travel to Essex which are the chief drains. For instance I need a book at the moment which has just come out, costing about £6. Actually I may be able to treat myself to this as I've been asked, with others, to do some examining of college scholarship candidates. This will be more rewarding experience-wise than financially. My W.E.A incidentally, as I think I told you is going better - as is my motor bike. How is your teaching, Mummy? Keep me informed on the problems/progress etc as it is of considerable interest & may even be <u>useful</u> in the future! Do you think a western-type educational system <u>can</u> be grafted onto India culture and institutions? I know you have your doubts about the possibility of this with regard to the British legal system.

I'm sure you'll have heard from Anne from now - you're last letter was worried about her, that's why I keep harping on the subject - she seems happy. I hope to spend a week-end with her before I go north on about 20th Dec. (with Richard)... Incidentally Granny now says she knows nothing about the 'Curse of Cromwell' (having already put it on Rev. Woodall!). She, Grandpa et al are weeping over Goodland's timber-felling [Goodland had bought the neighbouring farm, long inhabited by the Cold Comfort Farmish Barr family], as no doubt you've gathered. I think, as I've always thought, he's pretty ruthless - but there are fortunately millions of trees left. No doubt I'll notice that clump, in its absence, as I never did when it was there. I'll refrain from making parallels with human deaths when the familiar oaks in our lives are felled... etc!

*I've had a succession of meal engagements over the last few days and - as the Tyrolean landlord put it to Hoffnung, feel "truly fed up"! Last night I went to see the hemophileac boy, Bill. Every time I meet him, it brings back my good fortune in health. I get distraught when I have a headache or a tooth chips off (as it did the other day) - while he goes on with internal bleeding causing constant agony in his side. Breakfast I had with the Chaplain. He asked after you. We discussed the 'Indian Mentality' because he had been in discussion with Lord Franks who was giving his views on the subject. I only wish you'd been here! All I could do was refer Alec to your article - as I've already done with numerous others. You could certainly do a service to India (& England) if you explained to "the general public" how & why we differ. I tried to do a little of this to Ralph Robinson with whom I had lunch today at Linton Lodge. He was, as usual, telling us about his friends etc. & I was lapping it up. He recently played bridge with the Watneys "Of what we want is W*TN*YS". The pictures on the walls of the house were insured for 2,000,000 pounds alone! While the world goes on suffering...!*

Much love to you both from this leafless city, Alan

My mother wrote from Cherideo on November 24th 1964 Cherideo

Thank you for your letter and kind remarks on my article, Granpa said it was "interesting" and Granny made no comment at all, but I got £26.5.0 for it – rather an odd sum, perhaps they pay you by the words? Very much worthwhile, in fact I think article writing would be more profitable than books but I'm sure HTD will never take anything more of mine. Your turn now. I'm concentrating as much as I can on the Moghuls but still have no books from anywhere so am frittering my time rather, I'm translating the odd folk stories in between but to write an imaginative childrens book I need privacy and concentration and have this child coming to stay for a month so will get little of either. I hope to do it sometime though.... Rosemary arrives on Saturday and thats the end of our peace for a long time, but I shall somehow try to spend a couple of hours a day at my work. ... So glad the classes are still going, you can have the £45 I get when my book is published for photographing those records, can't imagine anything I would like to do more in my retirement than browse through them and I agree that it would open up a new scene to historians and be invaluable.
Alas the Nagas have not accepted the peace terms and we're expecting an invasion any minute – so it doesn't look as if we'll get much river after all.

My mother wrote to me on 26th November 1964 Cherideo

Got your letter yesterday and have just written to the bank asking them to transfer £40 to your account, also told them to let you have small overdrafts in future to tide you over crisises – your Oxford branch seem excessively suspicious, remember the trouble I had with them trying to prise five pounds out of them. Anne should have paid you back by now as she has had £45 from us since we left, I thought that would be enough until her pay came in.

The one that really worries me is Fiona. Could you please find out from her, or one of her friends what goes on and why she is short of money?… Don't bother to pay back the £40 until and unless your able it has been a heavy quarter for us too but by January things will have eased off and Anne be more or less self-supporting. ... I have had a reply from the National Library and sent for some books, so in about a month's time I should be able to start work, if they have any of them. A sort of staleness has set in with my work and I feel it's pointless and nobody will ever want to read any of it as there is nothing new for me to say and who is interested as you say in old Indian history. This is just a phase I expect, I think it is being out of the historical orbit and living in a vacuum here with not a soul I can talk to about the things that interest me, except Brenda but even she isn't keen on history. She feels exactly the same about her snails. Must hurry back to the Gita for reassurance on the subject of "achievement".

Yes Anne sounds happy, expect you will be at the party and will see Fiona there and be able to talk to her perhaps? I haven't quite decided about Christmas but think I'll probably send a cheque to you, to either give them as money or as record tokens if you think that best. A pity you couldn't have got the car going to take you home in but someone might be able to drive by the spring. Maybe Fiona would like a course of driving lessons as a present? Sorry to give you so much finding out to do but I feel so helpless and frantic sometimes here. ...

I wrote to my parents from Worcester College on 29th November

Thank you for your letter of the 15th - I hope your outing to the 'clean monks' was rewarding and hasn't landed you with malaria, or cost you a leg to a passing tiger or crocodile. I nearly wrote off to Evans-Pritchard asking him if he would like an account of the festival as it is just the sort of thing he is interested in. He himself was the first white man to witness several such ceremonies in Africa. I see him wandering around dreamily in Oxford quite a lot - looking quite disorientated in his old, undarned jersey & patchy corduroys. Unfortunately I never have the courage to go up and say 'hullo'.

Rosemary will be with you now so you will be leading the 'gay life' again. Are there any young men for her to chase? I hate entertaining people. When even a best friend turns up one begins to wonder what one does all day. On this subject, it is possible that Peter Goodden (the ebullient, Dr. Johnson like character who failed his English finals and is now teaching at a 'prep' school in Scotland) may come for Xmas to the Lakes. It is a long way for him to travel from Glasgow to Cornwall where he lives, and anyhow he finds his home situation very difficult. Unfortunately I will only be at home for a week myself - from about 23rd to 30th so don't know if he'll feel it's worth coming. Incidentally, I had a flying visit from Geoffrey Bromley a little while back - I may have told you - and invited his ex-girlfriend round to coffee on Wednesday. She is super-intelligent (got the top 1st of her year in English here Helen Garner's [Gardner's] *special pupil) and very like Geoffrey - bouncy, slightly sensual & big-boned and friendly. She is going to do a thesis on C17 ideas & myths about how the world began - the controversy over how long it took, the Garden of Eden etc. Very interesting I should think. I imagine there are a lot of folk stories about this in Assam?*

I was interested to hear about your plan for the Moghul book; it sounds sensible to me. In describing 'everything that led up to it' (i.e. to each battle) are you going to go into the economic, social, religious structure as well as the actual events & people? If so, are you going to divide them up into separate sections? Ideally, I think, it is best to write a narrative which brings in all the different factors rather than splitting them, though this is very difficult. Perhaps, then, one could have a more detailed analysis - say of the systems of agriculture, the kinship system etc - in Appendices at the end of the book for the more 'serious' readers. I realise however, that the kind of literary material which you are using may not give an appreciable amount of information on such matters. As for my writing an article for History Today or some such, I do often feel tempted to. And then I think that perhaps in a few months I will know a lot more about the subject, and anyhow that I don't want to start drawing on my reserves until I have to. What I mean is that once one starts writing one should produce a continuous stream, stay in the limelight etc. Either one has to have a glib tongue and considerable energy like Robert, or have accumulated a lot of material like Asa Briggs or Christopher Hill. Of course, one article would do no harm. It's probably that I've got the 'don's disease' - fear of criticism & committing oneself, combined with a measure of genuine humility & with a devouring curiosity which is reluctant to pause long enough to work rough thoughts up into printable form.

To quote Cyril Connolly in 'The Unquiet Grave' (have you read it?) - "The more books we read, the clearer it becomes that the true function of a writer is to produce a masterpiece and that no other task is of any consequence. Obvious though this should be, how few writers will admit it, or having drawn the conclusion, will be prepared to lay aside the piece of iridescent mediocrity on which they have embarked ... Every excursion into journalism, broadcasting, propaganda and writing for the films, however grandiose, will be doomed to disappointment. To put our best into these is another folly, since thereby we condemn good ideas as well as bad to oblivion..." This is probably the only time in my life when I will have enough confidence, conceit, optimism & freedom from family, work, money etc. worries to be able to think like this so I might as well make the most of it.

I've had an invitation to a party for next Saturday but don't think I'll be able to go as we have a party of boys coming down from the Borstal that day. They may not be allowed to come, however, since there's been serious trouble recently. One of the warders was killed when a home-made bomb composed of inflamable floor-polish & rags exploded in his face when he was opening a cupboard. No one seems to know whether it was intentional or not. Talking of atrocities etc. isn't this Congo business vile?[1] *If I were a Manley Hopkins I would write a Wreck of the Deutchland poem, instead I turn and bury myself deeper in my academic bolt-hole.*

---

[1] Part of the Congolese civil war, and particularly the Simba Rebellion in November 1965. See https://en.wikipedia.org/wiki/Simba_rebellion

It was Penny's birthday on the 20th. After I'd sent her a card (and a promise of a present 'to follow' - your book (she's the second person to whom I've promised it already & all my Christmas letters are going to take that form!) I suddenly realised it might be her 21st. I haven't heard from her for some time.

I'd rather books than driving-lessons for Xmas - I will only learn to drive when I really have to & would like to put it off till Daddy is home for good. But give the money to Oxfam - I have more than enough worldly goods etc. (after having asked you for a loan this isn't over-convincing!) Much love as always, Alan

1964 - December

My mother wrote from Cherideo on about 3 December 1964 (no date)

My dear Alan,
... Granny sent me my only fan letter to date (which she had opened, to save a 1/3 stamp she said but I didn't' quite follow this as she still had to send it!). It turned out to be from an old boyfriend I hardly remember so can't really be counted as an appreciation of the article!
My books have come from the Hakluyt Society so I'm dying to get down to them but have little opportunity with R. here, sometimes feel like chucking the Moghuls & trying to write a novel on the tragedy of this society – but Forster said it as well as anyone ever will & I could produce no "answers". According to Leach everyone in every society is working & planning for "power" but it seems to me that the impulse behind most people's action is the saving of pride – there is a word here "izzat" which is hard to translate – roughly "face" & the thing that everyone's life is directed at saving & enhancing... [rest lost]

The next indication of the progress of the thesis is in a long letter I wrote to Keith on 4th December from Worcester College. He had annotated the letter with comments, placed in square brackets.

Dear Mr. Thomas,
I wonder if I might see you sometime towards the end of next week – I will be going to Essex the week following and then home to the Lakes for a few days? Practically any time suits me.
I enclose a few snippets. Perhaps you would be interested to see, roughly, how accurate Ewen is & how many cases he missed in Essex. Considering the bulk & speed with which he worked the "Variations …." Indicates that he was seldom far wrong; he omitted some things, perhaps because he thought them too trivial, and in the actual clashes of translation he is right just as often as the Calendar. As for the new cases I have found, of the total 23, Ewen would have omitted 12 because they are recognizances & inquisitions (though, of course, they are valuable for us) while he missed 5 references from Gaol records – Calendars, Delivery Rolls etc – and, more importantly affecting his statistics, 6 indictments. He may, possibly, have omitted some of these (e.g. 23) because they refer to 'white' witchcraft. More broadly, he naturally left out quite a large number of indirect references to the treatments of people who, from the context, we can be certain were on trial as witches. I have not listed these. [K.T. 'Why not?']
In "Distribution of English Witchcraft: Assizes" I have very roughly [K.T. 'why roughly?'] summarized some of Ewen's findings – in an attempt to show how Essex compares with other counties. I think the whole process somewhat useless until distinctions are made between different kinds of records in different circuits (i.e. between indictments, list of witches in prison, depositions by a series of persons etc), between 'black' & 'white' witchcraft accusations (as I note, this biases the number from Chester for instance) and especially the survival of record. But we can go into the details elsewhere. I would prefer to refer readers to Ewen & leave it at that, [K.T. 'No'] but presume his figures must be partially incorporated? With the new cases (& the two printed in Appendix H. of Ewen) that brings Assize cases to almost exactly 500. A large enough figure for some interesting analysis I feel. I will be giving you some preliminary analyses [K.T. 'Not till data is established, at end] of these at the beginning of next term.

<u>Quarter Sessions.</u>
I haven't finished searching the Bundles or checking <u>all</u> of the Sessions records so my conclusions on the number & value of this source are tentative. Also I would be interested to hear how your search of

local archives [K.T. 'No'] has supplemented the somewhat scanty cases I've dug out of the printed records in Duke Humphrey & the cases sent in reply to my letters of enquiry. I've tabulated my present state of knowledge – but this is misleading in several ways. For instance, I'm not certain whether to count the number of persons accused [K.T. underlined accused], the number of depositions, every reference or what. For example under Derbyshire 'Black' the figure 6 includes five informations etc. from one case. Have you decided on this matter? It's obviously more important to distinguish 'black' and 'white' in these records since the former came up more often than in Assizes. [K.T. 'overlap?'] There should, ideally, be distinctions also between the different forms of 'white' – treasure-seeking, healing, finding lost property etc. Then one comes against the 'survival of records' problem again. A problem which has been vexing me is whether Middlesex Sessions Records (Jeafferson & later W & Le Hardy) are properly "quarter or Assize records? Ewen II quotes them as if they were Assize & it seems that Middlesex had no Assize courts like other counties. But the pamphlets (of the Record Office) in Duke Humphrey imply that they are Quarter Session papers – and the Middlesex Record Office certainly didn't complain when I called them that. (Incidentally I've written to them to ask if they can clear up the matter). Yet there are a high proportion of sentences of execution passed & the justices clearly met more than four times a year. Probably there is some easy explanation. I would be interested to know because the large number of cases to be found (some 86 when Ewen's Appdx H. is brought up to date with Le Hardy – and I'm sure many more if one went through the Calendars at the P.R.O) may be strong evidence against the predominance of Essex. For instance in Le Hardy's Calendar (which includes 7 recognizances for 'white' witchcraft – suggesting that this is a Q/S court or its equivalent) there are a total 17 references to witchcraft (10 recognizances & 7 indictments) within 5 years (1612-1618). Even compared to Essex this is a considerable number. Middlesex looks like the only county which might have anything like the volume of records – especially Q/S for Elizabeth's reign – that Essex possesses. [K.T. 'Do QS & Assize overlap?']

Essex, as you will see from the chart, has roughly 65 direct cases of witchcraft. A few more cases have turned up even since I compiled that figure, and it will end up as over 70. Some of these are long depositions & examinations (like the Aylett affair – a transcript of which I enclose; do you feel it is within my province? It's sad that M. Murray didn't have it – she'd have quoted it <u>in extenso</u>!) [K.T. 'please explain it to me!] but mostly they're recognizances to appear etc (only 9 are indictments for instance). I am analysing these by name, place etc. Naturally most of the cases appear in the Assizes, though there are some, especially concerning 'white' witchcraft, which don't. [K.T. 'Where do they come? Ecclesiastical?']

<u>Pamphlets.</u>

Looking through Notestein's Appendix I notice that there is a pamphlet I've missed. N. mistakenly attributes it to Staffs (there is no Burntwood or Barking in that county so I wonder where he got the notion?) and says that he was unable to find it. Ewen noted that it related to the notorious case (which I attach) of Mother Arnold. Lowndes gives no further information and I've looked at the various books on the open shelves in Duke Humphrey. [KVT. 'STC?' – i.e. Short Title Catalogue of Early Books] Perhaps you could keep your eyes open for it?

Hope this hasn't wasted your time too much,

I look forward to seeing you next week,

Yours sincerely, Alan Macfarlane

Keith replied the following day, 5th December

Many thanks for a v. intersting packet. (But don't start analysing until you have finished writing up the facts about the data). Would Saturday (12 Dec) at 11.45 be all right? K.V.T.

Unusually, at this period there are more of my letters surviving, and the next is also from me, dated on Monday 7 December from Oxford to my parents.

Thank you very much for the loan (and the two letters). I should be able to pay it back almost immediately as I get my £60 for the W.E.A. I asked them for some of it in advance over two weeks ago and they said 'yes' - since then we have been exchanging forms and nothing more has happened. Bureaucracy takes the place of corruption in this country! I'll try to find out from Fiona where her money goes - I wasn't at Anne's party so couldn't then. I got the impression from her letter that her grant hadn't arrived & that was why she was short. ...As for my amorous situation, I've got into a bit of a rut with Linda, very pleasant, but a little unfair on her and far from my usual Dittany/Heloise type frenzies. I got round to going to see Jill (Celia's niece) yesterday, or at least I found the Catholic Worker's College where she lives at Boar's Hill and found that her second name (which I'd been unable to read) is Walker. I've invited her to coffee. I still haven't heard from Penny. The girl who was doing an essay on witchcraft & who lives in Chelmsford has, on my mentioning it, got into the course which Penny is doing, a Diploma in the History of Art at the V & A.

I don't seem to do much here - tho every evening is full. On Saturday I marked examination entrances for the College. I feel guilty marking down people whom I know are just as intelligent as I was three years ago. Later in the week we will interview them. Part of the reward was dinner in High Table - very delicious too! The academic life slides its tentacles round one, you see! Yesterday evening I went to the College carol service, packed and inspiring. Why are carols so sad? Or at least most of the best medieval etc ones? I suppose because tenderness, awe and longing are close to sadness. Nearly all good folk-music is sad. This is the time, of course, when people begin, slightly, to feel guilty about the "Other 2/3rds" - Oxfam is launching another great appeal etc.

I hope that your feeling of staleness and inconsequence in your work has evaporated Mummy. I get it even here where I have no excuse with all my sources at hand, a fascinating topic and a multitude of interested & interesting people to talk to. Aren't there any books I can get for you here? - out of the money for your article for instance? (Richard confirming that he could take us North on 23rd said "Your Mother's Article ... read very well. A family symposium might be a possibility.") If only for this you ought to keep writing. But more importantly a) one has to keep creating b) I want to read what you write if no-one else does and I'm sure they will, anyhow. As for the stone wall of apathy, corruption, etc in India I suppose the only thing is to have a steel head to bang against it - steel because it is a) detached b) forge into an organized, well-informed and sympathetic machine. Pity one can't advertize for a Ghandi! Much love to you both, as ever, Alan

My mother wrote from Cherideo, date stamped 10th December 1964, re-directed to Poste Restante, Chelmsford Post Office, Chelmsford, Essex

My dear Alan,

Thank you for a long letter – we do appreciate your writing at such length when you must be sick of your typewriter by Sunday. I got my "History To-day" yesterday, I think they did me very well, in spite of writing about me as if I was dead at the end! I agree with Cyril Connolly, the only thing is that one's fear of not writing a masterpiece prevents one from even starting. ...You'll be starting off north soon, how I wish I was there "but I have promises to keep" – or try to, though I know in my heart I'm beaten before I start. Could you sometime go into Blackwells & ask if they got back the book "Indian Seamen" which they've again billed me for? Much love – Mummy

Keith's assessment of my progress is indicated in the supervisor's report which he wrote to the University on the same day that he had suggested we meet.

Supervisor's Report, 12th December 1964

[Degree of D.Phil. is noted, with B.Sc, B.Litt crossed through]

'Mr. Macfarlane is making good progress in his study of witchcraft prosecution in Essex, 1560-1680. He has combed the Assize records and has nearly finished working through the Quarter Sessions records. The archives of the ecclesiastical courts are the only large source which remains to be consulted before he can start analysing his findings. He is a very keen student and, although his exposition is sometimes rather careless, I expect him to bring his work to a satisfactory conclusion.'

My mother wrote to me from Nazira on December 13th 1964,
re-directed to Poste Restante, Chelmsford Post Office, Chelmsford, Essex

It's even more difficult than usual to work out if this will arrive in time to wish you a happy birthday, but you know whenever it does get there that we were/will be thinking of you on the day and hoping you will have some people you like with you. It's odd that I'm still so near your birthplace and it certainly doesn't seem twenty three years ago that I was sitting on the road verge clutching my stomach at one in the morning while Daddy tried to get the car we had borrowed started. We still seem to be fairly disorganised with cars that won't start and not much more money than then, but very conscious of our good fortune in you all – Rosemary and I were reading "If there were dreams to sell" for her English and discussing what we would buy and apart from that croft with the seals and otters I couldn't think of a thing I lacked. My birthday wish is that you will have as nice children (and I was going to say husband!) as I have – and as "The Grapes of Wrath" rather beautifully describes the mother, "mount pain and suffering like steps into a high calm". I'm reading it at last, have been saving it up, or dodging it, I don't know which, for ages. I'm glad you got the money, don't bother to pay us back but perhaps you could give Fiona a few pounds to buy presents, I still haven't worked out why she should be so short but she obviously is...

We're going to Delhi in January for ten days, to stare at palaces and make contacts I hope. I wondered if the lecturer in Indian History could be approached for contacts? I'll leave it to you to decide and do this for me if you think it wise, but it would be very nice to know of someone to turn to for advice and chit chat. I shall probably stay a week in Calcutta afterwards to do my final reading, and start on the book when I get back. I just hope to make a lively and readable story, a personality history showing the reactions of the Indians to Europeans and vice versa, serious scholars won't want to read it so there won't be any need for an appendix and there are masses of books with chapters called "The Agrarian system under the Moghuls" so I don't think I need add to them. Can't really think who will want to but you say you kindly will and people have made the dustiest and remotest past live convincingly and tempted an audience to be interested. I shall try, even if I fail I will never regret the time and trouble I've spent as its been fascinating. I hope the Edyes niece turned out to be nice, of course I remembered straight away that the name was Walker. ... Ceylon seems to be another sad muddle,[1] what a bitter harvest is being reaped everywhere from the colonialist sowings, but one can't lay the blame anywhere particular. This isn't a very birthday letter but you know it brings all our love and thoughts.

As I set off, presumably to Essex for another spell in the Record Office, I jotted down the following.

Waiting in a bus – Walton Street 13/12/64

Rhodedendrons brushed the waiting bus
A backscreen to the little play
The winter sky which had sucked all
The colours, carried Salvation Army carols

[1] Among other things, there was a cyclone over Ceylon during December 1964.

And the scent of soaked fields
Of the full brown river
Across the slates.
Listless conversation mingled with Bach
Nostalgia merged with emptiness
And a group of youths sidled, watching
How the collections for the band were treated.
The whole world seemed caught in
That restless web, of Yeats' poems on my
Knee, the clink of counted change
The moment of children being guided
To their seats. All the complexity
The crowded unmeaning
The silence of the babble of men
Seemed to come into that
Waiting bus.

Letter from Iris to Alan, Fiona and Anne, from Cherideo December 14th 1964

Quite a Christmas feeling here to-day with rain pouring out of a black sky, the first winter rain we've had for several years and very welcome to the garden … This is supposed to arrive on Christmas Eve and I'm imagining the house simply humming with light, colour, Telly, brown paper, smells of milk boiling over and toast burning, and the church bells ringing romantically over the fields. Rosemary is sitting on the carpet making paper chains which is the nearest we can get to it and Radio Ceylon is making its contribution to the Christmas spirit by playing an ancient version of Rudolf the Red Nosed Reindeer ceaselessly. We are all thinking of you and will toast you in the evening which will be about your lunch time and imagine you staggering from the table to the Telly to hear our not so little monarch – don't suppose you will be allowed to see even her at Such a Time! Nobody ever mentioned the weather but I'm dreaming of you...

Meanwhile I had gone off for a week's research at the Essex Record Office, and wrote my Christmas letter from the Chelmsford Public Library on 16 December. I remember it as a cosy place with a good local history collection and the occasional visiting speaker (including Noel Streatfield, whom I was asked to introduce!)

I've left my Christmas letter very late and I only hope it isn't held up. Whether you get it or not you know we'll all be thinking of you and wishing you happiness, long life (if you want it!), good health etc. Only one more Xmas will I have to write to wish you this (I hope).

Thank you very much for the birthday/Xmas cheque - though I'll write properly to thank you when I've bought something with the money and can tell you what it is. I don't quite understand about the driving instalment present. I get £5 (presumably birthday & Xmas?) & the girls get £2-10s for Xmas. Then do we all get driving instalments for our birthday also? Perhaps I'm just getting a bigger birthday present? I'm not sure how long I will be North - if Richard is driving down to Hertford on 28th it may be for only 4-5 days. Any post to reach me before Jan. 8th should go to Poste Restante, Chelmsford Post Office, Chelmsford, Essex.

How are/did the preparations for Xmas go? Did the Suzie-Wong type bamboo brothels induce the right atmosphere? I suppose you can't/didn't (in future I'll write in the future tense - excuse this if it's wrong) get up the river on the day but had to go to the Spree with Rosemary. Here the heart breaking decorations go up again, waking in people a vague uneasiness with their reminder of the need for Joy at something which they do not know. Records of choirs and lighted cribs appeal for charities and the Rolling Stones join in the benevolent rush to give gifts to Oxfam. If one stops to think for a moment this utter hypocrisy on one side, and the untold need and misery on the other tears one to pieces. And yet what do I do? Nothing. But we'll get off our favourite subject.

While in Essex I'm staying with another newly married couple (Kevin & Anne - Kevin is a sweet, beatnikish, slightly dazed & scruffy boy who lived for a while at 19, Chalfont Rd; he got a 2nd in P.P.E. and is now a reporter for the Harlow Chronicle - Anne, also R.C, is equally nice). They have a huge flat with a kind of studio attic. Unfortunately the buses are bad & take 85 minutes each way; but when my motorbike (lights being overhauled thoroughly) is ready this should be a great boon. It looks as if I'll be spending March-May inclusive in Essex delving into the fascinating Archdeaconry records. I saw Keith Thomas (my supervisor) on Saturday. He seemed happy with how things are shaping. The last week was a little interrupted by marking College entrance papers & oral examining. I didn't ask many questions but sat, clad in my jeans & old jacket, between Lord Franks and John Vaizey (the economist). The students obviously took me to be "one of them" and looked shocked when I did ask them anything!

I finally got round to meeting Jill Walker (Celia's niece?) on the final Sunday when I had tea with her at Boars Hill. She is tallish (probably a little taller than me), slim, walks nicely, wears sensible clothes, has an interesting and probably beautiful face, framed by medium-longish brown hair. She's intelligent, sensitive, a good sense of humour though of a generally serious nature, thoughtful, religious (R.C - though not bigoted) and "socially concerned". In fact very nice. Leaving Oxford on Tuesday I only had a chance to meet her for coffee on Monday but she is staying in London at a friend's flat so perhaps I shall see her again? But you know me. I fall in and out of love like records go in and out of the 'hit' parade! (Not that I'm 'in love' - yet!)

Any chance to read the Hakluyt stuff, Mummy? Don't despair with the Moghuls - you have one ardent admirer & reader anyhow! I have great plans for a combined "opus" on English local social history when you return, but will explain anon.

Sorry this is so tedious - especially, perhaps for Daddy, but can't summon up any Xmas feeling yet; though it was very beautiful riding through the little Essex villages this morning white with hoar frost - the red-faced labourers cutting their hedges and the ploughed fields jaggedly furrowed. All my best love to you both, as always, look after yourselves, Alan

On my twenty-third birthday, I wrote the following.

20/12/64 Birthday

How can one reach through the sticky sentiments
Of Christmas, the mock loneliness, the prettiness and trivia
To something permanent and true; man's eternal search
Seems again important. And as I write the faces of the many dead
Rise through the forests of beauty to sing
That in the depths and bitterness of winter
And in the snow and cold
And in the tears that have mixed with the dirt
Of station platforms and through the vomit
And blood of a thousand hospitals
Where the ulcered and lepered lie
Screaming curses on their god
As he tears the brain and paints
The heavens with the cloth of gold
And pulls the trees across the sky
The graves and the beggars on the pavement,
The movement of young girls, the sugared

Voice of mock pop singers, the bitterness
Of hurt lovers all these merge into
The agony and laughter that we know.
To feel velvet and to know the cold wind
To abandon the pen and let the sore
Heart moan to the moon: to feel that
Death rides each shadow and that laughter
Pulls back from the machine-given.
We cannot hold one another
Cannot compromise, nor fight,
Cannot feel nor think though we sneer
And scoff at other's who walk in humility
In their sorrow. And here I stand in my
Mock despair, no older, no deeper, no
Nearer God or Man, eaten up with myself
Slobbering before the feast of fame
And self-importance and yet groaning
Awestruck before the majesty of man's inconsequence
Horror at the balloon of ignorance & prejudice
On which we dance. Sleep on in your cosy
Irresponsibility or give and lose, suffer and
Shout and dance into the rolling years.
Pour your soul into God's bucket or man's
Pocket and let the wind numb the body
And man's whip, to scar your timid flesh.
Laugh and stand on Christ's side in the
Infinite tragedy of this deep folly.

My mother wrote to Alan, Fiona and Anne from Cherideo on December 22nd 1964

Hoping to get in one more combined letter before you scatter – Val included of course. You'll all be slumped round feeling anti-climactic I expect, but here were are right in the middle of the Whirl – i.e. trying to grind up some thick lumpy sugar to ice the cake with and decide whether to kill a poor old goose or dear little duck to eat up the river.

I wrote my last letter of the year to my parents from Field Head on 29th December

Thank you very much for your Christmas letter and also, formally, for the money. I received a pile of very welcome book tokens - as well as assorted useful articles of clothing. I hope to buy two kinds of books with the money tokens - anthropological and on the techniques of studying local history. I've already bought 'Teach Yourself' Local History - very elementary and naive but with some interesting bibliographies, and a chapter on 'Folklore & Sociology'. I am itching to get down to a proper study of Esthwaite valley - if there is enough material at the Record office and in the parish records. Still, perhaps, I'd better stick to Essex for now.

How was your Christmas? Ours went with its own pleasant rituals. The morning expedition to Hawkshead through the bitter fields to the sound of church bells and the return as the sun was rising over Latterbarrow, the Christmas lights refusing to work; the dismal flicker of lighted brandy on Christmas pudding; "my husband and I..."; the feeling of satiation from an enormous lunch; and at the back of one's consciousness a gnawing realization of all the millions who are still cold, hungry and homeless. Perhaps it was right that the B.B.C. should show one of the most bloody & brutal episodes of 'The Great War' (the Battle of Verdun with people torn to shreds by splintering shells etc) in the evening.

I am embarking hopefully on Justine when I arrived with Richard on the 23rd expecting this to be a quiet spell but in fact there has been much dashing here & there over snow-covered roads. On Xmas eve we went carousing at the Outgate Inn & Duck. At the latter there were abortive carols. On boxing day the girls went hunting and in the evening we went to a party at the Vicarage. Here I met a nice girl called Jane Wilkinson (she came to the house once in the summer with Pippa Manby) who is a speech therapist in London. She lives at Colthouse (the little group of houses just beyond Hawkshead on the Sawrey road) and is pretty, intelligent & fun. We walked round the Tarns the next day and last night to 'Tarzan in India'(!!) at the Ambleside flea-pit and then walked back! Meanwhile the others have been fairly busy too. Mike Doogan has been rushing around ... Grandpa (& Richard) have been also whirling round in the usual circle - meeting the Callendars at Beryl, meeting Beryl at the Callenders etc.

Meanwhile the snow it snoweth every day and the Tarns stay on the edge of being frozen enough to skate on. There have been some unimaginably beautiful scenes - the sun pinking the mountains and flecking the fir-trees with gold. I have done a good amount of walking and very little - if any - work which is perhaps a Good Thing. I go down south again this Sunday so my next letter will be from Essex. All this walking has been too much for the dogs and Pooch is hobbling around on three legs having strained the other. ... F is looking well & doing a fair amount of drawing. Mr Doogan is up and around, but has a stammer. ... Hope you can read this - Granny said my writing was getting very bad. Look after yourselves, much love, Alan

The work I had been doing on the Essex records, and my choice of Essex, was largely influenced by one work – the pioneering researches of C.L. Ewen. Without his seminal works on witchcraft assize records, I doubt that I could have embarked on using records which, as I record elsewhere, were extraordinarily difficult, though I might have been able to do so because the Essex Record Office had, by this time, made a calendar of their Assize records against which I was checking Ewen. Ewen not only transcribed the records for the different counties in the Home Circuit, but was invaluable in providing a detailed account of how the legal system, and particularly the Assize courts, worked, in a very long introduction with examples in his major book.

WITCH HUNTING

AND

WITCH TRIALS

The Indictments for Witchcraft from the Records of 1373 Assizes held for the Home Circuit A.D. 1559–1736

Collected and edited by

C. L'ESTRANGE EWEN

With an Introduction

LONDON

KEGAN PAUL, TRENCH, TRUBNER & CO., LTD.

BROADWAY HOUSE: 68–74 CARTER LANE, E.C.

1929

It was followed four years later by Witchcraft and Demonianism which I was unable to purchase, but used also.

Here are two examples from the book. The first is a gaol delivery in the exceptional Matthew Hopkins period in 1645 to which I will come later.

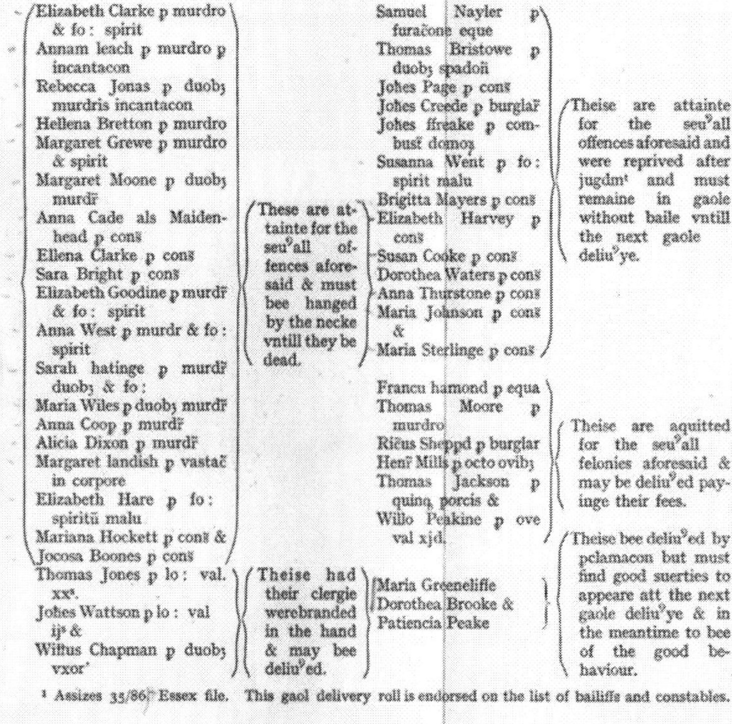

APPENDIX I.

Essex Gaol Delivery Roll, Summer 1645.[1]

ESSEX ʃʃ Delibačo gaole đni Regis coñ sui Essex teñ apud Chellmisford in eodm coñ dic Jovis decimo septimo die Julij Anno regni đni ñri Caroli dei grã Angli Scocie ffranč & hibnie Regis fidei defensoris &č vicesimo primo coram Robto comite Warwici Johe Barrington milite & Barronetto Martino lumley milite & Barronetto Henrico Holcroft milite Henř Mildmay de Wanstead milite Willo Conyers Ař & alijs socijs suis Justič dči đni Regis ad gaolam suam coñ sui Essex pd de prisonib; in ea existeñ delibãnd assigñ.

Elizabeth Clarke p murdro & fo: spirit
Annam leach p murdro p incantacon
Rebecca Jonas p duob; murdris incantacon
Hellena Bretton p murdro
Margaret Grewe p murdro & spirit
Margaret Moone p duob; murdř
Anna Cade als Maidenhead p conš
Ellena Clarke p conš
Sara Bright p conš
Elizabeth Goodine p murdř & fo: spirit
Anna West p murdr & fo: spirit
Sarah hatinge p murdř duob; & fo:
Maria Wiles p duob; murdř
Anna Coop p murdř
Alicia Dixon p murdř
Margaret landish p vastač in corpore
Elizabeth Hare p fo: spiritũ malu
Mariana Hockett p conš &
Jocosa Boones p conš
— These are attainte for the seu⁹all offences aforesaid & must bee hanged by the necke vntill they be dead.

Samuel Nayler p furačone eque
Thomas Bristowe p duob; spadoñ
Johes Page p conš
Johes Creede p burglař
Johes ffreake p combusť domos
Susanna Went p fo: spirit malu
Brigitta Mayers p conš
Elizabeth Harvey p conš
Susan Cooke p conš
Dorothea Waters p conš
Anna Thurstone p conš
Maria Johnson p conš &
Maria Sterlinge p conš
— Theise are attainte for the seu⁹all offences aforesaid and were reprived after jugdm^t and must remaine in gaole without baile vntill the next gaole deliu⁹ye.

Francu hamond p equa
Thomas Moore p murdro
Ričus Sheppd p burglar
Henř Mills p octo ovib;
Thomas Jackson p quinq, porcis &
Willo Peakine p ove val xjd.
— Theise are aquitted for the seu⁹all felonies aforesaid & may be deliu⁹ed payinge their fees.

Thomas Jones p lo: val. xx^s.
Johes Wattson p lo: val ij^s &
Wiltus Chapman p duob; vxor'
— Theise had their clergie werebranded in the hand & may bee deliu⁹ed.

Maria Greenecliffe
Dorothea Brooke &
Patiencia Peake
— Theise bee deliu⁹ed by pclamacon but must find good suerties to appeare att the next gaole deliu⁹ye & in the meantime to bee of the good behaviour.

[1] Assizes 35/86, Essex file. This gaol delivery roll is endorsed on the list of bailiffs and constables.

Robtus Griffeth p roboria. hee was attainted att Suff[...] in the xviij^th of his matę: reigne for seu⁹all rob[...] the highway but was reprived by a speciall warrant [...] matę: & was then ordered to remaine in gaole with[...] & must remaine in gaole according to the said order[...]

Maria Ashwood p murdř spuř. Shee is attainte for th[...] aforesaid att the last gaole deliu⁹ye but was repri[...] judgm^t: & must remaine in gaole without baile vntill [...] gaole deliu⁹ye.

Franciscus Smyth. hee is attainte for two seu⁹all robb[...] is reprived from execucon by the space of tenn d[...] ensuinge this 22th day of July 1645. And if before [...] hee pcure not a further reprive hee is then to be exec[...]

Maria Coppine. Shee is attainte for murder by witchc[...] was reprived after judgm^t: vppon desire of M^r. [...] minister & must remaine in gaole without baile vntill [...] gaole deliu⁹ye.

Elizabeth Codwell. Shee is attainte for murthering [...] bastard child but because shee is found by a jury of [...] to bee with quicke child execucon of her is to bee st[...] one month after her deliu⁹ye & then execucon to [...] of her.

Jacobus Langden. hee is acquitted of two seu⁹all rob[...] the highway but must remaine in gaole vntill hee [...] suerties to appeare att the next gaole deliu⁹ye & in t[...] time to bee of the good behaviour.

Edrus Orton. hee is comitted for that hee is ve[...] suspected to have robbed vppon the highway & must [...] in gaole without baile vntill the next quarter Sessio[...] holden for this County & then to bee bailed if the c[...] thinke fitt to appeare att the next gaole deliu⁹ye to b[...] for this county & in the meanetime to bee of [...] behaviour.

Johanna Rowle. Shee is acquitted vppon three seu⁹all [...] by witchcraft but must remaine in gaole vntill shee [...] good baile for her psonall appearance att the ne[...] deliu⁹ye & in the meanetime to bee of the good beha[...]

Anna Bragg. She was form⁹lie comitted by Sr Thom[...] for suspicon of murthering her bastard child, but [...] none . . . to psecute ag^t: her Sr Thomas Bowes is [...] examine this businesse & to baile her if hee shall t[...] to appeare att the next gaole deliu⁹ye & to bee of [...] behaviour.

Matheus Pett als Powell. hee was comitted by Rob[...] Esq. for diu⁹s misdeameanors & must bee sett att [...] the howse of correccon vntill the next Sessions to b[...] for this county.

Willus Gilford. Ignoramus. hee is deliu⁹ed by pclama[...]

[To fac[...]

The second is one of many hundred pages of abstracts of indictments. (Apologies for the quality, but it is a large, tightly bound, book.)

[illegible] Surrey Lent Sessions and general gaol delivery holden at . . . Commission dated 12 Feb., 22 Chas. I.

[illegible] Anne Jackson [erased] of the parish of St Saviour's, [illegible]ark Borough, widow, on 1 Feb., 22 Chas. I, at St S., [illegible]ed Sarah Gilbert, wife of George G., who languished [illegible] 14 Feb., 22 Chas. I, when she died at St S. *Endorsed.* [illegible] Burnham, Lettice Gately, George Hewett, George Gilbert. [illegible]mus.

[illegible] Essex Summer Sessions and general gaol delivery holden at Brentwood on 11 Aug., 23 Chas. I. Commission dated 12 July, 23 Chas. I.

[illegible] Jane Lavender of Navestocke, spinster, wife of Francis [illegible] N., tailor, on 20 June, 23 Chas. I, at N., bewitched Margaret [illegible], spinster, who was wasted and consumed. *Endorsed.* [illegible] Cole, Sarah Wyer. Billa vera.
[illegible] se non cul n^cr^ Q^a^.

[illegible] ——, on 1 Jan., 22 Chas. I, at N., bewitched Anne [illegible]kes, who languished until 1 Apr., 23 Chas. I, when she [illegible] at N. *Endorsed.* Thomas Hawkes, Winifred Norris, Ruth [illegible]bolt. Ignoramus.

[illegible]. Francis Lavender of Navestocke, yeoman, on 1 Jan., [illegible] Chas. I, at N., bewitched Mary Peirce, wife of Richard P., [illegible] languished until 1 Mar., 19 Chas. I, when she died at N. [illegible]*rsed*. Thomas Hawkes, Richard Peirce, Winifred Norris, [illegible] Sherbolt. Billa vera.
[illegible] se non cul n^cr^ Q^9^.

660. ——, on 1 July, 23 Chas. I, at N., bewitched Sarah [illegible]er, wife of John W., who was wasted and consumed. [illegible]*rsed*. Sarah Wyer, Joan Cole, John Stapler, Robert [illegible]bbe, William Small. Billa vera.
[illegible] se non cul n^cr^ Q^9^.

661. ——, on 20 July, 23 Chas. I, at N., bewitched to death [illegible] calves of William Hone of N., yeoman. *Endorsed.* William [illegible]e. Ignoramus.

I was able to find supplementary materials of his in several small publications through the kindness of his sister Mrs Williams, who gave me some privately published copies of his work which were annotated by him and contained some of his search notes.

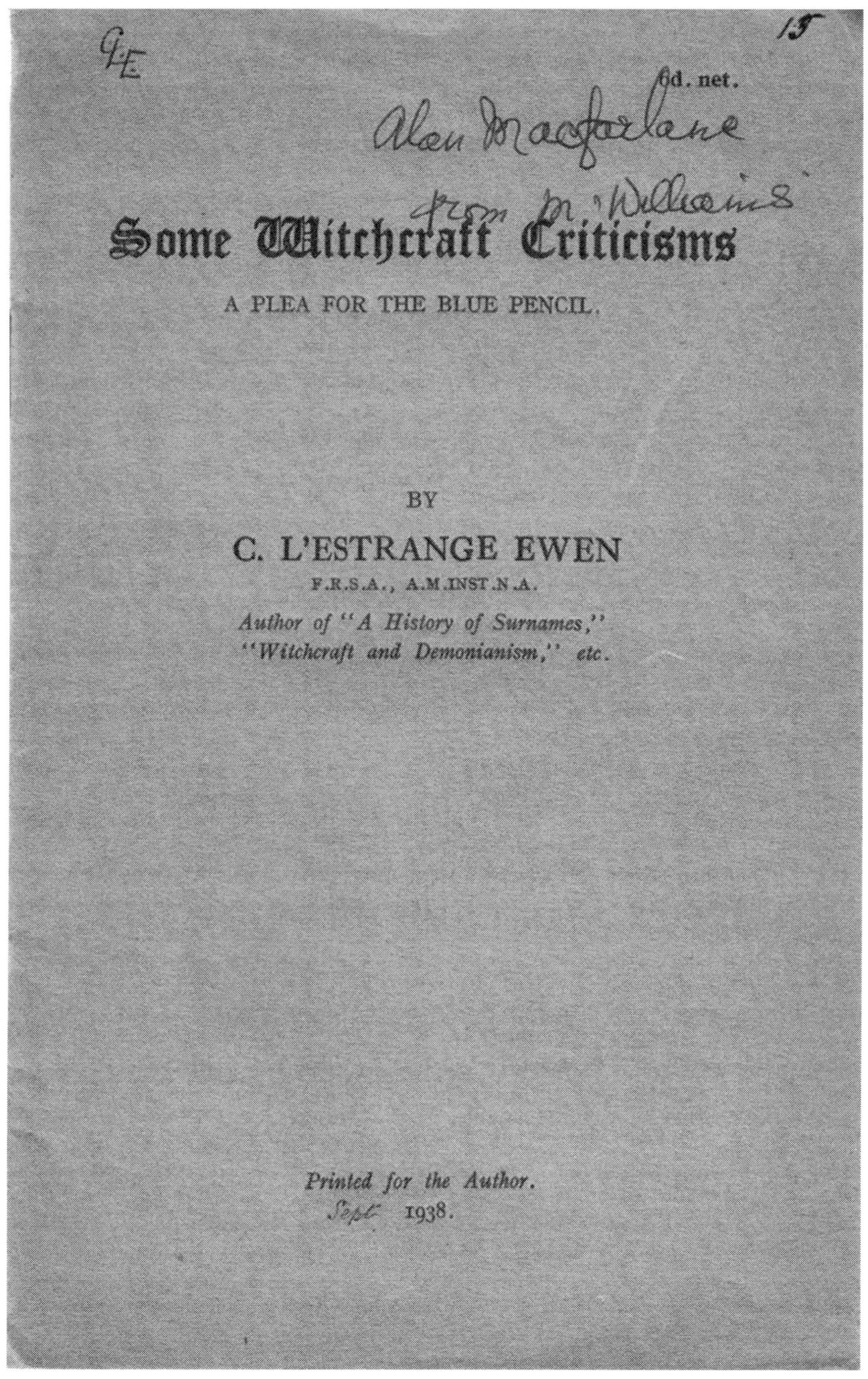

6d. net.

Some Witchcraft Criticisms

A PLEA FOR THE BLUE PENCIL.

BY

C. L'ESTRANGE EWEN

F.R.S.A., A.M.INST.N.A.

Author of "A History of Surnames," "Witchcraft and Demonianism," etc.

Printed for the Author.
Sept 1938.

1965

1965 - January

At some point, either at the end of 1964 or start of 1965 I sent Keith a plan of my next nine months work, which gives a good outline, for the middle and crucial phase of research, of the working through the primary sources.

OUTLINE OF WORK: Jan.1965.

8 weeks. Jan. Feb. **In Oxford:** cross referencing by name, place, subject etc. to Assize, Pamphlet & Q/S records. Legal & medical background; literature (1) on witchcraft (Scot etc) // Mid-March, **In Essex** -

8 weeks. March. April. Ecclesiastical records & preliminary attempts to trace individuals in selected areas.

6 weeks. May. June. **In Oxford:** cross-referencing of Ecclesiastical records & preliminary statistics of all legal sources. General writers on witchcraft.

2-3 months. July. August. September. **In Essex.** Final, direct (2), sources (borough, diaries, central (3) etc) Essex background to selected outbreaks, villages & persons.

October. **To Oxford:** Writing-up material.

(Obviously the above may, ~~obviously~~, have to be modified in practice)

Though I hope to produce a fair amount of written work before October, and to be analysing all the time ~~that~~ while fresh information is coming in, it is obviously dangerous to be too precipitate; only when all the sources have been examined can proper chapters be written.

(1) With the considerable amount of contemporary discussion and comment on witchcraft and associated subjects it will probably be best to keep working through Ady, Harsnett, Glanvil etc. all the time.

(2) As opposed to 'indirect' i.e. the background of individuals involved from parish records etc.

(3) P.R.O. and other London archives. I think we agree that I can't go very far into this.

January 4th 1965 Cherideo Iris to Alan

Afraid this is a day or two late as I've been sending in every day for forms without any luck. Thank you for yours written while waiting for Richard, I was relieved to get it and hear about Anne as there had been complete silence from her for three weeks, however I got a letter the day before yesterday. She sounded rather tired and jaded but it was probably just the mood of the letter. I wonder if you managed to dig yourselves out and get south again, though judging from the papers the south has had the worst conditions. Your lovely parcel of books arrived three days after Christmas which was wonderfully timed, and needless to say have been ecstatically received. Daddy pounced on Verrier Elwin but I've read the first three chapters and find it terribly entertaining, he has a delightful sense of humour which must have been the only thing that carried him through some of his experiences. I'm sure you will see yourself in him when you read it, his great desire to stay in Oxford and live the life of culture warring with his call to help the helpless and ignorant – of course I am more maddened than ever that I never met him. I'm reading Kierkegaarde (?) as well, a name I've heard referred to so often so it is nice to meet him at last, and am dying to delve into the other books but am spacing them out. … I get terribly depressed just frittering my days on knitting and silly chatter which is all I've done for the last six weeks. … We are also going to suggest that we finish a year early, i.e. this November instead of next, but there again he will probably refuse. We would spend the winter in India but in places relevant to my work or interesting in other ways and come home next spring – but this is only a dream. I've now accepted the fact that I'll never be able to collect folk stories from the villages or old histories, and the most I can hope for is to get my Moghuls done and perhaps another childrens book, which I have simmering in the back of my head – a sort of mixture of "The Secret Garden" and the Jungle Stories! I'm glad Jill Walker turned out nice, and hope it will prove a fulfilling friendship. Where have you got to with your witches, has any pattern emerged or have you reached a decision about that it was that "caused" them? One of Verrier Elwins ancestors was burned as a witch, Holman I think was the name.
Rosemary is full of stories about Khasi witches who still sit in caves mixing love potions and so on, I must go and visit one when I go to Shillong. The Khasis are a tribe well worth studying in depth... Are you going to keep on your room at Oxford when you go to Essex?

I wrote from Essex on 5th January describing a little more of that last Christmas when my grandparents were still at Field Head.

I'm sitting in front of a coal fire after an enormous breakfast at my digs in Chelmsford. I returned South on Sunday (by bus) and spent the night with Annie. After a week here in Essex I will return to Oxford for two months. I went to the P.O. to collect my mail and found your birthday letter among it, late but still very welcome - thank you very much. Incidentally, I wonder if you got the assorted books I sent out?

I was sad to leave the North again so soon, after a delightful break in which I eat and slept and flirted & did little else. There were some breath-taking days when the snow was still on the higher hills and the dead bracken glowed against the sky. For instance the day before I came down I went for a walk (with Jane Wilkinson) up Latterbarrow and through those pine-woods to the little tarns. There was something magical in the air; we saw some large wild deer and came upon a mysterious piece of string tied from tree to tree. This led off into the Forest Sauvage & we followed it until it ended in a clearing where we quite expected to find a gingerbread house with an old witch inside or King Pellinore's bratchet wound round & round a tree. We talked of unicorns and monsters, of Jenny Green Teeth who is a beautiful siren believed to live at the bottom of many Lake District tarns and to lure travellers into their depths with her green, weed-like, hair. Another day Val & I went with Stephen Grieve & Carol (who are thriving - S. is still on the verge of potting) to visit a hidden farm-house up behind the Tarns where Lanty Slee, a famous whisky distiller & smuggler, lived about 100 years ago. There is a long passage on him in Cowper's book on Hawkshead. (When you come home we must really get down to the local history of Esthwaite valley as well as Lancashire legends & folk-lore). It was a romantic cottage - beside it was the newly made grave of a greatly loved sheep-dog who had had to be shot because he had got in with a litter - and inside a couple and their young baby living on the dole (8 pounds a week!): also 11 piglets and a mass of old beams & walls.

Jane's party was quite good - lots of drink & food etc & I went with my Jane & so enjoyed it, but too many people were paired (Like Jill ?Sinnok - 2 weeks before her baby arrives) married or engaged for it to really explode. Talking of marriage I travelled down in the seat behind Alistair Grieve who is married to a German girl - most attractive (just like Dorothy - medium - straight blond hair, grey eyes, etc) and nice. A.G. is half-way through an M.A. (for which one has to write a thesis at London) on Rossetti.

My latest plan about my future is that after my official grant expires in October 1966 I will spend about 6 months either finishing off the thesis or turning it into a book - living off either writing or casual labour or what I can save of my grant - and then go abroad for six months (perhaps that reminds you of earlier resolutions!). My only new year's resolution is the purely selfish one that I will not become a slave to my work but get around a bit more - meet more people, do more things while I am young etc.

About the money I owe you - I'll keep it in reserve. I'll pay it back before the end of the financial year - I've got to as I'm not allowed to accept it - but will keep it for now in case of any crises - either mine or the girls. Thank you.

I'll contact the reader in Indian History as soon as I can.

Much love to you both,

Alan

My mother wrote to me from Cherideo on Jan 11th 1965

Thank you for your most amusing letter on Christmas, it made me very homesick. also for sending that letter of Mr Strachan's. It's nice to find another Roe fan, I would like his book eventually but not at the moment as I have a pile of reading on hand, for my birthday perhaps? I'll see if I can dig up anything for him in Delhi but I'm afraid the white ants will have eaten any pictures that might have existed. Our trip is fairly organised except that the Finneys keep changing their minds as to whether they're coming, did you think it a good thing to get in touch with either of those gentlemen whose addresses you gave me or not? Im sitting on the verandah waiting for Mr Remnant who is visiting this morning, we asked him if we could be released a year early, i.e. this November instead of next and he has come out to discuss this. It didn't sound very hopeful form his letter, or rather he is prepared to let us go on a reduced pension and this we shan't accept.... I got a letter from my agent the other day and the publishers have decided to cut out all the background material from my book, he is cross about this but I have rather lost interest. Afraid it will hardly hit the best seller lists in its present form, I hope I don't have to pay back any of the advance!...

I wonder if you saw Jill Walker or Anne or both... Has Rosemary had her baby? Have you seen Miss Faraday at all and when is Robert starting?[1] *I suddenly feel a great longing to be back for a week end to catch up on all the little things that can't be said in letters, your classes for instance, I wish I could attend one... are you permanently in Essex till March?*

Violet to Iris Field Head, Outgate, Nr. Ambleside on 12th Jan 1965

Richard's 44th Birthday

---

[1] Rosemary was Rosemary Collins, with whom (along with her husband Roy) I shared a flat during my postgraduate years. Miss Faraday was a former landlady. Robert was my uncle, Robert Rhodes James, who was starting a new career as a Fellow of All Souls College in Oxford.

My darling Iris – "The Shouting & the tumult Dies". & Daddie & I are left in a vacuum – It was a very happy time for us as everyone was cheerful & helpful & this was the centre of the local whirlpool – Steve Darbyshire & v. young attaché were nearly permanent – I find him marvellous company of the brand of Johnny Watson & I wish he were not such a rolling stone – Steven Grieves & his Carol – Manby's & 2 boyfriends – Tim Boddington – Tim Manby, Michael Doogan & our Richard – at all hours – en masse or singly – Daddie & I crouched by the fire & had little trays brought us while Fiona & Val coped in the kitchen. All I had to do was to keep my wits about me & see the food didn't give out! – Happy Memories – one party at the Vicarage & Alan insisted on donning his old jeans which needed urgently to be mended in a most vital spot – I had insisted on washing them before mending but he took them off the line & went off to the Vicarage with 2 shining safety pins – you know where & apparently one safety pin sprang open during the evening and pierced his – you know what – so he fled to Michael Doogan's room who lent him a new pair – Michael had to lend another pair to Pippa Manby who slipped on the snow/ice & split her right u behind!! Ann Johnson & Mike gave a New Year's Eve party at Jane's & everything was sumptuously laid on but it failed to thrill our young. – Alan's girlfriend – Jane W. – came to one orgy here & never spoke one single word & as she is not pretty one can't enthuse but he seemed smitten. Even Fiona remarked placidly "I can't think how anyone can be in a room full of people & not say something". Anyway she can walk as they walked home after the cinema at Ambleside & went to Latterbarrow his last evening – Poochie came back matted with bracken so they hadn't kept to the hard high road – She was sporting enough to drive him to Ambleside at 8 A.M – I offered to pay Fiona & Val's fares back by bus rather than this hitching but that would do away with the thrills & anyway I got Glaister to drive them as far as Ambleside – He had to come & re-do 2 of the steps as the post had cracked the cement & he has raised that wall at the end of the wall – only to the extent of stones available from that bit of wall – it looks v. nice. ... Actually she is a very nice girl & Joy was so happy to be here once more. Tansy is back as Jane has indulged in 3 kittens & the smallest was desperately ill with enteritis & Jane found Tansy too much in the way – you can imagine the mutual pleasure – I haven't seen Mrs Woodall – he was nosing round by his dustbins & we almost met – by mistake – his look of black hatred was quite revealing – I became stone blind – Pam goes for walks with Daddie – The new Floribunda roses have come & I've put them in yesterday so the front bed will now be full up – very first teeny tiny snowdrops – always a heart throb – Mr Doogan Died on Friday & I am going to his funeral this afternoon with Mr Callendar – for Michael's sake really – Robert starts off on his Oxford Adventure on 14th – I hope someone will be helping Angela.
Take care of yourselves – Lots of love from us both, Mummie

Another poem was inspired by a visit to see Jill Walker whom I describe as meeting at the Catholic Worker's College. I paid her a later visit and that may have inspired the following.

Catholic Workers College. Reflections 15/1/65

And if I had woven a web of fire
For the blue and the gold of autumn days
For the blood that mingles with the mire,
For the passionate depths of lost mystery plays
Or if I had sought through the forest shade,
Catching the stars of the weeded sun
Running or staring at the monstrous glades
Pulling the moss where the wild deer run
I had found a house of dream-grey stone
Where the birds sang down in their streams

And the music of water and of distant foam
And of lights and dreams
But I cannot move in the magic wood
It's depths turn to slabs
And the trees turn to tombs
Where the factories jolt up and stagger
Heaving on their oceans of sand.
And all that was fresh that was young
That was pure, sinks in the sound
Of the lute
And all that I hear in the cold of this night
Is the distant flute
Let it pour, let it come.
Let the song roar & run
Let the winds on moor blow free

But the empty house, with wainscot & mouse
No longer contains me.
For I move in a world of a different dream
Hard and noisy, good & clean
Where the mind leaps around
From mound to mound
Digging and delving and sorting.

I am split in two
So what shall I do?
You see I laugh at myself,
So do you!

There are obvious allusions again to Elliot (Wainscot and Mouse). The end is interesting – the final recognition of a split, a division, between the older poetic, unified self, and the new filing-system, researching, self.

My mother wrote to me from Cherideo Jan 22nd 1965 Iris to Alan

I've completely lost track of who I wrote to last, as you're the only person who writes at all regularly to me I really must keep some sort of account. I daresay your weeks slip past as soundlessly as mine do, though you seem to have a lot on your plate with tutorials as well, are you paid for these? You will soon be a world expert on the sociology of the Stuarts, one day when you have time could you send me a short resumé of some of the punishments meted out to witches – no hurry but I want to be able to show that the East was not especially sadistic or unjust in this line, an accusation always levelled at the Moghuls. One of my travellers met a male witch near Mocha who described how he had made a "bluyd" pact with the devil to supply him with sacrifices. However when his son and daughters died he got fed up and stopped the sacrifices so the devil visited him in the shape of a young fawn "his heate being soe extreame that it putt out his eyes" (1608). I don't know if the devil as a red hot fawn has cropped up before, I expect it has. Have you come to any conclusion about witchcraft, whether it was the remains of a pagan cult, psychological disturbance, clerical plot, or what? I wondered if the final shape of the thesis was at all clear in your head, with that vast amount of material I can't imagine how you will ever get it into any sort of shape, even with the few notes and cards I have in my little boxes I quail at the thought of "working it up" – I think I shall probably go on making the excuse that my research isn't finished year after year... How is the New FELLOW OF ALL SOULS?!

I wrote the following day, Sunday 23rd Jan 1965 from Worcester College

Dear Mummy and Daddy,

After the two letters last week an expected gap this one. I wonder what the verdict is as regards an early retirement (and also the cottage for the V.S.O. teacher)? I expect I'll hear tomorrow.

The national news has been full of the impending death of 'Winshton' all week, and half an hour ago it was announced that he was dead. People heave (secretly of course) a sigh of relief. I wonder if there'll be scenes of mass hysteria similar to those on Nehru's death and burial? Alec, our college chaplain, has a house overlooking the Bladon churchyard where W. will be buried and newspapers, B.B.C. etc have been badgering him for film rights. Poor little man, he's torn between the desire for decency and decorum, and the desire to make as much as possible for Bladon Church Restoration fund! The other calamity (?) was the defeat of Gordon-Walker which everyone says is "a slap in the face for the Labour party" etc. In fact I think (completely unqualified as I am) that it's merely personal dislike of the sombre G-W. In Oxford things buzz in their little way as the Franks and Roads (road through Christ Church meadow) commissions swing into action again.

Moving onto an even lower level, i.e. the insect-like life of A. Macfarlane, things are also fairly busy. The abortive attempt to find a soulmate in Jill has come to a somewhat uneasy stop (perhaps because she is already attached - perhaps because of the disunity arising out of an evening spent at a Christian Unity meeting in which I behaved somewhat irreverently and flippantly!). The search goes on. In the work line things also are busy - though my thesis tends to be neglected in the rush. My first tutorial was fun - at least for me - and having two people (one older than myself) treating one as God Incarnate was a definitely pleasant experience. The reverence won't last I'm sure when they discover my feet of clay - namely my loathing and naivity concerning all political/constitutional/event history. Still it's nice to be paid about £3 for doing an hour's enjoyable work! My W.E.A. is also slightly less tricky. Having started on Food I now launch out on epidemics and plague, with a multitude of gruesome illustrations from Defoe's "Journal of the Plague Year" & contemporary poets. Learning about the primitive ways in which plague was combatted and the way in which religious taboos and systems hampered attempts at reform may be useful if I ever do get out East. I have bought several books, including a reprint of a delightful "Boke of Chyldren" which is written by a doctor of the C16 and gives all sorts of fascinating cures for childish ailments. I'm testing - or going to - test them on Rosemary's brat!

On Tuesday I am, once again, going to talk about "cunning Men" - this time to a seminar held by Christopher Hill. C.H., incidentally, has finally been elected Master of Balliol, a great distinction, esp. for an ex-communist.

To natter on about my doings... Last night I went to a "Presbyterian Social", ostensibly to play my guitar (which I did a little) and, in fact, mostly to highland dance with a nice Dutch girl and to play party games - a refreshing change from the normal undergraduate parties. I will definitely take my guitar with me when I go round the world.

How are Brenda etc? Tell them to come & see me when they come home & give me a warning of the dangers & disappointments of the East.

Birds in the bare trees and quickly-melting snow. It will be spring soon.

Fondest love, Alan

I wrote to Keith on 27th January from Worcester.

Dear Mr Thomas,

Thank you very much for your letter. 2 p.m. on Saturday 13th Feb. will be fine for me.

I enclose a hasty piece on 'White witchcraft' for C. Hill's seminar. It doesn't pretend to analyse the major problems – the statistical changes (in Essex), attitude of the Church courts etc – but you might find something you've missed in it and we could perhaps discuss it, if there's any disagreement, when we meet.

I'm going to Beattie's lectures on social change in small-scale societies,[1] *and will let you know if this helps re. the major problem you mentioned; why systems of belief change over time.*

Yrs, Alan Macfarlane

Here is the first page of my talk for Christopher Hill's seminar.

[1] John Beattie was an Africanist and lecturer in Social Anthropology at Oxford. Keith Thomas had encouraged me to go to anthropology lectures.

THE CUNNING-MAN OR WITCH-DOCTOR IN TUDOR & STUART ENGLAND.

(Talk given to C.Hill's seminar. 25/1/65)

Introduction.

Robert Burton in his Anatomy of Melancholy [1] complains that "Sorcerers are too common,Cunning men, Wisards, & white-witches as they call them, in every village." If he is right they were an extremely widespread phenomenon and a study of their activities and the attitudes of various groups, particularly the clergy,lawyers & doctors, towards them will give us a revealing glimpse of village life during our period.
I would like to divide this study into three parts. Firstly an attempt to give some definitions of witchcraft & magic & to sketch in the relevant background in Europe & England. Secondly an analysis of the actual individuals who practised white witchcraft & their activities and finally a few words on their relationship to other professional groups.

Definitions & the European background.

"Of Witches there be two sorts; the bad Witch, and the good Witch: for so they are commonly called." wrote Perkins in his Damned Art of Witchcraft [2].The main way of distinguishing between the two were by means & ends. The'good' witch, or cunning man, healed people, found lost goods and generally helped people; whereas the evil witch did the reverse. A slightly more blurred distinction was that between the means they used to their end. Essentially 'white' witchcraft was the practice of a magical activity, it was an art which could be learnt, which was external & visible. It involved the use of medicines & spells, of circles, holy water or mirrors. On the other hand one was a witch,it was hereditary & inward. The Pact with the Devil, represented the sale of one's soul. One injured people purely by one's malice & evil wishes. Evil will was enough. Many contemporaries blurred the distinction as did the law, ~~but Hobbes~~ but it is important to keep it in mind. Perhaps it is best put by Professor Evans-Pritchard when writing about African witchcraft where he says "a witch performs no rite, utters no spell, and possesses no medicine. An act of witchcraft is a psychic act...~~The sorcerer, on the other hand, may make magic to kill his neighbours."~~[3] They (i.e.Azande) believe also that sorcerers may do them ill by performing magic rites with bad medicines." [3] These definitions are the hinge on which most of the controversies about the history of witchcraft; whether it was a'pagan survival', a figment of the fevered imagination of sadistic church-men of the fifteenth and sixteenth centuries or whatever.We can return to them in discussion if necessary.

1. Burton,Anat.Mel.ii.111.1.289. cited in A New English Dictionary... ~~ed.~~ Oxford 1928 under "White witch".
2. William Perkins, A Discourse of the Damned Art of Witchcraft...Cambridge,1608. p.173. (my notes. 659.a.)
3. E.Evans-Pritchard,Witchcraft,Oracles, and Magic among the Azande. (Oxford,1937).p.21.

I wrote again from Worcester College on Sunday 31st January 1965

Dear Mummy and Daddy,

Please excuse a letter written on typing paper, but I've got to send the enclosed and have no proper air-mail paper. I hope this reaches you before you set off on the Delhi trip, Mummy. I will keep writing and Daddy - who is presumably forced to stay on the garden? - can read them but it will be the last you hear from me for about a month. I'll try to make it a fullish letter therefore. (thanks for yours, which arrived yesterday).

About the enclosed letter first. Do write to the suggested names & to Ballhatchet. Don't get inferiority feelings; these people, no doubt, will be as anxious to meet people interested in the subject as you are. Ballhatchet is the Reader in Indian History at Oxford. The reference to 'Congratulations' refers to the write-up I gave you "author of.... etc"

Incidentally I went to Blackwell's and asked them to check about the book you sent back - they were, as usual, very vague, but said they'd let me or you know when they'd sorted things out.

This week has been a little disrupted by the arrival of Rosemary's baby, two weeks early. I wandered in to borrow something on Monday morning and found R in labour. Roy was out and the doctor couldn't come until 3.30 so I had visions of delivering the baby myself! The issue was complicated by the fact that it might only have been a bad stomach ache caused by eating 2 tins of cold baked-beans the day before! Finally she was ambulanced to hospital, and the baby, a girl (Rachel Elspeth) came half an hour afterwards. It's back here today, replete with hair etc & is really very sweet. Much jubilation. Birth & death seem to have been the dominating features. Angela is expecting this week-end, I believe, and of course we've all been mourning, as the B.B.C. etc put it, for "our greatest-ever hero", "patriot leader" etc. I was invited to watch the private Bladon church from the chaplain's garden but didn't go. (I've just heard there are long queues all through Bladon at the moment).

Talking of Robert & Winston, he's got a long front-page thing in the Observer on Randolph - as Granny will tell you. I haven't seen anything of him yet, but hear from another friend at All Souls that he's "fitting in".

I went to a poetry-reading session with Constantine Trypanis on Friday and found that my poems were "promising" and that one of the group even liked them and took away a copy. I'm almost tempted to launch-out and write an epic, à la Wasteland, based on Arthurian or other medieval legend. This quiet, in time, evening was somewhat of a contrast to the previous one when I took Linda to Cleopatra. Most lavish and rather enjoyable, mostly for its virtuosity & pageant. No real sex, sadism, tension etc. A real 'family' evening! This week the University dramatic society is doing Lear - I very much want to go.

I've now staggered through three tutorials, two with two people and one with one. Actually, I rather enjoyed them and was astonished to find that they actually wore gowns and hung (perhaps!) on my every word. If one did a lot of it & the government didn't take half of it (everything over £100 over one's grant is taxed by a half) it would be very lucrative - about 32/6 per person per hour is the rate. Also it's good for my general history; one certainly learns as much from one's pupils as they learn from one - (ugh! all those "one's"!)

I've just returned from another Linton Lodge meal with Ralph Robinson and am feeling very well fed. All my friends gang round to keep me in sustenance - another took me out to supper on Tuesday and David had me to supper last night. In the intervening times I alternate between fish & chips and home-made curries based on the Vesta, do-it-yourself, frozen-dried packet curries. Linda has a passion for Madras chicken curry, but the other evening I took her to have one which was so hot she couldn't eat it, nor could I. I think they'd spilt the curry powder.

I was interested in your mentions of witch folk-lore. In England the devil was more often cold, at least in his relations with the witch. He felt icy when embraced etc. I will gather together some stuff on cruelty to witches; I agree that it is very doubtful whether the West can sit back on its supposed superiority and tolerance. England <u>*was*</u> *milder than elsewhere (physically). Always one has to take into account mental cruelty and sadism, not just physical.*

I'm glad Jenkins replaces Remnant. Does this increase your chance of retirement? I expect that issue has been settled - probably to the negative - by now.

I hope you have a very profitable & enjoyable trip & that Daddy doesn't get ill etc. in the interval. I'm afraid this letter has been the usual self-centred drivel. But it carries all my love to you both,

Alan

1965 - February

My mother wrote from Cherideo on February 1st

My dear Alan,

Always a letter to thank you for – Anne has stopped writing altogether & F. back to occasional scrawls, so we appreciate the effort you make especially… My only distraction was to stagger through & listen to Churchill's funeral! How much more beautiful, dignified & organised it was than Nehru's, and how much less it moved me. Perhaps because though I admired Churchill I never really liked him, he so signally lacked the qualities I do admire – humility, tolerance and kindliness – to be a great war leader one can't afford to have them I suppose? I agree about Gordon Walker. I think Labour's doing fine, giving the country the shake-up it really needed instead of woolly clichés. … We're most impressed by your tutoring & addressing Christopher Hill, what are you doing about the tutoring money I would love to see you with your disciples grouped admiringly around. Sorry about Jill, perhaps you can continue to meet on a less intense level? I wonder if I will get to Delhi, only ten days away.

My mother wrote from Cherideo on February 8th

A slightly more cheerful scene here – I am up and headacheless, though still not feeling quite right, start to droop rather easily and sniff a lot. .... I'm sure we shall now pull up rapidly. I shall have to as I set off for Delhi the day after to-morrow, the prospect slightly appals me at the moment, rather reminds me of the way I felt when I did my last bit of research at the Bodleian, perhaps it is all a large neurosis, I did read somewhat that sinus headaches were a neurotic symptom – but what have I got to be neurotic about now?... My plans for Delhi are fluid to say the least, I'm hoping to find a good library and read all day and in the evenings do some sightseeing but whether this will work out I don't know – also hope to make some "contacts" who can perhaps lend me some books to bring back. Have decided to make my book three sections, 25,000 words each side and a lump of 40,000 in the middle, my problem is going to be how to keep it down to that amount, even that is a bit long with illustrations. ... I thought Richard's article in the Spectator on Public Schools rather good and fair, but it riled Brenda who couldn't believe that masters solemnly sat round in their common rooms fretting about the table manners of the hoi polloi they might have to open their doors to or whether "they" would know how to use the toilets! … I'm reading "In pursuit of the Millenium" at present and finding it fascinating but wonder how I dare to think of publishing anything when faced with such scholarship – it's only the thought of Robert that cheers me.

I attended my termly supervision with Keith Thomas on Saturday 13th February. The topics I wanted to discuss with Keith are indicated in my preparatory notes. (I think that the reference to tutoring for David Gallifant was asking advice about doing some supervisions for Hertford College, which I shall come to.)

K.V.T. 13.2.65.

– Cunning man paper.

– Cunning man refs.

To give.

Ian Maclaren.

Refs. misc. in Archdeaconry. (explain system)

1582 Pamphlet.

– ref. to Spectrum of Social Time. Bourvitch(?) (Can societies change time?)

- Gluckman. 'Gossip & Scandal' - Current Anth. June, 1963. (PG. IX. C. 62)

To ask.

Book. K.V.T – outline?

To discuss.

Beattie, Ardener etc.

– discussion with (Field – 'Search for…

– talks on witchcraft . . .

– David Gallifant – Antony.

✱– Nicholas Culpepper.

✱– Winstanley. // Scolding/quarrelling + abuse in words.

There is a reference to discussing 'Beattie, Ardener etc' and I also have notes on talks by Burridge, Beattie and others on a series of University Extensions lectures. These were important in deepening my understanding of the anthropological approach to witchcraft. It also shows that there was a lively interest in the subject at just this time.

ANTHROPOLOGICAL STUDIES IN WITCHCRAFT AND RELIGION

A course of eight lectures on Wednesdays at 8.15 p.m.

20 January	**Introductory** Dr. R. G. Lienhardt, *Senior Lecturer in African Sociology*
27 January	**Witchcraft and Zombies in a Changing African Society** Mr. E. W. Ardener, *University Lecturer in Social Anthropology*
3 February	**Confession and Belief in Witchcraft** Mr. D. M. McLeod, *Institute of Social Anthropology*
10 February	**Myth** Dr. K. O. L. Burridge, *Lecturer in Ethnology, Pitt Rivers Museum*
17 February	**The Eternal Brahmin in Indian Society** Dr. D. F. Pocock, *University Lecturer in Indian Sociology*
24 February	**Sectarianism** Mr. B. R. Wilson, *Reader in Sociology*
3 March	**Divination** Dr. J. H. M. Beattie, *Senior Lecturer in Social Anthropology*
10 March	**Shamanism: The Techniques and Function in Spirit Contact** Dr. A. J. Butt, *Lecturer in Ethnology, Pitt Rivers Museum*

COURSE TICKETS (price 12*s.*) **should preferably be obtained in advance** from the Secretary to the Delegacy for Extra-mural Studies, Rewley House, Wellington Square, Oxford. Tel. 57203

Tickets for SINGLE LECTURES are obtainable at the door, price 2*s.*

I wrote again on Worcester paper on Monday 15th February

Dear Mummy and Daddy,

Thank you for (a more cheerful) letter with news of recovering from illness. I hope you're both well and Mummy is reading this in Delhi. I also hope Mummy got my letter with the few "contacts" in it before she left. I look forward to hearing all about the trip in detail. I'm sorry to hear Rosemary is proving so worrying; I do hope you get something settled. I avoid these problems by remaining selfishly uninvolved - except on a superficial level. My main problem of that kind is Linda who I seem to make unhappy - because she's more involved than I am I suppose and is hurt when I try to withdraw. She's such a sweet little thing, but it really would be hopeless for us to think in terms of marriage etc - for numerous reasons, most of which will be obvious to you. Still, enough about those personal problems for now.

Anne didn't come down finally, partly because Julie had arranged to come that week-end, partly because she had a party on. I don't think she's either particularly miserable or happy - just a little restless & lonely. She's a far more sensitive and intelligent person than the rest of the flat girls and also than the male visitors. When I'm in Essex I'll be able to see more of her. She goes for her driving test on the 23rd.

I had a letter from David Porter the other day who sounded cheerful & guitar-playing, sports-car-messing-about with and busy with his law. He's doing his 'articles' at the moment. I can't remember if I told you that Charles Vignoles is engaged.

I had my termly session with my supervisor the other day (Saturday to be precise). This as usual, went well and I'm all set for further research. I'm half glad, half apprehensive that he's so fascinated in the subject that he's writing a book on it - with chapters on Astrology, Sorcery ('white' witchcraft, healing etc) and 'black' witchcraft. He's not going to touch on Essex, nor will he have any statistics and I'm sure will give me good advance publicity; but it's likely to be so good that it'll "take the wind out of my sails" a little at least. Still I mustn't become a jealous academic, more interested in my reputation than the pursuit of Truth!

You're (Mummy's) rough outline of the book seems sensible; what are the 3 sections going to be on - the 3 battles? Actually, I think you did explain in an earlier letter, but being hazy at this time of Monday morning, I've forgotten. I wouldn't worry too much about the scholarly trappings of N. Cohn in 'Pursuit of the Millenium' - they're less impressive when one knows the subject and can see how subjective and, often, mistaken he is. Still it is a fascinating book.

Yesterday was a beautiful day - as befitted St Valentine. I meant to go for a long walk but instead went to a Quaker Meeting and afterward a discussion at the same place on 'Science and Religion'. At the latter I met an interesting girl called Zoë Allen - her parents live in Birkenhead and are moving to Ullswater (Glenridding) next year. She's in her final year at St Hilda's reading P.P.E. (Philosophy, Politics & Economics) and veering towards sociology, social work etc. Very C.N.D. ish, committed, poetry-liking, art-studentish (she looks vaguely like Fiona) she's rather a poppet. (Her sister is a doctor in Madras married to a solicitor there). No doubt our friendship will founder in the same way as Jill & mine...

In the evening I went to coffee/beer/cake with Professor Habakkuk. (Prof. of Economic History) along with 3 other graduates. It was just a social meeting with him and his very sweet wife. Lady Clay, who he knows, proved a useful 'link'!

A very dull letter about my doings; but I can never summon any great thoughts on a Monday morning. I must get down to my W.E.A - all about 'Law & Order' this week.

Much love to you both,

Alan

My mother wrote from Delhi on Feb 18th

I'm afraid my intentions to write on the train came to nothing, I did complete two grubby wobbly letters and then gave up. I've been in Delhi five days now and still feel slightly dazed and wake up each morning wondering where on earth I am and why. ... The main thing is that I'm settled in at the National Archives where I tootle off every morning in a funny little car cum scooter and stay till about six p.m. when my head is like old blotting paper and quite unable to absorb more.

My father wrote from Cherideo on 25th February.

My dear Alan,

You will probably have heard from Mummy telling of her exciting journey and the fact that she has found some books that will help the work on the Moguls considerable. I must say I take my hat off to her the way she has stuck it out with frustration at every turn. She is a remarkable little woman. She left with a full three days train journey in front of her and she hadn't really recovered from her cold etc. John and Brenda are back and Mummy comes back early next week, thank goodness. I really go round the bend when she's not here. Anyway had drinks with the Finneys last night and they were full of their adventure, and said how well Mummy was looking, sleeping and eating. I must have a dig at her, it seems that being away from me does her good! My life is very hum drum at the moment, sort of "in between seasons" with nothing much doing in the garden or factory. I am actually going down the valley quite a way, to umpire some polo on Saturday. In a moment of weakness, I foolishly accepted to so and shall no doubt pay for it by not being able to sit down for weeks. I haven't ridden a horse for at least four years. We have a host of big noises descending on us during the next few weeks. Our new

Chairman Sir Owain Jenkins amongst them. We expect sweeping changes from him and I shall probably find myself being swept into retirement with his new broom, I hope so, we shall have to wait and see. Have had long letters from Fiona & Annie who both seem well and cheerful (letter from you also of course). Annie astounded me by saying that her bank balance was now "only £86.6" as she puts it. We all know where to go if we are on the rocks. Excuse the scribble Alan, my usual enterprising effort. Any ways takes all my love and hope all goes well. Daddy

I wrote several poems at this period. One I still remember writing, was written on toilet paper in the Bodleian library while I was suffering from a very bad cold. I read the poem, to some approval, at the poetry club I was then attending.

A cold. 27/2/65.

The influenza or the common cold
~~Lays low~~
~~Hobbes as well~~ in human mold
hows healthy.

The reason is, I'm sure you'll see,
It takes
~~All Mr Takes~~ us fever at reflex

And then the shimmering lights
The hotness stretching up into the brain,
The trickling, reaching tendons
of burnt flesh round the nose,
smeared with ~~moisture~~ & rubbed
sore by damp rags
/ ~~handkerchief~~.
The drug-handkerchief complex
The descent into magical pills
Rituals with bottles or jars
The loss of interest in ~~all~~
ideals
In beauty, sex, ~~thought~~ all
Except when the damn thing
will stop.
God puffs out in a sneeze
Woman evaporates in a whoop,
Purposive intellect moans to a
standstill
And friends became ~~enemies~~
Because they fail ~~to~~ ask us
how we are

[illegible] which before shook our
fancy into shaking Shakespeare
into shaking the darling
buds of Day;
Now beat, break through and
cut raw rust of our
reddened face.
Sleep which before slept,
slid and sealed the
casements of our souls,
now bubbles, claustrophobia,
crumpled-sheet distracts
upon us.

We are turned from men,
Nature leaves us a giddy
world
Into mouls, mooning our
self-pitying way back
into our mother's laps

Perhaps the influenza were
right?

[illegible]

My dear Alan,
My last morning here, I leave this afternoon for Calcutta, feel sad in a way, have got attached to this grubby little room and the sparrows who hop amongst the saucepans while we cook.... I met Dr Grover, whose name was given by Major Harrison whose name your professor gave me. I had got cold feet about getting in touch with him, couldn't find him in the telephone book and kept putting off trying to reach him but of course when we did meet he was charming and told me how much he could have done for me and I kicked myself. he is quite young and looks more like a rugger forward than a scholar and couldn't have been kinder, took me out to coffee and cakes, wrote the names of books all over the menu and then took me round to his pet bookseller who now can't do too much for me. He is going to write to me about more sources, and also knows of an early portrait of Roe ... His particular field is revenue and I think like most specialists he is surprised that anyone can imagine there to be any other, and looked a bit doubtful when I tried to explain the sort of book I was writing. I can't judge at the moment how much work I've accomplished here. ... I wonder if you could get the wheels moving about getting a gramophone for Fiona, I think that is what she would like don't you, it'll have to be H.P. I think so if you could make the arrangements we will pay you back. I'll leave it to you to decide on what make, rather better than the old one but not in the luxury class and reasonable light. I thought of the £15-£20 price range, but a bit more wouldn't matter. Rather better than your Gita, I still feel guilty about that. Can't get out of Fiona what she has done with the camera and film we left with her?

I wrote on Sunday 28th February, on Worcester College paper

Dear Mummy and Daddy,

Thank you very much for an interesting letter about the journey to Delhi & settling in - I hope things have gone as well since you wrote and your sight-seeing was successful. Are you finding much useful material in the Archives? It must be a rather desperate feeling - knowing that what you don't get now you may never get (I have the feeling sometimes in Essex, even though I know I'll be returning soon). And how are you managing Daddy (you're not expected to answer this question, at least not for a while!)

Here term rushes to its close - with only two weeks left - and Spring prickles underfoot though everything is very still and brooding. Today I went for a long walk, but couldn't find any wild-flowers in the bare fields and the beech-leaf coppices. But the wheat (or barley) which I always notice beside the river near the Victoria Arms (remember, we walked down past it crossing several stiles) is planted and about as long as grass.

You'll have probably heard that Annie failed the driving test. I hope she doesn't take it badly - she rather wants to pass I think, and it would give her confidence. I hope she'll come down & see me soon. I'll be leaving Oxford for Essex at the end of term for six weeks - he doesn't know it yet, but I'm hoping to dump some of my junk (books etc) on Robert. A book on Gallipoli - called "Winston Churchill and the Dardanelles" has just come out - by one Trumbull Higgins and dedicated to a (real) Lord Riddell. It couldn't be Robert under a pseudonym could it? The style & presentation (e.g. having long quotes) are similar - though it's not as racy as his usual stuff. If it isn't, I hope it doesn't spoil his market.

Today is the second anniversary (week) of my meeting with Zoë . I've seen her for short spells (lunch, coffee) etc. most days this week and like her as much as ever. But I'm not sure she's terribly struck on me. I've been slightly hampered in my pursuit of her by having an <u>*awful*</u> *cold - one of the most intense I can remember. It only lasted 3 days but I got through half-a-dozen handkerchiefs & 2 and a half toilet rolls in no time. It's nearly gone again thank goodness.*

I've been thinking a little more about the future etc. It strikes me that a combination of humanitarian/social reformer (worker) etc AND academic (intellectual) might solve certain problems. The temptations of the former are to
a) over-emotional involvement in one's schemes leading to narrowness, desperation frustration, (boredom possibly) etc. Also it would be difficult not to be patronising, conceited etc. Also, as far as one's effect was concerned, a maximum of intellectual training would prevent me wasting effort through wrong goals & uninformed 'emotional philanthropy'. A person with academic training & continued academic interests could gain strength from detachment etc.
b) On the other hand it is very tempting for an academic to become pig-headed, petty-minded, intellectually conceited, "knowing" and superior about others and lose all sense of proportion. He also suffers from depression - but of a different sort to the social worker - a gloom arising from self-consciousness, inability to communicate, guilt at a 'wasted' life etc.

Thus a combination of thought & action - in the manner of a Tawney or Schweitzer is the best. But how to attain it?

Any suggestions welcome. Forgive this outburst.

Look after yourselves. Much love, Alan

My next note to Keith Thomas is on 28th February, when I sent a card from Worcester.

Dear Mr Thomas,

Thank you for your note. We didn't have a date fixed, but I'd like a talk before I got to Essex. Could you manage 11.45 a.m. (or 2 p.m) Saturday 13 March? If not, perhaps sometime on Friday of that week?
I'm afraid I may not have any written work for you as there's no point at the moment (but <u>may</u> send a scribble along in advance). Yrs Alan Macfarlane

1965 - March

My mother wrote to me from Cherideo on 7 March

Back on my verandah with the sleepy Assam air sapping me of my energy and the Taj Mahal is a rapidly fading dream, amazing how quickly it all dissolves and one forgets the things one thought one never could.... I found Daddy very well and fat, ditto dogs, and the news that we shall almost certainly be leaving here this November. The last details have got to be worked out, but as far as we can gather the company are to give us full pay for a year and then our full pension so we really couldn't ask for more. I'm not telling the girls until we have seen Sir Owain just in case a snag arises, but I don't think it will. At first I felt a terrible sadness and emptiness, thinking of never seeing India again, never making my model school, collecting my folk stories and so on, but now I am happy about it. I don't honestly think I would have ever done any of those things, there is too much to be overcome and I haven't the time and energy. … Also there is to be a complete upheaval in the company as far as we can see Nazira is to go and it's going to be run from Calcutta, very ruthlessly, efficiently and cost-consciously so there will be no room anywhere for people like us. We haven't decided what we shall do until we find out about the tax angle, we may have to fill in time till March and then come home, in which case hope to get a little cottage on the south coast and drift home in a cargo boat. Lots of problems, Granny, dogs etc. but they will all be solved and I shall be able to help you with your thesis? I agree with your ideas of your future, and a job such as you visualise might be available here, there is masses to be done in social reform and research but the trouble is to find the two things situated side by side – also in a country where so many are jobless they are not keen on outsiders doing anything if they can help it. There is a school in Mussoorie for 1100 Tibetan refugee children and the only two European teachers have been thrown out though the Indians are apparently totally disinterested in the children. ... I bet the minute we step onto English soil you will all head for India! … I hope your Zoë is still living up to her good start, you'll have to find someone very tough for the sort of life you intend, physically and mentally, I certainly couldn't visualise Linda for instance in the role of social reformer or help mate.

Must write to Granny who now seems to have turned her wrath against Goodall and his pigs, I think it's time they moved. Do hope you'll find some digs and Roy a job …

My preparatory notes for the supervision of 13 March were:

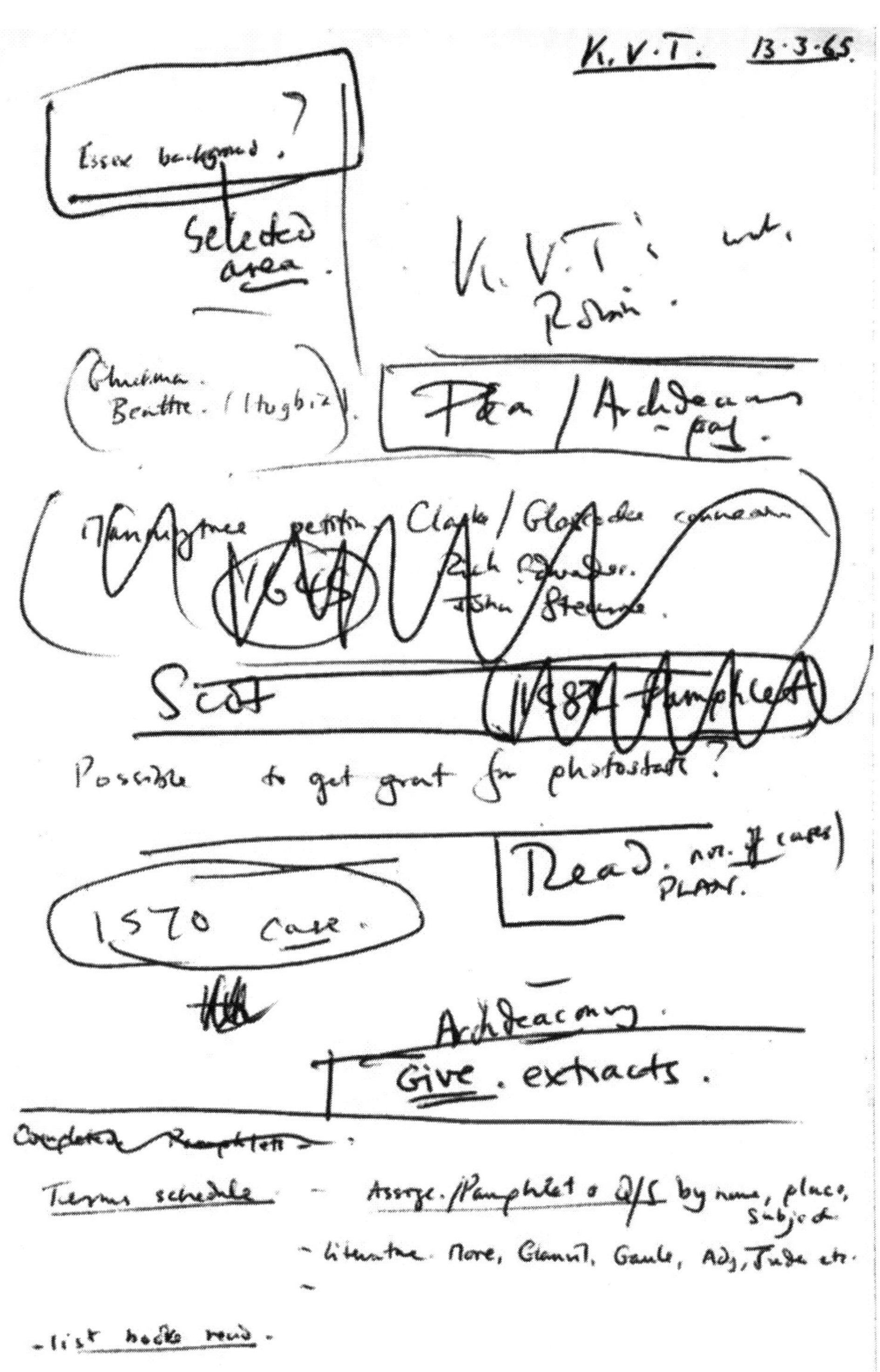

K.V.T. 13.3.65.
Essex background?
Selected area.
Scot
1584 Pamphlet
Possible to get grant for photostats?
Read.
PLAN.
1570 case.
Archdeaconry.
Give. extracts.
Terms schedule
- list books read.

As planned, I went off to Essex at the end of the term and my next letter, on Tuesday March 16th, was from the Poste Restante, Chelmsford Post Office, Chelmsford, Essex.

Dear Mummy and Daddy,

Back in Essex again as you see and quite glad of the change; my routine also changes and I gravitate between the Record Office, the Borough Library, my digs and the fish-and-chip bar. I hope to get away at week-ends & see people, e.g. Annie or the Sussex clan.

I won't get too excited about the retiring - in November - news just in case snags do turn up with Sir Owain, but it would really be <u>*wonderful*</u> *if you* <u>*did*</u> *come home then. (My thesis will probably be in a wilting state and need propping up, or more likely weeding, among other things). What are the plans for Granny? I'm glad also that the return journey from Delhi was easy enough. Don't worry about all the things left behind in India, no doubt one of us will carry on the good work ...*

I've ordered a gramaphone to be delivered in Manchester on April 1st - a nice Ferguson, fairly light & decent volume, with 1 yr guarantee £18-13-6 I think, at least if its' paid off on the H.P quite soon. Will send Fiona some records or equivalent & tell her that the present is there, in case she's in the Lakes. I thought it was best that way as she's usually at Manchester. Richard, Billy etc are all going to Field Head & they can take it up if necessary.

My digs problems have partly sorted themselves out. I'm staying on at 38, Park Town - at the top of the house - which is a good deal bigger, quieter & a nice view over the back garden. It also has its own kitchen; but it's going to cost £4 p. week. Still it saves me finding a place to dump my stuff this vac. Now I've got to find a place in Chelmsford; where I'm staying the next few days is 15/- per night, bed & breakfast (double room) & hence a little too expensive for a long stay. I've got a few ideas. Roy & Rosemary are moving on about 25th - to Rosemary's parents. Roy still hasn't got a job & has consequently been rather neurotic & depressed. Rosemary cooked a delicious good-bye meal on Sunday evening to which I invited Zoë. She (Zoë) has been a little upset because her grand-mother - who lived with the family - has just died & she had to go up to Liverpool for the funeral. I still like her enormously and hope to see her next week-end & in the Lakes. She's terribly gentle and thoughtful - but no milk-sop. She would be an ideal reformer's wife probably!

The end of term was the usual rush. My tutorials finished cheerfully enough & on the strength of them I went to dinner at Hertford college. The usual stomach-distending experience - sherry, two kinds of wine constantly plied to one, port & fruit, brandy & coffee & plenty to eat. Fun occasionally & nice to be able to be blasé about, but meanwhile "back in the refugee camp..."! My W.E.A. sessions have practically ended. At the last - on "Leisure" I played them some ballads on my guitar to which they cooingly listened. One of them very kindly gave me supper before the session. They really are very nice. Just two more - probably on witchcraft - next term. Now I can really get down to my thesis. I've got the most gruelling part ahead - going through the almost illegible archdeaconry records. How do you find the writing & language?

Sunday was a very pleasant day in fact as I also went for an 18-mile walk with the (sweet) Chaplain, paying my respects to W.S. Churchill at Bladon (where the chaplain lives) on the way. Just a few daffodils from Bladon school to commemorate all that energy ....

Must end now - or I will be locked in the Borough Library. Hope you can read this.

Much love to you both,

Alan

Iris to Alan 16th March Cherideo – to Alan, c/o 10 Weight Road, Chelmsford, Essex

Thank you for your letter, sad to think you won't be sitting in your cosy little basement room any more, you'll probably have to go hat in hand back to Miss Faraday. I'm hoping Robert will decide to move to Oxford, it'll be just the job for all my researching. Thank you for arranging the gramophone, but please let us know if you want another loan, now that Christmas, the car and Fiona's fees are dealt with we are surfacing again and the fact that the bank knows our provident fund will be coming at the end of the year will make them more understanding (actually they are very understanding as it is) We have now decided to come straight home in a cargo boat, calling in at south Indian ports, so will get there in January. I had planned a trip to Ankor Wat but instead we're spending the money on bringing Anne out to do the homeward voyage with us, and also sending Dinah home. ... Fiona will probably moan, but we will give her the equivalent amount next year when she finishes, and something to you too for that world trip. The main problem this year is the A.P's, I have either Exmouth or Dale Cottage in mind but they don't seem keen on either. … Apart from that I have been trying to sort out my notes, and am putting together another article for History To-day, haven't really much hope that they will want anything more about the Moghuls yet but it's a good way of getting myself organised for the first section of the book which I'm going to start very soon. It's amazing how much one knows and wants to include when one gets started, my problem is going to be how to keep the words within a reasonable limit. It's difficult to know exactly how much use my trip to Delhi was, but as its obvious I shan't get there again I wouldn't have missed it for anything. I think I'll write a better book for having soaked up the atmosphere of the Moghul buildings and gardens, I hope so anyway. The problem of your future seems to be exercising you, I can think of so much you could do here that would satisfy your every urge, i.e. in the Garo hills where fish farming, school work and anthropology would all be welcome, as Dr Verrier Elwin said everything about the Garos is terribly out of date. I think I'll put out feelers to see what openings there are, the only trouble would be the loneliness of having nobody of your own background to talk to but perhaps you could take on for a period of so many years. ... It is the big Hindu spring festival this week, my last Indian spring.

Hope leaving Oxford won't mean a break with Zoe – how is the motor bike these days? Most impressed with your dinners with the Master of Balliol.

Around this time I obviously gave Keith another piece of work, to which he refers in a letter of 20th March, probably just after the supervision referred to in my next letter. *re*. Chapter on Witchcraft & Puritanism']

Dear Alan,

You make some very interesting suggestions here, though as you say it is going to take a lot of research to resolve them. Working through Biblical commentaries on the Witch of Endor and similar passages in the Old Testament might possibly throw some light on the variation of opinion among differently inclined divines. But even that would be a long job. Then again is there any connection between the notion of a pact with the Devil and the Puritan Covenant Theology (see Perry Miller, etc)? But there are lots of things one can speculate about (I've put a few squiggles which we can discuss next time if you like.

Meanwhile two factual points.

a) Have you got the Fairfaxes sorted out from each other?
b) P.ii n.3. Burning was the penalty for petty treason by a woman (i.e. murder of her husband or employer) as well as high treason.

I hope to hear all about Essex next time – it should prove very rewarding when the Record Office lets you get down to it. I was disconcerted to be told by a man yesterday of an encounter with a (white?) witch in 1951. She was a cook in a house where was staying and the locals came with their problems to the back door – in Essex, of course. Yrs. Keith Thomas
P.S. Many thanks for the placebo cutting.

A page from the rough notes for the Puritanism and Witchcraft chapter is as follows (I later wrote a more polished piece as a possible appendix to the thesis, but I did not use it).

Possible links.
i) Geographical -e.g Scotland, New England, Sweden, England,.....
Within England - East Anglia.
Absence of persecution in Med'n Catholic countries - Spain, Italy etc.

ii) Temporal - After 1560 generally, & particularly 1640-60 when Puritans are in power in England.
Decline of witchcraft after 1660 in England.

iii) Attitude of specific Puritan writers, e.g. Baxter, the Mather's etc. Bunyan, Milton etc. + HOPKINS, Cromwell etc.

iv) ~~Geographical~~ Economic. If one loosely accept the Weber-type thesis & the theory of growing individualism & attacks on traditional & organic links in Puritan countries, then it seems likely that Puritanism & witchcraft were both manifestations of a stress in society.

v) Cultural & religious. The likelihood that Puritan upbringing with its stress on the Devil's power & the reality of sin, its gloom & fear & suspicion, its breaking down of the barriers between supernatural & natural, its fierce righteousness & belief in the importance of individual decision(despite predestination) all led to an atmosphere congenial for witchcraft.

vi) The attitude & conduct of Calvin(& Luther) in Zurich.(Cf 'Religion & rise!...' answer to this type of argument.

There are two implications in the above. Firstly that because witchcraft & Puritanism seem to coincide temporally & geographically one must be the cause of the other & thus, implicitly, to blame. ~~The other~~ Secondly that because believed in the reality of evil & spiritual forces & the need for seeking salvation they would thereby be persecutors. Are these valid ?

vii) James of Scotland, a Puritan, assumed to be a persecutor.

Obvious weaknesses in the links.
i) Geographical.
Why was Holland free from witchcraft persecution ? Why was Catholic Europe, especially France & Germany so badly infested with persecution? Can one draw a line between Catholic & Protestant Germany ? Why was there so little witchcraft persecution in America & Sweden except for the dramatic outbreaks at Salem & Upsala (?)? England seems to have suffered far less than, say, France. Was the persecution in East Anglia much worse than other parts of England - or is this due to the survival of records?

ii) Temporal.
It is assumed that persecution was worst in England after 1603 & especially after 1640. This does not seem to be so - see Ewen who shows that it was worst during the years 1560-1600, when it is difficult to show that puritans controlled the machinery. Again, James I, after an initial scare was fairly sceptical. The worst outbreak in the Interregnum was when local govt' had broken loose of central control & once Cromwell was in power he took steps to prevent persecution (esp. in Scotland)(cf here Robins theory that the whole thing was a delusion fostered by greedy rulers & churchmen). In Sweden the outbreak occurred over a hundred years after she had become Protestant & similarly in America it was ninety years since

I was in touch with Trevor-Roper during this period, as the following letter indicates.

From The Regius Professor of Modern History

History Faculty Library,
Merton Street,
Oxford.
Telephone 43395

22nd March, 1965.

Dear Macfarlane

Thank you for your letter. I am indeed holding my class next term, and I nearly said to you, when we met in the Bodleian quadrangle the other day, that I would be delighted if you would care to come. But I checked myself, since I thought that might put you in an embarrassing position. But since you have written, I write to say that I do hope you will come: you would certainly help it to go well. The class will be on Friday at 11 p.m. So I look forward to seeing you then and discussing other problems with you too.

Yours sincerely

Hugh Trevor-Roper

Alan Macfarlane, Esq.,
Worcester College,
Oxford.

My mother wrote to me from Cherideo on 23rd March
[Forwarded to 10, Weight Road, Chelmsford, Essex]

Thank you for your letter, and also for fixing the gramophone – but will pay this off ourselves, starting next month. Now that the bank knows we're retiring all should go swimmingly where overdrafts are concerned! So glad you're not leaving 38 Park Town though it does seem rather a lot of rent. I was thinking that Essex might be a good place for the A.P's to retire to, is there any chance of your being able to drag yourself from the Archdeacons doings to visit the local agents? We visualise a small, central house or flat with a little garden, within walking distance of shops and a bridge club if poss. Granny isn't apparently too well and has been told to rest so I don't like to think of her packing up and moving this summer so there isn't really a violent rush but you might make enquiries about the sort of thing Chelmsford has to offer and prices?

Going to Ankor Wat and Japan was going to be so expensive I really didn't feel justified in spending the money even if we had it, what with those millions still starving, I'd rather buy a couple of crofts and turn them into homes for poor little Manchester children if it comes to that. Also we are hoping to have Anne out to do the voyage back with us.... I wonder if you could get the rest of that course "Essential English for Foreign Students" from Blackwells and have it sent to me, I will send the necessary. ... Has your W. E. A. come to an end voluntarily or through lack of interest? … I've finished my article which hasn't come to life and makes me despondent about my book, but maybe it's just because I've read it through about a hundred times, seems just a mass of clichés and facts nobody wants to know. I think I'll send it to you to read first to see if I'm right. No letter from the Delhi prof. so perhaps he thought I was just a silly female after all, no answer from Ajmer Museum or the

National Library or anywhere else I've written to either. A book I want (but not if it's expensive) is called The Pearl Fishers by Hollis – the life of Franciso Xavier... I hope you've found somewhere to live & are happy.

I wrote on 24th March from c/ 10, Weight Road, Chelmsford, Essex

Dear Mummy and Daddy,

Thank you very much for your letter of the 16th which was forwarded from Oxford to the above address. I'll be at the above until 9th April at least so you can write direct if it'll arrive before then. You seem to more or less assume that you'll be coming home early - in January - which is really wonderful! Is it certain yet? Lucky Annie coming home with you. I'll be in the throws [sic] of writing by then. But there's plenty of time. I hope something turns up for Granny & Grandpa - if Robert moved to Oxford that would be ideal. What about Richard's vague offer?

Hope the writing goes well. Yes, there's always too much to go on & one is loath to waste the labour. [Elsewhere as well? I am already dreaming of a 3 volume work entitled 'Witchcraft & Magic in C16 & C17 England' - one volume of Essays on selected topics, e.g. John Dee, the magician, or 'Puritanism & Witchcraft', 1 volume on the folklore, myth, intellectual & philosophical principles of witchcraft; 1 volume on the actual individuals involved - an expansion of my Essex thesis. Still, we'll see how the first stage goes. One of the major problems is to keep one's mind narrow enough - for instance the ecclesiastical records I'm working on are full of fascinating stuff on all aspects of the moral life of the time - sex, suicide, drunkenness, heresy etc. and are an almost untapped mine. It is difficult to prevent oneself from getting sunk in the whole moral/spiritual life in C16, I wrote C17 villages. Perhaps I can do something on this - the broader background of village witchcraft - in my next thesis!] The Garo hills sound fascinating & I'm longing to read Elwyn [sic]. But I must do some anthropology before I go there - so it looks like at least another 4-5 years, except for a possibly flying visit. I'm reading with great enjoyment Beatrice Webb's "My Apprenticeship", her wit, fanatic application, religious feelings & social dedication make her fit to sit beside my other heroes - Tawney, Ghandi, Fl. Nightingale etc. Unfortunately she didn't like poetry. I find a few pages reading sets me up for the day - I feel inspired to great things. Nice to be so easily moved isn't it?! I'm also in odd moments reading the Penguin book of 'Georgian Poets', Housman, Graves, W.H. Davies etc. I find I've read quite a lot of them already, esp. as I've been having a go at Edward Thomas (who I like very much). The lines of Housman

Tell me not here, it needs not saying,
What tune the enchantress plays
In aftermaths of soft September
Or under blanching mays,
For she and I were long acquainted
And I knew all her ways.

have been going through my head. I've suddenly realised, for good, that I'm not a poet, but perhaps the ability to find illuminating relationships between objects & to fuse & blend into a creative new construction may be working in my history? Let's hope so!

I saw my supervisor last week. I can't tell what he thinks, but I think things are going quite well. I'll soon be starting the most exciting stage, analysing & writing up the material. I may have a few surprises for various historians - including Trevor-Roper, who wrote me a nice reply to an enquiry about whether I could go to his seminar next term.

While up in Oxford last week-end I also took Zoë out to supper on Saturday evening. I enjoyed it very much and I think she did, though I babbled somewhat. She's going to be in the Lakes for a few days at the end of the vac' so I hope to see her then. If I could ever be responsible & unbegrudging of my time enough to win her she'd make a wonderful wife. I've already (quite fatally no doubt!) suffused her with colours drawn from B. Webb! But have warned her of this. That would solve the problem of loneliness in the Garo hills; it would also be a strong combination to have a historian/social anthropologist to deal with India as it is and an economist, politician, sociologist to deal with it as it is becoming. The transition period & clash between cultures is going to be my subject I think (and hope) one day.

My motorbike is fairly stationary & will have to be re-licensed etc. Of course there's been the usual search through tennis boxes etc for the old insurances etc but I haven't found them & thus am having to start again.

Please forgive a nauseatingly self-centred & hearty letter!

Longing to see you, much love, Alan

Iris to Alan 31st March Cherideo
[Written to 10, Weight Road, Chelmsford, Essex]

Thank you for a very nice, and very long letter, I hope this will catch you before you leave Essex. Your plans for a massive work on Witchcraft sound fascinating, I hope I'll be able to help, somehow feel my Mughals will taper away when I get home, one's interest is definitely stimulated by one's surroundings and away from India her history will probably become as boring to me as it is to everyone else. The clash of cultures is the aspect of it that interests me most too but it's so tremendously complex that I haven't enough lifetime left to study it in. I sent off my article to History Today but haven't much hope of it, I was really wanting to put it towards Anne's fare! It was called "Two sixteenth century passages to India" and described the arrival of Babur and Vasco da Gama, rather facetiously perhaps and of course there was no room to follow up.

I know nothing about Beatrice Webb and always thought of her as a dreadfully bossy lady who overshadowed her much cleverer little husband – but I'm obviously completely wrong. There is to be a Hill University soon I'm told, for the Tribal peoples and probably situated in some salubrious and beautiful spot, so that might be an opening for you but I agree that you should probably have a diploma at least in anthropology – even if you never needed it in your actual work you can't have too many qualifications, particularly here. I wish every day I knew more in that line, I went to a school the other day which is in a Naga village, a little island of Nagas in the middle of the Assamese who have retained their language and dress and culture and yet settled down to living as plains people, I would love to study them properly and not just coo about their beauty and oddness. ...

I'm really terribly glad we're leaving at this moment, the company is going to be run by a lot of accountants in Calcutta and everyone here treated as pawns in their nasty little games – at least thats the way it would appear. ...

I feel the book I want to write now is a bitter, waspish Waughish satire on the whole shabby society – perhaps I will if I don't mellow in the Lake District air. That poem you quote of Housmans is one that is always haunting me too, especially when I feel homesick, that and "For I have promises to keep" and de la Mares "There is a wind where the rose was" seem much sadder than a lot of better poems and full of one's sense of waste and loss – though exactly what it is one has lost is hard to define.

I think you are right in saying that poetry is good for history, I'm sure it makes one aware of the wind that is blowing through the facts which is so much more important than the facts themselves. That is a terrible metaphor or rather simile, no metaphor – you can see how muddled my thinking is this morning – I wish I hadn't got this class on. It's just tiredness. ... and yet at once I sense you criticizing my own superiority and I can see it too, I <u>do</u> think myself superior to people like that and there are an awful lot of them here, the only way to cope is to be like Verrier Elwyn, just gently humorous – only it's very difficult! We both feel we shall be stepping into a saner world soon, but I suppose you meet that sort of tiny-mindedness everywhere. … Oxford must be beautiful this month, I hope you will have some walks by the river with Zoe and not feel the sadness of the lost springs of your life. Here the brainfever bird has started to call to brighten our nights. …

On earlier visits to the Essex Record Office, where I had started to work on the fairly difficult quarter sessions and other records, I had been aware that there was one large source which might prove very rich, but was also extremely difficult to use. This was the set of recently discovered archives of the Archdeaconries of Essex and Colchester, hundreds of thick books which had lain unused and perhaps unknown to scholars until they were deposited in the Essex Record Office only a little time before I arrived.

The ecclesiastical courts were the judicial part of the Church of England. They dealt with moral offences such as sexual offences, non-attendance at church and misbehaviour in the church and churchyard. They used a different procedure to those of the secular courts, consisting of depositions and without the use of juries.[1]

The difficulty consisted of various things. Firstly, there was the quantity of the records. There were two Archdeaconries, Essex and Colchester, as well as a number of other smaller jurisdictions. One of three pages of my list of the Archdeaconry of Essex will give an indication of just that one jurisdiction (ff stands for folios or pages and the ticks show which volumes I had read). It will be seen that there were various different classes of documents, 'Acts' (notes taken during a hearing – often very abbreviated and rushed in the form of a sort of short-hand, bits in latin, bits in English), 'Causes', that is cases between people, and 'Depositions', that is longer examinations transcribed in more detail. There were also 'Visitations', that is inspections of parishes, wills and other classes of ecclesiastical document.

[1] A description of the ecclesiastical courts in Essex and how they worked can be found at: http://linux02.lib.cam.ac.uk/earlscolne/reference/church.htm#overview

Archdeacon of Colchester. (2)

38. 8 Nov.1614-17 Sept. 1617. Sampford & Newport deaneries. D. Index loose. (202 ff)

39. 2 Mar. 1615/6 - 4 Nov. 1617. Colchester & Tendring deaneries. D. B.IV/155-171. Cl.XXIII/2-52. (187 ff)

40. 2 May 1616-7 Feb. 1620/1. Witham & Lexden deaneries. D. (220 ff)

41. 25 Nov. 1617-14 Dec. 1620. Colch. & Tendring deaneries. D. B. IV/172-187. Cl.XXIII/53-92. (197 ff)

42. 5 Dec. 1617- 7 Mar. 1623/4. Sampford & Newport deaneries. B.III/1-23. Cl.XXII/76-90; XXIV/2-53. (189 ff)

43. 18 Jan. 1620/1-9 Ap. 1623. Colch, Tendring, Witham, Lexden deaneries. Index loose. (187 ff)

44. 30 Ap. 1623-25 Feb. 1624/5. D. Loose index. (191 ff)

45. 18 Mar. 1624/5-10 Sept. 1627. D. Loose index. (332 ff)

46. 17 Sept. 1627-4 June 1629. D. Index at end. (184 ff)

47. 11 June 1629-8 Ap. 1631. D. (218 ff)

48. 20 Ap. 1631-20 Nov.1632. D. (246 ff)

49. 5 Dec.1632-5 June 1634. D. (230 ff)

50. 18 June 1634-18 Nov.1635. D. (216 ff)

51. 26. Nov.1635-29 Mar. 1637. D.VII/34-68. (263 ff)

52. 17 Ap. 1637-30 May 1638. D. (263 ff)

53. 14 June 1638-1 Oct. 1639. D. VIII/69-96. — unsuitable for microfilming

54. 23 Oct. 1638-26 Oct. 1641. D. (240 ff)

55. 30 Sept. 1663-14 July 1666. V.D. (256 ff)

Cause Books (D/ACC)

	Deaneries	Br.	Cl.	Nos folios
1 Mar. 1571		VI. 88.		231.
2 22 Nov. 1588 - 23 May 1593.				
3 18 June. 1593 - 17 May. 1596.				
4 20 May. 1596 - 21 Ap. 1600.				200
5 9 May 1600 - 10 Dec. 1601.		V 129.	XXV. 2-19.	183.
6 Ap. 1602 - 2 Oct. 1603.		V 129.	XXV 31-40.	
7 Jan. 1603/4 - 7 Feb. 1604/5.	Newport, Sampford		XXVII 80-5.	?
8 22 July 1604 - 1. July 1607.		V 129.	XXV 20-30.	
9 26 July 1607 - 7 Nov. 1609.				180.
10 27 Nov. 1609 - 20 Oct. 1624				" "
11 1 Dec. 1609 - 20 Oct. 1624	Witham/Sampford		XXV 67-93.	
12 8 Dec 1615 - 23 Nov. 1620.				
13 17 Jan. 1620/1 - 25 May 1627.				
14 14 June. 1627 - 11 Jan. 1631/2				
15 Jan. 1631/2 - 29 May 1634.		XII 53.		
16 1 Mar. 1636/7 - 29 July 1640.		IV. 18.	XXV 40-67.	

Depositions & Cognate documents (D/ACD)

EC date	Amount	Brown	Clark	Nos folios
1 Sept. 1587 - June 1592	1 vol.	II 151		60
2 Oct. 1612 - Dec. 1616	1 vol.	III 155-65	XXVIII 2-43	98.
3 Feb. 1625 - 18 May 1631	1 vol.	III 65-75		90
4 1626 - 1627.	[illegible]			40
5 1626 - Oct. 1639	loose papers			40
6 25 Mar 1631 - 30 Oct 1632	[illegible]			20
7 1633 - Oct. 1641	1 vol.	[illegible]		143

PTO for Visitations

The difficulty was of various kinds. Although there were some helpful transcripts of some of the volumes , there had been little analysis of how the courts worked, so I had to work out the procedure in some detail.

Secondly, I had to work out the various types of abbreviation. Some of these can be shown in a page from my mother's notebook a year later, as I taught her how to read the deposition books so that she could help transcribe some of them.

Archdeaconry Books.

Fatetur = he confessed
Prout = according as
Patet = open clear,
Dicta = the said Dr.
× Quesitus = judged ?
Testamenti = will
Monité = advised
Interessendum = to attend
Procuratorem = proctor
Suum = his
Quatenus = how far
Hoc die = that day
Quindenam = 15 days
Exhibendum = exhibit
Unde = then
Pronunciavit = pronounced
Emanet =
Sententia =
Restituit = restored
*Ecclesie = ecclesiastic
Sic = thus
Curatum = curate
Gardianis = guardians
Monitione = admonition
Perquisita = sought for
Examinavit = examined
Supra = above

The combination of latin, very rapid writing, unknown procedure rapidly summarized in standard ways, and bits of dog latin, led to the following kinds of documents – thousands and thousands of pages of this.

The example is from the Archdeaconry of Colchester.

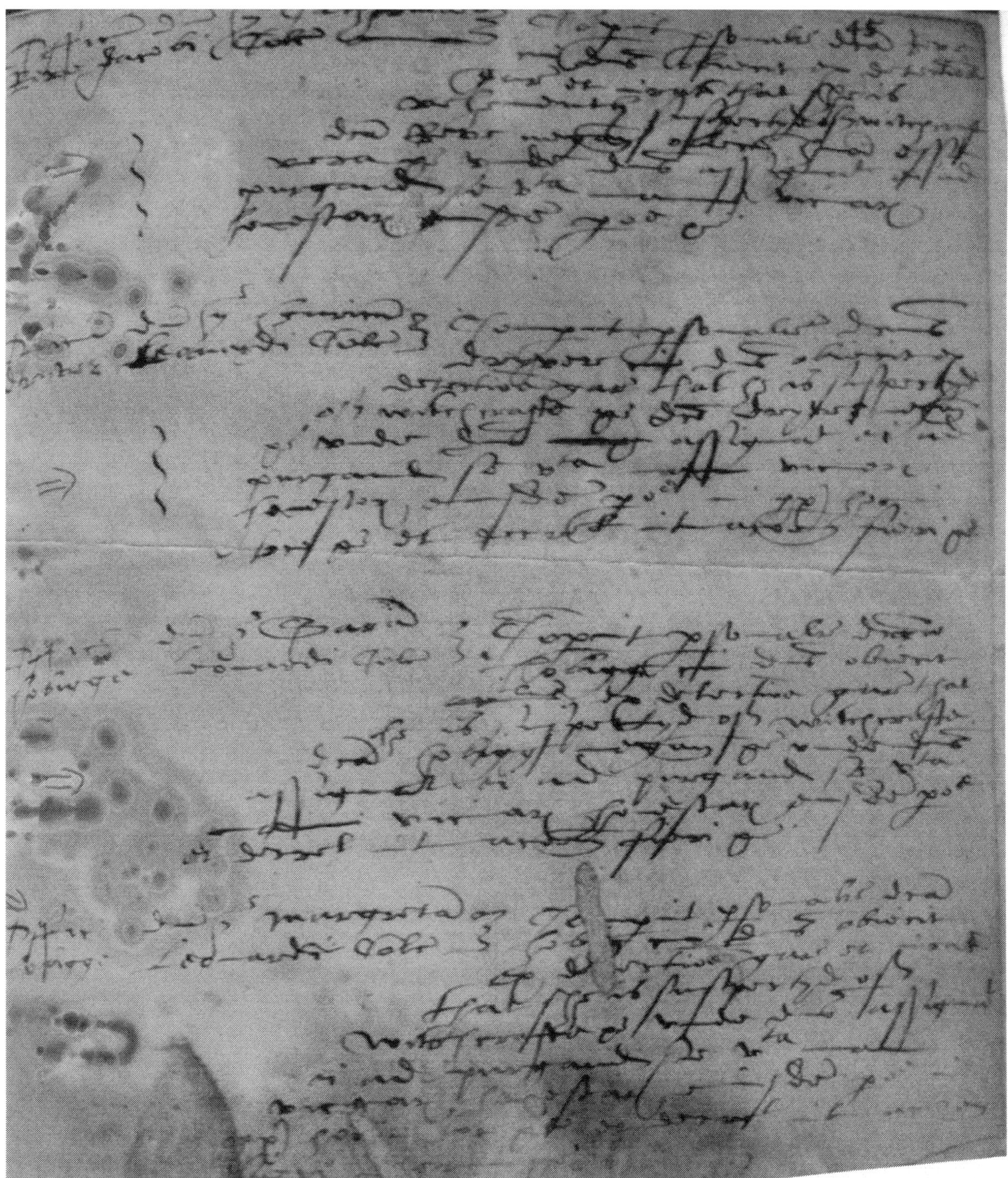

When I was first faced with pages like this, and the thought of having to search through the many volumes, for witchcraft related material, my heart sank. But I did it. The transcription of the above, in case readers need a little help, as I made it at the time, was:

D/ACA. 10 f. 45.

O.D.c. Catherina Reve Jacobi Colc / Co̅parint p̃sonalr dc̃a Reve cui dn̄s obiecit ex detectione quod et inuat that she is vehemently suspectyd of witchcraft dc̃a Reve negavit obiecta esse vera etc unde dn̄s assignat ei ad purgand se v^ta m.v.h. eisdem po^e etc.

O.D.c. Henricus Dryver Leonardi Colc / Comparuit p̃sonalr dn̄s Dryver cui dn̄s obiecit ex detectione quod that he is suspectyd of witchcrafte etc dc̄s Dryver negavit etc unde dn̄s assignat ei ad purgand se v^ta m.v.h. eisdem po^e in p̃d hoc in loco etc et decret intimacoem fieri etc.

O.D.c. Sara Hobigge Leonardi Colc / Co̅parint p̃sonalr dc̃a Hobigge cui dn̄s obiecit ex detectione quod that he (sic) is suspectyd of Witchcrafte dc̃a Hobigge negavit etc unde dn̄s assignat ei ad purgand se v^ta m.v.h. eisdem po^e et decret intimacoem fieri etc.

O.D.c. Margareta Hobigge Leonardi Colc / Comparuit p̃sonalr dc̃a Hobigge cui dn̄s obiecit ex detectione quod et inuat that she is suspectyd of Witchcrafte etc Unde dn̄s assignat ei ad purgand se v^ta m.v.h. eisdem po^e p̃d hoc in loco etc et decret intimacoem fieri in (stand) etc.

This contains the abbreviations, which would then have to be expanded and the latin translated.

An example of cases from the Archdeaconry of Essex is as follows.

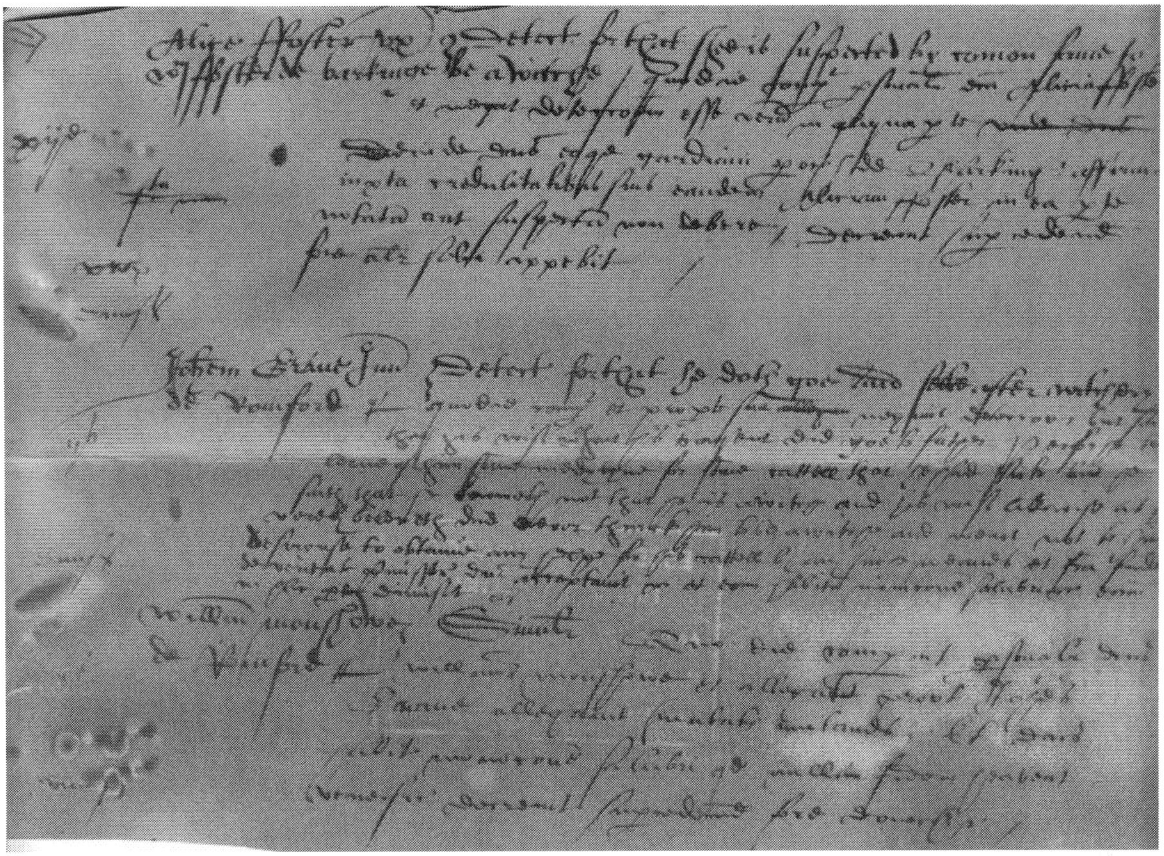

My early attempt to make sense of this is as follows:

Photo. 20. m.a. 559(A) 585(B) 879(C) 1) /ACA. 16. f. 56.

Alice Foster ux
Wm Foster de Barkinge } Detect ~~for that~~ she is suspected by comon fame to be a Witche/ quodie compt psnalr dea

xiid Alicia Foster et negat detectionem esse veram in aliqua pte ~~unde dus~~ (sic) Deinde dus eo^{e} gardiani pcch de Barking ~~affirmaverit~~ notatam ~~aut~~ suspectam non debere/ Decrevit

dimiss ⊗ sup ~~cedant~~ fore ~~abr..~~ ~~.ster~~ ...

Johem Crave Jun } Detect for that he doth goe
de Romford } and seake after witchery quodie compt

ii s. et pro pte sua negavit detectionem, ~~but~~ saith ~~that~~ his wife without his consent did goe to father Parfoche to lerne of him some medycyne for some cattell ~~that~~ he had sicke but he saith ~~that~~ ~~he knoweth not~~ that he is a witche and his wife likewise as he verely beleveth did never think him to be a witche and went not to him. ~~[illegible]~~ desirouse to obtaine any helpe for his catell by any suche meanes

dimiss Quo dus acceptavit ~~pte~~ et eum et fea ~~fide~~ de ~~veritate~~ ... in ~~hac~~ ~~pte~~ dimisit ei habita monicione salubri ~~pte~~ ...

Willm Moushowe } Simili quo die comparit psonalr (dcte)
de Romford } ~~[illegible]~~ William Moushowe et allegavit ...
et dus ~~Johes~~ Crave allegavit (mutatis mutandis) Et ...

ii s. Will. habita monicione salubri q^{e} nullam fidem ~~habeat~~

dimiss beneficio decrevit sup~~cedend~~ fore ~~donec~~ ~~pte~~.

The Act Books were the richest in terms of numbers, but occasionally there were fascinating depositions in the Deposition books, none more interesting and curious than this one – which shows the original and the three stages of my attempt to read it.

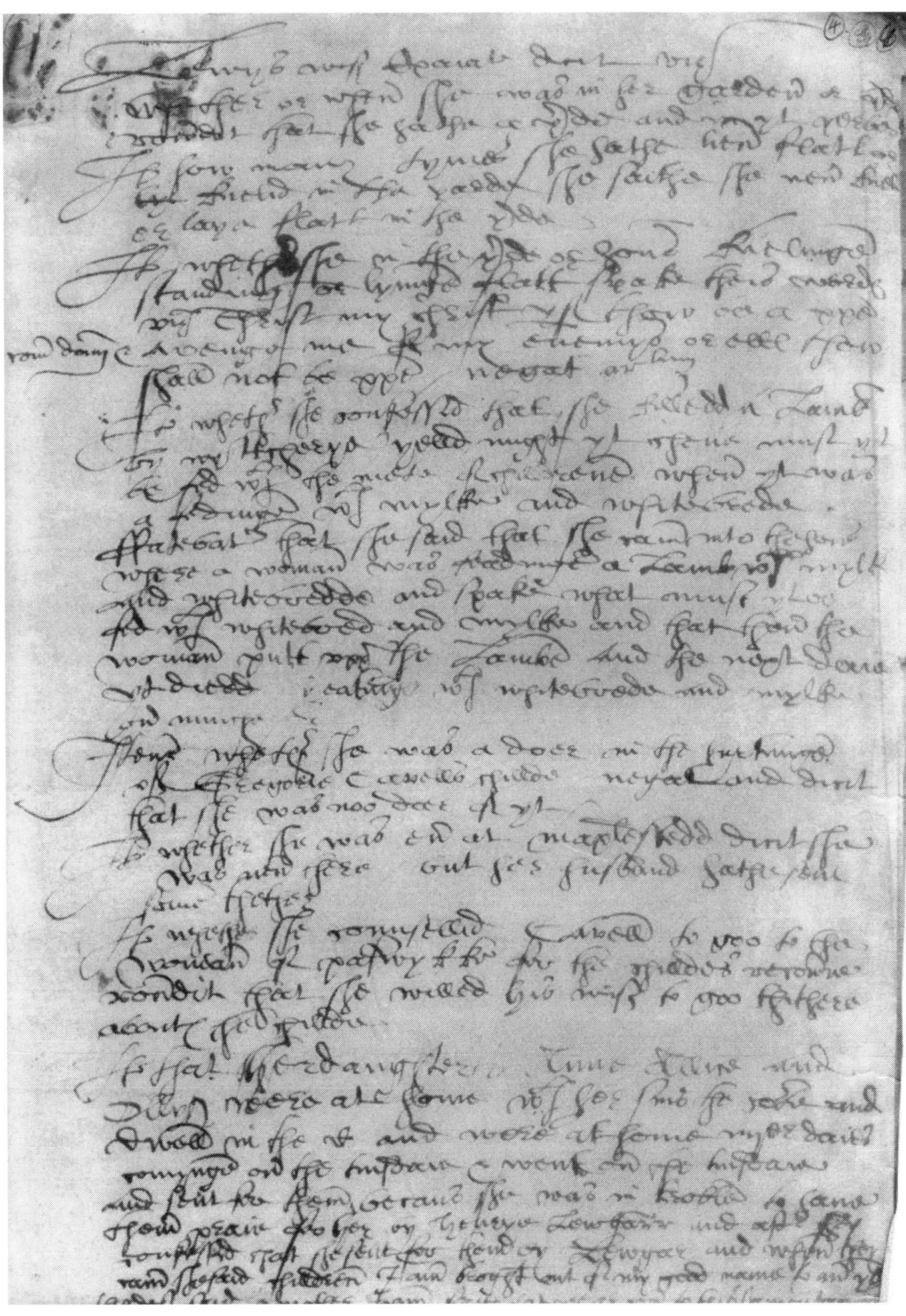

My first attempt at reading it was as follows:

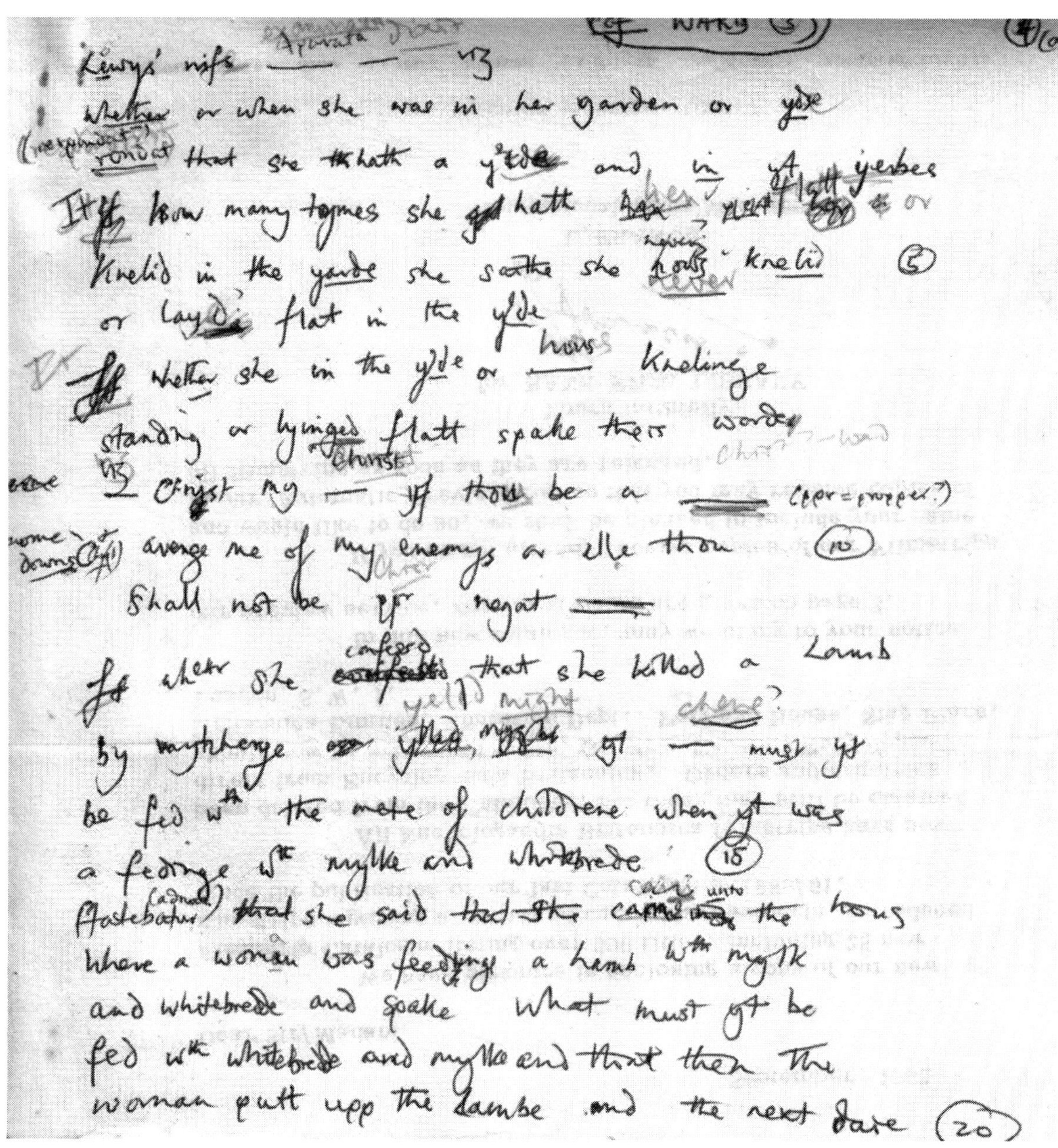

Kenys' wifs ——— ——
Whether or when she was in her garden or yde
that she hath a yerde and in yt yerbes
How many tymes she hath ... flatt
Knelid in the yarde she saythe she never knelid
or layd flat in the yde
whether she in the yde or hows knelinge
standing or lyinge flatt spake these wordes
Christ my — yf thou be a —
avenge me of my enemys or elle thou
Shall not be yr negat
whether she confessed that she killed a Lamb
by mythenge ... yt — must yt
be fed wth the mete of childrene when yt was
a fedinge wth mylke and whitebrede
that she said she came unto the hous
where a woman was feedinge a lamb wth mylk
and whitebrede and spake what must yt be
fed wth whitebrede and mylke and that then the
woman putt upp the lambe and the next dare

My second attempt was:

(4) Lewys wif Exa(m)i(n)at(ur) dicit viz D/AEA. 2. (Depositions)
Whether or when she was in her garden or y(ar)de
r(esp)ondet that she hathe a y(ar)de and in yt yerbes
It(em) how many tymes she hathe lien flatt or
knelid in the yarde she saithe she neve(r) knelid
or laye flatt in the y(ar)de
It(em) whether she in the y(ar)de or hous knelinge
standing or lyinge flatt spake theis wordes
viz Christ my christ yf thow be a xpe (xxe?)
come down(e) & avenge me of my enemys or elles thow
shall not be xpe / negat ar(ticu)lum
It(em) whethe(r) she confess(e)d that she killedd a Lamb
by wytcherye yelld might yt cheve must yt
be fed w(i)th the mete of chilldrene when yt was
a fedinge w(i)th mylke and whitebrede
Fatebat(u)r ~~that~~ she said ~~that~~ she cam(e) unto the hous
where a woman was feadinge a Lambe w(i)th mylk
and whitebredde and spake what must yt be
fed w(i)th whitebredde and mylke and ~~that~~ then the
woman putt upp the Lambe and the next daie

Finally I made a fair typed copy of this curious case.

D/AEA.2. DEPOSITIONS. (4)

Lewys wif Examined says viz
Whether or when she was in her garden or y(ar)de
she replies that she hath a y(ar)de and in yt yerbes
It(em) how many tymes she hathe lien flatt or knelid in the yarde
she saithe she neve(r) knelid or laye flatt in the y(ar)de
It(em) whether ~~of~~ she in the y(ar)de or hous knelinge standing
or lyinge flatt spake theis wordes viz Christ my christ yf thow be a
saviour come down(e) & avenge me of my enemys or elles thow shall
not be a saviour/ denies
It(em) whethe)r she confess(e)d that she killedd a Lamb by
wytcherye yelld might yt chene must yt be fed w(i)th the mete of
childrene when yt was a fedinge w(i)th mylke and whitebrede
(~~Fatebatur~~ Confessed.) that she said that she cam(e) unto the hous where a
woman was feadinge a Lambe w(i)th mylk and whitebredde and spake
what must yt be fed w(i)th whitebredde and mylke and that then
the woman putt upp the Lambe and the next daie yt diedd / (b)y

My fascination with these documents stretched well beyond the insight they directly provided on my thesis topic though they were important for studying the counter-actions against witchcraft and the activities of 'white' witches or 'cunning' folk.

I was aware that the desire to write a new kind of history, the social and mental history of ordinary people at the local level, could be pursued in a new way with ecclesiastical court materials. No-one to my knowledge had used these sources (though several of Keith Thomas's pupils who came after me, particularly Ralph Houlbrooke and Martin Ingram, would do so). I suddenly felt as if a whole new historical landscape had opened up before me. When I started to index the records for my three-village study, I worked out a numerical code for the small cards, and listed the subjects in the cases. This also gives some of the abbreviations used in indicating the process.

Code for ecclesiastical court cases: Essex.

CATEGORIES

1. Absence from Church/communion.
2.
3. Breaking Sabbath/service – by working etc.
4. Misbehaviour or church property.
5. Drink.
6. Swearing.
7. Sexual.
8. Clergy: duties, stipends etc.
9. Marital relations; husb–wife.
10. School.
11. Poor.
12. Baptism & Churching of Women.
13. Funerals.
14. Marriage service: weddings, licences.
15. Midwives.
16. Church Fabric – incl. fence.
17. Churchwardens.
18. Outside preachers.
19. Nonconformity and doctrine.
20. Not wearing surplice.
21. Church rates and rents.
22. Quarrelling, scolding.
23. Witchcraft.
24.
25. Keeping disordered company in house.
26. For standing excommunicate.
27.
28.
29.
30.

T = Testamentary.
? = Unknown.

Abbreviations.

penance/confess = to undergo p/c.
ex = excommunicated.
ex = stands ".
r.c. = receiving comm'n
det = detected for.
app = appears/to appear
rec = receive
p(x) = at next court
pen = penalty.
cont = continued at
cert = to certify
D = dismissed
n.a = non attendance
d/s = divine service
✓ = admits charge
X = denies charge
Δ = wife
E = Easter
E.C = Earl's Colne
P/4 = to purge with 4.

Sample Format

NAME, Xian. ①

first presentment/process

second presentment/process

third presentment →.

Vol. fol.
↓ ↓
7/20 ← R 3rd D → 14/2/1567
6/18 5v ← E 2nd A/T → 8/11/1566
6/80 ← F 1st. E → 4/9/1566

The density of information from this source for one village for three months, as well as the use of the classification system above, is worth illustrating briefly for the village of Earls Colne. This was done in late 1965 or 1966.

D/ACA.16. H.P. Acts(?)

16/119. 30/7/88.	g of HP.	Cert. of the repair of ch. windows + pavement pd	(16)
16/120. 30/7/88.	g of HP.	'our ch. lacketh glacing + certayne pavemente' (they are in the Queenes s'vice' Cit in pd)	(16)
16/120 30/7/88.	Δ ~~[illegible]~~ (ca) BIXTED	N.r. comn at Easter last. M by (w) Cont. Ex. (query 'what matters is in the house de wright')	(2)
16/120. 30/7/88.	HATCHMAN John +Δ.	S (i.e. n.r. comn at Easter last) J.H. Comp. + alleged that he at Easter laste and his wife receyved the holye Com at Easter laste paste' fid. fac. (1) +Δ.	(2)
16/120. 30/7/88.	FRAUNCES Wm.	S. (i.e. n.r. comn at Easter last) M by (w), (v + m)	(2)
16/120.v. 30/7/88.	old g of HP.	'that they have not given up ther accompt' M by (w) on Mr Pilbarrowe one of g's, Cont. T.p. in pd. Mr St John. has. (judge releases husband Mr Doctor Withers). (vom)	(17)
16/122.v. 30/7/88.	BARKER Dorothy.	'for keeping company wth on webb & that they are suspected of Incontinent life togither.' Cit. by (w). to appear pd + pay.	(7b)
16/122.v. 30/7/88.	WEBBE —	S. (i.e. incontinency with Dorothy Barker) Cit. in pd	(7b)
16/126.v. 4/9/88.	g. of HP	Penalty of Mr Pilbarrowe for cont. res. D & Mr St John. Cit. v + m. O in pd. (cited as formerly in pd)	(17)
16/128. 4/9/88.	BARKER Dorothy.	Examined + to appear. in pd.	(7b)
16/128. 4/9/88.	WEBBE —	*susp. of Incont. with Dorothy Barker. Cit. by (w) n.a.: Cont. + T.p. in pd.	(7b)
16/132.v 2/10/88.	g's of HP.	Cert. 'of repayring of ch. + pavement. + the same in pd (come for act)	(16)
16/133. 2/10/88.	g's of HP.	Cited this day. (exped. antea)	(17)
16/153. 2/10/88	Δ BOXTED — ~~[illegible]~~	ex query a Wright / What matters here / in the howse. 'boxted kepeth a woman daughter suspiciouslye as his s'vaunt and his wyfe complayned that she dyd weare her gownes and apparell and ~~that~~ she colde have, nothing but as the mayd wille' Cit. said boxsted vir et his maid in pd	?
16/133. 2/10/88.	FRAUNCYS Wm.	penalty for cont. res. to this day. Ex.	?

1965 - April

I wrote again on 1st April from 10, Weight Road, Chelmsford

Dear Mummy & Daddy,

No letter has found its devious way to me yet this week - but with my present extended 'forwarding' system I'm surprised anything ever finally gets here. I hope all goes well & Mummy is free from her recurrent illnesses. Also, how did the visit of Sir Owain go?

Here it has been warm & sunny for the last few days - so warm that I've begun reducing my layers of clothing - from 5 to 3. Cherry is out in Chelmsford & London & magnolia also & the crocuses are out in church-yards and the garden of Keats's house. The reason why I know about the latter is that I went up to London last week-end & visited it. I don't know if you've been there. It's a smallish C18 villa standing in 'Keats' grove' in Hampstead & surrounded by a small lawn, trees & crocuses. Somehow I'd expected something shabbier. The place was well arranged - just a few first editions, poems written & blank pages of Shakespeare's sonnets, plum trees where he sat & wrote the 'Nightingale' & locks of Fanny's hair. I dutifully following Thomas Hardy's precedent, sat on the rustic bench outside & wrote a poem.

I rang up Annie several times over the week-end but she appeared to be having a gay time - Grand National, Hamlet etc & was never in when I called. Any hope I had of staying the night was slightly dashed by hearing Fiona & friend were up - looking at pictures. I told them where I was spending the week-end but didn't see anything of them. I hope to see Annie this Saturday.

I'd been lent a key to a flat in Hampstead, but the person had given me the wrong one so was wondering vaguely what to do. I bought Orwell's 'Down & Out in Paris and London' (which Jill Walker had recommended) as I thought it might give a little practical advice! After reading of the appalling conditions of the poor in his time I felt more cheerful & was in a very susceptible frame of mind when I walked past a small group of beat-nikky types who were on a 36-hour hunger-strike on a pavement at the foot of Hampstead Heath. I decided to join them & to sleep out the night there. In fact it was a most interesting experience for various reasons. I never felt hungry although I did about 40 hours in the end. I only got a little sleep, though I was lent a sleeping bag. There were moments of intense beauty - looking up in the Salvador Dali-skeleton trees at night with the light shining up into them and one "lone star" shining over Keats's house. The dawn chorus - just as melodious as nightingales - and a walk over Hampstead Heath early on Sunday morning - when "All that mighty heart was lying still" and "the very houses seemed asleep" etc. Also the people were interesting - about 7 of them. Ages about 16-18, mostly from Hampstead & Highgate, very intelligent (hoping to go to University), sons of liberal, artistic, upper-middle parents. I spent a lot of the time talking to a sweet girl who was a sort of Dittany Stone. Very dreamy & in love with legends, Robert Graves, Tolkein, fairy stories etc. When I left to come back to Essex I nearly fainted twice - more from the heat than anything else I think. To think there are <u>millions</u> who face <u>far more</u> hunger all the time... Next week-end Father Borrelli is coming to Chelmsford (the man who works for the slum urchins of Naples) & I hope to see him before bussing (?) (Richard is driving from Iwerne) home.

Please forgive this egotistical letter.

Much love to you both, Alan

My mother wrote to me from Cherideo on 6th April Cherideo

Thank you for a letter describing your hunger strike outside Keats's house, it sounded romantic though in fact was probably awfully uncomfortable. I hope it wasn't because you were completely out of cash – you didn't say what the strike was about? It sounds so lovely at home, but the last April I shall miss my springs seem such a very little store but I shall enjoy them all the more I expect because of it. … but have a terribly intense programme mapped out – teaching, Mughals and preparing another childrens book. The mapping is all that has happened so far! I think I'll have to write you a joint letter in future, letter writing seems to take up so much of my time. I got a reply from Peter Quennell almost by return of post saying that the other editor was away but he would let me know about my article when he had discussed it with him – it doesn't sound too hopeful but I must say they are very polite and nice in that place, quite different from most editor one knows. I'm re-reading Tawney and feel so small, ignorant and incoherent by comparison, his knowledge and the strong, supple and moving prose in which he expresses it astonishes me at every sentence. I've had no reply from anyone I wrote to for books or information, the only two people who have answered are those English profs you put me onto, typical I'm afraid. Granny wrote yesterday, she sounds very cheerful and says she is feeling much better and seems delighted at the thought of us coming – Crowborough seems to be the place Richard has in mind but I hope he'll choose something central and near a bus stop. The gramaphone arrived for Fiona apparently, thank you so much, I will send you a cheque for 1st instalment in my next.

I then went north for Easter, my grandfather noted in his diary:
Sunday 11 April Billy & family leave Alan arrives

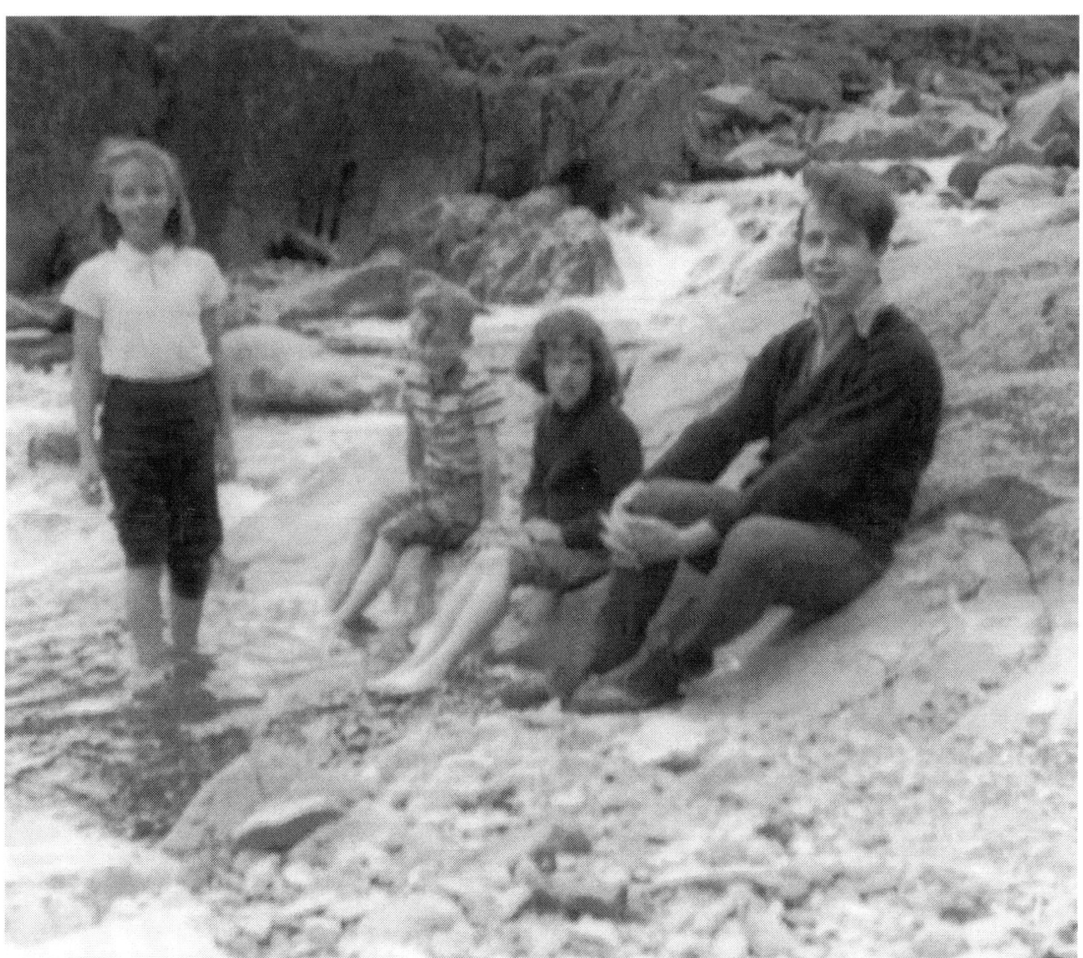

Cousins Caroline, Robin and Sarah with me

Granny, Aunt Julia and I

Monday 12 April Richard arrives
Saturday 24 April Alan leaves

I wrote from Field Head on 14th April.

Dear Mummy and Daddy,

My mail is being kept at Worcester from the 9th April onwards & I expect a letter of yours is waiting for me there. I hope all goes well. As you see I've sunk to a brief rest at Field Head, with its rituals of long meals, taking the dogs for walks, listening to the news every couple of hours etc. I am gently forging on with my witches - but having a holiday as well.

[Elsewhere as well: I was sad to leave Chelmsford in a way, I'd got rather attached to my routine and had had an exciting time mentally. I think I gathered together about 230 cases of witchcraft in all and I'm now putting them into a set form & putting them on cards. It is this and later stages, when I shuffle the cards around, that the real discoveries are made. In a v. interesting appendix on 'The Art of Note-Taking' by Beatrice Webb she says " I realise how difficult it is to convince students - especially those with a "literary" rather than a "scientific" training - that it is by just this use of such a mechanical device as the shuffling of sheets of notes, and just at this stage, that the process of investigation often becomes fertile in actual discoveries." She gives examples from her own writings of how, until she had shuffled things about there was no plan or seeming connection between all her facts and she had no idea of what her conclusions would be. I feel a bit like this. It's not until I start drawing maps & graphs that I'll have an idea of how witchcraft 'worked'. That will be the exciting stage. I think I'll have to do about 3 more months research on actual sources & the rest of the time

digesting, arranging & writing. As you know, it's frustrating and unhealthy just to absorb for too long. I'm also beginning to realise that this fairly strict training in how to extract, file & write-up information may be very useful in any social work I do. I have visions of putting all the inhabitants of Calcutta on cards - with their incomes, diseases, opinions etc tabulated in a statistician's nightmare! Anne says you're thinking of writing another children's book before the Moguls (?). The more you write the better, as one day the public will be crying out for it! Will it be similar to the last? Have you been told any date for the publication of the first? I wish they weren't leaving out the children - it really does spoil it.

I came up by bus, spending the night with Anne. Judy Ellis & Ginny (?) were there and we spent the evening trying to find a pub at Leicester Square not absolutely crammed with alcoholic Scotsmen, as it was the evening of the England v Scotland football match. We didn't succeed, but enjoyed joining in hearty Scottish songs. Anne & Ginny then went on to a film. Ginny is big, bouncy, enthusiastic & a little affected (= insecure) & friendly/good-natured. But I only saw her a short time. Anne was looking forward to going to the Beatles etc. the next day.

It's been drizzling almost continuously since I arrived, but it's still very lovely here; lambs, primroses &, of course, daffodils. I think I'm growing old & hardened as I no longer feel inspired poetically, no wild frenzies etc, just peaceful. I've been walking round Blelham tarn with Jane Wilkinson & I went with her to Peter Hall's party in the basement of Hawkshead Town Hall - quite fun, tho only a few of the regulars - Tim & Simone, Boddington, Linda Manby, Richard Brownson. The Beatles/Rolling Stones & food & drink etc. Jane is a v. nice girl - slightly wild & 'cool', but with a nice sense of humour rising from a disinterested amusement at human folly. I've had a long letter from Zoë full of her Irish hitching experiences (if it's as nice for Fiona - who, incidentally, sent a P.C. to say she'd arrived safely in Dublin - she'll love it). She's a good letter-writer and I'm longing to see her. Granny, as you'll know, is going down to Robert's 'Gallipoli' orgy so I'll have to stay up as long as is possible to be with Grandpa. Zoë is supposedly coming up on 22nd. Richard is here & as good-natured as ever & full of economics and journalism. He is looking round seriously for a house for G & G & is going to take Granny round likely places near Crowboroguh (Sussex) when she is South. Are you collaborating with Richard? Granny doesn't seem to like the thought of Essex.

Dipped into Ronald Knox 'Enthusiasm' - it looks fascinating. I must try to buy it. I hope you can read this scrawl - do say if it causes problems.

Look after yourselves,

All my love, Alan

One of the last poetic outpouring which I have saved was written on 19th April 1965.

Jane's kitchen after a party

Sausage frying and safely tabled toast,
A few half empty glasses
To remind one of the party,
Impatient children eating left-over
Easter eggs, nests of bright pebbles
Held in the hollow of chocolate.
All these disassociated images,
Caught in a web of the Beatles spinning
And tugging one gently back into life,
Faces drift from yesterdays,
Stalking into the kitchen of my mind
On cat feet, playing with my affections
As with a dead vole – and then all

The splendour of a peacock's
Tail – shot through with all the
Fury of emotion aroused, of sand
Streaming across the mountains
Shaping the waterfalls into rainbows
And the trees fermenting in the ground,
Spring's wine oozing into the soup
Of summer. When will the call
Come so that the sleep will be shaken
And the trumpet sound.
When will the splendour of a thousand
Golden days enrich again our shifting skies
And all the summer of youth & innocence
Drown itself in the greater glory of
The Word Revealed when Christ
Shall fall from the Cross and let
His soul's agony stain the flowers?
Then shall the mountains leap
And the heavens spark beauty,
Then shall the sons of man speak
An unutterable humility, and the
Broken limbs shall be mended.
Slowly, slightly the skies sombre
Fulfilment pulls the light down
It's back, revealing breasts and
Thighs of ivory, long-combing back
It's hair of light; pressing with
Iris-tender hands the smothering
Cries of our fevered brows.
Asleep the strong find themselves
Chained by the fire of Old forests,
Caught by their muscles in a band
Of blood, which flows down through
Their eyes and catches and tugs at
Their restless minds. I saw
The ecstasy breaking down through
The farms, rolling the trumpet
Through the boulders, and the
Sand of the seven riders. High
Above the thunder, and the
Moving of deep-down Evil. The
Splitting open of wounds, the appalling
Scream of shells and the batteries
Of force engage and maul,
And then the stillness of
Infinite distance and the tenderness
Of sunlight on music, of water
Blending into the leaves and
The reflections, catching long
Tresses of hair, and wide eyes

Reflecting naked feet and long limbs
And I felt hands stealing through
Sand; the gradual pouring out of
Desire; and when the wind dropped
The lake was completely still
And your heart in mine enfolded.
The conflict for a moment
Higher than the mountains and
Hidden from eyes in the deep moss
At a tree's foot.

A strange semi-poem indeed, filled with my usual mixture of borrowed ideas, obvious battles between sex and religion etc.

I wrote again from Field Head on Wednesday 21st April

Dear Mummy and Daddy,

Once again I can't answer your letter as it will be at Oxford; not much has happened around here so this will be short & dull in all probability, but I will be writing again shortly (to get myself back into my Sunday routine).

I'm sitting alone in the house (except for John Wright whose just breezed in). A car-load left half-an-hour ago with Richard, Granny & the girls (Fiona & Ray). Granny of course, is on her expedition to launch 'Gallipoli'. She's going to stay at Anne's Angela's etc & perhaps house-hunt at Crowborough with Richard. The general level of excitement has been raised by the fact that Lucy & Emma have just gone down with measles - <u>poor</u> Angela! Granny returns on Tuesday. Meanwhile back at the ranch... Fiona & Ray turned up yesterday you'll be relieved to hear. They'd lugged a tent round, but, because of the weather, been unable to camp & hence run out of funds & come home a week early. They loved Ireland, as no doubt you'll hear, but, as with all Fiona's expeditions, it was more an endurance test than anything else. They couldn't have added to their enjoyment by carrying 40 lb. rucksacks and wearing gumboots! Oddly enough they travelled over exactly the same ground as Zoë and were interested in her long letter describing it. Restless as ever, they've shot off to-day to see someone in Yorkshire for the day. I must say they look well on it - Fiona is looking v. pretty.

My one burst of social life was on Easter Sunday. After Easter communion in the beautifully decorated church & a chicken-lunch I was driven over to Troutbeck by Jane (Byrne) & spent the afternoon watching the Beatles & others (the session Anne went to). Then cocktails at Anne Johnson's - where we met Bill Critchley etc & back for a select party at Jane's till 2 p.m. Jane & Dusty seem as happy together as they ever will be, and being able to drive makes a tremendous difference to J. Last night I went to 'Wonderful Life' (Cliff Richard) at the Ambleside flea-pit. It was pretty dreary as a film but I went with Jane Wilkinson & going to the cinema is really the only alternative to walking round the Hawkshead lanes or carousing in the Queen's Head.

It was a miserable Easter as far as weather was concerned - occasional sunshine but mostly rain, hail and even snow. Poor campers! Hawkshead is 'developing' itself very rapidly to meet the growing hordes - a vast new car park for about 1,000 cars; a vast new coffee bar which will seat well over 100 when it's finished (there are already two going now - tho' they are very small); the road from Ambleside re-tarmacked & widened in some places. (I can hear you groaning to yourselves!) Fiona is planning to spend the summer in the Outer Isles renting a cottage/croft. I had been thinking of buying one (if cheap enough) so that I could write my thesis there. Perhaps if all the family want to go there we could get a couple? I really must go to Ireland too, it sounds gorgeous. Perhaps I'll go there instead of Greece this summer...

I've been for a series of 'literary' walks with Richard, usually discussions about our respective futures as writers. R really has been bitten by the bug I think. I hope your writing goes well. I haven't

done all the work I wanted to do, but nevertheless haven't done too badly. I return to Oxford this week-end & am looking forward to it. Zoë arrives in Lakes today.
Much love, Alan

My mother wrote from Cherideo on 22nd April
[addressed to Field Head, Ambleside and forwarded 28th April to 38, Park Town]

I think you and Granpa will be living on porridge and poached eggs unless Granny is back – I do hope all is well and that Roberts lunch was a great success, I'm longing to hear of the impact of his book. Granpas description of it as a story of unimaginable horror will surely make it a best seller. Please thank him for a letter we got a few days ago, don't seem to have had one from you this week but it's probably all this moving about. Anne said you had been staying there for a night, we are swithering[1] a bit now about the project to get her out. It seems unlikely that we shall have our provident fund in time to pay for the passage, and also I'm wondering if a trip on a cargo boat with a lot of old fogeys like ourselves (who else would be able to afford it?) would be worth the expense and have suggested that we give her a trip later instead – perhaps with Fiona or a young party. ... All my dreams are having to be abandoned one by one – seeing Ankor Wat, doing a tour of India, having Anne out, bringing the dogs home – it now seems that we shall just climb onto the boat, finis. However I'm still hopefully planning a long train journey round Buddhist shrines on my way to Calcutta and will cling to that until the last few weeks. My photos of Delhi came the other day and were very good really, not good enough for an article on the Mughals I had planned for the Sunday Times but a beautiful reminder of some unforgettable moments. I'll be sending them home with someone soon.

I have at last Got Down to my book, am writing the first draft of the first section and hoping my agent will interest someone in it, there are still lots of missionary sources to be consulted which I can't get here. Now I have started I want to write all day and emerge in a dream of Moghulistan which can't be very cheerful for Daddy. I am reading D.H. Lawrence and Tawney in between and my style veers from one to the other, my forte obviously would be parody as I am so quickly influenced by what I'm reading. When I stop to consider who will ever read my book I am tempted to fling it aside forthwith, but there is always the comfort of knowing you will bravely struggle through! Anyway results are beside the point, a rather nice poem of Tagores expresses what I hope to feel; "As my days pass in the crowded market of this world And my hands grow full with the daily profits, Let me ever feel that I Have gained nothing – let me not forget for a moment, Let me carry the pangs of this sorrow In my dreams And in my wakeful hours" (It looks better when printed in lines) ….

I wonder if you have started the thesis, the difficulty is to make some sort of shape of the mass of unco-ordinated facts, but with your trained mind that probably is taken care of. It still continue quite cool and breezy, I expect to hear some lyrical descriptions of spring from you from Lakeland, though it sounds as if it's been pretty wet. Crowborough appears to have fallen through but perhaps Richard has some other plans, we are all leaning heavily on him which is a bit unfair really. Lunch time, I'm sorry for a dull letter but I seem to be slightly dazed though I have no illnesses to report, in fact am heavier than I've been for about 20 years, probably middle aged spread actually.

I wrote from Worcester College on 27th April.

Dear Mummy and Daddy,

Thank you for the letter which was awaiting me on my return to Oxford. I hope the programme of work Mummy had mapped out has not caused a breakdown etc. It seems our family has a lot of energy - and isn't prepared to sit back & enjoy life. Fiona expends it on Irish bogs & slapping on paint, the rest of us on writing. Maybe it'll get one of us somewhere soon. But it's nothing compared to people like Wesley - who got up at 4 each morning to preach one of his 40,000 sermons at 5 a.m. and did so

---

[1] A Scots word for doubt, indecision, being in two minds.

until he was 85! Getting a few hours work done in the early morning - before interruptions begin - seems to be one of the secrets of most prodigious workers, for instance Flo' Nightingale & Beatrice Webb both did this; reading government Blue books before they were called to function as Victorian aunts.

I wrote to Blackwell's re. the book by Hollis (on Xavier) & they say 'we cannot discover the book listed in our catalogue': I'll try to see if it's in the Bodley or British Museum catalogue. It appears that our fields overlap: Sir Thomas Roe appears in several of my searches as quite an important Essex gent at the time of the witch trials there (e.g. Essex Review, xx, p.135: An Essex Worthy: Sir Thos Roe). How are the Moghuls/children's books going? You know I'm always interested to hear plans etc. Yes, do write joint letters if it will give you more time to write; though I'll be sorry not to get an individual one. Perhaps it might be better to send a carbon copy to one of us as I think one copy would get stuck at Fiona!

This has been the great week of Robert's book. No doubt G & G will send out reviews; the best was by A.J.P. Taylor in the Observer. I somehow feel that it's just missed the headlines. A good book, but not causing a controversy as far as I can see. It's too early to tell yet, it's still in the book-shop windows.

Yes, Tawney is magnificent. I'm just reading his essays - mostly on socialism/Christianity and he writes gloriously. Supposed to be because (partly) he was steeped in the bible. He is still, of course, the father-figure around here, largely because he was an inspiring man as well as a good historian. Compared to the usual fossilized professor he was (& is) a breath of mountain air (to mix metaphors) - in this way, & this alone, Trevor-Roper despite his spitefulness, is similar.

I walked over to see Zoë just before leaving the Lakes - over the tops from Rydal and it was hot enough to sunbathe at Grisedale Tarn. Her parents are sweet & took me out to dinner & the house, though small & new, is very pleasant. I travelled down with her by train on Friday & have seen a little of her. With her finals & all the pressures of Oxford we both feel a little insecure & this will be a testing period; if we come through it the relationship should be quite strong.

I've asked Granny to get the £7 odd pounds for my two weeks (or just under) from you. Hope this is O.K. Knock it off the Gramaphone H.P.

My new room is delightful - high up among the chestnut trees & with its own telephone & kitchen & Mrs Keen (landlady) very kind & motherly.[1]

Will write soon & again attempt to get back into Sunday ritual.

Lots of love, Alan

On 27 April I wrote a long letter from Worcester College to Keith Thomas.

Dear Mr. Thomas,

I hope your book progresses and you have been free from any further bouts of flu' etc. I wonder if I could come to see you some time in the next week or two? Saturday, 11.30 a.m. or after lunch are usually clear. Could you bear it if I bought a few Photostats etc. & we tried to sort out a few palaeogriphic jumbles?

I had a rewarding stay in Essex and almost finished the Archdeaconry records. Another week should see me through them. According to the 'outline of work' I sent you in January this term is going to be spent "cross-referencing Ecclesiastical records" & doing "preliminary statistics of all legal sources" & also doing further reading on "general writers on witchcraft". Next week I am giving a talk to the Devorguilla[2] *– probably on "Neighbourliness and witchcraft" (witchcraft as a cohesive & a fragmenting mechanism). I don't want to start the statistics until the very last moment – for obvious reasons – and therefore, like the talk on the cunning man, this will be necessarily impressionistic.*

---

[1] The room was at the top of the same house, 38, Park Town.

[2] The Balliol College history society.

I think you said you were interested in the relationship between trials in the different courts; whether people accused of sorcery or going to sorcerers were later accused of witchcraft, the interrelation of 'black' and 'white' etc. It is possible that one or two more cases may be found in the Act Books (I have finished the Archdeaconry of Colchester, but have not quite checked all of the Essex Archdeaconry) but I don't think this will alter the general impression. The Archdeaconry of Essex covers roughly a third of Essex & 44 Act Books survive. In these I found 124 cases of witchcraft or sorcery) as opposed to 111 in the 55 Act Books of Colchester). In these 114 persons were accused as follows: 13 for calling people witches, 34 for using sorcery (from burning animals to being or going to cunning folk, 1 for incontinence with the daughter of a suspected witch – the mother lived in his house, 1 for not communicating (his wife being suspected for witchcraft), 1 for wanting to be a witch so that she could revenge herself on her enemy, 1 for advising a witch not to confess, 1 for heresy & had a wife suspected of witchcraft (= misc. cases); and 62 for 'witchcraft' – often not specified. Of those 52 not accused directly of 'witchcraft' only 1 (who had gone to a cunning man) appears in any other court. He appears in both the Assizes and Quarter Sessions as having some livestock bewitched. Thus it seems that 'sorcery' was unlikely to appear in the civil courts.

*Of the 62 who are accused of 'witchcraft' 11 appear charged with this offence in other courts; 7 in the Assize courts, 2 in both Assize & Quarter Sessions, 1 in both Assize & in the 1589 pamphlet, 1 in the Maldon Borough records. Thus there are some fifty individuals who appear in the Archdeacon's Court & not elsewhere & vice versa it looks as if – this being a fair sample – there will be over 450 [*note in my hand: *'no. muddling cases with individuals. Prob. About 300 individuals'.] individuals accused in the civil courts & not occurring in the ecclesiastical. I will have to check the episcopal records before any conclusions can be drawn. 107/124 of the cases occur before 1603 & the proportion is even higher in the Colchester Archdeaconry. Hale prints 6 of these cases in his Precedents; you are very welcome to see the others whenever you like.*

I enclose some rather intriguing depositions from the end of the 2nd Essex Archdeaconry Book; as you see Elizabeth Lowys occurs both in the Act Book and the Assizes. Like the pamphlets it gives some interesting glimpses into the causal connections people saw between misfortune, possible causes for the witch's anger & the final act. It is also interesting for its early date – it antedates the more notorious 1566 trial & is thus the earliest for which we have detailed evidence.

Yours sincerely,

My mother wrote from Cherideo on 29th April

My letters seem to have been missing you but I hope this will catch you safely. You didn't sound as if you enjoyed the Lakes as much as usual, perhaps being away from the people and atmosphere of Oxford is what you miss. From what you say about cavernous great coffee bars the sooner we get that croft in the outer isles the better. Why don't you all go croft hunting this summer, we could pay for one in the spring of next year in time for you to retire to for your thesis. If only someone could drive there is the car waiting to be trundled round the highlands, I'm sure you could pass a test with a few lessons…

I'm ploughing on with my book, it's hard for the light touch I intend not to slip over into facetiousness, it won't be history at all in the way you mean the word, no juggling of cards to find new meanings and connections, just a story to be told. I aim at a modest 1000 words a day but can't always manage it when I have to go out…

Do wonder how Gallipoli hit the world. Is Zoe really coming to India? She must come and stay here if she gets this far, it seems a tremendously daring thing to do but crossing Afghanistan by hitch hiking will probably be a lot easier than Galway judging by Fiona's descriptions. She ought to read a book by Nicholas Woollaston called "Handles of Chance" in which he did much the same and wrote about it most engagingly. I hope the squalor won't horrify her too much. I can't quite make out if you have finished with Essex for good and will now be settled in Park Town? Of course I will pay Granny for your keep, to be quite honest I always do, perhaps she gets it twice over?! We can't enter into the buying of a house for them at this stage but could contribute a bit towards the rent, I really must write to Richard about it all. What are his plans as a writer, is he embarking on a book? Brenda Finney has a flat in Wimbledon, I'll get the address and you might go and see her if in London.

1965 - May

I continued to live out of College, but to make use of some College amenities, as shown in the battels for the Summer Term.

WORCESTER COLLEGE, OXFORD

Battels for Trinity Term, 1965

A.D.J. Macfarlane, Esq.,
Field Head,
Outgate,
Nr. Ambleside, Lancs.

	£ s. d.
Inclusive charge for Board and Lodging	
Meals in Hall	3. 0.0
Guests Meals	4.0
Guests Accommodation	
Boys' Club Cricket Party	
Buttery	2. 8.9
Kitchen	3
Coupons	1. 0.0
Gratuities	
Laundry	1. 10.6
Heat	
Gate Fines	
Postage	3
J.C.R. Scholarship	10.0
Damage	
Library-book Fines	
Junior Common Room	1. 0.0
College Clubs	4. 10.0
Graduate C. R. Battels	5.9
Graduate C. R. Subs.	10.0
College Dues	15. 0.0
University Dues	
Library Dues	2. 0.0
	31. 19.6*
Tuition Fee	18. 0.0
Key Deposits	
B.U. Provident Association	
Oxford Society	
Debtor Balance brought forward ...	
Prepayment for M.T. 1965	35. 0.0
	84. 19.6*

Credit:	£ s. d.
Prepayment for T.T. 1965 ...	25. 0.0-
Credit Balance of last account	
Scholarship	
Exhibition	
Dept. of Education & Science	40. 10.0-
Local Authority	
Caution Money	20. 0.0-

Balance Due to the ~~College~~ £ 10.6CR

Mr Macfarlane

Apart from reading and research, I also attended a number of research seminars in this term. Some were held by the newly appointed Fellow at All Souls, Robin Briggs, or the one by C.B. Macpherson on 18th May, titled 'Against Patriarchalism' with a reception hosted by Christopher Hill afterwards. Then there was a series run by Hugh Trevor-Roper. I have notes on a talk by Peter Burke on 'Neo-Platonism in C16-C17' to this seminar on 27th May, and a talk the week before by Rattansi on 'Cartesian Doctrine in England' on 21st May.

I gave at least two talks. One was to the Balliol history society, or Devorguilla society, which I had attended the year before. I had given an earlier version to one of my last two extra-mural classes.

WITCHCRAFT & NEIGHBOURLINESS.
W.E.A. 3/5/65
+ Balliol 'Devorguilla' Society 7/5/65.

Introduction.

I would like to talk about the idea of 'neighbourliness' or 'friendship' and how witchcraft beliefs acted within these concepts. First I would like to outline what 'neighbourliness' meant & how it worked, how it was expressed, between which people it flowed, the special occasions on which it was particularly emphasized, and the forces which preserved it as an idea. Then I would like to mention a few of the forces which during our period were undermining the old order, causing tensions and conflicts between people and groups. And finally I would like to outline how belief in witchcraft and accusations against specific people formed an important part of these relationships. [In our age where there are so many strains between different groups - the old and the young, those competing for jobs, those competing for power and education - and where there are many gulfs between the beliefs we hold and the actions we are forced to perform it is especially interesting and instructive to see how the Elizabethans and their descendants dealt with these problems.]

OUTLINE OF NEIGHBOURLINESS.

1. The groups involved; the need for.

The village was the frame within which the majority of the population carried on their life. Balanced on the edge of starvation, plague & warfare there was enormous pressure to work in close co-operation with one's fellows. Rejection from the group meant social, and possibly physical death. Intimate links of blood & cO-residence bound one in a complicated web of relationships. The ties obviously worked between different groups within a village; thus certain families, perhaps living near to each other, perhaps linked by blood, would co-operate more intimately. Women would lend and borrow from each other more freely than from men; there would be special obligations to the old. Children would, for a time, be under different pressure. Finally social classes would be divided, thus, for instance, yeomen would co-operate in farm work, etc., festivals and in a closer way among themselves than a yeoman would be expected to work with inmates of the poor-house or with the local gentry. [1]

2. Expressions of neighbourliness.

'Neighbourliness' was expressed in a host of ways in everyday life. In the physical field there was probably a considerable exchange of gifts, food, clothing, utensils, especially on celebrations or during periods of crisis. Loans of labour or farm equipment or food, like loans, a strict system of reciprocity. All articles were expected to be returned, or an equivalent given. The gifts and loans were both a way of cementing relationships & gave elasticity to the close-to-subsistence economy. [2] 'Neighbourliness' showed itself in many other ways. It brought obligations to give support in times of strong emotion. When a 'friend' was married, suffered a bereavement, had a child joy or sorrow ought to be shared by attendance at the

The talk was fairly short, but I expanded it a great deal by producing footnotes of almost equal length to the talk. Clearly I did not read these out, but they were an important chance to start to put my findings into a wider anthropological setting.

Notes. p.1.

1) For excellent general accounts of the importance of 'neighbourliness' in agricultural communities see Arensberg, Conrad M. and Kimball, Solon T. Family and Community in Ireland (Massachusetts, 1940). and Williams, W.M. The Sociology of an English Village; Gosforth (London, 1964). especially chapter 7. For 'neighbourliness' in the medieval village there is Homans, G.C. English Villagers of the C13 (New York, 1960) p.82 and passim. The importance of gifts and neighbourly feeling among yeomen is touched on in Campbell, Mildred. The English Yeoman (1942) p. 387.

And see: John Beattie, 'Gift Giving'.... New Society, (13) 27. Dec. 1962.

2) On gift-giving as a form of relationship generally there is M.Mauss, The gift..., trans. I.Cunnison, (London, 1954). The principle of 'reciprocity' & the relative unimportance of the actual article exchanged, as well as the occasions on which gifts reach their peak are discussed in R.Firth, Human Types (Revised edition London, 1958) pp, 89, 90 & 76. Gift exchange, in courtship, just one of its forms, are mentioned in Campbell, op.cit., p.303 and in G.G.Coulton, Medieval Panorama, vol.II (Fontana edition, 1961), p. 293. Examples of Mass food gifts on important occasions are given in F.G.Emmison, Tudor Food and Pastimes (London, 1964), p.53. One example of such exchange at the lowest level of society illustrates how one gift could be turned into another. Being examined in Essex in 1582 a villager said " that before Michaelmas last, she the said Ursley sent her sonne to the said Letherdals House, to have scouring sand, and sent word by the said boy, yt his mother would give her the dying of a payre of womens hose for sand:" incidentally, the loan was refused & shortly afterwards the refuser believed herself to be bewitched. A True and Just Recorde of the Information, Examination and Confession of all the Witches, taken at S.Oses in the countie of Essex.... (London, 1582). (Short Title Catalogue, 24922) A.3.

3) This would take some of the strain off the individual, responsibility, guilt & emotion would be shared. As anthropologists point out , in primitive societies where the boundary between the inner world of the self & the outer world of the community is not clearly marked, individuals can easily externalize & release their conflicts and emotions into the rituals of society (see for example M.Fortes in The Institutions of Primitive Society (Oxford, 1961) p. 90-1. But this also applies to less formal forms of association where the individual receives support - in gossip for instance. The comparative importance of the family/neighbours in ritual - for instance at birth thanksgiving or burial - during the middle ages and our period would help in sorting out the relative importance of the family & the village to the individual. It has been suggested that the village, rather than the family, was the most important social grouping in the middle ages, a suggestion based on the somewhat dubious assumption that while one flourishes the other must be weak. (J.Thirsk 'The Family' (review article) in Past and Present, 27, pp. 118,122) . With the attack on communal rituals around important events there may have been associated a withdrawing of one's relationships, which had previously extended throughout the village, and which gradually centred on the nuclear family. Witchcraft accusations - as we will see later - may have played a part in such a withdrawal.

4) 'Hospitality', the ever-ready 'cup of tea' and food for travelling or visiting neighbours, is a great virtue among Irish countrymen (Arensberg, op.cit., p. 77-8) Certain people, by virtue of their position, were supposed to offer more of this than others ; thus in the 1570's an Essex vicar was presented in the Archdeacon's court because he "doth not keep hospitality" (E.R.O. D/AEA.8. f.195) Contemporaries lamented the decline of this virtue and commented unfavourable on Londoners meannes as comparted to country hospitality. (M.St.C.Byrne, Elizabethan Life in Town and Country (London, 1934), p.34). People ascribed the decline in large part to the abolition of the monasteries; but it seems to be more generally one of the symptoms and products of the wider changing social organization.

5) John Addy, The Archdeacon and Ecclesiastical Discipline in Yorkshire 1598-1714, Clergy & the Churchwardens ~~gives a good account of how this worked~~ (Borthwick Institute (St. Anthony's Hall Publications No.24.1963) gives a good account of how much 'rumour' 'fame' and reputation entered into ecclesiastical process. People were often presented on 'common fame' or rumour & were acquitted if compurgators could be found who would swear to their good reputation. 'The

I wrote from Worcester College on 4th May

Dear Mummy and Daddy,

Thank you very much for two letters since I last wrote - one must have been slightly held up. I hope tea, Moghuls, animals etc. thrive. As you see I've still not got settled into my Sunday letter-writing schedule. Leaving all my leisure activities like Church, having a bath, visiting people, reading newspapers etc to that day I don't seem to get round to writing letters nowadays.

I'm sending out 3 paperbacks: 'The Crisis of India' & two on literary criticism - for the minister, I'll be most interested to hear what you think of the former, though I haven't read it myself. What is the 'breakthrough' in contraception you speak of - a new 'pill'? I thought the major problem was cultural not technical - the difficulty of getting people to use new methods; tho' obviously their reluctance will, to a certain extent, vary with the methods they are recommended.

Yes Zoë is planning to hitch to India: but naturally finding it difficult to find anyone else who is. She is a very self-possessed girl. If, however, she goes on to do sociology in October (where they require some practical work in the summer) she may not have time. Though undoubtedly more intelligent than me (I?) she is less organized, more spontaneous, less old-maidish.

Last week-end was 'May-morning'. I didn't get up for it but David Porter who came down with a friend from Manchester did. They stayed out all night, put bicycles on the top of college flag-poles etc. He has changed little, except for mellowing. He seems to enjoy being a solicitor in his father's firm. On Saturday evening we went out to the Tudor Cottage at Iffley and had a delicious meal - mixed grill, caramel crisp, wine etc. (Which reminds me, in a rash moment I invited two friends to come to dinner tonight and on Saturday & I've got to cook them a meal! Must buy 'Cooking in a bed-sitter'. I haven't any crockery, let alone food. Ah well, I expect they like baked beans...!) On Sunday I drove out on my motorbike with Linda & picked some cow-slips near Woodstock. A magnificent evening with 'cattle lowing over the lea' & great ridges of grey/cold cloud. My relations with L. are definitely a problem - a mixture of attraction and boredom; a wanting not to hurt (or be hurt) and desire for freedom. Still, I expect things'll sort themselves out.

I am thinking of croft-hunting this summer - so is Fiona.

Much love to you both, Alan

The following day, 5th May, I wrote another poem about Zoë on Worcester College notepaper:

For Zoë

No words, only the meaningfulness of a dreary moment
Remind me of you.
No visions, but the sameness of things when you are absent.
No songs, but the sigh of the drear wind and jumbled cries.
No dreams, but the growth of reality.

I cannot lure you to the cavernous growths I had prepared;
Growths where the lute and lyre, the honey and jasmine would have lulled you.
Instead, obstinately, intently, you move with
Hurtful reality. Forcing re-adjustment, refusing
To cloud into the untouchable untouching
Presence I had hoped. Unwilling, perhaps unable
To bring back awe and lost mystery into my life,
Yet making me yearn yet, making me
Drift from the tiresome moment to the
Everlasting instant.

I cannot sing or slobber, but only push
Back the lush growths painfully and uncover
Beneath them a weak, trembling creature
Which I offer you – my heart.

My mother wrote from Cherideo on 5th May Cherideo

Thank you for your letter from Oxford, where you must be glad to be back with a bit of space and your books again – I wonder where Granny put all those divans she bought, in your room probably! I haven't heard from her since her trip south which is rather surprising, I expect her version of the reception given to Gallipoli will be more dramatic than yours – but I hope it will sell well. One always gets the impression that Robert's scholarship is rather superficial but perhaps that's because he carries it lightly. The more I write on my subject the more I realise the limit of my poor little knowledge, the adjective I can see applied to my book in imaginary criticisms is "trivial" – which it is. I have at last got one of my books from Calcutta, "India" by Percival Spear who is one of the acknowledged specialists – it is very fair, straightforward – and dull, because the writing is so pedestrian, not to say repetitive. I wonder how important the words actually are in the writing of history? Indian history is so dramatic and full of such amazing people that to offer it to the public as a tame chronicle of events nicely balanced but sepia coloured throughout seems a pity. Better to be bitter and sometimes wrong like Trevor-Roper surely. Anyway I'm tapping on with my own bitter offering and have got about half way through the first section and enjoying it very much now I've really got started. I even dream Mughals at night so it must have seeped right into my subconscious. It's certainly a wonderful way of passing time, the days go whirling past and I'm practically unconscious of what is going on elsewhere – though thank goodness the border situation seems to be better .... By the way before I forget, I got a letter from Blackwell and my debit of 13/9 had turned to a credit of 5/- Is this your doing? Thank you very much if it is… I will send a cheque towards the H.P. in my next, do say if you are running into financial difficulties at all.

The meeting with Keith I referred to on 27th April with Keith was held on 8th May. I have some notes in preparation.

K.V.T. — to ask. 8/5/65.

[illegible] talk: [illegible]
[illegible] extracts [illegible]

Archdeaconry cases — could [illegible] allright?

[illegible] [illegible] courts: jury or judge decides?
Assizes: — process?
(LA [illegible])

Archdeaconry map.

check — '450' individuals
— mudding individuals
with cases, — prob
nearer 300
individuals.

what about all the cases where
a witch almost certainly comes
up — but no actual charge of w.

1. village. area. in depth: Hatfield Peverel.

Book of KVT

write [illegible] have a.
Extant visitation articles.
S.T.C. [illegible] — Church of England
visitation articles.
10198 — see

S.T.C. — after 1640. (Wing)
— interleaved in Bodley,
kept at desk in upper
Reading Room.

1662, 1667, 1680.

1716 — Norwich
1704 — Dent. Jean of York } still asking.

— see Laudian articles &
theory of T. Davies [illegible]

George Herbert: A Priest
to the Temple.

1604. canons.

Funeral sermons on nobility } hospitality
Visitation articles.
Literature about ministers.

— send refs re extracting
information.

E.G.R. Taylor — see
The Mathematical Practitioners
in C16 & C17 Eng.
— see biographies of
them — whether any
astrologers in Essex.

— see "Father" (Father [illegible])

John Gaule's — religion.

W.A. Bewes.
Church Briefs.
Fire of London caused by
Catholics.

The next letter to my parents is postmarked Oxford 10th May and on Worcester College paper

Dear Mummy and Daddy,

I'm nearly back into my old Sunday routine & consequently, since your letters usually arrive on Wednesday, there isn't one to thank you for. I hope all goes well - you must almost be beginning to think about starting to prepare to come home! How much junk have you accumulated & will you have to abandon any? In a selfish way, I hope you will be able to bring all the books you have, to add to the

Field Head 'library' - otherwise, I suppose, you could give them to some university or something. I wonder how the writing goes - it must get increasingly difficult as the days grow hotter.

Granny's 'grand tour' seems to have gone well - as you've probably heard - and Robert seems happy about the reception of Gallipoli. I had lunch with him yesterday - at the 'Turf' pub (you remember the one? - down a narrow alley-way where we had lunch outside once, under a sun-shade). He is very well & not looking as tired as usual. He is thinking seriously in terms of renting a house in Oxford & seems interested in the idea of letting G & G stay at Dale Cottage - for a minimal rent (perhaps contributed by assembled relatives) to pay the rates. He is going to talk this over with Richard next week & will presumably get in touch with you. Apparently the Crowborough venture was unsuccessful.

Oxford is looking exquisite at the moment - I can't remember seeing it look more lovely. The trees, startling in their young green half hide the medieval stone and the Banbury & Woodstock roads are rivers of pink and white foam-blossom. The evenings are full of strange, disturbing, scents "mixing memory with desire" and the wall-flowers are especially strong. Like butterflies, girls in summer dresses have emerged in scores and the willows caress the face of the river. Rupert Brooke, Matthew Arnold and Keats are the men of the moment! I have no particularly ecstatic love-affair 'on' at the present - but still see Zoë and Linda. The former is, naturally, immersed in her work, and hasn't much time to think about, for instance, how she is going to get to India. I wish I could help - or even go myself - but can't think of any bright ideas. She only has 3 months at the most, and not too much money, so can't afford to work on the way. If you know of any rich family needing a nanny or something on the boat out ... but then there's Annie also.

It's Monday, and no W.E.A , a very pleasant feeling. I'm still doing a fair amount of talking - tomorrow to a Graduate seminar, on Friday last to Balliol. The latter went fairly well I think, at least they asked penetrating questions for 1 and a half hours. The next day I went to see my supervisor, Keith, who seemed happy with the way things are progressing. As he said, our interests are so identical that he could write my thesis and I could his book! He really is a very exciting person to be in contact with; I am extremely fortunate. I let myself get a little over-tired last week - consequently depressed, but intend to relax a little more now. Keith agreed that writing-up the thesis at a croft in Scotland might well be a good idea, so I really may start hunting this summer. The draw-backs are (a) I don't know if I could stand the loneliness (& the darkness) (b) One has to be in Oxford during the terms, if not for the books, then to keep in touch with 'important' people. Keith didn't think a D.Phil. in social anthropology such a good idea, but we'll see about that.

Sorry this is a grossly self-absorbed letter, but I think of you. Fondest love to you both, Alan

My mother wrote to me from Cherideo on 12th May

Thank you for your letter, I was very impressed with your lecturing the Balliol history society, was Christopher Hill there? I do hope it goes off well. I had a long letter describing Grannys grand tour but haven't seen any reviews of Roberts book yet. Granny said there was a hopeful house in Crowborough but Richard didn't know if he could afford it though I should have thought a building society would have done most of the paying to start with. I would like to see them settled before the winter. Granny mentioned having lost that green blanket, thin thing, it should be with you because we brought it down when we last came and left it by mistake. I'll replace it if it has disappeared though.

I have churned out the first section of my book, I can't think how I could have written 20,000 odd words so quickly, it must be very bad but I shall send it home to my agent anyway. I was cheered by getting a letter from "History Today"[1] *saying they will take my article, Alan Hodge wrote this time and said it was excellent and that both of them had greatly enjoyed reading it. I must say they are charming people, even if somewhat vague – they say it will come out in the autumn but perhaps they*

[1] Iris Macfarlane, 'The Emperor Babur and Vasco da Gama, *History Today*, vol. xv, nos. 8, August 1965

mean next. It will nearly pay my train fare to Delhi which eases my conscience. I'm reading "Louis XIVth" by Vincent Cronin which is much boosted and a book society choice but I can't think why, it is very feebly written, Tawney has spoilt me I'm afraid and E.M. Forster who I'm reading for about the tenth time.

We had Peter Sehmer for the day on Sunday and I went to the service, a new padre and jolly, he is a keen mountaineer I believe; his sermon on the problem of suffering was not very inspired, in a country like India to have cliches about God's good time delivered in bright tones is irritating. Still one has to admit that it is Christians who do most about Indias suffering, even if they have odd ideas about its use. The break through in contraception isn't a pill, its called an intra uterine device and is fitted permanently by a doctor and removed when a child is wanted. The pill doesn't really suit the coolie mentality, one would have to hand them out daily and see them swallowed. ...

Thank you very much for sending the books for the minister and the one for me too, please count these as my birthday present. I read a review of "The crisis of India" in which he is said to advocate a form of communism, certainly one feels that anything would be better than the terrible resignation with which most of the people accept their hopeless lot, as Xavier said "I never cease wondering at the number of new inflections which, in addition to all the usual forms, have been added in this language to the ill-omened verb "to rob". The latest from here is the surrounding and imprisoning of the Vice Chancellor of Gauhati University, Dr Taylor, for six hours because he wouldn't alter the date of the M.A. examination! ... Have you started to write your thesis yet? I wonder if you found the answer to any of the questions you were asking. ... Any news of Roy and Rosemary?

My next letter was on 17th May from 38, Park Town, Oxford

Dear Mummy and Daddy,

Thank you very much for your letter. I'm glad the book has got started & is going well. Yes, I also find that when I'm writing I get absorbed and don't want to think about anything else. I don't want to sound patronizing, but I wouldn't worry about being 'trivial' or not having 'scholarship'. etc. I'm certain that good writing and imagination and sympathy are much more important. The people one reads are people like Tawney and Macaulay who write with vigour and confidence, firing their ideas with strong emotion. Of course, one has to avoid purple passages etc. but the tedious stuff that one has to churn out for theses is very far from readable. The tendency of small, finickity minds to reduce the tremendous personalities & movements of the past to their own dimensions, for instance turning the majestic struggles of the C17 to petty & sordid squabbles is all too evident. I myself, of course, have fallen into this way of thinking; obsessed with being objective and getting things right one abstains from generalisations, metaphors, comparisons and value judgements; carefully weighing each word to see if it has an ounce of emotion in it. Perhaps it's a good training but god forbid that one should bore the general public with it. Here endeth the peroration! The gist is, anyhow, have confidence; you can write better than 99% of the people here and have a curiosity and sympathy with the past which is almost absent among professional historians. It seems to me extraordinary that when one has the whole range of the human past - man's dreams, attitudes, nightmares, family life, attempts to control his environment by magic & religion etc. that nearly all history should be about a) the one and a half per cent of the population at the top of society b) about one narrow sector of their lives - either political action or now, to a certain extent, economic. Nor is there much awareness of the interrelationships between fields of human activity - between sex and economics, religion and the social system between myths and political actions, between kinship and religious ritual etc. This is the real value I find in reading anthropology. It deals with man in his totality and treats him as far more complex than historians do. I hope, of course to develope all this one day. For the next group I talk to I want to take one such topic - the relationship between magical belief and the economic/social environment. Incidentally this will bring in a good amount of folk-lore which no doubt you would find very similar to Indian mythology - about monsters, strange animals etc. There is a vast field for you to work on when you return to England!

No, I didn't put any money into your Blackwell's account. Perhaps it was just the book being returned.

Linda is well (& incidentally reading Verrier Elwyn 'Tribal Worlds' which her mother recommended her: I think I'll have to buy a copy it looks so relevant to my present thoughts). Zoë I still see, tho' we are now merely 'friends' I think.

I am going as bursar on a Borstal camp this summer - on the understanding that I will be allowed to do some reading as well. I went for a walk with the Governor of the Borstal (Eventhorpe, Yorks) on Saturday & he was a really first-class person & very amusing & tolerant & 'liberal'. Possibly another Elwyn? My friend Ralph who is commandant of the camp had me to dinner at the High Table of St Peter's College on Monday & on Tuesday I dined at High Table at Worcester. The society life is thickening! I have parties of Christopher Hill & Robert next week, not to mention fellows of Nuffield [Brian Harrison] *coming to supper etc. I'm not working so hard now (as I was getting a little over-tired) and have been for some delightful walks. I've never known Oxford so enchanting. We've had a heat wave and the evenings have been almost unbearably beautiful. On Friday, for instance, I went out to dinner at a C17 manor house north of Oxford where a friend (Euan) lives. Set on the river Glum* [Glyme] *in a wooded valley with cuckoos and doves it is a magical place - full of secret gardens, old court-yards and strange scents. A combination of the castle in 'I capture the Castle' and the landscape Powys describes in Love & Death. If one was going to meet an elf or Dittany Stone it would be there.*

I am off to Essex next week-end for a few days so forgive any delay in my letter.

Much love to you both, Alan

As my research progressed and I became increasingly excited by the combination of anthropological questions and newly discovered primary resources, in particular the ecclesiastical court records, I began to write to other researchers, both those of my generation in Oxford, and senior historians, asking them questions and firing off some theories. This developed more extensively after I left Oxford for the Lake District. With each of those to whom I wrote I would continue the conversation, but here I shall just reproduce the letters of that summer term.

Joan Thirsk

Joan was born in 1922, so she was the same age as my mother – thus about 43 when I met her. She was teaching in the Department of English Local History at Leicester, and later I knew her as the Reader in Economic History at Oxford. She was a wide-ranging regional historian, open to new sociological ideas, and a considerable inspiration and support. I had been to her on 19 May, when she had spoken at W.G. Hoskins' seminar on 'Sociology and History', and I wrote to her in some excitement the next day.

Dear Mrs. Thirsk,

As you are aware I found your talk in Dr. Hoskins' seminar most stimulating. As a pupil of Keith Thomas I am, of course, already a convert to the gospel of sociology/social anthropology. I have found in my own research into witchcraft that anthropological studies are far more rewarding than those by historians & my first reading of The Institutions of Primitive Society & the works of Williams, Homans and Arensberg in the last few months have added another dimension to my historical thinking. Above all I was excited by the idea of the interrelationships of phenomena, the study of the total social unit. As Mauss points out in his illuminating study of The Gift (London, 1954) "It is only by considering them (i.e. socieites) as wholes that we have been able to see their essence, their operation and their living aspect, and to catch the fleeting moment when the society and its members take emotional stock of themselves … Nothing in our opinion is more urgent or promising than reerach into 'total' social phenomena." (p.77-8). I can still remember my excitement when I realised that the organization of the church – for instance the actual lay-out of the seating – was closely interrelated with the economic structure of the village. Hence seating (should – does it?) differs depending on whether the village is enclosed or not etc. Recently I have been analysing the relationship between the concept of 'neighbourliness' – so important as Williams, Arensberg & others show – and witchcraft accusations. It seems certain that witchcraft beliefs were intimaely bound up with the ideal of 'friendship' and the attacks on that ideal by the various individualizing forces of he C16-C17. If you are, or become interested in this subject I would be delighted to send you the paper.

I hope you will forgive me if I make two very general addenda to your talk. The first is obvious; that by broadening economic history to take in all aspects of human activity one is not destroying the discipline but merely suggesting that it should be applied more widely, but more thinly. This is put badly, what I mean is that instead of thinking that one can completely answer certain questions – for instance the growth of population, or changes in prices – economic hisorians can make a partial contribution to a much wider range of subjects – for instance C. Hill has shown what can be done from the economic angle as regards the Church and no doubt one could contribute to studies of artistic, intellectual & certain largely untouched regions of social history (for instance marriage – as Professor Habakkuk has done) as well. Work along the lines of Homans (relating the agricultural and ecclesiastical calendar) and Thomas (relating concepts of leisure, labour and time to systems of production) is immensely stimulating. The new professors who ask for a break-up of the old specialization are hence not abdicating their power completely; by allowing others into their own field they break out themselves.

The second point seems to me to be the major draw-back of the 'sociological method' and it is a further reason for the impressionistic quality of such work (which I developed a little in my version of your talk). This is that sociologists/social anthropologists do not deal with their interrelationships over time. They can provide a functional analysis of how, for instance, a Melanesian society links its myths, economic system & religious organization but it looks at this statically. After a series of lectures on 'Social change in Small-scale Societies' by Dr. Beattie the anthropologist I was little enlightened on these problems. One can see how a belief such as magic or witchcraft, or an institution such as the Catholic Church worked at a moment in time. But when one relates various strands into a complex web of interacting forces it becomes all the more, rather than less, difficult to explain change. At least this is what I find. I wondered if you came across this difficulty & whether you know of anything in print which is helpful on this problem?

Having wasted your precious time for long enough I had better return to the ostensible subject of this letter! Could you plese jot down the cross-references which I have numbered at the end of the talk, and if you have the time, the correct quotation which I was unable to write down? Incidentally, if I have misrepresented you radically don't hesitate to put question marks etc. Of necessity the transcription was over-simplified.

I will be writing to Dr. Everitt shortly & will perhaps visit Leicester in the summer to look for witchcraft cases.

Finally, you mentioned that you benefitted from a year's teaching sociology. At the moment I am searching vaguely for just such an opportunity. I hope to do a Diploma in social anthyropology & had thought of London or Cambridge. If you do happen to know of any fund or course open to impoverished D.Phil. historians I would be most interested to hear about it.

Once again forgive me for taking up your time and thank you for the talk.

Yours sincerely,

P.S. Could you return my copy of the talk; I forgot to take a carbon.

To this I received this very full and helpful reply the following month.

45 Meadway, London, N.W.11.

Department of English Local History
UNIVERSITY OF LEICESTER
PROFESSOR H. P. R. FINBERG, M.A., D.LITT., F.S.A., F.R.HIST.S.
Telephone: Leicester 50000

29 June, 1965

Dear Mr Macfarlane,

Thank you very much for your very kind letter. Please accept my apologies for being so slow in replying to it. I have been trying to be an efficient secretary and organizer of the Past and Present conference, but my correspondence has suffered accordingly.

I have begun to get extremely interested in witchcraft so I shall be most interested to see anything you write on the subject. I learned from one of my students at Leicester that there is a certain amount of material about witchcraft in the parish chest at Scunthorpe, Lincs. Apparently one of the parsons put it together, but I am not quite certain whether it relates at all to the seventeenth century- probably only the eighteenth. However, I got the student to write down his information together with the address of the present incumbent so that if you ever find yourself extending the subject outside Essex you can make use of it.

Yes, I do not think one is weakening the argument for economic history as a discipline by broadening one's interests and taking in other fields of history. It looks as though some economic questions will never be satisfactorily answered unless we do so. And in any case, I believe in the unity of history, and in practice most other historians appear to do so, even though we all wear a label which suggests otherwise.

I agree with you entirely about the drawbacks of the sociological method which ignores changes over time. That is why I think that in the end it may be the historians who will best exploit the sociological method! However, there are sociologists who see the errors of their ways, and as an increasing number of sociologists and historians are changing places with one another at the moment, I would not be at all surprised to see a new theory of sociology being built up, or rather the present one modified once again. After all, the discipline, like anthropology, is undergoing change all the time.

I do not think it is possible to explain the causes of change without surveying the subject over a fairly long period, but even then one may not get very far, however accomplished an historian one may be, if one examines one society only. Surely this is where it becomes necessary to combine the sociological (i.e. functional) and historical methods and add yet a third-the comparative method. By comparisons one has a much better chance still at getting at the causes of change. Do read Marc Bloch's essay on Comparative History in his Melanges Historiques, vol. 1. He produces various examples of his own. I do not think I would have seen any order in the chaos of English rural communities if I had not had enough examples to enable me to compare. In short, I do not think you should be studying ~~withx~~ witchcraft in Essex, which is a fairly homogeneous county agriculturally speaking, but witchcraft in Essex, Leicestershire, Norfolk, and perhaps Westmorland!

I don't know any sources offhand of money for a diploma in Social Anthropology, butw would you care to write to Professor Raymond Firth at L.S.E., tell him your problem, and tell him that I have suggested that you write to him. He is a good friend of mine and has opened up the world of social anthropology for me. He is very keen that economic historians and social anthropologists should fraternize, and would help you, I am sure, if he could.

Sorry about the awful typing!

I am now going to go through your notes of my paper and will add comments and references where necessary.

With good wishes,

Yours sincerely,

Joan Thirsk

Joan Thirsk had taken the trouble to annotate my notes carefully and add footnotes.

My mother wrote to me from Cherideo on 21st May

I'm afraid this is a couple of days late, I got in a muddle and then couldn't get any forms. ... This cyclone in Pakistan is ghastly, it seems to happen so often and nobody ever seems to give warning, perhaps it will take Ayub Khans mind off invasion but the cost is rather high.[1] *The world seems in a more than usual muddle at the moment but one goes on hammering at ones typewriter and hoping for the best. I am getting through my work and think I will be finished in time to send it home with John Finney in about ten days' time and then will have to wait till I can get to another library again which won't be till I get home I suppose.*

It would be an excellent thing if Robert bought a house in Oxford for us to lodge in, I had a letter from Richard though saying he was definitely going to buy G & G a house so had better leave it to them to work out. I haven't seen a sign of Gallipoli but only see the Telegraph and I expect a sheaf of press cutting are on their way out. Richard said he thought Robert rather went out of his way to show up Morehead but otherwise it was very good. I wish I could help over Zoe but apart from keeping my eyes open for anyone wanting help on the voyage can't really suggest anything either, it's not really the right time of year for voyages and anyway I do wonder if she has the faintest idea of what trying to live in India on a shoestring with the hot weather to cope with as well would be like? There is nothing except a YWCA offering possible accomodation and they're usually booked up, I feel she would be better advised to wait until she could get a job and stay longer. I know she probably feels she could rough it but in an Indian city that would mean dysentery or worse.

Very little news as usual, I have been writing a bit and teaching a bit and walking through the sopping leech-ridden tea and haven't seen anyone. … we are picturing arriving in mid Jan with Granny having removed all the carpets and beds, luckily theres your sleeping bag which we shall have to crawl in in turn… How is Rosemary and Roy? (My grammar gets worse the more I write, I sometimes find myself unable to string together a logical sentence). If you retired to a croft to write your thesis you would have to take Poochie with you, and we would pop up at weekends, and as it would be

---

[1] Pakistan cyclone and build up to war.

the summer there wouldn't be much darkness anyway – I rather fancy the idea of writing my own book there too so altogether it would be better to stay at Field Head on your own and let us live on the croft! I keep trying to imagine the sort of life we will live, permanently on leave, it'll be very strange and take a lot of adjusting oneself to. Did Anne tell you she met Penny? Looking rather washed out she said, but going to Courtauld in the autumn, dear Penny, she was so vulnerable one felt.

I had sent Keith the piece I was giving as a talk on 'witchcraft & neighbourliness', as he wrote to me on Sunday May 23rd.

Dear Alan,

Many thanks for the enclosed, which I enjoyed reading. As always the main difficulty is the chronological one – why did it start and why did it stop? I think your approach <u>does</u> permit of an answer to these questions, especially to the second one, since informal accusations of witchcraft did after all continue to be made in country villages long after the law had ceased to pay any attention to them, and it was presumably in such villages that the ideals of neighbourliness survived longest. But the analysis on p.3 does obviously need a bit of tightening if it is going to satisfy objections of the kind made in the Dervorguilla. Of course the advantage of the detailed approach to the village you are eventually contemplating is that it would enable you to do just that.

Perhaps we could reserve detailed points (not that I have many) till we meet next? Meanwhile I'm glad to see things are going so well. Don't overwork. Let me know whenever you'd like a session (tho' I'll be away between roughly 20 May and 2 June.
Yrs Keith

My next letter was on 25 May, from 'A coffee bar in Hampstead'

Dear Mummy and Daddy,

Thank you very much for your letter. To answer your queries etc. first. As for the green blanket that also is a mystery - I must have lost it as I never remember seeing it. Sorry! Let me contribute towards another one. <u>Congratulations</u> on getting another article into <u>History Today</u> - I'm so glad. I tell everyone that you are going to be a great writer and this is the start. I intend to show your last article to Trevor-Roper some time. He gave me an autographed copy of one of his articles the other day and I said I'd send it out to you as you were an 'admirer' of his (I didn't say of his style) & he positively glowed. The article mentions Roe twice & I think he'd like your article (esp. the style). As I've said before, personally he's a very sweet man. As you'll gather my social life continues apace. I went to a party given by Christopher Hill on Thursday - for a visiting professor. It was rather enjoyable, and I even had an (no doubt drink-induced) offer from the editor of the leading historical journal (<u>Past & Present</u>) for an article. We agreed vaguely that when my research was a little further on something might emerge. On Friday afternoon Robert gave a party - 'champers my dear' - where the guests varied, me & his undergraduates to Sir Isaiah Berlin the political philosopher. He looked very well - so did Angela. I'm hoping to dump my books in his room when I leave in the summer - but he doesn't know about this yet! Finally, after Robert's party my '70-hours-work-a-week' friend [Brian Harrison] at Nuffield came to supper. He's very nice - though terribly tensed-up. He doesn't seem to have suffered from food-poisoning which is lucky as the frustration would have driven him mad!

As you'll gather from the heading, I'm off on my wanderings again. I decided I needed to look at some Essex records before I forgot how the writing works. I may take in Cambridge & the British Museum also. But have to be back in Oxford by Friday. I am seeing Jane Wilkinson today (you know - the one who lives in Hawkshead) and may see Penny on Thursday. I don't know if I'll get to see Anne this time. I ought to look up Roy & Rosemary too ... oh dear. My love life blossoms. Linda & Zoë still hold the centre of the stage but I had letters from both Penny & Dorothy on the same day last week saying they would like to see me / be in England soon (from Holland), respectively. Only yesterday the lists were lengthened by a girl called Isley - Lady Clay's niece. Very beautiful with big eyes & dark hair & very "arte nouveau" - goes around in purple & black lace & worships the Oscar Wilde / Rackham/ Beardsley generation. But she also works for £4 a week amongst spastics so isn't 'too too'. She's very like Fiona in temperament - quick tempered, warm and generous-hearted, artistic generally. I expect it's summer. The place, as I've said before, is magical at the moment. I picked some periwinkles for her hair. Next week is 'Eights Week', Oxford's most exciting time: college plays in the gardens etc.

Excuse this drivel but it was written against a background of a rather interesting conversation.

Much love to you both, Alan

*

There are numerous allusions to the influence of W.G. Hoskins in my letters. With his opening up of local history and study of Wigston Magna, he was a great inspiration. I attended his lectures and a seminar he ran on local history in All Souls. There is not much correspondence between us, and that of a cursory nature, but I shall just include the first of the four notes I had from him.

25 May '65

ALL SOULS COLLEGE,
OXFORD.

Thank you for yr card. I'm glad you liked the talk. When I return to Exeter, I'll see if I can find the script of my BBC talk on <u>Work & Leisure</u>. It was never published but I think I can find a copy in a few days' time.

I'm not sure I can find the York epitaph again, but I'll try.

W.G.H

My mother wrote to me from Cherideo on 28th May

Thank you for your letter in the coffee bar at Hampstead, I hope the tour was a success and you saw Penny... I am thrilled at the thought of having T. Ropers autograph, I <u>am</u> a great fan, I don't know enough to criticize the content of his work but his style is sooper – though I can hardly believe he really glowed at the thought of having a distant middle aged planters wife as his disciple! The proof of my article has come and gone, very quick so maybe they will publish it soon and I shall get the money. Another bill from Blackwells this time for 8/7 – I wonder if you could talk to them about all this sometime when you're in. ...

When one wipes the sweat from one's eyes and looks round it is to be dazzled by the beauty of the flowering trees which are a riot of scarlet of gold, and all the villages are floating in pools of pale purple water hyacinths. Seeing it all for the last time is breaking my heart, but I think I keep the sneaking hope that it won't be the last time, that I shall make masses of money out of my book and somebody will give me a vast great research grant to come back to India. This in fact would be impossible unless I learnt Persian – actually I have been thinking quite seriously of trying to do this – I wonder how difficult it is. I am more and more coming round to your idea that history is written in crop statistics and legal records and revenue assessment and not in travellers' tales or junketings at court, though it's a good deal easier in India to discover how people lived and what they thought about because they're living and thinking to a large extent in the same way now. I'm terribly impressed with the world you're moving in, Isaiah Berlin and Co., trust Robert too.

1965 - June

I wrote again to Keith Thomas on 5th June.

Dear Mr. Thomas,

I enclose a talk I gave to Trevor-Roper's seminar; (magic in C16 & C17); I expect it will all be familiar to you. My last impressionistic canter before I settle down to writing up the Essex material? I hope to start writing on the Quarter Sessions next week; this will be a model for the presentation of material from the different sources (which will be the first half of the thesis).

I spent a week in Essex & have finished the Archdeaconry Act Books – so the rough statistics I sent you on the Essex cases remain unaltered (I didn't find any more cases). I am even more convinced that a detailed study of a couple of villages will be very valuable; the archdeaconry records are very illuminating on this.

My main problems at the moment are 1) whether to write the thesis in Oxford, or to retire to a less hectic base 2) when to switch over to social anthropology – whether to do a Diploma before or after my thesis. {Perhaps I will consult the Oracle, E-P.

I wonder if we could meet sometime? Any time Saturday (12th) would suit me – or most days the following week. I hope your writing goes well.

Yours sincerely, Alan Macfarlane

My mother wrote from Cherideo on 7th June

Thank you for yours, I hope the lecture went off well also the visit to the authoress [K.M. Briggs], *neither of whose books I've read I fear. There has been a correspondence in the Telegraph about witchcraft, have been daily expecting you to appear, I missed the original article by Robert Graves which started it in which he apparently put forward the theory of it being an ancient cult – and was shot down by a lady called Rosemary Harris and someone else. I read a letter yesterday which was so pompous and longwinded I was about to give up when I saw it was from Robert! I hope that isn't the effect All Souls is having on his style. I know how you feel about knowing less and less, can you imagine how little you're going to know when you're my age?! Just about everything I put on paper is a generalisation that could be immediately contradicted, Indian history is particularly evasive as the British found to their cost when they tried to pin down the land revenue system, they sent questionnaires round and found that the land belonged to the king and also to the peasant and in a sense to the landlords and yet to neither and still most definitely to all. This flexibility was of course the strength of the indigenous system but maddened the earnest improvers and they busily set about straightening and destroying, how sad that anthropology was still a closed subject then. I shall love to help with your archdeaconry records, I am longing to get to original sources, I am sick of other people's interpretations of facts, particularly as they differ so widely and one just has to pick the one that suits one's own theories. It would be interesting to compare the village life of India and England in the 17th century and might help with answering the eternal question of what went wrong here…*

I'm sorry you and Penny have drifted apart, what you say about schools being more important than pictures is true – but what are schools for except to teach us to enjoy pictures and such? It is very difficult to get ones priorities right, I get maddened here by all the money that is apparently "wasted" on cultural shows and literary symposiums and such and yet the spirit must be fed as much as the body – and think how poor India would be without the Taj and Europe without its wonderful wasteful cathedrals built from the money that should have kept people from starving. Beauty may not be truth – is anything truth? – but it is essential surely – what does seem wrong is that such huge sums should be able to circulate among a small section of the community for their private enjoyment and snobbery. …

I wonder when you are starting your job[1] , I hope it isn't because you're short of money, you must be naturally but do try and get a bit of a holiday as well. I sent £5 towards the HPO but please let us know if you want more. Haven't heard from Granny for a long time, I hope all is well... the book I sent home was the first section of my Mughals, the introductory fifty pages with a synopsis of the rest, I'm now about to embark on another childrens book which I will probably write up on the boat.

As described in the letters to my parents, in the middle of my time, I found myself uncertain as to whether to switch from history into anthropology. I wrote to Christopher Hill on 7th June.

Dear Mr. Hill,

I wonder if I might come and talk to you sometime? I am leaving for the Summer in two weeks & can manage most times before then – for instance any time this coming Thursday, Friday afternoon, or in the following week. My problem is what to do after my thesis. I am hoping to study social anthropology – while remaining based on historical material. I am going to see the pundits on this – Mr. Thomas & Evans-Pritchard – but would very much appreciate any advice you cared to offer since you, as a true disciple of Tawney, are more aware than most of the problems of being both a scholar & a human being. Not all the academics I know can be recommended for their sensitivity to social need and suffering.

Incidentally, I think you might rather like this: On 8 August 1594 at the Essex Assizes Peter Francys of Hatfield Peverel labourer was charged that on '18 July, at Ulting said in public "corne wilbe deare and rather then I will storve I wilbe one of them that shall rise and gather a companie of eight skore or nyne skore toguither and will go and fetche yt owt wher yt is to be had I can bringe them wher corne inoughe is to be had and yf wee were such a companie gathered toguither who cann withstand us". Someone said "What can poore men do against riche men". Peter answered "What can riche men do against poore men yf poore men rise and hold toguither. Acknowledges."' Yours sincerely,

He replied the following day suggesting a meeting.

[1] The job was acting as Bursar on the Borstal camp.

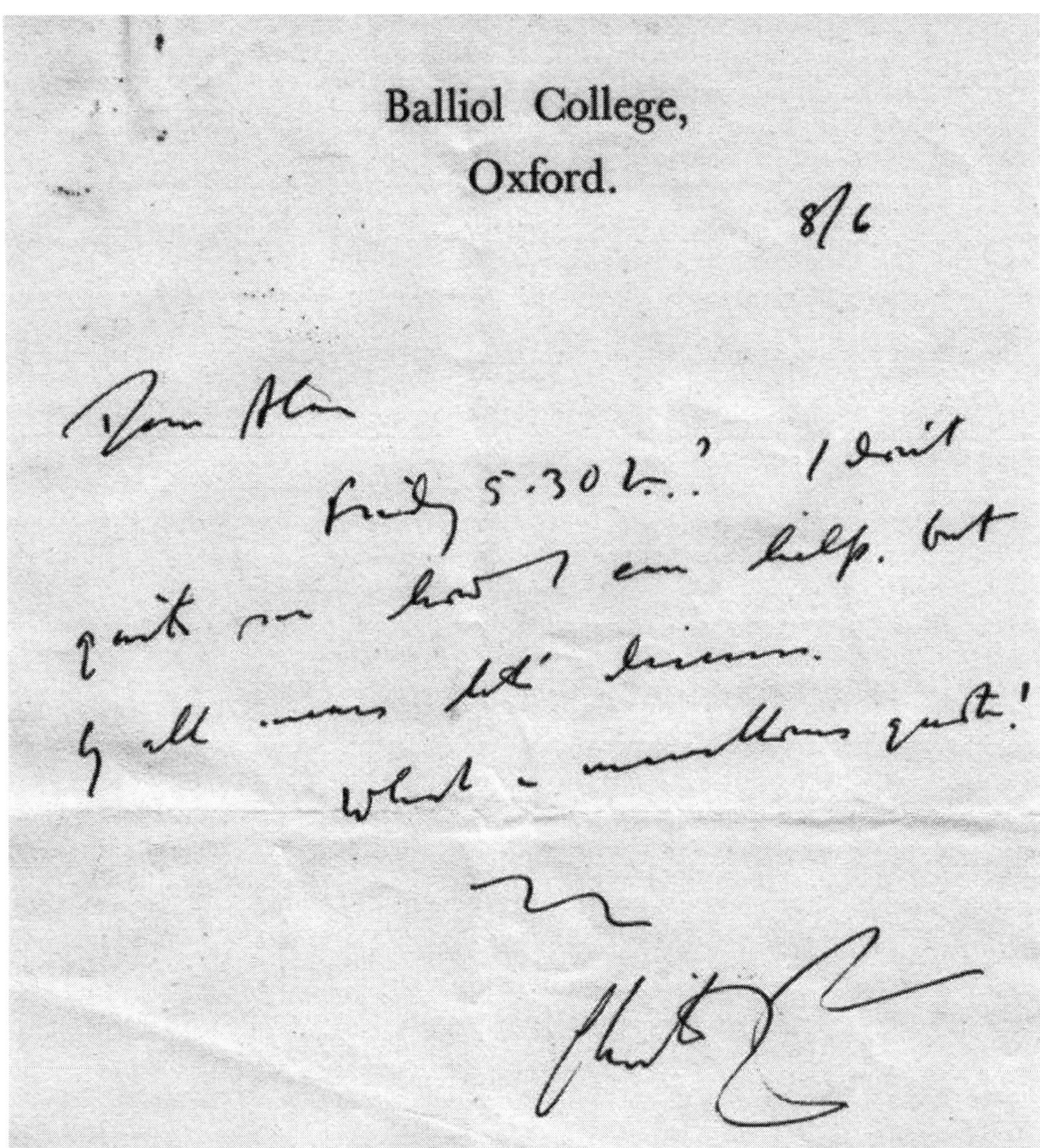

Balliol College,
Oxford.

8/6

Dear Alan

Friday 5.30 p.m.? I don't quite see how I can help, but by all means let's discuss.

What a marvellous quote!

Yrs

Christopher

[*Dear Alan, Friday 5.30 p.m? I don't quite see how I can help, but by all means let's discuss. What a marvellous quote! Yrs, Christopher.*]

I remember that we sat on a wooden bench in Balliol College quadrangle and Christopher gave me sage advice about 'not changing horses in mid-stream' etc. and advised me to stick with history until the end of my D.Phil. and switch later – he also gave me advice on possibly working in Africa etc.

It looks as if I was unable to make this time, and I have the following note, whose wording rather shocked me, but I have always remembered.

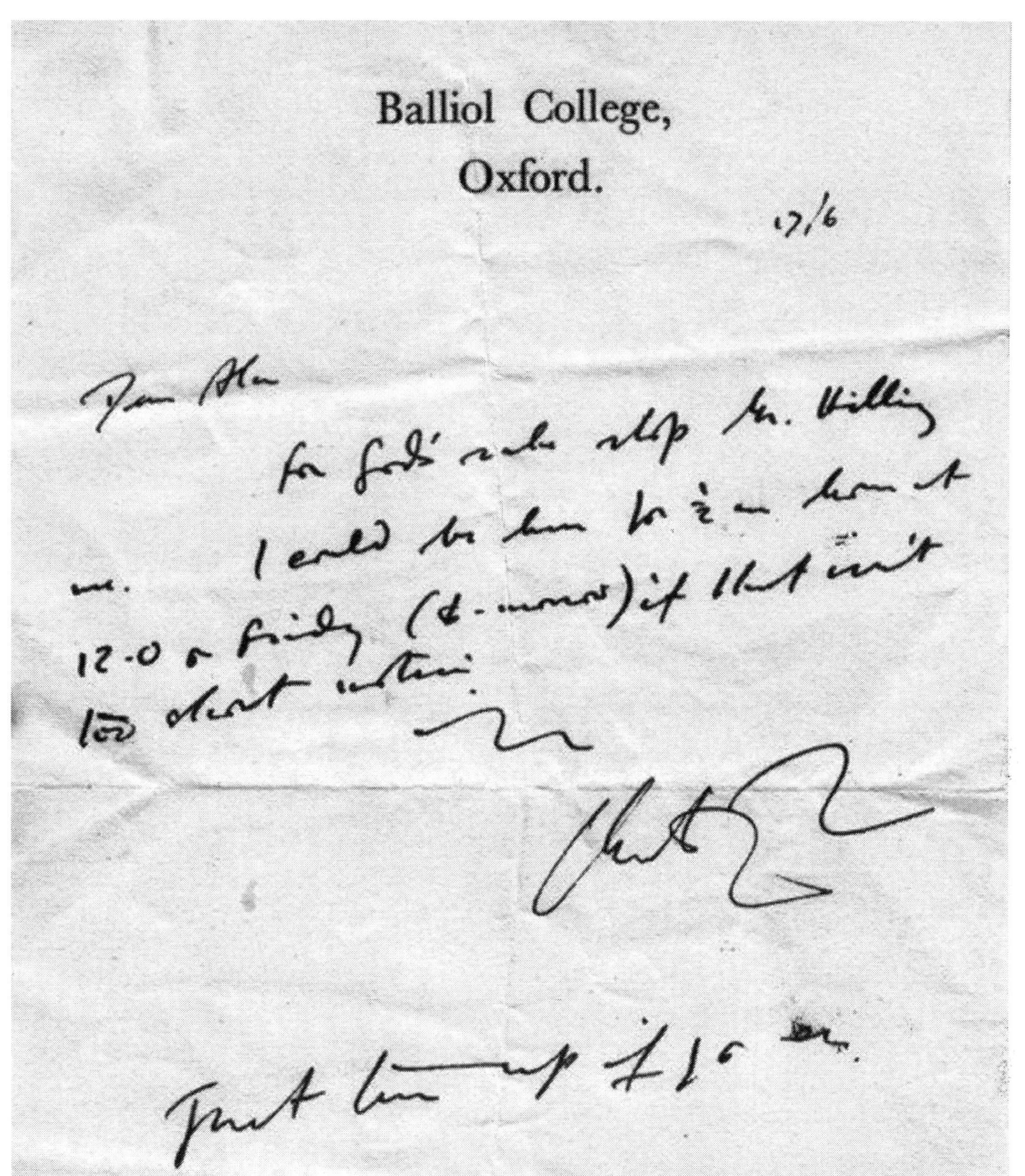

Balliol College,
Oxford.

17/6

[*Dear Alan, For God's sake stop Mr. Hilling me. I could be here for ½ an hour at 12.0 on Friday (to-morrow) if that isn't too short notice. Christopher. Just turn up if you can.*]

Edward Evans-Pritchard

As well as Christopher Hill, I decided to contact Professor Edward Evans-Pritchard about my future. I first encountered him when I started to go to lectures in the Institute of Anthropology in Oxford on the advice of Keith Thomas. By that time, 1964, E-P as he was known, was 62 and not very well – he died ten years later of, among other things, diabetes. I remember reading his various books, both on Azande witchcraft which greatly influenced my writing, and more generally on the nature and history of anthropology, as well as his works on Nuer kinship and religion from which I taught for many years. I remember him demonstrating the two types of causation in witchcraft with the story of the two spears that killed an animal among the Azande, as we stood sipping coffee in the Institute coffee room. And I remember being rather embarrassed when he invited me up to his room and asked me to sit near him on the sofa – until he explained he was very deaf.

As I became more interested in anthropology, and advised by Wendy James who was one of E-P's students, I sought E-P's advice. (Perhaps after the vividly remembered occasion when I helped E-P push start his car in the snow-filled car park on his way to give the famed lecture on 'History and Anthropology' at Manchester).

There are other memories – drinks at the Lamb and Flag over which he shocked me by telling me that my revered Verrier Elwin was a sex maniac and the inside gossip on the Oxford Professorship.

I wrote to Evans-Pritchard on 7th June.

Dear Professor Evans-Pritchard,

You kindly said that I might come and see you sometime and I hope to do this on Wednesday or Thursday morning if I may, if this is convenient. I had better remind you that I am doing a thesis on English witchcraft ("Witchcraft prosecutions in Essex, 1560-1680; a sociological analysis" under Mr. Keith Thomas. I have been working on this for some 18 months and have a little less than that time in which to submit it. Though my subject-matter is historical I have found that the problems and explanations of anthropologists are far more fruitful than those of historians such as Lecky, |Robbins, Lea et al.

I have become growingly interested in social anthropology in a more general way & increasingly convinced that, as you say in your Manchester lecture it will be a happy day "when a course of social anthropology, including some field research, is regarded as a valuable part of an historian's training". Consequently I had decided to do a Diploma and research degree <u>after</u> having completed my historical D.Phil. Wendy James with whom I discussed this matter suggested that my present thesis might be more valuable both to anthropologists and historians if I did the Diploma before I submitted it. She also pointed out the obvious fact that it will be difficult to find money for endless degrees. Do you feel that this would be advisable? Further, having done the Diploma would there be any chance of submitting the thesis as an anthropological one? I realise of course that, based as it is on purely documentary evidence this will rouse opposition.

But to quote you again "The fact that an anthropologist studies people at first-hand and the historian in documents is a technical, not a methodological difference." I am sure that the enormous bulk of evidence which I have (over 800 cases in Essex alone, cf. Nadel and Fortes' elaborate theories on the subject, in each case based on less than 15 observed cases) will partly make up for the impossibility of direct contact.

There is no need for me to stress the value of such a time study to anthropologists as a test of many of their synchronic laws. As Mrs. Wilson put it in 1951 "I long to read an adequate analysis of this problem (i.e. why witchcraft arose & declined in C16-C17 England) by some social historian aware of anthropological theory." The more training I have for this the better.

Of course I don't know whether the state would support me in another year's study, nor have I put this issue clearly to Mr. Thomas – though he did vaguely suggest, when I explained that I wanted to go on to do social anthropology – that I transferred to your faculty before I submitted. But I would very much appreciate your opinion & would feel better qualified to approach others after I had it. I think that the element of risk in the whole undertaking may well be a good sign; crossing borders is never easy.

I apologise for taking up some of your valuable time.

Yours sincerely,

At the bottom I made some notes in pen, which were clearly things I wanted to bring up in the meeting.

1. Check historical D.Phils in Institute.
2. Show graphs/maps etc.
   Questions
   (a) What point in changing before?
   (b) What chance of changing after?
   (c) Money?
   (d) India.

I had a swift reply the next day.

OXFORD UNIVERSITY

INSTITUTE OF SOCIAL ANTHROPOLOGY

Tel. 55971

11 KEBLE ROAD
OXFORD
8 June 1965.

Alan Macfarlane, Esq.,
Worcester College,
Oxford.

Dear Mr. Macfarlane,

Professor Evans-Pritchard has seen your letter of 7 June on his way to the station and he has asked me to tell you that he will be pleased to see you here to-morrow morning, 9 June, at 11 a.m. to discuss your plans. He cannot manage Thursday at that time as he has already an engagement at that time.

Yours sincerely,

Barbara Allany

Secretary.

My next letter to my parents was written on 12th June from Worcester College, Oxford

Dear Mummy and Daddy,

A delay in your weekly letters - so no questions to answer. I hope all goes well and the hot weather isn't too bad. I'm ploughing on with Verrier Elwin so will be living out with you in imagination at least. He seems an extraordinarily naive and innocent person, almost child-like and must have been extremely difficult for 'Government' to deal with. I do wish I could have met him. What has happened to NEFA now? Are there any anthropologists working among the tribes. I must say, more & more, reading about them, makes me attracted to the hill tribes. I wonder if there will be a chance of studying there by the time I've finished my thesis etc. - or whether the place will be a) changed beyond recognition b) under strict military control.

I ask the above with a reason. I have been having a soul-searching week talking to people & wondering about the next stage. I haven't seen the key man - Evans-Pritchard - but have talked to Christopher Hill and my supervisor. They all stress the difficulty of getting money to do a Diploma in Anthropology. Christopher was very kind and suggested that it might be possible to go to a university in Africa (or India) and teach history and at the same time do some anthropology. i.e. find a university where there was a good dept of social anthropology and do a diploma there. I wonder if there is anywhere where they'd want an English history teacher in India, where I could also do anthropology. The alternative - unless E-P is prepared to find the money or to allow me to change my thesis over before I do the D.Phil - is to finish my D.Phil and then live a garret-existence, writing & teaching to make ends meet, and doing a year's diploma before going out. In fact it would be only 9 months & if you let me live at Field Head during the vacations I wouldn't need to earn much. Anyway we'll see what happens. The present plan with your approval - is to move my base to the Lakes for the next year making occasional forays to Oxford, London & Essex to collect material, but for the most part to write there. It is made easier by the knowledge that you will both be back in the Spring since otherwise the Lakes are a little lonely.

I'm sending out a paperback of Macaulay's essays as a late part of Mummy's birthday present - you'll like the signature at the front.[1] *I've just been reading the essay on Warren Hastings. I expect you'll know it; fascinating and superb descriptions of the Indian character & law. Buying books is one of the many problems one has to face. Looking at the handsome, bound, collections of all the dons & of some of my friends I sometimes get restless! I suppose the trouble is that I buy expensive new books, whereas if I got them second-hand or off the 1/- stall I could build up a good collection much more easily. When you return - if you bring your books - we must put up some book-shelves (or possibly the APS will take theirs away) and start a proper library. The second-hand book-shops in the Lakes & Manchester should provide some cheap items & with a combined budget we might get some nice historico-anthropological fairy-books.*

Linda has disappeared to Majorca and I feel a little lonely in the evenings. After a year I would be a very hard-hearted monster if I wasn't more than a little attached to her! She wants to come to the Lakes, but I'd rather it was after you were back - if we're still going out - as Granny might react a little to her supposed "commonness". Zoë has finished exams as I said and is in the same position as I was. She is waiting to hear if she's got a state studentship. She will then do a year's course in sociology & then go to India. Perhaps we'll come out together? As you feared it looks as if the moment you step on to the English shore we'll all flee off to Assam! The croft-hunting I'll (probably) leave to Fiona. Next week (for 2 weeks) I'll probably go to London to check sources. By then I hope to have dispatched my massive luggage to Field Head...

Excuse this self-centred scrawl.

Fondest love to you both, Alan

I went for a meeting with Keith Thomas on 12th June. My notes in preparation for the meeting are as follows.

[1] Professor Hugh Trevor-Roper's signature.

12/6/65.

K.V.T.

1. Map of cunning men – check O.K.
2. Newbould – ref. (Eric Maple) – refs given to KVT?
   – looked up Timothy Crowther.
   – came across 'Salmon's' books?

---

3. Visitation Articles.
5. Ask re. civil courts Q/SR. – False/[illegible] to decode?
4. Hedingham – show where.

Returning to Lake – OK? – cf. Lancs witches (live in/record)

Social Anth: E-P: Hill-money.

Plan for thesis – general // + time (next vac') London/Essex.

Possible to get Ewen II. photostated? – cheaper?

Any criticisms of Devonshire talk? + T-R. talk.

How Assize to be calendared? – refer to E: I → o.k. (with maps interspersed)

My mother wrote to me from Cherideo on June 15th
[forwarded to c/o Miss A. Macfarlane, 27 Eardley Crescent, Earls Court, London, SW5]

Thank you for your letter, and also for a parcel of books which has just arrived, the English course and the Cowper Powys. All very welcome, I'm going to hie up to Shillong and show the minister of education the course and try to persuade them to adopt it, or something similar. I haven't yet started "Wolf Solent". I like to gloat over a new book for a week or two – you must let us help you with your Blackwells bill when you finally have to face the day of reckoning as you have spent an awful lot on me. I have read one of the Mughal books you mentioned and the other two sound as if they are along the usual lines, so I won't bother with them. I am more concerned with the European aspects of the period now, as the two are supposed to run parallel through the book until they finally collide. (Can aspects collide, this is the sort of sentence I'm forever struggling with, but I'm glad to note that other authors have the same trouble and don't bother to cope with it). I had three letters from Granny yesterday, maybe you are with her now, in which case tell her I'll be writing tomorrow.

I don't know what to suggest about your future because I'm not quite in the picture, if you have finished your research and still have another years grant couldn't you use it for your social anthropology course instead, and then you could write up your thesis next winter. Anyway your tutors will be able to advise you better, I do think anthropology would be an asset for the sort of work you hope to find, I saw an advertisement for work among the bushmen which would have suited you but it demanded anthropology – and out here the more qualifications the better. Verrier Elwin of course underplays the terrible loneliness one must feel living for years amongst a simple alien people, however attractive, and he was a saint anyway – but possibly you are too? An embryo one? It hasn't been a very nice week for me as I've been suffering from tummy trouble and it's been very hot and the combination depressing, specially as the tummy kept me awake at night However I'm much better to-day and able to face problems again. ... It would be interesting to study the structure of their [Naga] society but the language problem would be too much for me, my Assamese is so superficial... Do hope you found somewhere for your books, Robert didn't play obviously.

I wrote to Keith Thomas on 16th June on a Worcester College card.

Dear Mr Thomas,

Jut to assure you that I'll be carrying on as a straight historian for a little longer. E-P agreed that 'it was dangerous to change horses in mid-stream' but hinted at possible financial support (if your recommendation was forthcoming) for a Diploma after the thesis was finished. He wondered if you would ring him as you are working on magic etc.

My Quarter Sessions piece will have to be re-written in the Lakes after 3 weeks in London so I will be sending it in about a month.

I hope your work goes well this summer. We can perhaps meet in the middle of the vac'?

Thank you for all your advice and encouragement.

Yours sincerely, Alan Macfarlane

Paul Slack was one year behind me at Oxford and I remember vividly seeing him studying very hard in his final year as an undergraduate at a desk in the Old Bodleian. We became friends when he graduated and his choice of research subject for the D.Phil., disease and in particular plague, in the early modern period meant that we had much to talk about. He introduced me to the work of the demographic historians at Cambridge and we shared references and ideas. This team effort in graduate research, where several students informally keep a look-out for material for each other, is not as widely practised perhaps as it should be. But here is an excellent example.

Paul had given at a seminar run by a mutual friend, Robin Briggs. I missed the talk and asked Paul to let me see it. I made notes on it and then shared my thoughts with him.[1]

[1] By an extraordinary coincidence, Paul had digs for a year or more at 25, St Margaret's Road where I had spent the first half year after I returned to England in 1947.

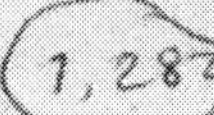

Epidemics in Some East Anglian Parishes 1538-1605. Paul Slack.

(Paper read to Briggs seminar. May '65)

(Sources for study. 138 parish registers 38 beginning 1538-40, and a further 57 1549-60)

1 The most obvious and general mortality-crises to emerge from an analysis of the parish registers of some 140 East Anglian parishes were those of 1558-9 and 1597-9. In the parish of St.Nicholas, Ipswich the total of deaths in 1556-9 was 45,35, and 33 in the years 1556-9 totals paralleled only in the 1603-4 plague. ....In the country parish of Dalham 34 people died in the years 1558 & 9 almost 16% of the population as estimated from the 1603 count of communicants. Even the 1605 plague did not approach this total. The late 1590's saw similar crises. Boxford and All Saints, Sudbury, in the years 1597-8 had mortality rates unparalleled in the period under consideration, and both show high death rates throughout the decade 1595-1605. The cause of these crises seems to have been famine - shown in the exceptionally high prices in Phelps Brown and Hopkins' price index - and epidemic disease following in its wake. 1556 and 1596 are the great years of dearth in Hoskins analysis of harvests.

.....There were differences in incidence, few parishes reaching the 16% loss of Dalham, and 5-10% being perhaps the normal, or three times the usual mortality rate at most. North, Central and Western Essex were similarly hit, Saffron Walden losing 175, a mortality three times the average, and double that of any other epidemic year except 1598. But the souther parish of Great Warley shows no sign of the famine or epidemic, and in the South East coastal area Bradwell-on-Sea and North Fambridge seem to have evaded catastrophe. The reasons for this are not clear - was population in this area sparse, or did grain supplies come from across the Channel? At Chigwell too, in the South West, the mortality rate was little more than average, though a concentration of deaths in November and December with 2 from the family of Fuller in November, suggests an epidemic.

In Norfolk, of the few parishes considered, only West Rainham escaped entirely.......

2. The high mortality of 1597-8 was not quite so general. ....The 7 Norwich parishes considered escaped completely. ....In Essex the 1597 crisis was more general, affecting Tillingham on the East coast as well as Chigwell in the West, Saffron Walden in the North, as well as Great Warley in the South. But the Norfolk...

3. The third great epidemic common to most areas of East Anglia was the plague of 1603-6, varying in date of incidence from area to area, and sometimes parish to parish. Again the variations in incidence are difficult to account for, perhaps being basically due to local differences in temperature and humidity which affected the plague flea. ......Only 100 communicants are given to St.Giles in the return of 1603 (i.e.Norwich AM), a figure which suggests that the mortaltiy was catastrophic in that year. .....It is possible that 1601 and 1602 with high death rates in many parishes in East Anglia - often with a peak in the Spring - were not years of plague but of some other infection perhaps connected with grain shortage. Lowestoft, for example, had a high death rate in the early months of 1602, and then heavy mortality in the summer of 1603, the latter being obviously caused by plague. ... 1604 saw a less heavy oubtreak in Bury ,with 13 of the 43 deaths states as those of children, a fact which recalls the plague of children in 1361. In Bury was in other parishes like Shotley, on the Orwell, plague followed on after a high death rate since 1597, a rate which had reached another peak in 1601. ......

4. Essex parishes present a simpler picutre. There is often high mortality in 1600-2, clearly here a hangover from the famines of the late '90s since plague does not generally occur until 1606. In the parishes of Bradwell-on-Sea and Tillingham and other eastern areas the mortality in 1600 was higher than any since the registers began. In Bradwell it was 3 times the average of the previous 5 years. In Beaumont-cum-Moze the Spring epidemic of 1602 produced a peak in

I wrote to Paul from Worcester on 18th June

Dear Paul,

Very many thanks for the loan of this – as you'll see from the string of questions I found it most intersting. I wonder what Hoskins main criticisms were? [Perhaps I missed the paper.] Apart from points of detail it seems an exciting approach to me, though I wonder how you are going to get to your next stage – people's reactions to plague. I'll give you any help I can from the witchcraft angle; people sometimes used magical remedies or accuses witches of starting a plague. But I'm not sure that 'Parish Chest' type evidence will give you evidence as to people's attitude to it. Did they commit suicide, worry, drink, rush to church, migrate, sprinkle their house with herbs and holy water, consult astrologers etc?

May I ask a few factual questions? What is the Howsen references (p.6) to people dying of starvation in the North? Who was Blomfield ("According to Blomfield" – p.9 btm)? Can one tell the age of those buried from the registers? Ie. children? Have you noticed any interrelationship between marriage/conception and the agricultural calendar – eg. Is it true that people tended to marry after the harvest was in and birth took place the following spring? What is your impression about pre-marital intercourse? Do deaths in non-plague years fall more heavily in certain parts of the year – e.g the cold months?

When I have finished gathering cases I would very much appreciate a look at your plague figures for Essex villages. It seems, at the moment, unlikely that it will be possible to establish any correlation between bad plague years and witchcraft accusations – but one might, and a negative answer is as important as a positive. In your paper you refer to the following Essex parishes: Saffron Walden, Gr. Warley, Bradwell-on-Sea, North Fambridge, Chigwell, Tillingham, Beaumont-cum-Moze, Grt. Clacton, Terling, Little Waltham, Chipping Ongar, Thaxted, Little Dunmow. Have you looked at any others? You will know from Erith's Essex Parish Records that quite a few other villages have registers – eg. Fifield and Stock (the only one mentioning a witch).

You ask whether population in South-East Essex was sparse (p.1). You probably already know the Ph.D. thesis of Felix Hull, Agriculture & rural Society in Essex 1560-1640 where he says (after having given a density table from the ship money assessment of 1638), 'All statistics for this period are so doubtful…'

Incidentally, talking of theses, you might just find something of interest in a London M.A. by E.G. Thomas (1958) 'The Parish Overseer in Essex 1597-1834' – ch. VI. 'Medical Relief. Medical contracts, inoculation, vaccination, lunacy'. Like Hull it is in the Essex Record Office. If you become particularly interested in Lowestoft you might contact James Campbell (tutor at Worcester Coll.) who lives there and takes a keen interest in its history from medieval to modern. He might have something on medieval plague. On medieval plague I'm sure you'll know J.F.C. Hecker, The Epidemics of the Middle Ages (trans. B.G. Babington, London, 1844) – I came across it the other day and it was just new to me.

I was interested in your speculations about malaria. Certainly there were some fever-like diseases, often called agues etc. exhaled by the South-East marshes. You'll remember the passage in Defoe's Tour where he describes how all the women on the Essex coast die off like flies and the men often have up to a dozen wives. It's tragic that one cannot learn the symptoms of the things of which people died – there may well have may well have been a number of different epidemics going round, spotted, yellow, black etc. I suppose there is no way of finding this out – except by chance references?

I look forward to hearing how you get on trying to relate plague incidence to religious attitudes, family structure, age groups, sex (were more women or men victims?), occupations, climate and harvests. It is in this linking that I'm finding the real difficulty with witches.

Excuse this long screed. I will be out of Oxford for about four months, but mail will be forwarded from the College. I look forward to a more detailed chat when I return.
Good luck with your stupendous task!

I wrote on Sunday 20th June

Dear Mummy and Daddy,

Thank you for your letter of June 7th. I am sitting in my room - bare now with all my precious files, notes, books and index cards in eleven tea-chests and trunks on the way to the Lakes. I was staggered by the amount of junk I have; like Granny I can't throw things away. Granny will have a horrible surprise when it all arrives! I will then stagger up in about two weeks on my motorbike with guitars, camp-beds, sleeping-bags, files, brief-cases etc tied on all over me.

My plans are now fairly settled. I went to see Evans-Pritchard on Tuesday [15th] *and he was very affable and kind - gave me coffee, beer etc. He advised me to finish my thesis and then to do a Diploma and hinted that money from some source might be forthcoming to help me. He seemed eager to read my work and kept pressing me to let him see it. While sharing beer with him & his colleagues I was introduced to Dr Pocock - reader in Indian Sociology. He seems a very nice man and I might well contact him to find out whether it would be possible to go out to do some field work there. One of the nice things about meeting the 'top' people is that they are 'in the know' about all the scurrilous stories about A.J.P. Taylor, Verrier Elwin etc. The same happened yesterday when I had tea with Trevor-Roper. He talks very well and I just sat open-mouthed and listened - which no doubt flattered him! He recounted his meetings with various people whose names are part of my mythology of history. Anyhow, to return to my plans, I will go to London for two weeks, then retire to the Lakes. I will have to go to Essex for a couple of months and - probably - come up to Oxford for a couple of weeks each term but it will be nice to have all my stuff stacked away.*

I had lunch with Robert at the Turf yesterday and he is 'on good form' - even expanded enough to tell me of one or two of his 'affairs de coeur' previously to Angela. He really is thinking of getting a house in Oxford for a while and even broached the idea of a houseboat to Angela - she was not amused! Richard is going down to stay next week-end to discuss the house for Granny & Grandpa.

Sorry I'm now writing in college and have mislaid my biro. Incidentally the Rosemary Harris you mentioned taking down Graves on witches was probably the wife of the College Egyptologist - John Harris: his hobby is witches and he gave a talk - I may have mentioned it - to the college society on the subject. Did you get to see John Freeman, if so was he interesting? The big political excitement of the last week has been the "Teach-in" - this is an eight-hour session of speakers talking about a set subject - on this occasion Vietnam. I only went for an hour, but Robert went for the whole session and was asked to speak, but didn't. The T.V. and press grossly exaggerated the heckling of Cabbot Lodge. I went with Zoë, who is much more politically minded than I am. She has now gone to the Lakes with about eight friends (including her American boyfriend). I hope to see her when I get up there in about two weeks. The more I see her the more I realise what a remarkable - gentle, sensitive intelligent, kind etc. person she is. Unfortunately there are a score of other people - many with more to offer than I - who think the same! Still, it appeals to my medieval chivalric, 'courtly love' side - to worship at a distance. I usually sign my letters Abelard! (Not quite appropriate of course).

At a drinks party I met an interesting Indian who I may visit when I am in London. He is writing a thesis on the Indian nationalist movement 1910-30. He recommended very strongly a book by Kosami (?) on 'The History of Indian Culture, Thought & Society' or something like that as absolutely brilliant. I had a quick look at it (at the moment its £2-10-0 in hardback - it might go into paper-back if successful) but didn't know enough to see whether it was good or not. Would you like it sent?

Oxford, just to make parting more difficult, is looking absolutely marvellous today. The gardens are roses and the trees a world of leaf-light and bird-song. There are recorders playing somewhere and the swans statuesque on the Lake. But I will be back...

I saw an enthralling film by Tennessee Williams 'The Night of the Iguana', Richard Burton as the "spooked" priest in the middle of the tropical forest. I must read his other plays - have you read anything by him?

I hope you can read this: I will report how Annie is. Fondest love, Alan

My mother wrote from Cherideo on 20th June

Thank you for a letter, perhaps your last from Oxford. I do hope you have managed to heave your books and files home somehow, aren't you going to have any holiday. Of course we would be delighted for you to make your base at Field Head, we have almost decided to fly home after all and be back for Christmas. None of the cargo boats seem to call at S. Indian ports which is the chief point of going in one, and Daddy is dying to have Christmas at home, not having experienced the delights of piles of greasy dishes stretching from the Queens speech till the Telly Panto! I hope they will give us our ten days local leave, which I will spend pottering round India looking at caves, and we'll then meet in Bombay.

You will have had your chat with Evans Pritchard by now and know whether you will be given a grant for your diploma course, if not don't bother too much, with a year's full pay, our provident fund and the profits from my book (?) I think we should be able to manage to see you through a year in Oxford without too much difficulty even if you don't get a grant. The trouble is we shan't be able to until after we come home which means you can't start this September as you probably would like to. I honestly think you would be better to do your diploma in England, the standard is much higher, and though I know Gauhati University has a department of anthropology I doubt if they know as much about it as you do already. I veer between wanting you to come out here and so some of the things I've left undone – studying the folklore and history properly and perhaps giving a hand with education – and hating the thought of the loneliness, frustration and pain you would experience. I don't think you have any idea of the suffering you would see all the time, you would neve be able to eat a thing. I don't really know what is happening in N.E.F.A. but Verrier Elwin in that letter said it was stiff with people and he would not advise going there. The new tribal univesity planned in Shillong would be a good idea, I'll find out about it when I go up, or there are the Tibetans. With a D.Phil. and a diploma you would have no difficulty in getting a job but would probably be poorly paid – however with a camera, Tape Recorder and your pen you would be able to make up in articles and books I'm sure. Both the Khasis and the Garos could do with systematic study – but goodness if you are lonely in the Lake District how could you stand living for years in wild hills with no outside resources? Perhaps with a Good Woman by your side it would be possible. … We had a quiet week-end, my tummy trouble has been worrying me a bit but I'm on various medecines and feeling better. ...

Paul Slack replied at length to my letter of 18th June. This inaugurated a lively and detailed correspondence which went on for some years, parts of which I will reproduce in later chapters.

St. John's College,
Oxford.

24 June 1965

Dear Alan,

Many thanks for the return of my essay, and for your interesting and stimulating comments thereon. If you don't mind I'll take your comments more or less in succession.

Hoskins's main criticism was that I assumed too readily that starvation and famine were fairly common occurrences in the sixteenth century, and did not refer to his article on this. His views are not very clear, but it seems to me that he would like to disagree with Laslett on the seriousness of crises of subsistence. I think he may well be right. As I tentatively suggested in the essay Goubert's famine picture for France does not apply to Norwich at any rate. But obviously I need to do a lot more on this. Norwich with its stores of corn may have been a special case, or it may be true that Norfolk as a whole was not so much affected by the bad harvests of the late 1590s. I don't yet know.

The Howson reference is: W.G.Howson: Plague, Poverty and Population in Parts of North-West England. Trans.Hist.Soc.Lancs+Cheshire. 1960.
Blomefield is the great 18th century historian of Norfolk (many vol. history on open shelves of Selden End near the V.C.H.s). I'm working on Norwich at the moment and it seems - as far as his reference to suspicion of the Queen (1579) is concerned, anyway, - that he had access to some sort of Chronicle roll that has now disappeared.

Accurate assessment of age at death and premarital intercourse depends on the tedious process of family reconstruction which is being pioneered in England by Laslett and Wrigley at Cambridge - they are shortly to produce a methodological handbook on English Historical Demography. According to Wrigley, whom I have met, as many as a third of all legitimate births were prenuptial conceptions. The number of illegitimate births is, of course much smaller. But pre-marital intercourse - in the sense of testing a wife to see if she would be fertile before you took the final step of marriage - seems to have been very common. I hope myself to do a small sample study in one or two parishes to find out how the age of death varied in epidemics. All I can say about this at the moment is that in Bury a large proportion of the deaths is the 1603 plague are noted as being 'infants' or 'children', as I think I said in the essay.

I have not looked very closely at the temporal spacing of marriages and births, but as far as I can see from a few parishes, marriages are commonest in Sept. or Oct. after harvest. The pattern of births is not so simple - there does tend to be a peak in the spring, but one parish I've just looked at had a consistently high no. in November. Pre-marital intercourse might be one obvious cause of this. On deaths you are right: the winter months are the chief death months unless some plague has come before and wiped out the aged already.

I do intend to make a close study of Essex as a special county, just as Norwich and London will be my special towns. So I hope to look at as many Essex registers as possible. I'll be glad to give you figures for any of them when I get them, just as I'd be glad to get any information from you on connections with Essex witchcraft. I have burial figures for the following Essex parishes already -starting at various dates, ~~and baptism record figures for those with asterisks~~: (Sorry: it appears I have no Essex baptism figures - I must already [illegible])

Bradwell on Sea, -
Tillingham
Dengie
Burnham -
Cold Norton
N. Fambridge
Stow Maries -

Little Waltham
Fairstead
Terling
Faulksbourne
Little Baddow
Great Clacton

Panfield
Stambourne
Toppesfield
Liston
Bobbingworth
Chipping Ongar
Moreton
Greenstead
Hadleigh.

Saffron Walden
Ashdon
Helion Bumpstead
Thaxted
Lindsell
Great Dunmow
Little "
Chigwell
Great Parndon

If you want any stuff on these let me know. It might be best to come and see me when you come back to Oxford unless I can send you anything specific.

Thanks for the two theses you mentioned. I didn't know about them and they may be useful, especially the Hull one, of course.

With regard to Malaria: Wrigley mentioned to me that Bradwell on Sea always had a high excess of deaths over births, clearly due to this disease. Defoe's description probably fitted there. There is an old article you might find of some interest on the malaria mosquito in England which mentions East Anglia especially: G.H.F.Nuttall and others: The geographical distribution of Anopheles in relation to the former distribution of ague in England. Journal of Hygiene Vol.I. 1901.pp4-44.

You're dead right about the difficulties of relating disease to other social phenomena. It's somewhat consoling to know that you have the same trouble. We must certainly have a long chat next term. I'm getting married in August so you must allow us to have you to dinner in our new flat sometime in September or October.

I hope you can understand this rather rushed letter, and I apologise for the atrocious typing. See you next term.

Yours,

Paul

As well as writing to me, my mother was also writing long letters to my two sisters and also, less frequently perhaps, to her father and mother. One of these is worth quoting, as it shows her concern and last minute plans as to the sharing of a house with my grandparents was effected. It was a painful wrench for everyone, but was handled satisfactorily.

My mother to her mother from Cherideo June 25th

Darling Mummy,

Delighted to hear about the house – I do hope nothing will go wrong as it sounds ideal. ... we have decided to skip the cargo boat and fly home and be back about 10th December... As for furniture, you must take everything you need, the only essential for us will be beds and either Fiona or Beryl could lay these in. ... I would like the rocking chairs if you could spare them, or anyway the one that Juno chewed for Auld Lang Syne. ... We are very grateful for all that you have done at Field Head, particularly in the garden – buying it has been the cause of all our troubles since but we don't regret it at all now and hope you haven't done so. I wonder if Alan is with you wrapped in his old grey blanket in the shed with dozens of dirty coffee cups round him which is the way I always remember him. ...

My mother wrote to me from Cherideo on 29th June

[addressed to Field Head, Ambleside]

I was so glad to get your letter saying your plans were stabilised and that E.Pritchard thought you had a chance of being helped with your anthropology. I wonder how long your thesis will take to write, and if you have discovered any significant "patterns" from all your little coloured pins, or came to any final conclusions about witchcraft generally. I'm longing to get home and talk about it all. As you will have heard Granny is probably moving in September, could you face staying on at Field Head with Poochie, you could put up a camp bed in the kitchen and bar yourself in at night. I'm very glad for Grannys sake she seems to have found a comfortable little house or rather Richard has, nice and close to Oxford and if she can get some bridge she should be happy, Granpa will be happy anywhere once he gets his routine established. We have definitely decided to fly home and will arrive about December 10th, havent got the details settled yet but talk of little else. If I make any money from my book maybe I'll be able to get back and see all the places I've missed, if not I shall carry a dream like picture of them about with me which is probably better.

Don't bother about any more Mughal books, I've shelved it till I get home, but do keep a note of anything specially good you hear of. I will write the first draft of my childrens book in the next few months, I can't seem to do very much in this weather. It is a strongly recognisable mixture of "The Secret Garden" and "The Jungle Book". I got a letter from Brenda yesterday saying she had just dumped my Mughals with the agents so await their gloomy tidings. ...

... I can't imagine Verrier Elwin being involved in "scurrilous stories", as you say he seemed a strangely innocent person, a type one meets very often out here, mostly in the robes of an ascetic admittedly with a childish unconcern about the Realities of life such as earning money and making a name. The respect accorded to voluntary poverty probably makes this possible. ...

I am deep in "Wolf Solent" at the moment, I wonder if you have read it, very Hardyish, full of dark incestuous crimes and unexplained relationships and deaths – the descriptive writing is beautiful – I love it. It's so nice to have a really long, lingering book that one can get right up to the neck in, and yet not tedious like those American novels. I still haven't seen a single review of Gallipoli, how is it going, do you know? I am going to see an Assamese historian friend this afternoon and will sound him outabout the chances of a European being able to do research or other work in NEFA – it needs someone there quickly as progress is engulfing the tribes and they will soon be wearing twinkle Terylene and decorating their houses with plastic flowers like so many of the Assamese do. Do find out from Fiona about the film from the camera we left with her, dying to know if those memorable moments after you got your degree are safe for posterity...

I wrote to my parents on 30th June, from the Waterloo Embankment in London where I was working on court records at various record offices.

Dear Mummy and Daddy,

All my mail is being held at Oxford at the moment so I don't know whether there is a letter to thank you for. As you see, I've made London and am now sitting about a quarter mile away from Big Ben waiting for the County Record Office to open. It is a beautiful morning - as it has been for the last few days - which almost makes up for the pneumatic drills, trains, dust and rush hour. On my left there is a man 'poisoning pigeons'[1] and further to my left the building into which Roy has just disappeared. As I forecast, I am staying with Roy & Rosemary made more convenient by their parents being away. Roy is a little frustrated by his job, but they have a cheap flat to move into and the baby is a honey. Roy is working for the Greater London Council - i.e. in local government. Tomorrow, if possible, I hope to spend the last two days of my visit at Annie's. I haven't seen anything of her yet. Last week-end I spent at Jane Wilkinson's (remember? - the Lake District girl) sun-bathing on top of their roof, at Hampstead and reading 'Lolita'. On Monday evening I went to a 'lonely hearts' club in

[1] A reference to a Tom Lehrer song, 'Poisoning pigeons in the park'.

Baker Street - appropriately enough situated in a Y.W.C.A. but rather heartily called 'The Coffee Pot'. Actually it is for decent types - young graduates and professional folk and it is a little rowdy - but then most groups of people (at least English) are, when consuming coffee while secretly hoping to meet the man/girl of their life. I went with an ex-Oxford friend whose offer to give me a lift home had to be cut short because he had his car stolen. Sad. As I've mentioned, my plans now are to spend the week-end at Oxford & crawl up to the Lakes next Monday. I haven't heard from Linda but presume she's arrived back safely. Apart from an abortive attempt to see 'The Knack' a new film with Rita Tushingham which is all the rage I haven't exactly hit the high spots - but then I'm here to work.

The work has gone quite well. As I've done practically nothing else you'll have to excuse a long description of it. I came principally to check witchcraft cases which I extracted from a translation of the Assize court rolls. These were housed in the Public Record Office - a grim building in Chancery Lane, surrounded by law books shops, inns of court, grubby snack bars and 'Zerox' photocopying machines. At the beginning, partly through my own stupidity, I had a disagreement with one of the lackeys who bring the rolls, and it didn't look as if I would get anything done, but the appearance of one of the 'Assistant Keepers', a "brass" who was very affable (old Oxford type you know) raised me in the eyes of the minions so that I was better supplied. In fact I got through about 80 rolls in 5 days; they are old parchment bundles of latin scrawl, but it shows that I've improved since I started this as, when I looked at them a year ago, I gave up in despair and now found them quite easy. The last few had only <u>just</u> been discovered - in a sack and they were crumbling to dust. It was like finding some dead-sea scrolls or something and most exciting. When I finished this I went to the British Museum (I expect you must have been there - very awesome, but magnificent) and after that the County Hall where I am currently trying to charm the pleasant custodian of the archives to let me see certain volumes of Church courts which are, because of their delicate state, technically "unfit for production". Working among these and other records I have become increasingly aware of the delicate pressures which come to bare even in strictly "academic research". If one has the right accent, comes from the right university, has contacts etc one can see things that others can't. In India it must be even more so. With strings all sorts of strong-room doors will slide open, where no amount of direct banging and pleading will open them. I must obviously gather as many 'contacts' and impressive qualifications as possible before venturing forth!

I've been travelling on the tube quite long distances and to deaden the rush-hour a little have been launching out into the very troubled sea of modern poetry - skimming through the Welsh earthiness of R.S. Thomas, the placid agonies of Elizabeth Jennings, the sunny waspishness of Lawrence Durrell and whirlpool of Rilke. This has been mixing with 'Lolita' - which, I expect you know, is absolutely superb and <u>most</u> amusing and sensitive - and a few books on anthropology and sociology to produce a very indigestible, glutinous mess of thought. But plenty of protein for the brain I expect! I am reading also Philippe Ariès "Centuries of Childhood" which is a fascinating book about the growth of the awareness of 'childhood', you must have a look at it when you return. Did you know, for instance, that Louis XIII learnt the violin when he was 17 months old?

Excuse this self-centred scrawl. I hope all goes well with you both and that plots, tea and flowers grow apace. Will write next, I hope, from the Lakes.

Much love to you both, Alan

1965 - July

I returned to the Lakes on 5th July and wrote on 9th July from Field Head Outgate

Dear Mummy and Daddy,

Please forgive a congested letter but I've got three letters from you (sent on the 15th, 20th & 29th) to thank you for and to answer - also quite a lot of travelling news. I do hope you are feeling better Mummy; Granny tells me you've had dysentery - why didn't you tell me? You must have felt awful. Poor thing. That's another reason for my staying in the Lake District. I'm so glad you're going to start the children's book, tho' I fear it may be a little swamped in preparations for departure. Which reminds me - It's wonderful that you're coming home in time for Christmas. I heard the news from Annie when I was staying with her & we're planning to meet you etc. It's rather lucky that I've decided to move here as I can look after the house for 3 months. I'm not sure about Poochie, however, as I'll still have to go down to Oxford and Essex for the odd week and don't know where to leave her; still we'll see. I've settled all my possessions in my room (except for the filing cabinet which is arriving today) and stuck up some maps & things & it looks quite nice. There are a growing number of books with which to line the walls, and my files are secure in the usual orange boxes. Granny, as she may have told you, has been going to Sales and among other things has bought a desk which I can put in my room.

As you'll have gathered from the address I've reached home after my wanderings. I spent Thursday & Friday night with Anne, then went to Oxford for the week-end and to see Linda & drove up on Monday. Anne is well & her hair looking very pretty. She was telling me about Alan, thou' I didn't meet him. As she's probably told you, we went out on Thursday - she got sick on too much Merrydown Cider. On Friday I went to Matta Hari (Jeanne Moreau) with the red-haired girl I met at the garden party at the end of last term. She's very sweet & bubbly, a very nice person to take out. Linda was well & very brown tho' she was recovering from gastric enteritis which she'd caught on the way back from Majorca. I feel rather guilty about her, tho' I probably flatter myself when I think that she misses me. She is still going out with her boss so I don't feel too awful. On returning to Oxford I found that my bike was still not working properly & the battery had run down again so I set off very pessimistically carrying a spare. I got about 50 yards & the first one appeared to run out! But it revived itself and got me, in a jerky fashion (for the last 20 miles the bike almost stopped every time I went round a round-about) some 90 miles. Then I put on the spare & hobbled up to the Lakes. Actually the engine went very well & I reached here at 7.45 after leaving Oxford at 11 - with one and a half hour stop on the way. The place is looking really lovely; the garden full of roses etc. (and, soon, raspberries & strawberries). Granny and Grandpa are looking terribly fit &, as far as one can tell, happy about the move (tho Grandpa grumbles). I went to see Beryl, Martin & Jean & consequently was invited to supper with Jane Buckmaster who had a rather fabulous ex-girl friend of Bill Critchley's staying. We ate steak - strawberries & danced (just 3 of us) till 1 a.m. Anne Johnson - looking very sweet - and Anne Hogg came for a short time. I haven't quite got myself settled in my routine yet, but will have to buckle down soon as I should send my supervisor some work soon. Yes, I'm still Bursar on the camp - which begins on 24th July

I'm glad you're enjoying (enjoyed?) 'Wolf Solent', no I've never read it, though want to read some Cowper Powys. Talking of books - I was glad to find that Margaret (the red-haired girl I mentioned) would take as her one book to a desert island "Cold Comfort Farm", she says that she visualizes herself as 'Flora'.

I'm not sure whether any patterns are emerging out of my thesis yet. I'm just about to embark on the exciting stage of hauling in the nets to see if I've caught anything. Having spent the first 8 months finding a likely stretch and making the net - i.e. deciding what questions to ask, I've spent the last 6 or so pulling the nets along; now we'll see whether I made the holes too big or too small. I can already feel a slight tugging and think that it may well have got a monster - the trouble is that a monster takes more than three years to capture. That's why I want to do a further degree (partly). I had a nice letter from

Joan Thirsk (a big noise in historical world) suggesting I write to her "good friend" Raymond Firth - professor of anthropology at London to see what he suggests. In some ways London would be a healthy change from Oxford. One snag is that I think I would be more valuable intellectually if I remained a historian in subject matter while a trained anthropologist - but this would be less use practically.

I'm hoping that Zoë will be returning today from a farewell holiday in Cornwall with her American boyfriend. But it may be next week she meant. I have missed her quite a lot (for me).

I hope you have good news re. the Mughals. Apparently (according to Richard) Gallipoli is selling well. Reviews of it are in the Listener etc. which Granny supposedly sent out to you.

Look after yourselves; won't be long now!

Fondest love, Alan

My mother wrote to me from Cherideo on 10th July

You really will have reached Field Head by now, I've been sending letters there for weeks so I hope some of them have reached you. I'm afraid you will find it a bit confusing trying to unpack your witchy notes in the turmoil of Granny moving, particularly as she seems to be bringing in a lot of new stuff. If she doesn't want the black leather sofa and chair we will have them, tell her, sounds most seductive, I can just see myself stretched out on the sofa with my disciples all round me twanging on two stringed instruments – my imagination is a bit muddled between holy men out here and what I imagine literary ladies do in salons at home! Your descriptions of your studies in London among mouldering parchments made my mouth water, its my dream to discover some secret hoard of historical material, I'm sure your thesis will provide some stunning new facts to rock the academic world – don't let Evans Pritchard or any of those crafty characters see it and pinch all your material. I have abandoned history for my childrens books which I'm enjoying writing though I see no great future for it, still its good discipline to write well within a limited vocabulary and I think a childrens book between every other would be a good idea – if one wrote the others? I finished "Wolf Solent" regretfully, it petered out a bit towards the end I thought but one had got so involved with the characters that it was sad to leave them. Do you see anything of Mrs Callendar?[1] I wonder how her writing is going. I have never read "Lolita" – the subject repulsed me I'm afraid but I must try it sometime.

I am feeling better at last, I seemed to have two lots of things wrong with my tummy and the treatment for one aggravated the other but both are now under control and I'm able to look around with pleasure again. I went to the bazaar on Wednesday to take some photographs, how I shall miss the colour and smells and beauty of Indian markets – the incredible variety of the faces, their unhurried absorption and grace, because of course they have all day to decide and the argument is half the fun. There was a man doing card tricks and Nagas and heaps of glittering glass bangles and spices and stalls of ruby red drinks – solid cholera probably but beautiful when sliding down the throat of a man in a gold silk shirt with green bananas slung round his neck like a garland. I am seeing everything extra large of course, as one sees it for the first and last time – and already there are lots of stalls full of cheap hideous printed cloth which everyone wants to buy and poison green plastic baskets instead of the bamboo ones they make themselves. The same story will be repeated here as everywhere, the old skills lost and then when it is too late the loss regretted. Both my schools are on their summer vacations for a month so I'm going to try to get the first draft of my book finished and then I can concentrate on them and on various other trips and thinks I want to make. …

Please don't bother to write every week while you're working on your thesis, you'll be sick of expressing yourelf, once a fortnight will do! Tim Edye wrote the other day, he had met Jill Walker who said how much she liked you and hoped the "rift" would be mended – this is his interpretation though, you probably know the situation better – in fact undoubtedly do.

---

[1] Mentioned previously as a Lake District friend.

I wrote again on Sunday 11th July from Field Head

Dear Mummy - especially (and Daddy),

Only four days since I last wrote so there's been no letter. But I'm writing now (a) to get back into my Sunday routine (b) to wish you a very happy birthday indeed; words are useless but you know we'll all be thinking of you on the 22nd and hoping that the next year will be wonderful for you both - it looks as if it may well be. I hope the books I sent have turned up & you find something to your taste. It may be presumptuous, but I feel as if I'm sending out vital intellectual injections to keep you from going to sleep. As you know, I'm sure you're going to be a 'great' writer (talking to someone yesterday I was placing you in the hierarchy somewhere between Jane Austen and the Bronte's!) once you've found your nitch. The problem is to keep your writing amidst ill health, daily intrusions and hopelessness. At least I have all your letters and when you return would like to piece them together to make up an account of life in India. Or perhaps you'd rather leave that 'till you write your autobiography? Have you thought of a title? I'm always finding lines of poetry to make nice titles, it's just the writing of the book that puts me off. But I haven't much to say at 23! I just hope a few people keep my more interesting letters. I've been sorting out letters to me & have masses from Penny/Julie etc. Returning to your birthday, I wonder how you'll celebrate? I do hope, at least, that you're feeling well on the day. I hear you're still not well. It must be awful - and makes me feel guilty for my ungrateful assumption of the right to good health. I've only had slight colds in the last 2 years - no headaches, insomnia, toothache, cancer, leprosy, V.D., etc. It's fantastic. And yet one still mopes and glooms around the place ... I can't think of any good advice etc - but then it's not my duty to do this, luckily!

Since I've been up I've seen a fair amount of Zoë. I went over for supper on Wednesday and she came here at tea-time on Thursday and stayed to mid-day the next day when I took her home and had lunch. Her parents are very nice - the father quiet and retiring, the mother friendly and amusing. They are cultured & gentle - like Zoë and there doesn't seem to be much mother-daughter tension. Z says she finds it difficult to make contact with her father & I can understand this. She is going down to London this week for an interview & coming in for coffee this afternoon on the way. She really is a delightful girl, kind, gentle, humble, amusing, sensitive, appreciative, etc. I could go on for ever. But neither of us really want to get involved I think, for a while and I'm not sure she could stand my self-centeredness and constant need of reassurance. She wants a dominating male, not one who starts leaning on her straight away. Still, with her interest in social problems, considerable intelligence, simpleness, unaffectedness etc. she really would be a marvelous 'Good Woman'. But idealization & hopeful thinking will not get me anywhere & I expect my butterfly heart will be set on some other "apple-blossom" maid next week!

Fiona arrived on Friday evening brought up by Rupert who is taking her down (armed with fishing rod, before she sets out to the Hebrides) today. She is very brown & seems fit & more mature. We've been having discussions about Ezra Pound, Art etc. I've almost accepted the fact that she's a nice person - something I wouldn't have done 3 years ago! I've asked her about the film; apparently Rupert has just got round to sending it off to be developed. She is very keen on classical music and comes & listens to Tanhauser in my room. Apparently the gramaphone is going well and she is fighting off the other inhabitants who try to use it. The usual scrum it seems at Parsonage Rd and the usual mixture of wanting to stay together - and longing for a 'place of their own'. I think they'll like the Isles, though I'm not sure they'll really be able to live off heather roots and mackerel or whatever! She seems to be working hard & loving painting. Incidentally, re. the gramaphone, you said "I sent £5 towards the HP" - was that to my Oxford bank or who? If it was in a letter, I didn't get it, but not to worry since things are going OK and I'd much rather you let me pay that £20 off & let me live here free to September (actually I'll be away half the time). Shall I give Granny some money? I won't till I hear from you.

It's a drizzly day, one of those days when one can't be sure whether it's heavy mist, or light rain and the whole valley is very silent. I went to Communion but didn't speak to Lindsay. Yesterday G &

G had a sherry party for their 47th wedding anniversary to which the Calendar's & Beryl came. We (Mrs C & I!) talking books of course.

It is really lovely being up here and I am longing for you to be back.

Hope you can read this!

Much love, Alan

I wrote on 18th July from Field Head, Ambleside

Dear Mummy and Daddy,

Thank you very much for your letter of July 10th - it only took four days to get here! I'm afraid my birthday letter will be very early. I expect this will also arrive before. I'm not sure whether you are being kind and considerate in asking me to write only once a fort-night - or are getting bored either with my letters or with writing. Since pride makes me decide it must be the former I'll go on writing once a week. I haven't started really full-time writing yet. When that happens we'll see. (but you'll probably be home anyhow). Actually I don't do anything on Sundays except write/see friends / have baths. Having said this, I realise that next week's letter I will be with the Borstal camp (where I go on Friday). I walked round the Tarns on Friday evening, the stillness and variation lovely, a bliss only broken by the yapping of 'Pooch' and clouds of gnats. Yesterday I sunbathed near Juniper Hill and looked down that magnificent view of Windermere. In the evening I collected Zoë who came over here to spend the night. She had been walking along Hadrian's wall when she had suddenly been informed that she had a "viva" (i.e. interview) on Monday. These are not common in the P.P.E. schools and mean she must be between degrees; of course we both hope it's between a 2nd and a 1st, which is the most likely I think. (Thus once again we will be similar). Luckily Jean McCormick ((?) was driving down to Dorset today & has taken her down to Gloucester. Zoë is as sweet as ever. I would like to persuade her to hitch up to see Fiona in the Hebrides with me - but I think she wants to go to Spain. She hitch-hikes around a lot - quite often by herself - another characteristic (i.e. independence, adventurousness etc) I admire tho' it's obviously risky. She also like me, wears jeans most of the time - but can look very "posh" also.

I'm glad there's progress on the children's book; will you finish it in India or here? I'm glad also your "mouth watered" over my description of mouldering parchments and that you wanted to discover 'some secret hoard of historical material'. This is just what I think I've done and I'm desperately anxious a) for some help b) to talk about it to someone. I will explain it all when you return, but let me give you an example. If one is trying to reconstruct the every-day life of villagers in the C16-C18, their attitude to marriage, birth, death, their relationships and groups, their anxieties and hopes and dreams, their incest and suicide, their poverty and amusements one has so far only been able to do this from literary sources - i.e. poetry, plays etc. which may well be an idealization & often doesn't deal with such common-place, accepted, matters. Alternatively people have made a start on the economic structure of life - rents, taxes, food-prices, population. No one has gone further. But I am <u>convinced</u> that with the ecclesiastical records (& enormous energy) one can do just this. Take a village - the total surviving records of everyday life would consist of about 50 pages for say the period 1560-1600. But the court records, the wills etc which have never been used will come to about 500 pages for that period - all details of family life, religious attitudes, drunkenness, insanity, obscenity, etc. Thus one has enormous detail ... But I must be boring you!

I hope you keep well, Mummy and everything goes fine on the garden for Daddy,

Much love, Alan

Raymond Firth in his office at the London School of Economics, around the age when he interviewed me for a place in 1967

Raymond (later Sir Raymond) Firth was, at the time I first wrote to him, aged about 63 (born in 1901) and a major figure in social anthropology and Head of the Department of Social Anthropology at the London School of Economics. He would become an important person in my life and a main teacher during my two years at the LSE. My correspondence with him is not particularly intellectual, though I learnt a great deal from his books. But it shows the way in which I transferred from history to anthropology and, more generally, the kind of strategies I was pursuing at this time. In any extended education such as mine, a good deal of effort was spent on worrying about and constructing the next part of the bridge ahead. These letters chart that progress and also show the trouble which Firth took to help me, despite his well-known ambivalences (which I discovered later) towards the Oxford anthropologists, in particular Evans-Pritchard.

The letters start off with an example of networking.

18/7/65

Dear Professor Firth,

I apologise for taking up some of your precious time, but Mrs. Joan Thirsk, to whom I took my problem first, suggested that I wrote to you. She pointed out that you have shown special interest in interrelating historical and anthropological studies and I found this out for myself from your stimulating chapter on 'Social Organization and Social Change', in Essays on Social Organization… It would therefore be needless, as well as impertinent, for me to argue for the need for an acquaintance with both disciplines. This is where I would like your advice.

I took a B.A. in history at Oxford and since October 1963 have been working for a D.Phil. under Mr. K.V. Thomas on 'Witchcraft Prosecutions in Essex 1560-1680: A Sociological Analysis' which I hope to submit in October 1966. During this I have necessarily had to immerse myself in anthropological writing on the subject and have found this most stimulating and helpful. I have discovered over 800 cases of witchcraft during this period and am now attempting to relate them to the social background.

I would like to be trained as a social anthropologist while remaining a historian in subject matter and am wondering how to achieve this. It is unlikely that the State would support me further and if I take a teaching job at a university this would not leave me time to do a further degree. I have talked with Processor Evans-Pritchard and am very attracted to the one year Diploma course at Oxford under the writer of 'Witchcraft among the Zande' but a) it is not certain that I could get funds, though the Professor hinted at this b) I have been in Oxford for some 11 years of my life and feel a change might do me good. The reputation of L.S.E. makes it my first alternative choice and thus I am writing to you.

The three questions which I would be very pleased if you could answer are:

- *a) If there is any Diploma in social anthropology lasting only a year, or any way, since I have read a certain amount on the subject, I could do the course in a year?*
- *b) If you know of any source of money to which I could apply to do such further training?*
- *c) a rather vaguer question: do you think I would be advised to do anthropological fieldwork after the Diploma or, if, as you say, "the anthropologist is using essentially the same kind of data as the historian does": (Essays …p.56) could finish training as a social anthropologist on historical material, say doing research on 'Kinship and Marriage' in seventeenth century Norfolk or some such?*

I am only 23 and unmarried so that this apparently endless state of intermediate status and protracted learning would not be too difficult.

I look forward to any help or advice you can give me and apologise again for worrying you with this personal matter.

Yours sincerely, Alan Macfarlane

My mother wrote to me from Cherideo on 19th July Cherideo, Iris to Alan [forwarded to me at Nutwith Cote, Masham, Ripon, Yorks, where I was at the Borstal Camp.]

Thank you for your very nice birthday letter which arrived a little early but it's impossible to time these things and it was most welcome. Your kind remarks about my literary potential were happily lapped up – but I'm afraid I see myself as a second class Enid Blyton and certainly have no intention of ever writing my autobiography – some chatty pieces on "My 25 years in Tea" for Woman's Own would be the absolute limit in that line. I have kept a selection of your letters, not all but the most interesting. I have got eleven chapters of my children's book written of the 18 I plan, it has kept me amused and will bring back to me, at any rate, Assam and the animals and birds – its about a "sanctuary" the children make in the jungle. I had a letter from my agent yesterday saying he had read the synopsis of the Mughals and thought it would make an interesting and entertaining book and would start to tout it round – not the wild enthusiasm I had hoped for but better than a blank refusal and I cheer myself with the fact that agents have to be cagey and not raise the hopes of inexperienced authors. The proof copy my Indian Legends isnt ready yet.

I do hope you will find you have that monster in your net, it is extraordinary to me that one could research away and not know what one was discovering – it shows how very little I know about research. I am toying with the idea of taking a degree by correspondence when I come home, to teach me how to organise my thinking a bit better and not chase so many red herrings and fritter my time. I hope you aren't too squashed in your room, we have big plans for making a sort of cupboard lined with bookshelves for you where Granny's linen is kept at the moment, opening out of your room, but hope it won't be too late to be of use. … Don't pay Granny as we have arranged to do so. I sent the £5 to your bank, and another lot this month I think. Let us know if you are short won't you?...

I have been visiting the local bazaars to take photographs and hope to have a reel ready by Thursday for Tom Poole to take home. It is rather difficult chasing reluctant Nagas through feet of slippery mud in the boiling sun – I didn't in fact manage to corner any Nagas but practically everything in an Indian bazaar is worth photographing. … As I told Granny I have decided to spend my last ten days in India seeing the Pepper Coast from Cochin to Bombay, full of history.

Raymond Firth replied at some length to my letter of 18th July

The London School of Economics and Political Science

(University of London)

Houghton Street, Aldwych
London, W.C.2
Telephone HOLborn 7686

22nd July 1965.

Dear Mr. Macfarlane,

I am interested in your letter of 18th July. I am indeed interested in the possibilities of integration of historical and anthropological studies where possible and think it an excellent idea that somebody with an historical training should take some systematic work in social anthropology. Your study of witchcraft prosecutions in Essex sounds very interesting indeed. In this connection you might some time get in touch with Dr. Audrey Richards of Newnham College, Cambridge. She has been conducting a contemporary anthropological study in a village not very far from Cambridge and would, I think, be very interested in your work.

Now for your questions. We have here a Postgraduate Diploma in Social Anthropology, but it is a two-year course and I do not think there is any provision whereby you could effectively complete the course with examination in one year. Unfortunately I do not know definitely of any source of funds to which you could apply to do such further training. It is perhaps possible that the Nuffield Foundation social science fellowships might meet your need. Perhaps this is what Professor Evans-Pritchard had in mind.

With regard to your field work question, I think that research among people of another culture does provide for the social anthropologist a kind of cultural jolt, so to speak, and perspective which are extremely valuable. There is no effective substitute for this. But for someone like yourself who wants to remain a historian (which I think is the right course) while having some training in social anthropology, I think it quite possible to do research on historical materials using the comparative framework of anthropology. In this connection, there is a paper by a colleague of mine, Dorothy Crozier, a historian with anthropological experience, on "Kinship and Occupational Succession", using 18th and 19th century materials. This was published in the Sociological Review of March 1965. Unfortunately I have no copy to spare but doubtless you can look it up. This, I think, gives some indication of possibilities parallel to your suggested study of 17th century kinship and marriage.

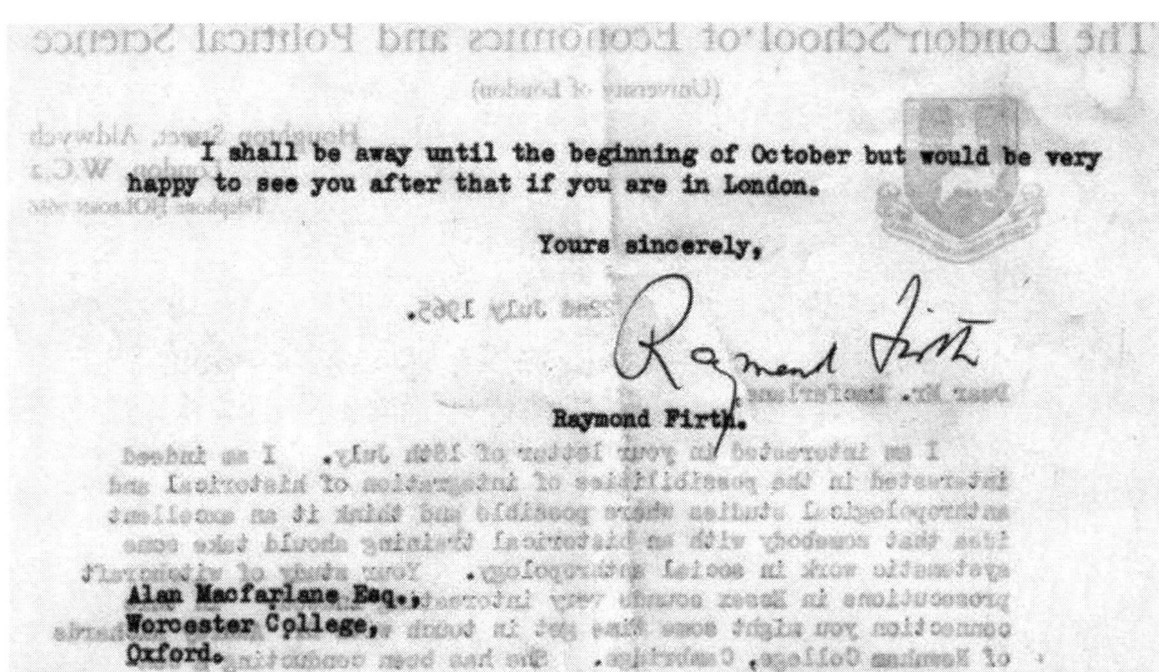

I shall be away until the beginning of October but would be very happy to see you after that if you are in London.

Yours sincerely,

Raymond Firth.

Alan Macfarlane Esq.,
Worcester College,
Oxford.

Friday 23 July Alan goes to camp - Grandfather's diary

The Oxford-Borstal camps, retrospectively, were an excellent educational institution. They involved a small number of undergraduates from an Oxford College going to camp for a week or so in the Yorkshire dales with a similar sized group of boys who were young offenders imprisoned in open prisons or Borstals. Then the group would return for a few days so that the undergraduates could share a little life in the Borstal. I wrote reflections on this as an undergraduate and attended such camps with a group from Worcester in my first and second years.

As a postgraduate I went with a group from St. Peter's College in my second year as a postgraduate, summer 1965, where my friend Ralph Johnson, who had been on at least one of the Worcester camps, was now located.

The detailed arrangements were sent to me by Ralph with additional notes on my duties as the Bursar.

OXFORD - BORSTAL CAMP, 1965

Dear Alan,

Our camp begins on Saturday, July 24th, and ends on Saturday, August 7th, when we leave Wetherby. Postal addresses will be as follows:

July 24 - Aug. 3	Nutwith Cote, Masham, Ripon, Yorkshire.	Aug. 3-7	H.M. Borstal, York Road, Wetherby, Yorks.
Telephone:	MASHAM (Yorkshire) 366		WETHERBY 2754

Please bring the following: ruck-sack (if you have one), washing kit and towel, electric torch, suitable clothes, including heavy walking shoes, plimsolls, swimming trunks.

There is one additional member of the Camp:

Robin Crossley	1 Geography	9 Otley Old Road, Leeds 16.

Please arrive at Nutwith Cote in time for supper on Saturday, 24 July, i.e. not later than 7 p.m. The most convenient trains and buses run as follows:

TRAINS:

London, King's Cross	9.00 a.m.	10.10 a.m.
York	12.05 p.m.	1.09 p.m.
York	12.47 p.m.	1.33 p.m.
Harrogate	1.25 p.m.	2.11 p.m.
Harrogate	1.51 p.m.	2.40 p.m.
Ripon	2.05 p.m.	2.54 p.m.

OR

London, St. Pancras	9.15 a.m.	
Leeds City	1.31 p.m.	
Leeds City	1.18 p.m.	1.37 p.m.
Ripon	2.05 p.m.	2.26 p.m.

(The two stations in Leeds are not more than 10 mins. walk from one another)

London, King's Cross	9.20 a.m.
Leeds Central	12.44 p.m.
Leeds Central	1.58 p.m.
Harrogate	2.30 p.m.
Harrogate	2.40 p.m.
Ripon	2.54 p.m.

BUSES: (Ripon bus-station is about 20 mins. walk from railway station).

Service 126 Harrogate railway station to Ripon railway station via Ripon bus-station. Service runs every half hour, taking 39 mins. for the whole journey, 35 mins. from Harrogate railway station to Ripon bus-station.

Service 127 Ripon to Masham via Grewelthorpe (ask to be put off at Nutwith Cote gate)

Ripon bus-station	4.45 p.m.	5.15 p.m.
Masham	5.21 p.m.	5.51 p.m.

OR

Service 146 Ripon to Masham via Well (This will necessitate a walk of 1½ miles to Nutwith Cote)

Ripon bus-station	2.35 p.m.	4.45 p.m.
Masham	3.19 p.m.	5.29 p.m.

If these transport arrangements present problems, or, indeed if you have any other queries please let me know.

Yours,

French Masham. 418.

NUTWITH BURSAR'S AIDE MEMOIRE.

NB there is no pa-ty line about all this: these a-e merely a numbe- of suggestions about points which have caused difficulty in the past. In pa-ticula- it should be noted that the Commandant is in cha-ge and what he says goes.

GENERAL DUTIES: The bu-sa- should make himself x -esponsible fo-:

(i) o-de-ing of food(see below);
(ii) a--angement of menus;
(iii) p-ovision of tentage and equipment-NB fo- wo-king pa-ties etc.
(iv) t-anspo-t a--angements fo- camp outings;
(v) liasing with bo-stal office- -e t-anspo-t back to the bo-stal;
(vi) e-ecting tents,lat-ines,etc(fi-st camp on site);
(vii) clea-ing up camp at the end of camp and the dismantling and sto-age of equipment(last camp on site);
(viii) P-og-amme: this will be a--anged by the bu-sa- in consultation with F-ank Theakston,but the bu-sa- should take on the -esponsibility of getting it into a cohe-ent fo-m,w-iting it out in full and ~~xx~~ making su-e that the-e a-ent any lacunae. It has been found helpful in the past fo- a notebook to be p-oduced(specimen enclosed) giving the detailed p-og-amme with notes on destinations of ~~xxxx~~ wo-k-pa-ties etc; one copy fo- the commandant and one copy fo- the bu-sa-. This should be made up in consultation with the commandant du-ing the p-elimina-y week-end. The-e should also be a menu book fo- the cooks.

MENU:

A specimen menu will be found in the enclosed book. The-e a-e no special dos and donts he-e,but as we a-e living on ha-d-raised cha-itable subsc-iptions some econmoy is necessa-y. The following a-e expensive and should be avoided except on the occasions shown:

(a) cold ham (sunday lunch to give cooks a -est)
(b) po-k pies (hike).

Food quantities: The following is a -ough estimate of the amounts to o-de-(if the camp is going well it should be necessa-y to inc-ease these towa-ds the end of the week):

Bacon: 2 to 3 oz pe- head pe- meal
Sausage: 3oz -ditto-
Cooked ham: 3 to 4 oz -ditto-
Stewing meat: 4 to 5 Oz - ditto-
Roasting meat: 5 to 6 oz -ditto- .

ORDERING OF FOOD:

(a) **G-oce-ies:** Bulk o-de- will be made befo-e you a--ive and should cove- the main non-pe-ishable items fo- ~~thxx~~ most of the camp. Any fu-the- needs(p-ovided the amounts involved a-e not too la-ge) may be easily obtained f-om B-ayshaws of Masham.

(b) **G-eeng-oce-ies:** These a-e ~~xxx~~ delive-ed twice a week f-om -ipon and the-efo-e some fo-esight is necessa-y. Delive-y days a-e tuesday and thu-sday o-de-s befo-e 10am that day(CHECK THIS-

OXFORD - BORSTAL CAMPS

ST. PETER'S COLLEGE - WETHERBY

July 24th - August 7th

could give you a lift – but please let me know by return if you want this

Commandant	Ralph Johnson		S.P.C.	R.
Bursar	Alan Macfarlane	5 History	Worcester College	
Cooks	Peter Raggatt	5 Biochemistry	S.P.C. & Dept. of Biochemistry, South Parks Road.	
	Trevor Hatchett	2 Maths	46 Amberwood Rise, New Malden, Surrey.	
House Master	D.B. Hamilton Smith		Wetherby	
Chaplains	Norman Davies		The Rectory Flat, 233 Court Road, S.E.9.	
Cricket team	Rory Geaghegan		Campion Hall	
Campers	Pat Brain	2 P.P.E.	Home Close, Yarnton, Oxford.	
	Robin Dixon	1 English	20, Cote Park, Westbury-on-Trym, Bristol.	
	+ Jim Golcher	1 P.P.E.	84, Aldridge Road, Little Aston, Aldridge, Staffs.	
	Tony Hills	1 Theology	109 Nuns Moor Road, Fenham, Newcastle-upon-Tyne, 4.	
	* Richard Hird	1 Geography	58, Deighlon Lane, Batley, West Yorks.	
	Tim Mead	2 Medicine	Highover, Gobblecote, Nr. Tring, Herts.	
	Tony O'Sullivan	4 Dip. Ed.	18, Grove Hill, Muswell Hill, N.10.	
	Ian Postgate	1 English	Coombe Hill, Highercoombe Road, Haslemere, Surrey.	
	* Neil Ridler	2 P.P.E.	The Rectory, Burlon Bradstock, Nr. Bridport, Dorset.	
	+ Tim Ward	1 Physics	Ellingham Rectory, Nr. Bungay, Suffolk.	
	Bob Whyte	1 Theology	158, Upper Grosvenor Road, Tunbridge.	
	Robin Crossley			

PLEASE NOTE

1. If any of you do not know each other please remedy this.
2. Sherry 6.15 p.m. June 15th in my room to meet everybody else; please do your best to keep this time free.
3. Will those coming up by transport (car/m/c) please let me know.
4. Further details later.

June, 1965. Ralph Johnson

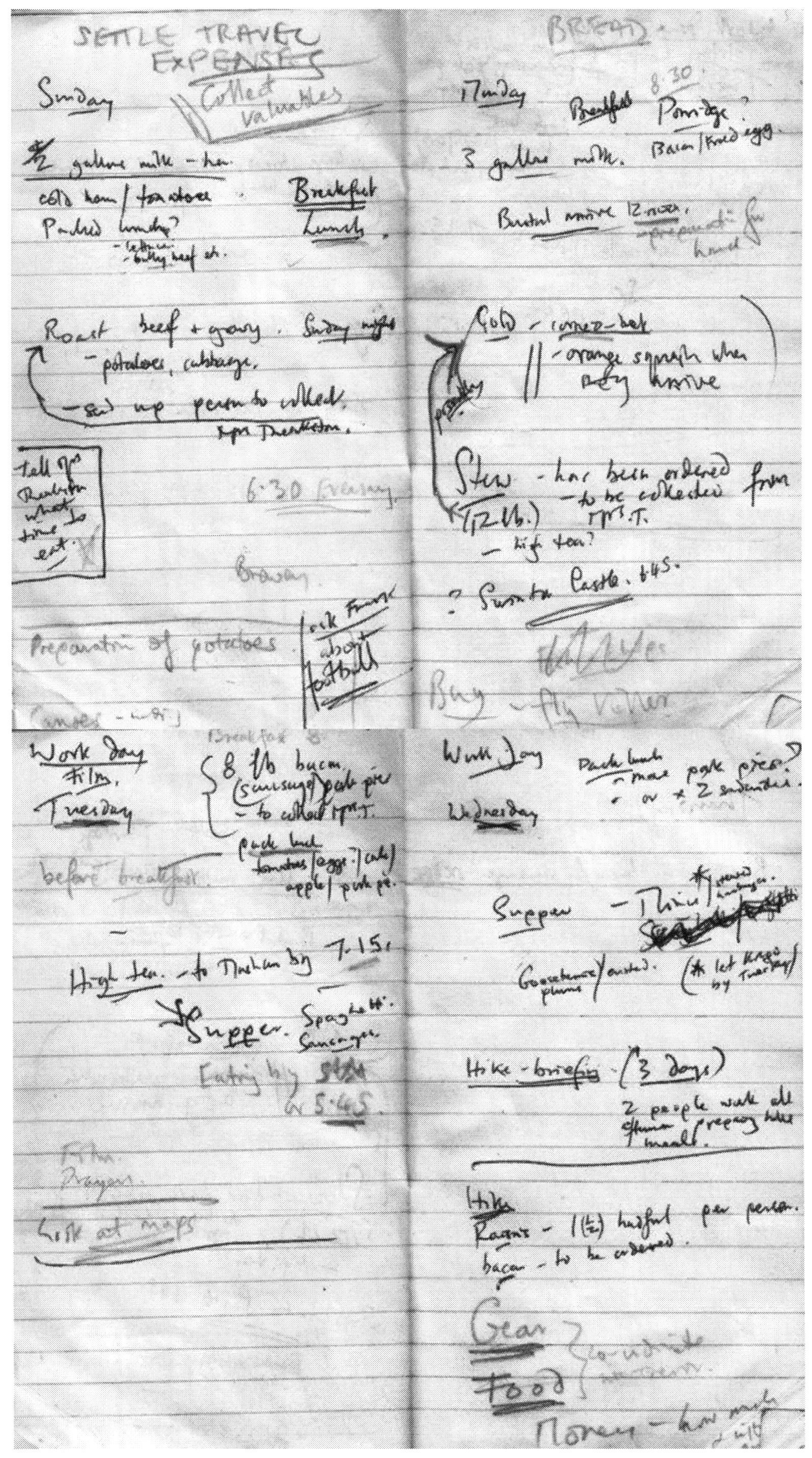

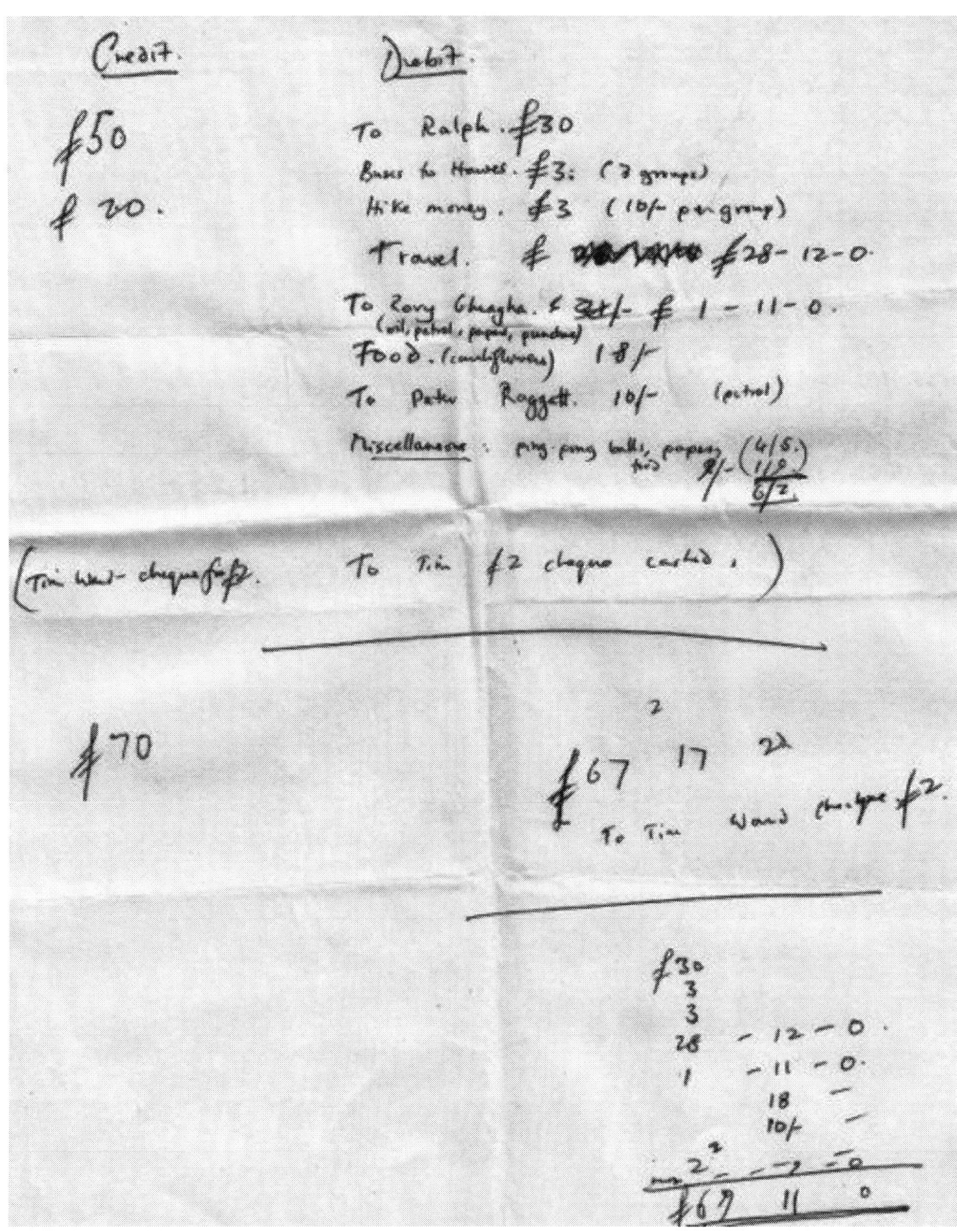

Credit. Debit.

£50 To Ralph. £30

£20. Buses to Houses. £3: (7 groups)

Hike money. £3 (10/- per group)

Travel. £ [illegible] £28-12-0.

To Rory [illegible]. £ 31/- £1-11-0.
(oil, petrol, paper, [illegible])

Food. (cauliflowers) 18/-

To Peter Raggett. 10/- (petrol)

Miscellaneous: ping-pong balls, paper, [illegible] (4/5. 1/9 6/2)

(Tim Ward - cheque £2. To Tim £2 cheque cashed.)

£70 £67 17 22

To Tim Ward cheque £2.

£30
3
3
28 - 12 - 0.
1 - 11 - 0.
18 -
10/- -
2 - 7 - 0
£67 11 0

Another scrap of poetry, written at the Borstal Camp is dated 24 July 1965

For Zoë
No gift

I cannot weave you patterns of delight,
Bring down the crowding stars of night,
I cannot sing across the mountainside,
Or boast with Priam in his pride.

All that I have – a seedy shape,
A haze of uncollected scenes,
A litter of suspicious rhymes
A handful of discarded dreams
An outworn voice in this an age of war
Protestingly forced to say
The things I cannot speak,
Of how your goodness, and the joy
Of meeting you were sweeter
Than the new-born hay
That the silences were longer
When you went away.
And only now could feel the moving
Of the clouds of which you'd spoke.
Where can I turn, what do or say
That I might win you?
What quest or deed could
Bring me on my knees
To turn the lonely whispering days
Into such a haze of wonder
With your presence?
Adrift, senseless, I roam; searching
For you. Aflame with other lusts
And the falling of soft hair and curved limbs
Alight with the power of kings
And future conquests. Yet amidst
All my plans and sudden desires
Aware of your gentle eyes
Dreaming of another world, your
Captive hands moulding mercy
To the moaning years.
All this I cannot say
Nor store one memory for the
Harvest pile & all is
Bitter with the breath
Of death …

My next letter was written on 25th July from the Oxford-Borstal Camp, Yorkshire moors

Dear Mummy and Daddy,

No letter has penetrated through to this remote spot this week; possibly I lost (or rather left behind) a letter which arrived at Field Head. Anyhow for once there are no questions to answer. I hope all goes well with you. Here I am sitting in the camp tent while two of my fellow-campers strum guitars - and the rain teams down. We are waiting for the gang from the Borstal to arrive. They come midday tomorrow so until then there is a slight vacuum during which we wander round the local brewery (owned by an old Sedberghian and sponsor of this camp) and 'get to know each other'.[1] *The St Peter's College undergraduates seem very pleasant. I am, I think I told you, 'Bursar' - which means I order*

[1] R.F. Theakston, owner of Theakston's Brewery.

food and collect in loose cash etc. I also get issued with £50 for incidental expenses - I had an idea of whipping off to the south of France with it ... It doesn't look as if I'll have to do very much, and during the 3-day hike on which they [go] *off I may go over to Patterdale with the commandant (Ralph) - he to see a Worcester friend who lives there, I to see Zoë.*

She is quite probably going to Spain before I get back from the camp so, with her 3 weeks social work I may not see for some time. She had to go down to Oxford, as I think I told you, to have a 'viva'. She was a bit depressed with it - and will hear the results in a week or so. I only saw her for a day before coming here. We went over to Sedbergh on the bike and I nostalgically showed her round 'the old school'. She says she wouldn't send her children to a public school (being left-wing) but liked it I think. I managed to avoid Marriot etc. Then we had a raspberry picnic beside a stream and climbed one of the nearby fells and back by way of Jane Buckmaster. It was a lovely day with cloud-and-sunlight, a mass of foxgloves and she was as sweet as ever. I find, much to my annoyment, that I miss her. She's not prepared to commit herself - and possibly I am not deep down. However she really is the nicest girl I've ever met. How many times have I said that?

We had a card from Fiona - it appears that she has set off to the Hebrides. I hope the weather is better for her than it is for us. Depending on various things - like what my tutor says about the first draft of my chapter - I might go up to see her. I pottered rounds some second-day [sic] *book-shops in Kendal & Skipton on the way over. In these little village places I should be able to build up a very cheap library, and one occasionally finds really good books. For instance I got a lovely bound cover of 'Forty Years in a Moorland Parish' by Rev. J. C. Atkinson which is a classic account of country life - especially folklore (witches) and old customs. With my book on Gosforth & Granny's book on Hawkshead we'll have the foundation for a library on the local villages. It really would be fascinating to study the beliefs etc of present-day Hawksheadians. One could draw little maps of 'gossip-chains' and charts showing what activities the Wright's had a finger in! How is your writing going Mummy? A copy of History Today should be arriving soon.*

Sorry, I feel a little apathetic and sleepy so this is a very dull letter. My first night on the corrugated-iron camping field was not as restful as it might have been!

Look after yourselves, much love,

Alan

My mother wrote to me from Cherideo on 27th July

Thank you for your letter, I certainly am not bored with hearing from you every week, I look forward all day to the mail, it's just that I thought with all your writing you might be bored having to do more. I expect a certain amount of flurry and excitement is becoming apparent at Field Head but I hope this isn't affecting your studies – anyway now I come to think of it you will be in your Borstal by now. I don't know how long you will be staying there but I hope it's a success and you don't get involved in too many problems. I had a letter from Richard about the house and I don't think there will be any hitches now unless, as he keeps darkly hinting, he decides to get married but even then he can presumably live at Haileybury.

I can think of nothing nicer than working on all those old records and do hope someone else doesn't get round to it first. The only snag would be spending my declining years in the Essex Records Office but perhaps I could collect them from nearer? It would be terribly exciting feeling the old villages come alive, and I think I have enough historical imagination but you could watch over that side and see I didn't gush. I had intended to make a study of an Assamese village this summer but haven't felt well enough, anyway it would take more than a few months to do it properly. I have nearly finished my book, it isn't of course what I'd hoped – I wanted to recreate in the jungle sanctuary the sort of magic of "The Secret Garden" and though I felt it myself I haven't made it work for others. I don't think anyone will publish it, as the idea (a commonplace out here) that all gods are one and that as I put it "it was the same god who walked the streets of Bethlehem and the forests of Brindaban" seems to shock the Christian mind. Richard would certainly be horrified – I think a few years ago you would have been too – and all those middle class mothers certainly would. A publisher out here might take it though as the idea is implicit in every Eastern religion. The only reasons (I think!) that I would like it to be published is that it sings the praises of Assam, and would be a sort of thank you offering. … My plans are now to fly to Madras, spend a day there (Clive country) and then go on to Cochin by air where I get a boat for a four day trip up the coast, I hope calling in at Calicut and Goa. I'm sure it will all fall through but it keeps us busy thinking it all out and if I can get some photos I could work up an article easily as every inch of the Pepper Coast is full of history. Have at last got a review of Gallipoli in Spectator that arrived yesterday, very good. …

Haven't heard from Fiona from the Hebrides yet but hope it isn't too disastrous a failure – if they can get a roof they will be all right. Zoe's parents must be a lot calmer and less hysterical than I am to let her wander everywhere on her own, but they probably have no choice! I do hope she got a 1st, what will she do after that? I think you mentioned Social Science. … Even more boring than usual to-day, it is very oppressive and I feel like a sack of damp salt, sagging and wet. Hope to write something brighter from Shillong.

1965 - August

My mother wrote to me from Shillong, Assam, on 5th August

As you see I'm up in the pines and the cool mists – what a relief to be away from that sticky heat for a bit too though it isn't cold here, still you can breathe. Somehow I feel much further away from you all, I suppose because I'm cut off from letters, I don't know how long your Borstal is lasting but do hope it is going well. Daddy and I drove up on Monday, Robert[1] let us bring the G.M's Plymouth and his driver but it refused to start in the morning and there was much pacing and cursing before we got going, the real reason for my trip and why we got the V.I.P. treatment was to see Dr Hughes the mission doctor up here. I didn't mention this before as I thought it might bother you all, but I have had all my tests now and it isn't the ulcers or other horrors that I visualised but simply persistent amoebic cysts and I'm going into hospital on Saturday for a ten days offensive against them. I just couldn't get rid of the pain and felt so miserable in the heat and watching my last hot weather go without being able to enjoy it that Tom Poole and Daddy decided to bring me up here for a thorough investigation. I had it yesterday and thorough is the word, one of the tests involved a piece of rubber tubing down my nose and then swallowed – you can imagine my horror at having to gulp down yards of rubber when I can hardly swallow a poached egg without imagining I'm choking. It was quite fascinating actually, as they siphoned the contents of my stomach up through this every fifteen minutes for two and a half hours, and one watched them turn from pale blue to green to sulphur yellow (hope you aren't reading this just before a meal). Luckily I had a very good book to read, "The Rector of Justin" by Auchinloss[2] and this kept me occupied, though as it has one of Gollanz's sulphur yellow covers I fear I shall never see one again without thinking of that tube.

The mission doctor, Dr Hughes is the one who operated on Daddy's appendix in 1942 – he does about ten operations a day and the hospital is crammed to very corner with patients but he moves through an impossibly long day with a radiant calmness and makes you feel as if your silly little troubles were all he had to bother about. He is the sort of man who would restore one's faith very quickly if one stayed with him, one forgets all the bitter things one feels about missionaries when meeting someone like him. ... I feel better already...

I got the Proof of my book[3] just before I left, it seems a poor little thing now and the illustrations rather dull so I don't think will do more than cover the advance. There is a new editor at Chattos who is an Oxford friend of my agents which is a good contact. Have brought the other book up with me with an idea of finishing it but doubt if I will. ... Will write again between enemas.

I wrote again on 8th August from Field Head, Ambleside

Dear Mummy and Daddy,

Thank you for your letter. Perhaps Mummy will be in Shillong when this arrives; I hope the visit refreshes you. I have arrived from the Borstal Camp and have comfortably embedded myself in the rituals of Field Head life; the 12 a.m. post, the vast lunch, the discussions of the enormities of the neighbours, the yapping of Poochie off for a walk and my cosy room filling up with books and files. Unfortunately I am running out of material and will probably have to do a lightening trip, Cambridge - Essex - London - Oxford starting next weekend and lasting about 10 days. I can't predict where my next letter will come from.

I arrived to find Mummy's History Today article had arrived. I enjoyed it very much. I wish I could write with such an easy touch. I reckon that I'm condemned to a rocky and fairly dull style -

---

[1] Robert Higham, General Manager.

[2] *The Rector of Justin* by Louis Auchincloss.

[3] *Tales and Legends from India* (1965).

perhaps the subject-matter will make up for this? After all, Marx, Freud, Einstein and other such heroes aren't exactly light reading. Anyway, about the article, as you said it was quite skittish - just right for the audience and fascinating. All the strange names and places confused me a little, but possibly added to the magic. I hope your other writing goes well. I am debating whether to write something for the same journal, largely for mercenary reasons. I hesitate partly out of a fear of being rejected, partly because of my lofty ambitions. When, in one's youthful pride, another book of the stature of 'The Interpretation of Dreams', 'A Discourse on Method', 'Das Kapital' or 'War and Peace' seems just round the corner it is a little upsetting to have to decide what the audience of History Today would like: I wouldn't even be allowed my precious foot-notes which I have spent so much time perfecting! Also there is my absurd idea that I should accumulate material as long as possible and then suddenly burst with its accumulated power onto a surprised (but delighted!) public. It is a constant temptation to let out a trickle, but any success would probably make such a trickle into a steady stream in a short time. I don't know if you follow this complicated dam metaphor. Talking of metaphors, you said that you were surprised that I didn't know what kind of fish or monster I had caught in my research net. It is a strange feeling, but I'm not sure that if one is doing really important work it is likely. I remember Beatrice Webb saying in her Appendix on The Art of Note-Taking (which is about filing systems) that she could never tell what her conclusions from interviews would be until she had sorted out all her separate bits of paper. One might change the simile and compare the process to oil-digging. For a year one constructs the derricks etc. and chooses a likely sight, then another year is spent digging down through layers of rock, the last year finds the researcher either wringing his hands over wasted time or with a jet of knowledge hundreds of feet high. To bore back two hundred or more years with only imagination and scattered, often misdirected, records as one's only aids is a risky business. The more exciting and worthwhile the problem, the longer will be the boring and the more impatient the world grows. It is very tempting to scoop up a little surface material (the simile is getting into trouble now!) to show the world (and oneself) that one is achieving something. But to disclose anything so complex and hidden as the structure of an extinct civilizations' beliefs requires enormous patience, energy and imagination. I hope you've got these, as I'm not at all sure that I have! Hawkshead might be worth studying in detail if church court records survive: the parish registers of burials, births and marriages go back to 1568. Research on Essex villages, so rich in materials, would not involve much time there. To 1 month spent in gathering material one would spend about 6 or more in analysing and writing-up. I may need your help before the thesis is over as I have found two villages with very good witches and records and will only have time to look at one ... But more of that anon.

I don't' think I mentioned that Professor Raymond Firth replied to my enquiry re. grants for research at London. The course is a 2-year one and he doesn't know of any funds other than those Evans-Pritchard spoke of. I would rather like to do the next part of my training somewhere other than Oxford, and will, if necessary live in a garret etc. About research he says "I think that research among people of another culture does provide for the social anthropologist a kind of cultural jolt, so to speak, and perspective which are extremely valuable. There is no effective substitute for this. But for someone like yourself who wants to remain a historian (which I think is the right course) while having some training in social anthropology, I think it quite possible to do research on historical materials using the comparative framework of anthropology." Thus plans to go to India are still in flux.

Sorry to talk 'shop' for so long. Zoë's future is still in flux also, depending on whether she gets a State Studentship. If she does she will do a two-year M.SC. if not a one-year Diploma in Sociology at London. We went for another glorious walk on Thursday. It was a warm but very gusty day with the clouds shaping the fells dark and light. We walked along Place Fell (the ridge that runs along the other side of Ullswater) and down into a secluded valley called Martindale. Then we caught a boat up the lake to Glenridding. Z is very well and has got over the slight disappointment at not getting a first.

Granny also is well, much better than she was. Surprisingly there isn't much strain or panic in the atmosphere (or perhaps I don't notice it, tucked away in my yew-tree level corner, descending only at meals). Jane Wilkinson came up for supper on Friday and is going to Switzerland for a couple of weeks tomorrow.

Much love to you both, Alan

Letter to Ian Green, 8th August 1965

Ian Green, a student at Worcester a couple of years behind me, had written to me after his finals in July 1965 to ask about doing a research degree. I replied on 8th August as follows.

Dear Ian,

Please forgive a typed letter. Thank you very much for yours. I'm glad you wrote as I love giving people advice or retelling my own experiences: I doubt, however, whether I can be of much help. It would be well worthwhile talking to Paul Hyams (who is now a research fellow at Jesus) or, perhaps even more valuable to David Palliser. ...

I will take your questions in order. As far as looking for other forms of employment in case I didn't get a grant I was very lazy. I didn't stand much of a chance of getting a State Studentship – probably far less than you – but decided to go round the world if I didn't get a good enough degree. I got as far as arranging various fisheries I was going to visit in Israel and India but that was all. I also, was advised by Harry Pitt to try for the Civil Service. I went for a gentle talk with the ex-Worcester man who comes round the college in the Spring to see what he can bag. I was amused by your day-mare of your interview as much of it resembled what actually happened with me. I didn't even bother to put on my little-worn suit and this, combined with my guileless answers and questions led him to say at the end. "I see Mr. Macfarlane, that you are an idealist. Very good. But we don't want any of them in the Service. You would only get frustrated. If you want to change the world, or even the Civil Service don't do it from <u>inside</u> that Service. Come back in a year or so and perhaps we can talk things over again." I may be being a little unkind, but that is the gist of the thing. Actually, my views of th subject have become a little tolerant since then. I think it is probably a bit silly to think, as I did then, that the 'world' was big and wicked, that business-men were ogres and the government in all its manifestations crooks. If I may quote David Riesman in the <u>Lonely Crowd</u> (a book I've only just read, and scarcely understand but absolutely fascinating for the historian)

'Partly as a result of this image of the businessman, many students at privately endowed universities have become reluctant to consider business careers, and, as more and more young people are drawing into the colleges, these attitudes become increasingly widespread... (Lonely Crowd, Yale paperback edn, pp23-1)

All that Riesman said about business I felt about the C.S. and even about the University. I suppose a large part of me still feels that University politics and life is a pretty nasty, introverted, business. It is only coming across people like James and Harry that persuades me otherwise. I don't think they would mind if you explained that you wanted to accept a State Studentship if you got one; Harry Pitt could tell you about this. Even if you go into the C.S. (or anything else) that isn't the end of an academic life if you are really interested. When my uncle went down from Worcester with a second ten years ago there weren't any State Studentships. He went into the C.S. and wrote history books (which they encouraged). Now, on the strength of these he is back – at all Souls. If you felt like it, he would, not doubt, be happy to discuss your problem. Again you might get him (Robert Rhodes James, All Souls College) as a tutor. He worked as a clerk in the House of Commons.

As an example I am hopeless. I entered for a Studentship in the off chance, but otherwise felt I would set off, romantically to search the world for God, a Vocation, a Woman etc. At 21 (or even 23) one can do this. But it is hardly the sort of thing that helps as advice...!

This partly answers the next question; when & how to choose a subject. I hadn't a clue. My interests (and even my interest in history generally – I was never very keen on the subject as it is taught in universities) have arisen <u>since</u> beginning research. I suppose I had a leaning towards social/cultural history and a definite fascination for a particular period (the C16 & C17). These combined to make *me want Christopher Hill as a supervisor and it was with this in mind that I went to him with some suggested subjects – Women, Witches and the Arthurian Legend in the C17. Now my head is buzzing with ideas and I feel I could set an army of researchers at work. If you ever feel like discussing this nearer the time, please don't hesitate. I'm out on a limb and would suggest topics like incest, kinship and marriage, suicide, insanity, magic, the sociology of the village, dreams and nightmares etc. etc. I am convinced that the big break-throughs in the next twenty years will be made by combining the approach and questions of anthropologists/sociologists (if you haven't read it, look at Thomas' article in Past and Present, no. 24) and the material to answer such questions at the local level – (see, as I'm sure you have, the works of Hoskins). Of course there are endless dangers. Too much of the former leaves one waving wild theories and shouting streams of jargon; too much of the latter and one sinks back into the V.C.H.[1] sterility of which even Hoskins is capable. But this is all a bee in my bonnet. I expect you have your own ideas. Perhaps you want to develop your vacation essay on the Interregnum bishop?*

As to the personal [side] of research, loneliness and inability to communicate, they are indeed present. Oxford can be a dreary place in the vac'. Things aren't nearly as bad as they were. There are now graduate societies and common rooms and a vastly increasing number of researchers _ Worcester has over 80 alone. I expect your work will take you away from Oxford some of the time and you're a sociable person, I think. But again, bound up in myself and my work as I am, I've never been very susceptible to loneliness; it would be worth talking to others.

If I can help at all let me know and good luck both in your future and with Lady Clay. I expect I'll see something of you there.

Best wishes, Alan

I probably met Richard Britnell at the Essex Record Office. I mentioned to him that I had notes on lectures by W.G.Hoskins and others. I sent these to him and he replied at length. He wrote me a long and very interesting letter about medieval peasantry, on which he was working. To this I replied at considerable length.

12/8/65 Field Head, Outgate

Dear Richard,

Thank you for an interesting letter and the references. I was specially interested in the Hunisett one as I met H. in the P.R.O where he was most helpful. I enclose an unpublished talk of E. Power's – I'm sure you'll know all there is in it (if you can read the abbreviations). The Visitation records, especially the famous 1397 Visitation of Hereford, seem to be the only means of getting at religion in everyday life, and even then it is the abnormal, or the immoral that we hear of. You say that 'anti-clericalism' sticks out a mile' and instance the constant presentation of clergymen in the manor courts for petty misdemeanours. The general impression of hostility and incompetence is deepened by the Visitation records – but I wonder what conclusions one can draw from them? It is difficult to decide what contemporaries thought of vices & misdemeanours which bother us. For instance, it is generally assumed that illegitimacy is heavily penalized in agrarian communities, yet this is not so in Gosforth (W. M. Williams, The Sociology of an English Village (London, 1964), p.65) in the C20 or Danby in Cleveland in the C19 (Rev. J. C. Atkinson, Forty Years in a Moorland Parish … (London, 1891), p. 5) What did people think of the priest's concubines therefore? Was it possibly an honour to be one? Was not the very involvement of the clergy in the every-day life and problems of the village a strength as well as a weakness? As you say, it is a fascinating problem.

It is indeed easy to over-estimate the stability and 'closedness' of the village up to the C17. Before Laslett on Clayworth we had little inkling of the amount of mobility. But there are a million problems. How far does social mobility – either horizontal or vertical – effect the rigidity either of social

---

[1] *Victoria County History.*

relationships or the system of values? Cannot a large number of peregrinating beggars etc. we'll be absorbed into a still closely-knit society? I have just read Jusserand's English Wayfaring Life but this does not help much. Tawney's study of C16 vagrants would probably confirm his opinion of the tight-knit parish organization since the national attempts to enforce the Poor Law, of course, stressed the necessity for people to be whipped back to their parishes and to be supported there.

I entirely agree about the value of looking at contemporary society – if possible vaguely similar, at least in productive system, to the one [one] is studying and then going back with certain problems in one's mind. I am finding a mass of stuff on suicide, gossip and scandal, attitudes towards time, women, leisure, drink etc. which I would never have noticed if I hadn't read a little sociology and social anthropology. The real problem seems to be twofold. Firstly to jolt one's mind out of its contentment with the clichés of social and economic history so that one has a series of problems, instead of pseudo-answers, in one's mind. Secondly to be constantly alert to the sidelights of history. By this I mean the unspoken revelations and premises for actions and statements which by their nature can only be traced indirectly. Thus one may be reading about a family sitting down to a meal and find that the men (master and servants) sit and eat together, while the children stand (as in the picture, p.8 of the Pelican Illustrated Social History:2 (Trevelyan)) and the women wait on the men and eat later. Here one learns something about the attitude towards servants, children and women – three fascinating and obscure subjects – as well as something about the function of meals. And so on … The difficulty is picking up these hints and tabulating them. The study of social attitudes, which is what I am really interested in, needs a new methodological foundation as it is infinitely more complex than the study of institutions which has been the core of historical writing to date. Thus I spend a lot of time messing about with little bits of paper & filing systems. The best sources for direct observations on the manners, customs and assumptions of a people are of course the works of foreigners or those who for some reason have had a 'cultural jolt'. Londoners would never bother to note that their women wore hats in the street only after marriage – but foreigners would (Van Meteren, quoted in Dover Wilson, Life in Shakespeare's England (Pelican, 1962), p. 27). The fascinating book I referred to about Danby in Cleveland (Atkinson) was written by foreigners describing medieval England. But they are only a beginning, of course. From the C16 on one has parish records and the detailed account of daily life in the, as yet untapped, ecclesiastical court records. This is where I hope to step in!

The other major problem as far as I am concerned is that of social change. It is here that historians can make their greatest contribution, I think, since, by definition, the study of such change is historical. But it is frighteningly complex. Sociologists and anthropologists have had a moderately easy time while studying communities in time cross-sections and have explained the function of various parts of society. But the unsatisfactoriness is becoming apparent (I think this synchronic approach is largely responsible for the ever-stable, unreal, impression Homans gives – tho' he could do nothing else), and the theories will have to be tested in motion. But when one sees a society changing it becomes immensely difficult to decide what alters what. Does the religious system reflect or shape the economic organization, do family structures condition or emerge from population change – you'll know the problems. And when one is dealing with social attitudes it becomes even more difficult. Were people more anxious in the C16 & C17 and was this the result or cause of changes in the economic system, the pressures of religious sentiment, the splitting of activities and functions, the reversal of roles? What indices for mental change, for anxiety and guilt has one? All that I have read so far, and it's very little I regret to say, gives me little hope of answers from the social sciences; they are hoping for answers from historians.

That is enough generalization and platitudes for now, I think! I will probably be in Cambridge next week (& also in E.R.O.) and if I'm not too rushed will try to look you up. Will also have a look at the Emma articles[1] so don't worry about them. I've got to check some witchcraft cases in the University Library.

I hope all goes well and you have a pleasant holiday.

---

[1] Copies of ecclesiastical visitation articles in the library of Emmanuel College.

My mother wrote from the Hospital in Shillong on 13th August

My dear Alan,

Here I still am on a grey afternoon with clouds literally swirling in at the door, half way through my course. The time isn't going too slowly now, have got into a sort of rhythm of writing, reading & dozing & the days slide by, though I feel I've been here about 3 months. Yours & Daddy's birthday presents arrived on my first day in hospital so couldn't have been better as I was feeling very depressed & cut off. Your selection as usual was perfect & I was thrilled with the "autograph"! I have only dipped into them, am trying to make them last as we're packed all our books & won't have anything till we come home (Daddy says another parcel from you is waiting for me.) I read "Warren Hastings" of course, & it was marvellous, even when wrong there is nobody so marvellous as Macaulay. Thank you very much. Daddy got me "The Pleasure of Ruins" which is sumptuous, you must have seen it – have found 2 "howlers" in the Mughal bit though, which gives me confidence for any I may make. I have also been reading a couple of books from the library, one Mughal, one "Kim" which I haven't read for years & is delicious. My course consists mostly of lying flat on my back – for about 5 hours a day – while they pump things into me – a "two-pronged attack" Dr Hughes euphemistically describes it, but I'll draw a veil over it! … The clamour will be rising at Field Head, don't let Granny do too much, she can always leave things for us to bring down. Fiona sounds happy but may find it palls, specially if the weather is bad, Granny says you are subsidising her, hope thats not true?

The next letter I wrote was on Sunday 15th August from Anne's Flat in London

Dear Mummy and Daddy,

Poor Mummy. I'm so sorry to hear of your awful rubber-tubes, enemas and illness. I do hope the treatment is not too awful and you are feeling better. Amoebic cysts sound horrible, will not the best treatment be coming home? It's awful to think that it might have been worse ... I do wish you had told me that you were in pain, tho' it would have worried me a little. I expect you will have returned from Shillong now, and be starting to gather together soon for the last move.

As you'll gather from the address, I've reached my first stopping place. I hitched down yesterday with Zoë. It was very difficult going, with a two-hour wait at Kendal before we could even get started. By the end of the day, as it got really dark, we were still eighty miles from London and I had visions (not unpleasant) of making a shelter of 'mud and wattles' at 'Gibbet's Corner' where we were stranded. But finally we got a lift from a nice Jewish couple and caught the last tube. Despite the bad hitching I enjoyed it very much - being with Zoë. I have seen a lot of her over the last week as she has had two college friends staying and I have been over every-day and we have been sun-bathing, walking etc. A wonderful golden week - one of those (like that last summer with my nymphet - Judy) which make up for everything else. But now Zoë is going to be in Italy for 3 weeks and then in Bristol for another three. And anyhow it seems that we can never be more than really close friends; which is perhaps the best thing. I shall miss her, but deep down am perhaps a little relieved to find myself still free. There are too many things to do and see before one becomes settled or confined. Zoë's parents are going out to visit Z's sister at the end of Nov/beginning of December and whether they are there or not Zoë said you should visit her. If you are in Madras, and felt like it do look her up - the address is
Dr Anthea Cooke (Allen is maiden name)
Prakash, Bishop Waller, Ave East, Madras, 4
She is married to a solicitor and I'm sure would be a sweet person and delighted to put you up. Z will mention that you might be around. Anthea will be having a baby in September so much excitement in the Allen household.

Anne is sitting a foot away and saying "what are you writing about". She looks well, if a bit tired. I may bus up with her next week-end. The flat is seething with Australians - useful 'contacts' for her proposed visit to the Kangaroo continent. There is the usual Sunday-morning inertia, very sapping on the will. One is so cut off in this vaguely shabby, deb world from anything except second-hand emotions, that it is difficult to be either sincere or committed to anything. It's like living in a 'Vogue' world of misty sentiments and other people's opinions. Anne rises above most of it. But the world of pain and unpackaged beauty is far, far away. Of course there is plenty of loneliness and frustration, but everything seems cloudy and half unreal. Perhaps it's just my bleary morning feeling.

My rapid tour is more or less organised. Monday-Wednesday in Essex, Thursday and Friday in Cambridge, the week-end seeing my supervisor & Linda in Oxford, next week back in London, perhaps staying at Roy & Rosemary's (their new flat). I haven't done as much work as usual recently so feel a big spurt (which will also shut out Zoë) is called for.

I do hope this finds Mummy completely better,

My fondest love to you both, Alan

My next letter was on Sunday 22nd August from Worcester College – 'in transit'

Dear Mummy and Daddy,

How are you both? I expect Mummy will be back from Shillong and I do hope feeling much better. We have all been thinking of you in this miserable illness and only wish there was something we could do. I'm having letters forwarded to Anne's, where I will be staying tonight, so maybe there will be a letter from you waiting for me there. In my rush round the archives of England I have lost contact not only with everybody but even of what's happening in the Great Big World - all the polio cases, wars, economic crises and other daily delights which enliven our lives ...

When I last wrote I was at Anne's flat. We spent the afternoon sun-bathing and walking across Hampstead heath. The mother of Anne's friend Judith is of Scottish descent and psychic and we had a most interesting discussion about second-sight, witchcraft etc. Its extraordinary how people who one categorizes and pigeon-holes as dull and normal (in one's conceited way) turn out to be full of interest and problems when one has a chance to talk seriously. On Monday I went up/down to Essex where I stayed with my usual motherly Irish landlady. I had three pleasant, if hectic, days and have now finished my biggest chunk (I hope) of records - the archdeaconry courts.

I also started making tentative probes to see which villages I should study in detail and have more or less settled on two. I am having some of their records microfilmed (this is the great thing at the moment, and the cheapest way. One can get a 400 page document which would take years to copy out done for £2) and thus will be able to work on them up in the Lakes. The only snag is that one needs a projector. A proper projector, which has mirrors etc and be used in semi-darkness costs about £200 but the expert said that a 35 mm stills projector (like Richards) would be just as good. Thus I will have to buy one. I imagine they are in £30 price range. It will be immensely useful for future work and save endless copying out & visits to places. Also I can show the slides which I bought for the W.E.A. I seem to remember you were contemplating getting a stills projector - are you still wondering about it? If you are perhaps we could go halves? I think I could manage to get one on the H.P. anyhow (with the money I got from teaching) but if you wanted one we might as well make a joint effort. I would hope to get it for work in November. I would consult Richard on the best buy. The microfilm may also answer your question about whether it would be necessary to spend a lot of time away from the Lakes if one took up local history. The answer would be no - hardly any.

Thursday I buzzed up to Cambridge where I checked a source in the University Library, walked down the backs, looked in 3 college libraries for documents, went to the Institute of Social Anthropology and talked to one of the teachers - had lunch with one of the students I met by chance, popped into the Folk Museum for a witchcraft chat and then came on to Oxford by the evening train! It was a lovely day and Camb. was really exquisite. I would be very happy there but the Inst. of Anthropology does not sound wholly attractive - a rather small, quarrelsome place possibly - no that's unkind. I think I've just set my heart on going to London....

Since being in Oxford I've seen a little of Linda. She's going out very seriously with her 'boss' and is contemplating marrying him and going to America in about 3 months. She has only known him properly for 6 weeks! I do hope she isn't hurt again. She really is very sweet. We went to the Beatles new film - glorious snubbing-of-noses at pomposity, officialdom and the boredom & unimaginativeness of modern life. They add a new dimension to living. Zoë is off I assume. I miss her. Much love to you both, Alan

My mother wrote again to me from Cherideo on 28th August

Taking this opportunity of writing a joint letter, chiefly because I'm out of my stride and trying to catch up... I wasn't sorry to leave Shillong, and was very happy to be home and have doggies, Miranda[1] *etc. pleases to see me – all fat and well. Immediately strode round the compound cursing the malis which shows how much better I am, haven't had the energy to garden for months. ..Have just finished "The crisis of India"*[2] *which I read with interest but slight irritation – he is absolutely right in everything he says but somewhere between the statistics and the sense of outrage India has slipped between his fingers. He has seen nothing but the poverty and degradation and doesn't seem to have noticed the beauty and gaiety, and though he continually (and rightly) blames the government for the present state of affairs, he doesn't blame us at all for the almost impossible state of affairs, he doesn't blame us at all for the impossible task we left them. My book will put the blame squarely where it should be – if it ever gets written! I didn't really mean my article to be "skittish", but my mission is to lighten Indian history so as to make it at least readable, the real scholars are such heavy going that only a handful of other real scholars read them! We definitely do want to buy a stills projector, if you can wait till December we could get one then, otherwise we could put down a deposit on an H.P. one but Daddy wants a good, powerful one, better than Richard's with some guard against putting the slides in upside down. Perhaps you could look round. I meant to warn you that a film would be arriving to be developed, and when it is ready could you please send anything that comes out to Dr T.W. Poole... No sign of the film that Fiona has had for a year and I wonder where the camera is? … Almost September and I've sent for my seeds and the egrets are coming back to the tennis court and the end is in sight, a horrible hot weather but perhaps just as well as it makes India a lot easier to leave! I've got my last ten days touring fixed, fly to Madras (will look up Zoë's people) and after a day and night there on to Cochin where I catch a boat to Bombay. I don't stop at Goa unfortunately but call in at Calicut and various other old imperial bases and might work up an article to pay for the trip if everything hasn't disappeared from sight. ...We hooted over the deb's dance, fantastic that that sort of thing can still go on and that sort of money still be wasted. Australia sounds a good idea though I am sad that my chicks are to fly from under my wings so quickly?!*

The correspondence which I had started with Paul Slack in the summer term continued through the summer vacation.

30/8/65 Field Head, Outgate

Dear Paul,

Thank you very much for your most interesting reply to my questions. As I am going to be writing my thesis in the Lakes and hence only making flying visits to Oxford to visit Keith I hope you'll forgive questions asked by letter. But first <u>*congratulations*</u>*, both on your marriage and on getting the Harmsworth despite your gloomy predictions. I am so glad things have sorted themselves out so well and I wish you every happiness. I would like to take you up on your invitation to a meal next term, partly to meet your wife, partly to discuss. I will get in touch when I know for certain which week I will be in Oxford; it will probably be about the second week of term.*

Before I discuss plague could I ask a few more questions? Firstly, have you come across any/many cases of suicide in any of your sources? Hoskins in a BBC talk he lent me said that suicide

---

[1] Miranda was a small deer.

[2] By Ronald Segal, published January 1965.

was 'very uncommon' in the C16 but when I asked for the basis for this remark he, quite naturally since all the proof he needed was silence, said 'that a long reading of C16 records from all sources has revealed very, very few instances indeed'. I see that he has a case in Wigston Magna (Midland Peasant, p. 187, Papermac ed'n), though he was evidently not interested in the subject as he leaves it out of the index. I've come across only a very few cases myself in connection with witchcraft and wondered if you're impression – since it is difficult for it ever to be more than this – is similar. I was interested in the reported remarks of Wrigley re. premarital intercourse. I'm sure you'll; know W.M. William's books – e.g <u>The Sociology of an English Village</u>, (1956) which gives statistics for the C19 and C20 & also statistics for the time of marriage. For instance on p. 196 he shows the commonest marrying month to be November (1572-1887) followed by June. March – a forbidden month – is fantastically low. One other, slightly more relevant, question. I am interested in the subject of syphilis & Nicholas Tyacke tells me that you have come upon records in Norwich which shed light on this obscure region. Are these the accounts of leper houses? Nich. Vaguely suggested that there were grounds for believing that medieval leprosy was in fact VD. Is there any truth in this? I haven't searched medical books: how frequent are cures for this disease? I've got some detailed cases of people with the disease – or alledged to have it by their spouses or future marriage partners. I've even a case of a person committing suicide from the pain; but none of people actually dying with it. Does this mean that it was less virulent than in the days of Beaudelaire? I can let you have my few refs. When you like.

I have finished reading through all the Archdeaconry records of Essex & Colchester but my eye, in its search for witches, doesn't seem to have caught much. Two isolated references are to various people dying of plague in 1610 (E.R.O. D/AEA.26. folio. 14) and to a man who said he had been unable to wash the surplice because 'he had the pox in his house a month or six weekes togither' (D/AACA. 51. F.67.v.) The second looks more like VD. Sorry, I didn't note the place or the second date.

A few general mentions of plague I've come across (I'm sure you'll have read them all, but it does no harm to double check:

J.C. Cox, <u>Churchwarden's Accounts</u>... (London, 1913), pp.317-9

R.W. Muncey, <u>The Romance of Parish Registers</u>... (London, 1933), pp. 100-3, 145

Reginald Scot, <u>Discovery of Witchcraft</u>, (Arundel, 1964 edition), passim, esp. 114, 248

George Gifford, <u>A Dialogue Concerning Witches and Witchcrafts</u>, 1593 (Shakespeare Assoc. Facsimile.1.193), folio. H.3

The last of these two are mainly about the supposed origins of plague in human malice. I have a section on witches supposedly causing plague which I can let you have when it is written up.

I wonder how your study of Essex parishes is going. Let me know when you have decided to do a 'sample study in one or two parishes to find out how the age of death varied in epidemics' as I can send you a list of those involved in witchcraft prosecutions in the villages so that you can keep an eye open for them in your family reconstruction. A quick look at the list of burial registers you sent me reveals that there were witchcraft cases in about ¾ of them. I myself am going to do a detailed study of one or two villages to try to work out how witchcraft was connected with kinship tensions, age-groups, other social deviation, religious affiliations, economic considerations etc. I have chosen Wivenhoe and Boreham so far and also Hatfield Peverel. The last does not have good parish records – but a splendid crop of witches and two detailed pamphlets. Boreham and Wivenhoe (I see their registers are omitted in your list: if you tell me what to count I can save you the work as I will be doing detailed work on them) have excellent records. They both have churchwarden's accounts from the mid C16 & are among the earliest parishes in the country to have poor relief accounts. On the latter you might find something of interest in F.G. Emmison, 'The Care of the Poor in Elizabethan Essex', <u>Essex Review</u>, LXIII, 1953, p. 7ff. Of course I will let you have anything I come across concerning plague, but any particular problems and questions you'd better let me know as my untrained eye will pass over information unless warned.

I hope this hasn't bored you. I find the whole subject most fascinating. Good luck with your work.

He wrote back at length on 23rd September, giving me many further ideas and references. [not included]

1965 - September

My mother wrote from Cherideo on 2nd September

My dear Alan,

I'm a little early in an effort to get back into a rhythm and haven't a letter to thank you for. I had one from Granny yesterday sounding a little worked up about the move, I hope she won't let it upset her but I'm sure she'll find the new place a lot easier to run. I hope you won't be too lonely without even Poochie there, I suppose you could go and sleep next door if necessary, feel I must have committed some awful parental lapse in making you afraid of the dark. I also got my History Today yesterday, my article was meaningless having read it so often but the cover was gay, though Mughal miniatures in reproduction aren't a patch on the original. I had a letter from Elek Books asking me if I would like to write the "scholarly text" on a book of photographs of Mughal India, they have apparently done a series called "Ancient Cities of Art" on Athens, Peking etc. Unfortunately I know very little about the architectural aspect of the Mughals, so I would have to read their previous books and see how scholarly I was supposed to be – they say they will meet me and show me these sometime – Robert here I come There was an excellent review of Gallipoli which yu probably read in H.T. which we read with tight smiles, mean spirited little people that we are. Actually there's nobody I'd like better to succeed than Robert and he deserves every bit of any credit he gets.

Have had a bit of a setback this week, more tummy trouble and the announcement by our Doctor Babu that he was going to give me another course of amoebic injections. However as he approached with the needle I got nervous spasms and couldn't face it, and when we sent for Tom Poole's stand-in he said it was nonsense, I couldn't possibly need more treatment, in fact he reckoned I had been given too much already and both my nerves and stomach needed a rest. So I've been given a mild tranquilliser and a mass of Vitamin pills and am feeling much better to-day. It's been very hot which hasn't helped, but now the rain has come again and everything improved all round – and the psychological effect of writing September at the top of a letter is vastly cheering. Only the political situation looks gloomy but I cannot believe that India and P[akistan] will really start a full scale war, it is difficult to fathom what they think they're up to, especially Pakistan who appears to be the aggressor – but who to believe? I've been reading a soothing book called "Chronicles of Fairacher"[1] to take my mind off my insides, feebly written, without an original thought or phrase but rather charming all the same, all about a Village School and the flower show and so on.

I read somewhere that Cambridge had had a project for some time to collect and sort out parish records from all over the country with a view to writing a new type of history – so perhaps we have been forestalled? I shall love just pottering round graveyards and going on outings with the local archaeological society and writing Rosemary Sutcliff's books – my literary aims are not high, although if I could do as well as R.S. I would be delighted. ... I hope you've managed to collect all the material you need to carry on, and the thesis progresses. You could surely write little pieces on "Familiar Spirits" or "A village witch" without letting out anything sensational or jeopardising your reputation – A.L. Rowse does and you could save your conscience by thinking of the many people to whom you would be giving interest and pleasure – even if they weren't the top scholars?

My mother wrote from Cherideo on September 11th

I have no idea whether this will get to you, everything is somewhat chaotic here at the moment and we haven't had any mail ourselves for ages. It has all happened so suddenly one can't really believe it is true, and rumours are flying madly and every second person one meets might be a paratrooper.[2] So sad,

---

[1] *The Chronicles of Fairacre* by Miss Read.

[2] The India-Pakistan War of 1965-6, centred on Kashmir.

so senseless, and as its impossible for either side to ever "win" one wonders how long their economies and arms will last out. don't worry about us though, if things become critical they will do another of their evacuations, this will be my third and last I hope. Actually I have decided to come home anyway, still not being quite fit and it being such a short time before we finally have to leave – but I don't know if I shall get a passage. All the children on their school holidays are stranded here and the first effort will be to get them away I expect – Daddy has gone up to Jorhat to-day to see what chance there is of an air passage. So maybe I will arrive before this letter. Hate to leave Daddy to face the crisises and what not but am not much help to him and it'll be one less worry to have me out of the way. He is going to ask to be relieved as soon as his replacement arrives which will be in another month with any luck so it shouldn't be too long a gap. We are wondering if our heavy luggage got through, it has to go down through Pakistan and left about ten days before the trouble by steamer so might have just made it – typical of us to lose everything – oh well one can't think about one's paltry possessions at a time like this when so many wretched people are suffering.[1] Perhaps it is just as well that this business has flared up at last, it seemed inevitable and something must now be done to settle it. Just wish it could have waited a little longer. One worries about the food situation here until the rice crop is ready in another eight weeks, and of course the tea industry will get badly hit, Daddy has another eight days' supply of oil to run his factory. As you can imagine all our thoughts have been on this, and much rushing to the wireless for news, though all the reports are so conflicting that one isn't much the wiser at the end. it is truly a sad way to leave India, one could really ring the necks of the politicians who for the sake of pride are plunging millions into chaos and starvation, but the very word "Kashmir" seems to spark off violent emotions beyond one's comprehension.

I got a letter from you last week, do hope you can keep the world from the door till your next grant arrives, you can take up to £10 overdraft and run up bills with Wright till we come home, he won't mind. Fiona will just have to manage on her £30 a month and cut out smoking and parties if necessary, it is a livable sum and she will just have to live on it. Please don't lend her any more. She seems to have had a wonderful time on Scarp[2] and I hope it will keep her peaceful and relaxed for several weeks at least, have been wondering about The Move and hoping it went off smoothly.

If I come home I shall probably spend a couple of days with Anne and then a couple with Granny before coming north, will of course ring you up. Was also amused in my last mail to get screeds from some historian who had read my article pulling it into little shreds – and have been composing a reply. Terribly pedantic old boy he sounds, keeps quoting from books I've never heard of and of course all my own source books are being scanned by the Pakistanis so it's difficult to answer him as exactly, but I have myself covered on most counts. How awful if I lose my notes, thank goodness I kept them with me and didn't send them with our heavy luggage as I had planned.

Really no news, and the fact that this letter probably won't reach you is a bit frustrating. Daddy is fine, he thrives on crisises and is a rock of assurance at a time like this. My tranquilisers are helping me considerably, not that I'm the least worried about Pakistan coming in here, they wouldn't do anything to us and would be only too anxious for us to go on making tea for them.

Don't worry about us – we'll be with you in no time.

On the same day, Sunday 12th September I wrote to my parents from Field Head

Dear Mummy and Daddy,

Another of my almost illegible, spidery, letters I'm afraid as there seems to be quite a lot of news. I will break this off in a moment to help Annie down to the bus-stop with her case. She has looked after

---

[1] The luggage was impounded and only finally released after a couple of years, thanks to the intervention of Erik Pearse, a friend from my undergraduate years at Worcester, who later married my younger sister Anne.

[2] A small, uninhabited, Hebridean island off Harris.

me very well and this is the least I can do. Then I will take Poochie for a short walk round by Outgate & back through the fields. I won't start describing the country now, it makes me sad, even tho' I'm here. September is such a beautiful month - the dried-blood (not my simile) blackberries in the hedgerows and the trees in the Bradley's drive their usual reds, yellows and browns. Still, the last one for you to be away from ... It really will be wonderful to have you both home to appreciate it with us. It's so much nicer to share this kind of beauty, beauty which no words can possibly capture. Most of the time I'm lost in my C17 world making the almost impossible leap of imagination & will to live within the minds of a lost civilization. But when I return to this land the mixture of beauty and horror is blinding. In the latter category comes this awful Pakistan/India trouble. I don't know if this letter will get to you. I don't read newspapers & we haven't a 'telly' now so I know very little of what's happening - even if I did the almost humorous (if the situation wasn't so tragic) & conflicting reports of the two governments would not give me much chance. It is the waste & stupidity of it all which strikes everyone here. Tolerance is now considered such a high virtue - esp. in religious matters - that it is very difficult to remember that people still hate each other. Meanwhile the money which should be going to the dying, the hungry, the lonely slips quietly into people's pockets or less quietly, down gun barrels.

Was it all inevitable as people imply? Is anyone to blame, or is it just something too deep to apportion guilt? Have you been effected much?

Last night we had a small party - Mike Boddington, the Manbys & all the other 'gang'. Actually it went rather well and people didn't drift off until after 2. Perhaps it was the Punch, which was made from everything we could find in the larder - chopped peel, dried raisins, bottled raspberries etc - and Merrydown cider, which kept them around! Unfortunately there were rather too many girls, tho' most of them were very young. I spent most of the evening with a very sweet child - she was 16 and looked much younger (at least her face did) from Grasmere. She is at ballet-school in Sussex & wants to be a ballerina. Her family is very complicated - a backwards sister, dipsomaniac (or semi-) father etc. Makes our family seem quite normal! Anyhow Susan (her name) very much appealed to my fatherly instincts. One exciting incident was when someone set alight to the 'put-you-up' which Granny has sent back from Crowthorne. There was plenty of smoke, but little fire. Actually we didn't know till this morning that it was not just an ordinary sofa. It hasn't done it much damage & now I have put it in my room instead of the bed: very much better.

The disembarkation went smoothly, tho' there were seconds when the T.V. tube looked like lost. Granny was extremely efficient - only Richard left something (his coat)! They are apparently happy in their new house and Tansy is going for long walks with Grandpa. Poochie is surviving well - if a little mopy. I will miss G & G very much.

Just after the party ended there was a little tap on the door - and Fiona staggered in. She had hitched down from Scarp and is off flat-hunting in Manchester tomorrow. She is absolutely bubbling over with Scarp and longing to go back. She looks exceedingly well - brown and fit. Earlier in the evening Val had rung. She is staying with Gill & sounds happy - she will be over for an afternoon so will give you fuller news when I see her.

In the rush of all the above I have forgotten the two most important matters - your health (Mummy) and your writing. I was afraid you might have a slight relapse - I do hope this was just temporary and you are feeling alright now. Am thinking of you. It should be getting colder now isn't it? I was so pleased to hear of the 'Elek books' offer; I'm sure you could do it very well, tho' I'm certain you could also do far more sensational things. Linda Manby was saying how much her mother praised your children's stories - incidentally. About my work; it is at a rather tedious stage where I'm having to summarise other people's findings as a background to my own - just introductory material, requiring simple, sensible, balanced judgements and summaries. But 2 hours a day I work on a village - the stuff I was telling you about, most exciting. I've written to the Cambridge Group for the Study of Population and Social Structure but they have no material for Essex. They come the nearest to my type of work - but they are more interested in straight economic/social problems - like population, harvests, size of families etc - whereas I would be more interested in religion, values, attitudes etc. We overlap, but I am not very impressed by what I know of them. A book should be coming out soon.

Zoë is in Bristol looking after autistic (?) children - mongols etc - and (I gather) finding it interesting. She hasn't contacted me for a while.

Hope you can read this. Much love to you both, Alan

On Sunday 19th September I wrote from Field Head.

Dear Daddy,

This will probably take ages to reach you - if it ever does at all - but if it does it's to cheer you up as you must be feeling a bit lonely and miserable - without Mummy. We still haven't much clue what is going on here, but will no doubt hear all this evening. No letters have arrived here for a couple of weeks so we don't know whether it's for health or safety reasons that you've decided it would be better for M to return. All we've heard was a telephone message from the Assam Co. to say she is arriving at 6.55 tonight. Anne is going to meet her and then ...? I will be up here till the end of the month (and could stay longer if necessary) and Val is coming over when I leave so Mummy would never be alone here. Still, we'll see what happens. Jill's sister was flown home with amoebic dysentery and apparently the cold weather cured her - perhaps this is what you're hoping? Anyhow, I do hope things are not too chaotic. Poor you, you'll have to organize all the packing etc. Still it all means you'll be home soon.

I have a friend from Oxford staying and he and I went over to Yorkshire to take Fiona part of her way back to Manchester. On the way we stopped at Whernside and climbed some of the way up it. There was a small river in the valley which was simply jumping with trout - it reminded me very much of the streams at Sedbergh, brown and peaty. Fiona has turned into the fisher(woman) of the family. She went down to Black Beck with Peter and they caught three small trout. I am a little cautious of going out at the moment as the water-baillifs are apparently very keen.

I am 'managing' fairly well - though the dustbin is rather full of empty baked-bean tins! There are a few technical snags - no drawing-room light as I broke the socket, the washer on the cold tap defective and so the tap has to be turned off with a hammer etc. Still, we'll get them all mended if Mummy is well enough to come back here.

Sorry this is a bit dull; I had a rather sleepless night last night as both dogs (we have Joy as well as Poochie for a while) sleep <u>on</u> my bed.

We are all thinking of you, Much love, Alan

P.S. I don't expect letters back - you must be very busy.

I had visited Lady Clay very frequently during my two years based in Oxford. But the fact that I moved to the Lakes meant that we had to keep in touch increasingly by letters. So there began a correspondence which lasted for ten years and includes dozens of letters on both sides. The one during this period which I shall include was written from the Lake District on 19th September.

Dear Lady Clay,

Please excuse a typed letter (I expect you prefer it actually as it is easier on the eyes). I hope all goes well with you and you are having a restful summer. No doubt your legions of relatives still drop in expecting lemonade and information about the rest of the clan. I wonder how the garden grows? Is it the time of roses now, or are yours all over? Here the miracle continues and the garden is still full of them. But otherwise it is undoubtedly autumnal, blackberries 'like dried blood' are on every hedge and the windfall apples litter the lawn. The house is full of the thick scent of stewing blackberry and apple which will soon drip through cloth to make jelly. The trees are on the edge of their autumnal ecstasy and the last of the harvest lies sodden in the fields. Perhaps that is enough lyrical description, the salute to Wordsworth has been made! But it is indeed very restful and lovely up here, I am very lucky.

I imagine you have been keeping up your hectic reading; I don't know where you get the energy to wade through all those huge volumes you wave at me every time I appear. When one is away from intelligent & interested people and the menace of Blackwell's overcrowded window the need to 'keep abreast' is less intense and one can just follow one's own whims. At the moment I am concentrating on the big names in American sociology – Margaret Mead, Erich Fromm, David Riesman, Ruth Benedict. They write about subject such as 'loneliness', individualism', 'anxiety', 'dreams', 'culture' etc. I find it all very refreshing after a long day struggling with my detailed but small-scale witchcraft problems. They are all interested in the Reformation and Riesman's Lonely Crowd and Fromm's Fear of Freedom (both in paperback) are most interesting on the Weber-Tawney type arguments about Calvinism and Capitalism. I think the real value of reading such books, as well as my social anthropology, is that it sets me a whole series of new problems which I then comb the seventeenth century sources to try to answer. For instance what was the rate of suicide, the incidence of pre-nuptial incontinence, the amount of anxiety, the attitudes to drink, sex, time, place, pain etc? when one starts to ask these questions it soon becomes apparent that the sources which historians have used up to now – mainly literary (plays, poetry, letters etc.) for a study of society are just not enough. On the other hand the really new sources, those such as probate inventories, wills, visual evidence etc. pioneered by Hoskins are again insufficient. They tell one a good deal about the economic structure, but what one is really after is what people thought and felt – how they reacted to their economic structure. Making lists of corn prices and population curves is very useful, but only indirectly. It still leaves one struggling with the central problems which concern the interrelationship between spheres of activity. How far was religion at the bottom of society related to the class system, to the family unit, toe the agricultural calendar, to the high mortality, to the age groups? How far did the changes in religious beliefs and church attendance, drunkenness, sexual deviation, gossiping and scandal, leisure activities (Lords of Misrule, feasts etc), school-masters, puritanism etc. etc. If they are related to information from wills, manor courts, inventories, surveys etc. they should allow a considerable reconstruction of everyday life. On the other hand, if one merely uses such sources (as is the temptation) one still gets a distorted picture. In my own subject I know this is true. If I based my knowledge of witchcraft merely on what appeared in village and county records, without using pamphlet literature and books to find out the opinions and analyses of the more intelligent contemporaries I would have a very lopsided picture. If is it not presumptions to say so, I think that Christopher Hill, brilliant and sensitive as he is to the 'indirect' assumptions, tends to over-depend on the literary/pamphlet material while the 'local historians' are tempted to dismiss this and go too far the other way. Ideally, I suppose, one should provide a framework (there is often a large and fascinating gap between what people think is going on and what is really occurring) by studying a small area in depth. But all this is speculation, I have only just embarked on doing all this and it looks like a long pull ahead.

As you can see I am getting plenty of time for reflection and writing. Despite finding that vital bits of information which I missed are three hundred miles away at Oxford, this is an ideal place to work. It looks as if my mother will be joining me very soon as she has just been flown home with amoebic dysentery and arrived in London yesterday. My father retires in December. I am busy making plans for my future, but will let you know all when I see you. Unless my mother is too ill for me to leave I hope to be in Oxford for a week in October and look forward very much to seeing you then.

Please excuse this long and extremely arrogant, not to say condescending (I didn't mean to sound as if I was 'explaining' things to you) letter. It's just that after all our discussions I feel that you are one of the few people who is really interested in history and to whom I can use a letter to sort out a few of my ideas on paper.

Very best wishes, Alan

My mother wrote to me from 25, Eardley Crescent , London on Tuesday 21st September 1965[1]

---

[1] Iris arrived late on Sunday 19th and was staying at Anne's flat in London.

My dear Alan,

Saving a phone call – have been wearing out Anne's machine and will ruin her if I go on! It was lovely to hear your voice, cheered me no end – as you imagine it has been a miserable end to India & I can't believe what has happened in the last few weeks, it's been a sort of nightmare. The contrast between the poor suffering Indians & opulent England is as amazing as always. I travelled 1st Class & they gave each of us (or tried to) enough food to feed a family for a week – ah well one will forget – & that is the saddest thing of all.

I won't be coming up this week, I went to the Tropical Diseases hospital this morning & have another appointment on Monday – they were very kind and sympathetic & the doctor said he wasn't keen to give me any more treatment but I'm seeing a different one on Monday & will know definitely then – they are all hopeful that a change of climate will cure me & so am I! Of course worrying about Daddy doesn't help, he must be so miserable & worried on his own – let's hope China will merely bluff & prod – I think probably it will. If things ease, he will be home next month as they're going to let him go as soon as his replacement (Ross) arrives. Knowing Daddy though he won't want to leave his precious people in trouble & I don't blame him, it's so horrible being cut off.

But I must stop moaning – I'm being cossetted and cared for by Annie but I think her friends are a bit bored with having an aged ailing female drooping round the flat! Granny wants me to go there afterwards, so I suppose I must – don't feel I have the energy but must try – they seem very happy & comfortable which is a relief. Fiona has rung several times & sounds cheerful & intent on marrying & populating Scarp – But it'll no doubt "pass"! She's coming down at the week-end. Let me know your exact plans so that we can meet before too long! I'll let you know the result of my Monday visit. Couldn't you leave Poochie with Beryl or Jane as I'm bound to be going north soon? Longing to see you & hope everything will be easier by then, don't worry about me, it's mostly tropical neurosis I fear. Lots of love – Mummy

Wednesday 22nd Sept. 65 Field Head.

My dear Zoë,

I promised a more sober and serious letter. After a fairly long day hammering out my thesis I'm not sure my brain is up to much, but here goes.

First – thank you again for your letter. I was fascinating by the details about the children and amused by antics of the anthroposophists. (hope your mail isn't opened). I feel terribly ignorant about mental illness; I really <u>must</u> get down to reading some psychology. I got as far as looking up some of the words you used, but when I found my 'Penguin Dictionary of Psychology' did not contain 'psychotic' or 'aphoric' I gave up in disgust. I really must master some basic psychology for the sake of my thesis if nothing else. I had a mildly lunatic letter and article from the Professor of Psychology at Birmingham and need <u>some</u> knowledge before I put him right. But all the books I have look so large and complicated … and psychology is in such an uncertain state at the moment anyhow. You didn't talk about the <u>treatment</u> of these children. How 'scientific' are the anthro[posophist]s? Do they rely entirely on 'lovingkindness'? Perhaps there is not enough known to do much else? How much chance is there of the various types of illness being cured – for instance is there any chance for David? I suppose they've got to discover the cause first. I imagine they try to notice significant variations in background, physical make-up etc. between different types – for instance, as you pointed out, 'psychotic' children with no obvious reason for their withdrawal tend to come from 'far more intelligent' homes. This seems to fit in with a remark (made in 1947 by Clyde Kluckhon, Mirror for Man, p. 155) that 'In the United States today schizophrenia is more frequent among the lower classes; manic-depressive psychosis is an upper-class ailment. The American middle classes suffer from psychomatic disturbance such as ulcers. Feeding problems are most frequent among children of Jewish families…" Have you come across any cases of schizophrenia? Can you get any of the children who live in a 'phantasy world (I see that this is more or less the definition of 'autistic') to relate to you any of their fantasy. I imagine *that one of the best ways to help them would be to try to get inside their world – but perhaps this is impossible. I mean to read Piaget & the Opie's books on the 'Lore, logic, Language' of children. How far back are there statistics for the mental health of children – have pre-war II records been kept, & if so, do they show any significant changes? I don't know why I ask you these questions – I expect the answer is in a book somewhere. I'm collecting examples of mental breakdown in the C16-C17 but have come across very few cases of children – do you imagine that there were mongols etc?*

What do <u>*you*</u> *do, meanwhile – apart from nursing? (& analysing them in the evening) – suppose there isn't much one can do but watch. What was the trip to home for older handicapped children across the Severn like? Do your children go on there? (You better keep this letter & answer these questions when you seem me!) I won't dwell on the anth---'s [anthropolosphists]. They sound more like my field than yours. The 'Miss Lake' of Outgate who their local secretary is a dear old woman –* <u>*very*</u> *old – who drives a little Austin up our narrow lane* <u>*very*</u> *fast and is so hunched up that she can't see over the dashboard. Often one meets an apparently empty car driving along. I always wondered what kept her alive – now I know it must be the prayers of the Anths!*

Any news of Anthea's baby yet? The war has lapsed just in time it seems.

No further news of my mother yet. I imagine she will ring tonight or tomorrow. My friend from Oxford, Peter, has gone and I am on my own. Julie the witch ex-girl friend – has decided that (as she is in the process of buying a book shop & is busy) she can't afford the time to come up. Consequently I'm getting lots of work done and making myself some delicious blackberry and apple stews as well. The most beautiful time is almost upon us. "Tell us not here, it needs not saying, 'what tunes the enchantress plays in aftermaths of soft September…" " beeches strip & storms for winter And stain the wind with leaves…"

My mother wrote to me in the Lakes from 27, Eardley Crescent on Thursday 23rd

I was very touched with the parcel of flowers, a sweet thought, they got here in good order most of them and the roses are by my bed luring me home as you say – but alas I don't seem to be able to get away for a bit. I feel much happier than when I last wrote naturally, the news being so much better, I felt Daddy would never get out but he should be able to make it now. Should also get some letters through though there'll be a vast great pile up.

I feel better in myself too, and am sure in a week or two will be back to normal, still can't quite make out what has been the matter with me. Robert has just rung up and suggested meeting for lunch but I hadn't the energy or clothes, he is dashing off to the States, on some very important business I expect, but I forgot to ask.

I'm just lolling about the flat trying to "find" myself, half of me seems to have been left in India but will gradually catch up I expect. Gorgeous weather which I don't see much of but is cheering, Anne has gone back to work after two days of watching over me, one of the girls is away on her gruelling social round so I have a bed. The other two seem quite pleasant if a little dull, or perhaps it's just that who rang up and why seems rather trivial to one fresh from the "front"! I don't think Anne is particularly happy here and is making plans to move out.

I have got all my notes with me but can't see myself getting launched on the Mughals again somehow – I nearly packed them in my heavy luggage which would have been a sad end to all that busy typing. There's a good chance our boxes will now get away and we might see them in about three months, I gather blankets are our chief need, I only have one rat-chewed one with me but will have to get an electric one when I come home.

Can't bring myself to describe my journey home, it was really quite simple but had the elements of a grand disaster for me. Can usually find something to laugh at on these occasions but this time nothing – except possibly some terrible, tanned rich holiday makers who got on at Rome and shouted to each other about the <u>*marvellous*</u> *beaches and stunning casinos and fabulous parties they had been enjoying and all the private planes they had chartered – as they were all quite young it made it somehow more nauseating.*

Hope you are all managing to enjoy the wide empty spaces of Field Head – and that the work goes well. Let me know your dates so that we can somehow manage to meet. Fiona is coming down tomorrow for the week end.
Thank you again for the flowers –
Much love, Mummy

On Sunday 26th September I wrote from Field Head.

Dear Daddy,

I don't know whether any mail is getting through yet, but am writing on the off-chance. Mummy seems to think there will be an enormous pile-up, but it might finally get through. How are things? I do hope you are not too miserable and chaotic. I wonder if my last letter to you, posted when they were still fighting, got to you? Mummy says you might be allowed home next month, I do hope that's true. It would be marvelous if you were both up here by the end of October. Any news of the luggage? It would be so easy for it to disappear down gaping pockets…

My humdrum life continues. A friend who came to stay called me the "Hermit of Field Head"! My only real conversation is with the dogs (Joy is staying here, along with Poochie). They get a bit bored with me sitting at my desk all day but we go out for a couple of walks a day. These often consist of blackberry-picking sessions. Goodland has cut down all the blackberries at the end of the lane, but there are a fine crop near the Boddingtons (on the short-cut to Outgate). You should taste my blackberry and apple stew! I almost live on it.

Peter [Goodden], my friend from Oxford now teaching at a prep school in Ayrshire, staying until Tuesday. He was great company – teases me about my pedantic, 'holier than thou' ways and, like Fiona, makes me feel an old woman! I get into such a petty rut of little pleasures & worries. It seems that I've inherited a considerable amount of anxiety from Mummy. I must say I sometimes wonder if all this sweat is worth it when my thesis will, no doubt, lie rotting and unread in some dusty library. But, on the whole, I enjoy the reading/writing life immensely – with the occasional jaunt on the motorbike (lying, with numerous faults, waiting for your return!) – or the occasional party.

I have more or less decided, with Mummy & your approval, that my next stage of training will be at London – probably doing a 2-year Diploma in Anthropology, then perhaps I will be ready to go out & look at a few of the world's problems. (By which time the whole N-E frontier of India will be closed I expect). I will finance myself either out of a scholarship, or work my way through. You have sweated for so many years giving me the best education in the world that, even if you offered, I would feel awful accepting any more help.

You'll have heard from Mummy I expect. She sounded more cheerful in her last letter – tho' she is missing you a lot. I do hope the examination tomorrow goes off O.K and she is able to come up here soon. Depending on her plans, I go for one of my 'Tours' starting next Monday – after a 3-days walking holiday with a friend.

Thinking of you, best love, Alan

In 1965 I noticed that a Professor of Psychiatry, W. H. Trethowan had given a talk on witchcraft. So I wrote on 13th to introduce my work. He wrote back a helpful reply on 17th. I then replied in detail to him.

26/9/65 Field Head, Outgate

Dear Professor Trethowan,

I enclose a M.S. of your talk to the Oxford Society. Thank you very much indeed for the loan of it and the gift of the offprint of your article on Demoniacal Possession. I look forward to reading your article in the British Journal of Psychiatry. If I appear to disagree on a few points this is only a reflection of how interesting I found your paper. I think you are on to a very exciting and important subject and hope you continue your researches into it. My comments probably reflect a difference in sources, rather than a basic difference in interpretation. At first one is struck, on reading the Malleus and works by Lecky, Robbins etc. by the sadistic, irrational side. But when one gets hold of the individuals involved and sets them in the web of contemporary tensions and relationships the thing becomes more understandable. Most historians, I am afraid, have concentrated almost entirely on the easily accessible pamphlet and other literary material and this gives a very distorted view. What people thought happened was not what did actually happen, nor does it give a very balanced impression if the more horrific and brutal cases are isolated from the countless episodes of a more prosaic nature. As you will see from the enclosed note from a recent draft chapter of my thesis, in the roughly 800 cases of witchcraft in the courts of one English county – Essex – there is hardly a case where either accuser or accused, as far as the records reveal, show symptoms of mental abnormality.

May I make a few comments on your paper first? I was interested in your remarks (p.3 – margin) about 'the omnipotence of thought'. In a sense, in a primitive society, this was based on a fact. Actions and attitudes were more closely interrelated than in our society; if a person harboured a grievance, even if it never resulted in obvious activity, it could harm the very closely-knit sentiment system. The distinction between the public and the private realm, the inner and the outward man was less clear than in our society. This whole problem is well discussed in Max Gluckman, Politics, Law and Ritual in Tribal Society (Oxford, 19565), pp. 242-7. What do you think causes this belief in children and schizophrenics? Is such a belief supposed to be a cause or effect of schizophrenia (if such a clear-cut distinction can be made).

You say 'Another opponent, Francis Bacon…'. Unfortunately, all the great thinkers obstinately refuse to be listed as either completely 'for' or 'against' witchcraft. To try to do so is the recourse of those who start with the assumption that the whole thing was irrational nonsense anyhow and therefore a few enlightened minds must have been able to rise above the fog. In fact everyone was born with some of the assumptions on which witchcraft beliefs were based: it was impossible for them to examine and shed all these. I think Kittredge is right when he says (pretty firmly) that 'To believe in witchcraft in the seventeenth century was no more discreditable to a man's head or heart than it was to believe in spontaneous generation or to be ignorant of the term theory of disease … The position of the seventeenth-century believers in witchcraft was logically and theologically stronger than that of the few persons who rejected the current belief.' (G.L. Kittredge, Witchcraft in Old and New England (New York, 1929, p.372). To take Francis Bacon, for example. It is very difficult to reconcile some of his remarks with the reputation he has for being a sceptic (see. The Works of Francis Bacon, ed. Spedding, (London, 1859), ii, 634, 641, 657-8. Like King James and most intelligent men of the time he was aware that there was a good deal of trickery, superstition etc. involved; but he hardly questioned that some causes of bewitching were true.

On p.9 you say that 'Professor Murray was able to produce a long list of the names of some of those in the British Isles who actually took part in these pagan rites'. Though Miss Murray is often unfairly attacked and her works most stimulating I wouldn't trust any of her very plausible theories one inch – especially the one about covens. I happen to have analysed some of her cases taken from the area I am studying, and on close examination they melt away as a clever fabrication. I suspect this is true elsewhere in Britain. (see. Alex Keiller, The Personnel of the Aberdeenshire Witchcraft Covens (1922) and under 'Coven' in R. F. Robbin's The Encyclopedia of Witchcraft and Demonology (London, 1959) for a few more criticisms. The 'pagan survival' theory rests on a completely ehistorical sense; she hadn't a clue from non-folklore sources, of what life was really like in the seventeenth century. Consequently it's all a most elaborate pattern, totally divorced from reality.

The trouble (or the main one) about the 'misogyny theory' is that it hardly fits chronologically. In England, anyhow, it was at a time when clerics were for the first time marrying, when women were rising in status in various ways (see K. V. Thomas, 'Women and the Civil War Sects', Past and Present, No. 13 (April, 1958) that witchcraft prosecutions took place. Nor have I found any evidence of sadistic outlets for repressed lust etc. It was usually women who accused women; there were few sexual details etc. Of course there are notorious cases on the Continent, but this does show that it was not an essential ingredient. While on the subject of sadism etc. you say (p.12) that 'the truly fanatical witch-hunter of any kind is someone who is himself possessed by strong sadistic tendencies'. Of course this may be the case, but it hardly stands as a generalization. In Africa it is not true (M. Marwick writes of a notable witch-finder 'the general impression I got of him was that he is very genuinely concerned with the growing incidence of man's wickedness (in the form of witchcraft) and that he considers it his divine calling to help man throw it off … From the mental hygiene viewpoint he probably does more good than harm. His function is comparable with that of a father-confessor or a psychiatrist in our own society …' 'Another modern anti-witchcraft movement in Eastern Central Africa', Africa, xx, (1950), p. 103; admittedly this does sound a good deal milder than Hopkins!) Incidentally, Reginald Scot's Discovery of Witchcraft was first published in 1584, not 1665 (as on p. 19).

As you must be aware it is a vast and complicated subject; there are many other points I would like to have discussed (for instance your stimulating suggestion, p. 12, note, that the demonologists, except for placing the unconscious outside the individual, foreshadowed many of the Freudian theories). But I must be boring you. One other reference, which I haven't read myself yet: G. Vandendrische, The Parapraxis in the Haizaman Case of Sigmund Freud, (Louvain and Paris, 1965).

I'm afraid the enclosed 'additional notes' are rather disjointed. [I then give the full titles to books by Hopkins, Ady and Perkins.]

I hope the above does not read too brutally. It is easy to criticize, but almost impossible to construct satisfactory explanations of why the whole extraordinary episode occurred. Anthropologists, who (as you will know) on the whole avoid or ignore Freudian theories of repression etc. haven't really provided a solution to why such beliefs occur in a specific culture at a specific time, though they have helped us to understand the function of witchcraft once it is there and the ways in which it becomes absorbed into other relationships.

Thank you once again for your help. Yours sincerely,

1965 - October

My grandfather's diary records all that happened to the family in this eventful month when my father and mother finally settled in Field Head.

Monday 4 October Alan arrives Visited RMA Indian Army Museum with Iris & V
Tuesday 5 October Alan leaves
Saturday 9 October Alan arrives Watched rugger match with Iris at Well Coll
Monday 11 Oct Alan & Iris leave for London
Wednesday 20 October Iris arrives
Sat 23 October Mac arrives in England & comes here with Anne.
Alan arrives
Sunday 24 Alan leaves
Monday 25 October Mac & Iris leave for Field Head
Friday 29 October Letter from Iris from Field Head

My parents arrived back from India looking tired and, in my mother's case, very ill. Their passport photos show how they had aged.

Now that they were back in England permanently, and I was living with them at Field Head, there are very few letters between us. My father was trying to find a job. At first he tried to find a paid job, but this proved impossible, so he worked voluntarily at Rydal Hall as a handyman and assistant. By early December my sister Anne had joined us. She and my mother then began to help me with the transcribing and indexing of records related to my Essex work on particular villages and ecclesiastical records. This was the first time I had spent such a long time with my parents since I was five years old.

My funding for a third year was still being negotiated as the next letter shows.

DEPARTMENT OF
EDUCATION AND SCIENCE
AWARDS BRANCH
13 Cornwall Terrace, Regents Park, LONDON N.W.1
Telephone: HUNter 1455

Your reference:
Our reference: UP.63/9154

18 OCT 1965

Dear Mr. Macfarlane,

With reference to your letter of 5th October, I write to say that our records show that your State Studentship was tenable for a course of study leading to the degree of B.Litt. and this is the first that we have heard of your proposed transfer to D.Phil. status, thereby requiring a third year. Would you please ask your supervisor to write to us recommending that your award be continued for the academic year 1965/66, to enable you to complete your approved scheme of advanced post-graduate research.

Yours sincerely,

(J. Wilson)

A. D. J. Macfarlane, Esq.,
Worcester College,
Oxford.

ADDRESS ✓

INVOICE

W. HEFFER & SONS LTD.

Booksellers and Publishers

PETTY CURY, CAMBRIDGE, ENGLAND

Cables: Heffer, Cambridge. *Telephone 58351*

Stationers: SIDNEY STREET Printers: HILLS ROAD

A. Macfarlane Esq., | E2 | 29th October, 1965.

Field Head,

Outgate, Nr. Ambleside, Westmorland.

	£	s.	d.
Verrier Elwin : Myths of the North East Frontier of India.	1.	0.	0.
Turner, V.W. : Schism and Continuity in an African Society.	2.	5.	0.
Arensberg, C.M. : The Irish Countryman.	1.	5.	0.
Verrier Elwin : When the World was Young.		5.	0.
Postage and Packing.		3.	0.
	£4.	18.	0.

35

For payment arrangements, see overleaf

1965 - November

Having decided to try to do a Diploma in Anthropology at the London School of Economics, I set about trying to find support funding. I first tried the Nuffield Foundation to see if I could get a Fellowship.

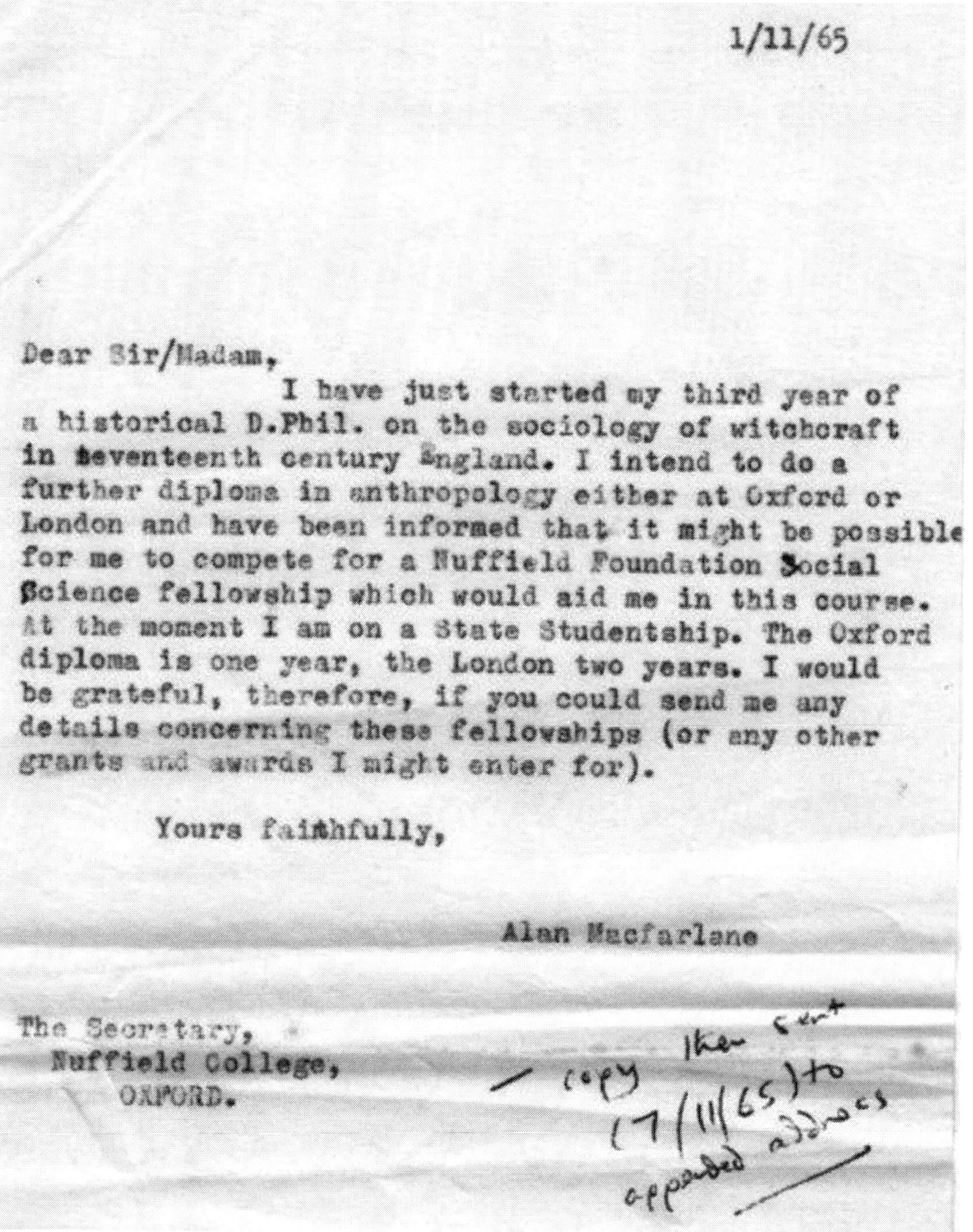

1/11/65

Dear Sir/Madam,

I have just started my third year of a historical D.Phil. on the sociology of witchcraft in seventeenth century England. I intend to do a further diploma in anthropology either at Oxford or London and have been informed that it might be possible for me to compete for a Nuffield Foundation Social Science fellowship which would aid me in this course. At the moment I am on a State Studentship. The Oxford diploma is one year, the London two years. I would be grateful, therefore, if you could send me any details concerning these fellowships (or any other grants and awards I might enter for).

Yours faithfully,

Alan Macfarlane

The Secretary,
Nuffield College,
OXFORD.

copy then sent (7/11/65) to appended address

There is a correspondence with one of my cohort of research students. Charles Phythian Adams was working on the social history of Coventry in the later middle ages. I remember walking across the Parks in Oxford as he explained to me something of the background to the newly formed Cambridge Group for the History of

Population and Social Structure in Cambridge and the new work by French social historians. My one remaining piece of correspondence with him for this period is a letter from me. It is very long and I have supplied some of the headings.

8/11/65

C Phythian-Adams

Field Head,
Outgate,
Nr. Ambelside,
Westmorland.

Dear Charles,

I hope things go well with you and Coventry flourishes. Whenever we meet we seem to be in a great rush so I'm writing to set down on paper a few stray problems which seem to interest us both. I realise that it is easier to write in this quiet spot than in the mental whirl of Oxford so won't expect anything back, though I would be fascinated to hear your views on the subjects I raise. But first a few references. I'm afraid I gave you the wrong reference (from memory) to the article of Dorothy Crozier - I hope you haven't tried to look it up yet. It should be 'Kinship and occupational succession' in The Sociological Review, March 1965 (not the Br.Jnl. of Soc. as I said). Incidentally, I'm sure you're aware that an A.L.Fotheringhame(?) is listed among the 'theses in progress' in the BIHS,1965, with 'Elizabethan Coventry' as his subject. I imagine this overlaps somewhat ? I notice that Hoskins uses Coventry quite a lot in his various articles, for instance he notes the Coventry assessments (Local History, p.103) of 1524,5. Was he unaware of the censuses ? If I remember you found them completely by chance. Have any more been discovered for any other towns in the C16 - I imagine Laslett would tell you if they had? Incidentally, if you haven't looked at it yet you might find something of interest on the elementary and three-generation family in Williams' book on Gosforth, pp.52,6. Apparently the latter is more common in the Cumberland village than in the country-side. I wonder if this was so in the C16 ? Have you found any explanations for the growth of ~~the growth~~ of non-nuclear families in C16 Coventry yet ? I don't suppose Hoskins was looking for this in Wigston Magna, but I wonder if he could have found any figures anyhow?

I have just been looking through my notes on ~~the~~ 'kinship and marriage' intending to write a snappy little account of problems and sources. But the size of the subject has overwhelmed me. Here are a few scattered reflections. First I'll list some of the problems bothering me, then, if I can, suggest how one might set about answering them. If you can suggest further sources (possibly more relevant to a town; I am principally interested in the village at the moment) or suggest more fruitful questions I would be most interested. The major probelem, as always, is that people never talk about things that are basic to their way of life; they assume them and hence basic relationships can only be studied indirectly, through their effects in other fields of activity. Thus I have approached kinship through a series of related topics. But first the direct approach.

The family.

To determine: size, age-structure, sex-structure, residence - how far distributed (both nuclear and extended), mobility - both vertical and horizontal, inheritance patterns, occupational sturucture - i.e. how often children follow parents, obligations (e.g. at birth, death and marriage), sanctions (e.g. parental curse, disinheritance, corporal and other punishments), specialized groups such as widows, orphans and unmarried daughters, relationships bewteen specific groups - e.g. between affines, changes over the time of all the above & relationship to other (e.g. religious, economic) factors.

Sources - any that will a) locate individuals - e.g. censuses, parish registers, wills, taxation. b) show the relationship between them - ecclesiastical and civil court, literary etc. In fact almost all local and other records.

Which of the following have you got for C16 Coventry ? Assize, Quarter Session, Borough, Manor, Archdeaconry, Episcopal, court records ? I assume you have the usual King's Bench, Chancery, Common Pleas and other central records, as well as the excellent census and taxation records. Have you used the ecclesiastical census of 1563 and the Liber Cleri of 1603 (or is this just restricted to certain parts of England , e.g. Wigston Magna - Provincial England, p.185).? Are there many wills for Coventry, I assume so - and what about inventories ? Strangely , the latter are fery scarce for Essex, the village I've chosen to study, for instance, hasn't got any. Are there any C16 rentals/maps/surveys of Coventry ? These are usually manorial so I don't suppose there was any manorial jurisdiction in Coventry was there? When do the churchwardens accounts start, and when the parish registers - I assume there are several parishes in C. and they differ. David Palliser seems to have found the borough administrative records for York useful, have they survived for Coventry ? I hope this doesn't sound too inquisitive - I'm not trying to do a take-over bid; I would like to know how far the records I have for my Essex villages are common to other places.

Who was present at;what economic arrangements were there - gifts and inherited wealth; what physical distance did they cover; how much social distance was there ; what were courting habits (e.g. it seems to have been necessary to get the permission of 'friends', was it also necessary to obtain parents consent); where did the couple reside - with her or his relatives, or by them selves (cf. Wilmott & Young); what age did they marry (cf. Arensberg on the social reasons for late marriage in Ireland); did the woman ever retain her maiden name, were children called after father or mother's names; what did unmarried children do; what were divorce, incest, adultery & fornication rates; how close could one marry, is the myth of 'great interbreeding' in villages true ? ; were'prohibited times ' observed and was there a favourite time for marriage (e.g. after the harvest); how high were re-marriage rates and did these often happen between the same families (ie. marrying younger sisters); what were the obligations towards in-laws - (e.g. I have come across a case of a man being sued for not paying for the burial of his mother-in-law. And so on <u>ad infinitum</u>. Once one had some facts one could test the various hypotheses of anthropologists (who have been obsesseed with this subject) and use marriage patterns as a clues to a number of other social relationships.

<u>Religion</u>.

How often did Puritanisa/ R.Catholicism run in families, and how far did it spread ? (e.g. did marriage carry it; can either be related, either as cause and effect, to any particular family pattern)

did the family become increasingly the focus for religious activity (as Hill would argue); who were god-parents and how strong a tie was it; in what ways did religious ritual reinforce family sentiment (e.g. how far was confirmation a puberty rite which exhorted family obedience, how far did sermons and the eucharist emphasize the importance of the Father); in what ways did religious rétual at birth, marriage and death influence the family - who were expected to appear, what gifts were given etc. In what, if any, did the clergy's family differ from those of the laity (larger, better educated, married who?). what was the effect of clerical marriage on the attitude to the family?

OEe's evidence here would tend to be mainly from Hill's sources - that is ecclesiastical records amd Puritan polémicists; these would be related to the kinship structure as established ffrom the above sources.

How did the occupational structure fit the family - were certain occupations followed by certain families, did the pattern in the agricultural/professional/commercial groups differ; what differences were there between sex and age groups in labour - e.g. did the women do domestic work, while the men went out, did the children start work very young and look after their younger brothers and sisters (cf. Mead, Coming of Age in Samoa), were certain jobs taboo for certain persons (as washing-up for early C20 men in Bethhall Green - Wilmott and Young); was the family, neighbour-groupp or village the 'leisure' unit - or was it divided into age-groups - e.g. it looks as if the 'family' holiday is a modern conception; were children looked after communally at all when the parents went to work, how developed was the system of putting children out to be nursed ? ; was there any tension between living-in servants and members of the family (e.g . I have cases of jealousy by the wife and of incontinency with servants) and how far was the servant system really another form of extended family (i.e. servants of friends were taken on and treated almost as children); what effects did changes in the economic structure - either temporary, e.g. famines - or permanent - e.g. price changes, growth of industries etc. have on the family ?

All the above sources are relevant - esp. anything dealing with servants,with children and with leisure.

Local officials and politics; authority and crime.

How far was theft, popular disturbances, suicide and mental breakdown, official positions (e.g. church-warden, JP,constables, borough and manorial officials), etc. related to families? How far did kinship/neighbourliness act as a sanction and as a preventive to deviation - and what alternatives were there? - how far were there feuds between families and what were the mechanisms (e.g. 'The Peace in the Feud') for preventing them?;what decisions were taken by the family and what by the community ; what local activities - e.g. road-mending,law-and order, sanitation,building, were undertaken on a family, what on a communal basis ? ; what were the mechanisms of decision within the family - did the father control all, or could a group of outsiders (e.g. the 'village elders') or a privileged relative (grandmother) or official (clergyman) influence the family ?

(4)

One could go on for ever - what effects (and what causes) went with the 'housing revolution' of the C16; did the increase in possible privacy help to strengthen the nuclear family against the community ? Why were there a large number of suicides among young men aged between 18-25 in Essex ? What were the effects of different agricultural and housing patterns (e.g. between forested, mountain, nucleated village and dispersed dwellings) ? etc. etc.

I do hope I haven't bored you too much. A string of questions isn't very exciting. But I wanted to clear my mind of a few of them, especially as I've got to write a piece on 'Kinship' for Raymond Firth. A lot of the questions are unanswerable, a lot are not well framed - still there might be some grain with the chaff. I am hoping to provide a few answers when I start a detailed study of an Essex village, using every kind of source (not just probate inventories) I can; perhaps Laslett has anticipated me?

I hope to be in Oxford early in December for a few days and hope we can meet then. I want very much to copy out any references I haven't got out of your 'exercise book', also to have a look at your large collection of books - not to mention discuss any of the above problems which interest you.

Best wishes,

(Alan Macfarlane)

Charles Phythian-Adams, Esq.,
60, Rectory Rd,
St Clement's,
Oxford.

The same day, November 8th, I wrote to Arthur Searle, then one of the Archivists at the Essex Record Office, with whom I would become friends for some years.

8/11/65.

Field Head,
Outgate,
Nr.Ambleside,
Westmorland.

Dear Arthur,

I said I'd send you a few suggestions for the Ingatestone exhibition. Though it probably won't be arranged like this, perhaps it is easiest if I give you some seventeenth century references by sources and you decide which are best.

Pamphlet.

The only C17 pamphlet is
A True and Exact Relation of the Severall Informations,Examinations, and Confessions of the Late Witches, Arraigned and Executed in the County of Essex........29 of July,1645.
(The copy I looked at was in Bodley, I imagine there is one in the B.M. I don't know whether it has any pictures,as the earlier pamphlets do, but the text is sufficiently interesting to bear reproduction).

Literary.

There are two passages in the Diary of Ralph Josselin, one in the printed one in the unprinted part; the references are given in Smith, The Ecclesiastical History of Essex, p.222,417. The second is quite interesting.
I enclose a xerox of one of William Lilly's astrological predictions concerning witchcraft in Essex - perhaps you know something more about the Ayletts of Maudlin Hall in Little Laver ?
There is also an extraordinary and very late case printed in the Trans Trans.Essex.Arch.Soc. n.s.xi(1911),pp.211-6, which purports to come from a Ms. contemporary diary; I imagine the original is lost.
If you had the energy you might like to trace a reference in Maple (paperback edition,p.182, second para.)to a seventeenth century astrologers book which'is in local hands' (presumably at Canewdon therefore; I haven't contacted Maple).The 'forgotten seventeenth-century wizard by name Neboad' is, I believe, in the Short Title Catalogue under Naibod.
Finally there are the works of Hopkins and Sterne. My version of Matthew Hopkins' 'The Discovery of Witches' (1647) is, I regret, from the reprint of his work by Montague Summers in 1928; there are quite a number of copies of his work, including one at Bodley and the B.M. I think.) John Sterne's work is rarer and deserves publicity. It is John Sterne, A Confirmation and Discovery of Witchcraft.... and the only copy is in the B.M. (C.54.e.6). Sterne's signature can be found, along with several other characters mixed up in the 1645 trial, in Q/SBa 2/46. There is an interesting account of the Chelmsford trial by Arthur Wilson, the steward of the Earl of Warwick, in Francis Peck,Desiderata Curiosa ,vol.II,p.476-7. (1779 edition)

Courts.

A ~~couple of~~ few examples from each court should give you scope.
Quarter Sessions: Q/SBa. 2/74 ; 2/76; 2/85 (E.R.O. Transcript,73);Q/SR. 328/94,106.

(2)

Assizes. It might be worth having the gaol calendar and gaol delivery roll of Assize 35/86/T (1645) copied – they are reprinted in Ewen, Witch Hunting and Witch Trials (in the E.R.O),p.222,230. Have a look through Ewen and see if anything cathes your fancy, for instance no.511 (Assizes 35/54/H) or 528 (35/58/T) – these are both slightly exceptional however; perhaps a normal indictment, e.g. 556 (35/63/H) would be better.

Borough. The obvious case is that at Harwich in 1633 (E.R.O. Transcript no. ?) (T/P. 86/7).

Archdeaconry.
All the following are D/AEA. (1604) 23. f.12.v. :(1619) 31. f.69 :
(1624) 34. f.79.v. : (1632) 39. f.29 :(1638) 41. f.220. I can give you the translations if you like; I think you'll find them all quite interesting.

If you want more references there are plenty to spare! There doesn't seem much point working out too many details of lay-out etc. yet. I should have graphs, maps etc. by the Summer. An obvious way of treating the subject would be to focus down from the whole county to a single year, a single person or a single village. The Hopkins episode, Deborah Naylor (see above Q/SBa.2/74 and Q/SR. 328/94,106) and Manningtree in the 1640's are obvious choices. Anyhow we can talk it over.

Hope this gives you something to mull over. I should be in Essex for a few days around the end of November. Please give my very best regards to Ron,Hilda etc. etc. and thank them very much for all their help on my last visit. Could you tell Hilda that regrettably my filing system has broken down and,like her, I can't locate the case of absence from church because the accused was out rowing (in the Archdeaconry court).

I look forward to seeing you all.

All the best,

Arthur Searle,Esq.,
Essex Record Office,
County Hall,
CHELMSFORD,
Essex.

On 11th November I heard back from the Department of Education that they had agreed to extend my grant for a third year.

DEPARTMENT OF
EDUCATION AND SCIENCE
AWARDS BRANCH
13 Cornwall Terrace, Regents Park, LONDON N.W.1
Telephone: HUNter 1455

Your reference:
Our reference: UP 63/9154

11 NOV 1965

Dear Mr. Macfarlane,

With reference to your letter of 23rd October, with enclosures, I am writing to say that, in view of your supervisor's recommendation, we can approve the extension of your State Studentship for the academic year 1965/66 to enable you to complete your post-graduate research studies leading to the degree of D.Phil.

I should explain that before your proposals to study at home and in Essex and London can be approved for State Studentship purposes, it will be necessary for you to ask your supervisor to write to the Department to confirm that your studies from Oxford form a necessary part of your approved programme of post-graduate studies and that he approves of your proposals. Your instalments of grant will then be sent to your home address upon receipt of a special form, as explained in paragraph 23 of the enclosed copy of "Education Information No. 3". Your grant would be based on the rate applicable for a student living at home, i.e. £380 per annum, but adjustments would be made for any period of study away from home, when you were able to state the exact number of weeks involved.

Payment of travelling expenses will also be considered if you will proceed in accordance with paragraph 12(C) of the memorandum.

/With

A. D. J. Macfarlane, Esq.,
Worcester College,
Oxford.

With regard to the Xerox copies and microfilms, we will consider payment towards the cost of these upon production of receipts and a certificate from your supervisor to the effect that these are essential to your research and that the information cannot be obtained from any other source. Any such payment would not in any circumstances total more than £20 over the whole tenure of your award.

Would you please confirm that your income of £120 during the academic year 1964/65 was from Workers' Educational Association classes. A prepaid label is enclosed.

Yours sincerely,

E W Hall

(E. W. Hall)

I wrote back a few days later.

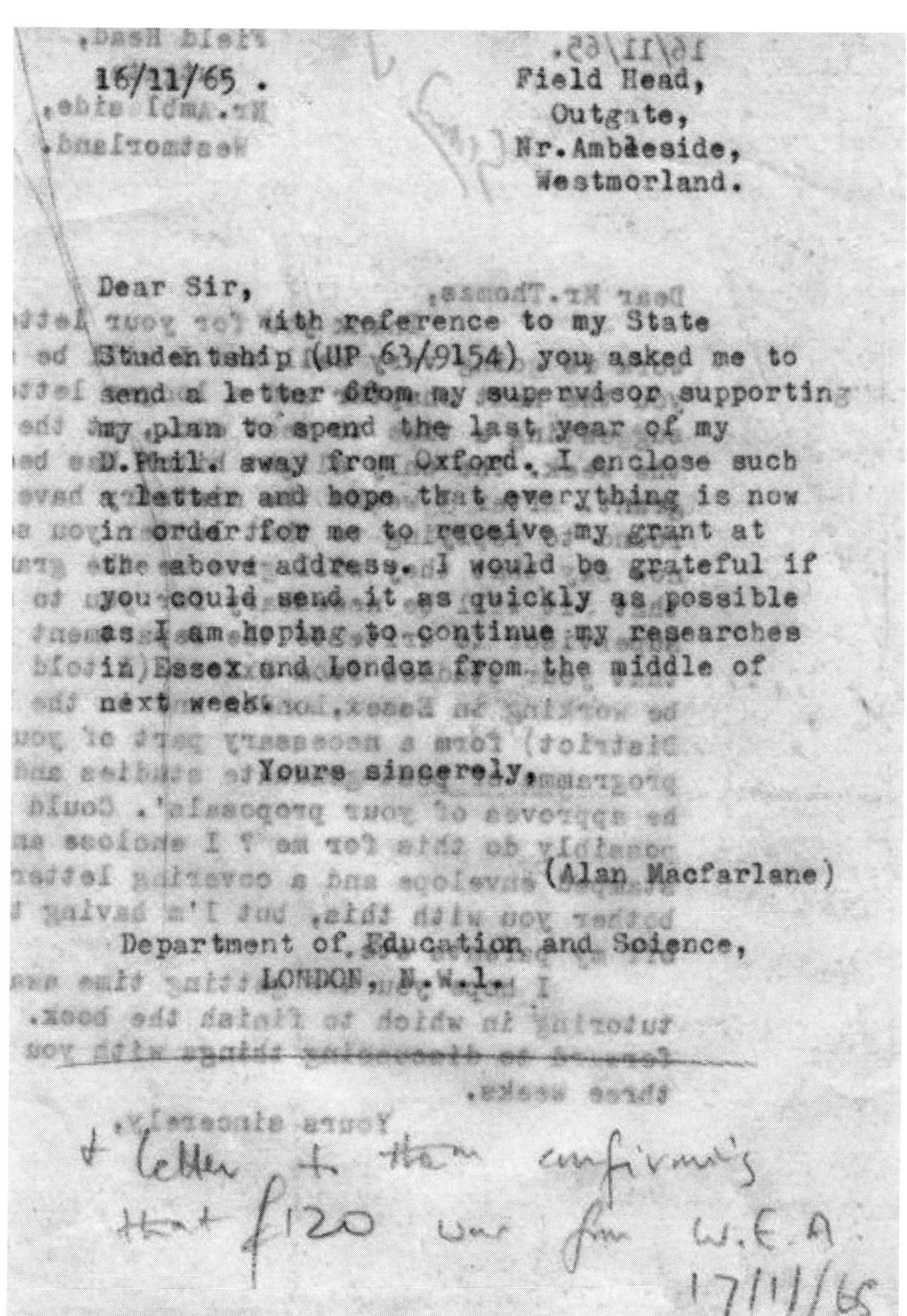
16/11/65 .

Field Head,
Outgate,
Nr. Ambleside,
Westmorland.

Dear Sir,

with reference to my State Studentship (UP 63/9154) you asked me to send a letter from my supervisor supporting my plan to spend the last year of my D.Phil. away from Oxford. I enclose such a letter and hope that everything is now in order for me to receive my grant at the above address. I would be grateful if you could send it as quickly as possible as I am hoping to continue my researches in Essex and London from the middle of next week.

Yours sincerely,

(Alan Macfarlane)

Department of Education and Science,
LONDON, N.W.1.

+ letter to them confirming that £120 was from W.E.A
17/11/65

I wrote to Keith Thomas on 16th November 1965 from Field Head

Dear Mr. Thomas,

Thank you for your letter. The work is going very well and I will send you the next chapter and a longer letter, suggesting a time to meet etc., at the end of the week. The only slight hitch has been my grant. After 3 weeks the ministry have just got round to replying to that letter you sent. They now say that they will give me the grant but that 'it will be necessary for you to ask your supervisor to write to the Department to confirm that your studies from Oxford (I told them I'd be working in Essex, London and in the Lake District) form a necessary part of your approved programme of post-graduate studies and that he approves of your proposals'. Could you possibly do this for me? I enclose an addressed stamped envelope and a covering letter. Sorry to bother you with this, but I'm having to borrow off my parents etc.

I hope you are getting time away from tutoring in which to finish the book. I look forward to discussing things with you in two or three weeks.
Yours sincerely,

I heard back from the Nuffield Foundation with disappointing news.

The Nuffield Foundation

Patron: H.M. Queen Elizabeth the Queen Mother
Chairman: the Hon. Sir Geoffrey Gibbs, KCMG *Director: Brian Young*

Nuffield Lodge, Regent's Park, London NW1

PRImrose 8871-9
Telegrams: Nuffound London NW1

CONFIDENTIAL

ENQ DDY/JT/GB 19th November, 1965.

Dear Mr. Macfarlane,

Thank you for your letter of the 15th November. I am afraid that it is unlikely that the Committee would relax its ruling regarding the age limit for the Sociological Scholarships. You may try, of course, but your chances must be slender in view of your age. I am afraid there is no other scheme in the field of Sociology. I am very sorry to have to send you such a disappointing reply.

Yours sincerely,

D.D. YONGE,
Fellowships Adviser.

A. Macfarlane, Esq.,
Field Head,
Outgate,
Nr. Ambleside,
Westmorland.

I then tried the Leverhulme Foundation.

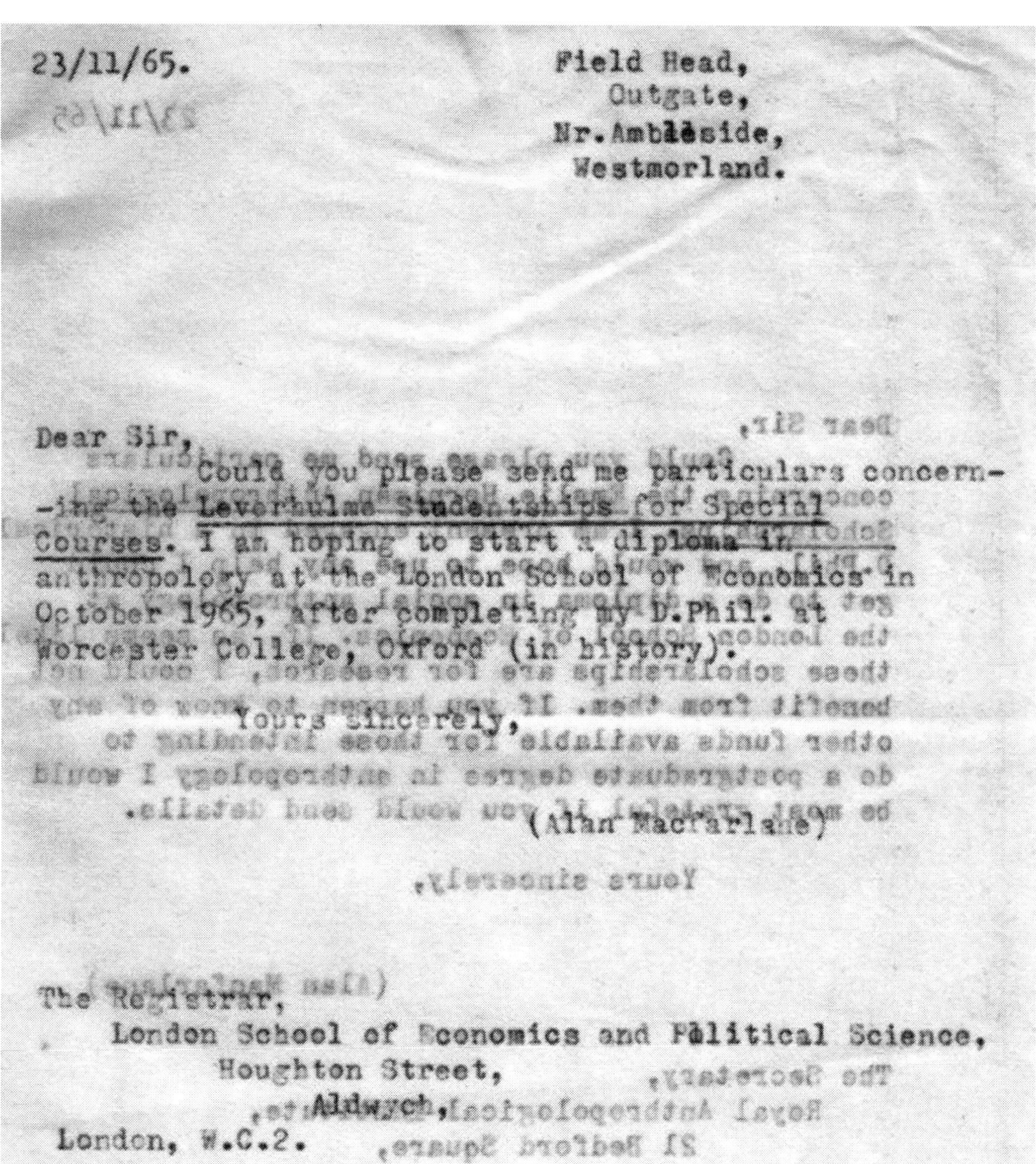
23/11/65.

Field Head,
Outgate,
Nr.Ambleside,
Westmorland.

Dear Sir,

Could you please send me particulars concern-
-ing the Leverhulme Studentships for Special Courses. I am hoping to start a diploma in anthropology at the London School of Economics in October 1965, after completing my D.Phil. at Worcester College, Oxford (in history).

Yours sincerely,

(Alan Macfarlane)

The Registrar,
London School of Economics and Political Science,
Houghton Street,
Aldwych,
London, W.C.2.

I wrote to Keith Thomas on 23rd November, Outgate, Nr Ambleside

Dear Mr. Thomas,

I enclose the next chunk of writing; I hope it is not too indigestible. As you'll see, the footnotes in the earlier section have become overweight, a fault emphasized by my inability to estimate how much room to leave at the bottom of the page. The reason for this is that I am loath to spend too much of my thesis outlining the legal machinery of the courts when there is so much material to deal with. The consequent cramming and argumentative footnotes aren't much better than dealing with the problems at more length. You'll also see that I've not interposed much interpretation of the facts; this will come later. I enclose a few xeroxes of maps in Felix Hull's thesis on agriculture in C17 & C17 Essex. Perhaps you will see some significance in the maps I've drawn; I haven't noted any very obvious correlations yet. Finally I enclose a letter from Ipswich which may interest you, I expect you know this already. My passage on Assizes outside Essex is the weakest part of the Chapter, and will possibly have to be re-written. As you'll see I've not been through the Ely records. I went to Cambridge, but Mrs Owen[1] said you'd spent a week there looking through them so it seemed pointless to duplicate. She

[1] Dorothy Owen, Archivist of the County Archives at Cambridge.

said you hadn't been through the Elizabethan material – pretty thin on the ground as it is – so I went through that and have one case which I can send you if you're interested. I would be most grateful if you could let me know about the other Ely stuff. You'll probably have been through Northern circuit recognizances also, which Ewen missed (Appendix 2).

Already the Appendices are growing and with the 200 odd cases from the Archdeaconry courts, nearly all unprinted, it doesn't look as if there'll be much room for the 480 odd correct Ewen 1 cases. (You'll see that I've abbreviated Ewen I to E.) Perhaps a very contracted list of cases will be necessary for the examiners?

As I told you on the phone, the Commissary records look as if they will be inaccessible by next October – all 15 tons of them! Thus my major chunks of material still to search are a) King's Bench b) Borough court. I'll also have to follow up some of the individuals we've already found – in local records. I've started analysing Hatfield Peverel and it is proving most fascinating. Though there are no parish registers there is a very detailed court roll 1556-1600 for the old Priory, now a manor. All the people involved in the witchcraft accusations – Wilmott, Waterhouse, Frauncis, Cocke appear here. There are over 1,000 references to Hatfield in the Archdeaconry records alone – and over 100 wills. Luckily I've managed to persuade my mother, just retired from India, to learn C16 handwriting and she is helping me with what, as you can see, is a pretty large effort of reconstruction. ... Hatfield [Peverel], *in itself, would be worth a book. I hope also to cover the next door village of Boreham which has poor manorial records but has both churchwardens accounts from 1560 and parish registers – and 4 witches.*

Incidentally in the P.R.O. in the Calendar of Carew Mss, 1575-1588, p. 425, nos. 610 I came across the following 'A Note of the Acts Handled in the last Session of Parliament, 1586' – May 16. The acts that passed ….. Against witchcraft and sorcery ….. (vol. 632, p.88) Have you any idea what this referring to? I haven't had a chance to follow it up yet. [in margin in Alan's hand 'Irish. See if same. P.R.O. Cal. St. Pap. Jas. I, vol.8, no.55, Notes for amendment of Witchcraft Statute']

I will be in Oxford on Friday and Saturday (26 & 27 Nov.) and could see you any time – at your convenience. But you probably won't have time to look at all this by then and perhaps the following Saturday (4th) or Sunday (5th) would be better. If you could drop a card in College (without a stamp – otherwise it will be forwarded) I will pick it up.

I hope all goes well with you and the book keeps moving. I look forward very much to discussing things. Yours sincerely,

It looks as if the piece I sent Keith was my first systematic sociological analysis based on the records. I probably sent him chapters on the Assize records and Quarter Sessions as well. Here I will include seven pages from the 30 page essay on Assizes, and leave on one side the 16 page essay on Quarter Sessions.

This was my first real foray into data analysis and the move from impressionistic to quasi-statistical analysis. Keith read it with his usual vigilance and his tiny pencil marks can be seen from time to time. The over-long footnotes, for which I apologised, can be seen at the start.

PROSECUTIONS IN THE ASSIZE COURTS.

I PROCEDURE.

As was seen in the previous chapter, witchcraft was a felony between 1542 and 1547 and again between 1563 and 1736. As such, supposed witches were tried at the Assizes. The records of this court consequently contain detailed information concerning prosecutions.[1]

Twice a year, in the Lent and Trinity vacations, two judges rode through the counties holding assizes of two to four days length in each county town.[2] A calendar of Justices of the Peace and other officials, which also included prisoners in gaol was first read.[3] Officials deposited their records: examinations and informations from the justices of the peace,[4] presentments from the hundred constables, and inquisitions from the coroners.[5] The grand jury was then called and sworn. It consisted of between thirteen and twenty-three lesser gentlemen from many of the hundreds.[6] They examined presentments and decided whether they were 'true bills' or should be dismissed as 'ignoramus'.[7] Bills passed by them provide the indictments which make up the bulk of the remaining material.[8] The court then divided into the civil and criminal sides, with one judge for each.[9]

The first indictment was then read and the named accused called to the Bar. The prisoner was asked if he pleaded guilty or not guilty, and the next was summoned until 'so many are arraigned as will serve for a petty Jury to pass upon at once'.[10] Those who confessed were put on one side until the time of Judgement.[11] The petty Jurors were then called by the Sheriff, their names read, and the prisoners given a chance to challenge them.[12] Witnesses against the accused were then publicly called for, and examinations of the accused taken before the justices of the peace

1. For a detailed discussion to these documents see the introduction to Ewen:1
2. This account is based on the Introduction to T.G.Barnes,(ed), Somerset Assize Orders,1629-40,(Somerset Record Society,vol.LXV), and Henry Twyford's contemporary The Office of the Clerk of Assize,(1676); all quotations are from the latter,unless otherwise stated.
3. Where material relevant to witchcraft prosecutions is to be found an example from Appendix 1 (Addenda and Corrigenda to Ewen) will be cited. For examples of gaol calendar references see Appendix 1 g(3). The gaol delivery roll, which is even more important in the study of witchcraft since it included the sentence passed on the accused, was a more formal document. Necessarily it was compiled during and after the trial. For a fuller discussion of these two records see Ewen:1,pp.97-8.

(for notes 4-12 see following pages)

were read to the jury, if they were evidence for the Crown.' Then if the Prisoner desire that any Witnesses should be heard for him, they must be called also, but they shall speak without Oath, unless the Fact be under Felony...' When the group of prisoners was large enough the jury retired

(notes from previous page)

4. Ewen:1, p.54 found neither examinations nor informations in the Home Circuit records, though he gave an example of the latter from the Assizes of the Isle of Ely. There are examples in the Quarter Session records (for instance Q/SR. 67/44-6), but deposition books for the Home Circuit must have perished. Detailed examples of examinations and depositions at the Assizes are to be found in the various Essex pamphlets; for their contents and accuracy see Ch. .

5. Ewen:1, p.60 remarked that 'one would have expected the coroner's rolls and inquisitions to be full of verdicts of death by witchcraft, but the writer has never seen any entry but felo de se, visitation of God, homicide, murder, or misfortune. Possibly, as in some of the gaol calendars, the word murder is used to include death by witchcraft.' Mr. R.F. Hunnisett of the Public Record Office informs the writer that in his reading of medieval and sixteenth century coroner's records he has not come across a verdict of murder by witchcraft. Ewen includes among his indictments some inquisitions (for instance nos.122, given in full transcript on pp.81-2) and he missed them occasionally (Appendix nos.1,7). These, however, are not taken from coroner's records.

6. The importance of the Grand Jury in a witchcraft prosecution was recognized by Richard Bernard when he wrote A Guide to Grand Jury Men, divided into two bookes: In the First, is the Authors best advice to them what to doe, before they bring in a Billa vera in cases of Witchcraft, with a Christian Direction to such as are too much given upon every crosse to thinke themselves bewitched. In the Second, is a Treatise touching Witches good and bad, how they may be knowne, evicted, condemned, with many particulars tending thereunto, (1627). From this it is clear that the grand jury could examine suspects and witnesses. Their responsibility was thus considerable. Bernard (p.25) states it explicitly when he says it is better to write Ignoramus than billa vera ' and so thrust an intricate case upon a Jury of simple men, who proceed too often upon relations of meere presumptions...' The final decision was with the jury of 'life and death', the petty Jury, a fact recognized by Perkins (Damned Art..., p.218) when he warned this jury not to shed innocent blood.

All punishments for witchcraft therefore needed the consent of a sizable group of the minor gentry. This argues against theories which place the total blame for prosecutions either with the superstitious lower classes, with the clergy, with the judges, or with individual 'witch-hunters'. It is thus important to determine when this group became sceptical. ~~The following graph~~ Table .. shows when bills were rejected as 'Ignoramus'. Occasionally this was on technical grounds, an incorrect bill had been proffered, but towards the end of the period we see a definite tendency to reject bills more frequently. It seems likely that this signified a change in the attitude of the minor gentry, now more sceptical of witchcraft prosecutions.

[for notes 7- 12 see next page]

\ All this should be in the text somewhere ? cf n.12

with a list of prisoners 'for their better direction and help of their memory to know who they have in charge'. Finally they returned and gave their verdict of guilty or not guilty, whereupon the Judge passed sentence.[1] Largely formal enquiries were also to be made as to the felons goods and whether he or she fled after committing the crime.[2]

Thus in the indictment we have a summary of the whole trial; the opinion of both juries, the sentence and details of the crime and those involved.[3]

(notes from previous page)

7. For the difference between a presentment and an indictment see Ch. p. (chapter on Q/S) and Ewen:1,pp.74-5. ~~There is only a slight difference.~~

8. Indictments are in Latin and on parchment. Usually there are separate indictments for different accusations against one person. During the interregnum they were in English. ~~They ought to include~~ County;Name, surname,address, and description of the indicted; the time and place of the offence; the name,surname, address, and description of the person offended or on whom the offence was committed (in the case of infants parentage and age ~~should be added~~); if the offence was not perpetrated on a human the kind, colour, value and ownership of the thing upon which the offence was committed should be included; the nature of the offence. Omissions and mistakes did not often cause the rejection of the bill. For a more detailed explanation and sixteen examples with their translations see Ewen:1,pp.75 seq. and for some abbreviated indictments Appendix (Addenda & Corrigenda to Ewen)

9. It was at this point that the Clerk of Gaol filed up the recognizances for the appearance of witnesses and accused (Twyford,op.cit., p.7); Ewen:1,pp56,7,prints two recognizances concerning witchcraft but omits them in his calendar of cases,examples will be found in Appendix (Addenda to Ewen,14).

10. Barnes,op.cit.,p.xviii, says this was usually 'seven or eight'; Twyford, op.cit.,p.10 says that the Judge decided the number.

11. Only a very few cases of a prisoner pleading guilty occur in the Essex records; see Ewen:1,pp.59-60 for examples of those who pleaded guilty and were neverthless found not guilty . For a general discussion of the numbers who confessed and pleaded guilty see the previous Chapter,p.16, note 1. No cases of the accused refusing to 'put themselves' on God and the country and hence enduring the 'peine forte et dure' (Twyford, op.cit., p.[illegible]) have been found in Essex.

12. The status and qualifications for service on the petty jury are a little obscure. If the Grand Jury consisted of the minor gentry it seems reasonable to suppose that they consisted principally of the yeoman and trader class. John Gaule implied this in 1646 when he argued that 'these Twelve good men and True' should not be Impannelled of the ordinary Country People: but of the most Eminent Physitians,Lawyers and Divines...'(Gaule,Cases...,p.194).This echoes Bernard's remark (cited n.6, on the previous page) about a 'Jury of simple men'. Writing of the Lincolnshire Quarter Sessions, Peyton explains that 'For the trial of prisoners at the bar, Hale states that fifteen days before the sessions, a general precept was directed to the sheriff to return twenty-four men, in order that twelve might be sworn should they be required. On the other hand, he describes as the common practice, a casual arrangement whereby jurymen were picked up in court as they might be needed.' (Pleas of the Crown, ii, 260-1)'. S.A. Peyton (ed), Minutes of Proceedings in Quarter Sessions held for Parts of Kesteven...... (Linc. Rec. Soc. vol. 25, 1931), p.lxxii. This probably applies to the Assizes equally well.

[For notes 1-3 see next page]

III. ANALYSIS OF CASES.

The following statistics are based on the indictments, inquisitions and gaol records (both calendars and delivery rolls) preserved for Essex. These somewhat different sources are treated as identical and are usually called by the group name 'indictment'. Indictments are by far the most numerous of the surviving types of record; there are half a dozen inquisitions and 23 persons mentioned in gaol calendars or delivery rolls alone.[1]

Types of offence.

Of the punishable offences listed in the witchcraft statutes the following appeared in the Essex Assizes.[2]

TABLE 2: Offences at the Assize court.

	Number of cases.	Number of persons involved
Invocation of evil spirits	28	29 (18-1645)
Using dead bodies for witchcraft	1	1
Treasure-seeking by "	6	9
Seeking lost goods " "	3	3
Injuring/killing people or property	460	270
Causing love	-	-
'Intent' to murder/injure	2	2
Fortune telling	1	1
'Consulting' witches	1	1
Uncertain	1	1

Some of the cases and persons overlap from different categories, for instance most of the persons under 'invocation' were also accused of 'injuring/killing people or property'. Thus the true totals of cases and persons in the Essex Assizes accused for activities associated with witchcraft are less than the sum of the above table. In fact some 503

1. Ewen in his statistics also does not distinguish these sources. The dates of the gaol record references are as follows: 1582,1582,1583,1585,1586,1609, 1619,1620,1626,1628,1631,1634,1634,1634,1638,1638,1639,1641,1644,1653,1656, 1659,1660. All these name individuals as witches who do not appear in the indictments. For a discussion of the process of making gaol records see p.1 above; for examples see Appendix 1,p.2.

2. For the Table of offences see Ch.2.p.7: for an explanation of the meaning of these offences was given on that page + there is another in the following pages.

other was the exceptional Edmund Mansell of Fingeringhoe, yeoman, otherwise of Feeringe, clerk. At Wivenhoe, by 'magic art', he burnt a barn, stable, and goods of a Wivenhoe man.[1] In half the indictments a verdict of guilty was found , but in the two cases where this was the only accusation the verdict was not guilty. Three of the cases occurred in 1582, the other three between 1587 and 1591.

Age distribution of accused and victims(human).

The age of the accused is never given and we can only infer from other sources or from their marital position that they were usually old enough to be wives or widows, and in three cases we know that they were young enough to be pregnant. The age of the victim, on the other hand, is often given, and where this is not so it is often stated that he or she is 'son of' or 'daughter of' another person. It seems likely that this was only done when the victim was a child. In the cases where death was caused, the following ages of victims are given: one unborn child,[2] one which languished from the age of seven days to a year old, children aged 3,3,3,6,9 months and 1,1½,2,2,3,3,3,4,4,4,4,5,5,5,6,8,8,9,10,11 years. From this an average age of 3 years 8 months appears. There were also two 'infants' and 46 'son/daughter of' persons . We only know the age of five children made ill; three of these were 1½ years, the others 1 and 7 years. There were 14 'son/daughter' and 1 infant.

TABLE 4: Age of people bewitched to death in the Assize records.

Period[3]	Under 3 months (including 'infants')	4 months and over (includes 'son/daughter')	Total for this period
1.	3	16	42
2	4	28	100
3	–	4	31
4	–	1	15
5	–	16	35
6	–	2	10
Total	7	67	233

1. There is a full transcript of this case E., p.85. Ewen was uncertain whether the other case of burning of a barn involved witchcraft (p.145.n.). However, the 1582.Pamphlet (D.7) makes it clear, in the remark of Alex Baxter that her spirits were employed and 'burnt Rosses with corn', that this was so.
2. E.145. Compare Elizabeth Frauncis who destroyed her own illegitimate child with a drink, before it was born, on the advice of her familiar (1566.P. p.318)
3. The numbers in the following tables represent the following twenty-year periods: 1. 1560-79 2.1580-99 3.1600-19 4. 1620-39 5.1640-59 6.1660-79.

nearly half the total, and the dominance of the agricultural profession. The cloth industry, represented by the 4 tailors and 1 weaver, only makes a slight appearance. It must be remembered that this table only gives us an indication of the social level of some 20% of the accused females.

TABLE 7: Occupation of the victims of witchcraft or their relatives.

Period	1	2	3	4	5	6	Total
labourer	2	3	-	-	-	1	6
husbandman	1	1	-	-	2	-	4
yeoman	6	1	-	-	8	1	16
gent	-	-	-	-	1	-	1
bricklayer	1	-	-	-	1	-	2
carpenter	1	-	-	-	-	-	1
fletcher	1	-	-	-	-	-	1
basket-maker	1	-	-	-	-	-	1
glover	2	-	-	-	-	-	2
tanner	1	-	-	-	-	-	1
sailor	2	1	-	-	2	-	5
weaver	1	-	-	-	-	-	1
smith	-	1	-	-	-	-	1
miller	-	1	-	-	-	-	1
butcher	-	-	-	-	1	-	1
mason	-	-	-	-	1	-	1
	19	8	-	-	16	2	45

Most striking in the above table is the high proportion of yeomen, over 30% of the sample, whereas the number of labourers has dropped considerably when compared to the table of the accused. This suggests a social polarization between accusers and accused. Another difference is that, though the occupation of fewer victims is known, 12 non-agricultural trades are listed as opposed to 6 for the accused. Together with the fact that 40% of the victims were in non-agricultural occupations, compared to 22% of the accused this suggests that there was a flow of accusations from small artificers and tradesmen towards agricultural workers. Once again, however, the cloth industry, here represented by the glovers and weaver, seems to be of no particular significance.

Marital position of accused persons.

It has been noted above that 9 of the 23 men accused of witchcraft had wives who were also witches. It is probable that one a number of occasions the fact that a person was married was not stated.[1] Thus it would be wrong

1. For a sample check of this from what we know from other sources see p.

(24)

with the highest figure in April. The deaths from these bewitchings were also highest in the spring, particularly in February, and sunk to a low figure in the autumn, reaching the lowest point in September. November, however, was a lone peak of high mortality.

FIGURE 2: Date of commencement of bewitching causing illness to humans.

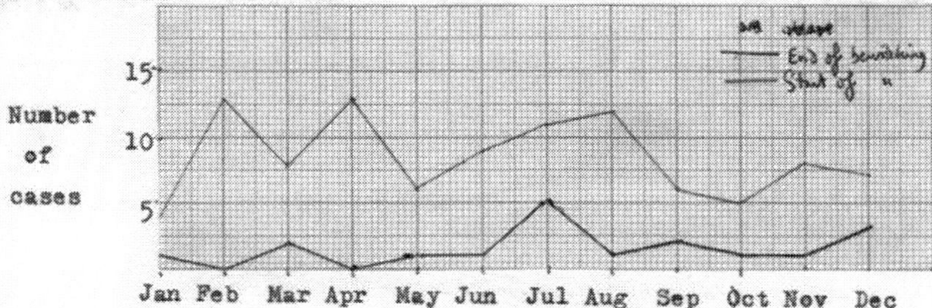

Again the spring, particularly February and April , were the most common months for the commencement of witchcraft illness and again the autumn, particularly September and October, were quiet months. The main difference is that July and August were also months of considerable activity in Figure 2. The date of the ending of witchcraft illness is not usually stated, since the victims were usually still languishing. It is interesting, however, that no-one recovered from witchcraft in the dangerous months of February and April, while there is a single isolated healthy spell in July.

FIGURE 3: Date of bewitching of animals.

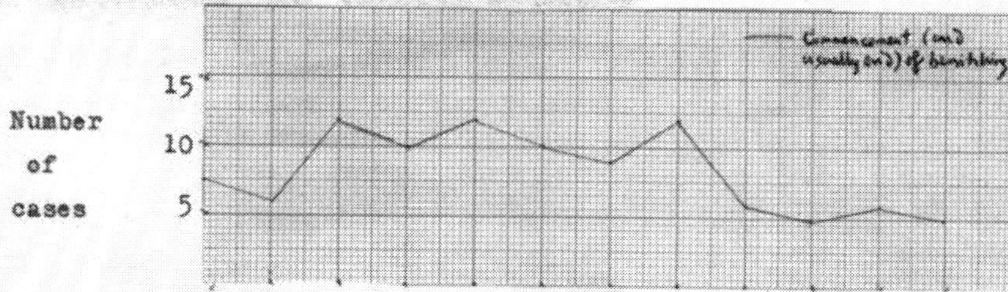

March to August was a consistently likely time for witchcraft to animals, while September to January show a uniform lessening of cases.

One interesting feature is the day of the month on which the bewitching or death was supposed to occur. A striking feature is the number of times the first day of a month is mentioned. For instance 1/6 of the 226 dates mentioned

At the same time I continued my correspondence with Raymond Firth about my work and future plans.

24/11/65

Dear Professor Firth,

It was most kind of you to see me in ~~November~~ October and I enjoyed our talk. You suggested that I might write a memorandum on 'historical kinship' with a view to discussing it with the other members of your group for the comparative study of kinship. This is an apology for not doing so. There are two reasons.

Firstly it seems to me that I know too little as yet either about anthropology or history to be able to write anything useful. I know roughly what anthropologists are interested in - from reading Young and Wilmott, Arensberg, yourself on 'Two Studies in Kinship', Williams on Gosforth, Turner on Schism and Continuity in an African Society etc. But it would be wasting your time to repeat the problems - size, residence, sanctions,succession, conflicts within, inter-marriage etc - concerning kinship. Nor can I yet give a clear account of how far there is historical material to answer the many questions one would ask. It is clear that parish registers, wills and manor court records (which record the succession to property) would be the basic materials for the actual kinship structure, while the ecclesiastical and other court records would illuminate conflicts and alliances between families and generally give the emotional content of the otherwise abstract structure. At the moment I am reconstructing two Essex villages in detail and hope to write a chapter on'kinship and marriage' in them. I would be most interested if you could give me your comments on it and I think it would be more valuable for you than a string of 'possible approaches' and 'possible sources'.

Secondly I have been thinking about your vague suggestion that I might (finances allowing) join your

(2) 24/11/65

group for the study of kinship. It was most kind of you even to think of including me and I fully realise that you cannot be at all positive at this stage. I also realise that it would be impossible for me to both receive money from this source and do the Diploma. But I have rather set my heart on acquiring proper training as an anthropologist. If I don't 'social frameworks' 'systems of sentiments' etc. now, I never will and would remain something of a dabbler - an expert in witchcraft and kinship perhaps, but with huge gaps where I knew nothing. I agree this is not a particularly sensible position but it is how I feel. Thus, assuming the School allows me to do the Diploma, I think I will take it. I am no further in obtaining funds from other sources yet - the Nuffield Foundation social science fellowships have an age limit of 28-40 and the secretary tells me there would be little point in my competing for them (I wonder why Evans-Pritchard suggested them?). No doubt something will emerge.

Thank you for all your kindness and I look forward to discussing historical kinship on future occasions.

Yours sincerely,

(Alan Macfarlane)

Professor Raymond Firth,
London School of Economics and Political Science,
Houghton Street,
Aldwych,
London, W.C.2.

The London School of Economics and Political Science

(University of London)

Houghton Street, Aldwych
London, W.C.2
Telephone HOLborn 7686

26th November 1965.

Dear Mr. Macfarlane,

Thank you for your letter. May I comment on the points you raise, in reverse order?

First, as regards the group for the study of kinship. This meets irregularly, perhaps once or twice a term on an evening, the members dine together and we then have a paper, usually discussing a piece of someone's research. I am not quite clear whether you realize this because your letter rather suggests that attending meetings of this group would be a sort of alternative to your Diploma work. This, of course, is not so. I can quite see that from your point of view the thing is to get a proper training as an anthropologist. When you say "assuming the School allows me to do the Diploma, I think I will take it" I am not absolutely certain whether you are referring to the Oxford one-year Diploma or to our two-year Diploma here. I rather assume the latter, in which case I would think there is unlikely to be any hindrance in your acceptance. Of course these matters are finally judged by committees, but your qualifications and case seem to me to be strong for admission.

As regards your first point, it seems to me that in due course your reconstruction of kinship and marriage in two Essex villages would indeed be of interest not only to me but also to our kinship study group. But I take it that this will be quite some time ahead.

Come and see me again, if you wish.

Yours sincerely,

Raymond Firth

Raymond Firth.

Alan Macfarlane Esq.,
Worcester College,
Oxford.

I heard in detail about the grant for my third year well into my third year, having been dependent on my parents for two months.

DEPARTMENT OF
EDUCATION AND SCIENCE
AWARDS BRANCH
13 Cornwall Terrace, Regents Park, LONDON N.W.1
Telephone: HUNTER 1455

Your reference:
Our reference: U.P.63/9154

29 NOV 1965

Dear Mr. Macfarlane,

With reference to your letter of 16th November, I am writing to inform you that the assessment of your postgraduate studentship has been revised and as from 1st October, 1965 the award will be

(a) approved fees

(b) a maintenance grant at the rate of £380 per annum, which will be paid in instalments of £95, £95, £95 and £95.

This award is subject to review at any time in the light of changes in your circumstances and is given on the understanding that:

(a) you will be required to devote at least 44 weeks of the academic year to approved full time study, otherwise, a proportionate reduction in grant will be made.

(b) your total income from other sources, including Scholarships etc. will not exceed £100 in the academic year 1965/66.

/As

A. D. J. Macfarlane, Esq.,
Field Head,
Outgate,
Ambleside,
Westmorland.

As you are studying away from Oxford, payment of your quarterly instalment of maintenance grant will be made if you will return one of the enclosed copies of Form 112F.UP duly completed.

In view of your income of £120 from Workers Educational Association classes during the academic year 1964/65, an overpayment of £20 has arisen for that year and this amount will be deducted from your October 1965 instalment. As you have already received a payment of £50 on account ~~this~~ the balance will be £25.

Any changes in your circumstances as outlined above, or, e.g. marriage or a change in your place of residence, should be reported to the Department without delay.

In writing to the Department on any matter connected with your postgraduate Studentship you should quote the reference number shown at the head of this letter.

Yours sincerely,

E W Hall

(E. W. Hall)

1965 - December

My mother wrote to me from Field Head on 2nd December.

My dear Alan,

OPF! [Our Provident Fund]. *Couldn't send you a wire – it arrived on Monday in the middle of a blizzard when the telephone had just been connected. All I could do was squeak at the Bank Manager but we were panting on the doorstep of the bank next morning & have since bought a Telly, Transistor, ordered a carpet & are off to get a canopied 4-poster bed! So if you want any assistance let us know, we'll pay off the projector. It all seems quite unreal & I think I shall soon tire of being able to go into a shop without wild calculations & tremblings at the knees – but temporarily its heady… Anne and I have been will-reading & needless to say she has learnt in 2 days what it took me 2 weeks to master!*[1] *Will try to get the shed finished but T. Edmondson hasn't reappeared as yet. Will ring him up. Am beginning to feel the pressure of Christmas weighing on my subconscious & must tackle some lists. I'm forwarding your mail to Worcester & hope that's all right.*

Do hope the work goes well & you are keeping the fleas at bay – longing to have you back to Ribena & chocolate biccys!

Must rush – Much love – Mummy

Another part of my correspondent at this time was with Hugh Trevor-Roper.

From The Regius Professor of Modern History

History Faculty Library,
Merton Street,
Oxford.
Telephone XXXXX 43388

3rd December, 1965.

My dear Macfarlane

I do not seem to have run into you all this term, and when I last saw you you were going off to some hermitage in the Lake District in order to work. How well did you work? I hope everything is going well. If you have time between now and the 13th December, when I shall be leaving, do call on me and tell me about your studies. I would very much like to see you again if you are free.

Yours ever
Hugh Trevor-Roper

A. D. J. Macfarlane, Esq.,
Worcester College,
Oxford.

---

[1] My sister Anne had left London and joined us to work with me in the Lake District.

Worcester College, Oxford 4th Dec. 1965 7 p.m.

Dear Professor Trevor-Roper,

Thank you so much for your letter, and the invitation to talk things over. Unfortunately I'm only in Oxford until tomorrow afternoon so I think this will be impossible. I wish I'd known you weren't too busy earlier as I've been wanting to see you, but hesitated since I imagined you had more important matters at hand. Could I come and see you early next term? I will write well in advance to fix a time. My witchcraft is going very well and I look forward to having your opinions on my theories. I hope all is well with you. May I take this opportunity of wishing you a convivial Christmas?

Thank you again for remembering me.

Yours sincerely, Alan Macfarlane

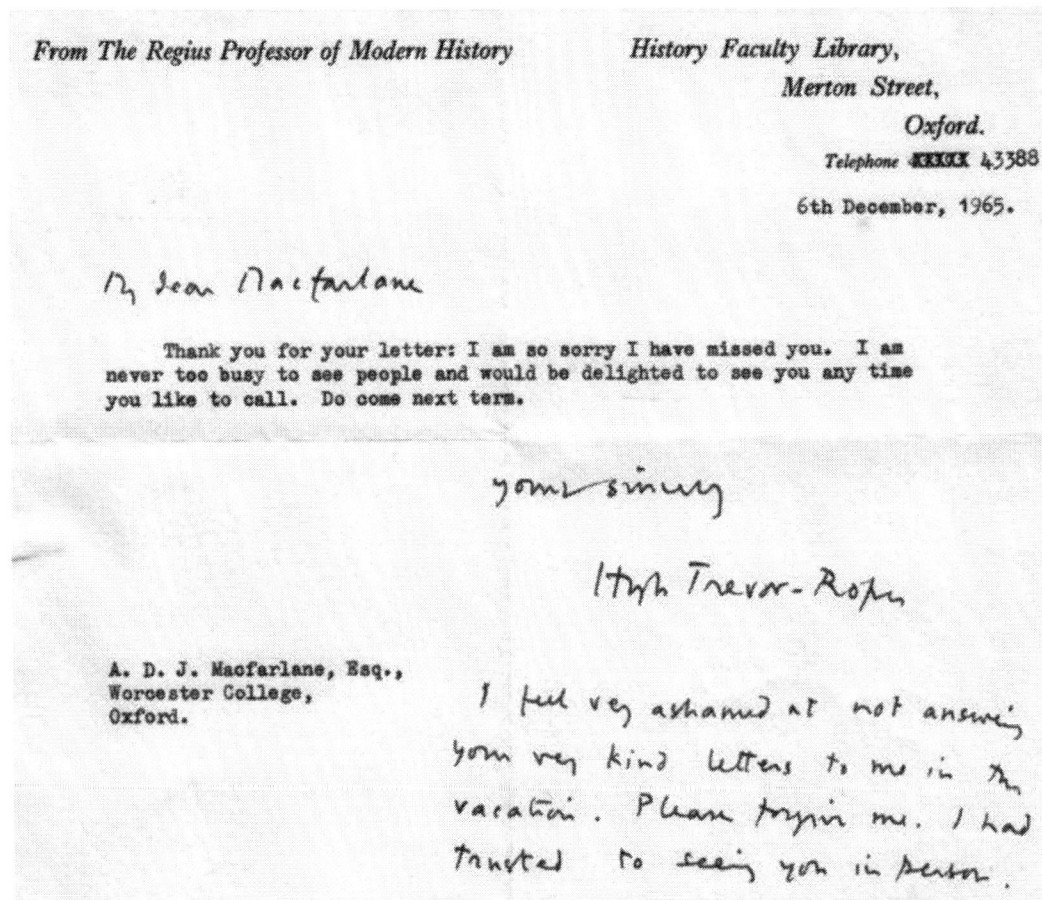

From The Regius Professor of Modern History

History Faculty Library,
Merton Street,
Oxford.
Telephone XXXXX 43388

6th December, 1965.

My dear Macfarlane

Thank you for your letter: I am so sorry I have missed you. I am never too busy to see people and would be delighted to see you any time you like to call. Do come next term.

yours sincerely

Hugh Trevor-Roper

A. D. J. Macfarlane, Esq.,
Worcester College,
Oxford.

I feel very ashamed at not answering your very kind letters to me in the vacation. Please forgive me. I had trusted to seeing you in person.

Friday 10th December 1965 Field Head, Iris to Alan

My dear Alan,

Thank you for two letters – a cri de coeur today which I'll deal with at the Bank to-morrow – if you haven't anything there I'll put some of OPF in – still have a little left! Of course we'd love to have Zoe for Christmas, Fred the Shed has been back & finished the main jobs so when Daddy has plastered the cracks & we've got a carpet down it'll make the cosiest little bed-sitter. Actually the shelves aren't in yet either but we're all working very hard to have everything done by Christmas and the strain is terrific – Anne & I went to a sale yesterday and I bid against myself for a table I didn't want & bought nothing else! We didn't get the canopied bed but another large one for £4 & 6 chairs for 9/- – all very furry & boardinghousish but we like them. We had an awful fright last weekend as the phone rang twice on Friday evening & then got cut off & we had visions of Fiona trying to get through to us while a homicidal lorry-driver lurked – actually it was awful & we could think of no way to get through to her. We sent her a wire & she rang on Saturday very surprised, & turned up later, & we drove her back to Manchester on Monday to save further neuroses. Anne is reading wills & we're waiting for H.P. [Hatfield Peverel] *with mixed feelings – we're slightly Terrified to be honest! Robert is giving a lecture in Kendal tomorrow & we might see him, perhaps take our hammer & sickle along as he's talking to the Tories. I got myself a coat & various other garments yesterday so that's me clad for the winter thank heavens, now a spot of something for Oxfam.*

Love to Rosemary & Roy & I hope the party is a success. It was nice of her mother to say those kind things about my book, please thank her for trying to help.

Everyone sends love, Poochie & the Cat are still in a state of armed neutrality & the snow has all gone.

Much love, Mummy

DEPARTMENT OF
EDUCATION AND SCIENCE
AWARDS BRANCH
13 Cornwall Terrace, Regents Park, LONDON N.W.1
Telephone: HUNTER 1455

Your reference:
Our reference: UP.63/9154

17 DEC 1965

Dear Mr. Macfarlane,

With reference to your letter of 4th December, I write to say that a draft for £25, in respect of the balance of your maintenance grant for the October quarter, is being sent to your bank in Ambleside.

I should explain that earnings from Workers' Educational Association classes, sponsored by the Delegacy for Extra-Mural Studies, are not regarded as income from University teaching or supervision, therefore the practice of halving any further income beyond the first £100 does not apply.

Yours sincerely,

R. Fowler

(R. Fowler)

A. D. J. Macfarlane, Esq.,
Field Head,
Outgate,
Ambleside,
Westmorland.

1966

1966 - January

Sister Anne my mother and I at Tarn Howes

I was now working solidly in the un-insulated garden shed in my parent's house. From there I started to plan ahead for various things I would need for my final thesis, including copies of maps and diagrams.

4/1/66

Field Head,
Outgate,
Nr.Ambleside,
Westmorland.

Dear Sir,

I wonder if you could give me any details about your ability to do plan copying ? I want to purchase about a dozen copies of an outline map, traced from an 1841 Essex tithe map in the Essex Record Office. I have already traced the map and wondered how I could reproduce some copies. Miss Grieve of the Essex Record Office staff suggested 'Industrial plan copying' which has been successfully performed for her with her maps of Chelmsford. The maps, as you know, are several feet in length and width.

Yours sincerely,

Alan Macfarlane

Messrs.E.N.Mason & Sons,Ltd.,
Arclight Works,
COLCHESTER,
Essex.

I heard back quite quickly.

THIS PAPER IS SUITABLE FOR DYELINE (DIAZO) REPRODUCTION

E. N. MASON & SONS LTD

COLCHESTER · ESSEX · ENGLAND Telephone: Colchester 5191. Telegrams: Arclight Colchester

YOUR REF.

OUR REF. RJL/JH/203/3/0297

7th January, 1966.

Mr. A. Macfarlane,
Field Head,
Outgate,
Nr. Ambleside,
Westmorland.

Dear Sirs,

We thank you for your letter of the 4th January and are pleased to inform you that we can undertake the reproduction of plans from tracings, by the dyeline or photographic processes.

Unfortunately, you omitted to state the size, type or number of drawings so that we are unable to give you a quotation but this we will be pleased to do on receipt of this information.

We can normally copy up to 40" in width by any length by the dyeline process.

We hope that we may look forward to your further instructions in due course.

Yours faithfully,
for E. N. MASON & SONS LIMITED.

R.J. LITTLE

A VENESTA COMPANY

I sent a postcard to Keith Thomas on 16th January from Field Head.

Dear Mr. Thomas,

I hope you had a pleasant Christmas and have had time to continue the book. Writing proceeds according to plan up here and I hope to have the first draft of the chapter on 'ecclesiastical sources for witchcraft prosecutions' with me when I arrive in Oxford next (22-23 Jan) week-end. I will deposit it in John's with an accompanying letter. Could you possibly have a look at it by the following week-end? I will be at the P.R.O. from Monday-Thursday & in Oxford Fri-Saturday (28-30 Jan). If you could manage anytime then could you drop a note in Worcester to that effect for when I come down on 22nd. Otherwise I can ring you if that (28-30) week-end is no good & we can arrange a time. Thank you. Yrs. Alan Macfarlane

I then wrote on 22nd January to Professor Trevor-Roper:

Dear Professor Trevor-Roper,

You very kindly said I might come and see you sometime this term. I will be in Oxford from Friday to Sunday 28-30 Jan. and 5-7 Feb. and wondered whether you would be free at either time? I'm sorry to only offer such restricted periods but, as You know, I am writing my thesis in the Lake District and consequently only pass through Oxford. I do hope we can have a talk as I would very much value your comments both on my present work, and on my future plans. 'Witchcraft' is progressing very well, but I find writing a strain all the same. When I finish, at the end of the year, I hope to go to the London School of Economics to do a diploma in social anthropology. People are always advocating that historians should be 'sociologically aware' but I haven't been able to discover anyone who is, in a tangible financial) way, prepared to back me. I imagine this is beyond even the long arm of a Regius Professor of History? Perhaps you think it would be a waste of time? I would be <u>most</u> grateful for any advice you could give me. I feel I am at a cross-roads, and though I feel I probably know what I should do I haven't much confidence in my convictions.

If you could see me I would be very happy. If you are very busy, perhaps I could write to you at greater length from my Wordsworthian fastness? I hope your many works all go well. I appreciate your continued interest in my work: it makes me feel slightly less isolated.

Yours sincerely, Alan Macfarlane

I received notice of a payment of my last year's grant.

DEPARTMENT OF EDUCATION AND SCIENCE

Curzon Street, London, W.1.

HYDe Park 7070

Ref: UP. 63/9154

The enclosed payment 26. JAN. 1966
in respect of

maintenance grant and
travelling

£32 - 4 - 0

is forwarded with the Secretary's Compliments.

A. D. J. Macfarlane Esq.,
Field Head.
Outgate
Ambleside
Westmorland.

Form 151F

One of my last poems was as follows:

*With Zoë – London – knitting.*_- 24 January 1966

The synthesis of your hands, flickering together
The threads of night and day, dark and white
Wool patterned by your presence
Into a new shape and substance
To Clothe me from the world's naked gaze
To bring me in moments of fear
When friends choke me with well-meaning
And the familiar becomes hostile –
And impulses no longer bring sensations
And the feet are wounded in the soft grass
Memories – of our meaningless friendship –
That I might strike down the flame
And bring peace to tormented minds.
That I might forget the I and You,
Swinging to the stars of ecstasy
In a passion obliterating: instead
Of this reluctant anatomizing of love,
This endless niggling, drawing and denying,
Demanding and pleading and hesitating
Towards the sympathetic smile.
I ought to sweep the autumn leaves,
Forget the first winter and remember
That there are a few bitter springs
Left to us: go your way, and
Push me on mine. No longer will
The hawthorn blossom, or the swans
Ride the level mist, but a lifted skirt,
Or a congratulation, tea after a cold walk,
Or a satisfactory footnote can still bring pleasure.
Soon will be the time for compromise and slippers.
And the end of living on the edge,
For a time, and then the lonely season,
When I remember. But shut away that time
And sweep me now into your arms
And spit me into the depths of
Forgetfulness…

I owed an enormous debt of gratitude to Hilda Grieve. She was the Student's room Supervisor at the Essex Record Office. I can still see her sitting at a raised table, perhaps behind a glass screen, with a special mat to keep her coffee well away from the documents. She was one of the leading figures nationally in palaeography, and her guide, with ample illustrations and parallel texts, to local palaeography was probably my major aid in learning how to read the almost impossibly difficult ecclesiastical. The formal palaeography of 'court hand' I had started in Oxford was of no use for this kind of work and without Hilda's patient help on a daily basis over the first few weeks, I would probably have given up. So it is a pleasure to find our correspondence around this time. I imagine I did not need to write in 1965, as I was on the spot, but when I retired to write up in the Lakes, I started to write to her.

Hilda Grieve, a few years after I met her.

My first letters were clearly after visits.[1]

[1] Hilda completed the mentioned study of Chelmsford, though I cannot find evidence that it was ever published.

c. 28/1/66.

Dear Hilda,

I hope to be in Essex on Monday for a couple of days and wonder if you could book me in ? I want to check a few ecclesiastical and other references. My witches and detailed study of Hatfield Peverel go well: even as I write my mother and sister are translating wills from the microfilms! Has Mr. Emmison been able to get the Boreham parish register for microfilming yet ? I would also like to have the Little Baddow register microfilmed - to 1603 - but will arrange that when I arrive. I hope all goes well with you and that you have had time to work on Chelmsford. I look forward very much to seeing you all: regards to Arthur, Ron, Nancy etc.

Yours,

(Alan Macfarlane)

1966 - February

Field Head, Thursday (no date, either 3rd or 10th) February Iris to Alan

My dear Alan,

Thanks for yours, glad your supervisor was pleased with yu – & that Linda is still baring up. the big news is that Anne past her test without tranquillisers or shots of cocaine – in fact she was remarkably calm which is probably why she past. We're all frightfully relieved but have no car for her to drive, the red Zephyr has gone & the green 1100 not arrived but the nice little garage man has lent us his pro tem so we're off to our last sale to-day – to get a typewriter I hope. I've decided to get Anne to type my book as it is practically incomprehensible as I type – hope you can spare her for those few hours? ...

What about coming up with Dusty on Friday? Shell House at Aldwych would find him I think. Very warm here now but no doubt the blizzards will have collected round the shed for your return, cementing just about to start & pink flamingos on the bathroom wall. Am reading Laslett & even I find him naive, we can do much better.

Looking forward to seeing you.

Much love – Mummy

Worcester College, Oxford 6.2.66

Dear Professor Trevor-Roper,

Just a note to thank you for your double kindness; first in seeing me and discussing my work/problems, second for the most generous gift of your book. Even if it looks as if I will have to work in a lift in the Hilton Hotel to work my way through a degree at London it was comforting to have your moral support on this.

I will be in Oxford in about six weeks and will call on you, if I may, as I very much enjoy our discussions.

I hope your book is a great success and that my namesake has no really telling arrows in his quiver.[1]

Thank you once again.

Yours sincerely, Alan Macfarlane

[1] K.B. McFarlane, Oxford medieval historian.

From The Regius Professor of Modern History

History Faculty Library,
Merton Street,
Oxford.
Telephone 43388

9 February 1966

Dear Alan

Thank you very much for your kind letter. I was very glad to see you when you were here, and I would certainly like to see you again any time you are here. But will I be here in "six weeks"? I fear that I may not be. It will be in vacation and I may well be in Scotland or abroad. But do anyway look me up if I am here. Meanwhile I will keep an eye out for any means of support for you in your project of working in London.

Incidentally I am re-writing for publication the paper I once wrote on the witch-craze. I wonder if there have been any special studies which I have missed, more particularly on trials on the Continent. Do you happen to know of any good recent work? Apart from the two studies by Bavoux (on Quingey and Luxeuil) I know nothing recent; but I may well have missed something. So if you do happen to know of anything, do please tell me.

+ Fèbvre's article

I suppose you are now buried again in your hut in the Lake District. I hope that work goes well in that isolated hermitage.

Yours ever,

H. R. Trevor-Roper

A. D. J. MacFarlane, Esq.,
Worcester College,
Oxford.

All the while I was working in the freezing garden shed at the bottom of our Lake District garden. In order to make this more efficient, so that I could be called if there was a phone message or for meals and coffee, I bought a red intercom. One buzz for the phone, two for coffee, three for a meal. Here is the purchase.

It can be seen that this was quite expensive - £50 or so by present prices.

DANson Park 1351

REF: RDP/JPC/EM/14

R.D.PIDGEON.
141,WELLINGTON AVENUE,
SIDCUP,
KENT.

Two Station Intercom Sets

Dear Sir,

It was with much pleasure that we received your recent letter expressing interest in our two station intercom system.

This system was, until recently marketed by a famous British firm who have now sold all their remaining stocks to us. We in turn are offering a set to you at nearly half the price it was originally sold for.

As you will see from the attached photograph the instument is a one piece moulding of unbreakable red polythene.

Communication is controlled by a two way switch on each instrument. This switch is pressed one way to call the other party, and the other way to speak. Calling is by buzzer which is housed inside the set.

The instruments are designed to operate over distances of up to 200 - 300 yards using only one 4½ volt battery. (Any 4½ volt battery will do but we particularly recommend Ever Ready No.126). Four wire telephone cable for connecting the instruments can be supplied by us at the rate of £2 per 100 yards.

Installation of the system is very simple and no technical knowledge or wiring experience is needed. Wiring and operating instructions including a diagram are included with the instruments.

We sincerely trust that the foregoing proves of interest to you and look forward to hearing from you further in the near future.

Yours faithfully,

R.D.Pidgeon.

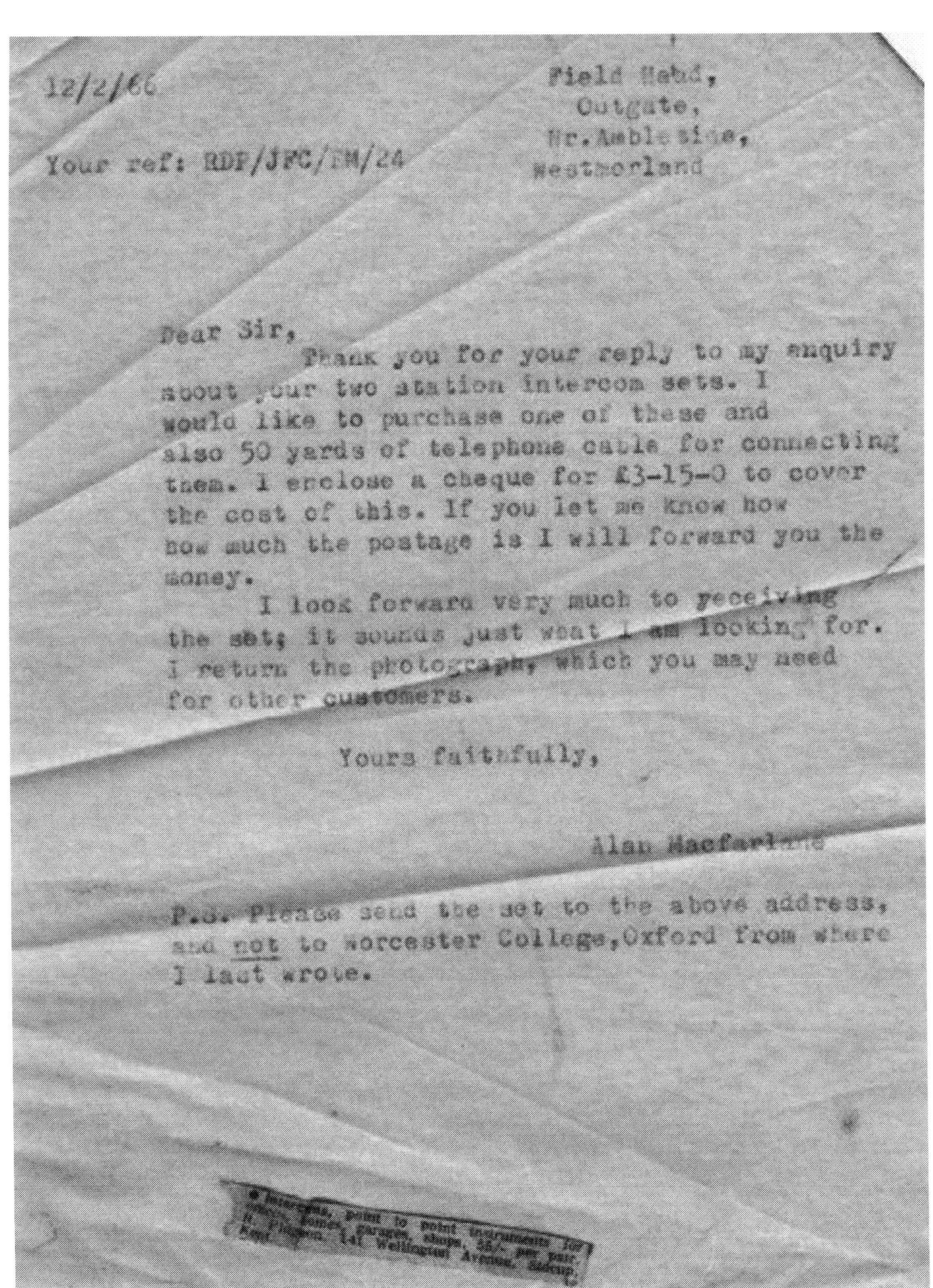

12/2/66

Field Head,
Outgate,
Nr. Ambleside,
Westmorland

Your ref: RDP/JFC/EM/24

Dear Sir,

Thank you for your reply to my enquiry about your two station intercom sets. I would like to purchase one of these and also 50 yards of telephone cable for connecting them. I enclose a cheque for £3-15-0 to cover the cost of this. If you let me know how how much the postage is I will forward you the money.

I look forward very much to receiving the set; it sounds just what I am looking for. I return the photograph, which you may need for other customers.

Yours faithfully,

Alan Macfarlane

P.S. Please send the set to the above address, and <u>not</u> to Worcester College, Oxford from where I last wrote.

Intercoms, point to point instruments for offices, homes, garages, shops, 55/- per pair. 141 Wellington Avenue, Sidcup, Kent.

A few days later I added another piece of equipment to hold my witchcraft cases on cards.

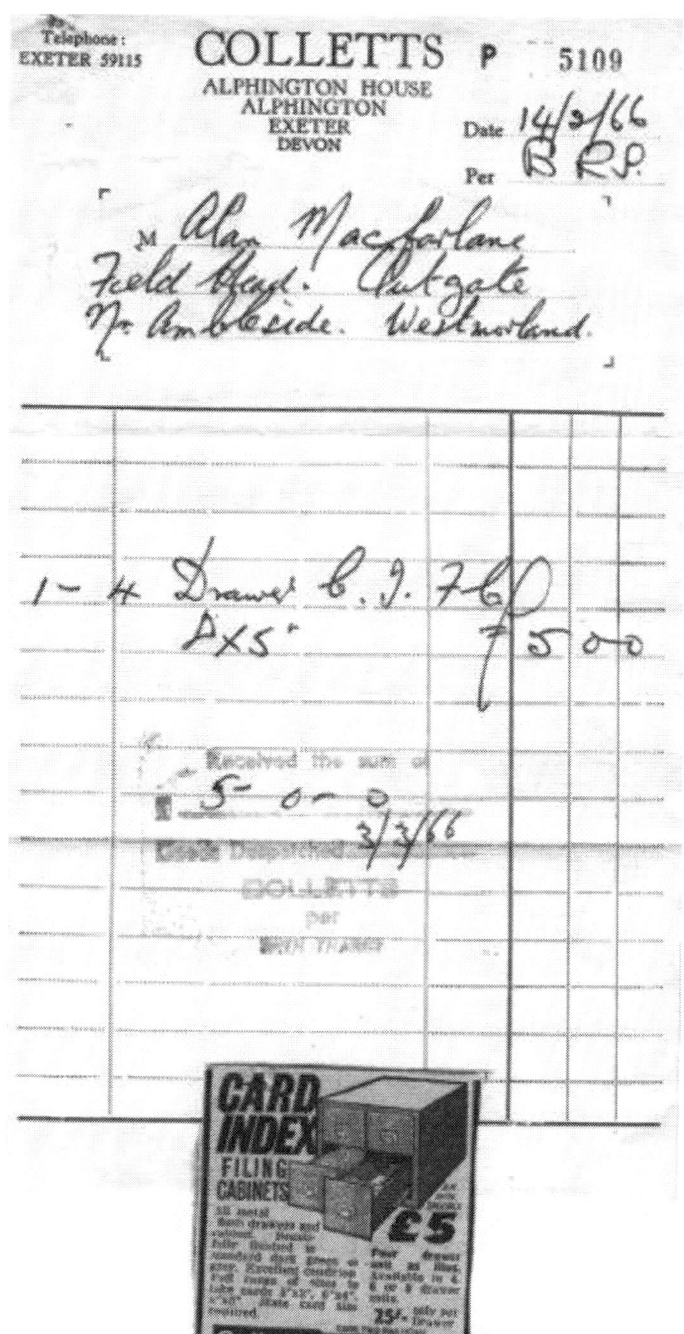

Telephone: EXETER 59115 COLLETTS P 5109

ALPHINGTON HOUSE
ALPHINGTON
EXETER
DEVON

Date 14/2/66
Per B R P.

M Alan Macfarlane
Field Head. Outgate
Nr. Ambleside. Westmorland.

1 – 4 Drawer C. I. 7" 8x5"		£5	0	0

Received the sum of £5-0-0 3/3/66
Goods Despatched
COLLETTS
per
WITH THANKS

Typewriters

I wrote again to Trevor-Roper on 16th February.

16/2/66

Field Head,
Outgate,
Nr.Ambleside,
Westmorland.

Dear Professor Trevor-Roper,

Thank you very much for your kind letter. It is always good for my morale and status within the family to get a letter from a Regius Professor. I do hope we will manage to overlap at Oxford. I will write as soon as I know exactly when I will be down.

You kindly said I might have your support in my bid to get financial aid for my London project, so I have taken the liberty of quoting you as a possible referee for a lectureship at Brentwood Training College. I do hope this was alright. I would have written and asked specifically, but there was a rush to get the form off in time. Also I think it <u>very</u> unlikely that they will bother you or be interested. I told them not to consider the application unless they were prepared to let me take an M.Sc. at London at the same time as teaching with them. I doubt if they will swallow this, even with your name behind it.

I'm afraid I don't know of much that's come out recently on Continental witchcraft. You'll know of J.C.Baroja's <u>The World of the Witches</u>,(1964)- mostly about Basque witchcraft - I'm sure. I've only dipped into it and wasn't very impressed. The only anthropologist he quotes is Mr.R.Benedict (meaning Ruth Benedict).You probably know also R.Delcambre, <u>Le Concept de la Sorcellerie dans le Duché de Lorraine au C16 & C17</u> (Waarg(?),1947,1949) and <u>Die Hexenprozesse in Franken</u> by Friedrich Merzbacher (C.H.Beck'sche Verlagsbuchhandlung,1957). Thee latter has, apparently, a very comprehensive bibliography. You will know that Notestein has just been reprinted. Though you are doubtful of its relevance a very good anthropological account has just been published; M.G.Marwick, 'Sorcery in its

Social Setting (Manchester,1965).

I can't remember if I ever told you the results of my hunt for that book by E.R.Snow, Secret's of the North Atlantic Islands which purported to reveal a hitherto unknown mid-C18 American witchcraft trial. This case was not in either of his other books - 'Tales of the Atlantic coast' or 'Amazing sea stories never told before' but these titles suggest he might well have written such a book - even though it is not mentioned in either the Bodley or B.M. catalogue.

I am interested to hear that you are going to publish your paper on witchcraft. As you know, we agree to differ on a lot of major interpretations,but perhaps this is because we work on different sources and different levels. You work on the branches and the broad outlines, I tend to get buried in the leaves. But both these are preferable to counting the twigs and small offshoots.(a metaphor borrowed, I expect you'll remember, from a conversation between Namier and Toynbee: I hope the comparison won't annoy you!).

Would it be presumptious to cite a few exceptions to points in the paper you lent me. You are probably going to alter it anyhow. On p.4. you say that the 'witch-mark', the insensitive spot which revealed the witch....was not recognized here(i.e. England). Of course the Newcastle 'pricking' episode was an exception - tho' this may be attributed to Scottish influence. In a number of English trials people search the witch for her mark but,in England, it was more often a protuberance or red spot, easily visible, than the dead patch which required pricking. The divided opinion on the subject (& attitude of puritan clergy) is nicely shown in one of the discussions at the Dedham classis where a minister moved 'how he might know a witche': 'some said she might be found out by serche in her bodie , some thought that to be fancy in the people easilie conc--eiving such a thinge and to be reproved in them'. (R.G.Usher, The Presbyterian Movement.... (Camd.Soc. 3rd.Ser.8. ,p.70).

On the same page you say that 'incubi and succubi were purely clerical inventions', and were not among the furniture of lay or protestant minds'. I think this is too strong. Of course the thing was systematized and spread by the Catholics, but the idea of sexual demons which assualted one in the night was much older and arose from the 'folk' mind. Perhaps it was the Church which united the two ideas. Certainly there were cases in England of a very similar idea . A nice case is quoted in J.S.Purvis, Tudor Parish Documents of the Diocese of York (pp.197-9 contain several witchcraft cases), (1948). A woman was tried for slandering 'that there dwelleth a witch within three houses at one time & five houses at another, & upon further examination, she confessed herself to be ridden with a witch three times of one night, being thereby greatly aston--ished & upon her astonishment awaked her husband'. (Ridden, I am told, is an euphemism). The devil was not far from an Incubus in the confession of Elizabeth Clarke before Hopkins.

On p.5. you say that the witch-mania was 'instituted, inflamed & prolonged....by organised religion', and on p.16 'What was needed was an anti-clerical revolution, a revolt of lay reason...' Of course this is a huge point & I can't deal with it here. But it is not true of England. Here, as I hope to show in detail anon, the Church courts were mild, the ecclesiastics not interested in finding 'witches' and the pressure for the punishment of witches came from their neighbours. Though it is satisfying to pin the blame on some particular group or institution no one was blameless. It is difficult, as you realize, to fit Italy - once the Church began to control persecution - into this pattern (or Spain). I think your solution, that persecution spread where the clergy had power but not discipline & where the laity lacked education and social strength is very ingenious. I must admit I find it difficult to find a hole in it.

As you know, we disagree over the interpretat--ion of Bacon and Selden's remarks. Perhaps this is because I am convinced that believing in witchcraft was not shameful or lunatic or even illogical. This is the horror of it. That sane, well-intentioned, logical men, men who reveal themselves to have been so like us in many ways, suddenly reveal both the awful consequences of putting any set of assumptions into action. Witchcraft belief also reveal that there is a great void between their world and our world, an abyss which we might never, otherwise, have noticed since it liesE in the unquestioned and unspoken depths of society, in the assumptions and pattern of thought of the age. It is terrifying that just as they were unable, for the most part to break out of this, so we must be committing awful atrocities because we also are based on assumptions we can never question. But enough sermonising. Perhaps we can talk over some of these points when we meet ? If you would like any statistics of the leaf variety, mainly on Essex (the sex, age,number, geography of, etc. witches) do please let me know.

Forgive me for taking up so much of your time. My regards, if you will pardon them, to your secretary, Carol.

Yours sincerely,

Professor H.R.Trevor-Roper,
History Faculty Library,
Merton Street,
OXFORD.

18 Feb 1966

From The Regius Professor of Modern History

History Faculty Library,
Merton Street,
Oxford.
Telephone 43395

My dear Alan

Thank you very much for your letter — and for writing so fully: I was delighted to read it.

I must confess that on reading my essay on witches, I was astonished to realise how much I myself disagree with it! I think I must have written it when I was too much under the influence of Lea and Burr. I agree with your criticism, and with your view that there was a difference of mental structure which Lea & Burr, I now feel convinced, overlooked. I am totally rewriting the essay. I didn't intend to republish it; but I have got myself into an irreversible position in respect of my essay on 'Religion, the Reformation & Social Change'. I have got to re-publish ~~it~~ that, and in order to make a volume of it have agreed to include other appropriate essays, including the one on witches. I have now rewritten half of it. If I may, I will send it to you when it is completely re-written.

I know Julio Caro Baroja: he is a real scholar. I don't know his work on witches, but I will look at it. The Mr R Benedict may be a mistranslation: Baroja is Spanish. His great work is on the Spanish Jews & Moriscos and, like Lea, he has been led into witches from the Inquisition, whose records he has studied. The evidence from Lorraine, I suppose, comes largely from Remy. Anyway, I am looking through the evidence again. (PS. Have now done so: I see it does not come from Remy but from local records).

I am much impressed by the little book I picked up

— quite accidentally — on the *Quais* in Paris. I think I lent it to you: *Procès Verbal fait pour délivrer une Fille Possédée par le Malin Esprit à Louviers*. This seems to me to shed real light, because the girl was *not* tortured and did supply minute *details* (unlike most English trials) of sexual activity. I think this is semi-fatal to the Lee-Burr Thesis. I have also had some discussions with psychiatrists at mental homes which confirms the conclusions drawn by the Vicomte de Moray, the editor of that text.

Anyway, I am most grateful for your observations and will pursue all the sources you mention (including Bacon & Selden).

I have come to some — provisional — new conclusions ('conclusions', in such a sense, must be the wrong word) which I would like to discuss with you.

The most important problem seems to me to be this: when did the *intellectual* substructure crack, & why? All the critics that I know of, including Wier, Spee, Scot, etc. etc., assume the reality of the demonic world even while doubting the genuineness of particular accusations. Lea ascribes the intellectual revolution to Balthasar Bekker (1691); but I think it must have been earlier. It seems to me that quite ordinary people, whose ideas must be at second-hand, are *genuinely* sceptical in the 1650s: e.g. Cromwell's soldiers in Scotland ('Witches, *if there be* such things ...'). Assuming, as I do, that it takes a generation for new ideas to become an attitude of mind, this would mean that *intellectual* scepticism began in the 1620s or 1630s. Perhaps this is too early; but anyway in the 1640s.

Now here I have a point to put to you. My <u>suspicion</u> is — based partly on analogy, partly on hunch — that some difference (whether recorded or not) probably arose on this subject between Presbyterians and Independents in the later 1640s. The Independents inherit so much from the 'Arminians' and the English Presbyterians were at that time so dependent on the Scots Presbyterians who, at that time, were fanatical witch-burners. But I cannot document this. Can you?

Lucien Fèbvre has some interesting observations on the general problem. He admits the intellectual revolution. He also dates the <u>public</u> expression of it in the 1650s — with Cyrano de Bergerac. But when was the revolution itself? He refers to 'la révolution copernicienne de <u>Bérulle</u>' — a phrase, evidently, of the abbé Brémond (I suppose in his splendid <u>Histoire du Sentiment Religieux en France</u>). But — although I have not traced the phrase in Bérulle — I suspect that it does not really refer to this subject (Fèbvre could be very random in his suggestive writing). Certainly Bérulle's <u>Traité des Energumènes</u> shows him to be completely conservative in this matter.

Incidentally, in Fèbvre's article ('Sorcellerie, sottise ou révolution mentale?', Annales 1948) there is a serious misprint, which misled me when I wrote my article. <u>Bossuet</u> is a misprint for <u>Boguet</u>: which makes

4

a great difference. When Fèbvre's article was reprinted after his death, in _Au Coeur Réligieux du XVIe Siècle_, the mistake was made worse. The editor, unwilling — I suppose — to allow that Fèbvre had thought it possible to dismiss Bossuet as an 'imbecile', re-wrote the words 'Un imbécile...' as 'Bossuet ...', thus redoubling the error and spoiling the sense. Replace 'Bossuet', when the name first appears, by the word 'Boguet' and all is clear.

I wonder if Grotius ever expressed an opinion on such a topic. I believe that Grotius' influence in England was immense, but it is not easy to trace.

I agree with you _entirely_ about the imprisoning effect of subconscious axioms. What is most terrifying to me is the easy way in which such axioms grow up, and their capacity to generate a momentum of their own. This makes the question, when do they begin to crack? all the more important.

yours sincerely

Hugh Trevor-Roper

I wrote to Arthur Searle, one of the staff at the Essex Record Office.

18/2/66

Field Head,
Outgate,
Nr.Ambleside,
Westmorland.

I hope things go well with you and Ingatestone progresses. Sorry to add to your burdens, but here are a few pretty pictures in case you want to stick any of them up. I hope they are fairly self-evident as it would take a long time to explain, via. a letter, to explain them. As you will see, they are mostly about Assize cases, though I have included a couple of maps and a graph from Quarter Sessions and ecclesiastical courts. Nearly all the ecclesiastical cases occur before 1600. The carbon part of a chapter on the Assize records includes some comments on the Assize graphs and tables, in case you want anything for blurb. It also includes statistics of women/men, age, type of injury inflicted, distance of witchcraft etc. You're welcome to use anything you think interesting, though it may all be a bit dry. I think the cases (the references to which I sent earlier) might liven them up a bit. If you are in a hurry for a transcript of any of them drop me a note as I have several copies of transcripts of them all. I don't know if you want any general observations on witchcraft, any moralising about 'those superstitious days'. I doubt it, but if you do there is plenty in Maple. I started a break-down of the 1645 pamphlet, showing the cross-accusations, and enclose this, though it's only very rough and incomplete. It shows the web of accusations which were built up.

Quite a lot of the witches died in prison and if you wanted to include a coroner's inquisition there are 5 between membrane 376-382 in K.B.9 838 at the P.R.O (m.378,379 are the ones not witches) - take your pick, they are all 1645 suspects and give age, widowhood etc. From the Jacobean Star Chamber records I enclose a summary of four cases. All of them are detailed and interesting, and I especially draw the attention of your readers to the examination of the counterfeiting victim of witchcraft in number 1 case (St.Ch. 8 32/13) before James I. As you will know, Samuel Harsnett, a native of Essex, wrote (admirably) on the subject in <u>A Declaration of Egregious Popish Impostures</u> (London,1603). Anyhow, I could go on for ever and you won't want more than a couple of graphs and two or three cases. I've left you the difficult task, to decide what to include! If you could let me have anything back when you have finished with it....

I wish you were doing the sixteenth century, then I'd load you with stuff on incest,suicide,v.d.,social mobility,kinship,insanity etc. as well. Perhaps, on second thoughts, its just as well....

It was nice seeing you all, if only briefly, and I hope to be down in four weeks or so. Please give my best regards to Ron,Nancy,Hilda etc. and thank them for their continued help. Meanwhile the factory churns on and my poor mother and sister wearily struggle their way through Hatfield Peverel wills.

Best wishes,

Sent to Arthur.

Arthur Searle,Esq.,
Essex Record Office,
County Hall,
Chelmsford,

<u>Assizes</u>
carbon of chapter on - pp. 10ff.
map of all cases
ten-year distribution of cases 1600-1600+ : 3 yrs with more than 12 cases
cross-village accusations
graphs of indictments at A: punishments for w. at Assizes : nos of persons accused

<u>Etc.</u>
carbon of appendix of St.Cha cases
diagram of accusations in 1645
ecclesiastical cases map

Patrick Collinson was referred to in my letters to others. His interest in ecclesiastical records overlapped with mine and he was part of the new movement in social history.

21/2/66

Field Head,
Outgate,
Nr.Ambleside,
Westmorland.

Dear Dr.Collinson,

I have been meaning to write to you for some time, but reading your interesting article on Field in Essays to Neale has finally spurred me on. I myself am working at Worcester College, Oxford on a D.Phil entitled 'Witchcraft prosecutions in Essex, 1560-1680; a sociological analysis' and this is due to be finished in October this year. I am in the process of trying to see correlations between prosecutions and other trends, one of which is puritanism. Your thesis on the 'Classical movement' was unfortunately on loan from the University Library when I was last there, but I have ordered it at the Bodleian. My first request is for permission to quote any small passages which may be relevant to my thesis, though, of course, I don't know what these will be yet. Secondly, Nicholas Tyacke (formerly of Balliol College) tells me that you are turning the thesis into a book: is there any chance of this appearing in the near future?

At the moment I am undertaking a detailed analysis of three Essex parishes, Hatfield Peverel, Boreham and Little Baddow. Though they were adjacent their experience of the classical movement seems to have been completely different.

While a presbytery was supposedly set up at Hatfield under Carew the other two vicars were dismissed in the Puritan Survey as 'unpreaching ministers'. I want to see, using all local records available - wills, manorial, parish registers etc. what this actually meant in these villages. Obviously the ecclesiastical court records are vital here and I have obtained a list of all suspected puritans in the three villages and hope to relate them to their economic and social background: to discover where they lived, what part they took in ecclesiastical affáárs (i.e. were they church-wardens etc), whether they intermarried, what expression their religious beliefs found in their wills etc. I wonder if you have undertaken anything of this type either in your thesis or since ? I would very much value your comments on the possibility of this approach and any suggestions for further problems or sources. Incidentally, do you know whether the Bishop of London ever did answer the enquiry about the number of communicants in the parishes in his diocese. In the Harleian Mss.(595) he promises to do so, but I have not been able to locate such a listing. Also, do you know if there is any equivalent to the Lincoln Liber Cleri edited by C.W.Foster (Lincs.Rec.Soc. xxiii) ? This was the enquiry about the number of communicants, made in 1603. I think this should be different from 'A viewe of the State of the Clergie within the Countie of Essex....' 1604 (B.M. 4705 d 22) or are they the same ? On the above two points the suggestion to ask you was made by Hilda Grieve of the Essex Record Office.

(2)

Apologies for bothering you with all this when you must be very busy, but it is very important for me to discover whether there was any link between puritanism and witchcraft. I am writing the thesis in the Lakes (at the above address) but come down to London for brief periods. Perhpps, if you are not too busy, we could meet and discuss sources and problems for the study of popular religion ?

Yours sincerely,

Alan Macfarlane

Dr.Patrick Collinson,
Department of History, King's College,
University of London,
Senate House,
Malet Street,
London, W.C.1

I wrote to Keith Thomas on 22nd February as from Worcester College

Dear Mr Thomas,

I enclose another chapter and some rather rough maps etc. there are several obvious difficulties in this section; the lack of comparative statistics for other counties, the possible haziness of examiners about ecclesiastical court procedure etc. I'm not certain whether the long description of Essex sources p. 14 onwards should be relegated to the bibliography. I'm not sure that a description is necessary for any understanding of the number and distribution of cases – but it takes a lot of room. It's probably a problem which will sort itself out. The last couple of pages would probably go in the second half of the thesis – in the chapters of subject analysis, but I thought you might be interested to see them. If you could let me have any rough comparative statistics of defamation cases I would be most indebted. I seem to remember that you had found a large number, but, as you see, they are rare in Essex.

I'm still working at King's Bench records, and will be moving on to chapters on Borough, pamphlet and central court (other than Assize) witchcraft. I should be able to let you have some suicide statistics quite soon. I'm also working on a couple of villages – Hatfield Peverel and Boreham in an attempt to reconstruct the economic, religious & kinship background. I never realised what an enormous amount of material there is, even for 1 village for 30 yrs. For HP. There are 100 wills or over, 130 folios of court roll, 1,000 cases in Archdeaconry court and about 20 in secular courts. I've even found my first suicide – in 1569, but not a witch, I regret to say.

I look forward to discussing things with you.

I hope all goes well,

Yours, Alan Macfarlane

I wrote again on 23 February

Dear Mr. Thomas,

Just a note to ask your permission to quote you as a possible referee for an application for money from a body known as the 'Covenantors' Educational Trust'. Would this be alright? They claim to provide assistance for those unable to obtain it elsewhere, but beyond this I don't know anything of them. Of course it's a long hope, but I'm at the stage of trying anything to get money to support me through my London M.Sc. in anthropology. The State, Nuffield Foundation and L.S.E. generally are unable to help, nor are Trevor-Roper or Firth.

The thesis progresses and I'm writing up the central records (St. Cha. K.B. P.C. etc) and literary and pamphlet sources. I will send down a further batch in three weeks or less if I may: I will also be down in about a month. I hope all goes well with your work.

I wonder what the significance of April, May and November as high suicide months is and why twice as many males as females committed suicide (so far this is only based on a small sample – i.e. the 79 cases occurring in K.B.9 in 1584)?

Yours sincerely, Alan Macfarlane

There is a card from Keith on 26th February

Yes, of course, do cite me as referee at any time (no need to ask in future cases!). I look forward to reading your next instalment. What you say about the months of suicides is v. interesting. In the 19th Century May & June were the peak months. We must talk about it when you come next. Keith

I wrote again to Trevor-Roper at the end of the month.

28/2/66 & P.C - suggesting look at newspaper reports (Notestein. Appx. C) to 1643, 1645, 1652, 1653 cases for Presb'n/Independent correlation

Field Head,
Outgate,
Nr.Ambleside,
Westmorland.

Dear Professor Trevor-Roper,

Thank you very much for your long and interesting letter. I would be delighted to read your re-written article when you have finished it. I wonder if, in exchange, I could quote you as a possible reference once again? Again I think it unlikely that you will be troubled, but I'm trying every source. This time it's a body called the 'Covenantor's Educational Trust' which claims that it provides money for those unable to obtain its elsewhere. I only hope I am not supposed to have pronounced views on bishops etc! Anyhow, I'm sure they'll appreciate your name.

Now, about the interesting points you raise in your letter. Firstly, thank you for warning me about Febvre's mistake (Bossuet/Boguet). Perhaps I was too hard on Baroja. I only read him on England where he varies between irritating generalizations - 'The English trials of the same period (i.e.late C16)....reflect a puritanical society in which hysteria could cause violent and dramatic action' - irritating because half-truths and superficial if meant to be explanations, and mistakes. On the same page (128) he says that 'In 1584 Bishop Jewell, in preaching before the Queen'....In fact Jewel had been dead for over ten years: the sermon (which he mistranslates - presumably because it's been through Spanish and back) was preached in 1559. Still, it's sugh a huge subject that's its difficult to be useful outside one's own little patch.

~~Yes, I found the book on '<u>Proces Verbal....</u>' ed. by De Moray, which~~ you kindly lent me, interesting. In England there are numerous examples of 'voluntary' confessions, the type which now usually take the form of people confessing impossible murders to the police. Usually these aren't so sexually besmeared as Continental cases (a very good case of such free, unprompted, witchcraft beliefs is discussed in Kittredge, <u>Witchcraft in Old and New England</u>, Ch.1). I don't know why sex played a smaller part in English trials than abroad: I suppose the two broad theories are a) that it was a more permissive society & hence people were less (à la Freud) bottled up & found less need to project into the current myths b) that a more rigid control was exerted and such confessions would not have been tolerated. I don't think either is entirely right. The problem is far more complicated and needs a study of dreams, attitudes towards illicit sex of various kinds and many other subjects before it can be solved. The most interesting study I know of the subject is by an anthropologist (M.Wilson, 'Witch Beliefs and social structure', <u>American Jnl. of Sociology</u>, 56, 1951, pp.307-313). She found that witch beliefs in two neighbouring tribes took completely different forms. In one there were hairy incubi and succubi and a strong sex element, in another there was a strong food motif, but no sex. Perhaps her attempt to relate these to the social structure of the two peoples fails - she suggested that one was dominated by food as a symbol of friendship and an object of competition, while the other had prohibitive incest taboos and a strong colour bar (the familiars were conveniently coloured white !). But she gets beyond simple theories that one tribe were hungry and the other sex-starved. The one with the sexual element was, in fact, far more permissive and allowed free love before marriage - outside the prohibited groups.

I'm afraid I don't know any remark of Grotius on the subject, nor

(2)

can I help with the Presbyterian/Independent correlation, this is your line much more than mine. I imagine Christopher Hill might have something on it, though he appears (perhaps ye has changed his mind) to have swallowed the Margaret Murray thesis (*Society and Puritanism*,p. 486). Unfortunately, no one, at least not in the higher levels of society, talks about witchcraft (in print) much and so it is difficult to guage views. Does silence mean acceptance or scepticism ? etc. I think Cromwell was fairly sceptical, as was the House of Lords (they gave a pardon for some of the Hopkin's witches - on the request of the local justices - House of Lords Main Papers,March 10 1645/6).Regrettable as it is, I imagine Trevor Davies would be the most likely place to find references.

As to the major problem, when did the intellectual pattern,of which witchcraft was a part crack, this is, as we all know, immensely complicated. For one thing it was not a straight case of'belief' against 'non-belief'. As with people who claim to be either 'religious' or'non-religious' today , in certain situations when emotions pull them in a different way they may act in a way totally opposed to their explicit beliefs. Throughout the whole witchcraft period there were people who claimed to disbelieve in witches. In witch-haunted Essex people could say 'I heard you say, if I did not mistake your speach that there be witches that worke by the devill. But yet I pray you tell me, doe you think there be such? I know some are of opinion there be none' (1593 - at the height of the prosecutions: George Gifford, *A Dialogue Concerning Witches and Witchcrafts* , reprinted 1931, B.4.v. The difference between private views and public action is well illustrated by Scot (*Discovery*,1964 ed'n,p.36) who says 'manie maintaine and crie out for the execution of witches, that particularlie beleeve never a whit of that which is imputed to them; if they be therein privatelie dealt withall, and substantiallie opposed and tried in argument'. I think this reveals one of the key problems. Though our only method of comprehending witchcraft is through our intellect, and though there is much that is subtly intellectual in the beliefs, in the end we are dealing with an emotional problem - something deep in subconscious assumptions. To understand it we must study it in action and not just listen to people talking about it. There is never a definite break on the intellectual surface, before which people 'beleeved', after which people 'disbelieved'. All the way through there were sceptics. Sometimes they were sceptics who might be expected to be otherwise. For instance in 1578 a suspected papist was, among other things, accused of 'spreading misliking of the laws by saying there are no witches' (*Cal.St.P. Dom.*,1566-1579, under Nov.5,1578). We can only isolate certain assumptions basic to a belief in witchcraft and follow them, watching how each one is attacked. Incidentally, one of the most interesting accounts I know of the struggle between new and old ideas is the account of Arthur Wilson's reaction to the Hopkin's trial printed in Peck,*Desiderata Curiosa*(1779),pp.476-7 , which I'm sure you'll know. It is extremely illuminating to watch his mind trying to reject his assumptions which, as Browne realised, were intimately interlaced with the most fundamental assumptions about God and the universe. Wilson reminds one of Manley Hopkins battling with God, and like Hopkins seems to fall back, spent and submissive.

One statistical way of finding out when beliefs altered is to look at the actual prosecutions. I have made maps and statistics of the treatment of accused witches in Essex which I would be glad to let you see if you are interested. They show a growing divergence from about 1620 onwards between the attitude of the villagers who made the charges and that of the minor gentry who comprised the juries. At first this took the form of an increasing number of acquittals and, if the person was punished, imprisonme rather than death. (excepting the the Hopkin's episode, though there were many indictments after that date, 1626 is the last known execution in Essex). Then, after 1646, there was an even more interesting gap. The jury began to throw out indictments as 'no true bill'. This went on until 1675, the last indictment. After that date there are still witchcraft suspicions in Essex, but the villagers, no longer supported by their social superiors, resort to ducking and other amateur methods. The turning point in the Church courts was about 1605, but this may be for technical reasons, from 1603 the State took over its function.

In brief, I think the most fruitful approach would be to try to isolate the necessary assumptions/conditions which make witchcraft not only intellectually tenable but of vital emotional importance. People won't kill and maul unless their 'climate of opinion' touches them deeply through their emotions. Among these conditions, conditions which can, I think, only finally be studied in the situations which generated them, that is, in England, in village life are:

a) The theory or assumption that all events can be related to persons, that nothing happens by chance and all is either the work of God,devils, or other humans beings. I think that the introduction of an impersonal,mechanist random element into everyday life, the idea of chance, needs study here. The personalized world allowed propitiation and counter-action, allowed all accidents to be understood and prepared for. How men came to accept purposelessness and pointlessness I don't know. But the acceptance, I feel certain, was of prime importance to the decline of witchcraft beliefs. I hope to develop this anon.

b) The idea of reciprocity - that every action,emotion, thought, had an effect somewhere; that humans were 'not Islands', but all a part of each other. That one man's thought or evil intent could hurt another, that we ~~are~~ are all each other's keepers. Apparently 'This is an example of the phenomena of omnipotence of thought a belief shared by primitives, schizophrenics, and children: that thinking harm can cause harm to be done.' (ms. addition to 'Demoniacal Possession' by W.Trethowan,Prof of Psychiatry at Birmingham, Q.M.M. Journ.of Birmingham Medical School vol.55. no.3.Dec.19 mostly pretty naive but one or two interesting ideas). This, obviously related to the previous point, I also hope to enlarge on one day.

I musn't take up any more of your valuable time. If you find any of the above points of sufficient interest I would be glad to have your opinions on thm. Otherwise I hope to discuss witchcraft and other matters when I come to Oxford. I will send a card when I know the date.

Yours sincerely,

Professor H.R.Trevor-Roper,
History Faculty Library,
Merton Street,
OXFORD.

1966 - March

The next letter I wrote to Keith Thomas was on 12th March from Field Head

Dear Mr. Thomas,

Thank you very much for your permission to use you as a referee when I like: I have made immediate use of this permission and cited you in an application for some extra-mural lecturing at London next year – I hope this is alright. I trust that your book is progressing.

As you see, I enclose a couple of short chapters. A third – on the pamphlets – is nearly ready, but I decided not to rush it. When this, and a brief chapter on the borough records, are completed the first half of the thesis should be finished (though it has all to be rewritten). I enclose a rough plan of the shape of the second half. I would value your comments as I'm not awfully happy with it – so much is left out – but can't see a better way at the moment. Section ii) a-f would all be short chapters of less than ten pages, attempts to find correlations between the material set out in part I and these subjects. I still don't feel much nearer to writing iii) b) (reasons for the growth and decline of prosecutions), but perhaps solutions will emerge as I analyse further. You will see that some of the appendices are very abbreviated; this is because I think that it would be best, finally, to incorporate quite a few of the lists of cases into one list by date – with columns for each source. I don't know if you think this would be a good idea.

There is a vague suggestion that I might be allowed to sample a few Commissary Act books, but this will have to be a last-minute addition as the P.R.O. keep putting a definite answer off. Otherwise I am through (except for a visit to Colchester) with primary sources for witchcraft and am now engaged in studying the background – parish registers, wills, other court records etc. I will be in London, Essex and Oxford over the next three weeks and wondered if we could meet at a time convenient to you? I will be in Oxford on Saturday 19th of March and the following Saturday (26th) and if you could manage either a note at Worcester (not stamped and 'to await arrival') would find me. If these are impossible I'll ring you when in Oxford and we can perhaps fix something.

As you see, I enclose a few figures from the Elizabethan coroner's rolls on suicide. These have got to be checked as I did them in a rush while noting deaths of plague (I now discover that Essex have been calendaring K.B.9 – which will help me cross-check), but I thought they would interest you despite their crudity. I hope to analyse further and correct them fairly soon, but I obviously haven't time to go into the subject properly. As it was partly through you that I became interested in the subject, I would be very happy for you to use any of the figures (when corrected) if you feel like writing on the subject. There is no need for me to comment on some very interesting patterns – e.g. age/sex figures for Essex. The major problem, as far as I'm concerned, is whether these are anywhere near the <u>total</u> figures. Equipped with names, date of death etc. I do hope to do a few samples in Essex to see how such deaths were registered in the parish registers, but I haven't enough cases from other sources (or the time) to do a cross-check the other way, i.e. see if misc. cases appear in the coroner's rolls – this <u>should</u> be possible however. Or instance, the case of John Brine or Brand of Great Hallingbury which I sent you does get recorded in an inquisition – K.B. 631 m.78. Unfortunately there is only one suicide in the three villages I am studying in detail (Hatfield P) and this is the village without a register – from other records it does appear that she was not a member of one of the established families anyhow. Of course, all this isn't too irrelevant to witchcraft, a map of suicides (which I should be able to make soon) will make an interesting comparison to the maps of witchcraft; or, it is obviously interesting to see whether suspected witches killed themselves: all I've noticed in this line is witch's <u>husband</u> who killed himself (apart, of course, from the attempted suicide of a witch in the Elizabeth Lowys of Great Waltham case – see appendix D/AEA 2 to the chapter on the pamphlets, when it arrives!). I look forward to another discussion, Yours sincerely

P.S. Please keep the suicide figures if they're of interest – I have another copy.

[Loose sheet attached]

Plan for second half of thesis.

- *i)* *Detailed studies of*
  - *a) Witchcraft in three Essex villages, 1560-1600 (Hatfield Peverel, Boreham, Little Baddow)*
  - *b) Anti-witchcraft activity: the cunning man, 'white' witchcraft.*
  - *c) Matthew Hopkins and the 1645 trial.*
- *ii)* *Witchcraft in relationship to*
  - *a) religious groups (puritanism,, clergy et)*
  - *b) medical factors (plague, types of illness caused etc)*
  - *c) economic change (poverty, famine, class, occupations)*
  - *d) kinship and neighbourliness*
  - *e) sexual factors; age tensions*
  - *f) personality/activities of accused and accusers*
- *iii)* *Explanations of witchcraft*
  - *a) the functions of witchcraft – as explanation, outlet for aggression and guilt, as rupturing force etc.*
  - *b) reasons for growth and decline of prosecutions*

Appendices, maps, graphs and bibliography

As I began to gather in the hundreds of witchcraft cases in Essex, and notice that they had a number of variables which I would like to cross-tabulate – for example age, sex, religion, geography, time, I began to wonder whether there were not devices which would help me with this. I went to see the Oxford computing service and they said that with only 500 or so cases and perhaps ten variables for each, it was not worth thinking of using a computer – which was very crude anyway at that time. But that I might use some other semi-computer form of device such as edge-punched cards.

So I started to do this. There was a system called 'Cope-Chat' cards, which I now discover was short for the Copeland-Chatterton Company, which made cards. You punched the edges and used something like a knitting needle to lift out cards which had not had the edges punched – or vice versa. The system is described in the scans below.

I remember spending a lot of time putting all the cases into the centre of the cards . I don't think that it helped greatly. As with computers later, by the time one had done all the tedious work of assembling the materials, one already had worked out the rough answer – but perhaps that is the function, to slow down and systematize thought.

Anyway, here is a little of the evidence for this activity – an expensive one in terms of my total research budget at the time and an indication of my desire to tinker with new technologies which would pervade my life

Here is the description of how it worked:

ASK COPE-CHAT

The COPELAND-CHATTERSON Co. Ltd.

GATEWAY HOUSE, 1, WATLING STREET,
LONDON, E.C.4.

TELEPHONE:
CITY, 2284/5/6.

TELEGRAMS:
COPE-CHAT. CENT.
LONDON.

REGISTERED OFFICE
AND WORKS:
STROUD, GLOS.

ALSO AT
BIRMINGHAM
BRISTOL
CARDIFF
EDINBURGH
GLASGOW
LEEDS
LEICESTER
LIVERPOOL
MANCHESTER
NEWCASTLE
SHEFFIELD

THE PARAMOUNT HAND OPERATED PUNCHED CARD SORTING SYSTEM

WHAT IT IS

Paramount Cards are punched with a series of holes along one or more edges. Each hole represents an item of information and is identified by either a numbered or lettered code. When the required information has been entered on the card the relevant hole is slotted with a pair of nippers similar to Ticket Collector's nippers. Slotting consists of making the closed holes into open 'V' shaped slots. Thus, when a needle is inserted through a batch of cards and the batch is raised, these cards which have been slotted at the needle position will fall away.

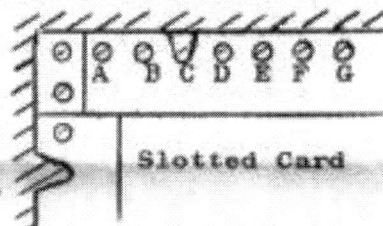

When sorting, the most satisfactory results are obtained by taking a convenient hand-full of cards and using the free hand to control the cards which fall out. Selection is quick and accurate; approximately one thousand cards can be needled through any one position in one minute.

FLEXIBILITY

Any reasonable size card or sheet can be used either singly or made up in various ways. Books are made for stores requisitions in which the Paramount duplicate is torn out and the original retained. Similarly, in an invoice set, Paramount is used to take care of analysis of sales by line, territory, town or traveller, etc. In many instances a Paramount card forms the last copy of a set.

MACHINE ACCOUNTING EQUIPMENT
THE PARAMOUNT CARD SORTING SYSTEM
VISIBLE INDEX AND STRIP INDEX EQUIPMENT
CONTINUOUS STATIONERY
PULL-AWAY SETS

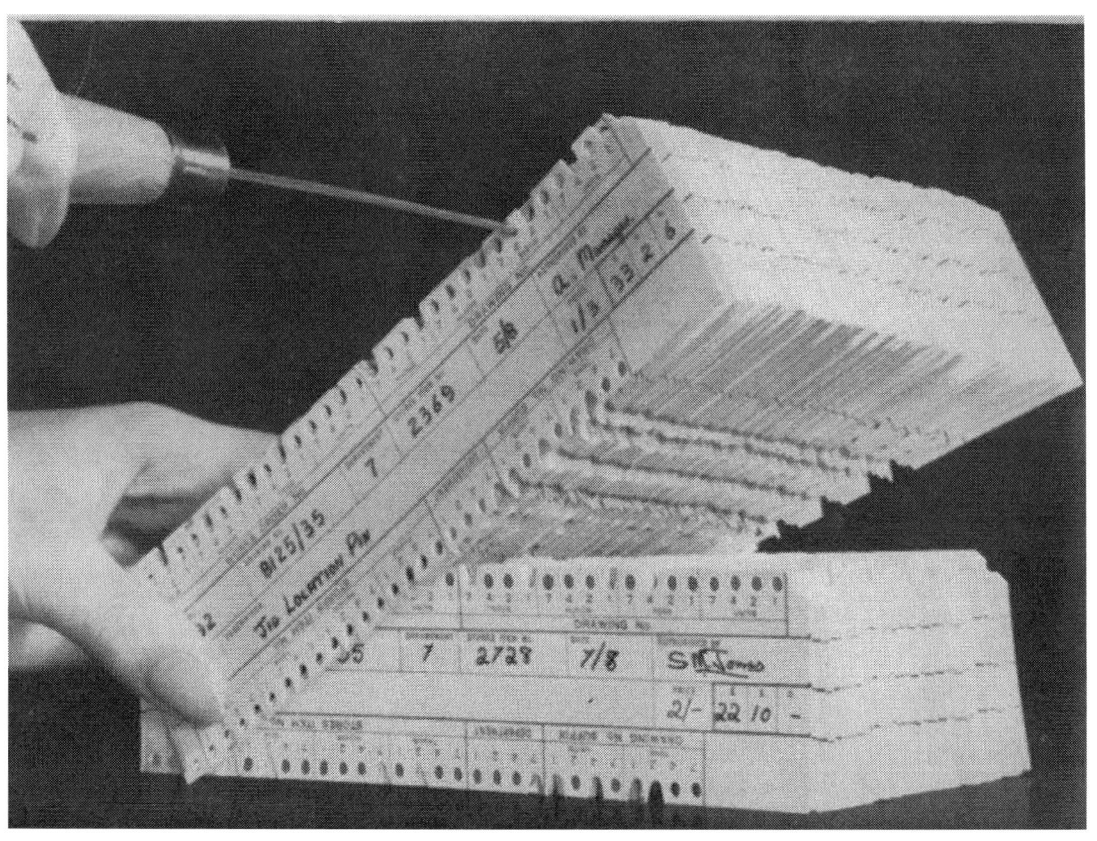

And my order:

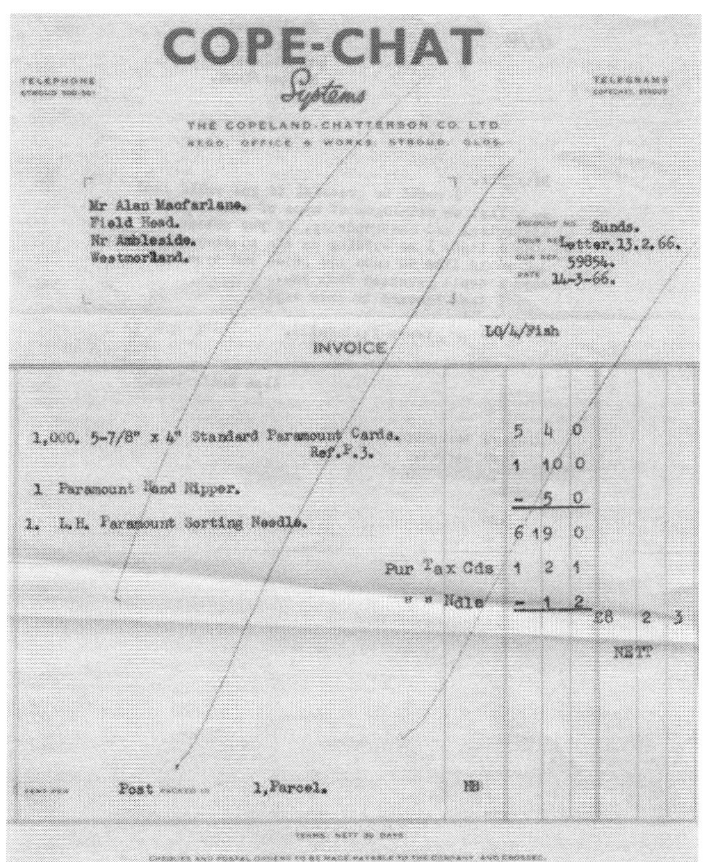

COPE-CHAT
Systems

TELEPHONE — TELEGRAMS

THE COPELAND-CHATTERSON CO. LTD
REGD. OFFICE & WORKS: STROUD, GLOS.

Mr Alan Macfarlane.
Field Head.
Nr Ambleside.
Westmorland.

ACCOUNT NO. Sunds.
YOUR REF. Letter.13.2.66.
OUR REF. 59854.
DATE 14-3-66.

LG/4/Fish

INVOICE

1,000. 5-7/8" x 4" Standard Paramount Cards. Ref.P.3.	5	4	0	
1 Paramount Hand Nipper.	1	10	0	
1. L.H. Paramount Sorting Needle.	-	5	0	
	6	19	0	
Pur Tax Gds	1	2	1	
" " Ndle	-	1	2	
				£8 2 3
				NETT

Post 1,Parcel. HB

TERMS: NETT 30 DAYS

CHEQUES AND POSTAL ORDERS TO BE MADE PAYABLE TO THE COMPANY, AND CROSSED.

In my search for funding to help pay for the course in anthropology at the L.S.E. I had written to the College of Arms to see whether I could get a part-time research job. I suspect this was a suggestion made by Hilda Grieve. I met with a Mr Woodward and received a letter from the Garter King of Arms himself.

The first letter I have, obviously after meeting a Mr. Woodward, is as follows.

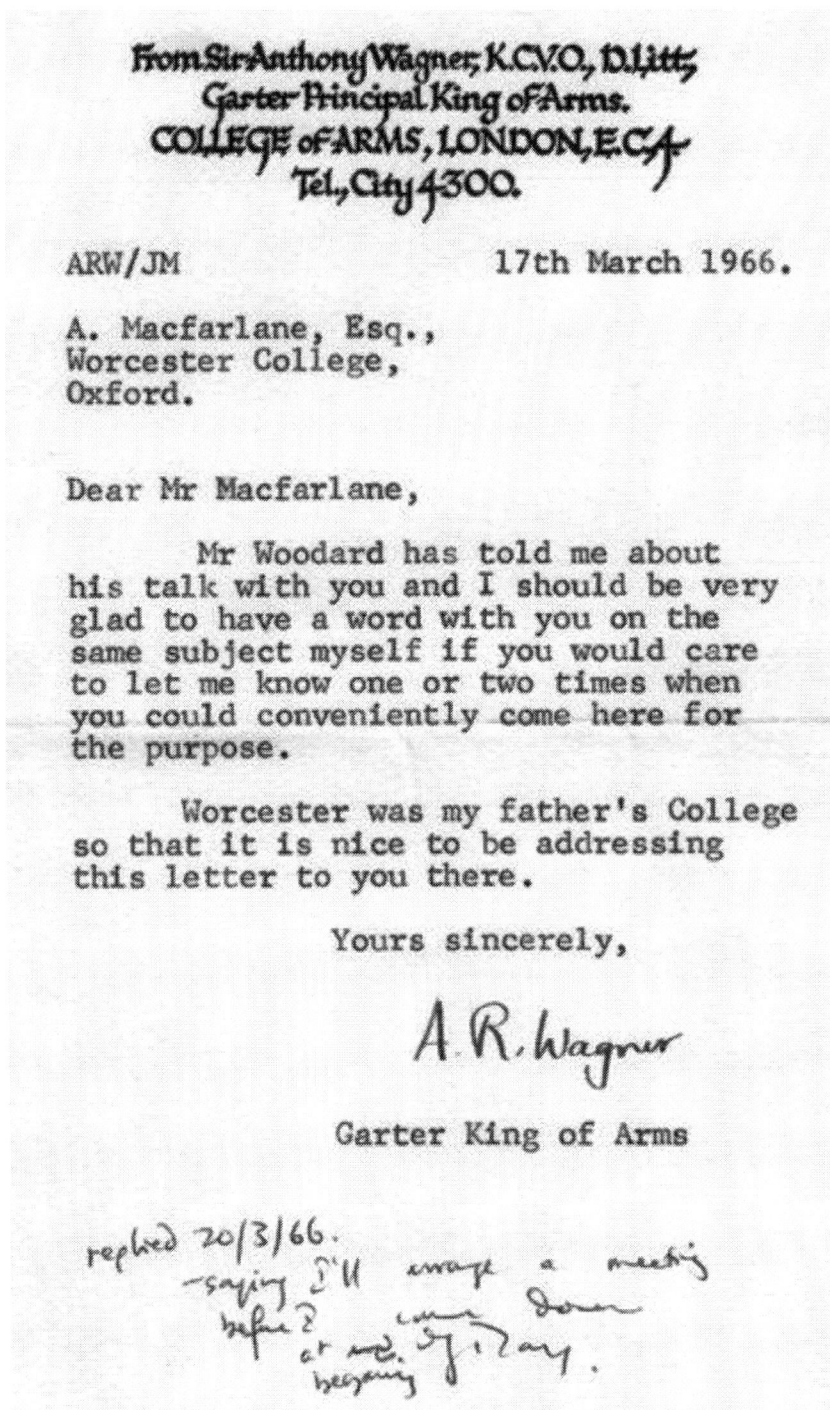

From Sir Anthony Wagner, K.C.V.O., D.Litt.,
Garter Principal King of Arms.
COLLEGE of ARMS, LONDON, E.C.4.
Tel., City 4300.

ARW/JM 17th March 1966.

A. Macfarlane, Esq.,
Worcester College,
Oxford.

Dear Mr Macfarlane,

Mr Woodard has told me about his talk with you and I should be very glad to have a word with you on the same subject myself if you would care to let me know one or two times when you could conveniently come here for the purpose.

Worcester was my father's College so that it is nice to be addressing this letter to you there.

Yours sincerely,

A. R. Wagner

Garter King of Arms

replied 20/3/66.
– saying I'll arrange a meeting before? come down at end. beginning of [illegible] 8 Jan[illegible].

I had a reply to my letter of 21st February from Patrick Collinson.

replied to 20/3/66.

University of London, King's College,
March 12th 1966

Dear Mr. MacFarlane,

I must apologise for leaving your interesting letter unanswered for so long. One reason for the delay lies in the many questions that you raise. There is so much that I should like to say in respose to some of these points that I think that it would be best if, as you suggest, we were to meet when you are next in London. I very rarely leave London these days. So let me know when you come to town and we can arrange a meeting. Another reason for this tardy reply is that the book to which you refer (on Elizabethan Puritanism) finally went to press yesterday. If all goes well (not a foregone conclusion) it should be out by about this time next year. No earlier, I'm afraid.

I am most interes ed in your subject, and have been ever since I saw how many references there are to witchcraft in the assize indictment slips at the PRO. If you do manage to get hold of my thesis you will see how much material it contains on Essex puritanism, but you will also see that I have not been able to do the close local research into individuals which you are developing. (I was covering the whole of England.) I shall be very interested to see your findings in due course. But I think that you will find a pretty clear picture in my thesis of the 'singular' and semi-separatist character of the 'godly' in Essex. This is used again in my book. And I shall draw on Essex archdeaconry material for a paper I am doing for 'Past and Present' on popular protestantism under Elizabeth. Yes, do draw on my thesis for any things which interest you. But I should be glad to be told what you propose to use.

I am sure the view you have of Hatfield Peverel, Boreham and Little Baddow, or rather of the incumbents, is the correct one. Carew wasn't at Hatfield for very long of course, and his position as donatee was precarious. He subsequently served two Ipswich donatives, and there is some fascinating material on his ministry there in the Norwich Deposition Books - see my thesis. His presbytery at Hatfield was, I think, a presbytery in inverted commas. I shall welcome a chance to talk about this. If you look at a dialogue by George Gifford of Maldon, A Briefe discourse of the ... countrie divinitie (1582) you will I think find a portrait of the ale-bench vicar of Great Baddow in the 'Atheos' of that dialogue. Certainly he is vicar of 'G.B.', and he and Zelotes are walking towards Chelmsford.

I look forward very much to meeting you.
Yours sincerely,
Patrick

The next letter was from Keith Thomas was written on 14th March

Dear Alan,

The briefest of notes to thank you for the package which arrived today and which I look forward to reading. The contents as usual look most intersting. Meanwhile there are two points I ought to mention. The first is that it would be very helpful if you could give me the roughest of indications as to when, at the present rate of progress, you expect the thesis to be finished and ready for submission. This is just so I can enter it in the terminal note for the History Board. If you could drop me a p.c. that would be fine.

The second is that I shall, I am afraid, be away from Oxford for the better part of the next fortnight. I'll be back by the General Election [31st March 1966] *and could see you over the weekend following (2/3 April) if that were possible. Otherwise perhaps you could offer some other dates thereafter. I am so sorry about this and do hope this isn't too inconvenient for you. It will be nice to see you again. Meanwhile I hope you are well and cheerful. The Lake District must be starting to be v. nice at this time of time year. Yrs, Keith*

I sent a card to Keith Thomas on 20th March, as from Worcester College, Oxford

Dear Mr Thomas,

You ask for a rough approximation as to when I'll finish the thesis. I hope to finish the final draught [sic] and send it to the typist in October. I don't know how long these people take and it'll have to be checked. So I imagine I will supplicate[1] *in January at the latest (illness/accident barring). I checked with the registry. I don't need to ask for an extension until June 1967.*

I hope the TLS goes OK. I suppose this new Waltzer book is psychological rather than sociological? I look forward to seeing you in March 31st. Yrs Alan Macfarlane

I shall just include scans of a few of the pages of the drafts I was producing for Keith. The first referred to in January, was a chapter on 'ecclesiastical sources'. This was 24 pages long and includes comments by Keith.

[1] To supplicate was to ask permission from the University to submit my thesis.

WITCHCRAFT PROSECUTIONS AT THE ECCLESIASTICAL COURTS

From at least the seventh century Liber Poenitentialis of Archbishop Theodore, witchcraft and sorcery cases had come under the jurisdiction of the Church.[1] Throughout the middle ages a considerable number of cases appeared before the ecclesiastical authorities, though punishments were usually of a non-physical kind.[2] Such cases were closely related to those for heresy and at the end of the fourteenth century were probably affected by the writ de haeretico comburendo. While the ecclesiastical courts still apprehended suspected sorcerers it is unlikely that a death sentence could be passed without parliamentary sanction.[3] During the fifteenth century scattered cases of ecclesiastical trial of witchcraft can be gleaned from the printed records, and others would undoubtedly emerge if a more systematic search of unprinted material were made.[4] As the amount of records increases in the first half of the sixteenth century, so do the number of known instances of trial.[5] A large proportion of all the cases before 1560 occurring in the ecclesiastical courts concern sorcery rather than witchcraft: none mention the Satanic compact and few include the malevolent destruction of persons and property.

1. For a further discussion of the interrelating jurisdiction of Church and State to 1500 see p. above: see also Notestein, Witchcraft, pp.29-30.
2. For cases to 1400 see Kittredge, Witchcraft..., pp.41,46,48,51-6; E.I, pp.6-9; H.G.Richardson, 'Heresy and the Lay Power under Richard II', Eng.Hist.Rev., li (1936), 4-5. A case from the 1397 Visitation of Hereford is mentioned in G.C.Coulton, Medieval Panorama, (Fontana ed'n, 1961), i.204.
3. This complex subject is inadequately discussed in Pollock and Maitland, History of English Law..., p.555; Holdsworth, History of English Law..., p.509 and Richardson, 'Heresy and the Lay Power....', 24.
4. For printed cases see E, p.10; Kittredge, Witchcraft...pp.37-9; James Raine, Depositions and other Ecclesiastical Proceedings from the Courts of Durham, (Surtees Soc., xxi, 1845), pp.27,29,33; William Hale, A Series of Precedents and Proceedings in Criminal Causes, 1475-1650..., (1847), pp.3,7,10,11,16,17,20, 32-3,36-7,61,63. An unprinted case of possible sorcery in 1499, involving an interview with 'Lez Gracious Fayry', was kindly brought to my attention by Mr. John Davies, formerly of Linacre House, Oxford; it is in the Lambeth Registers, Morton, II. f.113.v. Another unprinted case, the reference to which I owe to Mrs. Owen of the University Library, Cambridge, occurs in 1465 in an Ely Episcopal Register, G.1.5. f.133.
5. Yorkshire cases are referred to in A.G.Dickens, Lollards and Protestants in the Diocese of York, (Oxford, 1959), p.16 and Kittredge, Witchcraft..., pp. 34,65-71. There are a series of cases in Hale, Precedents..., 77,102, 107-8,139 and in Raine, Durham Depositions..., pp.45-6, and Visitations in the Diocese of Lincoln, 1517-1531, ed. A.H.Thompson (Lincs.Rec. Soc., xxxiii, 1940), i, xlix-l ; also in the Act Book of the Ecclesiastical Court of Whalley, ed. A.M. Cooke (Chethams Soc., n.s., 44, 1901), pp.22,67. and Ewen, II, p.446.

Cf. also Fincham, Eccl'l Ct. pp 119-120. early C16 St Alban's sorcery case.

Number and type of offences in the Essex ecclesiastical records.

Visitation articles listed a number of offences under the general heading of 'sorcery': for instance in the London episcopal articles of 1571 'any that useth sorcery, witchcraft, enchantment, incantations, charms, unlawful prayers, or invocations in latin' were to be presented.[1] Thus we find a number of different crimes in the courts. These are set out in table 3. below. A major division has been made between 'witchcraft' and 'sorcery', that is between 'black' and 'white' witchcraft.[2] This tests the hypothesis that while the secular courts dealt with maleficent witchcraft, the ecclesiastical authorities punished sorcery. The statistics show that this is by no means true for Essex, at least until 1603. Within 'sorcery' a major division is made between going to cunning folk for help, and actually being a wizard. Finally, there are some offences which do not fit into either category. Included in these are the seventeen defamation cases: calling a person a witch without sufficient proof. The defamation cases include the three 'instance' cases from the Deposition books; thus all the cases in the first two categories come from the Act books of the Archdeaconry courts, except for a dozen from equivalent records of the Bishop's Consistory. The number of persons, rather than each appearance of each person, is counted: hence a person might appear more than once (as we have seen that nine did) and only be listed once.[3]

TABLE 3: Types of offence in the ecclesiastical courts: number of persons.

Offence	Total	Example
WITCHCRAFT.		
'Witchcraft and sorcery' (of which 19 were probably sorcery[4], and 24 definitely witchcraft.[5])	128+7	D/AEA 8, f.23

(for 'sorcery' see over....

(notes from previous page)
2. D/ACA. 21. 3. See Appendix . 4. D/AED 3. f.113.v. ff.
5. See Appendix . 6. Including those in the Act books there were 17 in all though some of these were merely quarrels in which 'witch' was used, see p.

1. See p. 2. For a discussion of this distinction see p.
3. .... 4. Often it is impossible to tell from the accusation whether 'black' or 'white' witchcraft was meant: the figure 19 here is the total of men, or man and wife, accused of 'witchcraft and sorcery', men were more probably sorcerers than witches (see p.). The 24 'definitely witchcraft' accusations are those persons who also appeared at the secular court accused of witchcraft. It is possible, of course, that, like Margery Skelton (see bottom p.13 above), they were accused in the ecclesiastical court of sorcery and then accused of witchcraft.

In February and March I refer to chapters on literary sources and pamphlet sources and one I was hoping to finish on borough court records. The literary chapter was sixteen pages long, and has Keith's comments on it.

LITERARY SOURCES FOR THE STUDY OF ESSEX WITCHCRAFT.

Since most historians of witchcraft have based their works mainly on pamphlet accounts of trials, and on literary sources, that is upon accounts of witchcraft written in polemical books and in letters, biographies, diaries, plays and poems, it is important to see how accurate a picture these give of the witchcraft prosecutions.[1] Such sources are also important because they indicate contemporary attitudes towards such prosecutions.[2]

Diaries.

Sixteenth and seventeenth century English diaries are not numerous and even less numerous are the references to witchcraft in them.[3] The earliest Essex diary to be explored is that of the Puritan, Richard Rogers, born in Chelmsford and preacher at Wethersfield in north Essex from about 1575 to 1618. Though there were many witch trials in neighbouring villages,[4] there are none recorded from Wethersfield until 1626.[5] Nor are there any references to witchcraft in the diary, which covers the period February 1587-August 1590,[6] and Rogers' name does not appear in any of the known prosecutions.[7] One Puritan, at least, seems neither interested in, nor encouraging to, prosecutions.[8]

The next diary referring to Essex was also written by an extreme protestant, Arthur Wilson, for a time steward of the Puritan Earl of Warwick.[9] Wilson was present at the sensational trial in 1645 and he recorded his opinions of it. These are extremely sceptical and an excerpt will give

1. See p. above for a table of the sources used by subsequent historians.
2. It is obvious that a lifetime could be devoted to such sources and still some references to witchcraft be undiscovered.
3. This impression is based on the works of historians who have based their accounts of witchcraft on literary sources: Briggs, Pale Hecate..., cites no diaries in her bibliography, nor does Trevor Davies, Four Centuries...(though he includes two Scottish diaries: from his comparative reading of English and Scottish personal records Professor Trevor-Roper has the impression, which he has kindly conveyed to the writer, that Scottish writers were far more aware and frightened of witchcraft than their English counterparts). Notestein, Witchcraft..., Appendix C, only cites one English diary for a county other than Essex, a Lancashire diary referring to a case in 1674-5.
4. See map . Great Bardfield, for instance, the home of Edward Mason the sorcerer, was next to Wethersfield.
5. E.565,566.
6. Two Elizabethan Puritan Diaries, ed. M.M. Knappen, (1933). The other Puritan diary, that of Samuel Ward, fellow of Emmanuel College, covering the years 1595-1630, also omits the subject of witchcraft.
7. Since Wethersfield was in the Archdeaconry of Middlesex, there are no surviving ecclesiastical records for this period: this weakens the negative evidence.
8, 9 - see next page.

finding no satisfaction at the courts, the villagers took the law into their own hands.[1]

The general impression from the infrequent diaries would be that witchcraft prosecution in Essex was an infrequent occurrence; a subject to dismay or perplex country vicars, occasionally leading to an exceptional and bloody trial. There is no mention of the Assize or ecclesiastical prosecutions, hundreds of them, and no witchcraft is mentioned before 1645.

Minute and Committee Books.

The diaries of official bodies, the minute books, are likewise sparse and provide little evidence of interest in witchcraft. One such minute book is that of the Dedham Classis from 1582-1589.[2] Among the many matters discussed was the following:

> '6 May.1588 Mr.Salmon moved 'How he might know a witche, it was thought fittest to geve it over to some Justice to examyne it, and that there must be some usuall experience of evell effects to ensue of their displeasure and some presumption of the death of man or beast: some said she might be found out by serche in her bodie, some thought that to be fancy in the people easilie conceiving such a thinge and to be reproved in them.' 3

Salmon was not an Essex minister[4] and his name does not appear in any of the recorded Essex prosecutions.[5] It is interesting that the clergy thought that the matter should be handed over to the secular magistrates, and that they were divided on the witch's mark. There is no sign here of either marked scepticism or a persecuting spirit. While the possibility of witchcraft was assumed, there was already some doubt as to the tests which could be employed to discover the crime.[6]

A minute book of another kind and another body, was that of the Civil War County Committee. That these sometimes contained references to witchcraft we know: the Suffolk Orders include a payment for expenses incurred at a witch trial.[7] In Essex, however, despite the notorious 1645 trial, no mention

1.See p.7 n.1. for the development of this trend in the eighteenth century and later.
2. The Presbyterian Movement in the Reign of Queen Elizabeth,ed.R.G.Usher (Camden Soc.,3rd ser.,viii,1905): a unique document hence comparison with other parts of England is impossible.
3. Ibid.,p.70.
4. At least he is absent from Newcourt, Repertorium; all the information Usher gives (Presbyterian Movt, p. xlvi) is that he was a member of the Classis and lived at Everton.
5.There is nothing,except name,to connect him with the notorious John Salmon of Danbury, probably executed in 1587 :(See p. for the career of John Salmon.)
6. William Perkins, among others, later emphasized this difficulty, see p.
7. This was in 1645: Alan Everitt,Suffolk and the Great Rebellion, 1640-1660 (Suffolk Rec.Soc.,iii,1960),p.73. They may have taken an even more active part: in a letter to John Gaule, printed in Gaule's Select Cases of Conscience Touching Witches and Witchcrafts, (1646), A.3, Matthew Hopkins remarks that a minister in Suffolk was 'forc'd to recant (by the Committee)' his preaching opposing the discovery of witches.

The pamphlet chapter was 22 pages long and had Keith's comments on it.

THE MOTIVES, METHODS AND NUMBER OF WITCHES: EVIDENCE FROM THE PAMPHLETS.

Detailed, often verbatim, reports of the depositions of witnesses and the examination of suspects in witchcraft trials have occasionally survived in the form of popular pamphlets. Usually they describe trials at the Assizes and in doing so they provide three principal kinds of information for the historian of witchcraft. Firstly, they often give added information about those involved as accusers or accused; their age, their wealth, their personality and their relationships. Secondly, they indicate how witchcraft was believed to work; the power of cursing, the relationship of the supposed witch to her familiar or to the devil. Thirdly, they reveal the motives ascribed to witches and the actual incident which was believed to have prompted the bewitching. In giving these details, otherwise often inaccessible, they become one of the most important of all sources for the study of witchcraft.

Essex is fortunate in possessing several detailed pamphlets. Of the twenty-eight 'Major English Witch Trials as Recorded in Contemporary Pamphlets' listed by R.H.Robbins, five are from Essex.[1] A primary consequence of this has been an immediate assumption that Essex was a particularly witch-haunted county. Though this may be true,[2] pamphlets, in themselves, are a misleading indication of the density of witchcraft beliefs and prosecutions. Often a major trial, for instance that in Lancashire in 1633, produced no pamphlet: Essex Assize records show that peaks of accusations in that county do not necessarily coincide with a pamphlet. This is shown in the following table:-

TABLE 1: Assize prosecutions and pamphlets compared.

(Years with either 12 or more indictments, a pamphlet, or both)

Year	Number of Indictments	Pamphlet	Year	Number of Indictments	Pamph.
1566	4	P	1589	19	P
1572	16	-	1592	14	-
1574	15	-	1593	13	-
1576	12	-	1594	17	-
1579	13	P	1601	12	-
1582	18	P	1616	13	-
158[illegible]	35	-	1645	50	P(x2)

1. Robbins, Encylopedia..., pp.168-9.
2. See pp. .

Pamphlets (14)

suspect, onto the person who had precipitated the conflict in values. Such a shift was rationalised and made acceptable by making the witch's offence far worse than the original uncharitable act. For instance, the victim could argue that although he had refused a loan of 12d. for a woman's sick husband placing his kinship obligations before his neighbourly ones, yet this did not justify an act of homicide by witchcraft.[1]

Table 11: The supposed motive of witches, as revealed in the 1582 pamphlet.

Name of accused	Supposed motive	Folio reference
Ursley Kemp	refused nursing of child. a promised payment refused. refused a loan of 'scouring sand'	Av A2v A3
Joan Pechey	a food dole given to her is not of sufficient quality	A4
Ales Newman	refused 12d. for her sick husband	A7
Ursula Kemp	called 'whore' and other names	B2
Elizabeth Bennet	cursed, maligned and her cattle cursed her swine beaten and pitchforked	B6v B7
Alice Manfield	a thatcher refused to work for her unless he could get his master's permission	C6v
Eliz. Ewstace	her daughter threatened (being a servant)	C7
Cicely Celles	denied mault at the price she wants, her cattle hunted off a neighbour's land	C8v "
Ales Hunt	denied a piece of 'Porke'	D5
Ales Manfield	denied 'curdes' a 'greene place' in fron of her house made muddy by a neighbour's muckcart	D6v D7
Cicely Celles	refused the nursing of a child	D8v
Ales Manfield	refused a 'mess of milk'	E2v
Margaret Grevell	denied 'Godesgood' denied mutton	E2v E3
Eliz.Ewstace	geese driven off a neighbour's land and hurt	E4
Ursley Kemp	physically attacked	E5

2v
3

1. 1582.P. sig.A7: for a further discussion of these problems see pp.

Ursley Kemp physically attacked E5

The borough court chapter was shorter, just five pages, and again had Keith's comments on it.

WITCHCRAFT PROSECUTIONS IN TOWNS: EVIDENCE FROM THE BOROUGH COURTS.

We have seen that witchcraft prosecutions were widespread in Essex villages. The problem remains, however, of how far this was a rural phenomenon, and to what extent statistics, based on the Assize and other general courts, understate the true number of cases because they do not include cases tried in the independent borough courts.[1] It is clear that, in England as a whole, a considerable number of accused witches were punished in borough courts. For instanc Wallace Notestein lists over three dozen cases from all over England tried in the boroughs; among them five from Great Yarmouth, four from King's Lynn and five from Newcastle.[2] As this chapter will demonstrate, the known prosecutions could soon be increased by a search of the voluminous printed and manuscript borough records.[3] A particularly difficult problem is the amount of witchcraft prosecution in London. That there were prosecutions in both ecclesiastical and secular courts, from 1560 on, is evident.[4] It also seems that London was especially famous for its cunning folk; people travelled from all over Essex to visit them.[5] Without a detailed study, however, it is not possible to go beyond an impression that both black and white witchcraft were commonly prosecuted; such prosecutions never appear to have mounted at any one time into a holocaust similar to those in Essex in 1582 or 1645. There are no famous trials of 'the London witches' described in a contemporary pamphlet.[6] Yet accusations, of the kind we have been studying in Essex, appeared in a steady stream at the Middlesex sessions. For instance, if we take the years 1612-1618 as a sample, there were nine persons either indicted, or mentioned as suspects in a recognizance; all were for killing or injuring human beings by witchcraft and they came from Holborn, Tottenham, Smithfield, Hampstead and several other suburbs.[7] Over the same period, in Essex, there were 15 people prosecuted, three of them in Harwich, the rest at the Assizes: there are too many incomparable factors, for instance relative population and survival of records to make this a useful comparative statistic. It does suggest,

1. Ewen believed that these courts were very important; he suggested that as many cases were tried in 'independent courts' as in the Assizes (p.112). If Essex is a fair sample he greatly exaggerated their importance: the ratio was more likely about 1:8(see p. below)
2. Notestein, Witchcraft..., Appendix C.
3. Two Essex prosecutions are listed, another 22 have been added (see p. below). A factor of ten would give over 300 persons tried at borough courts throughout England, but Essex may be exceptional. Notestein only sampled printed records and others have become accessible since he wrote: for an example of cases he missed see R.H.Morris, Chester during the Plantaganet & Tudor Periods (Chester, 1893), pp. 187, 371.
4. For a summary of trials at the Middlesex sessions see p. above; for ecclesiastical cases discovered while searching for Essex prosecutions, p. .
5. See p. below.
6. Though it is impossible to be categorical until all the records have been thoroughly checked; as we have seen in Essex in 1584, a major trial may not produce a pamphlet.
7. Of course it would be wrong to think of London as a city in our sense, Hampstead, for instance, was a neighbouring village, probably little different from many Essex villages. This complicates the question of whether witchcraft tensions were exacerbated or undermined by the break-down of the obligations and social relationships upon which accusations were founded in the vill[illegible] discussion of thi[illegible]

I wrote to Trevor-Roper on 20th March.

Dear Professor Trevor-Roper,

I am writing on the off-chance that you will be in Oxford next week-end, though I expect, as you warned, you will have gone to your own particular brand of hermitage in Scotland. If you are in Oxford, and not too busy, on either Saturday 26th or Sunday 27th of March at any time (except Sunday evening), I would very much appreciate another discussion of history and historians, witchcraft etc. If this is forwarded to you in Scotland, please don't bother to reply. I'll try again next term. Meanwhile, may I wish you a restful vacation.

Yours sincerely, Alan Macfarlane

P.S. If you <u>are</u> in Oxford, could you please reply to Worcester College ('to await arrival' or they may forward it, anywhere – some has been forwarded to the Rev. Andrew Macfarlane in Kent!), thank you.

1966 - April

Supervisor's report 1 April 1966 by Keith Thomas.

Title: Witchcraft Prosecutions in Essex, 1560-1680; a sociological analysis.

Mr Macfarlane is now writing his thesis and hopes to be able to send the final draft to the typist by October. I think, however, that he will be lucky to get it finished by then. Most of his research is completed, but the arrangement and presentation of his thesis is affording him some difficulty. His preliminary drafts will need to be reshaped and polished quite substantially before they are ready for submission. His findings, however, are extremely interesting, and should constitute a real contribution to knowledge.

I sent a card to Keith Thomas on 4th April from Field Head

Dear Mr. Thomas,

Thank you for a stimulating supervision. You asked for the reference to the 1609 Essex survey – it is 'A Viewe of the State of the Clergie Within the Countie of Essex'... : a printed copy presented to the B.M. in 1895 (catalogue mark = 5105 d 22) and original in the P.R.O. 30/15/1/128. I've checked and the printed copy looks alright. It is used a lot in Hill, Economic Problems (e.g. pp. 68, 111, 140, 203, 218, 228) and is a most fascinating document. I hope to place and name the ministers anonymously referred to in the second half by comparison with the 1589 survey, the Archdeaconry records etc.

Yours sincerely, Alan Macfarlane

I worked closely with a senior Archives Keeper at the Public Record Office, Dr Roy Hunnisett. As with the correspondence with Hilda Grieve and Arthur Searle at the Essex Record Office, it shows how important it is to establish strong working relations with archivists if one is going to work effectively on their collections. They are the equivalent to 'gate keepers' and key informants who are so vital in mediating with other cultures in anthropology. Furthermore, archivists were generally working on the records themselves, so would be very aware of the difficulties and pitfalls in using them.

The letter I first wrote is a carbon copy. Unfortunately the right margin is slightly truncated.

7/4/66

Field Head,
Outgate,
Nr.Ambleside,
Westmorland.

Your ref:RFH/JG

Dear Mr. Hunnisett,

Thank you so much for letting me know about the new Essex Assize file. Though my heart ~~s~~inks at the thought of all my tidy maps and graphs as a pursuivant (?) of truth I am glad I seem to have got into a bit of a muddle over this, for though I noted it was missing from your card index C.L.Ewen (Witch Hunting and Witch Trials pp.124-5) either made a mistake in dating a file or else saw it before it became gummed up: I have followed him. I will sort all this out when I come down.

I have been meaning to write to you for some time on another issue - suicide. While searching for witches dying of plague in the coroner's indictments (K.B.9) I hastily noted down suicides for Essex and one sample year for the whole of England. The enclosed rough figures (I have subsequently checked them and there are a few corrections to be made) are the result. I thought they might interest you. Of ~~the~~ course they need much more detailed analysis - eg. the age group 10-19 needs a further breakdown - and various factors, for instance sex and month, need to be correlated. But, as you will see, there are already some interesting facts.

Two of the major problems worrying me at the moment are a) how complete are these figures, both in details and as a total of Elizabethan suicides ? b) how do they compare with medieval

(2)

figures ? As to totals, the only way I can think of checking is to find cases in other sources and then see if there is a coroner's inquisition. The only two I have found so far for Essex, in a parish register and a ~~...~~ manorial court, were bo echoed in inquisitions down to the last detail, t this is obviously too small a sample to give much confidence. One or two other cases must have come within exempt jurisdictions - for instance in Essex the manor of Writtle had its own coroner's inquests. I wonder if large towns such as Colche and Chelmsford also had such rights ? It shouldn' ~~make/it~~ be too difficult to find out and it will obviously make quite a difference to total statistics and to any theories about the stresses caused by conflict between urban and rural values etc. I wonder, also, if there was deliberate undervaluation of property to benefit relatives ? In a considerable number of cases inventories are given and these appear to be thorough.

As for the medieval period, that is your province. I see that you only found 3 (or 2) suicides out of 223 inquests in Beds (Beds. Hist. Rec.Soc.xli.)xxiii. Have you any theories why there should have been such a low number - apart from the one you suggest about the uncertainty of contemporaries in the many drowning cases(which unnertainty does not seem to have deterred sixteenth century juries from ascribing many drownings to suicide)? I have forgotten when you said inquisitions started registering suicides in quantity - was it the end of the C15 ? Perhaps there was a procedural or legal change then .

Sorry to bombard you with questions.

Thank you again for all your help.

Yours sincerely,

I wrote a card to Keith Thomas on Saturday 9th April from Field Head

Dear Mr Thomas,

Could we arrange another session? I'm writing so far in advance as I'll only be down one week-end and thus don't want to miss you. I'll fit my various London interviews in when I've heard from you.

Could you manage any time on Saturday 7th May (or Friday 6th/Sunday 8th) or, failing that, any time Friday-Sunday (13th-15th) the following week-end? I will send down a couple of chapters in two weeks' time. Yours Alan Macfarlane

I had a reply to my letter of 7th April from Roy Hunnisett. I include the first of five pages of this letter.

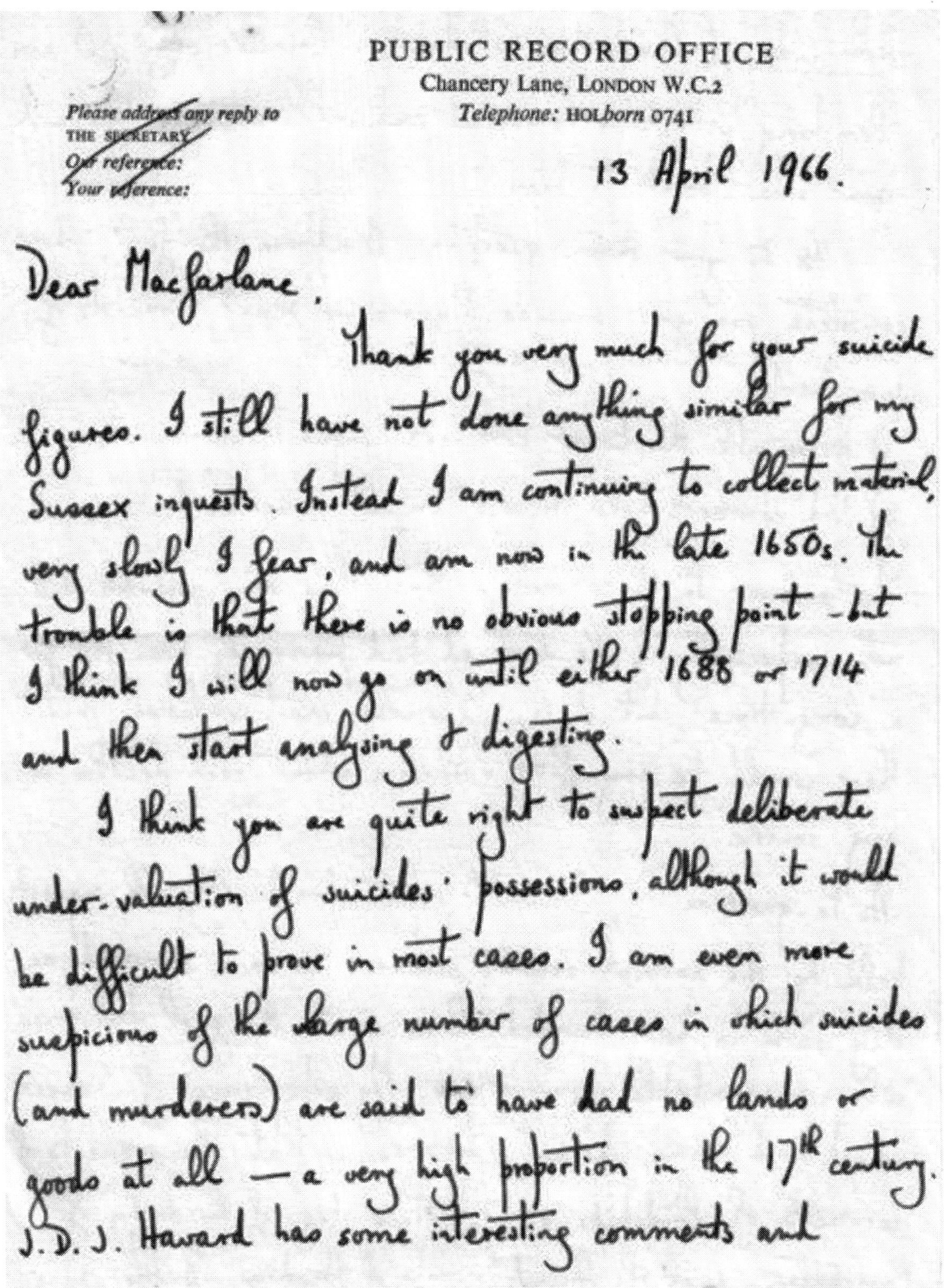

PUBLIC RECORD OFFICE
Chancery Lane, LONDON W.C.2
Telephone: HOLborn 0741

Please address any reply to
THE SECRETARY
Our reference:
Your reference:

13 April 1966.

Dear Macfarlane,

Thank you very much for your suicide figures. I still have not done anything similar for my Sussex inquests. Instead I am continuing to collect material, very slowly I fear, and am now in the late 1650s. The trouble is that there is no obvious stopping point - but I think I will now go on until either 1688 or 1714 and then start analysing & digesting.

I think you are quite right to suspect deliberate under-valuation of suicides' possessions, although it would be difficult to prove in most cases. I am even more suspicious of the large number of cases in which suicides (and murderers) are said to have had no lands or goods at all — a very high proportion in the 17th century. J.D.J. Havard has some interesting comments and

I wrote to Keith Thomas from Field Head on 20th April

Dear Mr. Thomas,

Thank you for your card. Friday 6th May at 2 p.m. will be fine; may I accept your kind invitation to lunch? Unless this is inconvenient and I hear from you I will call at your room at 1 p.m.

I enclose a couple of chapters; this concludes the 'Sources' half of the thesis and I now hope to move on to analysis. First I'll have to get Hopkins out of the way – a quick sketch (as I haven't much to offer in the way of new material or insights) should be completed by the time I come down. I'll bring it with me and perhaps we can discuss it at a later meeting. The analysis of my three villages, in depth, is proving most interesting – for instance it looks as if all the Hatfield Peverel witches and their victims lived on one manor, though it may be the fact that this also happened to cover the village rather than the fact that it was the old monastic foundation, that is significant. I ought to apologise for all the bits of cellotaped footnote: I don't seem to be able to anticipate how long (or over-long) my footnotes are going to be, but this may be a preferable method to continuing them on the next page.

Three isolated points:

i) Though I agree that the 'bloody flux' was probably too well known to be often ascribed to witches that it was <u>*sometimes*</u> *appears from the confession of Agnes Waterhouse in the 1566 pamphlet.*

ii) The additional Aylett references in the Ashmole Ms. 412 which you omitted from the list you kindly gave me are f. 13v, 16, 19v, 153v, 175v – this may save you going through it all again.

iii) I may remember wrongly, but when we were talking about animals I think you said that you had not come across any examples of butchers actually being presented for not baiting their bulls to death, in accordance with the law: there are two examples for Dec. 1975 in the Maldon Borough Records, (in the E.R.O) D/B 3 1/6 f. 192v.

I enjoyed your article in the T.L.S.[1] *very much and hope it was not too bitterly received in certain quarters. Still unable to get any support to do social anthropology at L.S.E. I, also, look forward to seeing whether 'the prevailing system of historical training can generate the intellectual flexibility necessary for the new history to sustain itself'!*

I look forward to your comments on the enclosed: I hope I've given you plenty of time to read them. Yours sincerely,

Rosalind Clay wrote on 21st April 1966 from Woodstock Road, Oxford.

---

[1] 'The Tools and the Job', *Times Literary Supplement*. I quote from the article in my letter.

~~21~~ 8st April
1966

121 Woodstock Road
Oxford.
Tel. 53093.

Dear Alan

Though you had to do without any written communication from me, I feel that you may have had telepathic messages, as I thought often of you — Far too much has been happening & I couldn't get peace for even a short letter, but your card this morning convinced me that I should have a try.

I shall be very glad to see you some time during the weekend of the 7th, but will warn you that my step-daughter may be in Oxford on 7th itself & she suggested coming at 6 to take me to dine out, so don't try then. (though she might cancel it)

I was with Oliver March 31st to April 8th (Totteridge — rather like Boars Hill. O has an acre of garden with cedars & masses of

Dear Alan,

Though you had to do without any written communication from me, I feel that you may have had telepathic messages, as I thought often of you - Far too much has been happening & I couldn't get peace for even a short letter, but your card this morning convinced me that I should have a try.

I shall be very glad to see you some time during the weekend after 7th, but will warn you that my stepdaughter may be in Oxford on 7th itself & she suggested coming at 6 to take me to dine out, so don't try then. (though she might cancel it)

I was with Oliver March 31st to April 8th (Totteridge – rather like Boars Hill. O has an acre of garden with cedars & masses of daffs.) & then 8th – 14th with Peter & Elizabeth & their 4 wild children at St Ives – Cornwall is a revelation – not like a piece of England at all & the coast enchantingly beautiful. St Ives is a high rocky headland, carved into 5 sandy bays, & huddled with houses perched one above the other & crammed into nooks – most of them reached by high stone stairs with painted balustrades – whole place full of colour – pink or blue houses, yellow rails & masses of creepers. The south coast is just as lovely – especially Mevagassey – An enterprising solicitor has turned a sort of pilchard packer into 16 flats, right on the beach so that the Atlantic thunders to within a few feet of one's bed – The sea is an irresistible spectacle to me, & my eyes get drawn to it even when there are no surf-riders – but there was. I found Peter Shore most congenial – very moderate, though I thought it wisest not to shatter the general impression that I had voted Labour (I voted Liberal). He is Junior Minister of Technology, under Frank Cousins - & the floor was thick with congratulatory telegrams. The eldest girl (nearly 15) is pretty & civilized but the 3 others ghastly noisy young savages. With completely animal manners – a pity. Elizabeth too has just let her looks go to pieces ^& that grieved me, but I managed to avoid giving advice of any kind. We took 11 hours in the car to get there & 9 to come back but the return journey (apart from the sight of Stonehenge in snow) was the more unpleasant as the children racketed & found & hollered – I got back on 15th. ...

The College dinner was last night, Mr Graham most kindly rang up & offered to meet me & take me down the steps. Which made all the difference. It was a marvellous evening for me, though there were far too many people & I had to sit between 2 strangers (Prof. Palmer & Dr Harris) – I didn't get on too badly there as one knew A.J.P. Taylor & Namier intimately & the other knew Prof. Toynbee – but I feared I was not going to see any of the dons I knew. However I had a long talk with Llewellyn Woodward (a v. old friend who had been seeing some of Rosemary's work), & then Mr Pitt & Roger Fulford & finally Mr Campbell who seemed in particularly gay spirits & promised to send me an offprint of his brilliant chapter on Bede. I had just read it that morning. It is a most wonderful piece of work. I did not get away till 11.40 & Lord Franks saw me to my taxi (a slight blow as Mr Campbell looked like doing this). These people have a real gift for making me happy. When Peter Shore's children want him to listen they seize hold of his chin & turn his face towards them. I have never before seen this trick & I told Mr Campbell I marked it at the time as suitable to apply to him. It was nice to apply to him. It was nice to see him in such a larky mood & I am thrilled about the offprint as I didn't really want to buy the book (almost entirely about historians like Polybius about whom I know nothing at all).

This term I have 4 English History girls (mostly London External degree) & 4 new Americans. I have masses to read & a stream of chatty interruptions. Sybil's graph is right up at the top as she was pathetic about missing me & also said she had been cutting down on cigarettes & for that reason had rudely contradicted everything I said – a handsome apology.

I picture you reading this as your prep just before you meet me – if you can read it.

I hope your writing is getting along. My son is still tinkering with his thesis but it sounds practically finished.

I shall miss Ian very much when he goes – I never expected to say that of any lodger, but he makes a good impression on everyone who meets him. I hope his very curious attitude will attract the attention of Mr Pitt or Mr Campbell or anyone who knows better how to receive the strange remarks he makes.

Garden very gay – I don't know how tall daffs stand themselves up again once they have been beaten to the ground – for that's what they have done,

Best wishes, Rosalind Clay

I have a carbon copy of my reply, dated 25th April 1966 from Field Head.

Thank you so much for your long letter – which I didn't read half an hour before coming to see you! Although this is a wonderful place to work I sometimes feel very cut off and start wondering, pathetically, whether all my Oxford (and London) friends have forgotten me. On these occasions a long letter from you restores me wonderfully. Thank you.

Please forgive this typed letter, but I think you'd find it easier than my handwriting. It's odd how bad handwriting seems to go with intelligence and character isn't it – at least it's comforting! Anyhow I won't write at length as I'll see you shortly...

I'm glad you enjoyed your Cornish venture – I really must visit the realm of Arthur. The very word Tintagel sends a pre-Raphaelite tingle down my sentimental spine. I love Devon and used to solemnly recite Tennyson to the breaking sea. But there are cloud-flecked days of daffodils and primroses and blue water between the silver birches when the Lakes are very magical, not awesome really like Wordsworth's vision but fey and strange. I visited Beatrix Potter's house (a couple of miles away) for the first time recently – enchanting. Jeremy Fisher's adventures happened on our local lake. Esthwaite.

My thesis staggers on and I've half written it, in a preliminary draught, now. I'm also employing my mother and sister in a microscopic study of three Essex villages during Elizabeth's reign: the kind of thing Hoskins did for Wigston Magna but, I hope, with a less narrowly economic approach. I'm finding out fascinating things about marriage, crime, sex, witchcraft, puritanism and their various highly complex interrelations. Will enlarge on this later.

Must plug on with my work, forgive such a short letter.

I look forward very much to seeing you. Regards to friends.

P.S. I wonder if the Thomas Hodgkin who wrote in the T.L.S. of April 7 is any relation?

I wrote to Keith Thomas from Field Head on 24th April

Dear Mr. Thomas,

Sorry to bother you again, but I wonder if you'd mind scrawling a note to the Secretary of the Graduate School and posting it in the enclosed. I have just applied for an M.Sc. in Social Anthropology starting in October of this year and the form says that 'All applicants should ask two teachers who are familiar with their work to write on their behalf direct to the Secretary…' Thank you.

I see you've roused a few old bears in the T.L.S. I note that Cooper, in a surprisingly generous manner, refrains from offering any suggestions as to English works which have succeeded or superseded Homans![1] *I'm seeing Wagner next week and hope to discuss the query he raises about the unreliability of parish registers: I don't know if he has any statistical support for his remark about wills – it doesn't appear that he has bothered to read Wrigley's various articles on the difficulties of using English material. I've done a quick check in one of the three villages I'm studying in detail and enclose the results. Obviously the families may have registered their children in a neighbouring church, may have been immigrants etc. etc. and this will emerge later (when I have more time to analyse – at the moment most of it is nobly being done by my mother and sister) – still I think it does suggest caution. I must tell Wrigley the glum news some time.*

See you on May 6th. Yours,

Card from Keith Thomas on 26th April

---

[1] Insert footnote on John Cooper and Homans.

Many thanks for your v. interesting letter re parish registers. You'll turn Peter Laslett's hair white, & Garter King of Arms will probably make you a Herald. See on Friday 6 May – 1pm for lunch. Keith. P.S. I've duly written to L.S.E. for you.

1966 - May

After a little more correspondence, and reading an article from Wagner in the *Times Literary Supplement* of 21 April on historical demography, we met on Wednesday 4th May. After that meeting I received the following offer of part-time employment.

From
Sir Anthony Wagner,
K.C.V.O., D.Litt,
Garter Principal King of Arms.

College of Arms,
Queen Victoria St, London, EC4
Tel, City 4300

ARW/JM

5th May 1966.

Alan Macfarlane, Esq.,
Worcester College,
Oxford.

Dear Mr Macfarlane,

Following our talk on Wednesday I write to confirm that when you come to London in October we should like you to undertake part time research work for us at the rates suggested to you by Mr Woodard which you have told me commend themselves to you. These are as follows - payment of 10/- an hour or if a day's work is done, £3 3s. for the day; Expenses if you are working away from London and from home at the rate of 2½ guineas a day additional to rail or bus fares.

I felt that we had much in common in our way of looking at things and if this arrangement goes well I hope we may be able to continue and extent it later.

I am sending you under separate cover a little book on the Records and Collections of the College.

I do not know whether you have seen my book <u>English Genealogy</u> but if not it might interest you.

Yours sincerely,

Anthony Wagner

Garter King of Arms.

Do let me know your relationship to M.R. James.

I had clearly discussed my relationship to the late Provost of King's and ghost story writer M.R. James with my grandfather. He wrote to me on 10th May explaining the connection.

10th May

Dearest Alan,

The family of Jameses may claim to be the oldest Colonial family in Jamaica + members of the family have been leaders both in its civil and military life.

The founder of the family ~~Capt~~ capt Richard James was an officer in the Penn + Venables expedition which conquered the island from the Spaniards in 1655. ~~Capt~~ capt Richard came from Glamorganshire

Brigadier Montague James, to whom the grant of arms, in 1772 by the College of Arms was made, was the eldest son of Col Richard James, who was the son of ~~Capt~~ James (of Glamorgan).

Col Richard James (b 1656 d 1759) had a brother (William (b about 1660) & it is from him that our family descends. The right to bear the arms was granted to the descendants of Col Richard and his brother William who married Anne James (d of Richard James)

See overleaf

William Rhodes James m Anne James

William Rhodes James m Juliana Wisdom

William Rhodes James m Rachel Anne Jarrett

1) William Rhodes James m 1st Mary Kerr Brown
2nd Caroline Pope

2) Herbert Jarrett James m Jane Caroline Vidal

Montague Rhodes James is the son of Caroline Pope + my grandfather (W.R.J) is the son of Jane Caroline Vidal –

I got a letter (which reached me in the trenches in France in 1915) from Mr Woods Woolaston Bluemantle saying that the descendants of William James are not entered in the pedigree of the family entered in 1823. He recommended that I should record our pedigree to date in the interests of the family + that the cost would not be great. I'm afraid I took no action but there is no doubt that we are entitled to bear the arms

Grandpa

It may have been as a result of a note from Harry Pitt that I looked out for the new S.S.R.C. [Social Science Research Council] awards – or I may have spotted them in the paper, as in the advertisement below. I then negotiated to get one for my two year M.Sc (later M.Phil) at the London School of Economics.

SOCIAL SCIENCE RESEARCH COUNCIL

RESEARCH FELLOWSHIPS AND FELLOWSHIPS FOR MATURE STUDENTS

Applications are invited for research fellowships in the social sciences from research workers who have completed the normal course of post-graduate research training, to undertake research in subjects affording scope for original work.

Candidates should normally be between 24 and 27 years of age and must be British subjects, normally resident in the United Kingdom.

The Fellowships are tenable at any institution in the United Kingdom acceptable to the Council.

Their value is between £950 and £1,175 per annum.

A limited number of Fellowships are also available for older graduates with experience outside the universities or research institutes, to enable them to obtain further training in the methods of research or on suitable courses of instruction at post-graduate rather than post-doctoral level. These Fellowships are tenable for up to three years. The conditions are similar to those for research Fellowships.

Applications should be sent to : The Secretary, Social Science Research Council, State House, High Holborn, London, W.C.1, not later than 10th May 1966.

I wrote to enquire about an award on 12th May.

12/5/66

Dear Sir,

I write to enquire whether I am eligible for any of the S.S.R.C. studentships (the most likely being the advanced course studentship). I took a B.A. (2nd) in history at the above college in June 1963 and since then have been engaged in research for a D.Phil. in history. This will be finished in October. I have been financed in this by a State Studentship. Having become very interested in anthropology (my thesis on witchcraft sociology took me towards the subject) I have applied to do an M.Sc. in social anthropology at the London School of Economics and Political Science commencing in October of this year. I see that in your booklet 'Postgraduate Training in the Social Sciences' you explicitly say (p.6) that 'the S.S.R.C. will also consider applications on behalf of eligible candidates who have graduated in other disciplines...' and I therefore wondered if there would be any objection to my competing for an award?

I realize that you do not handle individual applications, but would be grateful if you would send me a form A.C.S.2. Also I would like a copy of the pamphlet 'Postrgaduate Training in the Social Sciences' - I will send a remittance for this if necessary.

Thank you in advance for your help in this matter.

Yours faithfully,

Alan Macfarlane

I wrote to Keith Thomas from Field Head on 12th May

Dear Mr. Thomas,

Thanks very much for the loan of this: I've written off to them to see if I am eligible – will keep you informed. I see Raymond Firth is on the committee. [info re. S.S.R.C.]

Glad your Hobbes piece was greeted with such enthusiasm in the T.L.S.

Will send more witchcraft shortly.
Yours, Alan Macfarlane

I received a short card from Keith Thomas on 17th May

Have you noticed the enquiry about Miles Blomfylde in Notes & Queries, March 1966, p.105 (& also in T.L.S. if I remember aright)?

I have a carbon of a letter to Lady Clay. There is no date on the letter, but from the contents it looks as if it was written in May.

Nr. Ambleside, Westmorland, from Alan Macfarlane

Dear Lady Clay,

Thank you so much for your interesting letter – it was nice to hear from you. Please forgive a typewritten reply, but you'll probably find it easier to read than my progressively worsening handwriting.

Yes, I dropped Mr Pitt a note and he had a word with Ian. He doesn't think he's too bad. I hope he's (Ian that is) recovered his spirits. Even I get depressed sometimes at my vast ignorance and drive myself on to work too hard so that I get tired into the bargain. I suppose we are all (including you) just the anxious type – anxious of what other people think of us (even the Sybils of this world) and desperately attempting to keep abreast of the lasts books. Incidentally, I'm sure you'll have come across the new Population in History edited by D.V. Glass which is even at this moment staring at me accusingly from my bookshelf because I haven't got down to reading it. It's a collection of essays, some of them look very good, tho' masses of statistics: Habakkuk's on C18 population is included.

Yes Ralph Houlbrooke, despite his intenseness and booming voice (or perhaps partly because of them) is a sweetie – and quick mind. His thesis on Norwich ecclesiastical records should be most interesting. With parish records (cf. the new book by E.A. Wrigley (Introduction to English Historical Demography, Weidenfeld, 1966), the records of the church courts are undoubtedly going to be the most important source for historical studies during the next 10 or so years. They give detailed (and often delightful) glimpses into everyday social and religious life. But then, I don't have to give you a lecture on this, you saw a few excerpts from them in the W.E.A. lectures I lent you. I hope to do a study of puritanism in a few villages – to see what correlations there are between religious groups and such factors as sex, age, economic position, kinship links, size of family, length of residence in a village, village disputes etc. I think this might give a new depth to the old wrangling about puritanism and capitalism for though one will never be able to say finally a man was a puritan because – (he inherited land at the dissolution of the monasteries, he was the youngest son in a big family, he was a 'newcomer' to a village, he was a frustrated batchelor etc.) one should at least be able to show some correlation with something- even if, like Brunton and Pennington,[1] it is that the average age of puritans was five years older than that of middle-of-the-road Anglicans etc. Also it would be nice to know who exactly was supposed (& did) attend church, whether the eccl'l regulations re. the prohibited seasons for marriage were observed, what was the attitude to the local clergy etc. etc. this can only be done, I think, if one uses every single source and not just pamphlets and economic sources (as Hill tends to) or parish registers and censuses (as Laslett) etc. But enough of that for now. If you are at all interested I would be grateful for your comments when I have written something. At the moment I am just at the stage of reading hundreds of wills, manor court rolls, parish registers, archdeaconry records, subsidy assessments etc. I never realised how much material there was for one village just for the reign of Elizabeth. There is more than enough for a large book. I am attempting to cover three villages and have

[1] Brunton and Pennington books

enlisted the support of my sister and mother who read and analyse with me. We really need a computer with this detailed mass of information.[1] *It's all carried out in our garden shed which my father has kindly set up as a kind of local history factory and which is becoming filled with trays of index cards and files of every colour and kind. I have a slide projector and get my documents microfilmed and then turn them into slides and show them on a screen here. Articles I want, I send for Xerox copies from the Bodleian. In fact, apart from checking and one or two sources too large to photograph, this place is pretty self-sufficient. When I enter the shed I feel I am in a bathescope; by turning the right controls and selecting the write information I can slide back 400 years and peer out into the sixteenth century where witches and suicides, puritans and young wedded couples float past my curious eye. This world seems much more real than the C20, and much more satisfactory, since I only have to see what I want to see and I can sort and arrange things as one never can in real life. This probably all sounds vaguely monomaniacal, but if anyone would understand it would be you.*

I don't <u>really</u> think you need support – if I had half your knowledge and half your memory power I would be a far better historian than I am. All I can say is that you have helped and inspired me more than I can say. Anything more would sound gushing.

If you ever have the energy to write, please do. Our weekly chats are one of the few things I miss here. But there are many compensations, not least the snowdrops which are visible from where I write this. Of course I miss Oxford in stabbing moments, but it is too gentle and voluptuous a place (at the moment) for my ascetic soul.

Ill times may be; she has no thought of time:
She reigns beside the waters yet in pride.
Rude voices cry: but in her ears the chime
Of full sad bells bring back her old springtide.

The last verse of a poem about Oxford – do you know who wrote it? It sounds famous.
I hope to see you again in four weeks or so.

Card to Keith Thomas, 20th May Field Head, Outgate

Dear Mr Thomas,

Thank you for the Blomfield ref: will chase it when within reach of libraries. I hope book etc. go well. I will be sending two more chapters in three days but write to see if we can arrange a meeting – as you will be very busy. I will be in Oxford <u>Friday 3rd – Sunday 5th June</u> and would be happy to see you at any time on these three days. If they are impossible and you could manage Monday 6th, that would be feasible. Otherwise I'll be down again about 25th June. Writing, after slight crisis of confidence, is progressing well. Will write at greater length with my chapters. Yours sincerely, Alan Macfarlane

Letter from Keith Thomas 21st May 1966

Dear Alan,

Many thanks for your post-card. The Blomfield thing is not a reference so much as a request for information, as you will see if you look up <u>Notes and Queries</u> in the Ambleside (?) Public Library.

I'm not quite sure about my movements during the weekend 4/5 June so I think it would be best if we were to meet on the Friday (3rd), say 3 p.m. We can have tea in the middle. I look forward very much to your chapters. They always cheer me up.

---

[1] While I was still in Oxford I had enquired at the Computer Laboratory about the feasibility of using a computer to analyze my witchcraft cases. They said that given the number of cases (less than a thousand) and variables, and the primitive state of computing, it would be more efficient to use punch cards - which I proceeded to do.

Incidentally do you mind if I mention your name to the Cambridge University Press, who have asked me to suggest possible authors of history books which 'employ the concepts and techniques of sociologists, social anthropologists' etc? I'm not sure how tied up you are with Routledge,[1] but the C.U.P. are anxious to print as many tables, figures, notes, etc as you want. Anyway you can always say no, if they write to you. Yours, Keith

Letter to Keith Thomas on 22nd May Field Head, Westmorland

Dear Mr. Thomas,

The next two chapters; not too indigestible I hope. Another, on the 'Cunning Man in Essex' will be ready, I hope, when I come down.

I hope the section on religion has untangled itself; as you see, I haven't been able to really get past the problem of whether people used the magic described by contemporary writers. Like you, I have a conviction that they did mutter spells over their crops and their butter, and that the Reformation, in its attempt to cut away this substructure, left people in a vacuum, but it's almost impossible to prove. The only new fact I've come across concerns a much more prosaic matter, church attendance. As you know Laslett et. al. have suggested that the lower classes didn't go to church. I don't know if you know of any studies of this, if so, I'd be most interested to hear of them. In my reconstruction of village life in three Essex villages it looks as if I should be able to more or less answer this problem. For instance, in Boreham, a combination of churchwardens accounts, wills and ecclesiastical court records makes it possible to learn quite a lot on the subject. I enclose some very hesitant and preliminary figures on this.

I look forwards, as always to our meeting. Yours sincerely,

A letter to Raymond Firth indicates how determined I was to study anthropology.

[1] The first reference to a contract with Routledge and Kegan Paul to publish the book version of my forthcoming thesis on Witchcraft, finally published in 1970.

22/5/66

Field Head,
Outgate,
Nr.Ambleside,
Westmorland.

Dear Professor Firth,

You may remember that I came to see you last October about possible means of financing myself for a course in social anthropology at L.S.E. Thank you for your letter of November: I didn't reply earlier as there has been no progress in my various attempts to find financial backing. It is possible that you have seen my application to do an M.Sc. next year and,if so, you will know that whether I get a grant or scholarship or not I intend to study at L.S.E. as long as I am accepted. But you will realise that in order to pay back a loan from my parents I will have to do part-time work - probably writing or lecturing (I hope to turn my thesis on 'Witchcraft in Essex' into a book etc.) and this will detract from the value of my course at L.S.E. I would not bother you with all these details if it was not for the fact that one possible source of money has just offered itself.

My supervisor, Mr.Keith Thomas, and my college Senior Tutor both pointed out the possibility of a grant from the Social Science Research Council which, as you know, has,as one of its aims, the facilitating of transfer from arts subjects to the social sciences. I therefore wrote to the Council, pointing out that I had already received a State Studentship for three years and asking if this would disqualify me from a S.S.R.C. award (particularly the Advanced Course Studentship). In their reply they did not comment on this, but seemed to imply, by their suggestion that I 'consult the head of the department at the L.S.E and ask to be considered for nomination to one of our studentships', tha there was no obvious reason why I shouldn't apply. I wonder, therefore, if you would let me know the position, and whether you would consider me in your list of nominations?

Incidentally, my study of three Essex villages is progressing well and I am applying the methods of 'Family Reconstitution' pioneered by Wrigley and the Cambridge School, but, I hope, giving depth to this method by studying the religious,economic and political life of the village through the financial and court records which the Cambridge Group, in their concern about demographic history, tend to overlook. I am convinced that in all this anthropology will be of essential importance and that the contribution which such studies have for anthropological theories is considerable. But there is no need to preach to the converted: excuse my over-enthusiasm.

I will be in London on Thursday 2nd of June if you would like to see me about the above, and again at the end of June for a few days.

I apologise for taking up so much of your valuable time.

Yours sincerely,

Alan Macfarlane

22/5/66

Field Head,
Outgate,
Nr.Ambleside,
Westmorland.

Dear Professor Trevor-Roper,

I trust that you have had a good term and that you various and varied articles and books progress. You must teach me your secret of how you manage to do so many things at the same time. I am especially interested to hear how your class went: I only wish I had been able to attend it. I gather you gave a paper on witchcraft which I am sorry to have missed.

I realise that you will be very busy in Schools week, but I will be down that week-end and if you have any free time I would be most grateful of an opportunity for another discussion of witchcraft and allied problems. I will be in Oxford from the morning of Friday,3rd June to Sunday evening (5th) and could manage any time,I think. I didn't like to bother you on my last visit, as Carol may have explained, but hope to see you on this visit.

The thesis truddles towards its end and all my Wordsworthian fantasies turn into demons and sorcerers: fortunately,perhaps, I haven't been visited by any incubi or succubi.

Yours sincerely,

Alan Macfarlane

Card to Keith Thomas on 23rd May from Field Head

As a p.s. to my jottings on church attendance, have just calculated total population growth in Boreham during the period 1560-1600. Population, comparing births & deaths, went up almost 85% – by about 250 people. I wonder where they all communicated?! Of course many were too young and many must have migrated, but still … By 1584, 140 increase, these should have been old enough in 1600… Yrs Alan Macfarlane

I went down to see Keith for a supervision in the middle of May and during this visit I went to a dance in Oxford. There I met Gillian Ions, who was doing a one-year course in social science at Oxford, having previously done a degree in English at Manchester University. We fell in love and were married on December 25th of this

year. I will include some of my letters to her during the months of June to September, particularly the parts relating to my thoughts on work and the goals of my life.
The first letter in our correspondence is from Gill, on 23rd May 1966 from Oxford. I had clearly lent her a biography of Florence Nightingale after meeting her, which I had posted to her. She was attending Keith Thomas' lectures on political theorists etc. She ended 'Thank you for remembering me'.

Letter to Keith Thomas, 24th May, from Field Head

Dear Mr. Thomas,

Thank you for your letter: 3 p.m. on Friday (3rd June) will be fine – I look forward to discussing things then.

It was most kind of you to mention my name to C.U.P: one cannot have too many panting publishers, and, though Routledge have first option, it will be a stick to beat them with. Also, one day I dream of writing a great work on my three villages, a sort of Williams on Gosforth, plus Firth on Tikopia, plus Homans, plus Hoskins, maybe Cambridge would be interested in this. But for now must obviously confine myself to witches.

I enclose a few more cases, too late to put into my chapter on ecclesiastical sources: I think you might like one or two of them – e.g. those connected with the clergy. I wonder what idea about insanity the first case reveals? I don't understand the reference to rats and moles. Nor do I, yet, know what a 'slyenck' is – Chambers suggests it comes from the same root as sly/cunning. Nice case of a woman refusing payment or her whit witchcraft 'who can not be paid'.

Please keep the carbon account, from the same sources as the above, of a conventicle. Thought you might like the meeting at a religious woman's house etc.

I heard again from Hugh Trevor Roper towards the end of the month.

From The Regius Professor of Modern History

History Faculty Library,
Merton Street,
Oxford.
Telephone 43388

24th May, 1966.

My dear Alan

I was very glad to hear from you again and of course I would like to see you if possible.

It is unfortunate that you have chosen a weekend when I am going away into the country. I am actually leaving on Friday afternoon and I have rather a busy day on Friday. I have my class from 11 a.m. to 1 p.m., and am busy in committees and seeing people from 2 o'clock until I leave Oxford. So you will see that this only leaves three possibilities:

1. to call on me before 11 o'clock on Friday;
2. to come to my class;
3. to have rather a hasty lunch with me on Friday (I would have to leave before 2 o'clock).

Will you take your choice?

Had I known earlier, of course I would have asked you to come to my class and talk about your subject. But I am afraid they have already had a dose of that, and I am not at the moment sure what we will be discussing that day. But I do hope I will see you anyway.

yours ever

Hugh Trevor-Roper

Alan Macfarlane, Esq.,
Field Head,
Outgate,
Nr. Ambleside,
Westmorland.

I wrote back to Trevor-Roper straight away.

24/5/66

Field Head,
Outgate,
Nr.Ambleside,
Westmorland.

Thank you so much for your kind letter and for, once again, making time to see me: sorry to catch you at an especially busy time.

May I be greedy and choose options 2 <u>and</u> 3 ? I would very much like to attend your class, but don't suppose we will have much time to talk at it, so perhaps I could take you up on the invitation to a quick lunch? Unless I hear from you, I will assume that this is O.K.

I look forward very much to seeing you.

Yours sincerely,

Professor H.R.Trevor-Roper,
History Faculty Library,
Merton Street,
OXFORD.

I also heard from Professor Firth.

The London School of Economics and Political Science

(University of London)

Houghton Street, Aldwych
London, W.C.2
Telephone HOLBORN 7686

24th May 1966.

Dear Mr. Macfarlane,

I think what the S.S.R.C. office meant by their suggestion to you about a studentship was that Research Studentships (two years) and Advanced Course Studentships (one year) are not awarded individually but on the recommendation of a department which has been allocated a quota. I see no reason why, if you are accepted for registration, you should not apply to this Department to be considered for an award. But it is likely that the number of studentships available will be very small, so I should not put too much faith in your possibilities of getting one.

I would be interested to see you and learn of your work and will be available at 3 p.m. on Thursday, 2nd June. Perhaps you could let me know if you can come then.

Yours sincerely,

Raymond Firth

Raymond Firth.

I also wrote to Dr Joan Thirsk. This carbon copy, like others, is not perfectly aligned.

29/5/66

Field Head,
Outgate,
Nr.Ambleside,
Westmorland.

Dear Dr.Thirsk,

Thank you for your letter. I would be more than delighted to read a paper to your postgraduate seminar in Michaelmas term. Shall I send you a title - something general like 'Problems in the interpretation of English witchcraft' ? How long would you like it to last? I am especially glad to do this as it may give us a chance to have our long-delayed talk.

My thesis is about to be re-written and will, I hope, be ready for typing etc. in October. Yes, I'm still going to L.S.E. but will have,probably, to live garret-like existence and work in coffee bars etc. I have a contract to write a book and there is a possibility that I'll get a S.S.R.C. grant; I'm going to see Raymond Firth about it on Thursday But in practice it seems that the blending of history and anthropology is a long way off. My detailed analysis of three Essex villages is going well and the results to general problems - illegitimacy,crime,population are beginning to emerge. I'm a bit stuck on kinship however. With the huge amount of social mobility in the villages a family tree of all those living in Elizabeth's reign is terribly complicated and full of loose ends. You don't know of any historical studies of kinship in English villages do you ?

I hope your own work goes well and that you are enjoying an Oxford summer.

Yours sincerely,

I wrote to Lady Clay from Field Head, Outgate Nr Ambleside on 29 May 1966. The right margin has been torn, so a word or two has had to be guessed at.

Please forgive a typed letter: it will at least save your eyes from my scrawly writing. It was nice to hear from you again; I always love hearing from Oxford. I miss your garden in the Spring and those late Oxford evenings with the scent of wallflowers and old stone. It is very beautiful here with an apple tree frothing into pink blossom outside my work-shed and azaleas in full flower. I still gather bunches of flowers for disconsolate maidens but it rather spoils the Peter Abelard flavour when they have to be wrapped up in brown paper and cellotape and sent by post! Still, I will see my current Heloïse (actually she's called Zoë which at least has the same punctuation). At least I'll have one excuse for coming to Oxford next term as Joan Thirsk has just written to ask me to give a paper to her seminar: on witchcraft. When I'm at London it will be easier to get down for week-ends.

I hope Ralph Holbrook and Richard Fletcher appreciated your guided tour: they are both intelligent and nice people. I envied your trip to East Leach Turville; I think I visited it when I was staying in the Cotswolds before Schools – exactly three years ago now. Even up here I get a sinking feeling this week when I note in my diary that History Schools are starting. I hope Ian is still relaxed and doing a modicum of work. Don't you get involved and worried. Like me, you would not be a very good social worker, you identify with people too much. As I want to do social work one day this is a problem for me, but I expect one gets immunized and 'cold'. How do saints manage to remain compassionate and firm?

I was interested in your remarks about Church attendance. I enclose a note I sent to my supervisor on this problem; it might interest you. As far as I know it is the first attempt to give any C16 statistics of church attendance and though both figures and conclusions are extremely tentative seems worth pondering. It is even more curious that total attendance slightly declined during the period when I measured population in this village. Between 1560-1600 population had increased by 256 (deducting deaths from births registered); thus it had nearly doubled. Even by 1584 (people born before that date would be over 16 by 1600 and thus should have attended communion) it had increased by 140. Where did they all go, and if they didn't all move out of the village, why didn't they go to church? Incidentally, it might interest you that the pre-marital pregnancy rate was about 15% in this village in this period. I might even be able to write my dreamed-of article on 'sex and religion: their relationship in a sixteenth village'! I am at the moment particularly interested in violent crime – rape, theft, manslaughter, suicide etc – in the attempt to really see how wild a society it was; whether it was tightly controlled being very mobile, also very savage. Unfortunately, I don't know of any studies (in detail) of crime-rates in Elizabethan villages. But enough of that. We can talk it over on Sunday. Looking forward to seeing you.

As materials accumulated, a preliminary sort of such things – particularly letters, was made through a simple device. I had early in my undergraduate days bought a wire In/Pending/Out tray which has (in later reincarnations) accompanied me through the rest of my life. The question was, however, how to organize the numerous files of research notes, as well as letters and accumulated archives, so that one could find them.

One solution was to buy large filing-cabinets with suspended files. These, however, had two disadvantages. They were expensive to buy (for me) and they were very heavy to carry around at a time when I was not yet settled down. So at some point I came across another idea – the lateral suspended filing system, as illustrated below.

Roneo Organisation

RONEO LIMITED 131-133 Portland Street · Manchester

Central 4382

Furniture, Systems & Contracts Division

Our Ref: TGW/BL

Your Ref:

Alan Macfarlane Esq.,
Field Head,
Outgate,
Nr. Ambleside,
Westmorland.

31st May, 1966.

Dear Sir,

We refer to your recent postcard addressed to our Head Office and have pleasure in enclosing a Pricelist for Lateral Filing Equipment.

We would inform you that for any future information or supplies you may contact our exclusive Dealer for Westmorland and Cumberland who are:

Commercial Office Equipment Ltd.,
73, Duke Street,
BARROW IN FURNESS.

Yours faithfully,

T.G. Whittaker. Trade Sales Manager.

Business Machines · Roneo Neopost Ltd · Roneo Vickers Partitions Ltd

Roneo Vickers

LATERAL FILING - UNILINK SYSTEM

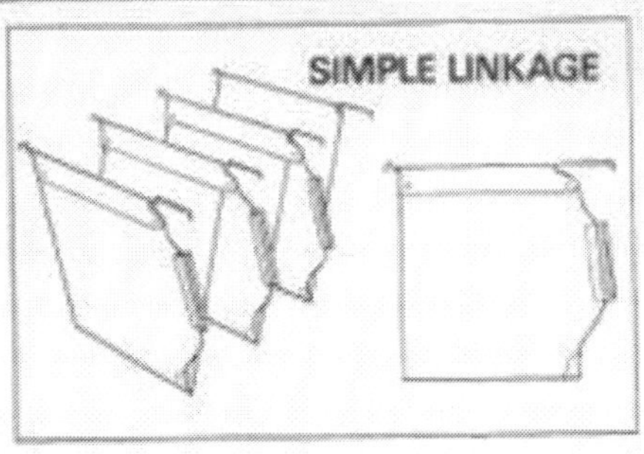

WIDE CAPACITY

Nothing could be simpler than the new Roneo Vickers Unilink System. At last, filing and finding become as easy as A.B.C. Just put two files together, slide in the link and Unilink is ready for efficient economical use. Check these Unilink advantages against **your** office systems and see how **you** can benefit.

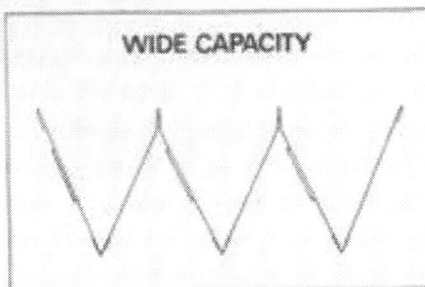

- Simple linkage.
- Quick assembly.
- Lightweight but strong.
- Cannot become unlinked when suspended.
- Whisper quiet in use.
- Nameholders slide-on easily and remain firmly in position.
- Economical price.
- Completely visible, easy-to-read nameholders.

What I did was to construct a simple wooden frame, and then attach curtain runners onto it. Onto the curtain hooks, by way of paper clips, I attached files, into which I put my papers. I filled part of the shed with these – never quite rivalling the quantity above, and later modified them to hang below a wallpaper hanging table when we moved to London. In effect I had created a cheap, easy to move set of filing cabinets – which were only later replaced when I moved to Cambridge in 1971 for my first real job, with real metal filing cabinets, of which I accumulated about ten in the end.

1966 - June

I heard back from Joan Thirsk on 1st June.

History Faculty Library,
Merton Street,
Oxford.
Telephone 43395

1 June, 1966

Dear Mr Macfarlane,

Thank you very much for your letter. Good, I am delighted that you can read a paper. I will put down the title you suggest. Will you say what date you prefer! It will be on Mondays at 5p.m. November 21 is free and some earlier dates between October 24 and November 21 have been offered to other speakers who have not yet made up their minds. Will you let me know whether there is any particular day you would like to choose?

Yes, I think that history and social anthropology will only be brought together by force of example, and your thesis will be one of the earliest examples. Perhaps in the T.L.S. ten years from now it will be quoted as a classic - a milestone on theway! I don't know a single work on kinship in a village. I think Alan Everitt's new book on the Community of Kent in the Civil War is a very good illustration of the importance of kinship in political history. Have you read it? It is not what you are looking for, but it shows that historians are moving towards an appreciation of the subject.

All good wishes,

Yours sincerely,

Joan Thirsk

I then wrote again to Raymond Firth.

6/6/66

Field Head,
Outgate,
Nr.Ambleside,
Westmorland.

Dear Professor Firth,

I really must thank you for your kindness in spending so much time last Thursday trying to sort out my possible future as an anthropologist/historian I feel guilty that I took up so much time but am very grateful all the same.

You asked me to let you know the gist of the correspondence with the S.S.R.C. I wrote to them on 12/5/66 as follows (I take this from a carbon):

> 'I write to enquire whether I am eligible for any of the S.S.R.C. studentships...I took a B.A.(2nd) in history at Oxford in June 1963 and since then have been engaged in research for a D.Phil. in history. This will be finished in October. I have been financed in this by a State Studentship.....and I therefore wondered if there would be any objection to my competing for an award?'

To this they replied (Miss H.M.Clay) on 17/5/1966 saying that they enclosed a booklet on the S.S.R.C. awards and that 'I would advise you to consult the head of the department at the L.S.E. and asked to be considered for nomination to one of our studentships. You do not have to supply the form ACS. 2 yourself. The College authorities have supplies of these.'

I would have thought that this reply a) implied ...

[bottom missing from carbon]

not about Research Fellowship but Advanced Course Studentships (hence the ref. to ACS 2). If they consider me ineligible now this must have been a mistake. Nor have I been able to find any specific ruling in the pamphlet on 'Postgraduate Training in the Social Scienc to say that a person in my position is not eligible. I realize, however, that, since this is a new project, everything has not been worked out clearly and I may have found an unintentional loophole.

Whatever happens, I would like to read anthropology at L.S.E. and very much appreciate any help you can give me. Please forgive my continued importunity.

Yours sincerely,

Alan Macfarlane

Professor Raymond Firth,
London School of Economics,
Houghton Street,
Aldwych,
LONDON, W.C.2

6/6/66

Field Head,
Outgate,
Nr. Ambleside,
Westmorland.

Dear Dr. Thirsk,

Thank you very much for your letter. I think November 21st will be fine for me - unless Professor Firth sends me off to Tikopia or somewhere to undergo a 'cultural jolt'. As far as I can see, it will be easy enough for me to come down from London so if the 21st. is already booked just give me another Monday. At this distance I have no fixed plans.

My interview with Raymond Firth was a little unsatisfactory and it looks as if there is no alternative to earning my way through the first year and hoping for help in the second. But as an admirer of Tawney, Webb et. al. I am rather (immaturely) excited by the prospect of reliving the early self-help/garret type of life: the main snag is that one cannot buy books.

The pattern of kinship in my villages is emerging a little more easily than I expected and when this is interrelated with crime, religion, economics (witchcraft) etc. should prove exciting. It's quite clear, for instance, that wills are a far better source for kinship than parish registers which surprises me slightly. Unfortunately all this has to be suppressed, more or less, while I finish off my thesis but I look forward to discussing it with you in due course.

I hope all continues to go well with you.

Yours sincerely,

My first, long, typed, letter was on 6th June 1966 from Field Head.
[I will include mainly work-related materials]

Dear Gill,

I feel somewhat overawed at starting what may prove to be an epic correspondence. When the Macfarlane-Ions (or vice versa) letters are published in 7 magnificent volumes with footnotes and appendices no-one will realize with what trembling the first typewriter taps were made. But enough of my coyness – at least its helped me get over the first sentence. How are you sweetie? At the risk of saying things that have been said ad nauseam (you said it didn't matter if one meant it): I miss you: I have been thinking of you: I don't really think that you're true and living: Oxford was just a startling dream and when I wake up to tomorrow… Even if I get a reply to this letter it will be impossible to believe it's really from YOU the Gillian Ions brushed against by chance on two summer evenings but who must now have gone. Oh dear, this must sound terrible. As you'll soon discover, I've got a vast (no – small) inferiority complex about my letters – at least to you – and will spend the whole time deciding whether to apologise or not. My mother has just buzzed me on the 'intercom' (from the house to my 'shed') and told me that they're doing a study of mental illness on T.V. Perhaps even now you're watching it? …

Writing a stern letter to my publishers (prospective) telling them that I would take my great contribution to knowledge elsewhere if they weren't brisker and more attentive. I can truthfully say, my dear Gill, that this is my thirteenth letter today and that I'm very tired….I'm also sending, under separate cover the collected works of Keith Vyvian Thomas – at least all I possess of them. Perhaps we can discuss them sometime. … The one on 'Anthropology and History' though it probabaly reads quite ordinarily to you was a turning point in my life and that on 'Time' also shook my historical foundations, Tillich-like, and showed me what one could be doing rather than discussing the price of turnips in West Cornwall or whatever theses are usually about nowadays. I hope one day to do the same kind of thing on 'Attitudes to Places'–showing how ideas of holiness/evil and the ritualization of place are related to the social system etc. But will discuss that at length some other time.

Though it would be wonderful if we were able to sort out each other's ideas even in absence I've never found letters to be anything but a poor substitute for conversation: even at full speed one is so slowed down and one always has the difficulty of only being able to say one thing at a time, while in speech, with inflection, one can say several things at the same time. Of course poetry is different, but I won't inflict any of my slush on you at this stage, Perhaps you'll be a scouring influence on my Aesthetic Aegean stable, not just squads but wild herds of undisciplined emotion trampling around. [A lot more sentimental writing follows.]

History Faculty Library,
Merton Street,
Oxford.
Telephone 43395

8 June 1966

Dear Mr Macfarlane,

Many thanks for your letter. I will put you down for November 21st. I should have asked you if you want to stay at All Souls, or will you go to your own college? Don't bother to reply unless you do want accommodation in All Souls.

I am sorry that you have not found a source of financial help. The only consolation is that ~~there are~~ lots of opportunities for getting part-time jobs in London – better than anywhere else. But it is a pity that you will not be able to devote yourself single-mindedly to your studies.

All good wishes

Yours sincerely

Joan Thirsk

The London School of Economics and Political Science

(University of London)

Houghton Street, Aldwych
London, W.C.2
Telephone HOLborn 7686

9th June 1966.

Dear Mr. Macfarlane,

I have your letter of 6th June. By the same mail I also had a note from the Secretary to the S.S.R.C. confirming that where a conversion course is involved, as in your case, they would see no objection to allotting a studentship to someone with more than four years' postgraduate study. The way is now clear for us to nominate you for a studentship and your name has gone forward for consideration. I do not as yet know how soon you will hear the result. I am sorry if I misled you the other day but I myself was not at all clear as to how the provisions regarding years of graduate study were intended to be applied.

I understand from the Graduate Office here that though your application was received quite some time ago, letters of recommendation regarding you have not yet arrived. Perhaps you could look into this.

Yours sincerely,

Raymond Firth.

Raymond Firth.

Mr. Alan Macfarlane,
Field Head,
Outgate,
Nr. Ambleside,
Westmorland.

Friday 10th June Field Head

A long three-page, typed letter.

My Dear Gill,

I've conscientiously made a little list (I love making lists – as you'll no doubt discover) of points in your letter I want to discuss. Also I've spent the time since I wrote storing up images and thoughts to share with you. … Comrade Gluckman could no doubt excel at explaining how a traditional ritual – for instance thanking you for your letter – helped give form to an otherwise incoherent jumble. Oh dear I don't know what I'm rambling about but before I forget, I now remember that Keith talked about Gluckman when I saw him and said that his Prefaces were extraordinarily egocentric. [lots of comments on the 'purpose and meaning of life' stuff and mutual interests in literature, poetry etc.]…

Thank you for Herbert's poem. I'm glad you enjoyed 'Time'. I suppose you use the word 'disassociated' intentionally of Herbert. Reading Eliot's essay on the Metaphysicals was another turning point in my intellectual life. Though it's no doubt laughed-at by professional academics it helped me enormously. I even tried to do a historical thesis entitled something like 'The Reasons for the Disassociation of Sensibility in the "Seventeenth Century'. Luckily, I was gently dissuaded as it would have been an impossible subject – yet, perhaps not by accident, you have revived what used to be my great obsession. I wanted to write a great work of synthesis – incorporating the tools of psychology, literary criticism, history and sociology and based on a study of the change that occurs in a) history in about the C17 b) in the poetic imagination – esp. of Wordsworth and others who feel they have left a fuller, more organic land (Yeats later became a substitute for me) c) the splitting and reorientation in every child.

This was one of the reasons I loved children's stories and why I wanted to remain a child as long as possible. Though it may sound simple, I'm sure that as a child one did have a more united attitude. The cracks and inconsistencies, paradoxes and ambiguities, for some reason, had not appeared. Everything was held in a 'lunar synthesis' ['T.S. Eliot: 'Rhapsody on a Windy Night' – 'Along the reaches of the street/ Held in a lunar synthesis, / Whispering lunar incantations / Dissolve the floors of memory/ And all its clear relations/ Its divisions and precisions/] One felt involved in everything one did and everything around. In fact one led a purposeful, if selfish and blind, existence.

In a sense I've been fortunate enough to be able to go on doing this. My work gives my life some kind of coherence, prevents an utter sense of futility and chaos overcoming me., I live for an ideal, or rather several ideals, and though they may be rather crazy and I often seem to let them get blurred they come back when I meet someone as sweet as yourself who is prepared to listen.

In a sense, this is why I was so attracted to anthropology. As a boy I was, I suppose, religious, though I almost feel embarrassed (?) at admitting it. I was also guilt-ridden (Interesting – another way in which we seem to overlap: we are both interested in guilt and subject to feelings of it).

…

Can I quote you something I mentioned when we were together? When I read this out to my mother she said – 'how badly expressed'! Perhaps she's right. But it's a great support to my feeling of second-rateness of intellect.

> *'The greatest minds, as they are capable of the highest excellences, are open likewise to the greatest aberrations; and those who travel very slowly may yet make far greater progress, provided they keep always to the straight road (i.e. tortoise and the hare) …*
>
> *For myself, I have never fancied my mind to be in any respect more perfect than those of the generality; on the contrary, I have often wished that I were equal to some others in promptitude of thought, or in clearness and distinctness of imagination, or in fullness and readiness of memory.' (Descartes, Discourse on Method, p.1)*

Most cheering, or, as you delightfully put it, hurrah! ?What I said to you when we were walking over the bridge together my ludicrously conceited remarks about being a minor genius, are built on the above. You need have no fear about being my intellectual inferior. I'm sure, though it's a pointless argument, that you're more intelligent', I.Q. wise, than I am. The only virtues or rather vices, I possess are a) compulsive work drive – probably arising (K.F. – will stand in future for 'Kitchen Freud' or over-simplified psychology, for which I have an addiction) partly from my feelings of guilt as I've said, to overcome anxiety. You will see the result when/if you come to stay.

I'm longing to show you my witches and filing systems of which I am needlessly proud. I love putting things onto different sized cards and will, no doubt, end up playing with 5x5 pieces of paper in the special ward of a mental hospital. Anyway, so far, it's been socially approved of in our filing-cabinet age, and I even have the sympathy and assistance of my mother and father. If you want a desk and typewriter to sit at, you are always welcome! Perhaps this is the modern-day equivalent of 'the sword in the stone', mysterious test and trial. If you can write the magic sentence on my "Remington typewriter you will become my princess!

My shed is a very magic place full of power and allowing me to look back deep into the past. But I'll tell you all about it some day. It was one of my lesser disappointments in Zoe that she never took much interest in it – which is a cunning way of putting pressure on you to show an over-stimulated interest in it.

[Lyrical descriptions of the Lakes follow.]

If I can borrow some money from my parents (as usual I'm broke) I will probably come down on Saturday or Sunday 25th or 26th: you finish exams on the Tuesday ….

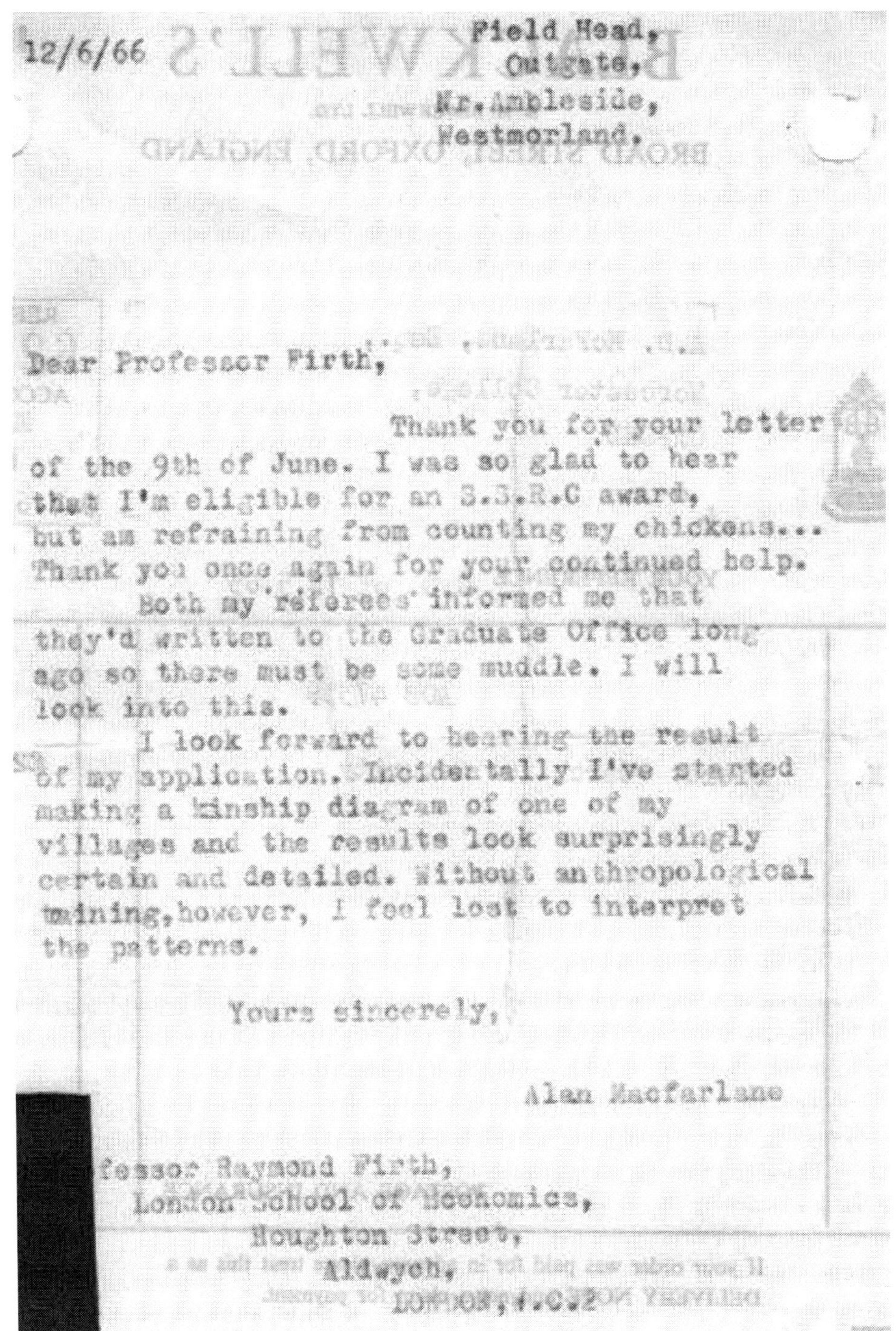

12/6/66

Field Head,
Outgate,
Nr. Ambleside,
Westmorland.

Dear Professor Firth,

Thank you for your letter of the 9th of June. I was so glad to hear that I'm eligible for an S.S.R.C award, but am refraining from counting my chickens... Thank you once again for your continued help.

Both my 'referees' informed me that they'd written to the Graduate Office long ago so there must be some muddle. I will look into this.

I look forward to hearing the result of my application. Incidentally I've started making a kinship diagram of one of my villages and the results look surprisingly certain and detailed. Without anthropological training, however, I feel lost to interpret the patterns.

Yours sincerely,

Alan Macfarlane

[...]fessor Raymond Firth,
London School of Economics,
Houghton Street,
Aldwych,
LONDON, W.C.2

Friday 17th June, 1966 Field Head, Outgate, Outgate Nr. Ambleside, Westmorland.

My dear Gill,
…Any excuse will sound feeble, but after a day on my thesis (I'm writing flat out at the moment in the attempt to get the first draft completed before I come down to see you) I don't feel like creating much further….

If it is really alright, I'll come down overnight arriving in Oxford at about lunch-time on Saturday 25th. My father's kindly lent me his car, though I feel a little guilty in indulging in this materialistic stimulus to pleasure, I will be a little more mobile. No more walks to North Oxford in Gill's jersey. The old, romantic, Alan finally recedes and the ruthless philanthropist emerges… If you're free perhaps we could have lunch together? … The real difficulty is, sweetie, that I feel, after your last letter, that I'd only be a nuisance. (I'd better warn you in advance that this is an attack of one of my worst/strongest emotions, a combination of self-pity (cf. comrade Lear) and a need for re-assurance (idem). [Further analysis of how the relationship was going in terms of other men in Gill's life.] [Various comments on the inefficiencies of L.S.E.]…

…both Routledge and Cambridge U.P. have written eager letters saying that they'd be prepared to sign contracts and give me an advance on a synopsis and a couple of chapters of my thesis. Thus, if necessary, I can start at L.S.E. under my own steam. The thesis itself is in a precarious state. The chapter I'm writing, a microscopic social analysis of 3 Essex villages and the role played by witchcraft in them, is fantastically complicated – it deserves a 3 volume work on crime, social mobility, illegitimacy, suicide, social sanctions, economic organization etc. to itself. Unfortunately I've got to condense it into 10,000 words! Still, I hope it'll make Keith pace around nervously for a while.

Letter to Keith Thomas 17th June 1966 Field Head

Dear Mr. Thomas,

I enclose a chapter on Cunning folk and a few more cases of witchcraft from Colchester records which you haven't seen. I am easy as to whether we discuss this chapter soon, or leave it until I've written my final 'first draft' chapter – on '3 Essex villages'. I will be in Oxford from Sunday 26th June until Thursday 30th and, if you would like this, could see you at any time during these days. Otherwise, I will be down again towards the end of July and we could fix a time then. Anyhow I'm sending this so that you will have plenty of time to read it.

I've just heard from Firth that I will be eligible for an S.S.R.C studentship – but that there's very fierce competition so don't know what my chances are.

Thank you for the tea and comments on our last meeting. I do hope the book is starting to roll again. I look forward to seeing you at the end of this month, or next. Yours sincerely,

I mention that I am sending two final chapters on sources. This probably included the following chapter. I will give one example here of what I did in every instance – type a first draft and heavily correct it, and then a new draft to show to Keith. This was ten pages long with an extra 7 pages of appendices.

The first draft was as follows.

Central Records of Witchcraft (excluding Assizes). (1)

A number of central courts and other bodies occasionally dealt with witchcraft cases. Since witchcraft only came within their cognizance by chance, for instance when it was allied to treason or slander, they cannot be used for statistical purposes. Yet some interesting points arise from these random cases, including indications of the attitude of the central government.

The Star Chamber.

From extracts and calendars of the records of the Star Chamber no pre-1560 cases have been discovered, either in Essex or England as a whole.(1) Nor have any Elizabethan cases been found, though there is little doubt that a search of the vast quantity of the unindexed material would reveal some. (2) The bundles for James I's reign have been calendared and some cases of witchcraft have already been printed by C.L.Ewen. He includes two Essex cases, but missed another two in the calendar.(3)

In only one of the four cases do we learn something more of the witchcraft activities of persons involved.(3b) In the second case (4) the accused sorcerer was Edwin Hadesley: a year later (1607) he was prosecuted at the Assizes for bewitching two people but was acquitted on both.(5) In none of the cases was a person simply accused of bewitching another, as happened at the Assizes. In the first the charge was fraud, counterfeiting the symptoms of being bewitched to earn money from sympathisers. Among the details of interest are a good description of a supposed witchcraft possession; the efforts of nearby preachers to heal the victim by prayer; the use of a sorcerer in the attempt to find a cure, and the large fee of twenty shillings paid to him; and the fact that the supposed victim was later examined before James I. Apart from the contorted state of Gregory Canneal in 1566 (6), this is the only known Essex case of 'diabolic possession'; on the continent this seems to have been a common feature of witchcraft trials,(7). The second case was one of deer-stealing and assault. It just happened that one of the suspected thieves also professed himself 'a Comon Coniurer' and tried to use his magic art to earn his release. He offered to show his accomplices to his accuser in his 'magik glasse, or familier and coniuring glasse'.Sorcery could have many uses, though this is akin to its use as a means of discovering criminals.(8) The third case, that of John Mountford vicar of Radwinter who believed that his enemies, in an attempt to oust him from his living, had conjured up 'fearfull and uglie shapes and formes of evill spirits or divills' is the most pronounced case in Essex of the merging of witchcraft and ghost beliefs. It also indicates another supposed function of witchcraft, to induce fear, and suggests something of the attitude of the clergy to the possibility of witchcraft activity. In the final case the dispute was over property: witchcraft only appeared incidentally as one of the means whereby a man was driven mad and hence gave away his land.

(1) There are none in the subject index to Select Cases in the Star Chamber, 1477-1544, ed.I.S.Leadam(Selden Soc.xvi,xxv,1903,1911) or in the P.R.O. Lists and Indexes No.xiii,1901,which is a calendar of proceedings 1485-1558.

(2) Only 31 bundles have been calendared and these contain no witchcraft cases (Star.Cha.7: press 13/104). A search of another (10) bundles revealed no cases (St.Cha.5 A.1- 9), but there are another 972 bundles. The labour involved in searching these would far outweigh the likely return. The 40 searched bundles reveal no cases while,if they are similar to those of James I, we could only expect one Essex case every 80 or more bundles. When the index has progressed beyond names and places this will be feasible.

(3) C.L.Ewen,Witchcraft in the Star Chamber,(For the author,1938),p.15,55. For a summary of the four cases see Appendix

(4) For simplicity these four cases will be dealt with as they are listed in the appendix (i.e.by documentary number rather than date)...

Second draft:

(1)

Central records of witchcraft (excluding Assizes).

(A number of central courts and other bodies occasionally dealt with witchcraft prosecutions. Unlike the cases at the Assizes, however, this offence only came within their cognizance by chance, for instance when it was allied to treason or slander. Such sources, therefore, cannot be used as a statistical indication of the amount of prosecution, yet they reveal some interesting facets of current beliefs, including an indication of the attitude of the central government.)

The Star Chamber.

From extracts and calendars of the records of the Star Chamber no pre-1560 cases of witchcraft have been discovered, either in Essex or England.[1] Nor have any Elizabethan cases been found, though there is little doubt that a search of the vast quantity of unindexed material would reveal some.[2] The Jacobean files have been calendared and some cases of witchcraft from them are already in print.[3]

There are four Jacobean cases for Essex,[4] but in only one can we discover from other Essex witchcraft records further details.[5] This is in the second case where the accused sorcerer was Edwin Hadesley:[6] a year later, in 1607, he was prosecuted at the Assizes for bewitching two people but was acquitted on both charges.[7] In none of the cases was a person simply accused of bewitching another, as happened at the Assizes. In the first the charge was fraud, counterfeiting the symptoms of being bewitched to earn money from sympathisers. Among the details of interest here are a good description of a supposed diabolic possession; the efforts of nearby preachers to heal the victim by prayer; the use of a sorcerer in the attempt to find a cure, a sorcerer who was paid the large fee of twenty shillings; and the fact that the supposed victim was later examined before James I. Apart from the contorted state of Gregory Cannell in 1566 [8] and the further

1. There are none in the subject index to Select Cases in the Star Chamber, 1477-1544, ed. I.S.Leadam (Selden Soc.,xvi,xxv,1903,1911) or in the P.R.O. Lists and Indexes,xiii,1901,which is a calendar of proceedings,1485-1558.
2. Only 31 Elizabethan bundles have been calendared (St.Ch.7) and these and the 10 original bundles (St.Ch.5 A.1-9), being searched produced no cases: there are, however, another 972 bundles. If cases appear in the Elizabethan records at roughly the same intervals as those in the Jacobean, we could only expect one Essex case every eighty or more bundles. Until a subject index has been made a search is impracticable.
3. C.L.Ewen, Witchcraft in the Star Chamber, (For the author,1938), includes two Essex cases,pp.15,55.
4. For these see Appendix .

For notes 5-8 see next page.

A diagram which, like others, I re-drew and used in thesis and book, is presented here in very early form. It shows the connections between those mentioned in witchcraft trials.

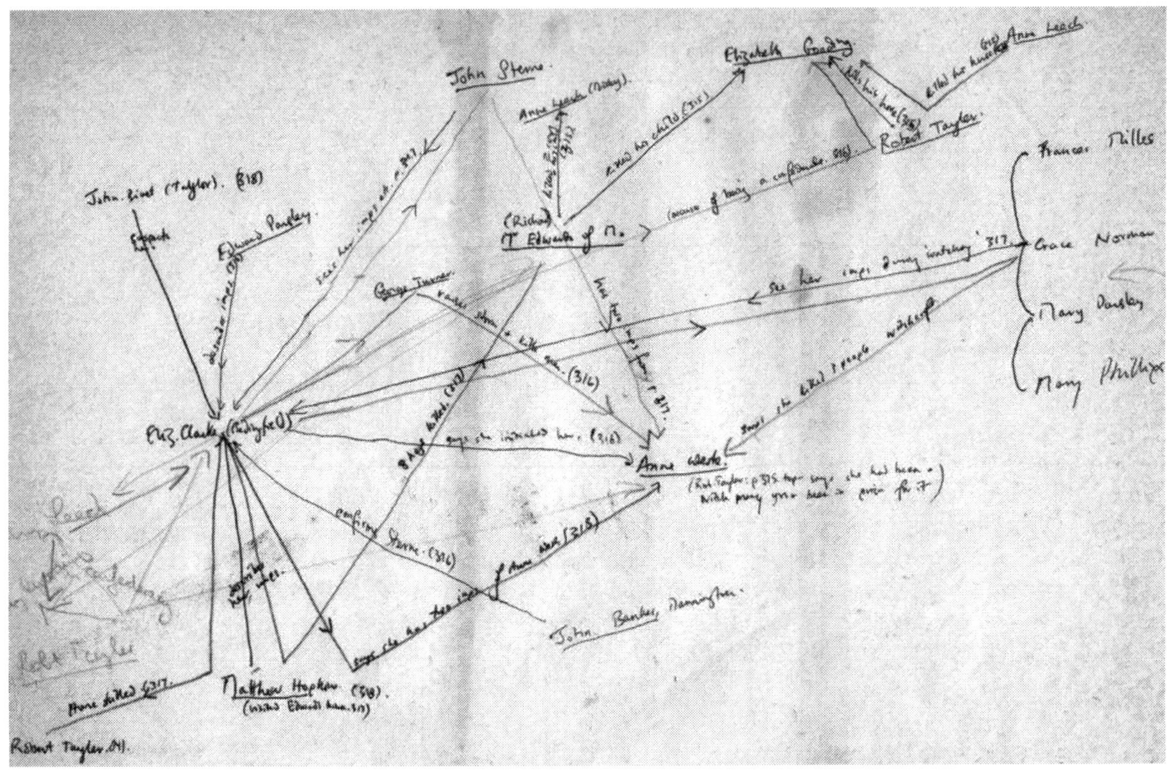

To Gill, 21 June 1966 Field Head, Wordsworthia

.... The post man doesn't come 'till about 11.30 as he has to swim various icy streams, fight a few dragons and the Snark and Boojum bird on the way – he's heralded by all the dogs in the valley and I then scurry out of my little shed where I've been sitting amidst my filing cabinets waiting and pretending to work…I love 'Four Quartets' and though you obviously know them well (probably much better than I do) you will probably get chunks out of them in my future letters.

I exactly agree with you about being able to conceptualize vague moods and thoughts into single lines or stanzas – usually of poetry. I have been going around for the last few days with a whole lot of these in my head – many from Eliot, e.g. 'words slip, slide, lose their meaning' and all that passage (I never get it quite right in my mind… but you know the piece with 'undisciplined squads of emotion' etc) ....

One of my Peter Pannery (in future = P2) attributes is that up to about a year ago I refused to read any poetry written after 1920 but wallowed mainly in Romantics, Metaphysicals & late Victorians (which includes Hopkins and Yeats) – I did read Eliot and Graves however. Now I'm beginning, albeit timidly, to widen my tastes (oh, I actually did read a few – ee cummings, Auden, R.S. Thomas) but am pretty hazy. I still prefer Donne to almost anything written since 1915.

Incidentally I think you were a little hard on Vaughan, Wordsworth and the childhood-fiends, just as Keith may have been on Rousseau (tho', from what I have heard, though the book still stares at me unread from my shelves, the author of the 'Confessions' can hardly be termed anything other than an 'uprooted neurotic') – both for the same reason, hindsight.

In our post-Freudian age it may be difficult to go around with a cheerful optimism about the naturally good man, just as it is difficult to think of childhood as calm and blissful or God in his heaven, or rather beaming benignly from Helvellyn. But perhaps it was alright then (a very tentative defence you see!)

My brain isn't really up to great thoughts at the moment – and anyhow you don't want chucks of tough dialect to chew on at the moment, just a bit of best Macfarlane delight, sweet and frothy to take your mind off things… I realize I will fail lamentably at this. Je suis un homme serieuse, unable to make the Little Princess happy….

… I will be down (car-surviving) on Saturday. I've got to see an old lady, who's leaving Oxford after lunch at about 12, but as I said, if I can meet you for lunch quick/slow depending on your exam position please let me know…
[several references and quoted poetry at end]

21.6.66 Field Head Outgate

My dear Gill, … also to say that I hope you enjoy after exams, my mother's book. Originally it was much more exciting, but the publishers hacked over half out – but she may be going to get that part published.

Organization: I will be staying down in Oxford until the following Sunday, i.e. 3rd July…. I will meet you at Worcester at 12.45 on Saturday.

1966 - July

With my sister, Poochie and horses

I wrote to Paul Slack, like me doing a D.Phil, in his case on plague.

5/7/66

Field Head,
Outgate,
Nr.Ambleside,
Westmorland.

Dear Paul,

Many apologies for not coming at the revised time on Sunday morning. Unfortunately a) I had food poisoning from a Chinese meal b) I had to return home to the Lake District that day. I couldn't find a 'phone number - have you got one ? A great pity as I would have loved a discussion. I hope the thesis goes well. I's longing to read it. When should it be finished?

A few stray references, which I'm sure you'll have, have collected under your name in my filing system and to prevent clogging I'm sending them here; excuse brevity of reference - don't hesitate to ask if anything is unclear.

Guildhall Miscellany,II,7, Sept.1965 A List of Works relating to....Plague
Cumb. & West'd Arch. and Arch Soc.Trans. o.s. xi, 'Visitations of the Plague..
C.M.Bouch & Jones, Economic....History of the Lake Counties,(1961),pp.80-1
V.C.H. 'City of York', p.159.
History Teacher's Miscellany,vol.v,pp.16,25. ; vol. vi,no.4, pp.50,71.
Essex Record Office, Maldon Borough Records D/B 3/3/207.
Bodley, Ashmole Ms.412 - Ms. index at end of.
~~###~~ P.R.O. Various die in early 1560's of 'le new ague' (K.B.9 604 m.97 e.g.) and 'the pyning ague' (K.B.9 627 m.226 e.g.)
Arthur Searle of the Essex R.O. told me that there was a detailed plague listing for Braintree for 1665 (I think), listed in Cunnington/Cunningham 'The Charities of Braintree' - sorry to be so vague.
Have you used manor court rolls at all?- e.g. those who essoin 'de malo venendo' - actually I've not come across plague in the two court rolls I've scoured.

I think you said you'd missed the Boreham parish register since it was only deposited recently - I enclose figures extracted from it for Elizabeth's reign, hope they are decipherable: sorry the period is too short for you now. You might be interested in a few rough graphs. Little Baddow is ~~###~~ next door to Boreham and it is thus interesting to see that mortality rates differ. Deaths of children are very crudely calculated from whether the register says 'son of' etc; you'll be aware of the dangers of this. Am just engaged in working out infant mortality rates for these two villages and could let you have these if you are at all interested. Incidentally I've proved, to my satisfaction at least, that witchcraft prosecutions do not coincide with peaks of mortality, at least in these two villages. Could you let me have these back when you've finished with them. Regards to mutual friends. Please excuse rather a breathless letter but I feel Keith's hot breath on the tail of my thesis - which is due to be finished within three months. Then off to L.S.E....

Hope to see you later this summer.

Best wishes,

I wrote on the same day to Brian Harrison

Dear Brian,

Just a note to say how much I have enjoyed reading your contribution to the P & P conference.[1] *All the problems you are studying for the C19 I am tackling for the C16 – which makes for interesting comparisons. Also congratulations on your letter to the T.L.S. about photographic facilities at the B.M. Hope it has some effect and that they don't outlaw you.*

Three Vague points.

a) Have you pursued the idea that drink/alcoholism is related to the amount of anxiety in a society (I'm sure you'll know of this, I came across it in Clyde Kluckhohn's Mirror for Man, p. 132 (Premier reprint, 1957): at one time I thought I might be able to use this for the C16 – but a detailed study of three villages (1560-1599, populations of roughly 300,400,500) has only revealed 4 cases of drunkenness in the church courts.

Re. Animals – have you studied the reverse of cruelty – buggery? I've got a lot of cases for the C16-C17, but haven't gone into the social attitude towards it yet. I gather that the prisons at the beginning of this century were full of offenders on this point.

c) How does cruelty to animals vary over Europe generally, between industrialised/agricultural countries, countries of different religious beliefs etc. Vast questions I just felt at the end of the paper that I wasn't quite sure what your answer to the most basic question of all was – i.e. what are the necessary and sufficient social conditions for a change in attitude towards cruelty to occur.

In relation to this I was interested in your suggestions about the growing anthropomorphization (?) of animals – reflected of course, delightfully, in late Victorian children's stories. this aspect, connected with the idea that God created the animals as well as humans and the Puritan influence especially interests me. The very human relationship of people towards their farm animals in the C16 (witness nicknames etc) appears a lot in witchcraft history. I can't decide whether it is the alienation from animals in towns which brings cruelty, or allows a final impractical, and sentimental attitude to emerge. Perhaps one should distinguish very clearly between cruelty through necessity – for which you obviously have sympathy – and sadism. torturing animals as an outlet takes one on to insanity etc: driving animals very hard takes one more into economic affairs.

Sorry I didn't mean to ramble. Just to say how glad I am that you're rolling into action. I'm holding back a bit longer though I have a projected book in the background. Will be off to do social anthropology in October, at L.S.E.

When is your book coming out?
Best wishes, Alan

To Gill, 7.7.66 Wordsworthia

....Yes, you are exactly right, my work is an attempt to prove to myself (and others) that all is not futility... It's that TIME thing again. My mania – and it can't well be described as anything else – for hoarding up useful, no I meant useless, information and then gloating over it is part of a drastic effort to make some impression, cause some little ripple on the surface (and other platitudes). It doesn't seem worth attempting to explain, in a note such as this, what it all means to me. But, darling, I hope you will be long-suffering with me. I have all the usual attributes of those who think themselves exceptional – especially a huge, concentrated, selfishness. You have broken though this more than almost anyone before, but you are treading a dangerous path (excuse the psalm-like analogies, I will be talking about the waters of plenteousness soon!). If you destroy my self-centredness and turn me towards you I will probably become a much more pleasant, and ineffective, human being. I don't quite know why I keep polarising like this. Perhaps love and genius aren't alternatives as I've always assumed. Help me to persuade myself. I'm sure you're the nearest I'll ever find to someone who could bridge the gap for me. Sorry, do you get the drift of all this?

---

[1] The annual conference of the Past and Present Society, whose journal *Past and Present* was the most exciting in my field.

Letter to Keith Thomas 13th July Field Head, Westmorland

Dear Mr. Thomas,

I enclose my last preliminary chapter, on '3 Essex villages'. I also enclose carbons of two tables which you are welcome to keep if you are interested; though the statistics are far from final I think they are accurate enough to show what is possible in this direction – they certainly took enough sweat to obtain! The chapter itself includes some extra statistics and discussions not strictly relevant to the thesis which I will cut out later, but thought you might be interested (e.g. social mobility from the Archdeaconry books).

Incidentally, I came across several references to collections 'for Virginia' in some Commissary records. Was this literally for virgins, and if so, why? For their marriage or what? Perhaps you've come across this.

I will be down, having started rewriting, about the 10th of August, but will write again to see when it would be convenient for us to meet. I hope your work goes well: I am longing to see your thoughts on the many problems of mutual interest. Thank you for your comments on the 'Cunning Men'. Yours sincerely,

I heard again from Professor Trevor Roper, from his holiday home in Scotland. He mentions in passing his wife Xandra.

CHIEFSWOOD,
MELROSE, SCOTLAND.
MELROSE 72.

16 July 1966

My dear Alan

Never eat meat-balls in restaurants, especially Chinese restaurants. I hope you have recovered. You will probably not need my advice after that experience.

I am glad all went well with Koenigsberger & I hope you will now be solvent next year.

I am living absolutely alone here until some of my family join me on Friday. I couldn't bear Oxford any longer. I find I can sleep here, not there. I am enjoying being alone, with no more exacting conversation than that of the gardener: and do not understand why Xandra makes such a fuss about cooking (to the extent, now, of fetching a Chinese cook from Hong Kong): I live on ham, tongue, pork pie, spring onions and strawberries & cream, cheese, white-wine and brandy, and I find that the preparation of meals takes no time or trouble at all, & I am working like mad on witches. If you feel in need of a change & can live on such fare, come & visit me. I should not entertain you: you would work on <u>your</u> witches next door.

I met a former pupil the other day, in Oxford. He was back from America. He said, you have a house in the North too. I said, yes. He said, In Westmorland I think. I said, no. 'Oh', he said, with affected <u>insouciance</u>, 'I thought I read a letter by you in the <u>New York Review</u> ...' I gave him a severe look (at which I am told I am very good) and he quailed and began hastily to withdraw: perhaps he had guessed wrong... I pressed him hard as to the origin of his conjecture: was it second-hand gossip or personal deduction. He insisted that it was mere personal deduction, on stylistic grounds alone. If so — & he seemed reduced to veracity (but after reading witches' confessions one can never be sure) — it is very alarming.

3

There is no anonymity left in the world.

Tell me one thing. What was the religious character of Essex in your period. Was it (like Lancashire) seething with popery? Why do you think that witchcraft trials were so common there?

I suppose you will not be in Oxford or London before I am, so it would be no use asking you to look up a book ~~x~~ or a point for me. I have promised to send in my completed text before leaving Chiefswood. It is desperate being so far from books. Hume couldn't find a text of Strabo in all Berwickshire, and Scotland is far less learned now than then.

And what a bore it is not being able to read Swedish or Hungarian! And having left the cellar-key in Oxford and being cut off, till Friday, from all

4

those half-bottles of champagne that I specially laid in for precisely such times as the present. And ... But there is no end to the crosses one bears in this Vale of Woe. I hope you are exempt from such tribulations in Westmorland –

yours ever

Hugh Trevor-Roper

P.S. I hear that Stone was in fine, pompous, boring form at the Past + Present + Anglo-American Conferences – 'pomping away on all subjects without discrimination' my source tells me — except on that one subject on which Miss Trollope challenged him, on which, it seems, he has now become suddenly silent . . .

Other letters came from Hugh Trevor-Roper. In them he made several references to Agnes Trollope. Agnes Trollope was an invented seventeenth century historian living in Westmorland. At some point, when Trevor-Roper realized I lived in the Lake District, to give authenticity to his letters with this pseudonym to the New York Review of Books, he would give me a letter, and ask me to put it in an envelope and post it in Ambleside. I did this, without reading them. One I have discovered was published in the *New York Review of Books* on April 28 1966.

The New York Review of Books

Communication from Buttocks

APRIL 28, 1966

Agnes Trollope, reply by Lawrence Stone

IN RESPONSE TO:

The Century of Crisis from the March 3, 1966 issue

To the Editors:

I have read Professor Lawrence Stone's most interesting article on the crisis of the 17th century (March 3), in which he touches—alas, too briefly—on an important fact, *viz:* that in Puritan England, and nowhere else, "for reasons which are at present wholly obscure," there was general practice of *coitus interruptus*. A friend of mine has also read to me (from behind a screen) the learned paper which the professor circulated to a recent *Past and Present* conference, in which he illuminated the problem of Social Mobility by pointing to the prevalence among the Puritan gentry of "anal eroticism."

I am engaged in a study of the English Civil War in Westmorland, in which my ancestors played an energetic part (on the puritan side), and I am anxious not to miss any of the penetrating and seminal ideas which Professor Stone so casually ejaculates, but which might, if correctly received, have a fertilizing effect on my researches. But being a somewhat oldfashioned spinster, I fear that I may lack expertise among these delicate details. May I therefore solicit Professor Stone's help? In particular, could he tell me where I may find contemporary documentary evidence about the prevalence of *coitus interruptus* in Caroline England and its apparent absence in other countries? I am not quite sure what *coitus interruptus* is, but it sounds like one of those things which foreigners do so much better than we. But perhaps I am exposing myself in too provincial a posture: We in Westmorland are admittedly regarded as sluggish and conservative: slow to warm up to any encounter, slow also to disengage.

(Miss) Agnes Trollope
The Quern
Buttocks
near Ambleside

To this, Lawrence Stone replied:

My wife has read to me (from behind a screen) the letter addressed to you by "Miss Agnes Trollope." Natural modesty and the Supreme Court forbid me to give detailed clinical answers in public to the intimate questions asked by "Miss Trollope." But let me suggest that she begin her historicopschologico-demographico-sexual education (so understandably defective in a provincial backwater like Buttocks near Ambleside) by a study of some of the works of Freud and N.O.Brown, Erik Erikson and Margaret Mead, T.H. Hollingsworth and E.A. Wrigley, Louis henry and Pierre Goubert.

Trevor-Roper asked me to reply to this, and here is my typed out (signed by me in Agnes' handwriting) letter.

copy

The Quern,
Buttocks,
near Ambleside,
Westmorland.

Sir,

I have just seen your issue of 28 April in which Professor Stone answers, or rather evades my question.

I asked for contemporary documentary evidence of alleged 17th century fact. The Professor fobs me off with 20th century psychological speculation. This will not do. I asked for Bread. I have been given a Stone.

Yours sincerely,

Agnes Trollope (Miss)

The Editor,
The New York Review of Books,
250 West Fifty-Seventh Street,
New York City,
New York 10019,
U.S.A.

Just to extend the story, which incidentally shows how I was given a privileged position within the gossip and quarrels of great figures in the generation above me and trusted with materials, here is an amusing account of how the Agnes Trollope fiction continued, as shown in an internet exchange.

View the h-albion Discussion Logs by month
View the **Prior Message** in h-albion's February 2006 logs by: [date] [author] [thread]
View the **Next Message** in h-albion's February 2006 logs by: [date] [author] [thread]
Visit the h-albion home page.

From: Christopher Thompson <ChristopherThompson@compuserve.com>
List Editor: Richard Gorrie <rgorrie@UOGUELPH.CA>
Editor's Subject: Agnes Trollope
Author's Subject: Agnes Trollope
Date Written: Tue, 21 Feb 2006 08:43:04 -0500
Date Posted: Thu, 22 Feb 2006 16:13:56 -0500

I am trying to trace published letters from the seventeenth-century historian, Agnes Trollope. I have found one in the New York Review of Books for 1966 but should be grateful if anyone knows of any further such correspondence. Many thanks.

Christopher Thompson

View the h-albion Discussion Logs by month
View the **Prior Message** in h-albion's March 2006 logs by: [date] [author] [thread]
View the **Next Message** in h-albion's March 2006 logs by: [date] [author] [thread]
Visit the h-albion home page.

From: AHORN302@aol.com
List Editor: Richard Gorrie <rgorrie@UOGUELPH.CA>
Editor's Subject: Re: Agnes Trollope
Author's Subject: Re: Agnes Trollope
Date Written: Fri, 17 Mar 2006 08:55:38 EST
Date Posted: Sat, 17 Mar 2006 11:03:04 -0500

I may be able to help with the inquiry you had some weeks ago. I remember Agnes Trollope as a tall, aristocratic country lady from the north west of England. She used to descend every few weeks on the manuscript room of the British Museum in the late sixties and early seventies to pursue her researches on the gentry of Westmorland. When she went into the tea room of the Institute of Historical Research, she made a striking impression with her hacking jackets and tweeds. Bindoff, Dickens and Hurstfield were, I believe, great admirers of hers. Her untimely death deeply saddened Lawrence Stone. Her unpublished papers were deposited in one of the college libraries at Oxford University.

Alice Horn

I wrote to my friend Arthur Searle at the Essex Record Office on 16th July.

16/7/66

Field Head,
Outgate,
Nr.Ambleside,
Westmorland.

Dear Aruthur,

Please excuse this bureaucratic letter (i.e. typed). As I will be pouring out later in this letter - or rather - will be holding back - I am, as usual, in love, or rather more so than usual and since the fair lady is question is staying at the moment and we are going for Wordsworthian rambles around the fells this leaves me little time to write letters (or pursue high thoughts re witches). Anyhow, I have time to thank you very much for your letter and for both Aylet/suicide and Maple references I was interested in them all. Suicide I hope to investigate when witches are over. The Maple reference was merely to find out who had the C17 astrological treatise he mentioned on p.182 (papberback ed.) of the Dark World. You know what I think of the book as a whole. Neboad is, Keith Thomas tells me, quite a famous astrologer called Naibod - several other of his works are more accessible so don't go out of your way to find out where it is.

I wonder how everything goes in the R.R.O ? I must say I miss those happy sessions buying tea, I mean coffee, with you and Ron and tearing unnamed individuals to shreds at the Fleece. It is possible that I'll get some money to do research at L.S.E. next year and in any case I hope to visit the R.R.)O frequently. My thesis is just

about to be rewritten; horrible thought.
This explains my long absence. I imagine I
will have to pay a fleeting visit before
October to check references, so I hope I'll
see you all then. Hope Ingatestone bun-fight
was a success and that parties of schoolchildren
haven't torn down all your marvelous drawings.
Am still working away on my various papers
on 'Syphilis and prosititution in C16 Essex',
'Insanity and bigamy in Hatfield Peverel' etc.
I look forward to your criticisms! Excuse
all this facetious bubble - I explained the
reason at the beginning. See how even Merlin
was bewitched in his old age... by a nymph.
My best regards to Ron and all mutual
friends, esp. Hilda. Thanks again.

all the best,

Letter to Keith Thomas 21st July Field Head, Westmorland

Dear Mr. Thomas,

I hope my chapter on '3 Villages' arrived safely and is not proving too stodgy. I enclose some receipts from the Essex Record Office for xeroxes, Photostats and microfilms of records. I wonder if you would be kind enough to write a note to the Dept. of Education and send it off in the enclosed envelope with the receipts? They said they would consider payment 'upon production of receipts and certificate from your supervisor to the effect that these are essential to your research and that the information cannot be obtained from any other sources'. Most of the xeroxes were of particularly difficult cases in the archdeaconry records and the microfilms were of wills, manorial, parish registers, churchwardens accounts etc. for my village studies. The former were made necessary by the fact that I had to keep a room in both Oxford and Essex during my visits there, the latter mainly because I am working at home. Actually the total comes to over £20 (which is all I can claim for) and does not include a certain amount of photographic work at the B.M. and P.R.O. I hope all this is in order.

I wonder if you will be back in Oxford on the week-end of Saturday-Sunday 13th-14th August? If you are, could we meet at any time on either day (or, if better, on Friday 12th?). At present I'm writing a chapter discussing the various possible interpretations of witchcraft – puritanism, medical etc. If possible, I'll let you have this well before I see you.

L.S.E. are proving as difficult as possible about my course. Having failed to tell me about the S.S.R.C grants at all, and then being muddled (Firth) about whether I was eligible, they have subsequently lost (and re-found after sending me two warning letters) your testimonial; changed my registration from an M.Sc. in social anthropology to a Diploma in Anthropology – without consulting me – which includes a considerable amount of physical anthropology and linguistics I believe; forgot to send me the application form for an S.S.R.C grant – they only sent it two days ago and the results are due out in two weeks; and now they've refused to let me do 3 hours seminar work a week for nine weeks in Nottingham, because internal students at London in no circumstances must leave the city! So much for the integration of history and anthropology.

Sorry to end on this peevish note, and to bother you once again. I hope your work goes well. Yours sincerely,

To Gill, 22.7.66 Field Head

....I enclose my outline for the W.E.A course as a substitute for discussion. Excuse the style and naivity of this pamphlet – it was written three years ago (nearly) when I was even more youthful than now – but you'll see how even then I wanted to interrelate (or, if you prefer correlate) different aspects of society. That was about the time that I first discovered social anthropology – which really excited me as a method of re-integrating fields of thought and activity, through my history, I had tended to split apart.
[Evidence in the letter that Gill had visited Field Head and met my parents.]

I wrote on 22nd July from Field Head to Trevor-Roper

Dear Professor Trevor-Roper,

It was <u>most</u> kind of you to write, and at such length. Thank you. I'm glad you're feeling revived on what sounds a delightful diet. I'm glad your insomnia has gone also. Perhaps the arrival of relations has disturbed your bachelor routine and elevated conversations with the gardener. It sounds as idyllic as the Lakes, and that is a high compliment. It was very generous of you to suggest that I might come to stay and work, alongside, on witches. Unfortunately I'm just off to Ireland for a few days holiday with Gill (the girl who tripped down, or rather up, your stairs) and so must, regretfully, decline. [1]

The main purpose of this letter, apart from answering yours, is to send you the enclosed (very faint I am afraid) carbon of a letter I have just had to send to Prof. Koenigsberger's colleague. As you will see there, L.S.E. are refusing to let me lecture at Nottingham – or rather the Secretary of the Graduate School is. She is a most incompetent and unhelpful woman. She failed to tell me that the Social Science Research Council were my most likely source of money, though I wrote to her twice asking for likely grants; she lost my testimonials; she almost forgot to send me an application form for a Social Science grand – and perhaps wouldn't have remember if I hadn't, by accident, aroused her over this Nottingham issue: now she says I mustn't teach. I've waved your and Prof. Koenigsberger's names at her, but she won't budge. I suppose there is nothing one can do. Since I am hoping to engineer social reform in India, I feel that I should not be daunted by such a small obstacle, but I don't quite know who to lobby. Please don't feel you need get involved: you have enough people to deal with already, including the Chinese and Prof. Stone. It's just so annoying that after everyone goes on moaning about the integration of anthropology and history (esp. the Professor of Anthropology at L.S.E. who has written a lot on the subject) they make it as difficult as possible for people to move from one discipline to the other. I feel almost tempted to pack it all up, become a pre-school master and really read myself into the sixteenth and seventeenth centuries.

I wish I could help you with references, but I fear that Ambleside is not renowned for its learned libraries. I'm sure it was better equipped when Dr. Arnold, De Quincey, Wordsworth, Ruskin and Coleridge all lived within 10 miles. Actually I've just discovered an excellent country-house library at Rydal Hall. It's not been catalogued and looks as if it has a fine legal collection of C17-C18 writers and travellers. It's now run as an Anglican retreat and the library is never used. If you think any of your references might be to the sort of book owned by a wealthy gentry family, or might be to works I've look at, don't hesitate to ask. I will be in Manchester for a morning on the way to Ireland (probably) and if I heard from you by Tuesday could look up a few things at the John Rylands Library – which I want to visit to see the original of the Minute Book of the Dedham Classis.

---

[1] This is the first named reference in this account to Gillian Ions, whom I had met in the Spring in Oxford and whom I married on December 25th 1966.

I hope your piece on witches goes well: I'm finding interpreting all my statistics incredibly difficult. to answer, every briefly (there will be a fuller discussion in my thesis) your two questions:
a) Witchcraft and Catholicism – I don't think the connection is very important. The only way in which it was important was that anything vaguely superstitious was termed 'witchcraft'. Thus, for example, any attempts to cure animals or humans by prayers etc. were called 'witchcraft'. This was taken to extreme lengths: people who said the Lord's Prayer were called witches by some. One example you might like was in March 1605 before the Bishop of London's Commissary (this is from a Correction book starting in March 1605, f.69, at present in transit to the Guildhall London and stored in the P.R.O. – where it has no call mark)

> *Elizabeth Chapman of Ugley, widow, was presented 'for disturbing their vicar reading Davids psalms in tyme of devyne prayer uppon the Sonday sevenight before St James daies laste in the fornoone and for that she audatiously in the audience of the Congregacon prayers beinge finished did advice their vicar to leave of his witchery coniuration and sorcery ... she admitted that she said 'that she prayed god that he did so as he sed', she further admitted that she struck the minister.*

I don't think people were called witches because they were Roman Catholics. As for the amount of popery generally, I wouldn't have thought the country was nearly as seething with it as Lancashire. the only statistics I know of are in an M.A. (London, 1960) thesis by M.O'Dwyer on 'Catholic Recusants in Essex, c. 1580-1600'. On p.24 he says that every hundred in Essex had active Catholics to the end of Elizabeth's reign, but the 'diocesan returns of recusants' in 1577 only had 60 Essex names. On p.43 he says that recusants lived in 115 and owned land in 83 more parishes of a total of 395 parishes. In the villages I've studied in detail, 3 in all, there seems to be little Recusancy. Measured in terms of church attendance (gauged from the ecclesiastical court records) in all three villages, numbering a total population of some 1,000 persons, there were, over the whole of Elizabeth's reign, only some half dozen likely Catholics, at the most. An analysis of wills (on the method of Dickens) shows that people stopped bequeathing their soul to the Blessed Virgin Mary in the early 1550s.
b) Why was Essex so witch-conscious? This is a huge question, of course, and I'm not sure that my whole thesis answers it. I'm afraid I'll have to refer you to the penultimate chapter which discusses whether it was 1) the medical background – plague and unknown disease. 2) the economic background – a very rapidly growing population, proximity to the London market, the introduction of the new draperies, huge amounts of migration, early enclosures hemming in population, etc. 3) the religious background – strong centre of Puritanism etc 4) the kinship structure 5) the manorial and neighbourhood system 6) the sexual and age groups and so on. If (and I think that the impression is heightened by the comparatively excellent survival of Essex evidence) Essex was exceptional, I think it was because of a combination of these factors. Sorry to be so vague, but it would take a long time to discuss all the issues in detail. No doubt you will have more than enough of such discussion before long.

As for the formidable Miss Trollope, I'm sorry to hear the proverbial cat is out of the bag. I gather Stone knew: for instance he sent a card to Keith Thomas to say that you were carrying on 'an obscene' and humorous correspondence in the New York Review. So Oxford must know.

Please forgive me for letting you down about Nottingham. I hope you have a restful summer.

There were further letters from Hugh Trevor-Roper.

CHIEFSWOOD,
MELROSE, SCOTLAND.
MELROSE 72.

22 July 1966

My dear Alan

I am so sorry about these difficulties. It looks as if Dr Bohm is an ass. I have written to Fryer & told him my opinion of Dr Bohm and said that my immediate reaction would be to suggest that you ignore her, keep to your original plan, and wait for the return of Prof Firth, whom Fryer & I could then get at first. I really believe that this would be the right course; but of course it is for Fryer to say, and he may not want to risk being left stranded. Anyway, I have told him that I will write to anyone whom he thinks that I could usefully approach.

Thank you very much for your answers to my questions. I wonder if Essex <u>was</u> exceptional, – 'seething in superstition' as Ewens says. ~~A~~ You make me think that it may not have been. After all, all these factors that you mention obtain elsewhere. ~~and~~ But intense puritanism, I feel, needs a challenge. There must have been something in Essex to <u>create</u> the puritanism – other than the puritan preachers! However, there are parallels abroad – Mecklenburg is one: and I can discover nothing about it, and there are no books on it in Bodley or the Nat. Library of Scotland. It is very kind of you to offer to look things up in the John Rylands Library; but I won't impose that on you!

The only hope now is to create Miss Trollope in the flesh. I am writing to a lady friend instructing her to telephone Stone as Miss T. yours very

Hugh Trevelyan

CHIEFSWOOD,
MELROSE, SCOTLAND.
MELROSE 72.

23 July 1966

My dear Alan

The more I think of Dr Bohm the more I think that, if supported by Fryer, you should stand firm. As I understand it (from your account of the regulations) you are right in law, and therefore they cannot deprive you of your award for doing something which is not excluded by the regulations. It is not for ~~Dr~~ Dr Bohm, as secretary of the graduate school, to make the law or to impose conditions which are not imposed by the law: she is a mere official and one cannot be too firm in keeping officials in their place. But you will see what Fryer replies.

Could you not get a female member of your household to ring Stone ('hold the line sir, a personal call from Ambleside') and say, in brusque hunting-field — or even kennel-maid — style, 'Agnes

Trollope speaking ...? and ask for a more satisfactory answer than has so far been given in the New York Review ... ?

But perhaps one battle is enough at a time.

Fryer has been appointed as professor [at Nottingham] in place of Koenigsberger; so perhaps he will feel that he owes it to his new status to give Dr Bohm a whack

yours ever

Hugh Trevor-Roper

To Gill, 24.7.66 Field Head, Lakeland

… I'm not highly strung – at least I don't think so (I feel that you know me better than I do myself, which is odd) – but I do tend to worry about things (e.g. the future, jobs etc.) and it is wonderful having someone interested to talk to, and in many ways, you are more practical than I am. Incidentally I'm very impressed by your efficiency re: Ireland. I'll have to stop being patronising about my filing systems etc…. In everyday living I'm a bit chaotic – where you can help me – while perhaps I can help plan, organize, work-wise….

Would you very much mind sweetie, if I used the rest of this letter to work out a few thoughts on a work-problem which is perplexing me? Perhaps we could discuss it, if you're interested? It concerns sin/guilt and the various explanations of pain/suffering.

It seems to me that when an Elizabethan villager suffered some mishap, say when his child died or was seriously ill, he would set about explaining this on one of four ways
1)An act of God 2) An act of the Devil 3) An act of a neighbouring witch 4) An accident. The explanation he chose would depend on a mixture of the following factors
a) the nature of the misfortune – the degree of pain, value of object destroyed, the amount known at the time about the origin of this particular illness etc. b) his relationship to the person/object hurt – e.g. he would need a more powerful explanation if it was his child or his leg, than if it was a neighbour's c)

the events leading up to the 'accident' – he would examine both his own behaviour and that of others for any clues or explanations: this links up with Gluckman's remarks about the extent to which the physical/social world are interlinked in a face-to-face society how nearly all events are given personalized causes how no events happen by chance everything is connected to the ethical system (thus natural phenomena can act as a powerful sanction – every event from harvest failure to stubbing one's toe can be interpreted to justify action or prevent deviation)

What I'm not clear about among other things is how far Elizabethans were prepared to accept that things might happen completely at random, and were prepared to dismiss them as the working of some mechanistic law (put in their terms as the result of the influence of the stars perhaps) rather than originating in evil will – either of themselves, neighbours or good and evil spirits. In a sense to ascribe a misfortune to God's will was merely to blame oneself – God was punishing one for a sin perhaps.

There was a considerable emphasis on this in Puritanism: for instance one Puritan in Essex [George Gifford] wrote that those who blame witches were shelving responsibility, people 'can by no means see that God is provoked by their sinnes to give the devill such instruments to work withall but rage against the witch', instead of realizing that it is 'their own wickedness' which 'hath provoked God to anger', they 'fly upon ye witch'. On the other hand, to ascribe misfortune to God is to admit that one doesn't know the causes and that, in a sense they are mechanical. It all depends on one's conception of God.

Thus, I think, though it's terribly difficult to show in a medieval village, when people said something was 'the will of God' ('it is the will of Allah'; cf.) they were merely shrugging their shoulders and turning away But was this a very satisfactory response to suffering? Perhaps blame for individual suffering was externalized and shared via. religious ritual? Perhaps the whole village would atone together – thus mourning etc. were much more communal. Perhaps during this period guilt/responsibility were internalized/individualized and one effect was the strain which resulted in blaming witches rather than bearing the burden oneself. Before such things had been dealt with communally: later they would be again widely distributed and alleviated both by the reintegration of people into groups and relationships, and by the development of mechanistic laws of causation (via. Cartesian philosophy etc). But for a while the guilt-load was highly and the methods of dealing with it and explaining suffering inadequate. Oh dear I wonder if I'll ever sort it out …?

26th July 1966

Field Head,
Outgate,
Nr.Ambleside,
Westmorland.

Dear Professor Trevor-Roper,

How kind of you to take such trouble over my struggle with Dr.Bohm and her minions - thank you for your two letters I've just had a nice letter from Fryer to say that he'll see what he can do. I agree with you, it might be better to wait until Firth returns. Even if the letter of the law is against me he may be sufficiently flexible to follow the spirit.

I wonder if you've managed to get your friend to phone as Miss T.? Unfortunately I've not been following the correspondence and thus it would be rather awkward to get a female friend to phone him (nor do I know where he is) I am off to Irèland for ten days from this evening but look forward to hearing how the strug le progresses when I return.

As for witches and puritanism..... I hope to leave those, like Stone, until my return. My interpretation of why Essex was strongly puritan would be vaguely along the lines of Michael Walzer's Revolution of the Saints - i.e. that there was enough insecurity and need for discipline etc. in society for people to need it without there being any particular opponents (R.C's etc) Still, its too large a subject for what is merely a note to thank you for your continued interest and support. I hope your writing goes well and that you have obtained the key to your cellar....

Yours sincerely,

I wrote to Lady Clay on 26th July from Field Head

Dear Lady Clay,

Funny how we always seem to decide to write to each other on the same day – perhaps psychic? Even as I type this perhaps you're writing - Anyhow, thank you very much for your long letter: hope you got my little p.c. in return. I'm off to Ireland for ten days from this evening so I'm replying now. This won't be very high-power stuff I'm afraid as most of my energy is being devoted to witches as the moment. Like all theses mine is at least a month behind schedule, but not to worry...

Sorry, for his sake at least, to hear of the death of K.B. Macfarlane – though he was a strange and frightening man. Have you seen any obituaries? What did he die of? I wonder who will take his place.

Sorry to hear that people have been criticising C. Hill. I think it's probably a measure of his courage (and, probably, narrow-mindedness) that people should find he doesn't drop all his egalitarian, anti-hierarchical principles once he is accepted into the Establishment. Only a very blind person could say that a book like Puritanism and Society (which I'm just reading) could have been picked up from his pupils. Though I think his sociology is home-spun and his sources are too limited to impressionistic pamphlet literature and secondary sources, I'm still convinced that he's the most stimulating historian on English C17 England since Tawney – though his influence, in the long-run, will be less than Hoskins'. His knowledge is quite incredible, especially when, as he claims, he employs no highly complex filing-system etc. I was interested to hear of your meetings with Mrs. Habakkuk: she is a dear. I would be interested to hear of his working methods. I expect you've read the massive 'Papers presented to the Past and Present Conference', stimulating but not shattering. Collinson's paper, for instance, used some very good sources, but did not attempt to answer any of the really exciting questions. He just misses, in my humble opinion, being very good indeed, both in his thesis and his other works. He talks about 'the sociology of religion', but his writing shows less evidence of sociological interest than Tawney's despite the enormous amount that has been written on the subject since Religion and the Rise – Still, perhaps I'm a bit prejudiced since he's stepped into my own particular plot, Essex Archdeaconry records...

I wonder why you get melancholy in August – the weather, the deadness of Oxford or what? I'm puzzling about melancholy generally at the moment – especially in the C16. Am trying to work out how much mental break-down, tension, anxiety, pain there was in the Elizabethan period & how people reacted to it. It's difficult to get statistics on this kind of subject. You probably know of various essays on social history, including one by Hoskins and interesting ones on prisons and medicine in Shakespeare Survey, no. 17 ed. Allardyce Nicoll (called 'Shakespeare in His Own Age', Camb. U.P. 1964). This has a little on illness etc. but not beyond what one knew already – that very little was known about most diseases; that there were masses of quacks; that medicine was very closely connected with astrology etc. I don't know where one would start looking for evidence for such subjects in the middle ages. Oh well, I've got enough problems to fill a life-time.

Mush rush off and put a tooth-brush and comb in a bag for Ireland. Hope to see you in early August.

Letter from Keith Thomas 27th July 1966

Dear Alan,

I have just got back from Cornwall to find your latest chapter, which I have not yet had time to read. I have however added a note to your batch of invoices and sent them off. I am a bit reluctant to fix a date in August as I am not quite sure of my movements at present (I may be in Wales then). I suggest that you give me a ring as soon as we get to Oxford and if I'm here I'll fix a time with pleasure. If not then it will have to be when you are next in Oxford. I hope this isn't too unsatisfactory for you.

What a lot of crosses you are having to bear for L.S.E. I do hope you get fixed up in the end. What is the Nottingham seminar you talk of?

All the best, Keith

1966 - AUGUST

Alan, Fiona, Anne, Iris

To Gill, 7.8.1966 Field Head

[Various warm endearments etc. and happiness over the success of the trip together to Ireland.]

...I don't know if you've taken down you typewriter. Otherwise I will bring it down when we move into our garret ... Talking of that happy event I was discussing it with my mother (who is fully approving as you know though she seems equally happy for us to get married in case you really do think it is delaying tactics on her part). She agrees that it would be nicer to furnish our own flat....

It seems that I will have quite a lot of next term – finishing my thesis, tutoring at Nottingham, giving a talk at Oxford, doing anthropology and thinking about starting my book. The typescript of the book does not have to be in until Dec. 1967 so I will probably write the bulk of it next summer.,..

Would you mind sweetheart, if I inserted bits of work into my letters? As you are aware, I very much value your comments and feel that you will make an enormous difference to my work. This doesn't mean that you have to start shivering and feeling all those feelings of inadequacy. I don't expect you to discuss Nietschke [sic] over breakfast or to be able to make telling comments about family reconstitution or demographic history: just to listen sympathetically and if you see any more obvious logical errors, point them out. ....

To quote Keith Thomas: 'The justification of all historical study must ultimately be that it enhances our self-consciousness, enables us to see ourselves I perspective, and helps us towards that greater freedom which comes from self-knowledge.' Perhaps this will excuse my rather emotional, and personal attitude to the subject.

May I quickly outline my idea for next term's talk to the Oxford seminar ? Say if you think it sounds uninteresting/impossible. I think it already has the title 'Witchcraft in Tudor and Stuart England', though I would prefer it to be something like 'Witchcraft and Conflict in Elizabethan Society'. I hope to circulate a stencilled set of notes on the actual <u>facts</u> of witchcraft - as far as they are known - so that people will be aware of the general outlines of the subject, the more notable authorities etc. The plan would be something as follows:

<u>Introduction</u>

<u>Types of conflict</u>: within the individual, between individuals, between groups; between social organization and ideals, between ideals, over economic, religious or other problems.

<u>Ex Extent of such conflicts in the C16-C17.</u>

Analysis of the situation in a village: age-conflicts, kinship-conflicts, religious, economic and other types: especial factors in the C16 precipitating these - e.g. attack on Catholicism, growth of industry, land sale, change in class structure, educational advance etc.

<u>Methods of dealing with conflicts.</u>

Vary with the type of conflict - value and amount of suicide, mental sickness, crime, religious drama/ritual, folklore & myth, joking/gossip, and other methods of settling dispute, providing an outlet for aggression.

<u>Witchcraft as an explanation of the feelings produced by conflict.</u>

Witchcraft myths explain a) conflict between beneficent God and personal failure b) feeling of insecurity and guilt at breaking ideals c) feelings of hate against those who make one offend

<u>Witchcraft as an outlet for conflict.</u>

The special situations in which witchcraft is valuable - when, in a traditional society, ideals are being challenged by more individualistic ethics; when there is no appeal possible to other methods of settling disputes; when aggression, suicide and many other outlets for conlict are either useless or taboo.

<u>Sources and problems.</u>

Necessity for studies of crime, suicide, alcholism, decision-making in village, mental breakdown, informal sanctions such as gossip/scandal, cursing etc; sources for such studies.

I wrote to Keith Thomas on 9th August from Field Head

Dear Mr. Thomas,

Thank you for your letter and for sending a note to the Dept. of Ed. Re. my invoices. As you see I enclose a couple more short, general, chapters which are the first half of my conclusion. I still have to rewrite the introduction, which was unsatisfactory, and write another concluding section on the English and European background. I hope to have this done by the end of month. I will just have to overlap into my L.S.E. course which is a nuisance.

There is no hurry about these chapters or the last one I sent you. I will probably be in Oxford this coming week-end and will ring to see if you are up. Otherwise I look forward to seeing you early in September. I do hope the book progresses. My Nottingham seminar is only some fill-in tutoring for one term which Trevor-Roper asked if I would like to do. No news of an S.S.R.C grant yet. Yours sincerely,

To Gill, Tuesday 11th August, 1966   Field Head

...Last night I slept on the shed floor in the sleeping bag... As I said on the phone we have various friends and relations staying which means that I retreat to the shed and work practically non-stop. It's going well at the moment but I still have to write the conclusion which will be rather difficult as most of my main contributions have been negative – showing that previous explanations are not satisfactory. ...

Haven't been reading anything outside my work just listening to your records when I feel tired.....

Having regaled you with the plan for my Oxford talk, I wonder, darling, if you would mind a few thoughts on next term's Nottingham tutoring? I will probably be seeing the Prof. soon and it would help if I jotted a few things down on paper I would very much appreciate your criticisms – e.g is this a little ambitious for 1st-year red-brick?

The tutorials, in which each student attends 8 and writes 4 essays, will have to be fairly factual and I can't work out reading or titles until I see a) exam papers b) syllabus c) facilities of Nottingham libraries- e.g. are there good periodical series as at Bodley ? (If not, I might get a grant to have some of the more important articles xeroxed and placed in the library). I roughly thought of setting 2 essays on each of the following topics, so that each person would write one essay on each - political,religious,economic, social/cultural. Its a bit of a farce since how a person can be expected to cover the whole of European political history for 200 years in two weeks I don't know. I only grazed the surface in 16 essays at Oxford - mostly political. Still, I suppose the best thing is to get them interested and excited and then they will read for themselves. As far as I am concerned, my two major aims would be to read the new psychological studies of religion (e.g. of Luther) and the new (French) sociological analyses of population and related studies, also learn something about the artistic and cultural history of the time.

The seminar subject, as I told you, will be 'Religion and the Rise of Capitalism', based on Tawney/Weber. Tawney's book, in itself, should stimulate them and it should allow me to do some reading on broad lines which I've always wanted to do. Roughly, I thought the plan might be (again each person would write 4 essays, alternate weeks).

Weeks 1/2 . The Tawney-Weber thesis outlined: analysis of the methods of argument and proof, types of evidence adduced etc.

Weeks 3/4 Modifications and developments of this thesis - criticisms and studies inspired by, e.g. 'Rise of Middle Class', work of C.Hill, Walzer and various studies of Puritanism: possibilities of further work and study of how far the thesis explains the European background.

Weeks 5/6 Wider extensions of the thesis: other distinctions between agricultural/industrial society and other attempts to explore the links between usually separated aspects of society: how illuminating, in the European context are the following ?
competitive - co-operative : multiplex-segmental relationships: Talcot-Parsons's pattern variables (status, ascription/achievment) diffuse/specific roles: affective/affective neutrality in playing roles: collective/self orientation etc):gemeinshaft/gesellchaft: mechanic/organically solidary (Durkheim); society based on status/contract: kinship/stratificat-ion dominated society: sacred/secular (Von Weise): traditional/bureaucratic (Weber): patriarchal/industrial (Stalin): capitalist/feudal (Marx): folk/urban (Redfield): tradition-directed/inner-directed (Riesman): asking 'why((Purposive)/asking how (impersonal)(Macfarlane!?): closed/open (Popper, Fromm).

Weeks 6/7 The problems and methods of studying this type of subject: sources available (specifically European): especial problems of studying interlocked social change/social attitudes: problems of testing hypotheses - what constitutes an 'explanation' and 'proof'.

Of course the above bonesw will look more appetising with a little flesh on them in the way of quotes, pictures etc. Perhaps my enthusiasm will make up for the somewhat speculative tone to all this....

Love you darling, and miss you. See you soon.

Alan

A few days later I heard again from Hugh Trevor-Roper.

Chiefswood,
Melrose, Scotland.
Melrose 72.

12/8/66

My dear Alan

Yes, I have been in vigorous correspondence with Fryer; but it is he who has softened up, or battered down, the tiresome Dr Bohm: I can only claim to have egged him on to the fray while remaining myself unexposed. I am very glad all is well and hope all will continue well.

I may call on your aid soon: I am thinking that poor Miss Trollope had better die, and have drafted her obituary notice for The Times. Would you post it from Ambleside if I sent it to you, in the name of Alan Basset (you will see why)? I think not till Sept — one must wait till the Silly Season is over before entering on serious matters like this. Besides, I shall have to draft a follow-up letter from 'A Friend' giving a brief, sympathetic character-sketch. I wonder if I could get that past my old bête noire (or rather, I am his) Sir William Haley.

I have finished my essay on witches, which is now almost as long as your ~~essay~~ thesis. But I may have to go down to the BM to check some last references. I have just read Julio Caro Baroja, <u>The World of the Witches</u> (which you mentioned to me). I'm afraid my opinion of Caro Baroja has slumped in consequence.

Let me know your movements & come & see me when you can

Yours ever

Hugh Trevor-Roper

I replied on 22nd August from Field Head.

Dear Professor Trevor-Roper,

How nice to receive your letter when I returned from a week's tour to Oxford and London. Thank you. My absence will, I hope, excuse my tardy reply. Of course, I'd only be too delighted to post off any of my mother (aunt ?) Agnes' letters, funeral notices etc. I am so sorry to be informed of her death, but agree that her rapacious wit and biblical references will probably be better appreciated in Heaven than in the New York Review...

Am slightly anxious to hear of your massive essay on witches, but perhaps we will not overlap too much if you are dealing mainly with Europe. I have just been checking references at the B.M. - what a pity I couldn't have helped. Oxford, of course, is buzzing with the death of my namesake and the vultures are picking over his unpublished notes. I wonder if a riot of medieval publications will spring up now that his shadow is gone.

I visited Fryer on the way down. He was more than amiable, perhaps because he felt a little guilt at a) having to ask me to do half my tutoring on fourteenth and fifteenth century European history of which I know nothing - because they have no-one

scarcely only paying c. £2 per hour...

Still, it is good experience and any money will come in handy if I don't get a grant. I've just signed a contract with Routledge for a book on witches to be completed next year so feel slightly more cheefful. Dr. Bohm has gone away on holiday, perhaps worn out with guilt and shame....

I will be in the Lakes until the end of September, and then go to live in London. I hope to be in Oxford frequently and do hope it would be alright for me to come and talk over our mutual interests. If you are ever travelling via the Lakes and could call in for a meal or a night please don't hesitate. It's far from palatial, but not quite a cell in the rocks.

Yours sincerely,

To Gill, 22.8.66 Field Head

[Assurances and endearments…]

…I am a terrible coward about missing people – I suppose a result of my often severed and wounded childhood…. I wanted to use this letter partly to discuss thoughts and ideas, but feel a little tired. I find it a great help discussing things with you: you have a much quicker, and more agile and correlating brain than I have. A combination of these qualities plus your enthusiasm and sensitivity added to my doggedness, organizational abilities and concentration should make some pretty big work possible. I must say, it would be tremendous if we could do a historical study (over a period of about 200 years) of changes in personality and basic assumptions – using things such as suicide, mental breakdown, magic, religious ritual etc as indices and relating these to changes of a broader kind in society – mobility, roles, status, classes, sex, age, occupational groups etc. One has to draw the limit, unfortunately; perhaps this would be dictated by the material. Meanwhile, the whole would be related to the most urgent needs of our present society and help us to a framework of understanding modern social problems. Oh darling, it is wonderful to have met someone not only delightful to be with but interested in many of the same things.

Letter to Keith Thomas on 25 August from Field Head

Dear Mr. Thomas,

I wonder if you could just have a quick look at the enclosed suggested method of doing the appendix of witchcraft cases? If (& the Notes for Writers of … D.Phil. Theses..' does not quite make this clear, p.5) the 100,000 words includes the appendices I am going to be very short of space. I don't want to take up more than 7,000 words (i.e. about 10 words per case) in the appendices – which means a very bald summary. Do you think I have the essential details? Do you think any of the cases – e.g. any of those from ecclesiastical, borough or Star Chamber deserve quoting at any greater length? As it is, anyone wanting to pursue the ecclesiastical cases, for instance, would have to go off to Essex and master the procedure and palaeography of the Archdeaconry records before he could read them. Still, it looks as if I have no alternative.

Could you let me know what you think as soon as possible as I want to finish the appendix before I go to London.

I was furiously writing during this period and also working on the appendices. The next, and to me particularly significant, chapter was on '3 Essex villages'. This was very long (33 pages) and the closest I got to real anthropology.

The First page was as follows.

THE SOCIAL BACKGROUND TO WITCHCRAFT PROSECUTIONS IN THREE ESSEX VILLAGES, 1560-1599.

Witchcraft prosecutions, it has been suggested,[1] were related to tensions at the basis of society. In an attempt to study how such accusations were correlated to other social phenomena, to religious, economic, kinship, and neighbourhood groups, and to other manifestations of conflict, crime, illegitimacy, suicide and mental breakdown, a microscopic analysis of the local records of three Essex villages has been undertaken. These are the adjacent villages of Hatfield Peverel, Boreham, and Little Baddow.[2] As will be seen in the maps of the distribution of prosecutions throughout Essex,[3] Hatfield was exceptional in the number of prosecutions which took place there, while Boreham and Little Baddow were normal. The names, references and dates of the witchcraft prosecutions in these three villages are set out in the following table. In all, there were 14 persons prosecuted at the Assizes in these three villages, 14 out of a total of 290 prosecuted at that court for the whole of Essex.[4] Thus we are studying in these three villages only a fraction of the widespread suspicio[n] circulating in Essex.

TABLE 1: List of Suspect Witches in Three Essex Villages.

Name of suspect	dates of trials	courts	reference (p. i[n] appendix)
Hatfield Peverel.			
Lora Winchester	1566	Assize	
Elizabeth Fraunces	1566,1572,1579	Assize, Quarter Sessions	
Agnes Waterhouse	1566	Assize, Quarter Sessions	
Joan Waterhouse	1566	Assize, Quarter Sessions	
Joan Osborne	1567,1579,1587	Assize, Archdeaconry.	
Agnes Francys	1572	Assize	
Agnes Bromley	1576	Assize	
(Elizabeth Lorde	mentioned as a witch in 1579 pamphlet)		
Agnes Duke	1584,1589	Assize	
Joan Cocke	1584	Assize	
~~John Heare/Jenny~~	~~1589~~		
Elizabeth Pillgram	1587	Archdeaconry	
Mary Godfrey	1587	Archdeaconry	
John Gosse and wife	1587	Archdeaconry	
John Heare/Hore/Jenny	1589	Assize	
Boreham.			
'Mason's wife'	1566	Archdeaconry	
Mary Belsted/Middleton	1566,1576,1594	Archdeaconry, Assize	
Margaret Poole	1576	Archdeaconry	
Agnes Haven	~~1594~~ 1593	Assize	
Little Baddow.			
Alice Bambricke	1570	Assize	
Alice Swallow	1570	Assize	

1. See pp. above.
2. See map .
3. See map .
3. See p. above.

One other page shows my attempt to investigate family relationships.

~~3 Villages~~. (26)

Kinship,marriage and witchcraft.

Investigators of the subject have found that in many societies witchcraft beliefs are related to the kinship structure, that accusations reflect tensions between certain members of the family.[1] Though there is a little Essex evidence that such strains occasionally precipitated prosecutions,[2] a detailed study of kinship and witchcraft in Boreham does not lend any support to theories that witchcraft prosecutions were related to conlicts in kinship organization.[3] In Hatfield Peverel there was certainly some blood relationship between the witches themselves. Elizabeth Fraunces was given her familiar, she confessed, by her grandmother.[3] Agnes Waterhouse was the mother of Joan Waterhouse and sister to Mother Osborne, another notorious witch.[4] It seems likely that Agnes Frannces was related to Elizabeth Fraunces. Yet there is no suggestion, either in the confessions of the witches themselves, or in local records, that they were related by blood to their victims.[5] Whenever their victims were talked about it was as a 'neighbour' rather than a kinsman. This impression is confirmed by a study of kinship in Boreham. The total results are too complex to set out here,but, so far, it has been impossible to trace even the most distant kinship ties between witches and victims. The following digrams give a few examples of this negative evidence.

FIGURE : Kinship and Witchcraft in Boreham,1560-1599; selected families.[6]

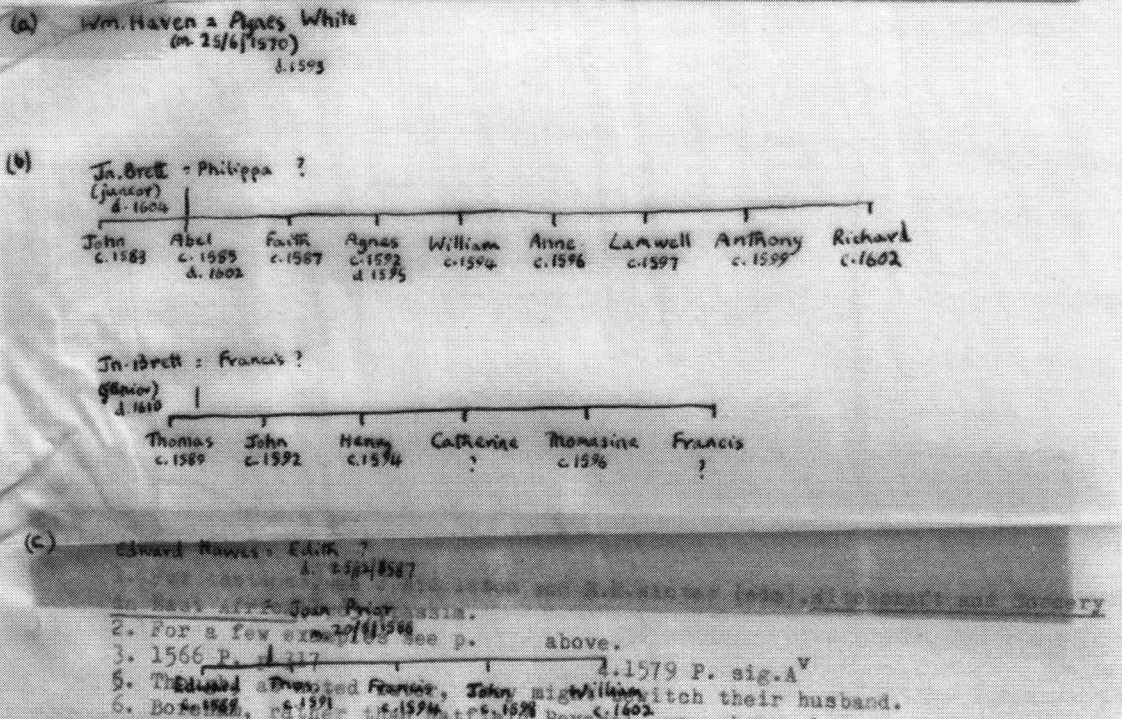

(a) Wm. Haven = Agnes White (m. 25/6/1570) d.1593

(b) Jn. Brett (junior) d.1604 = Philippa ?
John c.1583 | Abel c.1585 d.1602 | Faith c.1587 | Agnes c.1592 d.1595 | William c.1594 | Anne c.1596 | Lamwell c.1597 | Anthony c.1599 | Richard c.1602

Jn. Brett (senior) d.1610 = Francis ?
Thomas c.1589 | John c.1592 | Henry c.1594 | Catherine ? | Thomasine c.1596 | Francis ?

(c) Edward Hawes = Edith ? d. [illegible]
Joan Prior 20/1/1566
Edward c.1569 | Thomas c.1591 | Francis c.1594 | John c.1598 | William c.1602

2. For a few examples see p. above.
3. 1566 P. ... 4. 1579 P. sig.A[v]
5. Th... might ... witch their husband.
6. Bo..., rather than Hatfield Peverel ...

I mentioned that I was sending another draft of the first half of my conclusion. This was 17 pages and was annotated by Keith. The first page is as follows.

POSSIBLE EXPLANATIONS OF WITCHCRAFT PROSECUTIONS.

Witchcraft and medicine.

It has been suggested that witchcraft prosecutions reflected the incidence of illness,[1] ~~(it has been argued)~~ that the sixteenth and seventeenth centuries were times of plague, high child-mortality and, as yet, undiagnosed disease, and that whenever an ailment could not be explained by medical theory it was attributed to witches, both by physicians and their clients. Obviously this does not explain why there ~~should have been~~ was a growth of witchcraft prosecutions in the second half of the sixteenth century, since it is difficult to show that plague or disease were not endemic in the middle ages. But it could be argued that improving medical knowledge, as well as a decline in certain forms of sickness, especially bubonic plague, at the end of the seventeenth century, does explain the decline of prosecutions.[2] The examination of Essex evidence does not support any such theory. Rather, it destroys any correlation between plague, medical improvements and witchcraft beliefs and prosecutions.

An analysis of the types of illness attributed to witches in Essex showed that they were usually of a lingering variety and that they were not normally accompanied by any particularly strange symptoms.[3] Witchcraft was not an automatic explanation of any unusual illness, mental breakdown or womb-diseases leading to paroxysms for instance. Much illness and many deaths were explained without reference to witches.[4] A majority of the cases of death or illness supposedly caused by witches were of adults: high child-mortality was not, in itself, a cause of prosecution.[5] Nor do medical factors explain change over time. Many villages had prosecutions before 1600, and none after that date.[6] It would be impossible to show any radical change in health conditions in villages before 1660. Nor does the incidence of illness begin to explain why ~~some~~ approximately three out of every four Essex villages witnessed no prosecutions, nor why Essex seems to have been particularly witch-conscious.

1. For instance by Kittredge, Witchcraft, p.5 and Parrinder, Witchcraft, pp.99-100. Contemporaries also argued that witchcraft beliefs were related to medical ignorance, cf. Bernard, Guide, p.168 and Ady, Candle, pp.103-4.
2. It is equally arguable that there was no appreciable improvement or growth of knowledge in medical matters at the village level until the later eighteenth century: overcrowding may have worsened conditions, cf. Hoskins, Provincial England, p.148.
3. For statistics of the duration of illness attributed to witches see p. above; for some of the symptoms of witchcraft victims see p. below.
4. This is discussed with reference to three villages on p. above.
5. For the age of victims of witchcraft see p. above.
6. See map , p. .

I wrote again to Lady Clay in reply to another letter from her.

24/8/66

Field Head,
Outgate,
Nr.Ambleside,
Westmorland.

Dear Lady Clay,

Please forgive a tardy reply to your letter - for which many thanks - but I've only just got back from staying in London. It was, as always, lovely to see you and discuss our many mutual interests. Thank you also for sending a sheaf of notes and references. Anything to cast a faint ray amidst the gloom of my ignorance on later medieval Europe is more than welcome. I am going to leave reading on the subject - except for books I want to read or re-read (e.g. Southern - though a little early) until the last minute. As long as I provide an up-to-date bibliography, give them an idea of the sort of questions they are going to be asked, and give them encouragement, I think they can hardly complai

Glad to hear that you've been getting out - with Mr.Higham - though I'm sorry to hear that your swimming caused you pain. Still, you are not quite reduced to the state of my haemophiliac friend who was in agony for several days after playing darts with me! I'm also glad that you're pupils did well on English II. Incidental my uncle , whom I met yesterday on holiday at Cartmell, spoke tenderly of you - so you can bask in the thought that your pupils remember you. Robert is a little overworked at the moment, writing books on Churchill (instalments of which are coming out in the Observer in Sept. I think) for N.A.T.O and an Ensor period on the whole of Europe. You may be interested to hear that my mother was brought up (or went on holidays with) the Wallace-Hadrill family and knows the author of the <u>Long-Haired Kings</u> quite well. In fact, I think we may be distantly related. I must look him up sometime.

As you see, I enclose some carboned notes from a couple of articles by Wrigley, Laslett's accomplice. Please keep these if they are of any interest - I have copies. Some of it will be a little garbled through my omissions, but you may learn something interesting. A more recent printing of some of the more digestible material has recently appeared in the Ec.H.R. for 1966 (last issue) in an article by Wrigley entitled 'Family Limitation in Pre-Industrial England' which I haven't had time to look at properly. Though the work he is doing is not for me, too statistica and two narrlowly concentrated on the economic and population angle, I am sure it is a major breakthrough in historical studies. The sonner he begins to use other sources - esp. wills - the better My thesis is now entering its final draft and the mound of indigestible rubble is being levelled to make a green sward of interpretation for Trevor-Roper and my other examiner to gambol on. Its very depressing to h ve to leave out material which took months to collect, but perhaps I will be able to use it on another occasion...

See you in September. Best wishes,

I sent a card to Keith Thomas on 25th August from Field Head

Dear Mr. Thomas,

Thought you might be interested to hear that I've just received a letter to say I've got an S.S.R.C. award for next year. <u>Many</u> thanks for all your support in this (as also for a most enjoyable tea/discussion during my last visit to Oxford). Hope the book thunders on ….

Yours, Alan Macfarlane (P.S. have received £20 for photographic expenses: thanks)

1966 – September

To Gill, 4.9.1966 Field Head

....Interested to hear about your money 'blockage'. Unfortunately, I'm rather the same. While I try to be efficient in other personal matters – e.g. letters, my work, birthdays etc. (though not clothes, as you may have guessed!) I just don't seem to have the desire to organize myself financially, I don't keep accounts ,or budget, or know anything about stocks and shares or know when I am going to be bankrupt or anything. Perhaps I will get round to this when we are married out of sheer necessity?...

I am getting a bit better now: at least I'm claiming for all the things to do with my grant, something I considered below me about a year back. Money strikes me as so boring, and accounting so tedious – at least that is my conscious excuse, but, no doubt, there are deeper and danker explanations possible of our attitude. Under Firth – who is especially keen on economic life in primitive society – I may learn something about the cultural implications and background to an attitude to money. But, of course, one can be intensely interested in economics generally and yet, in one's daily life, hopeless. Tawney, for instance, pioneered economic history in this country, yet he was hard up most of his life and (I imagine) disorganized – at least he was personally very untidy and refused (on principle) to invest: this isn't quite the same thing, of course. ...

The trouble about next weekend is that my parents are taking the car up of Scotland on Tuesday to look for a croft and may not be back by then. ...

.... Here is a short passage I especially like. It's quoted as the heading to the Conclusion of Christopher Hill's Society and Puritanism.

'I pondered all these things, and how men fight and lose the battle, and the thing that they fought for comes in spite of their defeat and when it comes turns out not to be what they meant, and other men have to fight for what they meant under another name.'

William Morris, A Dream of John Ball, chapter 4.

I feel that could be a text, half disillusioned, half fatalistic and hopeful, for one's life.

It reminds me of a favourite passage in East Coker. [18 lines quoted]

'So here I am, in the middle way, having had twenty years –
Twenty years largely wasted...
For us, there is only the trying. The rest is not our business.'

Hurrah! Good old Eliot! He exactly captures my foundering mood of hopelessness as I try to break through my limited and limiting emotions to write something of value sub specie aeternitate. I wonder if he knew that he would be looked up to as one of those 'whom one cannot hope to emulate'? I wonder why you and I, sweetheart, derive so much stimulus and encouragement from reading about great and noble people... Is it something weak in us, I wonder, or does everyone gain a sense of elation like that?

[I then quote a passage on mental illness and other topics in social psychology from Keith Thomas, 'History and Anthropology' article, and include the detailed bibliography to accompany it.]

Glad that my future Prof. is interested in suicide. I really must get hold of E.R. Dodds' book ['The Greeks and the Irrational']. ... *Goodness, I am going to have fun delving about in social anthropology/sociology/social psychology next year! Integrating these with history should keep us both busy for a few years to come ...*

Of course there are considerable problems in dealing with such topics – perhaps that's why (partly) historians have not dealt with them at all. The more interesting and basic the attitude to be studied the less likely there is to be any written record of it. This makes the C16 and C17 centuries particularly fruitful since they were a time of social change when people began to attack all the traditional organizations and beliefs. The whole structure of society and consequently of the heavens as well, became changed. The interrelations between different sectors of life economic, religious, political etc became changed.

Not only this, but every relationship with other people, within the family, between different professions, etc. became altered. The incredible width of such changes – from altered perceptions of 'reality', to new sanctions and pressures to action, from altered responses to changes in time, place and pain to new methods of taking decisions, resolving conflicts, expressing emotions socializing children – don't seem to have struck historian with full force.

The real problem is how to study these changes and gauge their importance as well as their cause and effect I wonder if that paperback on 'Attitudes' helps at all? What one wants are indices which can be applied to written records. The historian obviously can't ask questions and therefore depends on using facts written for another purpose as indices (a favourite word you see!) of unspoken attitudes.

As far as I can see, there are two major sources for sixteenth and seventeenth century society. There are the pamphlets and literary sources, puritan manifestoes and poems, plays, letters etc. Naturally, these are lively, but they can give a very distorted impression. For instance, I've shown in my thesis what a distorted impression literary sources taken alone give of Essex witchcraft: they underestimate it enormously; people took witchcraft prosecutions for granted and therefore did not comment on them. The other major source are official records legal and local – which record facts. These provide a statistical basis, within reason for a number of subjects but again they distort since they do not give the emotional background to the problem. One would never know what the villagers attitude towards sex was from merely working out how many illegitimate children there were.

A third source combining the two, and hardly used, are the ecclesiastical court records. These record moral offences and people's remarks and justifications of such offences – they cover the lower part of society and include subjects such as gossip, drunkenness, sex, obscenity, marriage, religion etc. This is what Mummy is working on. They are incredibly detailed and incredibly difficult to read. I think, in combination with the other two sources something might be done to chart the ethical 'atmosphere' of pre-industrial society and its transition to industrialism in a way that has never been attempted before.

One necessity is for a 'model'. Unless one has <u>*some*</u> *idea of what one might find the clues are missed. Of course, the danger is that one will see what one is looking for and history will be merely a mirror as it has been so often before. Nevertheless, unless one has* <u>*some*</u> *problems and driving interests, the facts all have equal interest and it is impossible to select. I hope that anthropology will provide such a model – that is a theoretical outline of an agricultural society against which to compare C16-C17 England.*

Sorry, this sounds like a W.E.A. lecture but it does me good to get it all out of my system occasionally; thank yo for listening so patiently…

I wrote to Sir Anthony Wagner, Garter King of Arms, to inform him of my grant.

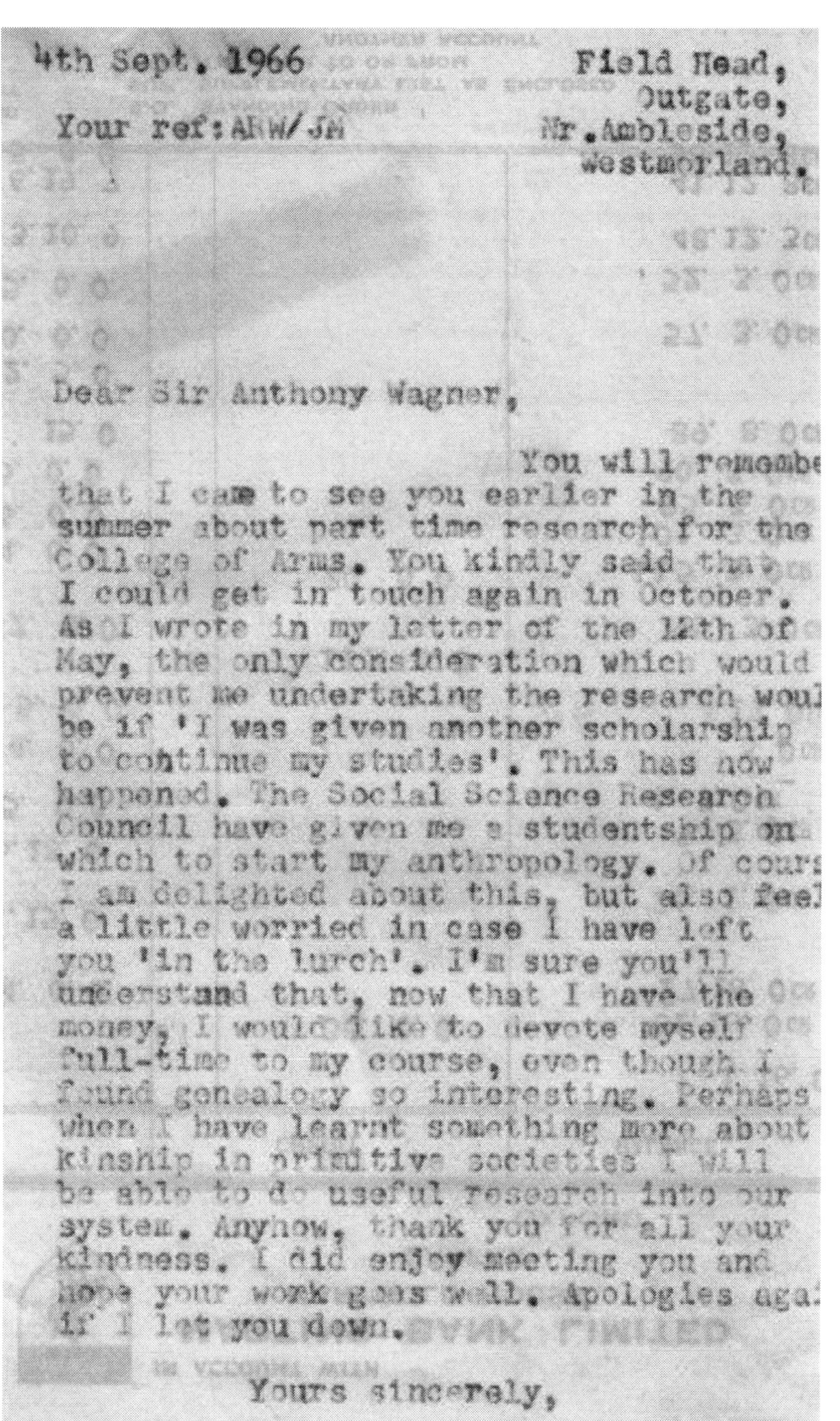

4th Sept. 1966

Field Head,
Outgate,
Nr. Ambleside,
Westmorland.

Your ref: ARW/JM

Dear Sir Anthony Wagner,

You will remembe[r] that I came to see you earlier in the summer about part time research for the College of Arms. You kindly said that I could get in touch again in October. As I wrote in my letter of the 12th of May, the only consideration which would prevent me undertaking the research woul[d] be if 'I was given another scholarship to continue my studies'. This has now happened. The Social Science Research Council have given me a studentship on which to start my anthropology. Of cours[e] I am delighted about this, but also feel a little worried in case I have left you 'in the lurch'. I'm sure you'll understand that, now that I have the money, I would like to devote myself full-time to my course, even though I found genealogy so interesting. Perhaps when I have learnt something more about kinship in primitive societies I will be able to do useful research into our system. Anyhow, thank you for all your kindness. I did enjoy meeting you and hope your work goes well. Apologies aga[in] if I let you down.

Yours sincerely,

I wrote to Hilda Grieve on 4th September 1966, from Field Head

Dear Hilda,

It seems a long time since I was last at the E.R.O. so just drop a line to let you hear how things are going. I hope to be able to get to Chelmsford more often from London next year and look forward to seeing yu all then. I wonder how your work is going? Does 'Chelmsford' inch towards the publishers, or are you still trying to untangle the late middle ages? I was most impressed by the map etc. when I was taken round Ingatestone.

My thesis goes quite well. The whole of the first draft is written and, though it needs fairly extensive modification and simplification, I see the end in sight. I should get it off to the typist by

December. My supervisor, Mr. Thomas, seems pleased. I have stuck my neck out and signed a contract with Routledge & Kegan Paul for a book on 'Tudor and Stuart Witchcraft' to be delivered by the end of next year. I am still proposing to do anthropology at the London School of Economics next year, to see if I can't save sociological history from the amateur hands of Laslett et. al. I have been fortunate enough (after a long tussle) to get a Social Science Research Council studentship for next year. Not exactly a vast amount – on a par with a State Studentship – but more than I ever hoped for and puts off my spare-time work in a coffee-bar for another year at least. I am still very grateful to you for the concern and active help you gave me in trying to find support. Garter was very nice and it was an experience meeting him, even if I'm not going to work for him. I'm also supplementing my income a little (only enough to get my thesis typed) by a term's lecturing (one day a week) at Nottingham university. ... you have all been terribly kind and also you, particularly, Hilda, have been one of the major inspirations of my thesis. I hope my acknowledgement will finally repay some of your labour. I imagine you will be too busy to read the proofs of the thesis, but very much look forward to your comments when it is finished....

I wrote to Keith Thomas on 5th September from Field Head

Dear Mr. Thomas,

I enclose an introduction and concluding chapter to the thesis – parts of each you have seen before but I've pruned desperately. If we could discuss these on my next visit to Oxford, probably in early Oct. that would be fine. I'm now in the process of re-writing and cutting down: very exhausting I find it.

Thank you for your suggestions re. the appendices. I agree that the cases should include a very brief summary. The trouble is that with about 1,000 cases to list I can't really allow myself more than 10 words per case – even that's 1/10th of the thesis space gone. When one has stated date, place, name, reference, verdict, there is little room left. Still, will see what I can do.

To Gill, 6. 9.1966 Field Head

Once again I've surrendered to the attraction of the comfortable sitting-room rather than the shed and the typewriter – so you'll have to excuse a scribbled letter, the fatal act was when Daddy put on one of your records, and it was too lovely to leave. Also, after 6 hours on the typewriter I'm quite glad to get away from it.

[poetic and melancholy descriptions of autumn]

I think I told you that Granny had had an haemorrhage and is now in hospital. She is/was having morphia & transfusion and they may have to operate. My parents , who were going to look for a croft today are staying till they hear what happens in case they have to go down to see her. They may leave here for Scotland on Friday or stay here he week-end.

… Revision of my thesis is enormously exhausting emotionally: hacking about one's own writing and reducing weeks and months of work to a few lines I find very harrowing; I'm glad to find that even K.V. Thomas admitted that he found it 'thick work' – i.e. exhausting. But I think the worst chapters (the first two I wrote) are nearly reshaped and considerably reduced and as I progress towards the chapter I wrote recently things should become easier. But it will definitely take me next term to finish writing/appendices/maps etc. which means I will have to have a room big enough to fit all my clobber into, even if there is nothing else in the flat except a bed… Anyhow, if I'm going to spend the major part of my time in London, I'll want to have my files etc. with me. Will you have a lot of things to take down? At least I won't have too many clothes!... I will be seeing you in three days (I hope)…

I heard from the Garter King of Arms.

From
Sir Anthony Wagner,
K.C.V.O., D.Litt,
Garter Principal King of Arms.

College of Arms,
Queen Victoria St, London E.C.4
Tel, City 4300.

AW/NN. 7th September 1966.

Alan Macfarlane, Esq.,
Field Head,
Outgate,
Nr. Ambleside,
WESTMORLAND.

Dear Mr Macfarlane,

Thank you for your letter of the 4th of September.

I must confess I am much disappointed at this news, since I was looking forward to working with you, and have kept the place for you, though there have been other applications, but of course I understand what has happened.

Have you ever been able to work out your relationship to M.R. James? I should like to know if so.

Yours sincerely,

A. R. Wagner

Garter King of Arms.

To Gill, 13.9.66 Field Head [Post-card]

Sorry to sound so depressed on the phone – I am feeling better now. I don't know why I was missing you particularly badly last night, but even poor old Erik, who kept trying to cheer me up with a continual flow of bright remarks, began to irritate me. … Now I'm back in my work schedule and making blackberry and apple mush and so I'm feeling better. Also, I've just heard from S.S.R.C., that they made a mistake about my grant – it should have been £500 for 2 years! Honestly isn't bureaucracy lousy! ... In two years we should be quite well off. Haven't heard anything from my parents yet.

[Gone croft-hunting in Scotland].

To Gill, 14.9.1966   Field Head

… Also, I enclose a proposed budget for next year. If you would like to make notes on it and send it back – or keep it and we can discuss it when I come down. We may have to be even severer that I've suggested… We've also our mutual overdrafts to pay off, and wedding/Christmas expenses. Oh well, I'm sure we'll manage. I also seem to have to support my sister (to whom I've got to send £5 this afternoon)… [Various discussion of possible budgeting in London].

Trevor-Roper's next letter alludes to a letter of mine which has been lost.

8 St Aldate's Oxford

TEL 47202

16. IX. 66

My dear Alan

You really must not mix *quite* so many metaphors! '... her acid pen cutting back the pompous growths...' Are pens acid? do pens, or acid, cut back? can growths be pompous? and ~~it~~ is pomposity cut back? If your thesis is written like this, and I examine, then alas, I shall fail you on literary grounds alone (as I would fail most of my Oxford colleagues). Alas for the English language! Will no one save it? Winston Churchill says that, at Harrow, he was taught the structure of an English sentence, 'which is a noble thing'. But now, I fear, such essential noble studies are overlooked: one must talk the fashionable jargon of sociology — especially, I fear, in St Johns — even if it is illiterate. The examiners in last year's History Schools reported that the candidates knew all about the social import of heresy but had not the faintest idea about the heresies themselves; and when I asked a graduate student whether he had no desire to write well rather than badly, clearly rather than obscurely, musically rather than ~~cacophonously~~, discordantly, pungently rather than obtusely, with lapidary brevity rather than with windy prolixity, he genuinely did not know what I meant. I find this very dispiriting.

But I must reassure myself. Occasionally one discovers, separable from the great mass of sinners, eternally doomed to literary perdition, a few Elect saints: an infinitesimal minority who nevertheless have not bowed the knee to that monstrous, faceless, formless Baal. Read the excellent front page article in the current TLS, on that Belgian fascist. It is by Cobb; who also wrote a brilliant piece on Furet et Richet and the _Annales_ (and, earlier still, an excellent character-sketch of Georges Lefèbvre in _Past & Present_). And perhaps there are others who, on the Great Day of Judgment, will be summoned before the Throne of Grace and pass smugly into that eternal bliss which (as the Fathers of the Church tell us) is enormously enhanced by the spectacle and sound of sinners cast down to eternal torment, and their wailing and gnashing of teeth.

Do come and see me next week. I am off to Scotland, via London, tomorrow, to lecture gravely on history in Glasgow and make a demagogic public speech in Galashiels. I return – if my plans hold – by the night-train on Saturday night and should be back here on Sunday afternoon. Telephone me on Sunday and I am sure [we] can find a time to meet: I would love to see you.

Do you know anyone who could gay up Oriel, _vice_ Gough? Are you still in love with Calcutta?

Yours ever Hugh Trevor-Roper

To Gill, Saturday 17.9.1966   Field Head

I love you. I could end the letter there, as I've now said everything I need to say and the essence of genius is simplicity etc. But a new ribbon on my typewriter, which makes everything stand out beautifully tempts me to go on making footprints of type on this virgin paper. … I'll be coming down within three days of you getting this. (Incidentally – just to show how certain I am that I will get you

in the end, and all that goes with you, I am not taking a carbon of this letter, since I will, no doubt, be filing all our letters away: in relation to this, you'll be interested to hear that my pea-size brain has thrown up one of its occasional bright ideas. I've designed a new filing system for record cards of any size. It involves the use of huge numbers of empty tomato boxes and I've spent the afternoon in Kendal collecting these. I reckon that on the 24 boxes I bought this afternoon (each costing 2d. and taking as many cards as 2 single-drawer filing cabinets at £2-2-0 each) I've saved nearly £100.
... Still talking about organization, I enclose a scrap on Critical Path Analysis. With the difficulties of moving shed I almost feel like investigating this further. Could you send this back in your next letter? Do you know anything about it? I'm getting interested in computers (a rather arrogant thing to say – perhaps it would be more proper to say 'computers are getting interested in me!' – I can just hear them chatting about me over their morning cup of diesel-oil 'almost as good a brain as a computer' they might say, 'pity about his memory, tho'. Still if they knew that I'd restarted doing the Memory Course for which I paid £8 at Oxford as an undergraduate and then gave up because it took too much effort away from Schools, they might take back the last remark. ...

Keep your eyes open for flats. I you could buy a newspaper or something like 'The Queen' or 'Dalton's Weekly' (the latter more likely) and make out a list of cheap places we could do a tour. [Travel down Thursday, flat-hunt, return north on Sunday with parents, following Thursday or Friday - finally go to London.]

I wrote to Lady Clay on 17th September 1966 from Field Head

Dear Lady Clay,

The letter I promised in my card – though it will be rather short I am afraid. My thesis is at its most fraying stage and after a day of appendices I don't feel like writing at all. Still, it cheers me so much to hear from you that I want to precipitate another letter by writing to you. It was nice to hear all your news. Hope the writing of your Elizabeth talk went O.K. It should be peanuts to you – except that you know too much. I've got to that stage with my thesis. What really exhausts me is having to discard so much information that has taken me months to extract, to summarize it all into a half-truth which I might have guessed at the beginning. I find it very difficult to be sure that I'm really doing anything worthwhile. One gets so close to the subject that it is impossible to decide whether one hasn't just buried oneself in some pile of silt at the bottom of an unimportant tributary to the historical stream – and other Trevor-Roper-like metaphors! (I have to eschew any colourful or high spirited writing in my thesis – so you'll have to beware muddy rhetoric in my letters) Anyhow, the main point is to say that I hope that September has restored your good humour, and that with the trees turning to the melancholy slaughter of autumn you feel revived. When my eyes blear open from their appendix-gummed state I vaguely notice leaves turning incredible reds and golds and the autumn beginning to toast the bracken. But even being in love isn't enough to raise me from my witches for more than a sniff of the Twentieth Century. Still, the thesis goes very well and I should have nearly half of it written in final form, and the rest in a fairly advanced draft by the time I go to London.

I think you know my plans. I have got a Social Science Research Council grant for the next two years (they made a mistake at first and told me it was only for one) – £500 p.a. Not much to live in London and keep a wife on – but I can hardly grumble having resigned myself to working as a lift-boy to keep myself. I really am excited at the prospect of learning something about social anthropology and sociology. I'm sure it will be a great help to my seventeenth-century studies. I would, finally, like to (among other things) do a study like that of Le Roy Ladurie reviewed in last week's T.L.S. – did you find his introductory essay intersting? I enclose draft chapter – it will have to be tightened up and cut down – on witchcraft in three Essex village. This is my first attempt at village sociology. I would very much value any comments – suggested sources or problems – you would care to make on it. Perhaps you could hold onto it until the beginning of October when I should be in Oxford and when I will collect it from you. Please don't bother to read it if you find it trying – rough chapters out of theses

must be most irritating to read – but having been launched into local history by your enthusiasm for Hoskins over 4 years ago, I would value your comments.
Hope to see you soon. Look after yourself.

I wrote to my sister Anne, who was living in France.

Sunday 18/9/66

Field Head,
Outgate,
Nr.Ambleside,
Westmorland.

Dear Annie,

I don't seem to have written for a long time, so here is little of my latest news. I expect you've heard most of it from Mummy. How are you? I think of you often and plow through the monster letters that are brought in wheelbarrows to field head. Glad you've made contacts in Paris; hope you'll manage to re-make them when you return from Cannes. Look forward to hearing about La Dolce Vita - probably turn out to be much like Waterhead on a sunny afternoon; crowds of over-fed, under-exercized, neurotic and anxiety-ridden families escaping from the towns and setting about trying to enjoy their leisure. Are there really masses of long-haired females in bikinis like Birgit Bardot ? Wonder if Erik contacted you before you left Paris, he said he was going to. Field Head must feel very distant.

My major news is Gill - whom you haven't even met and whom I am going to marry on 20th Dec. I know you'll like each other. Mummy has probably given you a pen picture so I won't add my enthusings. Anyhow, she's a poppet and bosses me around in a nice way. I'm annoyed that all my plans have been thrown out and that I've got to put my schedule forward five years, but still.....Am training her to analyse wills, touch-type, note books etc. so perhaps we'll make up lost ground ! I do hope you'll be back in plenty of time for the wedding. It is going to be delicious chaos. I have at least 250 people I want to invite and will be meanwhile finishing off my thesis in the shed. In fact Gill suggested that we had the honeymoon in the shed - which shows how well she knows me! Mummy will need help and I want you to be around; do come back as soon as you can. You'll have heard my other news also I expect; I,ve got a grant for another two years (£500 p.a.) to do anthropology at London and a book contract for the end of next year. So all your work on Hatfield Peverel, the Wilmotts etc. will be appearing before a startled public in not too long a time. I have several new filing systems now and the shed is filled with orange/tomato/cardboard/cornflake/cigarette and other boxes, as well as a new framework filing system which I don't think I had when you were here. Mummy is gamefully struggling away with archdeaconry records and I'm generally getting my egotistical way in all things. I hope to go down to London next week-end to get a flat in London and to visit Granny in hospital. I expect you've heard that she is recovering well. It'll be nice if we can find an attic somewhere as then you can come down to London and stay. I hope to be in the Lakes for the holidays, and the room will then be free. Still, musn't count my chickens.

Must back to my thesis appendices which are driving me bleary-eyed. Thinking of you. Have a happy autumn.

Lots of love,

I replied to Sir Anthony Wagner on the same day, drawing on my letter from my grandfather (reproduced above on 10th May).

18/9/66

Field Head,
Outgate,
Nr.Ambleside,
Westmorland.

Your ref: AW/NN

Dear Sir Anthony Wagner,

Thank you for your letter of the 7th of Septmeber. I'm sorry that I made you turn away applicants, but hope that you'll find someone to help you. I would have enjoyed working for you.

You asked for my relationship to M.R.James. It's more distant than I thought. I was misled by my uncle, Robert Rhodes James (whose just been writing in Observer Colour supplement on Winston Churchill in the '30's) who sometimes claims to be closely related. Anyhow, may I set out the relationship as explained to me by my grandfather, William Rhodes James, in a recent letter ?

leaving out the earliest, Jamaican, Rhodes James',

William Rhodes James m. Anne James

William Rhodes James m. Juliane Wisdom

William Rhodes James m. Rachel Jarrett

1) William Rhodes James m.a)Mary Kerr Brown.
b)Caroline Pope

2) Herbert Jarrett James m.Jane Caroline Vidal.

M.R.James is the son of Caroline Pope and my grandfather's(W.R.J) grandfather (W.R.J) is the son of Jane Caroline Vidal.

My grandfather got a letter in the trenches in 1915 from Mr Woods Woolaston suggesting that he register his pedigree.

P.T.O

To Gill, 19.9.1966 Field Head

I'm in the middle of packing up my files so please excuse just a couple of sentences of scrawl …[I quoted the following approvingly:

'The more books we read the clearer it becomes that the true function of a writer is to produce a masterpiece and that no other task is of any consequence. Obviously though this should be how few writers will admit it, or having drawn the conclusion will be prepared to lay aside the piece of iridescent mediocrity on which they have embarked! (Cyril Connolly, The Unquiet 'grave, p.1) …

I hope to get to your office by 5. 30 p.m. on Thursday perhaps you could buy all available local newspapers and those which more specifically advertise property?

During the late autumn I wrote rough drafts of the conclusion and introduction, which were revised considerably before the thesis was submitted. Writing these two chapters is always particularly tricky and has to be done when the body of the thesis has been completed. There was a second, formal, conclusion, which I may also have written in draft at this time. It is fifteen pages long and was annotated by Keith Thomas. The first page is as follows.

CONCLUSION: WITCHCRAFT IN A WIDER CONTEXT.

A study of Essex has shown that witchcraft prosecutions were far from peripheral to the life of villagers. Perkins wrote (because) 'witchcraft is a rife and common sinne in these our daies, and very many are intangled in it...'[1] and Gaule attacked the multitude who 'conclude peremptorily...that witches not only are, but are in every place, and Parish with them....'[2] These general impressions were echoed for Essex by Sam's remark in Gifford's Dialogue that 'there is scarce any town or village in all this shire, but there is one or two witches at the least in it.'[3] Some cases are listed in the appendices to this thesis, and detailed study suggests that this was less than one third of the actual suspected acts of witchcraft. From all records we know that witches were accused in of the 400 Essex villages during the period. At the peak period of accusation some 13% of all the cases occurring at the Assize court concerned this offence. A detailed study of all offences committed in three villages showed witchcraft to have been one of the most common charges. (Behind the formal accusations), the occasional glimpses afforded by the pamphlets suggest a background of complicated and widely held [set of] beliefs and activities related to witchcraft. Cunning folk and magical counter-action against witches absorbed much of the interest and time of villagers. It may well be asked whether Essex was exceptional in all this, or was the whole of England living in a world of witchcraft and magic, which has only escaped the notice of the historian because of his lack of interest in the subject? If Yorkshire in the later nineteenth century was saturated in witchcraft beliefs so that it was 'difficult to exaggerate the dimensions of that element of folklore'[4], how far was this true in the earlier period?

Conclusion: Notes.(1)

1. Perkins, Damned Art, p.1.
2. Gaule, Select Cases, p.4, v
3. Gifford, Dialogue, sig.A4
4. Atkinson, Moorland Parish, pp.73-4.

The first draft of the introduction was about 13 pages long and again annotated by Keith Thomas. This is the first page.

CHAPTER I **Introduction: definitions, sources, and problems.**

i. Definitions.

It is notoriously difficult to make definitions of the terms 'witchcraft','sorcery', and'magic'. Yet, since different uses of these words have caused many of the disagreements between historians of these subjects, it is essential that their meaning should be made clear.[1] This is especially important when the historian is forced to make analytical distinctions which were not made by members of the society in which such beliefs occurred. If it is generally true that,

> 'No social phenomenon can be adequately studied merely in the language and categories of thought in which the people among whom it is found, represent it to themselves', 2

this is especially the case when analysing witchcraft beliefs in sixteenth and seventeenth century England. Not only did different authorities define terms in incompatible ways, but definitions also varied over time. 'Witchcraft' meant something different in 1700 and in 1560. It meant different things to ordinary villagers and to literary authorities, ~~Terms were also used with a different connotation by ordinary villagers from the meaning ascribed to them by literary authorities~~, who often based their definitions on continental works of demonology. We shall, therefore, first discuss the definitions employed by modern students of witchcraft; then investigate how far contemporary Englishmen, that is to say those living in the sixteenth and seventeenth centuries, employed such distinctions in their discussions of the subject; finally, the meaning ascribed to various terms, for the purposes of this thesis, will be stated.

The classic distinction between witchcraft and sorcery in Africa was first outlined by Professor Evans-Pritchard in the following words.

> 'Azande believe that some people are witches and can injure them in virtue of an inherent quality. A witch performs no rite, utters no spell, and possesses no medicines. An act of witchcraft is a psychic act. They believe also that sorcerers may do them ill by performing magic rites with bad medicines.' 3

p.1

1. K.M.Briggs, Pale Hecate's Team(1962), p.3, discusses various definitions and suggests the effects of defining terms differently. Among other recent discussions are those of C.L.Ewen (Ewen I, pp.21-24) and G.Parrinder, Witchcraft (Pelican edn., 1958), pp.11-13.
2. G.Lienhardt, Social Anthropology (2nd edn., Oxford, 1966), p.123.
3. E.E.Evans-Pritchard, Witchcraft, Oracles and Magic among the Azande (Oxford, 1937), p.21.

Witchcraft - final writing up 1966-7

October 1966

To my parents from 44 Ridge Road, London 1st October 1966

Well, have arrived safely and am sitting comfortably, well fed, well-dressed and surrounded by acres of books and tables and files. Bliss! But I miss Field Heed and the Lakes all the same, and especially both of you. Thanks would be too paltry to express my debt to you both: but I really am terribly grateful for everything you have done for me from waking me every morning at 7 a.m. (or a bit later!) to cutting my hair; from providing delicious meals, to helping me so magnificently in my work. If my work ever comes to anything it will be in a large measure due to you. I will always remember this last year as one of my happiest. Before too lyrical, but really, thank you – it was wonderful. ..

I wrote to Keith Thomas on 2nd October from 44, Ridge Road, London, N.8, the flat to which we had just moved as I started my course at the London School of Economics.

Dear Mr. Thomas,

I wonder if I might see you to discuss the introductory and concluding chapters which I have sent? Also, I could bring down the appendices which are completed; in thesis condition, I hope. As you see, I am now established in London, and mail will reach me at the above address. I start at L.S.E. on Monday.

I intend coming up to Oxford on one of the next three week-ends... Will be interested to hear re. progress of the book etc and hope you've had a productive autumn and I look forward to seeing you,

Yours sincerely, Alan Macfarlane

The first was written to Paul Hyams, who had been reading history at Worcester with me as an undergraduate and had then gone on to get a Research Fellowship. We had shared tutorials in the last year, though he had done better with me and obtained a first.

Letter to Paul Hyams, Jesus College, Oxford on 3rd October, from 44, Ridge Road, London. N.8, , 3 October 1966

Dear Paul,

I have been meaning to write for ages, but now that I know that you must be back from Israel (how was it? exhilarating I hope), and in Oxford, I really have no excuse. Meeting you briefly in the street at the end of last term reminded me how much we had to say to each other. I was especially delighted to hear of your enthusiasm for anthropology, but more of that in a moment. First, news. How are things with you? ... What is it like to be a 'baby' don? I envy you in many ways. How goes the thesis? Are you writing any learned articles? If you ever have time, drop a line to the above address where I am now resident. I'd love to hear. My main news is engagement to Gill – the girl you met me with. You'll be getting a formal invitation to the wedding soon...

As I may have said, I'm just embarking on a 2-yr. Diploma in Social Anthropology at L.S.E. I started there yesterday. I've been fortunate enough to get a 2-yr. Social Science Research Council grant and, with Gill's grant/salary as a Probation Officer we should just scrape through. I'm doing a term's tutoring, one day a week, at Nottingham University, helping them out on European History from

1400-1700 – god help them! In my spare time (of which I seem to get a fair amount on this course – exams aren't until next year (1968)) I'm finishing the thesis – which has been written once, but parts of which have to be re-drafted and the bibliography made. Also I've got a contract to write a book on witches – but that hasn't got to be completed for over a year.

About anthropology: I would be interested to hear your views on its utility to historians. Have you a lot of ideas beyond Keith's article? Are you working on any particular lines. So far I've made a tentative study of suicide, of the religious/economic/kinship/social system in three Elizabethan villages –concentrating on crime and Puritanism; then there is witchcraft of course. I couldn't have started to study the subject if I hadn't had the works of anthropologists as a theoretical model. I'm now looking around for a subject for a short dissertation instead of 2 papers of my Diploma. My new supervisor, Prof. Schapera, suggested the historical study of incest regulations – with particular reference (of course!) to sixteenth-century Essex. As a starting-point for a general study of the relationships between religion and sex, e.g. of subjects such as the force of taboos, the sexual effects of the Reformation, the structure of kinships, and the methods of settling dispute in the church courts this might be worth investigation. Do you know of any studies for the middle ages? Do you think it would be possible to do such a study for your period? Beyond general remarks about the huge number of prohibited degrees in Holdsworth, Pollock & M et. al. I haven't come across much of use.

I think this brings up a subject of wider importance. Though I'm convinced that anthropology would provide a whole new range of subjects, as well as new ways of looking at old problems (e.g. millenarianism, the feud, feudalism etc.) I'm not sure that it is <u>really</u> possible in any period in English history before 1540, to do an ideal anthropological study. As I see it, the basic feature or contribution of modern anthropology is to show the relationships between normally separated fields of study – e.g. the economic significance of religious ritual, the emotional significance of legal proceedings, the social significance of each etc. Though broad studies are possible for medieval Europe – e.g. similar to Mauss, <u>The Gift</u> – I think Homans' attempt showed that the documents do not allow a detailed reconstruction of peasant/village life.

To interrelate, one must be able to study a group of people, e.g. a village, a manor or monastery, in <u>more than one</u> of its activities. One must be able to study <u>the same people</u> in, say, their religious activities, and their economic. Ideally a number of different sources should bear on the same person. Now, after 1540, or better still, after 1560, in ideal conditions, one can fill in at least 3 major portions of a villagers life – probably more. His religious from ecclesiastical court records, which (in Essex at any rate) show whether he attended church, his attitude to birth, death, marriage etc – and from wills: his social from the above and from the very extensive evidence to be found in parish registers, court records (partic. Assize and Quarter Sessions and Coroner's Inquisitions): his economic from various subsidy assessments and manorial records (the latter, contrary to popular fallacy, seem to me to be just as good for the C16 as they had been for earlier periods). Obviously there may be other good sources – churchwarden's accounts, Laslett-type listings etc. But the above are the main ones.

Now, I know that if I only had court records – and these diminished by the absence of quarter sessions rolls and, before the C14, ecclesiastical court records – and very occasionally instead of roughly decennial subsidy assessment; no wills; no parish registers; manorial records perhaps, I just couldn't have started to study, without huge distortion – or by using Homans' techniques of quoting C19 French evidence or evidence from other parts of the country – the <u>total</u> situation of my three villages. Even with all the evidence one has there are huge gaps – no real indication of attitudes except by using other things (e.g. suicide, illegitimacy, witchcraft) as indices. But at least it's possible. Do you think I'm being unfair on your period? I would like to be convinced, although, of course, I now have a vested interest in the Elizabethan period as the earliest period for which intensive rural sociology can be carried out. But perhaps I'm wrong.

I won't bore you with any more Paul. I will be in Oxford sometime this term and will try to look you up and perhaps we can discuss these further. Otherwise, perhaps I'll see you at that oldest of all anthropological get-togethers, the monogamous wedding where affines and agnates form a structurally

significant gathering to cement their kinship obligations and to re-orientate their social relationships, i.e. my wedding! From the borders of the realm of jargon and mystery I leave you... Have a good term.
Yours, Alan

I wrote to Keith Thomas on 5th October from Ridge Road.

Dear Mr Thomas,
Thank you for your note. yes, Saturday 15th at 2 p.m. at St Johns would be fine – I will meet you then unless I hear to the contrary. Incidentally, my new supervisor, Prof. Schapera, suggested as the title for a dissertation (to be submitted as part of my diploma – a year this coming March) 'Incest in C16-C17' Essex – how does that strike you? Perhaps you could make some suggestions re. reading – if there is any – when we meet?
Yours, Alan Macfarlane

To parents from 44, Ridge Road, 16th October 1966

... Oxford was as wonderful as ever... I saw Keith for a little over 2 hours – as usual it left me with a mixture of awe and depression and elation. He only made trifling criticisms of the two chapters I had given him and seems to think that I should not submit the thesis before the summer, but I'll see about that. he says his own book is at about the same stage as my thesis. Autumn in Oxford was most invigorating and it was reassuring to find so many people who remembered one. Incidentally I met Hilda Grieve, the head of the Essex Record Office, in London, and was sad to hear that she had retired from being supervisor. ...

1966 - November

I heard from Trevor Roper in a letter dated 5th November.

My dear Alan,

How is your work at Nottingham?... I don't suppose that you have time to visit Oxford. But if you do, I hope I shall see you...

You tell me that you have signed a contract with Routledge for a book on witches. I hope it was a good contract, and that you are not going to be mulcted by Michael Hurst, who has contrived to interpose himself between author and publisher in other cases.... I have completed and sent in my huge essay on that subject: 30,000 words I fear. I don't think we shall compete. You nibble at the Essex grass-roots: I float in the stratosphere, surveying, through iridescent, distorting mists, the slowly revolving globe from china to Peru, or at least from Constantinople to Glasgow. ... If you really want to see my essay – though I assure you that it will teach you nothing and you will probably dissent, pricking my iridescent, aerated soap-bubbles with your whetted witch-needle – of course you may. the trouble is that it is so chaotic: I doubt if I have a readable copy. But I suppose that in due course I shall have a proof.

Yours ever, Hugh Trevor-Roper

I wrote back to Trevor-Roper on 13th November, from Ridge Road

Dear Professor Trevor-Roper,
.... The thesis progresses though I fear that it will not be completely finished and ready for submission until my final statutory term – next Summer. Doing anthropology and growing older has rather disturbing effects on my previous thoughts and I keep reshaping the whole structure of the thesis – which is rather fatal at this stage. Perhaps I can write it as I want it in the book. No, I'm not under

Michael Hurst's aegis – I think he is editor of the Political History series and I was intending to join the social history series – but Routledge have suggested that I would get better treatments in America if I publish as a semi-general book outside a series. The whole publishing world is, of course, a strange jungle to me and the mysterious creatures that roam there, emitting weird prehistoric cries, are still to be identified. Any help you can give me in the way of advice from your own experience is gratefully received.

I'm glad the witchcraft essay is off to press. You must have done a lot of work up in Scotland. Yes, I don't think we'll overlap much, but when you do have a proof I'd like to see it if this would be alright. I will be in Oxford next Sunday and Monday (20th, 21st) and if you are free at all on either occasion would like to call in. I'm giving a talk to the Habakkuk/Thirsk seminar on at 5 p.m. on Monday...

To Trevor-Roper, from 44, Ridge Road, 22nd November 1966

Dear Professor Trevor-Roper,

Thank you so much for tea and sympathy on Sunday. I enjoyed, as always, hearing anecdotes of the great whom I have never met. I'm writing now to ask whether you really do think it would be worth my trying for the Oriel fellowship? Considering that I have not published anything, being intent on hoarding intellectual capital, and that I will need another year to finish my course at L.S.E. – as far as I am concerned an essential condition – do you think I've still a chance? Of course you can't make predictions, but if you <u>*do*</u> *consider it worthwhile I've decided to postpone Calcutta. I haven't seen the Oriel post advertized anywhere, so if you think it worth a try, perhaps you could let me know to whom I should make application?*

My talk to Thirsk's seminar went without too many eruptions, though I could scarcely see some of the other students at the vast green baize table at All Souls.

I look forward to your advice on the above. Thanks again for hospitality, please thank Lady Alexandra for me,

Yours sincerely,

Alan Macfarlane

From Trevor-Roper, 25th November, 1966

My dear Alan,

Thank you very much for your letter. I did not answer it till I had had an opportunity of making enquiries in Oriel, which I have now done. The answer is that certainly an application from you would be accepted, even though you might make it clear that, if elected, would could not take the post for a year. Other things being equal, they would certainly prefer someone who could come next year, but if you were thought to be the best candidate an arrangement could no doubt be made. So this proviso should not deter you from applying if you want to do so.

I do not think that you should be deterred by that fact that you have not published anything. Otherwise will not doubt be in the same position. But you should of course have a testimonial from your supervisor who has seen what you have written for your thesis. I will certainly be pleased to help you in any way I can.

So in answer to your question. I do think that you have a chance. You should apply in writing to the Provost. Theoretically the closing date for the application is tomorrow, but this will not matter if you apply fairly soon. You should write to the Provost saying that you have heard that they have advertised the post and that you would like to be considered, and you should give an account of your career and the names of two referees, one of whom should be your supervisor. Perhaps the other one should be someone from Worcester College. I will be on the committee, so I can speak for you there without the necessity of a formal reference.

So I hope you will apply if you have decided that you will not blame yourself afterward for postponing Calcutta!

Yours ever,

P.S. I have followed your advice and written to Charles Phythian-Adams too.

Letter to Erik, from 44, Ridge Road on 26th November 1966

.... Half of me yearns to get buried in piles of old manuscripts and books with their distinctive smell, and to spend the rest of my life there. This is really what I do in London actually. The world of witches and the sixteenth century is much more real to me than the present; magic more important than moving staircases; tubes less noticed than the strange cavorts of my sixteenth century villagers. ... Last week-end I went to Oxford to give my long-dreaded talk to a history seminar at All Souls... I had tea with Trevor-Roper (Prof. of history) and he made some rather tempting suggestions job-wise which I'll say more about if they come to anything. Next day I met my other likely examiner, Prof. Evans-Pritchard. He's a real sweetie, just my idea of the absent-minded, dishevelled, shrewd and highly distinguished Professor. He's one of the few people I've met whom one could say definitely 'This is a great man – possibly a genius'. He's one of the two greatest social anthropologists produced by Britain this century – with Malinowski; almost on a par with Weber and Durkheim. ... I'm also writing about a chapter a week of my thesis. Today I finished a chapter which once excited me very much – showing that there was a widespread organization of witch-doctors in Elizabethan village, plotting where they lived, how far their clients came etc. Should throw a cat among the historical pigeons. ...

From Trevor-Roper, 27th November 1966

My dear Alan,

I wonder if you are applying to Oriel or not.

I now know a bit more about the field. As often happens, a flood of last-minute applications has strengthened it. There are (in a total field of 28, 9 of whom I regards as non-starters) 8 candidates in your position – i.e. who have not yet taken the degree of D.Phil or published anything; so you would not be at all exceptional. On the other hand there are some fairly formidable candidates too. So I think that your chances, though as good as any of the 8, are diminished by these last-minute heavyweights.

I have absolutely no idea what the Fellows of Oriel really want for the college. I know what I want – someone fairly young who will help to revitalise the place. But perhaps they don't want to be revitalised: perhaps they will prefer one of the applicants who is aged 60 and who, having spent a roving life in business and journalism, sees Oriel as a place of rest... They may dislike this excellent candidate's Left-wing views, that candidate's Methodism, another's field, another's age. So, as they are more numerous than I, they will – if they agree among themselves – prevail, and at present I regard the issue as entirely open. I do not suppose that the strongest candidate will necessarily win!

In these circumstances you must be guided entirely by your own view of your own interest. The one thing which makes me pause in urging you to apply is not any question of the result – that is the luck of the game – but the last remark that you made on leaving my house: that if you were to apply and succeed, you would – or might – blame yourself afterwards for having been diverted into an easy course. I don't want to be the cause of your self-reproach!

Yours ever,

Hugh Trevor-Roper

To the Provost of Oriel College, Oxford, from 44, Ridge Road, on 29th November 1966

Dear Provost,

I have heard that Oriel College will be electing a new Fellow in Modern History shortly and I wonder if I could apply for this post? I am sorry to be late in applying, but I have only just discovered that the Fellowship is open.

I read History at Worcester College and took a 2nd (viva for a 1st.) in Trinity term 1963. Since then I have been working for a D.Phil. on the subject 'Witchcraft prosecutions in Essex, 1560-1690; a sociological analysis' under Mr. Keith Thomas of St. John's College, Oxford. I hope to submit the thesis in Trinity term 1967, the last term before an extension is needed. Meanwhile, I have started a two-year Postgraduate Academic Diploma in Social Anthropology at the London School of Economics; I am being financed on this by the Social Science Research Council. My teaching experience is limited; I took some tutorials on sixteenth and seventeenth century English history for Hertford College in 1965; I gave a course of 24 lectures for the Oxford Delegacy of Extra-Mural Studies in 1964-1965 – on the same subject; at the moment, concurrent with anthropology, I am doing three essay classes a week at Nottingham University (on the same period in European history). As you can see, my special interest is in the sixteenth and seventeenth centuries; as an undergraduate I did the economic documents paper on this period and the 'Cromwell' special subject (under Dr. Gough of your college).

If I were elected I would only be able to take up the Fellowship at the end of my anthropology diploma, i.e. in October 1968. naturally, if this occurred and there were teaching problems I would help in any way I could. I do feel, however, that it is important for me to complete my present course. I do hope this does not debar me.

I have asked Mr. Keith Thomas of St. John's College and Mr. Harry Pitt (of Worcester College, my tutor as an undergraduate) to act as my referees.

Yours sincerely,

Alan Macfarlane

To Harry Pitt, from 44, Ridge Road, 29th November 1966

Dear Harry,

So sorry to miss you last but one week-end, but terribly pleased to hear you (and Keith) are coming to the wedding. I very much look forward to seeing you then. If you want directions (though you've been there before, of course) or possible accomodation etc. do let me know. Theoretically, however, it has been arranged so that one can get there and back in a day. (Gill and I will be wearing suits – so dress is optional).

I'm mainly writing this note to ask if I may, once again, quote you as a referee? It's been suggested to me that I try for the forthcoming fellowship in Modern History at Oriel College and though I think I'm an outsider with a very slender chance there is nothing to lose. They may debar me altogether since I've stipulated that I want to finish my anthropology – which only leaves me free in Oct. 1968. But, if they consider me I would be most grateful if I could use your name? Please say if for any reason you would prefer not to do this, however.

Anthropology/thesis/Nottingham etc. are going well. Gill is reading Middlemarch with vast enthusiasm. Hope term ends well.

Regards to Alec and James,

Yours ever,

To Trevor-Roper on 29th November, from 44, Ridge Road, London, N.8

Dear Professor Trevor-Roper,

Thank you very much for your letter which I have just received on my return from Nottingham. I've taken the plunge and written to the Provost of Oriel. Thank you very much also for the offer of your far from inconsiderable support; without it I don't think it would have been worth my while applying. More than your support, however, I value your continued interest.

I will keep you informed as to developments at my end, though you'll no doubt be far better informed than I am.

Incidentally, I came across a reference to an E.C. Trevor-Roper in a family bible of my grandmother's – next to it was written 'Aug.16' – she was apparently the daughter of Maria Hockin Stirling, and related to Admiral Hockin and the Earl of Glencairn. (My mother's mother is a Swinhoe.) Wonder if all this connects up on your side?

Thank you again for taking so much trouble.

P.S. I have just received your second letter; once again thank you for spending your very valuable time on writing. As you say/imply, my chances are very slim. I think they were from the start, actually, as I can't see them wanting a budding social historian with a definite leaning towards such heretics as Weber and Durkheim. Still, I think I'll still apply; it'll be good practice seen at the lowest level and I always enjoy an excuse to visit Oxford. Also I may learn a few more details about that fascinating field for anthropological study, the tribal groves of academia. I must say I feel rather relieved that the conflict in which I found myself at first – between Oxford and Calcutta – is more or less resolved. I won't feel as I bind leper's sores that I missed a wonderful opportunity. It's very difficult. I love Oxford, and I love history; but I'm also young and idealistic and convinced that I'd be a beter don and person after a few years among <u>*real*</u> *peasants, instead of the romantic creations of Hoskins et. al.*

Still I mustn't' waste your time with rambling. Though defeated in theory, I look forward to the contest. I think the only possible line is to stress my apparent weakness – i.e. my intention to shake history up a little by applying other insights to it.

Thank you for your concern.

I wrote to Keith Thomas on 29th November from Ridge Road

Dear Mr. Thomas,

Thank you for your moral and verbal support at the seminar the other Monday. Hope I didn't expose too many flanks to the enemy. I'm <u>*delighted*</u> *that you can come to the wedding; Harry Pitt has a deep suspicion of the North of England, so don't be dissuaded by mountain mist etc too easily. We're getting married in suits – so dress is optional. I'll alert all the second-hand book dealers in the district!*

I'm really writing to ask if I can again make use of your kind offer to act as a referee. I'm trying a long shot and applying for a fellowship at Oriel College when Gough leaves. They may debar me before I start since I won't have ended my anthropology until 1968, but there doesn't seem to be anything to lose. As you know I have the backing of Miss Trollope[1] *I would be* <u>*most*</u> *grateful, if the application comes to anything, if you could write me a testimonial or whatever they need. I do hope this is alright by you.*

I haven't been sending you chunks of the thesis since I think it will be best, as you suggested, if I give you the completed, checked, version; this should be ready in March. I'm doing about a chapter a week – but all my naive assumptions are being rather shaken up by anthropology.

Hope all your work goes well.
Yours, Alan Macfarlane

I also wrote to Ian Campbell. I had last written to him at the start of my doctorate, in January 1964, so this letter written just after I finished at Oxford takes my story on from there. The letter is a carbon and not dated, but appears to be in late November.

Dear Ian,

---

[1] Hugh Trevor-Roper's pseudonym in a correspondence with Lawrence Stone in the New York Review of Books.

Please excuse a typed letter – but you will probably be so surprised (guilty? - for no reason) to hear from me that you'll overlook attempted efficiency. It is literally years since I've written. What prompts me now, apart from the usual Christmas sentiments, is partly curiosity to hear how you are getting on, partly that this seems to be more or less a turning point in my life and I thought I'd let you know my news. Anyhow, Ian I hope everything goes well with you.... Are you married? How is Pat?....

As regards Sedbergh friends – to get the old school tie out of the way first. I met Charles Vignoles with his wife in Oxford the other day – they are both teaching. Geoffrey I think has gone into the Borstal service. David Porter I still see occasionally – he is a fully-fledged solicitor in his father's firm, has a red sports car, is pursuing a girl and is generally contented. Stuart Black was up here the other day – he wants to work on yachts and was looking very natty in polo-necked jersey etc. He is going out with Gill L. – one of my first flames if you remember. Alan Barnes is in Australia; David Badger was killed in a motor-bike accident; Weedy Savory was up – he is working in the armaments division of the Civil Service and still spends most of his time killing animals and birds. Well, I don't want this to sound like the Old Boys sections in the Luptonian, so will end. Incidentally, I expect you'll have heard that Marriot is leaving this year and Dave Alban becoming house master of Lupton. At least the cooking should be better if the story about him marrying the Hart House cook is true!

About myself. I haven't quite forsaken my dreams and ideals of my youth, though they become narrowed. I've just finished three years doing a doctorate at Oxford on the history of witchcraft – which I think I must have told you of. The thesis will need another couple of months to finish and I will submit it early next year. It has led me into weird crevices of the human should and I have got interested in a host of sociological and psychological problems. I have signed a contract to turn the thesis into a book next year – and if this happens it is going to be printed in America, so keep your eyes open in the bookshops in about 18 months' time! I spent last year at home, working in the garden shed at the bottom of the garden which I fitted up with lights, heating, filing cabinets, my own invented form of a lateral suspended filing system, microfilm projector, tape recorder etc. I even got my sister (Anne) to work as my secretary/help for a small salary and my parents – who have retired from India – to help part-time analysing mortality rates etc. in the sixteenth century. It was most exciting and I think, if I have time to finish the work, I will have made quite a break-through both in history and sociology. Anyhow the year was well spent, but now my life has changed radically. With my yearning to go to India, I decided that I should do some training in anthropology, so I am now at the London School of Economics doing a 2-year diploma in Soc. Anthropology.

This is, of course, only putting off the evil hour of decision. I'm still planning to go to India, if only for a couple of years, to see what there is to be done. I think population problems will be my final resting place, but in what capacity I don't know. But I'm also very attracted by the academic life and have a desire to become a Professor at some beautiful tree-shaded old city like Oxford. Anyhow, anthropology is fascinating – among the most fascinating peoples I study being the Kwaktiuls (?) and other tribes around Vancouver Island!

I've saved my most important news until last – this being the reason above all, for this letter. I'm getting married on my birthday Dec. 20th. The wedding is at Hawkshead parish church – I'm not sending an invitation as there isn't much likelihood of your being able to attend and I don't want to cadge a present. But think of me! ....

This letter will also have to serve as a Christmas card, so VERY HAPPY CHRISTMAS and also HAPPY BIRTHDAY on 16th Dec. All happiness in what you are doing.

Yrs. ever, Alan

December 1966

St John's college, Oxford, 1 December 1966 Keith to Alan

Dear Alan,

Many thanks for your letter. I thought your paper was admirably delivered, and I should like to discuss its implications with you some time. Keep the thesis until you have completely checked it all, if you like, but do leave time for any minor alterations if you want to make them after my comment! I take it that you now plan to submit it the end of Trinity term.

As for the Oriel Fellowship, I hadn't ever realised that you had the academic life in mind, as I had always thought you intended to go back to India....

To parents from 44 Ridge Road, 2nd December 1966

... I don't seem to have done much else but work recently. I want to get the thesis as nearly completed as possible by Christmas and I am hammering away at it. It's a grisly business dissecting and surgically cutting away great chunks which were so lovingly nurtured. Still I hope it will read better. I've got about 2.3 of the way through which is better than I had hoped. This leaves little time for anthropology, unfortunately. ..

6th December 1966 44, Ridge Road, London, Alan to Keith

Dear Mr. Thomas,

Thank you very much for your letter and for writing to Oriel. I do hope I haven't put you in an awkward position. Of course, Brian Harrison would be a much better bet for Oriel and I would be very happy to 'lose' to someone from whom I have learnt the rudiments of filing system techniques. I'm still set on India, actually, and am prowling round the School of Oriental Studies sniffing for grants, but the Oriel fellowship, at one time, looked a golden opportunity. T-R suggested that I tried for it when the field was light, but it has thickened and I am pretty well resigned. But I won't, I hope, be pestering you for too many references for a while.

Yes, I'll try to give yu as much time as possible to correct the thesis. I will, I hope, be submit it at the end of the Trinity term.

I've managed to persuade Schapera to broaden the 'incest' dissertation a bit – I may now cover kinship and marriage in my three Essex villages a bit.

From Trevor-Roper, Oriel College, 12th December 1966

My dear Alan,

Alas, I have to tell you that although you reached the semi-finals, you have not reached the finals, in the contest for the dubious honour of succession to Gough at Oriel. I am very sorry, and feel slightly guilty, having encouraged you to enter; but with necessity, as Simonides (I think) says, even the Gods cannot contend; and today, at our second meeting, when we reduced the list to the last five candidates, it was clearly impossible to go further in support of one who, for good reasons, could not have taken up the post for another year.

I should explain that, when I first made the suggestion to you, I had just had an agonised appeal from Christopher Seton-Watson who told me that the field was very poor and that the only possible candidate was one X (whom I knew and thought impossible); and he therefore begged me to encourage applications. But at the very last minute there was a rush of heavyweights which made the issue very different: hence my shamefaced second letter. On seeing the final list, I very much doubted whether you had any chance; but as no battle is lost till it has been fought, I didn't despair. However, as I say, today's vote put you out, and I hope you will forgive me for having persuaded you to expose yourself to this honourable defeat. Allow me to console you (if it is any consolation) by saying that it is a defeat which everyone has (I think I incurred it three times), and that you are in good company among your own contemporaries.

Who Oriel will choose, I do not know. If you saw the elector, you would realise that anything might happen. At times I have almost thought of entering Agnes Trollope. There might be difficulty about her sex, and when it came to an interview, but I would still give her even odds if she had good referees, such as could no doubt be found in Westmorland, or even in the B.M.

I hope you will take this, as you seem to take everything, in good spirit, and that I shall be a better adviser, and a more effective patron, in some later battle.

Thank you very much for your Xmas card.

Yours ever,

Hugh Trevor-Roper

Letter to the Provost of Oriel, from 44, Ridge Road, 13th December 1966

Dear Provost,

I wrote to you some two weeks ago asking if I might apply for election to a Fellowship in Modern History when Dr Gough retires. I gather that one of my referees, Mr. Thomas, has heard from you, but since I have not had a confirmation of my letter, or any correspondence from you, I wondered if a letter had gone astray. I will be leaving London for three weeks on the 17th December, after which date all mail will be delayed. I am writing all this in case you have written to me and are wondering why I have not replied. If this is not the case, please ignore this letter.

I look forward to hearing from you at some point.

Yours sincerely,

Alan Macfarlane

From the Vice-Provost of Oriel College, 14th December 1966

Dear Mr. Macfarlane,

I thought it best to let you know at once that, after giving your application the most careful consideration, in a very strong field, our committee has decided not to include your name in the short list for candidates for the history fellowship.

Thank you for letting us consider you for this appointment.

Yours sincerely,

C. Seton-Watson

To Trevor Roper, from 44, Ridge Road, on 15th December 1966

Dear Professor Trevor-Roper,

Thank you for your most kind letter; it, alone, made my attempt at the Oriel Fellowship worthwhile. Thank you, also, for all your help and encouragement. At this stage in my career the important thing for me is not to succeed, or find some cosy nest, but rather to feel that someone is interested in what I am doing. It therefore not only brightened a few grey London weeks to feel that, however remote, I might one day return to the polished tables of Academia, but also gave me great pleasure to feel that you had some confidence in my abilities. This makes me sound very dejected and alone. Actually, if anything, I am over brimming witch (sic) confidence and am conceited enough to think that one day Oriel will regret their decision. On the evidence before them, however, they were, of course, right. As I said in a previous letter, the present method has at least taken the decision off my shoulders. I do hope your pessimistic fears concerning the abilities of the electors prove false and a reasonable man is chosen. Actually, I have a friend, far more experienced and competent than myself, who has also entered. If he succeeds I shall rejoice, since he has helped me often; if he fails I will be in very good company indeed.

I am leaving London for the Lakes tomorrow. My mind is slightly distracted from witches for I marry in 5 days – on my 25th birthday. I think I must have told you already: the girl is the one who fell up your stairs on one occasion. I am not really in a fit state of spiritual preparation to get married – as you can judge from the fact that I suggested 'Luther's Hymn', 'Jerusalem' and 'Hark the Herald

Angels...' as appropriate for the wedding service. The tone of gentle disapproval which the vicar's letter conveyed was superb! Miss Trollope, if not running her basset hounds with the Coniston foxhounds, will surely be among the confetti-sprinklers...

Thank you again for all the time and trouble you have taken, especially re. Oriel. I look forward to seeing you next term, when I will call in if I may.

Yours sincerely

Keith Thomas and Harry Pitt came to the wedding in Hawkshead Church on 20th December.

All from left:
top row - Father, Gill's father, Lesley (Gill's best woman)
middle row - mother, Gill's mother
front row - grandmother Violet, Gill, Alan

27. 12. 66 St John's College, Oxford Keith to Alan

Dear Alan,

Harry and I thoroughly enjoyed our trip to the Lake District. It was a very nice wedding, and I hope you had a good Christmas honeymoon. This is just to say that my wedding present turns out to be too big for the post (don't get excited; it's very dull), and I shall therefore hold on to it until you appear in Oxford. Let me know when you are coming, and bring Gill if possible. Valerie and I would like it very much if you could both have supper with us. Yours, Keith

Trevor-Roper wrote on 30th December 1966 from Chiefswood, Melrose, Scotland

My dear Alan,

Many thanks for your letter: it is very kind of you to accept my bungling attempt at Oriel so charitably and I admire your equanimity. Your letter arrived on what I deduced to be your wedding-day, viz on 20 Dec; so I looked desperately around for a wedding present, but these rural solitudes are not the best place to look. I ended up by looking in my own shelves, only to decide that half my books here are too dear to me to give, and the other half too unworthy to be received. so you must accept this letter in lieu, at least as an interim contribution, and I shall hope, later, in a more favourable milieu, to find a more appropriate offering. Meanwhile, I send you my best wishes, or, as you would say, to judge from the Freudian lapse in your letter, my best witches. As for the Fellows of Oriel, I hope that they will regret their decision more than you do. I think that perhaps it was anyway the wrong thing for you; whether it is wrong for them will depend, to some extent, on whom they do choose. I think I can identify your friend. Anyhow the great thing is that you don't seem too upset by the affair, and I hope that will find the place that you want: to which if I can help you, I shall be very self-satisfied, having, as I do, great confidence in you. .... I greatly look forward to seeing the result of your work. Do take some trouble to write it in beautiful, lucid, lapidary English prose. No subject is so arcane or so rebarbative, so technical or so trivial, that it does not deserve that trouble, and if we take no trouble to write, why should anyone take the trouble to read us? ...

Final Writing Up: 1967

January 1967

I wrote to Keith Thomas on 9th January from 44, Ridge Road

Dear Mr. Thomas,

Thank you for your note. I'm so glad you enjoyed the wedding; I was delighted that you were able to come. May I take you up on your kind invitation to supper? Gill and I be coming down to Oxford for either 28-29 Jan or 4-5 Feb. and wondered if any of these four evenings suit? Otherwise, we will be coming down later in the term. Perhaps, also, you would have time to talk witchcraft on one of these days? I'm not sending you anything more until the thesis is quite finished, but there are a number of problems I would like your advice on you said that there were a few points in my talk which you'd like to discuss. I could also collect the appendices I left with you.

I think you mentioned that you would be holding seminars at Oxford this term, similar to those last year. I wonder if you could possibly send me the time & date &, if possible, subject/speaker, as, with your permission, I would very much like to attend one or two if I can get away from L.S.E. The historical seminars at London University, under Bindoff and Neale, are dreadful & there seems to be nothing stimulating here.

Hope the book progresses,

Yours, Alan Macfarlane

P.S. You'll have heard my fate at Oriel: thanks for your trouble, anyhow.

Keith Thomas wrote back on 10th January 1967

Dear Alan, Many thanks for your letter. It would be very nice if you and Gill could come to supper with us on Saturday 28 January, at 7.30. I do hope you can come (we are not free the following weekend). We could even talk about witchcraft after dinner if that wasn't too barbarous: I only had one or two points, and they needn't take more than 5 minutes. Alternatively we could arrange something else when you come.

Here's the programme for the class this term. You'll see there's still one blank date, which I shall have to fill myself unless I get a bid from someone. Any offers?

I hadn't heard from Oriel, but I'm sorry, and I hope you won't be discouraged. Yours, Keith

I wrote to Keith Thomas on 13th January from 44, Ridge Road

Dear Mr. Thomas,

Thank you very much for your letter and the programme. yes, Gill and I would love to come to supper on Sat. 28 January at 7.30 p.m; I look forward to seeing you then and having a short chat about witchcraft afterwards.

I'd be delighted to read a paper if you still haven't got anyone for February 21st, though I imagine you have plenty up your sleeve. Actually what I really want to hear is your paper on 'Suicide' which we missed last year. If you would like me to do something – and I think witchcraft has been rather flogged at the seminar level – I could do something along the same lines as Ralph Houlbrooke, i.e. on marriage. As you know, I'm doing work for a dissertation on incest and marriage prohibitions in the period combined with a discussion on the anthropological approach to marriage and kinship and examples from the Essex records and my study of three villages it this be of interest. I'll quite understand, however, if you feel that one session on marriage is enough. If possible, I'd like to come to the sessions on Feb. 7 and Feb. 14. If you would like something on marriage, perhaps you could think of a title – something on the lines of 'Incest and marriage in Elizabethan society'.

Hope the term goes well.

Yours sincerely, Alan Macfarlane

P.S. I have a lot of material on sexual matters in the sixteenth century – illegitimacy, prostitution, buggery, rape, pre-marital intercourse, and obscenity etc. If you think this is not too frivolous I could do something on 'Incest and sexual offences in the C16' rather than marriage....

Keith Thomas wrote on 14th January from St John's College, Oxford

Dear Alan,

Many thanks for your letter. It was splendid of you to be so ready to help with the seminar and I should have jumped at your offer, which sounded most appetising. Unfortunately I was rung up only yesterday by Anne Whiteman with a quit unsolicited suggestion, which you'll see enclosed. It is an interesting subject on which she says she has some new material and I readily accepted, never dreaming that you would have time to help me as well as do your London work. Anyway I hope we can lay your paper on a future occasion. Meanwhile we both look forward very much to 28 Jan.

With many thanks, Yrs, Keith

To parents from 44 Ridge Road, 15th January 1967

... I will also, if I may, send the carbon of my thesis by registered post. If you could possibly correct the worse errors of grammar and spelling, I would be terribly grateful. That will probably be in a couple of weeks or so. I will send full instructions....

I wrote to Trevor-Roper on 15th January from 44, Ridge Road

Dear Professor Trevor-Roper,

How very nice to get your long and most entertaining letter. I regaled my family with it, as usual – good for my prestige, and a pleasure for them. I was very touched by the kind things you said; as I've said before, for a struggling graduate in the no-man's land between University and an academic trench, it is most comforting to know that the generals are interested (o.k metaphors?). I will take to heart your advice re. style, though I'm afraid it's a little (late) for my thesis which is now completed. I shall have to check the footnotes, draw maps, and compile the bibliography, but the text, thank God, is finished. I feel very much in sympathy with Francis Hutchinson when he wrote about witchcraft:

'As the very Nature of the Subject carries both Horror and Difficulty, polite Men, and great Lovers of Ease, will turn away their thought from it with Disdain' (Historical Essay, 1718, p.vii)

perhaps it is just writing a thesis that is exhausting, but I think I chose a neurotic subject. Still, it was very fascinating, and I don't regret the choice at all. I'm looking forward very much to seeing your essay on the subject: did you find it a particularly difficult topic? Still, you seem to glide through amazingly intricate tangles with enormous ease; I couldn't <u>begin</u> to write books on either Hitler or Medieval Europe. After four years I still feel I know hardly anything about witchcraft in one county. This probably sounds timid to the extreme; an acute example of the academic fear of being contradicted. I expect it is, but what is the cure? Also, what is the cure for the jargon mania? I agree absolutely that it is intensely annoying to be faced with whole sentences which appear to mean nothing, as I constantly am as an anthropologist, but I see little hope of avoiding some technical terms. For instance, I couldn't, as an anthropologist, avoid using terms like 'agnatic', 'affinal', 'matrilineal', 'sibling', if I was discussing kinship in Elizabethan society, merely because it would take far longer to describe anything if I did. Where does one draw the line? When a word has already been coined? Is it jargonistic to talk *of status, social mobility, projection etc.? I didn't want to get off onto this tack – but [if] you know of any good rule by which one can avoid jargon I would be eternally obliged. ...*

I won't drivel on any longer since you must be very busy indeed. Talking of work – I wonder if you could tell me, since you may be intimately concerned, how long examiners like to have in which to read a thesis? Obviously, the longer the better, but what would be a reasonable time?

I do hope that we will be able to meet soon. May I wish you a very rewarding term, free from trouble from those you have etc. Thank you again for your generous letter.

Yours sincerely,

Trevor-Roper wrote to me on 22nd January from 8 St Aldate's Oxford[1]

My dear Alan,

Thank you very much for your letter. I am so glad that your thesis is finished. I agree with you and Francis Hutchinson about witchcraft – in fact I nearly used Francis Hutchinson's phrase as an epigraph to my essay, which is now in proof. It is a depressing subject; and yet if the 'horror' depresses, the 'difficulty' attracts. I am so glad to have tackled it. I hope I have said something new about it. I am sure you have, and I shall be interested to see whether your well-timed thesis has blown up my airy generalisations. I hope not. I assure you that it is no very admirable quality that takes me into these tangled thickets. As Dr Johnson retorted to Boswell, who credited him with 'courage' for going 'sliding in Ch Ch meadow' when he should have been waiting on his tutor in Pembroke College, 'Courage? No sir: stark insensibility'.

You ask how long examiners like to read a thesis. I think that a month is a fair allowance. They are seldom free to read it when it first arrives—theses tend to be presented in term—and so they have to wait and find time. Then they generally need to do some checking. Then they have to find a date for viva convenient to them both. However, they are usually reasonable people and if you have a particular time-table problem, say so in our submission to the Registry. The Board is thoroughly accustomed to applications, especially by Indians, for 'late submission' (so that they can scribble to the last minute) and 'early viva' (so that they can catch an available dhow or catamaran back to Bombay or Madras). This can be very inconvenient – especially when they time it, as they sometimes do, so that the examiners would have to do everything between Christmas and the New Year. However, the Board tries to co-operate, only insisting that its approval of such courses is subject to the convenience of the examiners, whom we never commit to an unreasonable time-table. It is always convenient to the Board if a supervisor suggests examiners. We don't necessarily appoint the suggested examiners but we generally do, and suggestions are always a help; so you will probably discuss possible examiners with Keith Thomas.

As for 'jargon' the rules—it seems to me—are very simple. First, one must distinguish between 'terms of art' and 'jargon'. At least I make this artificial distinction. 'Terms of art' are agreed, exact definitions, necessary to the discussion of an esoteric subject. The terms you mention ('agnatic', 'affinal', 'matrilinear', 'sibling') are such terms and there is nothing wrong with them at all, or with any other such terms. I simply think (a) that the terms should be 'agreed' between writer and reader explicitly if they are unusual terms, and (b) that they should be respectable, properly constructed, euphonious terms, as simple as possible, not fanciful neologisms or grotesque hybrids. 'Jargon' is (to me) something quite different; the use of pompous clichés, or second-hand conglomerations of words stuck together in habitual postures, when it is perfectly possible to use a clean, simple word or phrase. Thus where you or I would naturally say 'enter' or 'go', your Jargonaut, when in full sail, would just as naturally say 'effect an entry' or 'proceed', as if it were better English, and raised his social or professional status to say so. I'm afraid that many writers really do seem to think that this kind of

---

[1] Also published on pp. 135-139 of *One Hundred Letters from Hugh Trevor-Roper* (2014) edited by Richard Davenport-Hines and Adam Sisman

long-windedness is necessary to their status, just as rat catchers now, in our status-bound society, call themselves 'rodent operatives' and dentists 'dental surgeons', etc. etc.—and graduates 'postgraduates': a revolting word which I refuse even to use, but which I have tried in vain to exclude from the vocabulary of the university.

In 'jargon' I also include metaphors which are not sensed as metaphors: i.e. metaphors which are so dulled by use that they create no vivid comparable image but only elongate the phrase. I make it a rule never to use a metaphor unless, with my mind's eye, I see the action or object from which I draw the image. I have just seen the Jargonauts, sailing in the good ship Jargo, which however, for them, has a certain florid Hindu decor and tramples down the waves like its kindred vessel the Juggernaut, and uttering horrible, polysyllabical, prosy meaningless noises as they plough through the inky Black Sea towards the Gold Fleece of journalistic success. What is the point of a metaphor if it is not really a metaphor at all—if it creates no image in the mind of the reader (because there has been none in the mind of the writer), but is merely a means of taking longer to say something? It is for this reason that I hate mixed metaphors. A mixed metaphor is proof that the writer has not seen the images; for if he had, the two images would have cancelled each other out in absurdity. For instance, if I were to say that some scholar of whom my opinion was low (I fear there are some) was a poor fish, not worth powder and shot, it would be self-evident that I had not seen him as a fish at all: the phrase would have been, to me, mere jargon.

Why do I feel so strongly, indeed passionately about this? Even as I write, I feel myself to be somewhat absurd. But I have my reasons. It is not merely that the English language—all language—is to me something beautiful which deserves to be treated well: it is also a moral question. Clear language is the expression of clear thought and muddy language is the slime which obscures thought, concealing the slovenliness, the crookedness slovenly, crooked minds and excusing the indolence of indolent minds. Indeed, it can be worse than that: it can excuse cruelty, vice, crime thing. All the great crimes of our time have been palliated, perhaps made possible by jargon. The use of phrases like liquidate' by the Bolsheviks 'pass on', or 'send to the East' by the Nazis, instead of 'kill', 'send to the gas chambers', made it possible for a whole bureaucracy to organise and carry out mass murder without even admitting to themselves what they were doing. Slipshod language, opaque meaningless metaphors, not only excuse the mind from the rigours of thought, they protect the conscience from the sense of responsibility. I feel morally revolted by totalitarian (or other) double-talk—that is what really maddened me in China—and since double-talk is impossible if language is used exactly and clearly, this is to me a compelling reason for insisting on exact, clear language.

And yet, I do not want language to be purely dry, neuter, antiseptic. It is too noble a thing for that. It is capable of warmth, light, subtlety, power. I want it to realise these capacities. But even in realising them, it must not slip into jargon. Fortunately, the safeguards are already there. Thanks to metaphors, images, language can move in more than one dimension and living metaphors, since they reinforce and vivify the intended meaning, cannot by definition obscure it. Only dead metaphors can do that. They are the unfailing resource of cant and hypocrisy.

Do you doubt my comforting equation? Then try reading some 17th century sermons, preferably Scotch. They never let one down. Try the letters of Samuel Rutherford. There is a metaphor in every sentence, and every one is stone-dead. He never draws his images from the peel-tower or the yew tree, the oatmeal or the salt beef, the gannet or the grouse: it is always from the fish-pools of Hebron, the cedar and the cypress, the gourd and the hyssop, the flamingo and the quail. And the whole work, of which edition after edition seemed edifying to generation after generation of your compatriots, is nothing but nauseating cant from beginning to end.

If, as an anthropologist, you are faced with whole sentences which appear to mean nothing, don't despair; they probably do mean nothing and can therefore be ignored. Life is short, and those who will not take the trouble to write clearly cannot properly expect to be read.

Do please call on me. Tuesday is a bad day for entertaining you, as it is our servantless day, and Xandra hates cooking; also it is the day when we have a 'business lunch' at Oriel and guests aren't

allowed. But I would give you a very dull dinner in college to show you what you have escaped. Otherwise take a chance and telephone me: I am likely to be in Oxford on Tuesdays.
Yours ever Hugh Trevor-Roper

P.S. Have you ever read George Orwell's essay 'Politics and the English Language' which is published in his volume of essays Shooting an Elephant and Other Essays? It says everything that I believe on this subject.

I wrote to Trevor-Roper on 31st January from 44, Ridge Road

Dear Professor Trevor-Roper,
Once again, thank you for a most amusing, and helpful, letter. I don't know how you find the time to write at such length, and the energy to write with such vitality. After a day at the L.S.E. I feel completely worn out. Today was particularly hectic – I gather there may be some repercussions in the Press since amidst the surging crowds opposing the new Director an aged Porter was killed – or rather, suffered a heart-attack from which I think he died. Anyhow, this is just going to be a short note to ask if I may really take up on your kind invitation for dinner at Oriel. I wonder if you are free on February 21st? ... I realise that you will probably be fully booked, but it would be nice to meet. I could then bring up the matters you discuss in your letter.
Yes, I've read 'Politics and the English Language' - wonderful.
I hope to see you soon. Thank you, again, for writing.
Yours sincerely,

February 1967

I wrote to my parents on 19th February

Dear M & D.,
... The day at Oxford was generally very enjoyable. I had lunch in the senior common room at Balliol and for the first and last time (probably) waived hullo across a crowded room at the Master (Christopher Hill); afterwards we had an amusing discussion about why he persisted in believing in Margaret Murray etc. In the evening I went out to dinner with Harry Pitt and we had a most invigorating argument. I saw David in the afternoon. Oxford was, as always, very lovely.

Trevor-Roper wrote to me on 6th February from the History Faculty Library

My dear Alan,
I am extremely sorry, but dinner on February 21st is now impossible. Since I wrote to you we have accepted an invitation to dine with the President of Trinity that night.
But I hope we shall nevertheless see you. At present I have no other engagements that day, so do come between 3 and 5, or, if you prefer, come to tea at my house at 5... Yours ever, Hugh Trevor-Roper

I wrote to Trevor-Roper on 28th February from 44, Ridge Road

Dear Professor Trevor-Roper,
This is a very tardy note to say that I very much enjoyed seeing you last week and only wish we could have had a longer talk. I wonder how the session with the gentleman from Prague went? Anyhow, I very much appreciate even a few minutes in your very busy time-table. Perhaps you will be kind enough to let me come down to one or two of your graduate seminars, if you are still holding them,

and we could then have a chance for a longer meeting. I was also sorry not to be able to see the proofs of your 'Encounter' article on witches. I look forward to reading the final version.

I hope you have a restful vacation; I presume you will be retiring to the Scottish house. You seem to be very over-worked at the moment, if th piles of letters on your huge table are anything to go by!

Thank you once again for listening to my problems.

Yours sincerely,

March 1967

Trevor-Roper wrote to me on 2nd March 1967

My dear Alan,

I was delighted to see you the other day, even for so short a time. I have had to retire to bed, which is very inconvenient as I am just about to give a lecture in Paris and then go to Rumania. So please forgive a hasty, dictated letter in answer to yours.

Of course I would have given you the proofs of my Encounter article on Witches had I had them by me. Since you are so kind as to express this interest, here they are. The text is not quite the same as the text which will be published in the book, and of course 90% of the footnotes have been left out. But do read it in this form if you like. Would you be so kind as to return them to my secretary for me... Of course I would be delighted if you would speak to my summer seminar. What would you like to talk about? May I write to you again when I am up?

Yours ever, Hugh Trevor-Roper

Trevor-Roper wrote to me on 8th March from the British Embassy, Paris

My dear Alan,

Many thanks for your letter, which reached me just as I was leaving Oxford. I had a hasty recovery followed by, or even coinciding with, a precipitous preparation for travel. However, all is now well. I have delivered my Parisian lecture and am none the worse for either the scrimmage or the exertion; and tonight I begin the long train-journey to Belgrade, where I am spending two days before going on to Bucharest. Meanwhile, I hope that my essay on Witches will not drive you into paroxysms of disagreement. If it does, I shall ask you to come to my seminar and disagree publicly for the enjoyment of the audience.

Of course I would be delighted to see you there. But I must admit that I am a little frightened of your suggested subjects. The general title of the class is 'Intellectual Movements in 16th and 17th century Europe', and I propose to include Platonism, Socinianism, Scepticism, perhaps Cartesianism, Paracelsianism, (Allen Debus, of Chicago, I hope will do that), & no doubt witch-beliefs which, to keep up the polysyllables, we could describe as Demonianism. All these, I think, can be described as intellectual movements. But your proposed subjects, Sex and Death, interesting though they are, are hardly in the same category. They are rather social attitudes than intellectual movements, and would seem more suited – unless re-baptised with polysyllabic abstract names ending in -ism – for a different course in which other talks would be on attitudes to money, time, servants and such things.

So what do we do? Wait, I think, is the answer, and see what second thoughts occur to you, as you meditate on social anthropology in L.S.E., to me as I meditate on anti-Trinitarianism in its Transylvanian home of Cluj, formerly Clausenburg. I have always longed to visit it. I have a romantic image of it in my mind. No doubt contact with the reality will be a deception – as in Persia, where I arrived, across hot and dusty deserts, to look at the fabled city of Shiraz, the home of Hafiz and the Persian poets, and found that it was like Godalming.

Yours ever, Hugh Trevor-Roper

I wrote to my parents on 12th March from 44, Ridge Road

Dear M. and D.,

Since I wrote a few days ago this will only be a note. It is principally to thank you, Mummy, very much indeed for all the trouble you took over th thesis. I really am very grateful. From this you will gather that it arrived safely. I've not been through all your suggestions, but I agree with nearly all the amendments I've looked at so far. It really is a great comfort to have had someone else go through it. It must have taken you a great deal of time – I hope you didn't feel it was all wasted.

Trevor-Roper wrote to me on 29th March from the History Faculty Library

My dear Alan,

I have stopped for two days between Moldavia and Scotland. Thank you very much for sending back the essay on witches, and for your comments. While you chew on my theories I will chew on your criticisms, but I will give one or two immediate answers, as far as I can do in my enfeebled state: for both my mind and body are etiolated by whirligig rotation.

First, the word 'witch-craze'. This is a term of art which I use deliberately in order to evade those pernickety little arrows of yours which come whizzing out of your piddling little county of Essex. Throughout I distinguish between 'witch-beliefs', which I leave to you and your pig-bound peasants, and 'the witch-craze', which is the high, metaphysical, system, which subsumes and vitalises them; the majestic intellectual confections of a Bodin, a del Rio, a Voetius.

Secondly, the mountains. I did realise, of course, that there are no very high mountains, no moon-wracking Tenerife, in the outskirts of Chelmsford. My point is that it is in the mountain areas that the beliefs are invested for reasons of social fear with the name of heresy. That done, the craze, once defined, is applied elsewhere. I entirely agree that a map would be desirable, and I have long ruminated on one; but I am always defeated by the statistical difficulty The available records would, as far as I can see, show a cluster of trials in the Alps and Pyrenees up to the end of the 14th century; then a movement outwards and northwards until, in the later 17th century, Bayle could write that the Northern countries were worse than Savoy and Switzerland. But while this general impression is very clear, I do not believe that statistical precision is available, and therefore in the end I decided that it was better not to construct a map which was bound to be somewhat impressionistic.

I plead guilty to the printing slips, but I rebut, with genial unconcern, your objection that 'the first English law was 1542 – the second 1563 (not 2)'. What I wrote was that the Scottish law was in 1563 and that 'the first general English law' was passed 'in the previous year' (i.e. 1562). I regard the law of 1542 as being particular, not general, in that it merely punished certain specific acts, not witchcraft generally – the interpretation of Notestein.

I am too tired to begin another sheet. I will write again when, in the repose of the Tweed valley, I have forgotten the exertions of the Danube. Yours ever, Hugh Trevor Roper

April 1967

I wrote to Trevor-Roper on 16th April from 44, Ridge Road

Dear Professor Trevor-Roper,

Thank you for writing, even if your remarks about me and my 'pig-bound peasants' seemed slightly more acid than I had expected. My comments were not 'criticisms', at least not meant to be, but just

comments. Perhaps the distinction is too fine. Anyway, it was very kind of you to write when you were obviously so tired by your 'Grand Tour'. I hope I shall have a chance of hearing how it all went. I will only be in Oxford twice this term, I think, both in connection with my thesis. Perhaps, if you have time from your busy schedule, I could call on you. But perhaps I am banished to my pig-sty? I must say I find the witches of Hatfield Peverel preferable to those of Bodin's imagination.

If you do ever find (time) to drop me a line, perhaps you could state the dates when your Encounter articles will appear as I would like to include the references in my bibliography. I presume your seminar will be at 11 a.m. on Fridays as usual.

May I wish you a profitable term, meanwhile I sit here sharpening my 'pernickety little arrows'!
Yours sincerely, Alan Macfarlane

Trevor-Roper wrote to me on 19th April from Chiefswood, Melrose

My dear Alan,

I fear that my genial observations – I don't recollect their form, and I hope they weren't 'acid': they were genially intend – about your pig-bound Essex peasants have disconcerted you. But he who loves peasants must love their pigs, and she who hates her peasant neighbours must bewitch their pigs. Peasants and pigs are inseperable; and what God has joined together, let not man, by mere literary fastidiousness, dissever. I do not doubt for a minute that the witches of Hatfield Peverel were more engaging than Bodin's succubi; but the essential thing is that they are different. Yours live in the world of witch-beliefs, his in the world of the witch-craze; and I don't understand why you object to the latter word, which is a distinctive term of art (in German, Hexenwahn as distinct from Hexenglaube). You, in Essex, deal with the one; I, in Bavaria, Mecklenburg, Hanover, Scotland and Lorraine, with the other. Of course I admit a connexion: without the witch-craze, as revived by the new Fathers of the Reformed Church, would the clergymen in all those Essex vicarages have been so sure of the diabolical influence at work in their pig-styes? I know you are going to contest this, but I am going to argue back; and perhaps you will you will prevail by producing some knock-out detail from a hitherto unknown document in a parish chest: in which case I shall have to yield gracefully. But it will be too late, even then, to alter my essay. What I have written I have written, as Pilate so insouciantly said. When it will be published, I can't say: all I know is that Macmillan give their provisional date of publication as mid-August, and that Macmillan have stipulated that Encounter publish their version near to that date: I suppose in the July or August number.

So enough, for the time being, of witches. The argument can continue when we meet. When will that be? My class is now on Wednesday at 11.0. (received an appeal from the Chairman of the Board, when I was in Rumania, to change from Friday to Wednesday; and argument being difficult across the intervening Carpathians, I yielded). I am coming down to Oxford on Friday 21 April & staying till after my first class, on 26 April; but immediately after that, I am returning, to Scotland to strike a blow for liberty here, and not return ing to Oxford till 11.0 a.m. on the following Wednesday; after which I shall stay in Oxford till the end of term.

I am beginning to recover from Rumania. It takes time: time, solitude and the therapeutic noise of falling water. Why does one travel to these countries? So I ask myself each time on my return. Caelum non animum... But no; for I did enjoy Rumania – I suppose I even enjoyed China in a perversely, intellectual way – simply because I learned so much; and one can bear a lot if one is learning. On the other hand some of the things that one learns are so depressing.

The most dispiriting of my experiences was lecturing in Rumania. They insisted that we lecture at all three universities. It was a very macabre experience. The undergraduates who (we were told) would flock to any lecture by anyone from the West, were excluded. Only professors of mature age, anchored to orthodoxy by their salaries, were present. No questions – or even informal discussions of the subject – were allowed. At Cluj, where we positively asked for questions, the Chairman formally invited questions, but in a tone of voice that made it quite clear that instructions had already gone out that no questions were to be asked; and none were. If we attempted to discuss the subject in casual conversation afterwards, dead silence ensued, broken by some hasty observation about the weather. As I spoke, and looked at the closed faces before me, I felt that this was an episode from Kafka. Nobody in that room wanted to be there. We were all prisoners. Neither Dimitri Obolensky[1] *(who was my companion) nor I wanted to lecture. None of our audience wanted to hear us. If any wanted to hear him, it was unlikely – given the difference of our subjects – that they wanted to hear me, or* <u>*vice versa*</u>*. Those who might have wanted to hear us, were excluded. We were all involved in an elaborate ritual, prisoners of a system of make-believe. For of course none of them believed in the system to which they so ceremoniously conformed. Almost all of them were sophisticated, Paris-educated scholars, who spoke perfect French (all conversation, lectures, etc. were in French). But equally none of them dared admit, by so much as a flickering eyebrow, that he had ever entertained a non-Marxist or deviationist idea.*

Some carried their conformity better than others. Some were clearly broken before they were bribed; others rejoiced in the discovery that conformity brings power, perhaps even freedom – as in the concentration-camp, where <u>*Arbeit macht frei*</u>*. (In fact, the most distinguished Rumanian historian was offered the alternative of the Chair of History at Bucharest or the concentration-camp: like Gyges in Herodotus, he preferred to survive). I now feel that I have seen the whole range of academic corruption, the extended spectrum or gamut of* <u>*la trahison des clercs*</u>*.*

I must stop: midnight strikes: it is the hour of the Sabbat in those Essex pig-styes; I will not detain you as you strain your eyes (or at least your <u>*oculus imaginationis*</u>*) from Ridge Road to Hatfield Peverel. Yours ever, Hugh Trevor-Roper*

Trevor-Roper wrote a postcard on 20th April from Chiefswood, Melrose

I wrote last night saying I didn't know when Encounter was publishing my essay. This morning I have received a copy of Encounter for May: it contains the first half of the essay, and threatens its readers with the second half next month. HRT-R

Letter to Erik, from 44 Ridge Road on 21st April 1967

... I hope to see the Oxford crowd in a week or so when I take the bibliography of my thesis to be vetted by my supervisor. I am handing it in on June 7th, so keep your fingers crossed for me. I had a long letter from Trevor-Roper yesterday. We are having a row about witchcraft, as I expected we would. His theories are out this month in <u>*Encounter*</u>*. It could well turn into a full-scale academic war since there are a lot of methodological questions at stake; the 'New History' with its anthropological/sociological bias is coming under fire a lot, and my thesis is a representative of it. ...*

I wrote to Keith Thomas on 25th April from 44, Ridge Road

Dear Keith,[2]

I enclose a re-written introduction (in which I've shelved the problem of definitions), a slightly renovated second chapter, a completely new chapter on 'Rise and Decline' of w. prosecutions, a new, short, appendix, and the 'Abstract'. I will be sending the bibliography in a couple of days. I wondered if you could possibly have a quick look at these before I send them to be typed; I am not altogether

---

[1] A Russian born historian (1918-2001) who became a Professor of Russian and Balkan history at Oxford.

[2] This was the first letter in which I wrote 'Dear Keith'. Even after he had attended my wedding in December of the previous year, I continued to write to 'Mr. Thomas' as I had for the previous three years since he started to supervise me. The change may be linked to the fact that Gill and I had been to a private supper with Keith and his wife Valerie at their house on 28th January, which further broke down the status gap between us.

happy with the new chapter on 'Rise and Decline'. Would you be able to do this and see me as early as Sunday or Monday or Tuesday 29th April - 1st May? If this is too soon, perhaps you could suggest a day or time later that week. The sooner I can send the stuff off to the typist, obviously, the better. If you could suggest a time and place, I could manage anything between 11 a.m. and 8 p.m. on any of th above days.

I hope your Indian trip was a great success. I'm longing to hear about it. Looking forward to discussing witches,

Yours sincerely,

P.S. I suppose we had better discuss examiners etc.

Card from Keith, St John's College, 27 April 1967

Dear Alan,

Many thanks for your chapters. I have a huge back-log of other stuff & you don't give me much time but I'll try to be free for Tuesday 2 May at 2 p.m., if you can come then. Keith

30.4.67 44, Ridge Road, London Alan to Trevor-Roper

Dear Professor Trevor-Roper,

Thank you very much for your long letter in which you succeeded in mollifying me and my pig-bound peasant friends. I must say, I continue to be amazed at the way at which you find the time/energy to write such long letters to unimportant people like myself. Most dons I know live in the world of snappy post-cards, unless they are directly discussing work and it is therefore a very pleasant surprise to find someone who can describe his travels with such gusto. I was both amused and horrified by your account of the 'Kafka-like' situation in Rumania. I look forward to seeing what the situation is like in India. Keith Thomas has just returned from some lectures there (with Richard Cobb) and I should get some amusing stories from him. Before he even went there was a typically Indian correspondence. He was asked to suggest some subject that would be appropriate to the problems of India today although located in the English seventeenth century. When he suggested 'Attitudes to famine and disease' the university authorities replied politely that this was rather irrelevant to India's current problems and couldn't he talk about 'The Gentry' instead! In a way one can see their point – too near the bone etc. But academics seem singularly blind in many ways. All this talk of India will show you that I'm still thinking of going there. The choice is really between spending an idyllic two years in a remote hill-tribe at the foot of the Himalayas studying myths and social structure in an unchanged setting amidst the incredible beauty of that region, or becoming involved in politics, famine, and disease by studying problems of change and population in India itself. The former appeals to my senses and intellect, the latter to my heart and my wife. Perhaps I will end up doing neither – as assistant lecturer in Tudor history at a Red-brick university!

As you see I'm avoiding the subject of witches since I want to launch my main attack when I've read the chapter in your book – which may dissolve the onslaught into a hymn of praise (like detergents clearing the menacing oil-slicks). The point about my objection to 'witch-craze' incidentally was not to the use of a differentiating term for the intellectual system as opposed to village beliefs. It's just that it is one of the terms, along with 'epidemic', 'persecution' and so on which are highly emotional and pre-judge the issues. 'Witch-craze' suggests both that the believers were 'crazy' and that it was a temporary 'craze' or aberration, like marbles or mini-skirts, a sort of perverse fashion. It may, in fact that been both these, but I just think that in a subject so engulfed in emotion, it is necessary to avoid emotional words and phrase as much as possible. you will see what I mean from the cold-blooded prose of my thesis!

Yours sincerely, Alan Macfarlane

May 1967

I wrote to Keith Thomas on 3rd May from 44. Ridge Road

Dear Keith,

Just a note about thesis regulations, but let me thank you first for tea and comments. I appreciated both very much, although the latter tend to make me a trifle depressed at this stage. Still, I'll dip in my tar-barrel for a final coat.[1] *Anyhow, I fully realize how much trouble you have taken and am most grateful.*

I've looked at the Examination Statutes and the forms sent me by the Registry and there doesn't appear to be any mention of how examiners are chosen. I imagine the Board will ask you informally for suggestions. All that you appear to have to do is send a certificate (which I will bring with me at the end of May) to say that I've spent six terms in Oxford 'pursuing my research'. Otherwise, all I have to do is have 3 copies of the thesis at the Faculty Office, and a cheque for £25 at the University Chest (and a note from my college). The Board meets on June 8. I will be up at the end of May to have my thesis bound.

Yours, Alan Macfarlane

I wrote to Keith on 20th May from 44, Ridge Road

Dear Keith,

I wonder if you would be kind enough to sign the 'Supervisor's Certificate' part of this form? Thank you.

Everything is under control at this end and the thesis is back from the typist and I'm correcting a rather massive number of mistakes made by the typist and getting maps and diagrams ready. I hope to deliver the copies to the binders in about 10 days. Luckily I obliterated T-R. from the bibliography since my inclusion of his June article in Encounter[2] *may prove anticipatory!*

Any success with the examiners?

I hope all goes well with you – I trust you not too caught up in examining this year.

Yours ever,

Trevor-Roper wrote to me on 20th May from the History Faculty Library

My dear Alan,

I agree and yet I don't agree about the use of language. I mean, dry, toneless, antiseptic language is no doubt best for mere intellectual analysis. The only book I have been able to read right through, with unfailing interest, about the extermination of the Jews under Hitler is R. Hilberg, The Destruction of the European Jews, which is also the longest; and I could red it precisely because it was written in that cold analytical style. On the other hand, on such a subject, the emotional consent is merely disguised, not excluded, by stylistic austerity. And such austerity, it seems to me, is not always legitimate, or at least not the only legitimate form. At times, the mind must take the risk of judging or history becomes meaningless and human responsibility atomised into insignificance. 2 + 2 = 5; and the witch-craze of the 1620s was a craze, not a natural expression of the cosmology of the time. You don't agree, but I am going to stand on my own ground, blow you never so loud on your archaic anthropological blow-pipe.

---

[1] Keith has warned me not to 'spoil the ship for a ha'porth of tar', ie. to make sure everything was as sound as possible - a final effort in checking and grammar.

[2] Encounter article

Now that the experience is behind you, would you tell me what you feel about the excursions to Nottingham? I ask because the situation recurs. John Hale at Warwick wants such assistance (survey of European history 1400-1600). How did it work out? What in fact did they pay you (so that I may compare rates) was it satisfactory? Do you, in retrospect, think that you gained by the experience? I will treat you as a corpus vile, a guinea-pig, a patrol sent forward to report on the terrain. Is it a howling wilderness or does it flow with milk & honey?

I have been ill off & on with some disagreeable virus for some weeks and am now going to Scotland for a week, to picnic on anti-biotics at Chiefswood; but I shall eke the antibiotics out with champagne and return, I hope, cured next week-end. I hope you are well.

Yours ever, Hugh Trevor-Roper

Keith Thomas wrote to me on 26th May from 1967 St John's College, Oxford

Yes, do alter it – though perhaps I ought to initial the alteration? (Call in when you bring it up, perhaps?) Did I ever ask whether the Hearth Tax returns were any use for social status of Essex witches & accusers? Forgive my memory: we probably talked about them. Keith

I wrote to Keith Thomas on 28th May from 44, Ridge Road

Dear Keith,

Thank you for your card. Sorry to keep plaguing you, but perhaps you could change the terms to 'six' and initial it, and send the form on in the enclosed envelope? Also, I wonder if you'd sign the application for early examination – I don't know how long they normally take, perhaps not more than two months anyhow. But I may be in the Outer Hebrides from mid-August and don't want to have to rush back to Oxford. Both forms are to go, like the thesis to the 'Secretary of Faculties' – but I'm not sure whether this means the Secretary of the History Faculty in the Faculty Library, so perhaps you could address the envelope. (I've just noticed the early examination form has to be in by Wednesday, so I'd be grateful if you'd post it soon.)

About witches in Hearth Taxes. I did have a look for the 1645 suspects and accusers (a sample) in the 1662 hearth Tax, but didn't come up with anything interesting. As you know, there are only a handful of Essex cases after 1650 and it would be impossible to get any statistical evidence. In a county like Wilts. where the accusations came later, it might be more hopeful. Hope this answers your query.

Thanks, in advance, for signatures etc. Yours,

I wrote to Trevor-Roper on 28th May from 44, Ridge Road

Dear Professor Trevor-Roper,

How nice to hear from you. I was so sorry to hear that you were ill (though I had heard dramatic stories of you delivering speeches in Congregation and then being carried out with a temperature of 104 from other sources!). I do hope that a well-balanced course of anti-biotics and champagne have indeed cured you. The thought of reading 400 pages of description of witchcraft among the peasants and their pigs will probably be enough to send you fleeing to Chiefswood again! When does the book appear? Masses of people at L.S.E. keep asking me 'what I think' of your Encounter article, but I'm reserving my opinions until the full version appears, as I said. I don't think, at the moment, we can pursue the matter about language much further. Like you, I agree yet disagree., I'll just be interested to hear whether you think my complete omission of words like 'persecution', 'epidemic', etc. and my horribly cold-blooded analysis of accusations makes my account 'meaningless'. I was amused, however, to hear that I was likely to blow on my 'archaic anthropological blow-pipe'. Having discovered the dictionary definition of archaic to be 'primitive, antiquated, no longer in ordinary use' I assumed that you meant the subjects of anthropological study, rather than the approach,. In optimistic moments our tutors try to persuade us that anthropology is a 'science', a more systematic and rational way of looking at societies than the 'old-fashioned' common-sense approach of historians etc. Not that I necessarily agree... But I would tend to argue that anthropologists, in their analysis of witchcraft beliefs anyhow, are at least 50 years 'ahead' of historians, if one can speak like that. Already most historical writing is beginning to look incredibly naive and unambitious to me – but perhaps that is merely because I am getting older and wiser. But enough of that side-track.

You ask about Nottingham. I wrote Fryer a longish letter stating what I thought was wrong with the teaching system – or a few items at least. Probably very presumptuous of me, but it was done, I hope, in the earnest desire that it might help him. I've got a copy of the letter and his rather evasive reply in the Lakes and will gladly let you see them if you're interested. I'll be up there in a couple of weeks and will send them then. They do not bear on my own enjoyment of the situation. To tell the truth my feelings are mixed. I'm sure it was a very useful experience and I'm sure that anyone who has done a very little university teaching would benefit. My trouble was that I grudged the time from my anthropology. I think if the student was really interested in what he was tutoring – i.e. going to teach that subject later on, or doing a thesis on it at the moment – then it would be fine. Jumping from Essex Witchcraft to Pacific islands to Gustavus Adolphus was a bit confusing. What I really did enjoy was teaching Religion and the Rise of Capitalism which overlapped with economic anthropology. As for the students – they left little to be desired. They were extremely intelligent and willing to learn. Given a better and more ambitious teaching system, they could have done very well instead of spending most of the time feeling a trifle frustrated. I expect Warwick is different. I saw hardly anything of the rest of the staff – probably my fault – but a pity. As for pay, they gave me £50 for ten sessions of 3 seminars a time. Then when they got your letter, Fryer took me aside and promised me another £20. Then (I like to think partly caused by my letter, but I doubt it) a cheque for another £50 mysteriously arrived. So, finally, I was handsomely paid – £100 for 30 seminars (admittedly I had to spend a day travelling to get to them). If there are any other details you want, do let me know.

Has Agnes Trollope's obituary appeared yet?

I wrote a postcard to Keith Thomas on 30th May from 44, Ridge Road

Dear Keith,

Thank you for your card. As I have an anthropology exam. in a week I don't think I'll be able to call in for a special visit to Oxford, unless there is something urgent you want to talk about. I'm happy at my end. If there is anything, I could come up on Friday afternoon, any time between 2.30 and 4.30, if I get a card from you on Friday morning.

Yours, Alan

June 1967

Keith Thomas sent me a card on 1st June 1967

No, don't bother then. It's just that I had thought you would be showing me the final version before handing it in. Keith
P.S. I posted your letter.

I wrote to Trevor Roper on 13th June. The address incorporated the fictitious address of Agnes Trollope - Field Head, Outgate, Nr. Buttocks, Westmorland

Dear Professor Trevor-Roper,

I enclose the letters which I said I'd send. Sorry the carbon is on such a messy piece of paper. re-reading my remarks and Fryer's reply I think that perhaps I applied too high a standard –that of

Oxford. It just seemed a pity that a new University should be a rather shoddy version of an old one rather than something new and exciting. I think his 'sensible' reply was all that my impertinence and idealism deserved.

Could you return these at your leisure? Thank you.

I do hope the end of term went smoothly. I'm having a rest in Agnes Trollop country for a week; cuckoos, buttercups and no witches to disturb my rest. I feel much recovered.

With best wishes,

Yours sincerely,

Alan Macfarlane

Trevor-Roper wrote on 15th June from 8 St Aldate's, Oxford

My dear Alan,

Thank you for sending me this correspondence. Whether you will have achieved anything will depend, I suppose, on Fryer, whom you have met and can judge, and I have not met and therefore cannot judge. Perhaps he did not much like the criticism but perhaps he will nevertheless do something to meet it. It is depressing that you should have found these predictable faults. I am afraid that English universities will go the way of American universities unless people are constantly vigilant at certain key points: the absolute necessity of books, the importance of personal contact and dialogue, the necessity of personal thought, independent judgment, clear writing. I think you were right to make these points, and I don't think that Fryer's reply necessarily indicates resistance, although we are all a bit resistant to criticism, especially when status-conscious, as most professors are.

I envy you being in the country. I feel as one who hath been long in city pent. But I shall escape soon.

I'm afraid I shall not read your thesis as an examiner. Your supervisor recommended other names, out of which we have chosen two.

Forgive a hurried letter. Come & see us again soon.

Yours sincerely,

July 1967

I wrote a postcard to Keith on 1st July from 44, Ridge Road

Dear Keith,

I will be coming up to Oxford on July 12th (Wednesday) for my viva and wondered if I could possibly see you at all for a few minutes? The viva is in the morning, so I could manage any time between 2 p.m. and 6 p.m. – the earlier the better, really.

Will fully understand if you are busy.

I hope to see you.

Yours,

Alan (Macfarlane)

Keith wrote a postcard back on 4th July from St John's College

Dear Alan,

Will you lunch with me in College then on 12 July? Come to my room at 1 p.m. or whenever your ordeal is finished. Keith

Letter to Lady Clay from 44, Ridge Road, 9th July 1967

Dear Rosalind,

Very many thanks for your most welcome letter. I'm afraid this will not be a proper reply. It is really a note to say that my viva (before the anthropologist Evans-Pritchard and Christopher Hill – I'm delighted with the choice) is on July 12th - Wednesday, at 10 a.m. I wondered if I might call in at some time? I'm having lunch with Keith Thomas and wondered if you couldn't manage any of the following times.
11.30– onwards, 2.30-3.30 or 3.45-5.0? Perhaps you could drop a card to college, or ring them, making sure they leave in my pigeon-hole and don't post it on, if any of these are impossible. The morning one may well be impossible if the viva drags on ... Anyhow, I hope I shall be able to see you. ... Went to Don Giovanni at Covent Garden last night with Tito Gobbi – still feeling slightly dazed!

Will give you the rest of my news when I see you. Oxford, and especially your garden, will be a refreshing change from Tubeland.

Best wishes,

[Lady Clay replied to say all the times were convenient.]

My mother wrote to me on 12th July from Field Head

We are thinking very hard about the poor old prospective doctor of phil. today, I'm afraid I didn't realise the viva was so important or I would have written in time to cheer you on. We are thinking of ringing up tonight to find out how it went and I do hope they'll soon put you out of your agony. ...

The outline of the thesis I presented can be seen from the table of contents, and the help I received from the acknowledgements.

The thesis was organized as follows:

WITCHCRAFT PROSECUTIONS IN ESSEX, 1560-1680;

A SOCIOLOGICAL ANALYSIS.

- - - - - - - - - - - - - - - - -

A.D.J.MACFARLANE

- - - - - - - - - - - - - - - - -

Thesis submitted to the Faculty of Modern History in the University of Oxford for the Degree of Doctor of Philosophy. 1967

TABLE OF CONTENTS

TABLE OF MAPS, DIAGRAMS AND FIGURES.

MAPS

DIAGRAMS

FIGURES

LIST OF TABLES

List of Tables (continued).

Acknowledgements.

Three acknowledgements cannot be omitted. The first is to my Supervisor, Mr. Keith Thomas of St.John's College,Oxford. Only a few of the many ideas and references he contributed have been specifically acknowledged and it is therefore necessary to state that this thesis owes an incalculable amount to Mr.Thomas's vigilance and insight.

Secondly, a considerable part of the research for this thesis would have been impossible without the superb facilities offered by the Essex Record Office. Indexes, transcripts, and, above all, the generous help of Miss Hilda Grieve and her charming assistants, made research at Chelmsford far more profitable and pleasurable than it would otherwise have been. I thank the County Archivist, F.G.Emmison, and all the staff.

Finally, my own nuclear family are to be thanked. They not only provided the background of a restful year in a garden shed in the Lake District, but also expert assistance in the analysis of the social background to witchcraft prosecutions in the three Essex villages used as a sample.

I wrote to Keith on 13th July from 44 Ridge Road

Dear Keith,

Just to thank you for a delicious lunch (raspberries and cream are a treat in garden-less N.8) and, more importantly, to say how very grateful I am for all your guidance over the last three years. I don't know what would have happened to my thesis without your encouragement and enthusiasm and the constant contact with someone interested in the same problems meant more than I can say. I also appreciate all the time and trouble you took correcting my appalling grammar and faulty logic.

I do hope that I will be able to repay, in part at least, all your help. I every much look forward to reading the draft of the book – it really sounded very exciting.

Thank you again – for everything.

Yours, Alan

My mother wrote to me on 14th July from Field Head

My dear Alan,

A line to add to the squeaks on the telephone – we were thrilled to bits of course – if anyone deserved it you did, in fact you should have a D.Phil. and Bar! Every time I get a pain in my stomach thinking about Rosemary I remember and feel warm and soothed and happy again. You will probably have a much delayed nervous breakdown now that the tension has suddenly relaxed. Let us know when we can collect Great Grannys moth-eaten mink and see you collect.

15.7. 1967 St John's College, Keith to Alan

Dear Alan,

It was very nice of you to write. I feel faintly sad that your thesis is finished, as I enjoyed our sessions together so much. But I am delighted it made such a good impression and renew my warmest congratulations. I always thought it was very good and it is nice that other people think so too.

How lucky you are to have the Lake District to which to retire. We hope to be in York at the end of August/beginning of September and will have the car. I'll give you a ring if we ever get near Ambleside, but I expect you'll be in Scotland then.

Let me know at the end of the summer if you have any more thoughts about the Cambridge conference.[1] *No hurry as I shan't be able to start on my piece till Christmas time anyway.*

Yours, Keith

16.7. 1967 44, Ridge Road, London, Alan to parents

Dear Mummy and Daddy,

Thank you very much for your two letters. Thank you, much more, for all your support and help without which of course, I could not even have begun to think of doing the thesis. The enclosed abstract indicated a couple of the ways in which you both helped – but I can't begin to say how grateful I am for everything you did. Anyhow, it is over now and I can't say I am sorry. Having carefully prepared myself for all sorts of questions the viva, finally, was only a formal one – as I said on the 'phone. We all dressed up and met in 'Room 13' – rather an inauspicious start. But they were both very sweet and immediately told me that I needn't worry about the questions they would ask me since they both thought the thesis was excellent and would recommend it to the Faculty Board as worthy to be accepted. E-P. then compared a few points in the thesis to the Azande and Christopher Hill made the point about 'what happened before 1560' and 'was society really so integrated and neighbourly before then?' I think both of them had minor points to make – but felt that it would be better to discuss these in a slightly less formal atmosphere. So both of them suggested that I went and see them later in the Summer if I ever visit Oxford. E-P. also bought me a drink at the Mitre later in the morning which was kind of him. The whole session only lasted 20 mins! I then had lunch with Keith who was delighted. I'm afraid there is still a considerable amount of ritual to go through. In mid-October, at the next meeting of the History Faculty Board they will receive the examiner's recommendation and (automatically I believe) give me permission to supplicate – ie. to dress up and go through the ritual in the Sheldonian. So it will probably not be until October or November that you will have to don ancient furs etc. I will also be collecting my M.A. We both feel a little anti-climaxish – but I will endeavour not to have a delayed nervous break-down. As you see, in fact, I am off onto all sorts of other subjects...

After the viva we went off for a drink at a nearby hotel and talked about anthropology and the future. I was now at the L.S.E. where E-P knew most of the

---

[1] The Association of Social Anthropologists conference, organized by Mary Douglas, and held at King's College, Cambridge, in 1968, to which both Keith and I presented papers, both of which were published.

senior anthropologists. E-P invited me to come down to Oxford for a longer talk, and I arranged to do this.

The arrangements and the talk are described below – basically I went down and spent the day from about 11 am until 6pm with E-P in full flow. Whether he felt I was a visiting anthropologist to whom he was imparting the sacred oral history of the Oxford Anthropology Tribe, I do not know. But it certainly felt like that. There is a good deal bordering on the libellous in what he told me, so the following is just for private consumption – and highly biased. But I felt enormously privileged to be eaves-dropping in this way. It is a mark of my interest that I clearly sat down straight away to write down some fieldnotes, even if abbreviated. As will be seen, there is wisdom and gossip, bitterness and humour in all of this, and it is important to remember that he was in considerable pain as we walked, lunched and talked.

25/7/67

44, Ridge Road,
London, N.8

Dear Professor Evans-Pritchard,

You kindly suggested that I might call in on you on my next visit to Oxford and I wondered if you would be free at any time on Friday-Sunday, August 4th-6th? If you could suggest a time/place I will endeavour to be there.

Thank you, incidentally, for helping me so gently over my viva ordeal.

I do hope I will be able to see you.

Yours sincerely,

Alan Macfarlane

OXFORD UNIVERSITY
INSTITUTE OF SOCIAL ANTHROPOLOGY

Tel. 55971

51 BANBURY ROAD
OXFORD

27/7/67

Dear Macfarlane

I shall be at the Institute on Friday morning Aug. 4 but not on the Saturday or Sunday. Can you try to be there by 11.0 o'clock.

We have a garden party at my home (see telephone book) – 4-30 6-30 tomorrow, Sat, July 29. Come if you can.

Yours sincerely

E. E. Evans-Pritchard

30/7/67

44, Ridge Road,
London, N.8

Dear Professor Evans-Pritchard,

Thank you for your letter and for your kind invitation to your garden party on Sat. July 2[illegible] I'm so sorry I couldn't come up to Oxford for the latter but we had visitors in London - but I do appreciate the invitati[illegible]

I will endeavour to be at the Institute by 11.0 o'clock on Friday 4th August and look forward to seeing you then.

Yours sincerely,

P.S. I wondered if the Institute library might possibly like this copy of my thesis abstract - anyone interested coul[illegible] then look at the original in Bodley.

I had written a long letter to Ian Green on 8th August 1965 in reply to his question about doing research. He was still wondering what to do in a long letter he wrote to me on 24th July, 1967. Although this is nearly a year after I finished my period at Oxford, it reflects on a number of issues of doing a doctorate and seems worth including here as part of a reflective postscript, particularly relating to the all-important question of the choice of a supervisor.

30/7/67

44,Ridge Road,
London,N.8

Dear Ian,

How nice to get your letter - and thank you for your congratulations. I must say I am heartily glad I'm through with witches - though now I have got to turn it into a book and I've embarked on another thesis - this time on kinship and marriage in the seventeenth century - at the L.S.E.

I'm glad you found Ghana so rewarding and enjoyable; as a budding anthropologist I would very much like to hear more about your time there and perhaps we can talk about it when I next visit Lady C. I will give you all my news then -e.g. of my marriage etc.

I have been thinking about your questions. As to the question of a supervisor, I think it is probably very much a matter of temperament. If you are at all like me, it will be important for you to have a good supervisor. The point is not really how often one sees him but the fact that for two or three years he is almost the only person who can provide a link with the outside world. He alone knows what one is doing; speaking for myself, one becomes very deeply involved with one's supervisor, he becomes an alter-father. His encouragement can tide one over barren stretches and his criticisms, if misplaced, could have a devestating effect. I think, therefore, that it is important to be careful whom one has. I don't think that one need like a supervisor - but one must respect them. Thus I was incredibly fortunate in having Keith Thomas-a man of incredible energy and intelligence who took a great interest in what I was doing and commented at all stages. The important thing is, I think, to have someone who is himself working on lines similar to ones own - so that he is facing similar problems and excited in one's answers. I don't know if Bennett fits - as I said it doesn't matter if you don't like his manner. The question is whether he a)knows the sources b) is prepared to bake a certain amount of time going over one's work c) is enthusiastic. May I suggest a few other people who would supervise you on the sort of subject you are interested in? Christopher Hill is an obvious choice - he is a very nice person, and obviously very intelligent. I think, however, that possibly he is too relaxed a supervisor - i.e. he is too gentle and nice and too involved in his own work. Perhaps this would suit you. On the Restoration period Anne Whiteman is very conscientious and knows the sources - but I don't know if you want one of Oxford's inimicable meticulous and very careful workers. Trevor-Roper himself would be, I think, your best bet. As you know, he started a thesis and wrote a book on Laud & is particularly interested in Church-State relationships. I've only spoken to one person who was supervised by him, but he was full of praise. From my own experience, he is a person of boundless energy and enthusiasm and prepared to go to endless trouble over a person he likes and feels deserves it. Obviously he is a little awe-inspiring and can be very bitter and nasty. But on a personal level he is usually charming. He also is obviously an unbeatable 'contact-man' - i.e. very useful if you want to go on as an academic. The main thing is that you would have to realize that he he is very sensitive and needs to be approached with mild deference. It might be worth your while to write to him before you are summoned and ask for his advice about a choice of subject. Not only would he have some useful ideas, but he likes being consulted. One other person who I don't know is the newly appointed history fellow of Oriel college. I gather that he is fairly dynamic and bright and wrote a thesis on some aspect of the Restoration Church. T-R. is a bit suspicious of him, but he might be good. I'm afraid I don't know his name. The main point against him is that it is not a very good idea to have someone who has just become a Fellow since he will be very busy working out his lectures, tutorials etc. and may not have enough time/be experienced enough to supervise one.

As for subjects of research, as you know, our views on what is interesting and important tend to be rather difficult. People who you might write to and who are more in your line are Ralph Holbrooke (were you his year at Worcester?) he is working on ecclesiastical history and is good on the sources/problems. A letter to Worcester College would reach him. A friend of mine who is just completing a thesis (under Anne Whiteman - he could tell you what she is like as a supervisor) on the Arminian movement in England in the early C17 is Nicholas Tyacke, formerly of Balliol College (a letter would be forwarded to him from there) who is now an assistant lecturer at London University. He might have some ideas. If you are interested in the Elizabethan period, the obvious person to contact is Patrick Collinson(Dr.) also of London University (Dr.Patrick Collinson, Dept. of History, King's College, University of London, London,W.C.2) - you might read his new book 'The Puritan Classical Movement' (or is it 'Elizabethan Classical Movement'?) first - and this would give you some idea of his interests.

You'll get to know the various bibliographies etc. as you go along; at this stage it might be worthwhile - if you can get to a library - to have a look at the 'Theses in Progress' section of the Bulletin of the Institute of Historical Research. But I wouldn't worry if you are still vage by October - I changed my subject after 5 weeks of the term.

As for subjects - I still think that if you read some of the classical accounts of the sociology of religion and then tried to answer the problems posed by taking a small region - say a county or a few villages even - you would find much more than if you took a whole movement or trend. Incidentally, if you are at all interested in Quakers, the Quaker records, especially the Books of Sufferings, at the Friends House, London, have hardly been touched and would possibly make the basis for a most interesting thesis. If you wrote to or went to the Society of Friend's Library, Friends House, London,N.W.1. they would tell you more. The records really are excellent and, they tell me, unexplored.

Do write again if further questions arise.

See you next term.

With best wishes,

August 1967

I wrote to my parents on 8th August on 44, Ridge Road

... We both went away last week-end. Gill to her parents who are very well, and myself to Oxford. I had a very refreshing week-end, including many of my old rituals (lunch with Ralph and David at

Timms;[1] *fish and chips in Walton Street etc.. the high-light was 7 hours of conversation with Evans-Pritchard on Friday. he took me out to lunch (we were first quietly ejected out of a snooty restaurant because we were both scruffy) and then back to his very shabby but delightful home just outside Oxford. He is a very sad old man – a bit like Grandpa with his dog and slippers – a diabetic, deaf, his wife recently committed suicide & 5 children to look after. But he was full of hilarious and extremely racy anecdotes about my supervisor, Malinowski, Frazer & others. Have jotted some of them down – but I'd better not send them in a letter as they are very libellous! ...*

I'm afraid I can't say exactly when my D.Phil./M.A. ceremony will be. I think, probably, either at the end of Oct. or beginning of Nov. I've got to be passed by the History Board first – to whom the examiner's report back. I will find out as soon as possible.

Lots of love from us both to you all,

Longing to see you,

I took notes on the seven hours of conversation with Evans-Pritchard.

[1] Timms was a boathouse when I was at the Dragon School, but later combined this with a restaurant.

Only parts are legible, so I shall transcribe just a few selected items of a personal and advisory kind, omitting a good deal of very funny, but somewhat scurrilous, comment on leading anthropologists. Evans-Pritchard was, in many ways, the pinnacle of British social anthropology in the middle of the twentieth century and from his many encounters and a long an combative life was well placed to observe the quirks and qualities of his contemporaries.

Evans-Pritchard 4th August

Personal – fear of death – no – Catholicism
- illness – diabetes

- discussion – general – re. mad dogs etc.
- house = scruffy, lots of children, guitars, 17 tortoises (couldn't bear to see them in market) [I remember these – and asking E-P whether it had not occurred to him that by buying up the tortoises he was not just encouraging the trade…] – chickens, over-grown; German maid – problems of selling – driver – cautious [presumably we drove somewhere and I noted E-P as a cautious driver]

<u>Personal</u>

- committee/admin work = 2-3 hrs a day [I was shocked at this load, but later experienced it myself, on a larger scale, in Cambridge]
- v. shaky, slow, considerable pains
- ribald humour & infectious spluttering humour. "I've seen death close too often to be very afraid"
- fairly straight Catholic line on contraception
- gives non-lecture at Chicago = they ask him over – he wants money but won't give lecture: therefore they advertise & then cancel lecture

<u>Fieldwork</u>
Necessity of – yes.
Dangers of tape-recorder – get too much information
Importance of <u>texts</u> & of getting enough biographical information

2nd-class minds & their progress [this may have been a comment about the fact that both E-P and I had received seconds in our Oxford History finals – and this was no bar, since many who got firsts burnt themselves out]

- need to go back to Comte & Montesquieu & for intellectual breathing space [E-P gave lectures on the History of Anthropology, which have been published, and start with Montesquieu. For some years I did a similar course, also starting with Montesquieu, in Cambridge – and indeed found that the broad historical roots were important]

= holiday at Butlins last yr – [I asked E-P why he went for his holidays at an Irish Butlin's Camp, usually the abode of people other than Fellows of All Souls, Oxford, and he replied that "it is the one place I can be certain I shall not meet any of my colleagues"; I guess the reference to the Irish bogs refers to the sale of some land he held in Ireland?]

- doesn't matter if my books are torn to pieces
- I'm not going to make any further intellectual contribution [a sad remark at the age of 62, but probably related to his illness and the pain which he was suffering even as we walked and talked; he had already written several immortal works, of course]

Letter to Evans-Pritchard.

8/8/67

44, Ridge Road,
London, N.8

Dear Professor Evans-Pritchard,

Please forgive my delay in writing to thank you for all your kindness and hospitality last Friday, but I've only just returned to London. I'm sure I don't need to tell you how much I appreciated all the time you spent on me, or how much I enjoyed our discussions. It was certainly the most delightful part of a delightful week-end at Oxford and I am most grateful. The day I was thrown out of the 'Ox and Cellar with E-P' will provide a memorable anecdoxte for the days when I become a teacher! It was most kind of you to offer to read the proof of my book and when it reaches that stage I will most certainly take advantage of your kindness. I hope that I will see you again before then.

I do hope that your have recovered from the stomach-pain you were suffering and that you will have a very enjoyable holiday in the marshes.

Thank you again, for everything.
Yours sincerely,

September 1967

From Alan to Erik, from Field Head, 4th September 1967

Dear Erik,

... My witchcraft thesis is finished and I was viva'd by Christopher Hill the Master of Balliol and Evans-Pritchard, Professor of Anthropology, in July (forgive me if I've already told you all this). The viva only lasted 20 minutes and I'm glad to say that I passed. I take my degree in November (4th I think). It is a great relief to have it over though, as with essay crises, new crises soon follow. I'm turning the thesis into a book, as you know, and am also half-way through an M.Phil. in anthropology on 'Incest and other sexual offences in sixteenth century England' or some such. ..

1967 - October

I received notice that I could supplicate, that is receive, my doctoral degree.

UNIVERSITY REGISTRY
CLARENDON BUILDING
BROAD STREET
OXFORD

26 October 19 67

Dear Sir,

I have much pleasure in informing you that the Board of the Faculty of Modern History has granted you leave to supplicate for the Degree of

Doctor of Philosophy

A notice to this effect will be published in the *University Gazette.*

Will you please make your arrangements for supplicating for the Degree through the proper officer of your College.

Yours faithfully

[signature]
Secretary of Faculties

To A. Macfarlane, Esq.,

1000:—8.65.

1967 - November

I received my degree on 4th November.

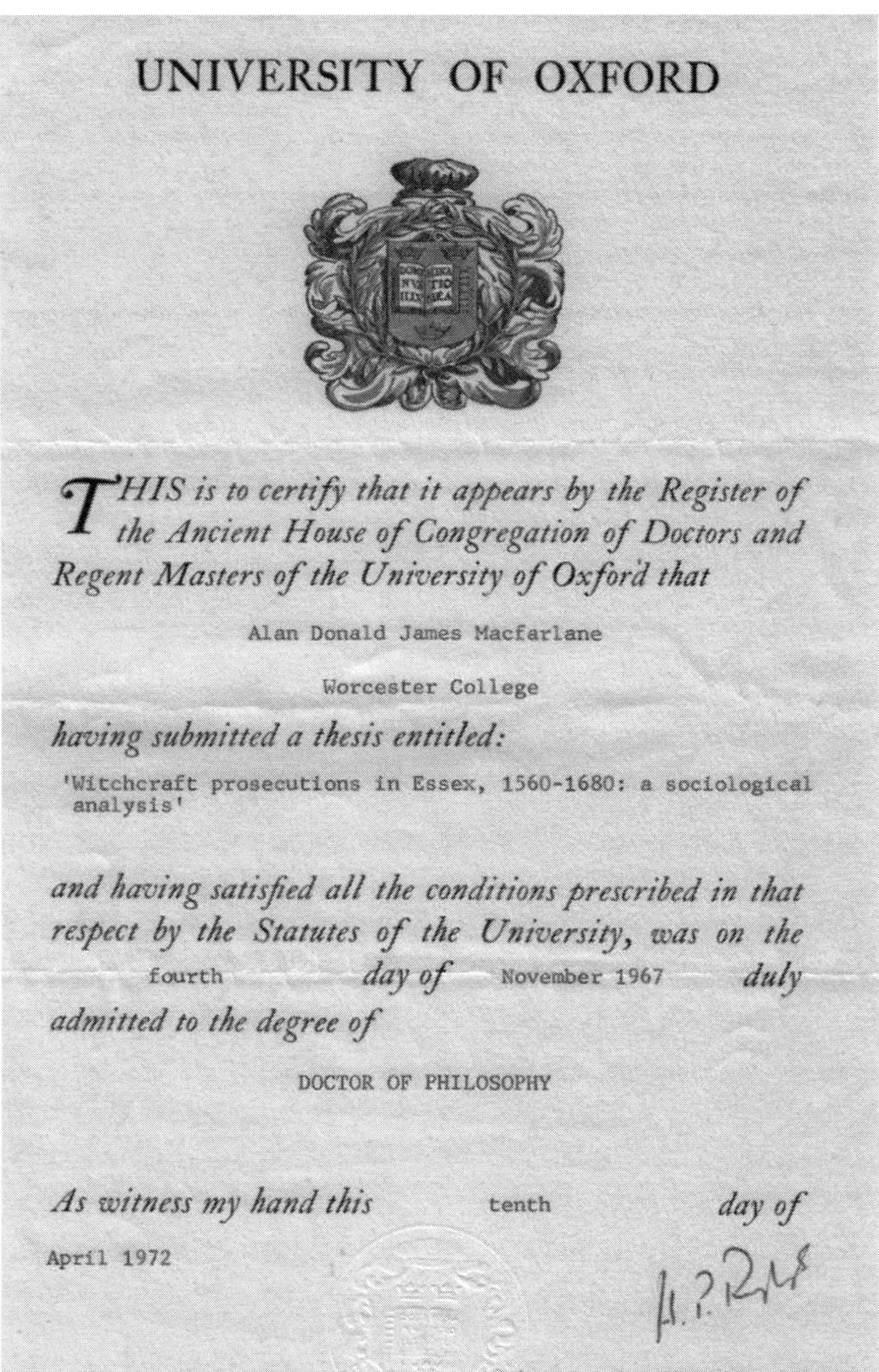

UNIVERSITY OF OXFORD

THIS is to certify that it appears by the Register of the Ancient House of Congregation of Doctors and Regent Masters of the University of Oxford that

Alan Donald James Macfarlane

Worcester College

having submitted a thesis entitled:

'Witchcraft prosecutions in Essex, 1560-1680: a sociological analysis'

and having satisfied all the conditions prescribed in that respect by the Statutes of the University, was on the fourth *day of* November 1967 *duly admitted to the degree of*

DOCTOR OF PHILOSOPHY

As witness my hand this tenth *day of* April 1972

Assistant Registrar

Trevor-Roper wrote on 8th November 1967 from Oxford

My dear Alan,

... I'm glad that the scientifically chosen examiners approved your thesis; as I am sure that any right-minded examiners would have done. Naturally, since Christopher Hill has repeatedly declared his faith in the True Word of Margaret Murray, I am a bit sceptical of his qualifications, which I cannot get him to exhibit in discussion of this delicate question; but I don't really hold even this against him. I hope I shall see your thesis when it appears from the press of Messrs Routledge (I hope it is Routledge and not Weidenfeld & Nicolson).

What are you doing now? Have you finished your work at LSE? Are you going to Calcutta? Or has matrimony adjusted the Benthamite springs of action?

I am sorry to report – but you may already have heard the sad news locally that Miss Agnes Trollope passed away in the autumn. I was with her at the end. Her last words were, 'don't let the poor bassets starve'. I am doing my best, but the cost of hound-meat is disagreeably high. I have been asked to edit her Nachlass – also to write a brief memoir of her in the press. I would like to do so, but am terribly pressed for time: too many committees, too many lectures, can't even read; and what is the point of life if one can't read? On this – as on all else (except for one thing, which you won't guess, so don't try) – I agree with Gibbon.

I hope you have made proper practical – i.e. economic - arrangements with Routledge. They are good publishers. I have only once failed with them, and that was because I didn't realise the extremely complex religious situation in the firm. But that won't (I think) trouble you.

I am escaping from committees on 25 Nov, by the drastic expedient of flying (I detest flying: it is pure torture to me, every minute) to China.
Yours ever, Hugh Trevor-Roper

Letter to Gill's parents (John and Mary) from 6, Milverton Road on 12th November

Please excuse a short scribble but I just wanted to say how sorry I was you weren't able to come to the ceremony. Also to assure you that you didn't miss much! Although I enjoyed wearing my scarlet and blue gown and it was nice seeing old friends etc. the weather made it a rather dismal day. It drizzled steadily and a cold wind blew through the medieval quadrangles. My father was upset because he had forgotten his camera and there were long waits between events. A pity - since Oxford can look really lovely at this time of year.

I wrote to Trevor-Roper on 19th November 1967 from 6, Milverton Road, London

Dear Professor Trevor-Roper,

How very nice to hear from you and how kind of you to send me an offprint of the essay on the Witch Craze. The only fact which marred my pleasure was to hear of the recent death of the much-esteemed Agnes Trollope. If I had any black-edged writing paper I would have written on it. Please send my sincerest condolences to her family and any of her basset-hounds still surviving on the scraps from the Regius Professor's table. the only consolation is that she was briefly mentioned as one of the angels of light in a recent review in The Sunday Times. I should have realized then, of course, from "The late Miss Agnes Trollope" but I was so distracted to find myself described elsewhere in the article ("they dogmatise about unverifiable sexual practices, and invoke the analogy of Congolese tribes..." – I was just off to give a talk at Balliol two days later on 'Problems in the sexual life of the Tudor and Stuart period'!) that I missed the implications. But since her arch enemy had discovered her real identity, perhaps there was nothing else for it.

Thank you very much for your advice about Routledge's. The only trouble I anticipate is not religious – but nepotism: all the directors appear to be called Franklin. I hope to have the typescript to them by March.

I am still at the L.S.E., – just finishing an M.Phil. on "Marriage & sexual attitudes in Tudor and Stuart England" and preparing to go out to India. Not Calcutta, I fear, but probably the Assam hills where I was born. I feel sad that the moving stair will pass me by and realize that I may never be able to return to Oxford. But feel that I would feel I had betrayed myself if I didn't at least try to get away at some point. Fortunately my wife feels the same. London is miserable in many ways and I miss my Oxford friends & autumnal trees etc very much – not least my awed visits to the Regius Professor's lodgings – but find anthropology continuously exciting.

I'm sorry you are weighed down by committees, lectures etc. You shouldn't write such long letters to 'unimportant persons' like myself – then you would have more time to read. Even I find little time to

read and I've got no teaching! I hope, anyhow, that once the dreaded flight is over, China revives you. I wonder why you've been drawn back to a place that frustrated you so much? If you ever have time to drop me a post-card (or, even better, a letter) I'd love to hear how you get on (also my father collects stamps). Hope you are equipped with your 'Sayings of Mao'!

Again, thank you for writing and sending Witches.

With best wishes,

Yours sincerely, Alan Macfarlane

P.S. Enclose a dingy/dirty xerox of my thesis abstract – which I hope you'll keep with best wishes.

1967 - December

Trevor-Roper wrote again on 29th December 1967 from Chiefswood, Melrose, Scotland

My dear Alan,

Thank you very much for your letter of 19 Nov. I hardly had time to read it, or its enclosure – the abstract of your thesis – before leaving for the Far East on 25 Nov. But we are now back: in fact we got back just in time for Christmas, having spent a fortnight not in Red China (I will never be allowed back there) but in the Republic of China – i.e. Kuomintang Formosa [Taiwan] – and a week, on the way back, in Bangkok and Angkor. I greatly enjoyed Formosa, which was quite different from my expectation, and almost reconciles me to the new American Co-Prosperity Sphere (as the Japanese used to call it) which is being defended in Vietnam. Certainly it is, in every way, preferable to the grim, monotonous, terrorised conformism of Red China. As we skirted the hills of Assam, I cast a loose thought towards you. I hope you enjoy returning thither: they looked tempting to me, from the air (but almost any terra firm is tempting when seen from the air), after that infinite, dreary, dusty brown plain of India. We flew out by the new SAS Trans-Asian Express which goes from Copenhagen to Bangkok, stopping only at Tashkent. Anyway, while you are there if you will keep in touch (a) with books, (b) with me, I will keep my eye fixed on the moving stair for you.

Your abstract makes me want to read your thesis, but I suppose it will appear in your book, to which I look forward. Routledge will produce it well and Colin Franklin will take trouble with it. Do the index yourself – or use domestic labour – and in detail, so that the index reads as another chapter and the reader discovers in it gems he has missed in a too perfunctory reading of the text. At least that is the ideal!

My essay on Witches is to appear separately as a Penguin. I have added a brief, brisk foreword sharply re-defining the territory between us in view of the incapacity of your supervisor to read what is clearly stated on the first page of the text!

Miss Trollope's death was a sad blow to many. I have had several letters deploring it, including one from Professor Stone of Princeton.

I have no objection to studies of sexual practices so long as they are based on verifiable evidence, not on the ipse dixit of some Gadarene sciolist[1]; but I want to know how the facts are known, and trace the argument by the known processes of scholarship, from which here is no escape, no appeal. It is because Christopher Hill sometimes (e.g. in his Intellectual Origins of the Puritan Revolution), Stone generally, and Laslett always skips these processes, and flouts these canons, that Miss Trollope and I occasionally demur!

Yours ever, Hugh Trevor-Roper

1968 - January

[1] Sciolist - a person who pretends to be well informed.

I wrote to Trevor-Roper from 6, Milverton Road on 14th January

Dear Professor Trevor-Roper,

Very many thanks for your interesting letter of 29th December. I very much enjoyed hearing of your journey to and from Formosa and envied your few days in Angkor. Oxford must always seem very small and sheltered after these excursions, although it has its own powerful currents. I was touched by your offer to keep an eye on the 'moving stair' for me. I've a suspicion that when you have read my two forthcoming books this offer will be withdrawn, however. I will be caged among other snarling beasts like Laslett and Stone, classed as one of the 'Gadarene sciolists'. I try to justify this in my mind by arguing that you and I use 'scholarship' in different ways. For me 'scholarship' is something more than precision of footnotes, logical consistency in the text, and style. There must be a breadth of vision, and imaginative understanding of the period and what is significant in it, which many 'scholars' in the narrow sense of the word do not have. Perhaps this is an idiosyncratic usage. But for me K.B. MacFarlane, for instance, or even, perhaps – though I don't know his work well – Maitland, are not scholars, whereas Tawney (who often made mistakes and made fairly wild guesses on occasions) <u>is</u> a scholar. Some people, like you, I find difficult to classify – e.g. C.H[ill]. Often one is convinced and there is such an immense abyss of lack of sympathy and understanding shown – e.g. in his bits on the 'Witch Cult' which is, I see, repeated in his latest book – that one has doubts. Actually it is difficult to think of many historians of this century whom one can whole-heartedly admire. The self-importance of those whom I come across at the I.H.R.[1] is amazing and the dreariness of their seminars beyond belief. I mustn't go on as this will sound very arrogant. But I felt I had better warn you that, poised between disciplines, I find most present historical debates very arid. If nothing else, the growing battle between self-styled 'New' and 'Old' schools of history should prove lively. I hope that our friendship will not end if we find ourselves temporarily ranged on opposite sides. In the fight against pomposity and academic small-mindedness I like to think we are each using different weapons in the same cause.

I look forward to the Penguin on witches although, as we have both made clear, our work hardly overlaps. My book should be ready for the publishers at the end of April or before.

I will be in Oxford to give a talk on Tuesday January 30th & the following day. I don't suppose you'll be free, but if yu are on either morning or afternoon, perhaps we could meet for a few minutes. If I don't get a card in the next few days I'll assume you are fully booked up.

Again, thank you for writing. Hope all goes well with your work.

Yours sincerely,

Trevor-Roper wrote back on 16th January from the Savile Club 69 Brook Street W1

My dear Alan,

You really <u>must</u> use language more exactly! Scholarship is something quite definite. Of course it is 'more than precision of footnotes, logical consistency in the text, and style'. (It is also a good deal less: it has nothing to do with style). But it does not include 'breadth of vision', imagination etc. Scholarship is technical accuracy and understanding of the rules of evidence within a discipline: nothing more. Historical scholarship consists of knowing and understanding the sources and problems handling the evidence aright, perceiving its value, reasoning correctly. It is not the sum of a historian's equipment, but it is necessary to him. Firth was a fine scholar <u>and</u> a good historian; so was Namier; but there are fine scholars who are not good historians, because they lack breadth or penetration (like Firth's pupils Godfrey Davies and E.S. de Beer), and there are historians who are not good scholars, but have other gifts, like Tawney and Hill, both of whom have insight and intellectual power but not scholarship. Laslett and Stone are, in my opinion, neither good historians (for they lack understanding and sympathy) nor scholars – they get their facts wrong, misquote their sources, use slipshod methods.

---

[1] Institute of Historical Research, London University.

Elton is a scholar; Plumb, I think, not. Gibbon was a scholar and historian, Macaulay a historian but not a scholar.

Who are the self-important historians of the IHR?

I don't know on which side I am on in the alleged battle between Old and New Historians. I don't really know what it is all about and can't get very interested. My complaint against the avant-garde sociological anthropological historians is not their aims, which I approve, but their methods: their refusal to correct their history by means of exact scholarship. They are like Margaret Murray (mutatis mutandis). They need the scholarship of a Ewen (who was a scholar but not a historian).

I would be delighted to see you on 30 or 31 Jan. I am theoretically on leave, but should be in Oxford, I think. Will you ring me on arrival if we haven't fixed a meeting before? At present I am a little uncertain having just arrived from Scotland and not yet being sorted out.

Yours ever, Hugh Trevor-Roper

We exchanged a few further letters until the later 1970s, but I will end the correspondence about my thesis with a last letter written from London on 3rd February 1968

Dear Professor Trevor-Roper,

Many thanks for your chastening letter of 16th January. I think I really agree with you about scholarship – except that I don't think the division between historian and scholar is as absolute as you make it. To be able to 'handle the evidence aright' or 'know and understand the sources and problems' is not something that can be mechanically learnt. It requires imaginative sympathy. But I don't want to embark on that discussion at the moment. the point of this letter is to apologise for not contacting you on 30th or 31st. In the event my visit to Oxford was shorter and more rushed than I had expected and I felt it would be rude to suggest specific limited times. I did in fact ring on Wednesday morning, but you had already left home. Next time I visit Oxford perhaps we can fix something definite in advance – then I can plan my other engagements round it. I was very sorry not to see you as I always enjoy our meetings very much.

I do hope your numerous projects go well and that your room is not too thick in piles of papers.
Yours ever,

The book, as it was published in the summer of 1970.

Witchcraft
in Tudor and Stuart England
a regional and comparative study
Alan Macfarlane

Thanks and acknowledgements

I would like thank Sarah Harrison, Fabienne Bonnet and Sir Keith Thomas for carefully reading and commenting on this text.

I would also like to acknowledge the copyright ownership of all materials quoted in this volume. If any copyright owner would like a fuller acknowledgement, I hope they will be in touch and I will do so.

Printed in Great Britain
by Amazon

66901838R00281